OXFORD HISTORY OF
ENGLISH LITERATURE

Edited by
BONAMY DOBRÉE *and* NORMAN DAVIS
and the late F. P. WILSON

THE OXFORD HISTORY OF
ENGLISH LITERATURE

ENGLISH
LITERATURE
1815–1832

BY

IAN JACK

OXFORD UNIVERSITY PRESS
New York and Oxford

FOR JANE

PREFACE

THE brevity of the period considered in this volume will surprise no one who is acquainted with the remarkable wealth and variety of the literature produced between 1815 and 1832. Even so, the plan of the present series has led to the exclusion of a number of the most important books published during these years. Since the General Editors wished as far as possible to avoid dividing the work of individual writers into segments, this volume contains only incidental references to Blake, Crabbe, Jane Austen, Wordsworth, Coleridge, and Southey. For the same reason the principal treatment of Macaulay, Carlyle, and other Victorian writers who were already active by the later 1820's is reserved for the succeeding volume. In the case of Scott and Landor a division has proved unavoidable: while their prose writings are discussed here an account of their poetry must be sought elsewhere.

Much has inevitably been excluded, but there is one subject about which I should certainly have said more: the relation between poetry and the visual arts. Twenty or thirty years ago the very notion of such a relationship was out of favour with many critics, and the same writers who would praise a poem for the precision of its 'imagery' would use the term 'pictorial' in a pejorative sense. That perhaps makes it the less surprising that when I began this book ten years ago I was quite unaware of the importance of this aspect of literature in the early nineteenth century. But as I read my way into the period I began to find it becoming more and more interesting. In the end I discovered that so much material was accumulating round the central figure of Keats that I determined to reserve the subject for an ancillary study, *Keats and the Visual Arts*.

A great many people have helped me at one time or another. I must first thank the General Editors, who have been generous with their time and their suggestions. Mr. James Maxwell has read several chapters in typescript, while other chapters have been seen by Professor John Butt, Dr. J. C. Corson, Professor John Jordan, Mr. Neville Rogers, Professor Peter Butter, and Mr. Andrew Rutherford. Several of these scholars have given me the benefit of their advice in spite of serious differences of critical opinion. Further assistance has been provided by Mr. David Joslin, Professor W. H. Clemen, Dr. A. N. L. Munby, Professor Randolph Quirk, Mr. Derek Roper, and Mr. John Morris. Mrs. George Gordon was kind enough to entrust me with the late George Gordon's material for an edition of the Shelley letters which once belonged to Thomas Jefferson Hogg. It is most unfortunate that ill fortune and the capricious working of the law of copyright made it impossible for this fine work of scholarship to be published, and I am glad to have had an opportunity of consulting it.

Throughout my work I have made continual use of the *Cambridge Bibliography of English Literature*. In common with every other student of our literary history I have reason to salute the labours of Mr. F. W. Bateson, Mr. George Watson, and their collaborators.

The greater part of this book was written while I was a Fellow of Brasenose College, Oxford, and I should like to record my gratitude to that Society and to two better scholars than myself who made my Fellowship possible, the late Hugh Last and the late David Nichol Smith.

I. J.

Pembroke College, Cambridge
28 October 1962

CONTENTS

CONTENTS

I

THE LITERARY SCENE IN 1815

WHEN Wellington defeated Napoleon in 1815 England was already beginning to suffer from the reaction that seems to be inevitable after a great war. As the publisher Charles Knight put it in his *Passages of a Working Life*:

The great Captive had scarcely sailed from Plymouth to his rock in the Atlantic, when thoughtful men began to feel that the millenium of universal peace and love was not quite close at hand. France could only be kept quiet by foreign occupation; Spain was trodden down under the feet of a drivelling idiot called a king; Poland was manacled to Russia; the dream of Italian independence was at an end when Austria was to rule over four millions of the Lombardo-Venetian Kingdom. Promises made in the hour of danger had been violated when Peoples had won safety for Crowns. Twenty years of war appeared to have produced little real and imperishable good. Such were my thoughts at that crisis, and they were those of many who would willingly have given themselves up to the general exultation at the prospect that peace had at last been securely won. (i. 167.)

The writer of the preface to *Blackwood's Magazine* for 1826 gives an account of the situation after Waterloo from the Tory viewpoint:

When we started, in 1817, the party to which we have always been attached was sadly in want of literary defenders. While the excitement of the war lasted, the paper pellets wherewith ministers were pelted, were of little moment; for the nation was too deeply engaged to think seriously of such things. The ardent spirits were abroad; and the stake played for was too deep to allow those who remained at home to be diverted from the game by anything less serious. When peace came on, the reaction which men of sense anticipated—the change which Lord Castlereagh's phrase so admirably expressed—'the transition from a state of war to a state of peace',—was productive of more domestic misery than was remembered for a long time in England. Thousands thrown out of employment—the usual channels closed—no others as yet adequately opened—were of themselves sufficiently dreadful; but when to them were added the dreadful seasons of 1816 and 1817, when the crops failed all through Europe, it is no wonder that an unparalleled degree of distress was the consequence.

It is not surprising that Byron should have succeeded Scott as the most popular poet of the day. When he turned from verse to prose after the appearance of the first two cantos of *Childe Harold's Pilgrimage* Scott was not only bowing to a superior poetical talent: he was also acknowledging that Byron's poetry suited the temper of the new age better than his own. While their country was fighting for its life Englishmen were excited by the zest and vigour of Scott's poetry, but as soon as they began to taste the bitter fruits of victory they turned to Byron and the poetry of revolt and disillusionment. As Bulwer Lytton pointed out in *England and the English*:

> The public, no longer compelled by War and the mighty career of Napoleon to turn their attention to the action of life, could give their sympathies undivided to the first who should represent their thoughts. And these very thoughts, these very sources of sentiment—this very satiety—this very discontent—this profound and melancholy temperament . . . the first two cantos of *Childe Harold* suddenly appeared to represent. They touched the most sensitive chord in the public heart—they expressed what every one felt . . . Sir Philip Sidney represented the popular sentiment in Elizabeth's day—Byron that in our own. (Book IV, chap. ii.)

As Bulwer Lytton recognized, Byron's poetry was greeted with 'an enthusiasm which his genius alone did not deserve'. Although the development of Wordsworth's reputation was much quieter and more gradual, it was this which constituted the most important literary phenomenon of the time. On their first appearance, contrary to the usual belief, the *Lyrical Ballads* had been reasonably well received; but the preface which Wordsworth was persuaded to add to the second edition was a serious mistake. For all its eloquence, and the brilliance with which it emphasizes some of the profoundest truths about the nature of poetry, on the central issue of the language which the poet should use the preface is both confused and unhistorical. As a consequence ordinary readers were uncertain what to look for in the poems themselves, while literary journalists seized on Wordsworth's pronouncements on the subject of diction and stigmatized them as heretical. This helps to account for the fact that *Poems in Two Volumes*, in 1807, received so much less than their due. The harm done to Wordsworth's reputation by the preface is particularly evident in Jeffrey's review of *The Excursion*. 'This will never do', he wrote. 'It bears no doubt the stamp of the author's heart and fancy; but unfortunately not half so visibly as that of his peculiar system.' Since *The Prelude* remained unpublished until the poet's death it was principally by *The Excursion* that his contemporaries had to judge his stature as a philosophical poet, and fortunately for Wordsworth there were a few younger men for whom its appearance marked an epoch in English poetry. For Keats in 1818 *The Excursion* was already 'one of the things to rejoice at in this Age': it constituted the evidence by which he endeavoured to decide, as his own epic ambitions were beginning to develop, whether Wordsworth 'has in truth epic passion'.

A precise indication of the developing views of a leader of the *avant garde* at this time is to be found in the successive versions of Leigh Hunt's poem, *The Feast of the Poets*. In the first version of 1811 (in which Moore is more highly praised than any other living poet, while Scott and Campbell also receive qualified approval) 'that Wordsworth' is given short shrift: Apollo laughs scornfully as Wordsworth recites 'some lines . . . on a straw, Shewing how he had found it, and what it was for'. In 1815 it is a different story. Although the satirical passage is retained we notice that when Wordsworth accedes to Apollo's request to stop trifling and give 'a true taste' of his art he is at once acclaimed as 'the Prince of the Bards of his Time'. In a long note now added to the poem Hunt says explicitly that Wordsworth is 'capable of being at the head of a new and great age of poetry'—indeed he is already, although unfortunately he abuses his great powers and clings to a dangerously one-sided theory of poetry. In the version of 1832 the satire on Wordsworth is removed altogether; yet it is interesting to notice that in the preface in which Hunt now deals with most of the subjects previously discussed in the notes, and which must be taken as expressing his considered views on the language of poetry, Wordsworth's theory about diction is still regarded with some suspicion.

During the 1820's, when people seriously interested in poetry had had time to study *The Excursion* and reconsider the earlier poems in its light, Wordsworth's reputation was gradually rising. In his incomparable series of literary character-sketches, *The Spirit of the Age*, Hazlitt reports that 'the tide has turned much in his favour of late years. He has a large body of determined partisans.' That was in 1825. Three years later John Stuart Mill discovered Wordsworth's poetry, with the memorable results recorded in his *Autobiography*. In *England and the English* Bulwer Lytton tells us that by the time of Byron's death there had already been 'a growing diversion from Byron to Shelley and Wordsworth' and insists that by 1833 Wordsworth has become 'influential to a degree perfectly unguessed by those who look only to . . . popularity' as a guide to the importance of poets. By 1835 Hartley Coleridge was able to write, only a little prematurely, of the 'complete victory' of Wordsworth's fame: 'he may at least feel assured', he wrote in a letter in September of that year, 'that no Great Poet ever lived to see his name of so full an age as Wordsworth has done'. In 1839 Wordsworth was given an honorary degree at Oxford, while in 1843 he was appointed Poet Laureate. Keble and Arnold, who were among his strongest supporters at Oxford, did a great deal to ensure that belief in the poetry of Wordsworth should be one of the principal articles of Victorian orthodoxy.

Coleridge's fame was also growing at this time, though his major creative period had ended even more definitely than Wordsworth's. 'Christabel' and 'Kubla Khan' were published in 1816, and the authorship of 'The Ancient Mariner' was first publicly acknowledged in *Biographia Literaria* in the following year. Coleridge was of course already well known as a lecturer, while his conversation was legendary. Keats met him once on a Sunday walk in 1819:

> In those two Miles he broached a thousand things . . . Nightingales, Poetry—on Poetical sensation—Metaphysics—Different genera and species of Dreams—Nightmare—a dream accompanied by a sense of touch—single and double touch—A dream related . . . Monsters— the Kraken—Mermaids—southey believes in them—southey's belief too much diluted—A Ghost story—Good morning.

'I heard his voice as he came towards me', Keats comments, 'I heard it as he moved away—I had heard it all the interval.' It was a voice that many men and women were to hear during these years. Charles Knight describes the impression that Coleridge made on him in his autobiography: 'To me, then a very young man, the outpourings of his mighty volume of words seemed something more than eloquence; and I went away, half crazed by his expositions of the power of the human will in producing such effects upon matter as were once ascribed to magic.' Coleridge was to remain one of the great seminal minds of the century, though it was through the intermediacy of others that his ideas were most often to find effective expression.

As the poetical reputation of Wordsworth and Coleridge rose, that of Robert Southey (the third of the 'Lake Poets', as they were nicknamed) sank steadily. He had succeeded Henry James Pye as Poet Laureate in 1813, having more or less abandoned the serious writing of poetry some years before. When he published *The Poet's Pilgrimage to Waterloo* in 1816 his enemies were moved to republish *Wat Tyler*, his early revolutionary drama— just as Dryden's enemies had republished his *Heroic Stanzas* to Cromwell in the 1680's. The only poem of importance that Southey was still to write was *A Vision of Judgement*, which gave Byron the hint for his great satire. As a writer of prose Southey remained in the first rank, but his political views were so unacceptable to the younger writers that it was impossible for them to do him justice in this respect. Although he always repudiated the label 'Anti-jacobin' and was very seriously concerned by the problems of the unhappy years following Waterloo—'We are arrived', as he once wrote, 'at that state in which the extremes of inequality are become intolerable'—yet the horror of revolution which he shared with many Tories too often led him to condone oppression. The liberals regarded him as the supreme example of an intolerant renegade: 'Those who have undergone a total change of sentiment on important questions', as Hazlitt wrote in his review of *Wat Tyler*, 'ought certainly to learn modesty in themselves, and moderation towards others; on the contrary, they are generally the most violent in their own opinions, and the most intolerant towards others.'

Except Scott, who belonged to the older generation, and De Quincey, an instinctive Tory from the first, most of the major writers considered in this volume were aware of a deep cleavage in political opinion between themselves and their elders. Today the situation is familiar, having been repeated in the 1930's, when most of the younger poets belonged to the Left and joined in deploring what they regarded as the reactionary politics of their literary leader, Mr. T. S. Eliot.

There was a similar division between the two generations in their attitude to the Church of England. Southey was a whole-hearted Church of England man, distrusting nonconformity and hating Roman Catholicism. In his dread of anarchy he looked to the Church as a focus of social organization. His book, *Sir Thomas More: or . . . Colloquies on Society*, helped to make the Tractarians believe that the dissolution of the monasteries was the ultimate origin of the diseases afflicting nineteenth-century society. Although Coleridge had a much subtler and profounder mind than Southey, his allegiance to the Established Church was hardly less passionate. For him (as Mill pointed out in his admirable essay) 'the long duration of a belief' was at least 'proof of an adaptation in it to some portion or other of the human mind'. It was his 'greatest object . . . to bring into har-mony Religion and Philosophy', and accordingly 'he laboured incessantly to establish that "the Christian faith—in which", says he, "I include every article of belief and doctrine professed by the first reformers in common", is not only divine truth, but also "the perfection of Human Intelligence"'. Wordsworth's attitude to Christianity is harder to determine, but there is no doubt that by 1815 he was strongly in favour of the Established Church. 'Wordsworth defended earnestly the Church Estab-lishment', Crabb Robinson recorded on 24 May 1812. 'He even said he would shed his blood for it. Nor was he disconcerted by a laugh raised against him on account of his having before con-fessed that he knew not when he had been in a church in his own country.' When he revised *The Prelude* in his later years he exerted himself to give a Christian colouring to speculations which had originally had nothing to do with Christianity. Scott was brought up in the Church of Scotland; yet though he soon rebelled against the austerity of Presbyterianism and was never a deeply religious man, in later life he was a strong sup-porter of the English Church on moral and political grounds.

It is not surprising that the young men who grew up during the Napoleonic wars had a very different view of the official religion from that of the middle-aged men who had grown up at the time of the French Revolution. Except De Quincey—who was odd-man-out among the younger writers, as Hazlitt was among the older—the younger men were all hostile to the Established Church. The sceptical and irreverent passages of *Childe Harold* and *Don Juan* caused the deepest offence and led many religious people to consider their author the arch-enemy of Christianity. If he had lived longer it is possible that Byron's attitude to the Christian faith might have been modified, but it is unlikely that anything would have brought him to respect the English Church of the day. Unlike Byron, Shelley had a marked capacity for abstract speculation: his hatred for the tyranny with which Christianity had come to be associated was compatible with a deep respect for many aspects of Christ's own teaching: but for the Established Church he had a profound hatred. Keats instinctively turned away from the drab forms in which Christianity was known to him towards the Greeks and their 'religion of joy'. Leigh Hunt and Hazlitt were his guides to a region in which the delights of the imagination and of the senses were welcomed and cultivated instead of being (as he felt) stifled by puritanical austerity.

When we turn to the prose writers we find the same tendencies. Hunt was strongly anti-Christian as a young man, Christianity presenting itself to him in the guise of the Establishment, with the *Quarterly Review* as its organ. He considered the doctrine of eternal punishment a barbarous monstrosity, and gradually evolved an eclectic religion of his own. His views are suggested by the title of a book he published in 1832, *Christianism; or Belief and Unbelief Reconciled*: in 1853 he revised and expanded it as *The Religion of the Heart*. Throughout our period most members of the Church of England regarded Hunt as a dangerous and impious person. Hazlitt belonged to dissenting stock, his father being a dissenting minister and a friend of the Dr. Price who delivered a famous sermon in support of the French Revolution. Hazlitt himself was educated at Hackney College but refused to enter the ministry. In general he may be described as a deist: in Haydon's painting, 'Christ's Entry into Jerusalem', Hazlitt is portrayed 'looking at Christ as an investigator', and that is a fair representation. He distrusted the Established Church as the focus of Tory repression. Lamb's attitude to Christianity was often discussed by his friends:

His mind [as Coleridge once said], never prone to analysis, seems to have been disgusted with the hollow pretences, the false reasonings, and absurdities of the rogues and fools with which all establishments . . . abound. I look upon Lamb as one hovering between earth and heaven; neither hoping much nor fearing anything. . . . His faith is in a state of suspended animation . . . Lamb, say what he will, has more of the *essentials* of Christianity than ninety-nine out of a hundred professing Christians. He has all that would still have been Christian had Christ never lived or been made manifest upon earth.

Peacock (with whom this brief summary must conclude) seems for the greater part of his life to have remained a consistent pagan. No writer of the time gives a better satirical representation of the absurd extremes of right-wing opinion. The chorus of Messrs. Feathernest, Killthedead, Paperstamp, and Anyside Antijack in *Melincourt*—'The church is in danger! the church is in danger!'—is precisely the rallying-cry of the *Quarterly*, there termed the *Legitimate Review*. Just as the liberal and sceptical tone of some of the most gifted writers of the day was partly responsible for frightening the authorities into an inflexible conservatism, so the intolerant attitude of the supporters of the Establishment drove many able men into a more definite opposition to the Church than they might otherwise have adopted.

These and the other conflicts of the time are best studied in the pages of the great Reviews. Coleridge pointed out that the founding of the *Edinburgh Review* in 1802 constituted 'an important epoch in periodical criticism', and its significance was not confined to the realm of literature. For the historian and the student of literature alike the long sets of the *Edinburgh* and its successors form an incomparable quarry of material, a quarry which has not even yet been worked with the thoroughness that it deserves. The prestige of the Reviews was very great. In an age of discussion they were among the chief channels of discussion. At times their influence was comparable to that of Parliament itself. Their editors were important men: the Tories originally hoped that Scott would edit the *Quarterly*, and Canning himself was part-author of the main article in the first number. Writing for the Reviews was a very different matter from writing for the newspapers. When Lockhart was editor of the *Quarterly* Scott told him that a 'connection with any newspaper would be disgrace and degradation'. The question of who should succeed Jeffrey and Gifford was discussed with almost as much seriousness as that of who should succeed to the Premiership. No man of letters exercises a comparable influence in this country today. As Carlyle put it, the *Edinburgh* was regarded as 'a kind of Delphic Oracle, and Voice of the Inspired,

for great majorities of what is called the "Intelligent Public"'.
It seemed as natural that Jeffrey should make the transition
from editing the *Edinburgh Review* to being a Judge of the Court
of Session as that he should have made the transition from being
an advocate to editing the *Edinburgh Review*. The motto of the
Review, 'Iudex damnatur cum nocens absolvitur', gives a foretaste of the severity for which it was to be applauded and
deplored.

The men who founded the *Edinburgh* had no idea that it would
live so long or attain such power. At thirty-one, Sydney Smith
was the eldest of them: the rest were in their twenties. By founding their *Review* in a city whose sympathies were overwhelmingly
with the Tories, Jeffrey and his friends provided a much-needed
outlet for liberal opinions. Yet although the *Edinburgh* soon
became associated with the Whigs, it should be noted that it
was not begun as a party organ. The first number, in which
Pitt is highly praised, disappointed those who had expected
'blood and atheism and democracy'. In the early days Scott was
a contributor, and as late as May 1807 we find him inviting
Southey to follow his example. On 6 December the following
year Jeffrey asked Horner to write something, 'only no party
politics, and nothing but exemplary moderation and impartiality
on all politics. I have allowed too much mischief to be done
from my mere indifference and love of sport; but it would be
inexcusable to spoil the powerful instrument we have got hold
of, for the sake of teazing and playing tricks.' At this point
Jeffrey was no doubt worried by the prospect of a rival Review;
yet the passage is revealing because it shows his growing sense
of responsibility, his awareness that something started almost
light-heartedly had grown into a powerful instrument of potential good. He would of course have distinguished between
'party politics' and certain specific political reforms: indeed
Horner's description of himself as a man 'who cares very little
about men or parties, except as connected with the fate of
leading objects', sums up the attitude of most of the Edinburgh
Reviewers. To appreciate the value of their Review, as Sydney
Smith was later to point out,

the state of England at the period when that journal began should
be had in remembrance. The Catholics were not emancipated—
the Corporation and Test Acts were unrepealed—the Game Laws
were horribly oppressive—Steel Traps and Spring Guns were set all

over the country—Prisoners tried for their Lives could have no Coun-sel—Lord Eldon and the Court of Chancery pressed heavily upon mankind—Libel was punished by the most cruel and vindictive imprisonments—the principles of Political Economy were little understood—the Law of Debt and of Conspiracy were upon the worst possible footing—the enormous wickedness of the Slave Trade was tolerated—a thousand evils were in existence, which the talents of good and able men have since lessened or removed.

It will be noticed that Catholic Emancipation was by no means a Whig preserve: on this issue Pitt and Burke were on the same side as Fox. The *Edinburgh* deserves every credit for not turning into a mere Opposition journal, automatically attacking what-ever the Tories supported. It took what it considered to be the liberal and enlightened line on every major public issue. But in particular it stood firm against the excesses of anti-Jacobinism and never ceased to assert the importance of the great figures of the French Enlightenment who were the spiritual ancestors of its own contributors.

Two reasons for the spectacular success of the *Edinburgh Review*, as Scott pointed out, were its independence of book-sellers and the fact that its contributors were invariably well paid. As Sydney Smith told Constable in 1803, it was a matter of notoriety that 'all the reviews are the organs either of party or of booksellers': he added that if Constable would give his editor £200 a year and his contributors ten guineas a sheet he would soon own the finest Review in Europe. Generous pay-ment was to be the rule with both the great Reviews. Writing for them was in every respect an attractive proposition. The contributors enjoyed—and often abused—the advantages of anonymity, but when they pleased they were always at liberty to let their authorship be known. When he published his article on Milton in 1825 Macaulay became famous overnight: until the appearance of the first volume of his *History* in 1849 his celebrity as a writer was almost entirely due to his contributions to the *Edinburgh Review*. The same was true of the economist J. R. McCulloch. 'Almost all my reputation has been built upon my contributions to the Review', he told Jeffrey's successor Macvey Napier at the beginning of 1830, 'and the understand-ing that I had the undivided task of furnishing such articles gave me an influence and consideration which I . . . valued highly.' In his *Life of Scott* Lockhart gives a startling example of the power of the Edinburgh Reviewers. Having received the offer of £1,000 for the copyright, the scientist Thomas Young 'was actually preparing for the press' his lectures on the wave-theory of light, 'when the bookseller came to him, and told him that the ridicule thrown by the *Edinburgh Review* on some papers of his in the Philosophical Transactions, had so frightened the whole *trade* that he must request to be released from his bargain'.

A modern reader of the Reviews is struck at once by the length of the articles and the variety of the subjects discussed. The reviews of poetry, novels, and other imaginative writing which are of most interest to literary historians form a relatively small proportion of their contents. They are to be found among articles on historical works, political pamphlets, scientific treatises, biographies, and books dealing with what we should now call sociology. While the Reviews had their specialist contributors, we notice that men like Jeffrey and Brougham were capable of writing on a very wide variety of topics. The Scottish system of education and the literary societies that were a feature of life at the Scottish universities encouraged the habit of speculation on a wide front. Jeffrey had in a high degree the advocate's ability to get a subject up very quickly: if he did not know everything, he had the air of knowing everything. One cannot read far in the *Edinburgh* without concluding that literature gained as well as lost by being juxtaposed with other matters in this way. It lost because political feeling often unfairly influenced literary judgements—though this is much more evident in the *Quarterly* than in the *Edinburgh*. It gained because literary questions were discussed in a context and in a manner which took it for granted that they were of serious concern to all educated people. Preciosity was avoided, though occasionally at the price of brutality. It is pleasant to find none of the narrowness which is almost inevitable in a purely literary Review. From the first the *Edinburgh* was highly selective in its treatment of new books. Freed from the obligation to deal with publications in which they were not interested, its contributors were at liberty to expatiate on those books which seemed to them of real importance. Often (it must be admitted) the work under review served merely as an excuse for an essay by the reviewer; but since he had a great deal of space at his disposal, he had every opportunity to summarize the book as well as developing his own views on the subject with which it dealt. 'I will try the life of Lord Burleigh', Macaulay wrote to Napier. ' . . . However bad the work may be, it will serve as a heading for an article on the times of Elizabeth.' In another letter he comments that Lord Nugent's *Memorials of John Hampden* are 'dreadfully heavy' and acknowledges that he has 'said as little about it as I decently could'. Coleridge was surely right to approve of this practice of 'supplying the vacant place of the trash or mediocrity wisely left to sink into oblivion by their own weight, with original essays'. The length of some of the articles is astonishing. Many of them run to ten thousand words: Macaulay's essay on Milton, nominally a review of the *De Doctrina Christiana* (first published in 1825), is some 22,000 words long: while his essay on Bacon, which contains some 50,000 words, takes up 104 pages and is about a quarter of the length of the present book.

The *Quarterly* was founded in 1809 to oppose the liberal politics of the *Edinburgh*. As Scott wrote in a letter, 'no genteel family can pretend to be without the *Edinburgh Review*; because, independent of its politics, it gives the only valuable literary criticisms that can be met with'—with the result that 'the disgusting and deleterious doctrines' which it contained became familiar to readers who lacked the opportunity of reading an equally powerful exposition of the views of the Government. 'In Edinburgh or I may say in Scotland', Scott told Gifford, 'there is not one out of twenty who reads the work that agrees in political opinion with the Editor, but it is ably conducted & how long the generality of readers will continue to dislike the strain of politics so artfully mingled with topics of information & amusement is worthy of deep consideration. But I am convinced it is not too late to stand in the breach.' The possibility of an alternative Review was discussed for some time, John Murray the publisher being the moving spirit. The line taken by the *Edinburgh* on the Spanish war did a great deal to bring matters to a crisis. Jeffrey and his colleagues believed that France was invincible: however much Englishmen might admire the heroism of the Spanish people, they argued—an admiration epitomized by Landor's joining General Blake's forces in Spain as a volunteer—they were bound to accept the conclusion that 'the Spaniards will be defeated, after a gallant and most sanguinary struggle'. This was not the view that Wordsworth had expressed in his *Tract on the Convention of Cintra*. Scott was so indignant at what he regarded as the defeatism of the *Edinburgh Review* that he cancelled his subscription.

There was no originality in the planning of the *Quarterly*. It was a tribute to the merits of the formula evolved by Jeffrey and his associates that when Scott and Murray had analysed the reasons for the success of the *Edinburgh* they could find no major improvement that could be incorporated into its opponent. Most of Scott's comments on the general conduct of the *Edinburgh* (apart from its politics) reveal wholehearted admiration:

> One very successful expedient of the Edinr. Editor & on which his popularity has in some measure risen [he wrote to Gifford] is the art of giving life & interest even to the duller articles of the Review. He receives for example a criticism upon a work of deep research from a person who has studied the book and understands the subject & if it happens to be written . . . in a tone of stupifying mediocrity he renders it palatable by a few lively paragraphs or entertaining illustrations of his own. (*Letters*, ii. 104.)

The main difference between the Reviews followed naturally from the origin of the *Quarterly*. From the first it was a party organ. Scott foresaw that its influence might be lessened if it became too evident that it was 'conducted intirely under ministerial influence', but suggested that this might be minimized 'by labouring the literary articles with as much pains as the political & so giving to the review a decided character independant of the latter department'. Yet the motive behind the founding of the *Quarterly* made it unlikely that it would provide the fair and unbiased literary criticism which Scott was demanding. If he himself had accepted the editorship, as the most influential of the promoters of the new Review desired, something might have been done; but Gifford was not the man to ensure any semblance of impartiality.

When one considers the attitude of the *Quarterly* to such matters as parliamentary reform, Catholic emancipation, university reform, and foreign affairs, it is impossible not to be reminded of the *Anti-Jacobin*, and in fact there was a marked continuity between contributors to the two journals. Canning, the *éminence grise* behind the new Review, had been among the principal contributors to the *Anti-Jacobin*, as had George Ellis and Gifford himself; so it is significant to find Scott exhorting Ellis to 'take down your old Anti-Jacobin armour, and remember your slashing blow'. The *Anti-Jacobin* had been the light-hearted diversion of a group of brilliant young men: no one had looked to it for a judicial impartiality. Its strong political bias, without its genuine high spirits, was transferred to the *Quarterly Review*. From the first some of the most determined of the *Edinburgh*'s opponents were highly critical of its rival. Southey complained that the *Quarterly* was 'a little too much in the temper of the *Edinburgh* to please me', and although he became one of the most constant contributors he was never wholly to approve of the way in which the *Quarterly* was run. He said on one occasion that he would 'rather be hanged without that Anti to my denomination than pensioned with it'. Yet it was of the essence of the new *Review* that it should be partisan, and even vehemently so: just as it was that the Government 'should upon topics of national interest furnish the Reviewer confidentially & through the medium of the Editor with accurate views of points of fact so far as they are fit to be made public'. Croker, for example, 'went for the foundation of many of his essays to the men who alone could rightly know all the facts with which he had to deal, and thus in many cases an almost complete draft of the political article was supplied by the Duke of Wellington, by Sir Robert Peel, by Lord Stanley (Derby), or by some authority of equal weight on the question of the day'. It was therefore inevitable that the tone of the *Review* should be over-whelmingly political. In this the *Quarterly* was as characteristic-ally English as the *Edinburgh* was Scottish: every Englishman is at heart a politician, as every Scotsman is at heart a critic.

Croker was described by Andrew Lang as an 'Anglican berserk' and the connexion between the *Quarterly* and the Church of England is of the first importance. While the *Edinburgh* was generally associated with an undogmatic, sceptical approach to theological matters, the *Quarterly* (like Southey) 'lived much with the lawn-sleeved'. Its task was to maintain sound constitutional principles, and not the least of these was the inviolability of the Established Church. When a detailed history of the *Review* is undertaken this matter will demand care-ful investigation, but it is at once evident that the great majority of the contributors were strong supporters of the Church of England and that two or three papers in the *Quarterly* often served as stepping-stones to a comfortable bishopric. The clue to the virulence of the *Quarterly*'s attack on one writer, compared with its leniency towards another whose work might seem at least equally objectionable from the point of view of conventional morality, is often to be found in its belief that the one is basically orthodox, the other free-thinking or 'jacobinical'. One of the wisest observations in Burke is that it is a matter of great difficulty to decide how far an abuse should be tolerated, for fear of the greater harm that may come from a drastic reformation. At this period the defenders of the Church and of the established order as a whole were often driven by an exaggerated terror of innovation to defend the indefensible. In *Melincourt* Mr. Vamp, the editor of the *Legitimate Review*, addresses a new recruit in the following words:

You see this pile of pamphlets, these volumes of poetry, and this rascally quarto: all these, though under very different titles, and the productions of very different orders of mind, have, either openly or covertly, only one object; and a most impertinent one it is. This object is two-fold: first, to prove the existence, to an immense extent, of what these writers think proper to denominate political corruption; secondly, to convince the public that this corruption ought to be extinguished. Now, we are anxious to do away with the effect of all these incendiary clamours. As to the existence of corruption . . . a villanous word . . . we call it *persuasion in a tangible shape* . . . we do not wish to deny it; . . . but as to the inference that it ought to be extinguished—that is the point against which we direct the full fire of our critical artillery. (Chap. xiii.)

Peacock here uses no more than the legitimate exaggeration of the satirist. Scott's hope that the Quarterly Reviewers would not 'forget the Gentleman in the Critic' was destined to be disappointed. If, as he believed, the public was 'wearied with universal efforts at blackguard and indiscriminating satire' in the *Edinburgh Review*, the advent of the *Quarterly* merely gave them a choice as to who was to be assailed. As Southey had written in his *Letters from England* in 1807,

Criticism is to a large class of men what Scandal is to women,— and women not infrequently bear their part in it;—it is indeed Scandal in masquerade. Upon an opinion picked up from these journals, upon an extract fairly or unfairly quoted,—for the reviewers scruple not at misquotations, at omissions which alter the meaning, or mispunctuations which destroy it,—you shall hear a whole company talk as confidently about a book as if they had read it.

By an irony of history Southey's accusation—like Copleston's brilliantly ironical *Advice to a Young Reviewer*—damages the

Quarterly, to which both men were to be contributors, more severely than the *Edinburgh* and the *British Critic*, which were the targets of their attack. And it is difficult not to feel that the men who wrote in the *Quarterly* lacked the excuse of the first contributors (at least) to the *Edinburgh*. They were not young, and they were not in opposition. While the two Reviews are of equal importance to the student of history, the literary importance of the *Edinburgh* is much greater than that of its opponent. While Southey and Scott were almost the only first-rate men of letters who wrote regularly in the *Quarterly*, the *Edinburgh* had a constellation of talent including Hazlitt, Macaulay, Carlyle, and Jeffrey himself.

Long before the appearance of the first number of the *Westminster Review* in 1824 Jeremy Bentham and James Mill had discussed the need for a Radical Review to oppose both the *Edinburgh* and the *Quarterly*. The founding of the new Review is described in the *Autobiography* of John Stuart Mill. From the first it had been 'a favourite portion of the scheme' that the Radical Review should analyse the reasonings of its opponents, and to the first issue James Mill contributed a long criticism of the *Edinburgh Review* from its commencement. Beginning with a penetrating characterization of periodical literature in general, he went on to give a Radical interpretation of the British Constitution and to relate the conduct of the two great Reviews to this pattern:

He held up to notice its thoroughly aristocratic character: the nomination of a majority of the House of Commons by a few hundred families; the entire identification of the more independent portion, the county members, with the great landholders; the different classes whom this narrow oligarchy was induced, for convenience, to admit to a share of power; and finally, what he called its two props, the Church, and the legal profession. He pointed out the natural tendency of an aristocratic body of this composition, to group itself into two parties, one of them in possession of the executive, the other endeavouring to supplant the former and become the predominant section by the aid of public opinion, without any essential sacrifice of the aristocratical predominance. He described the course likely to be pursued, and the political ground occupied, by an aristocratic party in opposition, coquetting with popular principles for the sake of popular support. He showed how this idea was realized in the conduct of the Whig party and of the Edinburgh Review as its chief literary organ. (*Autobiography* of J. S. Mill, Chap. iv.)

This exceptionally able article was followed by a continuation by John Stuart Mill in the second issue and by an equally shrewd analysis of the conduct of the *Quarterly* in a later number. It is hardly surprising that the advent of the *Westminster Review* created something of a sensation. Most of the Whigs were furious, while the Tories were astonished to find the *Edinburgh* appearing almost respectable by comparison with the whole-hearted iconoclasm of the new Radical Review. More will be said about the *Westminster* and its contributors in the last chapter, when the time has come to survey the literary scene in the late 1820's and early 30's.

From the literary point of view the Magazines of the time were hardly less important than the Reviews. The *Gentleman's Magazine*, to which Samuel Johnson had so often contributed, continued to appear throughout our period and far beyond it. By 1815, however, its appearance was distinctly antiquated: it was an obvious relic from the days of bohea and full-bottomed wigs. Although the *Monthly Magazine*, which had begun in 1796, had at first promised well, it soon became tame and unadventurous. It was when *Blackwood's Magazine* fell into the hands of Lockhart and John Wilson in October 1817 that a new chapter opened in the history of the Magazine. That was the opinion of Charles Knight:

The new era of Magazines may be said to have commenced in 1817. In that year 'Blackwood's Edinburgh Magazine' startled the London publishers into a conviction that for a new generation of readers more attractive fare might be provided than at some of the old established *restaurateurs*, whose dishes were neither light, nor elegant, nor altogether wholesome. When Blackwood was started— apparently without any very correct knowledge that something was wanted in periodical literature beyond political bitterness—the old magazines and their new rivals had gone on without much deviation from the hackneyed paths in which they had first walked. (*Passages of a Working Life*, i. 265.)

De Quincey agreed with Knight in regarding *Blackwood's* as an important innovation. Writing to its publisher in 1830 he pointed out that the Tories had always been in the habit of following rather than leading the way, giving as examples the *Edinburgh* and *Quarterly Reviews*, 'the two London Universities' (University College and King's College), and 'the cheap bodies of popular literature' provided on the one hand by the supporters of Reform and on the other by the conservative upholders of the established constitution. 'I doubt . . . whether there has been one exception', he wrote, 'beyond that of your own journal. You unquestionably had no precedent, though you have since had so many followers.' De Quincey considered this the more creditable because, whereas the *Quarterly* had from the first been 'a pet child of the family', *Blackwood's* had been obliged to make its way 'as a foundling or an adventurer would'. In fact the adventurous young Scotsmen who ran *Blackwood's* had more in common with the founders of the *Edinburgh* than with those of the *Quarterly*. Where they differed from Jeffrey and his companions was in the temper of their minds. Whereas the founders of the *Edinburgh Review* had certain measures of reform which they were eager to promote, and usually managed to restrain their love of mischief to gain these ends, it is hard to escape the conclusion that for Lockhart and 'Christopher North' mischief was an end in itself. It is true that they were convinced Tories; but they were also inveterate bullies. Their idea was an excellent one: to produce something less ponderous than the *Quarterly*, a nimbler periodical which should not give the impression of having been written throughout by a number of very senior and very disgruntled members of the House of Lords. They were even prepared to make concessions to readers whose classical education was imperfect: as the editor remarked on one occasion, translating a quotation in a footnote, 'everybody is not bound to know Greek'. *Blackwood's* deserves commendation for publishing short stories and serializing longer works of fiction— a practice incompatible with the nature of a Review. Several of Galt's books, including *The Ayrshire Legatees*, first appeared as serials in *Blackwood's*, as did two books by Michael Scott, *Tom Cringle's Log* and *The Cruise of the Midge*. The *Magazine* also included a good deal of literary criticism, some of it (including some of the articles on novels) of a high standard.

Two pieces of professedly literary criticism which were by no means of a high standard appeared in the issue of *Blackwood's* for October 1817, however, and ensured for 'Maga' a high circulation and a bad name in literary history. The 'Translation from an Ancient Chaldee Manuscript' is an allegory in pseudo-Biblical language describing the conflict between the publishers

Blackwood and Constable from a Tory point of view. At this time of day it is difficult to understand why a crude piece of pleasantry of the sort that one might find in a school magazine should have caused such a sensation in Edinburgh. For the worst passage, that on the cripple James Graham Dalyell, Blackwood was obliged to pay damages out of court. Although he seems at first to have been taken aback by the outcry, Blackwood was one of the first men to discover the important truth that lies behind so much gutter-journalism today, that every pound paid in damages represents a large accession of new readers. The authorship of the Chaldee article was industriously concealed, but we now know that the idea was Hogg's, while Lockhart and Wilson were the principal writers. The justice of Lockhart's description of himself as 'the scorpion, which delighteth to sting the faces of men' is borne out by the series of articles 'On the Cockney School of Poetry' which began in the same issue. Over a period of several years a running fire was kept up against Leigh Hunt and a number of other writers known to be associated with him. 'Z' maintains that it is presumption for such a poetaster to publish verse when men of the calibre of Wordsworth and Byron are writing. The most curious aspect of the criticism is its basis in snobbery. 'All the great poets of our country have been men of some rank in society', 'Z' wrote, 'and there is no vulgarity in any of their writings; but Mr. Hunt cannot utter a dedication, or even a note, without betraying the *Shibboleth* of low birth and low habits.' There is perhaps just a grain of truth in this remark, but when the reviewer moves from Hunt's poetry to talk of 'the extreme moral depravity of the Cockney School' he completely loses our sympathy. It is interesting to notice that Blackwood softened the attack in the second edition of this number, and that in January of the following year 'Z' himself was disingenuous enough to write: 'When I charged you with depraved morality, obscenity, and indecency, I spoke not of Leigh Hunt as a man . . . I judged of you from your works.' Blackwood's own attitude to these attacks is manifest in a letter which he sent Thomas Cadell in April 1823, when the latter expressed his concern about the attacks on Hazlitt: 'The public will be completely on the side of the Magazine for attacking such a nest of infidels and profligates as Hazlitt, Hunt, Byron & Co. who are daily outraging not only private character, but every thing sacred & civil. So far therefore from there being any thing discreditable in the Magazine having attacked such a vile person as Hazlitt it will rather be considered as the reverse.' After reading some of the personal abuse in *Blackwood's* it is extraordinary to come on the preface to Volume XIX, for the year 1826:

Before we appeared, the art of criticism was indeed a truly miserable concern. The critic looked upon the poet as his prey. The two were always at daggers-drawing. The insolence of reviewers had reached its acme, and absolutely stunk in the nostrils of the Public. Yet still there was a power in the rancid breath to taint, if not to wither. Men of genius were insulted by tenth-rate scribblers, without head or heart; and all conversational criticism was pitched on the same key with that of the wretched reviews. We put an end to this in six months. A warm, enthusiastic, imaginative, and, at the same time, philosophical spirit, breathed through every article. Authors felt that they were understood and appreciated, and readers were delighted to have their own uncorrupted feelings authorized and sanctioned. In another year the whole periodical criticism of Britain underwent a revolution. . . . The authority of the Pragmatic Faction was annihilated, and no Zany-Zoilus in the Blue and Yellow could any longer outcrow the reading Public.

The whole history of criticism cannot show a more flagrant instance of 'men of genius' being insulted by 'tenth-rate scribblers' than the attacks on Keats and Hazlitt in 'Maga'. Perhaps the fact that they were not 'gentlemen' was taken as an excuse: their initial offence, certainly, was their association with Hunt. 'The two great elements of all dignified poetry', 'Z' observed of Hunt's writings, 'religious feeling, and patriotic feeling, have no place in his mind. His religion is a poor tame dilution of the blasphemies of the *Encyclopaedie*—his patriotism a crude, vague, ineffectual, and sour Jacobinism. He is without reverence either for God or man.' Voltaire would have been amused by the Christian spirit with which the anonymous libeller set about bullying his victims into a more religious frame of mind. It is hardly worth detailing the attacks made in other numbers—attacks which led Murray to give up the London agency for 'Maga', and for which Blackwood was more than once obliged to come to a settlement with the men whom he had libelled (as he was with Hazlitt). Perhaps too much has been made of the attacks on Keats and Shelley by biographers in the hagiographical tradition. In some respects Lockhart and his associates were merely reverting to the rough-and-tumble of the early eighteenth century, which survived in Edinburgh longer than in the south. But the anonymity and the flagrant inconsistency of the attacks leave a bad taste in the mouth, and it is impossible to forget that whereas the attackers were men of only moderate talents, secure and prosperous for the most part in their worldly positions, the attacked were men of genius who were struggling for a livelihood if not, like Keats, for life itself. A man who could describe Keats, after his death, as 'a young man who had left a decent calling for the melancholy trade of Cockney-poetry, [who] has lately died of a consumption, after having written two or three little books of verses, much neglected by the public' and add that 'he wrote *indecently*, probably in the indulgence of his social propensities', has won critical immortality of a sort, and it is an effort to remember that Lockhart was also the author of a remarkable biography and of some intelligent literary criticism.

As the *Edinburgh Review* led to the *Quarterly*, so *Blackwood's Edinburgh Magazine* led to Baldwin's *London Magazine*. The original editor, John Scott, was himself a considerable man of letters—his *Visit to Paris in 1814* and *Paris Revisited, in 1815*, are unusual and perceptive books—who had already had the experience of running a newspaper called the *Champion*. His object was to present the same mixture of essays, poems, criticism, and general comment as might be found in *Blackwood's*, which he considered 'a great improvement . . . on the general run of magazines' because it had 'a spirit of life, not usually characterising such publications'. As we read the *London Magazine* we notice that its contributors are more often pseudonymous than anonymous, and that we are being encouraged to feel that we are in the company of friends. The contributors' dinners seem to have been organized with the definite aim of giving the writers a sense of community, and Lamb makes it clear how much this meant to him. Certainly no editor has ever gathered round himself a more brilliant circle of writers. It was in the pages of the *London Magazine* that De Quincey's *Confessions* first appeared, as well as the *Essays of Elia*. Much of Hazlitt's *Table Talk* had the same origin, while poems by Keats, Clare, Hood, and John Hamilton Reynolds may also be found in the *London*, as well as numerous contributions by Hartley Coleridge, Darley, and Allan Cunningham. In reviewing, the aim was to be fairness uninfluenced by political passion: while Scott himself and many of his contributors had strong liberal sympathies, his magazine differed from *Blackwood's* in being as far as possible from a party organ. A particular feature of the criticism was the belief that 'more pains should be taken to search out for the beauties than the faults' of the books criticized. Whereas the Edinburgh Reviewers often aspired to write their criticism against some sort of framework of critical and aesthetic theory, the Londoners were more empirical. In this respect—rather surprisingly—John Scott believed that *Blackwood's* had made a noteworthy advance: 'It has done important service to the cause of taste and truth by its poetical criticisms . . . [by showing] a just and quick feeling of the elements of poetical beauty and power: it has vindicated . . . several neglected and calumniated, but highly deserving poetical reputations . . . the subtlety and delicacy of which cause them to escape the grosser vision of the . . . Edinburgh and Quarterly Reviews.' It would be hard to find a passage throwing more light on the transition from one kind of eighteenth-century criticism to one kind of nineteenth-century criticism. At first Scott hoped to avoid conflict with *Blackwood's*, but he soon found that this was impossible. The poets particularly commended in the first half-dozen numbers of the *London* are Wordsworth, Keats, Shelley, and Clare, and Scott soon felt it his duty to defend the 'Cockneys' against the assaults of his rival. At the end of 1820 Charles Brown wrote delightedly to Keats telling him that Scott 'is doing a thing that tickles me to the heart's core. . . . By some means . . . he has got possession of one of Blackwood's gang, who has turned King's evidence, and month after month he belabours them with the most damning facts'. In his first open attack on 'The Mohock Magazine' Scott took as his motto the words 'They do but jest—POISON IN JEST—no offence i' the world.' The subsequent story of how Scott was killed in a duel by John Christie (deputizing for Lockhart) is part of literary history. It may be summed up by saying that the editor of the most brilliant magazine ever produced in England was killed because he dared to expose the libels published by a cowardly and dishonest rival. After his death the publishers Taylor and Hessey took over the *London*, John Taylor himself acting as editor with the assistance of Thomas Hood. For another three and a half years there continued to be some outstanding contributions, although Taylor

offended some of his contributors by revising their work: then
came a sudden decline, and the *London* was just an ordinary
magazine. There is no need to say more about its astonishing
heyday at this point because a great deal of the literature discussed in later chapters made its first appearance in its pages.

Colburn's *New Monthly Magazine* was founded in 1814 to
oppose Sir Richard Phillips's *Monthly Magazine*. The 'Address
to the Public' prefixed to the first six issues in June of that year
directly attacks the *Monthly*, 'whose Editor, nursed in the School
of Jacobinism, commenced his career as a promulgator of Paine's
Rights of Man, and who, with all the consistency of our pseudo-
patriots, has of late years been one of the most zealous wor-
shippers of that Moloch, Buonaparte. The political poison so
artfully introduced into every department of that work [the
Address continues] and mixed up with a due proportion of
ribaldry and irreligion, was calculated to produce a mischievous
impression upon the minds of the unthinking and inexperienced.'
To all this the new *Magazine* is to be the antidote. In fact
a number of different phases may be traced in the history of
the *New Monthly*, and it was under the editorship of Thomas
Campbell, which started in 1821, that it began to be of literary
importance. In the preface to his first volume Campbell informs
us that he has 'no pretensions to rank among the periodical
publishers of the time, who struggle for the honour of directing,
or deeply influencing, political opinion. It does not follow'—he
continues—'from the general utility of political discussion, that
it should invariably pervade every species of literary compilation, or that there should be no calm spot in the world of
periodical literature where all minds of common charity and
candour may meet without the asperities of party feeling.' The
fact that Colburn paid Campbell £500 a year, as well as providing him with a sub-editor, demonstrates very clearly the
possibilities which publishers were now seeing in magazines.
But a timid man seldom makes a good editor, and the difference
between the *London* and the *New Monthly* may be stated by saying that whereas John Scott had wished to avoid bitterness and
party conflict if he honourably could, Campbell was determined to avoid controversy at all costs. As a result he failed
to stamp his own character on the magazine which he edited.
He was deeply disconcerted at having published an article
which had given offence 'on the other side of the Atlantic', and

the passage in which he acknowledges this has some interest as a document in Anglo-American literary relations. Yet it must be admitted that Campbell and his publisher succeeded in finding able contributors. 'Colburn is making magnificent offers', we find Miss Mitford writing to a friend on 12 December 1820. 'He has proffered twenty guineas a sheet (five more than Hazlitt gets for the "Table Talk" in the "London") to Horace Smith (one of the "Rejected Addressers", you know) for any contribution, prose or verse, and he will give Talfourd his weight in gold rather than part with him.' It is not surprising that Hazlitt transferred his *Table Talk*: his fine essay 'On Going a Journey' appeared in the *New Monthly* in January 1822, and a good many other of his best essays first appeared in the same periodical. By 1831–3, when the Countess of Blessington's 'Conversations with Lord Byron' were serialized, Bulwer Lytton had become editor and the *New Monthly* had ceased to be a 'quiet spot' and become a hurricane centre. As one looks through the volumes today, the change is very welcome; but Colburn's public had come to expect *belles lettres* without controversy from this particular periodical, and Bulwer Lytton's reforming zeal was too much for them. After three eventful years he resigned and made way for Theodore Hook.

The independence of the *New Monthly* was frequently jeopardized by Colburn's determination to promote the sale of his own publications, and it is interesting to notice that both the *Athenaeum* (1828) and *Fraser's Magazine* (1830) made a point of their avoidance of literary 'puffery'. An advertisement for *Fraser's* published soon after its commencement emphasized that 'The Journal is not connected with any large publishing house, and the public have therefore a guarantee that its opinions will neither be sold for lucre, nor biassed by self-interest.' But an account of these two distinguished periodicals belongs to the next volume of this *History*, and it is time to say something of the importance of the leading publishers.

The names of Archibald Constable and John Murray will always be remembered when the *Edinburgh* and the *Quarterly* are mentioned, and indeed the great publishers of the nineteenth century deserve the same sort of attention as the great patrons of the Elizabethan Age. 'A literary man of the present day', wrote a journalist in the *News of Literature* for 10 December 1825, 'would as soon think of seeking patronage from the Emperor of

Austria, or setting forth the talents and the virtues of the Spanish Ferdinand, as of placing his hopes of a hearing with the public upon the foremost nobleman in the land'; and he went on to point out that 'this change has brought the publishers of books into an attitude of the greatest importance and honour;—it has made them the connecting link between the people of England and that which has made, is making, and shall continue to make the people of England superior to the people of every land where intellect has not the same unbounded scope.' In fact patronage was not dead: men like Sir George Beaumont and Lord Holland did a great deal for writers. But it is true that it was now through the publishers that the great majority of authors earned their living. As in most periods, it need hardly be said, the writers of the age had very different opinions of the middlemen on whose services they depended. Thomas Moore recalls a conversation 'chiefly about the profits booksellers make of us scribblers' at which John Wolcot ('Peter Pindar') asserted that booksellers 'drank their wine in the manner of the heroes in the hall of Odin, out of authors' skulls', while in 1833 R. H. Horne had some hard things to say in his curious *Exposition of the False Medium and Barriers Excluding Men of Genius from the Public*. The chief complaint made by the man who was to publish his epic at a farthing[1] as a protest against the public's lack of interest in poetry is that publishers place too much reliance on the opinion of ill-qualified 'readers' and are excessively unwilling to take risks: once a new writer or a new vein of writing has won favour they will compete for the publishing rights: novelty is too dangerous. The impression that we form when we read the histories of the great publishing houses of the period is very different, and although it is difficult to know how much allowance should be made for the fact that these were uniformly written on behalf of the firms themselves, we are likely to conclude that the authors of the period were on the whole fortunate in the men of business with whom they had to deal. It was to the advantage of writers that the trade was expanding at this time, and becoming more competitive: one of the advantages of publishing a successful Review or Magazine was, indeed, that it attracted authors. In May 1821 Thomas Cadell wrote to William Blackwood: 'I sympathize with you . . . with regard to

---

[1] Horne's instructions were that only those who pronounced the title correctly were to be given *Orion* for $\frac{1}{4}d$.

Murray's procuring the publication of almost all the new Works of consequence, which, I conceive is occasioned by the extensive literary connexion attached to the publication of the "Quarterly Review".' It was Constable who had made this discovery, with the *Edinburgh*, and this is only one example of his flair for discovering and directing the public taste. 'To Archibald Constable', Cockburn wrote in his *Memorials*:

the literature of Scotland has been more indebted than to any other bookseller. Till he appeared, our publishing trade was at nearly the lowest ebb. . . . He rushed out, and took possession of the open field, as if he had been aware from the first of the . . . latent spirits, which a skilful conjurer might call from the depths of the population to the service of literature. Abandoning the old timid and grudging system, he stood out as the general patron and payer of all promising publications, and confounded not merely his rivals in trade, but his very authors, by his unheard-of prices. Ten, even twenty, guineas a sheet for a review, £2,000 or £3,000 for a single poem, and £1,000 each for two philosophical dissertations, drew authors from dens where they would otherwise have starved, and made Edinburgh a literary mart, famous with strangers, and the pride of its own citizens.[1]

It was not only the literature of Scotland that was indebted to Constable, and Scott was wholly in the right when he urged him to make memoranda of his life and dealings because his career had been 'of uncommon importance to literature'. Every book about Scott is also a book about Constable, whom even Lockhart (who treats him unfairly) refers to as 'the grand Napoleon of the realms of print'. Apart from Scott's own writings, the publication of which forms the dramatic central plot of his career, Constable made a speciality of 'curious and valuable works relative to the history and literature of Scotland' and there is justice in his claim to have been the first publisher 'who took a deep interest in securing and preserving all books relating to Scottish literature'. It is natural that it should have been to him that Lockhart wrote, at the end of 1814: 'I have been amusing myself with writing a novel, and as it chiefly regards Scotland, I should wish to have it printed in Edinburgh. I am

[1] Archibald Constable (1774–1827) began life as a bookseller's apprentice in Edinburgh. In 1798 he began to publish pamphlets and sermons on his own account, and soon he was interesting himself in periodicals. In 1802 he started the *Edinburgh Review* and began his association with Sir Walter Scott. In 1826 he became bankrupt through the failure of his London agents. His *Miscellany* is mentioned in Chapter XV.

sensible that much has been done of late years in the description of our national manners, but there are still, I apprehend, many important classes of Scotch society quite untouched.' Although in the end Constable did not publish any of Lockhart's novels, a list of the books on Scottish subjects which he did publish would be extensive and impressive. Nor were his activities confined to Scottish books. What he regarded as his 'greatest speculation' was his purchase of the *Encyclopaedia Britannica* in 1812: by 1826, when he sold it to A. & C. Black, it had grown and improved greatly under the editorship of Macvey Napier. The appearance of the first volume of *Constable's Miscellany* in 1827, dedicated to George IV, marked an important era in Constable's own career and in the development of the cheap literature which was to be so striking a feature of the Victorian Age.

John Murray resembled Constable in having his Review and his best-seller of genius.[1] Like other leading publishers of the time he realized that to treat publishing as a profession need not make it less profitable as a trade, and as the historian of the firm points out, about the year 1815 'Murray's drawing room was the main centre of literary intercourse' in his quarter of London. 'Men of distinction, from the Continent and America, presented their letters of introduction to Mr. Murray, and were cordially and hospitably entertained by him; meeting, in the course of their visits, many distinguished and notable personages.' Among the pictures of authors whom he had published there were in his drawing-room portraits of Byron, Scott, Coleridge, Southey, Lockhart, and Crabbe. It was at Murray's in 1815 that the American George Ticknor made the acquaintance of Moore, Campbell, Isaac D'Israeli, Gifford, and Humphry Davy. There is a tradition that the idea for the Athenæum Club was first discussed in Murray's drawing-room, and Humphry Ward points out in his *History of the Athenæum* that the five 'persons of acknowledged literary eminence' mentioned by Croker in his letter to Davy about the founding of the Club were all 'habitués of Murray's literary assemblies'. In an interesting little

---

[1] John Murray (1778–1843) was a Scot who emigrated to London. For a short time he acted as Constable's agent, but in 1809 he started the *Quarterly Review* in opposition to the *Edinburgh*. In 1812 he moved to Albemarle Street and became acquainted with Byron. His publication of Mrs. Mariana Starke's *Guide for Travellers on the Continent* in 1820 led to his well-known series of guide-books. Byron's Memoirs were burnt in the grate in his parlour.

book called *Bibliophobia* the bibliographer T. F. Dibdin tells us that Murray was 'among the very first booksellers of his day who treated authors, of character and connection, with the respect due to gentlemen'—a statement in which the qualification is hardly less revealing than the principal affirmation. As soon as he read *English Bards and Scotch Reviewers* Murray conceived the desire of publishing something of Byron's, and he soon became the publisher of *Childe Harold's Pilgrimage* and most of his other writings. He also became the recipient of a great many of Byron's letters—letters which were not intended as a private correspondence. As Moore points out in his biography, 'to keep the minds of the English public for ever occupied about him' was 'the constant ambition' of Byron's soul and 'in the correspondence he so regularly maintained with his publisher, one of the chief mediums through which this object was to be effected lay'. Since, as Moore goes on to explain, Murray's house was 'the resort of most of those literary men who are, at the same time, men of the world, his Lordship knew that whatever particulars he might wish to make public concerning himself, would, if transmitted to that quarter, be sure to circulate from thence throughout society'. In Chapter II I shall suggest that something of the tone of *Don Juan* may be attributed to the fact that Byron had Murray's circle in mind as an audience—a small circle of intelligent, classically educated, men of the world. If this is true it is ironical that what Byron called Murray's 'cursed puritanical committee'—an odd description for a group of men including Moore, Hookham Frere, and Hobhouse—were obliged from the first to warn the publisher of the danger of being associated with such a poem. Although Murray published the first few Cantos, they did not bear his imprint, and no review of any part of the poem appeared in either the *Quarterly* or the *Edinburgh*. 'I am sorry to say it is a book which I could not sell on any account whatever', Blackwood wrote to Murray from George Street, Edinburgh. It was only after careful consideration that Murray's legal advisers were satisfied that copyright in so scandalous a publication would be valid in law:

> Through needles' eyes it easier for the camel is
> To pass, than those two cantos into families

—as Byron himself complained, near the end of Canto IV. The

later Cantos were published by John Hunt, Leigh Hunt's brother, who was to be prosecuted in 1822–3 for publishing *The Vision of Judgment*. But Murray was to be the publisher of most of Byron's writings, and the connexion between the poet and the publisher continued after Byron's death with the publication of Moore's *Letters and Journals of Lord Byron*—and continues to this day. With *Emma* in 1816 Murray became Jane Austen's publisher, and while she calls him 'a rogue of course' we notice that in the same breath she calls herself a mercenary author. Murray was also the publisher of some of the works of Coleridge, of Southey, of Hookham Frere, and more suprisingly of Leigh Hunt. He produced a great many travel books, Napier's *History of the Peninsular War*, and the English translation of Mme. de Staël's influential book, *De l'Allemagne*.

William Blackwood was another of the important publishers of the day.[1] 'Like the other publishers of the age', as Mrs. Oliphant remarks in her *Annals of a Publishing House*, 'it had been Blackwood's desire from the beginning to make his place of business a centre of literary society, a sort of literary club where men of letters might find a meeting-place.' Like Constable, Blackwood specialized in books of Scottish interest. The article by Jeffrey on 'Secondary Scottish Novels' in the *Edinburgh Review* for October 1823 deals with a dozen books, including seven by John Galt and three by Lockhart, and every one of them had been published by Blackwood. Blackwood also published Susan Ferrier's *Marriage* and *The Inheritance*, with their acute satirical descriptions of the Scottish scene. His poetical list was less distinguished, but it included numerous volumes by James Hogg, 'The Ettrick Shepherd', as well as a good deal that no one continues to read, such as the poems of 'Christopher North' and 'Delta' (D. M. Moir, the friend of De Quincey). Perhaps the most popular of all the poems that he published was Pollok's *Course of Time*, a work which resembles *Paradise Lost* in two respects, and in two respects only: it is written in blank verse, and it takes for its subject the whole significance of human history. It was a common joke that Blackwood never met an author without inviting him to contribute to his *Magazine*, and it is

[1] Like Constable, William Blackwood (1776–1834) began life as an apprentice-bookseller in Edinburgh. After periods in Glasgow and London he started publishing on his own account in Edinburgh in 1804. A few years later he was the principal founder of the *Edinburgh Encyclopædia*.

noticeable that most of the memorable books which he published were by contributors.

If anyone should ask which Magazine of the period published most that was later to be reprinted in volume form, however, the answer would certainly be the *London Magazine*. Taylor and Hessey were never a large firm, but they published an extraordinary number of valuable books, and the fact that they never made much money should serve as a reminder that publishing good books was no more a certain road to commercial success in this period than in any other. From their *Magazine* they republished De Quincey's *Confessions*, the *Essays of Elia*, and a great deal else. They also published two of Hazlitt's most notable series of lectures, *The English Poets* and *The English Comic Writers*. They published Keats, and they published Clare. Like other publishers of the time they sometimes behaved with considerable generosity towards writers in whom they believed: when Keats went to Italy in search of health, he went with money lent him by his publisher. R. H. Horne explicitly exempts Taylor and Hessey from his censures on the publishing houses of the day. It was Taylor and Hessey who reprinted Cary's translation of Dante, which had at first been poorly produced and which had attracted little notice: when Coleridge recommended it to them they responded by bringing out a beautifully printed edition, as well as disposing of the pocket edition which was the only book that Keats took with him on his Scottish tour. Horne insists that Taylor's superiority to his fellows was due to the fact that he did not employ a 'reader', and it is true that Taylor was himself a literary man, and a fine judge of poetry. There is no doubt that he made improvements in the text of Clare—notably in that of his finest volume, *The Shepherd's Calendar*—and while Keats was angry at his slight bowdlerization of *The Eve of St. Agnes*, it is quite possible that Taylor also suggested one or two minor improvements in the text of his poems.

One reason for Taylor and Hessey's lack of commercial success may have been the fact that they did not interest themselves in novels. If they knew a great writer when they saw one, Henry Colburn of Conduit Street knew a best-seller, and novels were his speciality. 'The first of the gambling publishers'—as Michael Sadleir describes him in the second volume of his bibliography, *XIX Century Fiction*—Colburn

regarded every author as having his price and the public as gullible

fools. He cared nothing about book-design, nothing about craftsmanship. Cheapest was best, so long as the leaves held together. . . . He
had no literary taste of his own, merely an instinctive sense of the
taste of the moment. In consequence . . . he published on the basis
of quick turn-over, and made a fortune for himself by sheer topical
ingenuity. . . . Impervious to snubs; cheerful under vilification, so
long as insults meant more business; thinking in hundreds where
others thought in tens, Colburn revolutionised publishing in its every
aspect. . . . He developed advertising . . . to a degree hitherto
undreamt of. He had his diners-out who talked up his books at
dinner-tables and soirées; he debauched the critics and put
them on his pay-sheet. . . . He was a book-manufacturer, not a
publisher.

Some of Colburn's authors, such as Bulwer Lytton, were men
of high abilities; but the majority were merely concerned to give
the public what it wanted. We think of him not as the publisher of Hazlitt's *Spirit of the Age* but as the imprint on a thousand ephemeral novels of the time. Longman, with his partners
Hurst, Rees, Orme, and Brown, is remembered for his com-
mercially accurate estimate of the value of the second edition
of *Lyrical Ballads* as zero. He published *The Excursion* at a loss,
in a handsome quarto; and was also responsible for producing
a good deal of the work of Coleridge and Southey. Some of
Scott's poems, in which he had a large share, had proved much
more profitable—as had the poetry of Thomas Moore. The firm
had a good reputation. As Moore wrote in his diary, 'there are
few tributes from authors to publishers on record more honourable, (or, I will venture to say, more deserved) than those that
will be found among my papers relative to my transactions for
many years between myself and my friends of the Row'. Other
publishers who can only be mentioned here are Charles and
James Ollier, who published *The Cenci*, *Prometheus Unbound*,
and the (pre-Elian) *Works* of Charles Lamb, and Edward
Moxon, most agreeable of minor poets and most honourable
of publishers.

The fact that some of the leading publishers were enlightened
and even generous men does not mean that the profession of
letters was an easy one at this time. Then, as now, the advice
of the seasoned practitioner to the young aspirant was that of
Mr. Punch to those about to marry. When the Quaker poet
Bernard Barton told Charles Lamb that he was thinking of

resigning his position in a bank in order to devote himself to writing, Lamb replied in a famous letter:

> Throw yourself rather, my dear Sir, from the steep Tarpeian rock, slap-dash headlong upon iron spikes. . . . The Booksellers . . . are Turks and Tartars, when they have poor Authors at their beck. . . . I have known many authors for bread, some repining, others envying the blessed security of a Counting House, all agreeing they had rather have been Taylors, Weavers, what not? rather than the things they were. I have known some starved, some to go mad, one dear friend literally dying in a workhouse. . . . Keep to your Bank, and the Bank will keep you.

It was not merely because Barton was a bad poet that Lamb gave him this advice—indeed he had a fondness for Barton's poetry: he was simply speaking from his own experience as a writer. Byron gave Barton the same warning: 'Do not renounce writing', he wrote on 1 June 1812, 'but never trust entirely to authorship. If you have a profession, retain it; it will be, like Prior's fellowship, a last and sure resource.' Scott repeatedly gave similar advice to those who asked for guidance. And here is what Leigh Hunt wrote in his *Autobiography*, after a lifetime's experience:

> Nor was I able, had I been never so inclined, to render my faculties profitable 'in the market'. It is easy to say to a man—Write such and such a thing, and it is sure to sell. Watch the public taste, and act accordingly. Care not for original composition; for inventions or theories of your own. . . . Stick to the works of others. Write only in magazines and reviews. Or if you must write things of your own, compile . . . Do anything but write to the few, and you may get rich. There is a great deal of truth in all this. But a man can only do what he can, or as others will let him.

The considered judgement of perhaps the most complete professional of the time, Southey, also deserves to be heard. Writing to John Murray in August 1812 he gave it as his opinion that 'literature in almost all cases is the worst trade to which a man can possibly betake himself', though he commended it as a pursuit for men of fortune and leisure. For his own part, he adds, he has never regretted his choice of a literary career; but this is because it has brought him many friends and the good opinion of many of 'the best and wisest and most celebrated of my contemporaries'. If he lives another twenty years—he adds—

then literature will give him 'fortune'. In fact Southey lived for more than twenty years longer, but literature never gave him a fortune, though it did provide him with a competence. It did less for many of his contemporaries.

Of course a number of writers did make spectacular profits at this time. Even before the advent of Scott very high prices had occasionally been paid for best-selling novels. According to Sir Samuel Egerton Brydges (an unreliable witness) prices as high as £1,500 and £2,000 were on occasion paid to Maria Edgeworth and Sydney Owenson (later Lady Morgan), and it is certain that the latter received £1,200 for *Florence Macarthy*, a novel of little merit that retains some interest because of its portrayal of Croker as Conway Townsend Crawley. But it was Scott who made the writing of romances 'big business'. By 1818, according to Lockhart, 'the annual profits of his novels alone had, for several years, been not less than £10,000'. Early the following year Constable agreed to give Scott £12,000 for his then existing copyrights. In 1821, when Scott had already earned at least £10,000 from *Ivanhoe*, *The Monastery*, *The Abbot*, and *Kenilworth* (four books written in little more than a year), Constable agreed to pay him 5,000 guineas for the remaining copyright in these works. Two years later the publisher bought Scott's copyright in *The Pirate*, *The Fortunes of Nigel*, *Peveril of the Peak*, and *Quentin Durward* for another 5,000 guineas. Lockhart sums up the rather complicated position as follows: 'He had thus paid for the copyright of novels (over and above the half profits of the early separate editions) the sum of £22,500; and his advances upon "works of fiction" still in embryo, amounted at this moment to £10,000 more.' It was not without good reason that Scott once told Moore that his books had been 'a mine of wealth' to him. One can only guess how much he earned by his pen during his lifetime, but something like £100,000 would seem a conservative figure; and the value of money was much greater in Scott's time than it is today. Nor did his earnings cease with his death: about the beginning of 1833 we find Cadell advancing Scott's executors £30,000 on the security of Scott's copyrights and literary remains. After this the sums made by other novelists come as something of an anti-climax, yet it is interesting to notice that Susan Ferrier earned £1,000 from *The Inheritance* and a considerably larger sum from *Destiny*. At the end of 1815 Godwin tried to persuade Constable that two and three thousand pounds had on occasion been paid for novels. We know as a fact that Blackwood gave Lockhart £1,000 for *Reginald Dalton*; while Horace Smith received £500 for *Brambletye House*, and then a further £100 from Colburn on account of its high sales. G. R. Gleig was paid £750 for *The Chelsea Pensioners*. In his diary for 24 September 1837 Moore describes how Richard Bentley has been to visit him at breakfast-time, 'full of impatience and ardour for something of mine to publish,—a light Eastern tale, in three volumes. Scene, Circassia; events, founded on the struggle of that people against Russia, and price £1500, with two-thirds of the copyright my own.' As this record of an unwritten novel may serve to remind us, there was little correlation between the merit of a novel and the sum which its author was paid. Scott was a man of genius, but the effect of his romances was cumulative and he made more from some of his inferior books than from *The Heart of Mid-Lothian*. By the time of her death Jane Austen seems to have made less than £1,000 from her novels.

A few works in prose, other than novels, made a good deal of money for their writers. Travel books and books about foreign countries were particularly popular. Lady Morgan received £2,000 for her *Italy*, published in 1821. When Harriet Martineau was in America a publisher advised her to 'Trollopize a bit, and so make a readable book'—the reference being to Frances Trollope's *Domestic Manners of the Americans* (1832). Soon after her return to England she was besieged by publishers, and her *Autobiography* contains an amusing description of how Bentley, Colburn, and Saunders (of Saunders and Otley), three men 'notoriously on the worst terms with each other', all called on her independently one November morning. Colburn went so far as to offer her £2,000 for a book about America and £1,000 'for the first novel I should write', and was both disappointed and astonished when she said that she preferred to accept a less extravagant offer from Saunders and Otley. Two remarkable transactions were Constable's payments of £1,000 each to Dugald Stewart and John Playfair for two treatises on 'The Progress of Philosophy' and 'The Progress of Mathematics and Physics' for the *Supplement of the Encyclopædia Britannica*. In 1816 Murray offered Croker no less than 2,500 guineas for a three-volume work on the French Revolution, but Croker declined the task. Five years later Murray paid Lord Holland £2,500 for

Waldegrave's *Memoirs* and Walpole's *Memoirs of the last Ten Years
. . . of George III*—a lavishness which he lived to regret. A much
more valuable property was that in Mrs. Rundell's *Cookery*, for the
copyright of which (when it was no longer a new book) Murray
was glad to pay £2,000—a reminder that literary and commercial values no more corresponded in this period than in any
other.

Poetry could also pay, as Scott had demonstrated before he
took to writing in prose. In 1807 Constable had paid him 1,000
guineas in advance for *Marmion*, 'without having seen one line
of it'—a price (as Scott later acknowledged) 'that made men's
hair stand on end'. According to A. S. Collins, Scott received
£4,000 for *The Lady of the Lake*. For half of the copyright of the
very inferior *Lord of the Isles* he was given 1,500 guineas. His
successor as the most widely read poet of the day also received
very large sums. Murray paid Dallas, to whom Byron presented
the copyright of the first two Cantos of *Childe Harold's Pilgrimage*,
£600. For Canto III he paid £2,000. No less striking are the
sums paid for Byron's Tales. Murray offered Byron 500 guineas
for *The Giaour* and paid the same sum for *The Bride of Abydos*
and for *The Corsair*. For *The Siege of Corinth* and *Parisina* Murray
offered 1,000 guineas. Byron considered his offer of 1,500 guineas
for Canto IV of *Childe Harold* too niggardly, and asked for 2,500
guineas. For the three tragedies, *Sardanapalus*, *The Two Foscari*,
and *Cain*, he had received £2,710. Although Murray was from
the first very uncertain about *Don Juan*, he paid 1,500 guineas
for the first two Cantos (with the *Ode on Venice* thrown in) and
2,500 guineas for Cantos III–V and three of the tragedies together. After his quarrel with Murray (one notices) Byron did
not manage to get anything like these prices from his later
publishers. Other poets were also generously paid, on occasion.
In 1819 Murray gave an incredulous Crabbe £3,000 for the
Tales of the Hall and the remaining copyright in his earlier
works—a purchase (it must be admitted) that did not prove
profitable. In December 1814 Longman had signed an even
more remarkable agreement with Thomas Moore: 'Upon your
giving into our hands a poem of yours of the length of "Rokeby"
you shall receive from us the sum of £3,000.' Hazlitt's observation that Moore 'ought not to have written Lalla Rookh, even for
three thousand guineas', is fair criticism; but the poem sold
spectacularly well and neither poet nor publisher is known to

have repented of the bargain. It is perhaps more surprising that Milman should have received 500 guineas each for *The Fall of Jerusalem*, *The Martyr of Antioch*, and *Belshazzar*. But most astonishing of all was the fact that Bernard Barton should ever have earned enough by his writings to contemplate leaving his bank. When he was dissuaded from taking to literature for his living, his fellow Quakers, regretting that his fine faculties should be wasted on a humdrum occupation, raised a large subscription to enable him to devote himself to poetry. Of the very different fortunes of Wordsworth, Shelley, and Keats there is no need to write. Keats made little and Shelley next to nothing, while it was only when he was an old man that Wordsworth began to make a little money from his poetry. This must act as a reminder that even in a period when there was undoubtedly 'money in writing', what paid was what was in demand, or what happened to catch the public fancy. Sometimes a good book sold well: as often—or more often—it was a bad one that proved successful. The quality that makes a book a best-seller is one thing, the abiding principle of life that makes it last is another: only occasionally, as with the best of Scott and the best of Byron, are the two one.

As already suggested, however, much the surest resource for a writer lay in contributing to the great Reviews and Magazines. That is why it is so much easier to point to the great prose writers of the time than to the great books that they wrote. Southey once told J. T. Coleridge that 'the most profitable line of composition is reviewing', adding that he had not yet received as much for his three-volume *History of Brazil* as for a single article in the *Quarterly*. By paying contributors to the *Edinburgh Review* ten guineas for a sheet of sixteen pages Constable had trebled or quadrupled the price paid by the older Reviews. It should also be noted that Jeffrey had considerable discretion and was free to pay valued contributors more than the standard rate. 'You shall have twelve guineas if you please', he told Francis Horner as early as May 1803. Soon sixteen guineas a sheet seems to have become the minimum standard rate, two-thirds of the articles (according to Jeffrey) being 'paid much higher, averaging from twenty to twenty-five guineas a sheet on the whole number'. In this matter, as in others, the proprietors of the *Quarterly* were content to follow the lead of the *Edinburgh*, seldom quite catching up. 'The *Quarterly* pays me well', Southey wrote in 1810, 'ten guineas per sheet. . . . And now for the bulky "Life of Nelson" . . . [I] am to be paid double. This must be for the sake of saying they give twenty guineas per sheet, as I should have been well satisfied with ten.' For his first contribution he had been paid £21.13s., but according to the writer of a retrospective article in April 1909 'his rate of payment was soon raised to 100 l. an article'. While this is probably an exaggeration, one has only to recall that he wrote altogether ninety-five contributions for the *Quarterly* to see how important a part this regular work played in the economic pattern of his life. If he had been prepared to act as editor he could have added greatly to his income—Scott told him that he could earn an extra £500 per annum in this way. Here again Murray was following Constable's lead. For editing the *Edinburgh* Jeffrey had been offered £300, 'a monstrous bribe' that he had been unable to refuse. For editing the *Quarterly* Gifford seems at first to have been paid £200 a year, though in 1811 he was given a congratulatory present of £500 and about 1813 his stipend was doubled. 'The only fault I ever taxed you with in pecuniary matters', Gifford wrote to Murray near the end of his life, 'was with that of being *too liberal* to me.' When Lockhart took over the editorship of the *Quarterly* he began with no less than £1,000 per annum. In the realm of the Magazine it was *Blackwood's* that led the way in generous rates of payment, but the *London Magazine* went even further, with the result that the *Confessions of an English Opium-Eater* were published south of the Border. The *New Monthly* also paid very generously. It will be seen that a professional man of letters could not afford to turn his back on periodical writing. 'The state of literature is painful and humiliating enough', Beddoes wrote to Thomas Forbes Kelsall in 1825—'every one will write for £15 a sheet.' Writers temperamentally unsuited to this form of composition were obliged to conform. Even those who had reason to curse both their houses had little option but to choose between the *Edinburgh* and the *Quarterly*. When in September 1819 Keats decided to try to earn his living as a writer he resolved to ask Hazlitt 'how the figures of the market stand' and to 'write on the liberal side of the question, for whoever will pay me'. Instead of living on hopes, he would 'get employment in some of our elegant Periodical Works'—anything (one may conjecture) except *Blackwood's*. And so we find George Darley, whose dream it was to be a Fellow of Trinity College,

Dublin, supporting himself by contributing to the Reviews and writing mathematical text-books. 'The profession of an author' enabled him to live, though not to earn enough to achieve the stable domesticity for which he longed.

Such being the position of the writer, how many books were published at this time, what kind of books were most in demand, what did books cost, and who bought them? To the first of these questions no reliable answer can be given. In 1791 James Lackington had estimated that more than four times as many books were being sold as twenty years before, and the Reviews of our period are full of complaints about the number of books now 'pouring from the presses'. Yet the number of books published then looks small beside the figures for today. In 1957 more than 16,000 new titles appeared in Great Britain, as well as almost 6,000 reprints of older books. Between 1815 and 1832 the annual average seems to have been something between 1,000 and 1,500. Unfortunately there are no statistics on which a firm estimate can be based, but it appears likely that the number of books published annually was increasing fairly steadily at this period and that the effect of the slump of 1826–7 was less dramatic than might have been expected.[1] If we can rely on Charles Knight's statement that 'in 1853 there were three times as many books published as in 1828' (*Passages of a Working Life*, iii. 195), it becomes evident that the curve of the increase rose fairly sharply in the early Victorian period, with the result that there was an enormous difference between the number of books published in the mid-nineteenth century and the number of books published a hundred years before. In the same passage Knight gives an analysis of the categories of books sold throughout the whole period from 1816 to 1851; since no analysis

[1] The best figures available for the years 1815–1825 seem to be those provided by the certified copies of the lists of books entered at Stationers' Hall which were sent to the Librarian of the University of Cambridge. These give the following approximate totals: *1815*, 1,121; *1816*, 1,176; *1817*, 1,207; *1818*, 1,174; *1819*, 1,290; *1820*, 1,170; *1821*, 1,062; *1822*, 1,390; *1823*, 1,264; *1824*, 1,258; *1825*, 1,346. The lists for 1826–7 are incomplete, but the total for 1828 (the last year for which a complete list is available) is approximately 1,377. For the years from 1826 onwards we can refer to the annual list provided by Bent's *Monthly Literary Advertiser*. Since the figure for 1828 is approximately 854 it is clear that this list is much less complete than that derived from the records at Stationers' Hall; but the figures for 1826–32 confirm the impression of a general increase in the number of books published. They are as follows: *1826*, 902; *1827*, 920; *1828*, 854; *1829*, 1,080; *1830*, 1,154; *1831*, 1,150; *1832*, 1,172. It will be noticed that Knight's figures appear to be even less complete than those in Bent.

is available for individual years his figures are reproduced
here:

Works on divinity	10,300
History and geography	4,900
Fiction	3,500
Foreign languages and school-books	4,000
Drama and poetry	3,400
Juvenile books	2,900
Medical	2,500
Biography	1,850
Law	1,850
Science (zoology, botany, chemistry, geology, mathematics, astronomy, natural philosophy)	2,450
Arts, &c. (antiquities, architecture, fine arts, games and sports, illustrated works, music, genealogy and heraldry)	2,460
Industry (mechanics, &c., agriculture, trade and commerce, political economy, statistics, military)	2,350
Moral sciences (philology, &c., education, moral philosophy, morals, domestic economy)	1,400
Miscellaneous	1,400
	45,260

Whereas these figures for the number of books published in
our period are necessarily approximate and uncertain, about
the cost of books at this time there is no uncertainty. Books were
very expensive. In the *Edinburgh Review* for October 1824 Henry
Brougham wrote on the education of the poor as follows:

The first method . . . for promoting knowledge among the poor,
is the encouragement of cheap publications; and in no country is
this more wanted than in Great Britain, where, with all our boasted
expertness in manufactures, we have never succeeded in printing
books at so little as double the price required by our neighbours on
the Continent. A gown, which any where else would cost a guinea,
may be made in this country for half a crown; but a volume . . .
better printed . . . than could be bought in London for half a guinea,
costs . . . less than five shillings at Paris.

By the later twenties the movement for cheap literature recorded in the last chapter of this book was beginning to gather
momentum, and Knight claims that between 1828 and 1853 the
average price per volume fell by about 5*s*. There was certainly
need for a reduction: the stiffness of the prices prevailing early
in the century is the more striking when one remembers the high

value of money at this time and the fact that most books were sold in boards, so that those who required a permanent binding had to pay a further sum to the binder. A small book of verse, such as Hunt's *Descent of Liberty*, usually cost about 6s. The two volumes of Clare's *Village Minstrel* cost 12s. Byron's *Doge of Venice* and *The Prophecy of Dante*, in one volume, also cost 12s. *Endymion* (a handsome book) cost 9s., while *Lamia, Isabella, The Eve of St. Agnes, and Other Poems* cost 7s. 6d. In 1821 a five-volume collected edition of Byron's poems cost 35s. Histories and biographies were sometimes very expensive: Hallam's *View of the State of Europe during the Middle Ages* was first published in two volumes quarto at 4 guineas, though a cheaper edition was soon available. The *Life of Hayley . . . by Himself* also appeared in two lavish quarto volumes at 4 guineas. Even the third edition of Moore's *Life of Sheridan* cost a guinea and a half. An octavo volume of criticism, such as Hazlitt's *Lectures on the English Poets*, cost about 10s. 6d. In 1826 the two volumes of *The Plain Speaker* were priced at 24s. Allan Cunningham's *Songs of Scotland*, in four volumes, cost 36s. Nor were new editions of old books always much cheaper: the two volumes of Moore's edition of Sheridan cost 28s., while Taylor and Hessey charged 36s. for their handsome edition of Cary's translation of Dante (the pocket-edition costing 12s.). Periodicals were also expensive: the *Edinburgh* and the *Quarterly* cost 6s. a number: the *London Magazine* began at 2s. 6d. but soon went up to 3s. 6d.

But it was novels that were most expensive. *Waverley* and *Guy Mannering*, in three volumes, cost a guinea each (the more usual price at this point being 15s. or 18s.), as did Godwin's *Mandeville* in 1817 and Susan Ferrier's *Marriage* the following year. But Scott and his publishers led the way to still higher prices: *The Antiquary* and *Rob Roy* each cost 24s., while with *Kenilworth* in 1821 we reach the three-volume novel at a guinea and a half that is so characteristic of the period. Whereas Lister's *Granby*, in 1826, cost 27s., Horace Smith's *Brambletye House* imitated Scott in price, as in everything else. The convention that a novel should appear in three volumes, which suited the publishers and the proprietors of circulating libraries, became a tyranny to the men and women who wrote them. It did not suit the genius of John Galt, for example, who tells us explicitly in *Rothelan* that he is 'most desirous of sending out two rather than three volumes' but that his publisher insists that the public 'would now be just as likely to buy a ten-tom'd tale of householdry, in the Richardson style, as a bi-form historical romance'. 'Vol. I', 'Vol. II', and 'Vol. III' became the fashionable equivalent of the Aristotelian Beginning, Middle, and End—and too often (it must be confessed) this artificial unity in trinity was the only unity that the book possessed. Only when a novel was no longer new did editions appear at a lower price. When *Waverley* and its successors had been on the market for some time editions were produced at a guinea. It was towards the end of our period that cheap editions of popular novels began to appear at 5*s.*

There were many people who were willing and able to pay these high prices for books. Apart from the circulating libraries, which consumed a considerable part of each edition of a successful novel, thousands of individual readers paid a guinea and a half for each of the later (and inferior) Waverley Romances. It was a time of great inequality of incomes, the period which Sir Arthur Bryant has called 'The Age of Elegance' but which the Hammonds considered as part of 'The Bleak Age'. While hundreds of thousands lived in abject poverty, tens of thousands were by our standards extremely well-to-do, and to them the high prices of books were no embarrassment. It must also be remembered that before the invention of the cinema, of radio and television, some knowledge of contemporary literature was regarded as appropriate among the upper classes and was therefore obligatory for the newly rich and the socially ambitious. In making literature 'news' the great Reviews played an important part, and fortunately we have some fairly definite figures for the circulation of the *Edinburgh* and the *Quarterly*. In 1814 the circulation of the *Edinburgh Review* was estimated at 12,000, while four years later it reached its peak of 13,500. According to Samuel Smiles the *Quarterly* was selling 12,000 copies by 1817, and 14,000 copies a few months later. The importance of the Reviews at this time becomes apparent when we realize that a great many readers saw each copy that was bought—'Murray ... prints 10,000 and fifty times ten thousand read its contents', Southey once wrote with pardonable exaggeration—and compare their circulation with that of *The Times* in 1816, which was only 8,000 copies a day.

It is perhaps more surprising how well poetry sometimes sold. By 1825 *The Lay of the Last Minstrel* was in its fourteenth edition, 33,000 copies having been disposed of. *Marmion* was equally successful, *The Lady of the Lake* even more so. When only 10,000 copies of *Rokeby* were sold in a month the poem was regarded as a failure. 4,500 copies of the first two Cantos of *Childe Harold's Pilgrimage* were sold in the first six months, while the sales of Byron's later poems greatly exceeded this. Of *The Corsair* Murray wrote that he sold 'on the day of publication—a thing perfectly unprecedented—ten thousand copies'. The circulation of *The Pleasures of Memory*, by Samuel Rogers, was even more remarkable. The first four editions were very small, but then the publishers scented success and the poem reached its nineteenth edition in 1816, by which time more than 23,000 copies had been sold. Rogers's *Italy* and his *Poems* of 1832 seem to have been produced in editions of 10,000 copies. It is clear that this was a period when poetry was in demand, and when people were prepared to pay for it. Exciting tales in verse, with unfamiliar settings, such as those of Scott, Byron, and Moore, were particularly popular. Long poems containing a mixture of description and reverie, with a generally religious tone, also found a ready public. It may be doubted whether there has ever been so welcoming a public for poetry in England, except perhaps at the height of Tennyson's hey-day. Many readers of this *History*, people genuinely interested in literature, will not have read a poem of a hundred lines published during the last year. In the early nineteenth century this would hardly have been conceivable. Yet we must again remind ourselves that some of the poetry that sold most widely was extremely inferior, while much that was best attracted hardly any notice. If poetry was popular, it was not because men of genius were producing great poetry—though it may have been partly because two men of genius, Scott and Byron, were prepared to produce the kind of rhetorical poetry that appealed to the reading public. The poems of Bernard Barton were absurdly popular: the list of subscribers to his poems bears witness to the invincible philistinism of English society, from Windsor and Lambeth to the wealthy manufacturing cities of the North. Charles Knight tells us that in the middle or later twenties 'except in a few rare instances, mediocrity was essentially necessary to a great literary success'. As Knight points out, the unreadable *Omnipresence of the Deity*, by Robert Montgomery—'the wrong Montgomery'—went rapidly through five or six editions, while *The Excursion* was slow to reach a second edition. Keats's great volume of 1820 sold very poorly. Shelley soon abandoned all hope of finding an audience for his poetry—a bitter disappointment to a man who had hoped to become 'the trumpet of a prophecy'. Even within the work of one particular poet extrinsic factors often did more to determine the sale of a volume than the value of the poetry which it contained. The best of Clare's work published in his lifetime is to be found in *The Shepherd's Calendar*, which sold very poorly, whereas his first book, *Poems Descriptive of Rural Life and Scenery*, which was at best promising, went into several editions. As one would expect, the sales of novels were even greater than those of poetry. Ten thousand copies of *Rob Roy* were sold in the first three weeks. Even more astonishingly, 7,000 copies of *The Fortunes of Nigel* were sold in London by half-past ten on the morning of publication—a reminder of the importance to publishers of the growing rapidity of travel. Thirty-five thousand copies of the 1829 collected edition of the Waverley Novels were sold each month.

It is not surprising that so many writers commented on the growth of the 'reading public'. The phrase itself seems first to become current about this time. In *The Statesman's Manual*, written late in 1816, Coleridge insists that he is writing only for 'men of clerkly acquirements' and goes on to express the wish that 'the greater part of our publications could be thus directed, each to its appropriate class of readers'. But this is now impossible (he continues): 'For . . . we have now a Reading Public . . . a strange phrase . . .; and yet no fiction. For our readers have, in good truth, multiplied exceedingly, and have waxed proud. It would require the intrepid accuracy of a Colquhoun to venture at the precise number of that vast company only, whose heads and hearts are dieted at the two public ordinaries of literature, the circulating libraries and the periodical press.' The situation that Coleridge looked on askance provided men as various as Scott, Byron, and Cobbett with their opportunity. In his review of the Third Canto of *Childe Harold* in the *Quarterly* for October 1816 Scott himself observes that 'reading is . . . so general among all ranks and classes, that the impulse received by the public mind on such occasions is instantaneous through all but the very lowest classes of society, instead of being slowly communicated from one class of readers to another, as was the case in the days of our fathers'. 'We present a spectacle of what, perhaps, was never before seen in any age,' Henry Southern wrote in the introduction to the first volume of the *Retrospective Review*; '. . . that of a whole nation, employing nearly all its leisure hours from the highest to the lowest rank in *reading*—we have been truly called a READING PUBLIC.' In a similar vein the writer of the editorial of the *Athenaeum* for 12 February 1828 remarked that 'the reading public . . . may now be said to include all who are above the condition of the merely labouring classes'. Even if we concede that the taste for serious reading was not quite as widespread as men like Henry Southern supposed, it is interesting to speculate on the numbers represented by the phrase 'the reading public'. Reviewing Crabbe's *Tales* in the *Edinburgh Review* for November 1812, Jeffrey praises him for addressing his poetry to 'the middling classes of society', defining these as 'almost all those who are below the sphere of what is called fashionable or public life, and who do not aim at distinction or notoriety beyond the circle of their equals in fortune and situation. In this country', Jeffrey comments, 'there probably are not less than two hundred thousand persons who read for amusement or instruction among the middling classes of society. In the higher classes, there are not as many as twenty thousand.' When he reprinted the essay in 1844, Jeffrey changed his figure for the higher classes to 30,000 and that for the middling classes to 300,000; but his conclusions remained unchanged:

It is easy to see . . . which a poet should chuse to please for his own glory and emolument, and which he should wish to delight and amend out of mere philanthropy. The fact too we believe is, that a great part of the larger body are to the full as well educated and as high-minded as the smaller; and, though their taste may not be so correct and fastidious, we are persuaded that their sensibility is greater.

The whole passage illustrates Jeffrey's flair for sociological observation. When he suggests that middle-class readers should not aim at imitating the taste of their social superiors and that writers should provide them with literature dealing with people of their own class, he shrewdly anticipates the course of nineteenth-century literature as a whole and shows himself well prepared to appreciate the genius of Dickens. By November 1844 it was to be possible for Thomas Hood—that least aggressive of men of letters—to write to Peel, then Prime Minister, regretting the omission of Literature from the Queen's answer to a civic address and remarking that 'whatever differences may obtain in society, that will be an unlucky one which distinguishes a sovereign from a reading public, rapidly becoming a reading people'.

It was not only the printed word that was in demand. One of the most striking characteristics of the period was the vogue for lectures. The popularity of lectures outside universities seems to have been a new thing towards the end of the eighteenth century. Samuel Johnson, who might appear to have been born to be a lecturer, had a low opinion of lectures as a mode of instruction and never delivered a lecture in his life. If he had lived fifty years later he would have been obliged to turn lecturer. The first public lecture on Shakespeare (as distinct from a paper read to a private literary or debating society) seems to have been that delivered by William Kenrick in 1774. Soon a complex of causes, including the ferment of ideas produced by the American wars and the French Revolution and the growing public interest in science, led to a steadily increasing demand for lectures. A number of the most important prose works in our period came into existence in this way.

Coleridge had begun his career as a lecturer in Bristol in 1795 with the object of disseminating Truth by lecturing on politics. Things did not go smoothly for him: in a letter he complained that 'two or three uncouth and unbrained Automata have threatened my Life' and that the 'Genus infimum were scarcely restrained from attacking the house in which the "damn'd Jacobine was jawing away"'. In 1808 he gave a very different set of lectures to a very different audience, lecturing on poetry at the aristocratic Royal Institution, which had been founded to encourage 'the application of the new discoveries in science to the improvement of arts and manufactures'. Admission was by ticket, and the lectures took place—or were intended to take place—at 2 p.m. In 1811–12 Coleridge gave another course of lectures on poetry in Fetter Lane. On this occasion Crabb Robinson complained that each alleged lecture was an 'immethodical rhapsody': Coleridge was the Pindar of lecturers. Encouraged by the success of another course which he gave in 1812, sponsored by Sir Thomas Bernard, Lady Beaumont, and William Sotheby, and by that of a later series of lectures in Bristol, Coleridge played with an odd scheme for 'a *system* of private Lectures with Discussions afterwards, conveying all the information that a gentleman ought to have . . . which if realized would secure me 600£ a year'—the sort of Academy that might have provided Aristophanes with the material for another *Clouds*. On occasion, it must be admitted, Coleridge's audiences had a good deal to put up with. In his 'Literary Reminiscences' De Quincey gives us a picture of Coleridge lecturing—or failing to lecture—that seems to be only a little highly coloured:

Thus unhappily situated, he sank more than ever under the dominion of opium; so that, at two o'clock, when he should have been in attendance at the Royal Institution, he was too often unable to rise from bed. Then came dismissals of audience after audience, with pleas of illness; and on many of his lecture days I have seen all Albemarle Street closed by a 'lock' of carriages, filled with women of distinction, until the servants of the Institution or their own footmen advanced to the carriage-doors with the intelligence that Mr. Coleridge had been suddenly taken ill. . . . Many in anger, and some in real uncertainty whether it would not be trouble thrown away, ceased to attend. And we that were more constant too often found reason to be disappointed with the quality of his lecture. . . . His lips were baked with feverish heat, and often black in colour; and, in spite of the water which he continued drinking through the whole course of his lecture, he often seemed to labour under an almost paralytic inability to raise the upper jaw from the lower.

We are reminded of one of the reasons for the popularity of lectures at this time by Coleridge's observation that 'a history of *Philosophy* . . . is a desideratum in Literature'. On many subjects about which books are available to us little had then been written. This was true, in some degree, both of the History of Philosophy, which Hazlitt chose as the subject of his first course of lectures (delivered at the Russell Institution in 1812), and of the History of Literature, on which he lectured on several occasions. After the first of these lectures on Philosophy, Crabb Robinson—that inveterate lecture-goer, to whom we owe much of our information about lectures at this time—complained that Hazlitt seemed 'to have no conception of the difference between a lecture and a book'; but he quickly improved. One of the most interesting descriptions of Hazlitt lecturing is by Thomas Noon Talfourd:

Mr. Hazlitt delivered three courses of lectures at the Surrey Institution . . . before audiences with whom he had but 'an imperfect sympathy'. They consisted chiefly of Dissenters . . . who 'loved no plays'; of Quakers, who . . . 'heard no music'; of citizens devoted to the main chance . . .; of a few enemies . . . ; and a few friends. . . . The comparative insensibility of the bulk of his audience to his finest passages, sometimes provoked him to awaken their attention by points which broke the train of his discourse, after which he could make himself amends by some abrupt paradox which might set their prejudices on edge, and make them fancy they were shocked. . . . When he passed by Mrs Hannah More with observing that 'she had written a great deal which he had never read', a voice gave expression to the general commiseration and surprise, by calling out 'More pity for you!'

Three of Hazlitt's most important books, *The English Poets*, *The English Comic Writers*, and *The Dramatic Literature of the Age of Elizabeth*, consisted of lectures for the Surrey Institution. We hear a good deal about the *Lectures on the English Poets* from Crabb Robinson, who often listened to Hazlitt before proceeding to Fleur de Luce Court to hear Coleridge on Shakespeare. It is an important series because it is perhaps the only course of lectures on poetry ever delivered in this country which is known to have had a demonstrable influence on a great poet. Keats turned up for the first lecture an hour late, but he did his best not to miss another, and the influence of Hazlitt's observations on poetry is to be found in more than one of the most illuminating passages in his letters. The fact that Keats mentions that he met many people whom he knew at these lectures suggests that Talfourd exaggerated the predominance of Dissenters in Hazlitt's audience; yet there can be no doubt that the vogue for lectures owed a good deal to the Dissenters' passion for self-improvement. It is ironical that a man who had refused to enter the Dissenting ministry should so often have found himself addressing Dissenters on subjects connected with philosophy and morals.

Not everyone shared the Dissenters' taste. Lectures were among the few manifestations of human nature excluded from the charity of Charles Lamb. The first scene of Byron's poem *The Blues: A Literary Eclogue* takes place 'Before the door of a Lecture Room' and satirizes the passion of the day, prompting the reflection that but for women the lecture might not so long have survived the invention of printing. Peacock's Dr. Opimian is characteristically forthright on the subject of lectures. 'I agree with Dr Johnson', he remarks, 'that little is to be learned from lectures. For the most part, those who do not already understand the subject will not understand the lecture, and those who do will learn nothing from it. The latter will hear many things they would like to contradict, which the *bienséance* of the lecture-room does not allow. I do not comprehend how people can find amusement in lectures. I should much prefer a *tenson* of the twelfth century, when two or three masters of the *Gai Saber* discussed questions of love and chivalry.' But by the time when *Gryll Grange* was published, in 1860, it was far too late to protest against the habit of lecturing. In the *Edinburgh Review* for October 1824 Brougham had emphasized the importance of lectures in the education of the poor. 'The institution of Lectures', he had written, 'is, of all the helps that can be given, the most valuable, where circumstances permit; that is, in towns of a certain size. Much may thus be taught, even without any other instruction; but, combined with reading, and subservient to it, the effects of public lectures are great indeed, especially in the present deficiency of proper elementary works.' These are the words of the man whom Peacock satirized as 'the learned friend', and Brougham's was the opinion that proved dominant as the century wore on. In 1838, we are told, Adam Sedgwick delivered an unofficial public lecture on the beach at Tynemouth 'to some 3,000 or 4,000 colliers and rabble (with a sprinkling of their employers)'. Sir John Herschel was told by a friend who had been there that it was 'impossible to conceive the sublimity of the scene' as Sedgwick

stood on the point of a rock a little raised, to which he rushed as if by a sudden impulse, and led them on from the scene around them to the wonders of the coal industry below them, thence to the economy of a coal field, then to their relations to the coal owners and capitalists, then to the great principles of morality and happiness, and at last to their relation to God, and their own future prospects.

But with Sedgwick's lecture we have crossed the border into the Victorian Age. It is time to turn back to consider the poetry written in the years immediately after Waterloo.

II

BYRON

BYRON had an extraordinary heredity.[1] His father, who died when the poet was three, was an incorrigible gambler and spendthrift, the eldest son of Admiral John Byron, 'Foulweather Jack', one of the most colourful figures in the history of the eighteenth-century navy. His mother, Catherine Gordon of Gight, was a descendant of King James the First of Scotland. She was a passionate, ill-educated woman, and although she tried to do her best for her son he was often to blame her for the tempestuous course of his later life. He was born with a slight malformation of the right foot, and as a result he was slightly lame: a disability which he allowed to prey on his mind. He inherited the title on the death of his great-uncle, 'the wicked Lord', who had killed a man in a duel and then retired to live at Newstead with his mistress and a single servant in circumstances that recall the novels of the Brontës. There were traces of insanity on both sides of the family and marriages between cousins had been unhealthily common.

After his early years in Aberdeen, Nottingham, and London, he was sent to Harrow, where he proved himself a wild and

[1] George Gordon Byron (1788–1824) was born in London and became the sixth Lord Byron at the age of ten. Before going to Harrow he was educated privately and at Aberdeen Grammar School. At Cambridge he led a wild life and kept a bear to teach the Fellows of Trinity good manners. In 1809 he took his seat in the House of Lords, published *English Bards and Scotch Reviewers*, and set out on his travels with a Cambridge friend, John Cam Hobhouse. He returned two years later, having swum the Hellespont and visited Lisbon, Cadiz, Gibraltar, Malta, Greece, Smyrna, Ephesus, and Constantinople. In 1812 he twice spoke in the Lords, published the first two cantos of *Childe Harold*, and became a prominent figure in Whig society. Two years later he married Annabella Milbanke, who accused him of insanity and left him. In 1815 his interest in the drama led to his being appointed a member of the sub-committee of management at Drury Lane. Soon his financial and other embarrassments obliged him to flee to the Continent, where he visited Shelley in Switzerland and wrote *Childe Harold III*. Later in 1816 he travelled to Italy, where he heard that Claire Clairmont had borne him a daughter. The first two cantos of *Don Juan* were published in 1819. In April of that year Byron met the Contessa Guiccioli and became her *cicisbeo*, living with her a good deal in the next few years. In 1822 he was present at the cremation of Shelley's body. In January 1824 he landed at Missolonghi to join the Greeks who were fighting for their independence. He died of fever on 19 April.

ungovernable boy. He was a good athlete and boxer and had
a passion for reciting his own poems and speeches. As his nickname—'The Old English Baron'—bears witness, many of his
schoolmates considered him a snob: it is said that on one occasion, when another boy pinched his ear, he threw something at
him shouting that 'that would teach a fool of an earl to pinch
another noble's ear'. From Harrow he went to Trinity College,
Cambridge, and towards the end of 1806 he published his first
volume of verse, *Fugitive Pieces*. The subjects of the poems in this
collection provide a conspectus of his life up to that point: there
are poems dealing with school and Cambridge, poems to male
contemporaries written in terms of fervent friendship, and a
great many addresses to Marys, Julias, and Carolines. A clerical
friend considered a description in one of the poems 'rather too
warmly drawn' and Byron was persuaded to destroy almost the
whole impression: only four copies are known to survive. The
next year, however, he produced an enlarged and expurgated
edition, '*vastly* correct and miraculously chaste', entitled *Poems on
Various Occasions*. This volume was followed by *Hours of Idleness*,
a slightly better collection of lyrics the publication of which had
momentous results. A few weeks after he had completed a satire
called *British Bards*, of which (in its original form) no complete
manuscript or printed copy survives, Byron heard that the *Edinburgh Review* was intending to notice his poems, and he awaited
events with keen anxiety. The review, when it came, was devastating. Byron had mentioned on his title-page that he was a 'Minor',
and the reviewer made fun of this in a manner very characteristic
of the *Edinburgh*, pointing out that minority could not be pleaded
in mitigation of the offence of voluntarily publishing a volume of
inferior verse. 'The poesy of this young lord', the reviewer wrote,
in sentences which Byron was never to forget,

belongs to the class which neither gods nor men are said to permit.
Indeed, we do not recollect to have seen a quantity of verse with
so few deviations in either direction from that exact standard. His
effusions are spread over a dead flat, and can no more get above or
below the level, than if they were so much stagnant water. (xi. 285,
January 1808.)

'Mediocribus esse poetis': it is the last charge that an ambitious
young poet can stand. Several years later, discussing the effect
that unfavourable reviews were thought to have had on Keats,

Byron wrote that 'a savage review is Hemlock to a sucking author', adding (with pardonable yet characteristic egotism): 'the one on me . . . knocked me down—but I got up again'. He got up fighting, and the remainder of his life as a poet was to be (in Pope's phrase about himself) 'a warfare upon earth'. He extended and rewrote *British Bards* and published the result as *English Bards and Scotch Reviewers* in March 1809.

It would be a mistake to suppose that in writing a formal verse satire Byron was reviving an obsolete type of poetry. More satires of this kind seem to have been written in the early nineteenth century than a hundred years before, although no poet of genius now came forward to make it his own. Byron makes it clear that he is acting as *locum tenens* for Gifford, 'the last of the wholesome satirists': his immediate models are *The Baviad* and *Maeviad*, Mathias's *Pursuits of Literature*, and the satires of Charles Churchill, while the wording of the Argument reminds us that *The Dunciad* was also in his mind as he wrote. As the form of the poem suggests, Byron is aligning himself with critics of a conservative cast. The standards that he upholds are close to those of the *Anti-Jacobin* twenty years before, and it is not surprising to hear that he regards the present as the age of 'the decline of English poetry'. Referring to Wordsworth and other poets of the day he tells us that each of them

like other sectaries . . . has his separate tabernacle of proselytes, by whom his abilities are over-rated, his faults overlooked, and his metrical canons received without . . . consideration. But the unquestionable possession of considerable genius by several of the writers here censured renders their mental prostitution more to be regretted.

The passage continues with a fine eighteenth-century sentence: 'Perverted powers demand the most decided reprehension.' Yet it must be admitted that Byron shows himself an imperceptive critic of his contemporaries, since he attacks Wordsworth, Coleridge, Southey, and (in some degree) Scott, and reserves his praise for Crabbe, Cowper, Rogers, and Campbell and a number of very minor poets indeed. It is significant that Bowles, the favourite of Coleridge's youth, receives a particularly severe castigation as

> The maudlin prince of mournful sonneteers.

Bowles was a poet without a trace of genius who happened to

anticipate the new sensibility, and Byron was to come into conflict with him later on the question of the merits of Pope.

There are successful moments in *English Bards*. Byron is unfair to Wordsworth (as he soon realized), yet in referring to him as a poet

> Who, both by precept and example, shows
> That prose is verse, and verse is merely prose

he scores a legitimate satirical point and makes it clear that it was the theories propounded in the preface to the *Lyrical Ballads* that particularly annoyed him. On occasion he can hit off the conciseness which is characteristic of Pope, as in the line

> Believe a woman, or an epitaph.

But there is a monotony and an occasional stridency in the poem which Pope avoided: there are not enough variations of pitch and tone. The formal verse satire is no medium for a young poet: it is not surprising that Byron at the age of twenty could not compete with Pope at the height of his powers. He wrote the poem, as he later acknowledged, when he was 'very young and very angry', and it would hardly be an exaggeration to say that he spent the rest of his life meeting, and liking, the men whom he had attacked. After four editions had appeared he was persuaded to allow his satire to go out of print. For us it remains of interest as an index to his early poetical views and as a reminder that conciseness did not come naturally to him. His satiric triumph, when it came, was to be due to the discovery of an idiom that encouraged expansion and digression rather than compression of the Augustan kind.

Soon after the publication of *English Bards* Byron took his seat in the House of Lords; he then set out on a tour of Europe. While he was abroad he wrote *Hints from Horace*, an 'Imitation' in Pope's sense of the word which is technically superior to *English Bards* and which (unlike the earlier poem) contains one or two passages that might be mistaken for the *Essay on Criticism*. But it was the other poem that he began on his travels that was to prove momentous. The first stanzas of *Childe Harold's Pilgrimage* were written at Jannina in Albania, on his return from a visit to the tyrant Ali Pasha. Byron was in a state of 'extreme discontent', but he was stimulated by his novel experiences and reminded by the mountains which surrounded him of his early boyhood in Scotland.

As the reviewers pointed out, it is difficult to say to what kind of poetry *Childe Harold* belongs. When he published the first two cantos in 1812 Byron described them as 'merely experimental', acknowledging that the poem had 'no pretension to regularity'. On another occasion he said that it was 'a poem on *Ariosto's plan, that is to say on no plan* at all'. Its most obvious affinities are with the travel-book, and it is interesting to remember that Byron's companion Hobhouse was engaged on his *Journey through Albania*, which was 'prepared in frequent consultation' with the poet. In view of the problem of a suitable form for a long poem which faced the poets of the early nineteenth century, it is interesting to find Byron using this popular and unpretentious type of book as his starting-point. As the *Quarterly Review* remarked:

Few books are so extensively read and admired as those which contain the narratives of intelligent travellers. ... If ... this species of information be so attractive ... in prose ..., by what accident has it happened that no English poet before Lord Byron has thought fit to employ his talents on a subject so obviously well fitted to their display? This inadvertence ... is the more extraordinary, because the supposed dearth of epic subjects has been, during many years, the only apparent impediment to the almost infinite multiplication of epic poems ... [Apparently] the followers of the muse have ... intentionally rejected the materials offered by a traveller's journal as too anomalous to be employed in a regular and grand composition. (vii. 191, March 1812.)

It we compare *Childe Harold* with the *Odyssey*—a comparison suggested by the reviewer—we are struck by the fact that Byron's hero, unlike Homer's, can be removed from the poem in which he occurs. In spite of Byron's claim to have introduced the Childe 'for the sake of giving some connection to the piece' it is surprisingly easy to detach most of the passages dealing with him from the rest of the poem. After the first fifteen stanzas of Canto II, for example, which contain no reference to the Childe, he is introduced by the following words:

> But where is Harold? Shall I then forget
> To urge the gloomy Wanderer o'er the wave?
> Little recked he of all that Men regret

—surely one of the most inept transitions in all literature. The Childe is next mentioned at stanza xxxi, after a series of reflections which every reader has supposed to be the poet's own. At

times one is tempted to wonder whether the Childe was part
of the poem as it was originally conceived. Perhaps he was an
afterthought. It may be significant that the first man to see the
poem in England, R. C. Dallas, merely describes it as 'a great
many stanzas in Spenser's measure, relative to the countries he
had visited'.

Whether or not the Childe was part of the original plan, his
function was no doubt to enable Byron to express with impunity
views which were frequently unorthodox and revolutionary.
After the highly controversial stanzas about the Convention of
Cintra, for example, Byron continues:

> So deemed the Childe, as o'er the mountains he
> Did take his way in solitary guise.   (i. xxvii)

Yet there is an amusing piece of evidence that the publisher
himself found it impossible to distinguish between the poet's
own sentiments and those supposed to be attributed to Harold:
in reply to a note about one particular passage Byron replied:
'The "he" refers to the Wanderer and anything is better than
I I I I always *I*.' When Byron claimed, in an addition to the
preface, that the Childe was designed to show how 'early per-
version of mind and morals leads to satiety . . . and disappointment', he was obviously trying to reply to his reviewers. He was
telling them what, perhaps, he should have done, or what he
may at some time have thought of doing: not what he in fact
did. In a suppressed passage of the preface he came nearer
to admitting the truth: 'My reader will remark that where the
author speaks in his own person he assumes a very different
tone . . . at least till death had deprived him of his nearest con-
nections.' Nothing could be more revealing than the qualifying
clause—unless it be the fact that in some passages of the manuscript the protagonist is called 'Childe Burun'—the old spelling
of Byron's family name.

The character of the Childe helped to make the poem famous.
As the *Edinburgh Review* pointed out, 'there is . . . something
piquant in the very novelty and singularity of that cast of misanthropy and universal scorn, which we have . . . noticed as
among the repulsive features of the composition'. Nothing could
be more revealing than the collocation of the words 'repulsive',
'scorn', 'misanthropy', 'novelty', 'piquant'. The fog of uncertainty surrounding the Childe's identity added to the fascina-

tion—as did the fact that he differed so markedly from the usual
poetic hero of the time. To recapture the impression that the
Childe made in 1812 one cannot do better than to look into
Campbell's immensely popular poem *Gertrude of Wyoming*, whose
hero wins a girl's heart by describing his travels:

> And well could he his pilgrimage of taste
> Unfold—and much they lov'd his fervid strain—
> While he each fair variety retrac'd
> Of climes, and manners, o'er the eastern main.

Perhaps Byron decided to offer a counter-blast to Campbell's
insipid hero, who made his appearance just before Byron left
England. The Childe also contrasts piquantly with the hero of
Beattie's *Minstrel*. The sub-title of this poem, which Byron knew
well, is 'The Progress of Genius', and Beattie explains that his
object is to 'trace the progress of a poetical genius . . . from the
first dawnings of fancy and reason'. The hero, based on the poet
himself, is 'no vulgar boy'—a marked contrast to the Childe
'Who ne in Virtue's ways did take delight'.

Today we are likely to agree with the writer in the *Quarterly
Review* who said that 'so far from effecting the object for which
he is introduced, and giving some connection to the piece', the
Childe 'only tends to embarrass and obscure it'. In Cantos III
and IV, which appeared separately in 1816 and 1818, it is no
longer possible to distinguish between the Childe and Byron
himself. As he acknowledged in the preface to Canto IV, he was
'weary of drawing a line which every one seemed determined
not to perceive'.

In Canto III the guide-book element has almost completely
disappeared. Byron once called it 'a fine indistinct piece of
poetical desolation', and to none of his other poems does his
description of poetry as 'the lava of the imagination, whose
eruption prevents an earthquake', apply so well. He was, as he
said, 'half mad' when he wrote it, 'between metaphysics, mountains, lakes, love inextinguishable, thoughts unutterable, and
the nightmare of my own delinquencies'. The mountains and
lakes, like the metaphysics, were partly due to the influence of
Shelley, of whom Byron was seeing a good deal at this time, and
who was urging him to read Wordsworth. The theme of Society
and Solitude which is so prominent in this Canto is one of the
master-themes in the poetry of Wordsworth—and it had also

appeared in *Alastor*, which Shelley had written a few months before. Although there is some vulgarization of Wordsworth in Canto III, and some philosophical nonsense, it is clear that the intoxication of his own griefs and the influence of Shelley did Byron's poetry much more good than harm. The verse moves more urgently than before. Instead of the *andante* of Cantos I and II we find a swifter movement which sometimes reminds us of *terza rima* and anticipates the most successful English poem in this metre, Shelley's *Ode to the West Wind*:

> Still must I on; for I am as a weed
> Flung from the rock, on Ocean's foam, to sail
> Where'er the surge may sweep, the tempest's breath prevail.

A new vividness of phrase appears in the description of a ruin

> All tenantless, save to the crannying Wind,

while there is also a new imaginative power in the imagery, as in these lines on ambitious men:

> Even as a flame unfed, which runs to waste
> With its own flickering, or a sword laid by,
> Which eats into itself, and rusts ingloriously.

In Canto IV Byron is no longer under the influence of Shelley, though it has recently been argued that the direct influence of Hobhouse has been exaggerated. As Byron himself pointed out, there are 'no metaphysics' in Canto IV: instead the element of the travelogue is again prominent. Byron said that the Canto was designed 'as a mark of respect for what is venerable, and of feeling for what is glorious'; and Hobhouse not only wrote the illustrations and notes, but even provided Byron with a list of eligible subjects (mainly artistic and historical). The political and religious views expressed in the Canto are also much less challenging than those in III, which had driven Scott to fear that 'the termination will be fatal in one way or other, for it seems impossible that human nature can support the constant working of an imagination so dark and so strong' (letter to J. B. S. Morritt, 22. xi. 1816). The *Edinburgh Review* was delighted with the change, remarking that 'it is not enough to say that the veil is torn off. It is a nobler creature that is before us.' The average standard of the verse is higher, perhaps, than in any other Canto, yet Canto IV hardly challenges the description of major poetry, as Canto III occasionally does.

While it is impossible to recapture the excitement of the original readers of *Childe Harold's Pilgrimage*, it is not difficult to understand its appeal. Byron's sensibility differed less from that of the average cultivated reader of his day than did the sensibility of Wordsworth or Shelley. Readers of Scott, Campbell, and Rogers turned to him with quickened pulses, but without the sense of being completely lost which most of them felt on reading *The Excursion*. His main theme consists of great commonplaces suggested by the history and the picturesque beauty of the places he visits. He displays many of the instincts of the successful journalist: he picks out precisely the features of the country through which he is travelling which are likely to hold the reader's attention—the scenes of battles and other famous events, a bull-fight, the life of the women. His descriptions are given piquancy by the mysterious and embittered character of the Wanderer and the shock of his unconventional views on religion, politics, and morality—views which had led the first publisher to whom the poem was offered to reject it. 'When we read the . . . sarcasms on the "bravo's trade"', commented a writer in the *Quarterly Review*, 'we are induced to ask, not without some anxiety and alarm, whether such are indeed the opinions which a British peer entertains of a British army.' Even those of the original readers who were most deeply shocked by the opinions expressed in the poem took it for granted that it was a masterpiece. Today indifference to many of the topics discussed is a greater danger to its reputation than anger and indignation ever were. We no longer feel surprised, as its original readers did, at seeing such sentiments set out in resonant Spenserian verse. To understand the sensation which the poem caused we have to remember Byron's own remark, 'If ever I did any thing original, it was in *Childe Harold*.' It is interesting to notice that one reviewer after another stressed the originality of the poem. As the *Quarterly* remarked, Byron was receiving 'that fame . . . which is chiefly and most justly due to one who, in these exhausted days, strikes out a new and original line of composition'.

Parts of *Childe Harold* 'date', but not as markedly as the series of Tales which began to appear between the publication of the first two Cantos of that poem and Canto III. Yet in their day these accounts of adventure and unhappy love—most of them based on true stories which Byron had heard in the course of his travels—were immensely successful: they poured through the gap made by *Childe Harold* and established Byron as the successful rival of Sir Walter Scott. A thousand young men made conversation, like Captain Benwick in *Persuasion*, by 'trying to ascertain whether *Marmion* or *The Lady of the Lake* were to be preferred, and how ranked the *Giaour* and *The Bride of Abydos*; and moreover, how the *Giaour* was to be pronounced'; and while Anne Elliott replied by venturing to hope that Captain Benwick 'did not always read only poetry', the young lady in *Jane Eyre* who 'doated on the Corsair' was more representative of her sex. Mme. de Staël had advised Byron to 'stick to the East', saying that 'the North, South, and West, have all been exhausted; but from the East, we have nothing but Southey's unsaleables', and the exotic settings of these poems—most of them were written during the only part of Byron's adult life to be spent in England —give them a technicolour quality which had a great deal to do with their success. Their heroes resemble the Childe in being passionate men at odds with their environment, and Byron's readers were quick to identify them with the poet himself. 'He told me an odd report', he wrote in his Journal one day: 'that *I* am the actual Conrad, the veritable Corsair, and that part of my travels are supposed to have passed in piracy. Um! people sometimes hit near the truth; but never the whole truth.' This subjective element is particularly evident in a passage added to *Lara* after the completion of the first draft:

> His early dreams of good outstripped the truth,
> And troubled Manhood followed baffled Youth;
> With thought of years in phantom chase misspent,
> And wasted powers for better purpose lent;
> And fiery passions that had poured their wrath
> In hurried desolation o'er his path,
> And left the better feelings all at strife
> In wild reflection o'er his stormy life.   (323–30)

The Tales were written swiftly and without much revision, 'amidst balls and fooleries, and after coming home from masquerades and routs', and there is an air of improvisation about them—a pace and a panache—which reminds us of their origin. Most of them are written in tetrameters of the kind which Scott had made fashionable, and on occasion—as in *The Prisoner of*

Chillon (1816)—Byron handles the metre with very considerable skill. Those which are written in pentameters, such as *The Corsair* and *Lara* (both 1814), more often resemble Charles Churchill than Dryden, yet sometimes (as in the passage just quoted) Byron reminds us of Dryden and his contemporaries, just as the Regency period as a whole occasionally recalls the Restoration. It would be easy to mistake some of the better passages in these poems for late seventeenth-century heroic verse, while many of the weaker passages would be completely at home in *The Rehearsal*.

Little need be said of Byron's lyrics, although two or three deserve their place in any anthology. In *Hebrew Melodies* (1815) such a resounding failure as 'Jephtha's Daughter'—

> Since our Country, our God—Oh, my Sire!
> Demand that thy Daughter expire

—must be set beside the mastery of 'She walks in Beauty, like the night', of which the first stanza (though not the third) might be the work of one of the Caroline masters of the lyric. Of the lyrics scattered among Byron's longer poems the incantation in *Manfred* deserves particular mention for its compelling power. 'So we'll go no more a roving' has something of the mystery and the ageless passion of an anonymous song. Byron did not persevere enough with the lyric to find an individual voice, and at times he is astonishingly obtuse in his handling of language and rhythm, yet it is impossible not to regret that he did not write more often in this form. He resembles Burns more than anyone else, but he was a Burns without the sustaining inspiration of a popular tradition behind him. Too often his lyrics remind us of the minor and minimus writers of the later eighteenth century.

Byron's neo-classical sympathies may also be examined in certain of his dramas, though not in the first which calls for attention. He himself described *Manfred* (1817), which was begun while he was working on the third canto of *Childe Harold*, as a work 'of a very wild, metaphysical, and inexplicable kind', and he considered it 'not a drama properly—but a dialogue'. Manfred himself is the only important human character, for the Spirits of the Earth and Air, which speak choral verse which reminds us of Shelley, have much more important roles than the Hunter or the Abbot. The subject of the drama is the last days in the life of a man who has discovered by his own experience that

> The Tree of knowledge is not that of life.

He is haunted by the sense of having destroyed his sister Astarte, whom he has passionately loved. Although he dies unrepentant, he is not dragged off to Hell: instead he proclaims that it is 'not so difficult to die'. While *Manfred* owes a good deal to the story of Faust, its deepest sources of inspiration were Byron's love for his half-sister Augusta and the profound impression made on him by the Alps. One has only to look into the Journal which he kept during his travels in the autumn of 1816 to see how closely these scenes were associated in his mind with his unhappy passion. At this time external objects became for him the types and symbols of his own experiences and moods, and something of the urgency of the verse in *Manfred* is due to this: Manfred tells us that his own actions

> Have made my days and nights imperishable,
> Endless, and all alike, as sands on the shore,
> Innumerable atoms; and one desert,
> Barren and cold, on which the wild waves break,
> But nothing rests, save carcasses and wrecks,
> Rocks, and the salt-surf weeds of bitterness.   (II. i. 53–58)

It is not surprising that Byron, having scored a partial success with a drama written in defiance of all dramatic tradition, should have decided to see what he could do in the way of a real drama: a drama at least potentially adapted to the stage. Nor is it surprising that he should have resolved to turn his back on the realm of the subjective and make an attempt to write something less directly personal. Everyone had noticed that Manfred was just another example of the Byronic hero: he would now attempt to avoid the familiar type. To this end, he decided to emulate the classical dramatists. 'My object', as he wrote in a letter, 'has been to dramatise, like the Greeks . . ., striking passages of history as they did of history and mythology.'

Byron's attitude to the drama provides a parallel to his attitude to non-dramatic poetry. Just as he had attacked the Lakists and extolled Pope, so in an age of Elizabethanizing he turned his back on Elizabethan models. He believed, as he repeatedly pointed out, that great drama cannot be written 'by

following the old dramatists, who are full of gross faults, pardoned only for the beauty of their language'. It was necessary,
rather, to write 'naturally and *regularly* . . . like the Greeks'. As
he put it in a letter to Murray written on 16 February 1821:

> It appears to me that there is room for a different style of the
> drama; neither a servile following of the old drama, which is a
> grossly erroneous one, nor yet *too French*, like those who succeeded
> the older writers. It appears to me, that good English, and a severer
> approach to the rules, might combine [to produce] something not
> dishonorable to our literature.

He was convinced that Shakespeare was 'the *worst* of models,
though the most extraordinary of writers'. In this quest for 'a
regular English drama' there was one modern writer who seemed
to him to have pointed the way. 'It is more like a play of Alfieri's
than of your stage (I say this humbly in speaking of that great
Man)', he remarked of *Marino Faliero* (1821), while in September 1821 he acknowledged explicitly that his 'dramatic system'
was 'more upon the Alfieri School than the English'. It would
be interesting to know what exactly he said when he defended
Alfieri in conversation with A. W. Schlegel, but his general
attitude is easy to make out. It was not only Alfieri's dramatic
technique that appealed to him: he was equally impressed by
his political beliefs. Sismondi tells us that 'every high-minded
Italian who lamented over the humiliation of his country, was
united to [Alfieri] by bonds of mutual sympathy', adding: 'Thus
was the taste for the noblest species of tragedy mingled with the
love of glory and of liberty.' Byron would have been proud to
have occupied the place in the history of the English drama
which Alfieri, with his 'Tragedies of Freedom', occupied in that
of the Italian.

On the question of the style suitable for tragedy Byron had
views as radically opposed to those common in his day as his
views on dramatic themes and structure. 'Do not judge me by
your mad old dramatists', he once wrote, 'which is like drinking
usquebaugh and then proving a fountain.' In *The Two Foscari*
(1821) he drew attention to his 'avoidance of rant' and to the
'compression of the speeches in the more severe situations'.
'What I seek to show', he added, 'is the suppressed passion,
rather than the rant of the present day.' On another occasion
he claimed to have 'broken down the poetry as nearly as I could

to common language'. Here, as often in reading Byron's critical observations on the drama, one is reminded of Mr. Eliot's attitude a century later, and it is interesting to find, as early as *Manfred*, a passage which could readily be mistaken for the later poet:

> And they have only taught him what we know—
> That knowledge is not happiness, and science
> But an exchange of ignorance for that
> Which is another kind of ignorance.   (II. iv. 60–63)

Unfortunately Byron is no more completely successful in the idiom of his dramas than in their construction. Although there are fewer long speeches in his plays than in those of many of his contemporaries, they are far more numerous than in the work of Shakespeare, while the style of his dramatic work is by no means as close to the spoken English of his day as that of the Elizabethans is to theirs. Yet while it must be admitted that Byron did not succeed in establishing himself as a major dramatist it remains true that he wrote several plays of note, while his critical assessment of the problems facing the English dramatist is one of the shrewdest in any period.

One of the things that appealed to Byron about the classical form of drama was that it seemed to offer him the prospect of release from the prison of subjectivity; yet it was by chance and not premeditation that he came on the form by which he was to escape into a larger world of the imagination. One day in 1817 he took up a copy of a lighthearted poem called *Whistlecraft* and found the following lines:

> I've often wish'd that I could write a book,
> Such as all English people might peruse;
> I never should regret the pains it took,
> That's just the sort of fame that I should chuse . . .

Whistlecraft was the work of one of the most gifted amateurs in the history of our literature, John Hookham Frere.[1] A former

---

[1] The full title is as follows: *Prospectus and Specimen of an intended National Work, by William and Robert Whistlecraft, of Stow-Market, in Suffolk, Harness and Collar-Makers. Intended to comprise the most interesting Particulars relating to King Arthur and his Round Table*. John Hookham Frere (1769–1846) was the eldest son of a Norfolk gentleman of antiquarian interests. At Eton he was one of the main contributors to a talented periodical called *The Microcosm* and formed a lifelong friendship with Canning. After being elected a Fellow of Caius College, Cambridge, he entered the Foreign

contributor to the *Anti-Jacobin* and a translator of genius, he had been fascinated by Pulci and had been inspired to attempt an English equivalent of the *Morgante Maggiore*. Byron was fascinated by Frere, as Frere had been by Pulci, and quickly dashed off *Beppo* (1818) in *ottava rima* 'in or after the excellent manner of Mr. Whistlecraft'. He thought of dedicating it to Frere, but refrained, rightly fearing that Frere would disapprove of some of his satiric allusions. Whereas the readers who had looked for politics in *Whistlecraft* had been wasting their time, in *Beppo* we find satire as well as joking. When we turn from Frere's poem to Byron's we move from a world of fun to a world of mischief. The fact that *Beppo* is 'A Venetian Story' does not prevent Byron from glancing satirically at English life. With a fine impartiality he satirizes England for being different from Italy and Italy for having something, after all, in common with England.

Byron seems to have realized that he had made an important discovery. 'If *Beppo* pleases, you shall have more in a year or two in the same mood', he wrote in April 1818; and when Shelley heard a reading of part of *Don Juan* later in the year he described it as 'a thing in the style of *Beppo*, but infinitely better'. While there can be no doubt that *Don Juan* is 'in the style of' the earlier poem, however, it raises questions which do not arise in the case of its predecessor: we are bound to ask what kind of poem *Don Juan* is, and what Byron had in mind as he wrote it. In spite of his references to 'the regularity of my design' and his claim that

> My poem's epic, and is meant to be
> Divided in twelve books

it is clear that he started without any definite idea of how he would finish. That is not the way to write an epic poem—or a mock-epic. 'You ask me for the plan', he wrote to Murray, 'I *have* no plan. . . . The Soul of such writing is its licence.' But he did have a general idea of how the poem should continue—or might continue. 'I meant to take [Don Juan] the tour of Europe', he wrote after completing the fifth canto, 'with a

Office and became M.P. for a pocket borough. In 1797 he joined with Canning and others in producing the *Anti-Jacobin*, to which he contributed some brilliant *jeux d'esprit*. In 1799 he succeeded Canning as Under-Secretary of State in the Foreign Office, but his diplomatic career came to an end because he was blamed for the disastrous decision to retreat to Corunna in 1808. In 1812 he married, settling in Malta four years later for the sake of his wife's health. Scott visited him there in 1831.

proper mixture of siege, battle, and adventure, and to make him finish as *Anacharsis Cloots* in the French Revolution. . . . I meant to have made him a *Cavalier Servente* in Italy, and a cause for a divorce in England, and a Sentimental 'Werther-faced man' in Germany, so as to show the different ridicules of the society in each of those countries, and to have displayed him gradually *gâté* and *blasé* as he grew older. . . . But I had not quite fixed whether to make him end in Hell, or in an unhappy marriage, not knowing which would be the severest.' How long it would take him to describe the Don's adventures he had not decided: the poem would be in 12 cantos, or 24, or 50, or 100, or even 150.

It is difficult to decide what Byron's object was as he wrote the poem. It is clear that he wished *épater les bourgeois*, less clear whether he had any further objective. When he tells us that *Don Juan* is 'the most moral of poems', adding however 'if people won't discover the moral, that is their fault, not mine', is he merely joking? These questions are difficult to answer because the composition of the poem was spread over a number of years and changes of mood and intention must be allowed for. Some of the claims that he made for the poem were made with his tongue in his cheek: on other occasions he was rationalizing after the event. Yet it seems safe to underline the importance of a passage in Canto x:

> Oh for a forty-parson power to chant
>   Thy praise, Hypocrisy! Oh for a hymn
> Loud as the virtues thou dost loudly vaunt,
>   Not practise!

Don Juan's visit to England, which results in some of the most pointed satire in the poem, gives Byron a chance to commend hypocrisy:

> Be hypocritical, be cautious, be
> Not what you *seem*, but always what you *see*.

He addresses the English public directly, in these words:

> You are *not* a moral people, and you know it,
> Without the aid of too sincere a poet.

Like most major satire, *Don Juan* had its origin in indignation. Byron told the Countess Guiccioli that he wrote the first two cantos in Venice at a moment when he was 'soured by a swarm of slanders and injustices', to avenge himself for 'those undeserved torments'. This helps to explain his emphasis on hypocrisy throughout the poem, and the way in which the word 'Cant' recurs so often in his own references to *Don Juan*: 'As to the Cant of the day, I despise it. . . . I will never flatter Cant. . . . I will not give way to all the Cant in Christendom.' He came to regard all hostility to his poem as a refusal to face the truth. 'The truth is that it is TOO TRUE', he once wrote, 'and the women hate every thing which strips off the tinsel of *Sentiment*.' He particularly attacks 'the cant which is the crying sin of this double-dealing and false-speaking time', while in the preface to Cantos VI–VIII he asserts that 'the degraded and hypocritical mass which leavens the present English generation' is incapable of facing the truth. Such had been the outcry when the first two Cantos were published that Cant was momentarily victorious: 'The cry is up', as Byron acknowledged, 'and Cant is up.' It is fitting that this Poem against Cant should be dedicated to Robert Southey, Laureate to George III and the man who seemed to Byron to sum up all that was most objectionable in an age of venality and time-serving. References to Southey in *Don Juan* are almost as numerous as references to Cibber in *The Dunciad*.

There is less danger of the modern reader's overlooking the morally shocking passages than of his failing to notice the passages which struck most contemporary readers as politically shocking. From the point of view of the average reader of the *Quarterly Review* it was a seditious and inflammatory production. This was quite deliberate on Byron's part: 'With these things, and these fellows', as he wrote in a letter, 'it is necessary, in the present clash of philosophy and tyranny, to throw away the scabbard.' The preface to Cantos VI–VIII is particularly revealing, with its bitter justification of the bitter stanzas on Castlereagh, 'a minister . . . the most despotic in intention, and the weakest in intellect, that ever tyrannised over a country'. In the mourning for his death Byron saw nothing but 'the nauseous and atrocious cant of a degraded crew of conspirators against all that is sincere and honourable'. By this point, it is clear, he had come to regard *Don Juan* as a campaign fought against the forces of oppression. 'The hackneyed and lavished title of Blasphemer', he wrote in a letter, '—with Radical, Liberal, Jacobin, Reformer, etc.—should be welcome to all who recollect on whom it was originally bestowed.' All these terms were certainly bestowed on Byron, whose poem gave offence by its anti-imperialism, its anti-royalism, its anti-clericalism, and its leaning to pacifism, no less than by its free tone on moral and religious questions. Alfieri had been the Tragedian of Freedom: now Byron was writing a comic epic with the same serious intention.

The most audacious parts of the poem are its digressions, and any account of *Don Juan* which ignores these passages is bound to be misleading. Byron flaunts them in the reader's face: 'But to my subject—let me see—what was it?', as he observes at one point: 'Oh!—the third canto, and the pretty pair.' Although the digressions sometimes swamp the main narrative, as in Canto III, they are so essential to Byron's intention that we seldom resent them. The introductory passages at the beginning of the cantos are bound to remind us of Fielding, who was clearly in Byron's mind as he wrote his 'comic epic poem in *verse*'; but at times we are reminded even more unmistakably of Sterne. When Byron draws attention to a daring transition with the words—

> .   .   how odd are the connections
> Of human thoughts which jostle in their flight!

—it might be the author of *Tristram Shandy* who is speaking. Byron reminds us of Sterne in his alternations between gaiety and gravity, in the confidential tone in which he discusses his book with the reader, debating points of literary criticism and morality, in the apparent shapelessness of his plot, and in the mischievous way in which he stands things on their heads and is determined to cheat the reader of the expected 'stock response'. Like Sterne, Byron presents himself as a broad-minded philosopher who has seen farther than the common run of mankind. Juanism has something in common with Shandyism and in many ways *Don Juan*, a poem unfinished and unfinishable, stands to the tradition of English poetry as *Tristram Shandy* stands to that of the English novel.

The idiom of *Don Juan* is the idiom of *Beppo*. Having left the Spenserian stanza of *Childe Harold* behind him, Byron is visibly rejoicing in the potentialities of the new stanza, its pace, its informality, and the licence it gives for digression. At times the measure itself seems to become an inspiration to him and the wheels catch fire with the rapidity of their motion. Unlike the pentameter couplet, *ottava rima* is a form which encourages a free play of fancy and makes for inclusion rather than exclusion, suggesting acceptance of the poet's first thought and a hastening on to its successor rather than scrutiny and revision of what has first presented itself. Byron quickly attained a remarkable fluency in the metre, making it so much the expression of his own personality that he could do with it as he pleased. The final couplet is well suited to epigram, and he specializes in bringing things down to earth at the end of the stanza:

> Think you, if Laura had been Petrarch's wife,
> He would have written sonnets all his life? (III. viii)

The skill of the rhyming contributes greatly to the wit of the poem. Byron likes to use the yoke of rhyme to jerk together the most incongruous concepts, such as cosmogony and mahogany, or potato and Cato (a rhyme that is so much a favourite that he uses it three times). In the art of rhyming surprisingly he was a pupil of Butler and Swift, and some of the most 'Hudibrastic' rhymes in the language are to be found in *Don Juan*, such as intellectual/hen-peck'd you all, Alonso/go on so, and oddest he/modesty. There are also occasional violent enjambements, such as hence-/forward, and the following—in the account of the shipwreck in Canto II:

> Started the stern-post, also shattered the
> Whole of her stern-frame, and, ere she could lift
> Herself . . . (II. xxvii)

As for the diction, what the *Edinburgh Review* said of *Beppo* is equally true of *Don Juan*:

The great charm is in the simplicity and naturalness of the language—the free but guarded use of all polite idioms, and even of all phrases of temporary currency that have the stamp of good company upon them,—with the exclusion of all scholastic or ambitious eloquence . . . good verse, entirely composed of common words, in their common places; never . . . one sprig of what is called poetical diction . . . running on in an inexhaustible series of good easy colloquial phrases, and [falling] into verse by some unaccountable and happy fatality. (xxix. 303, February 1818)

No word in the language is too familiar or too commonplace to be used in this poem, which contains such humdrum words and phrases as mortgage, Patent Blacking, vermicelli, soda water, menagerie, indigestion, really, hencoops, Five per Cents, butler,

cheese-paring, ready money, bagged, billiards, thereanent, old
newspaper, affidavit, solvent, portmanteaus, income tax, super-
cargo, beefsteak, post-obit, damme, guts, cough, breakfast, non-
suit, raising cash, emetic, entrails, broth, jugular, blankets,
cookery, phthisical, clap-trap, grand-dad, quiz, valet, teaspoon-
fuls, annuities, and gastric juice. Of many of these it may be
said, as Byron says of 'broth', that it is 'A thing which poesy
but seldom mentions'.

The use of 'the language of every day' in *Beppo* and *Don Juan*
has nothing to do with the theories of Wordsworth: Byron's use
of familiar diction is that of an aristocratic writer conversant
with classical literature and the English poets of the early eighteenth century. He is aware of the different 'levels of style', and
is deliberately choosing to 'wander with pedestrian Muses'. It
is significant that the Horatian motto of *Don Juan—Difficile est
proprie communia dicere*—had already been the motto of *An Epistle
to Dr. Arbuthnot*. It is to the work of the Augustans that one must
look for English analogies to the style of *Don Juan*—and not
least to the *Alma* of Matthew Prior.

Several of his friends assure us that the style of *Don Juan* is an
echo of Byron's conversation at its best. That is what he himself
claims:

> I rattle on exactly as I'd talk
> With anybody in a ride or walk. (xv. xix)

If we look into his letters and journals we find the soil from
which the poem grew. Some explanation of the remarkably sure
tone of *Don Juan* may be found in the fact that Byron's letters
to John Murray were habitually read out to the publisher's
friends, or passed round among them, so that he knew that he
was writing for a small group of intelligent and sophisticated
people. *Don Juan* seems to have been written with just such an
audience in mind, an audience of witty men of the world. As he
tells his story Byron catches perfectly the tone of conversation:

> I had my doubts, perhaps I have them still,
> But what I say is neither here nor there:
> I knew his father well, and have some skill
> In character—but it would not be fair
> From sire to son to augur good or ill:
> He and his wife were an ill-assorted pair—
> But scandal's my aversion—I protest
> Against all evil speaking, even in jest. (I. li)

Don Juan's visit to London gives Byron a particularly good opportunity for exploring the resources of colloquial diction, and he by no means limits himself to idioms 'that have the stamp of good company upon them'. A writer in the first number of the *London Magazine* made the suggestion that Byron may have used the 'New and comprehensive Vocabulary of the Flash Language' in *The Memoirs of James Hardy Vaux* to supplement his own knowledge in some of the more aggressively 'familiar' passages—such as, perhaps, the ironical requiem pronounced over an English soldier:

> Who in a row like Tom could lead the van,
> Booze in the ken, or at the spellken hustle?
> Who queer a flat? . . .   (XI. xix)

But often all he had to do was to put the most obvious vulgarities of speech into verse:

> 'Oh Jack! I'm floored by that 'ere bloody Frenchman!'   (XI. xiii)

—a line that Kipling must have envied. Yet the delight of the poem lies in its variety, and beside such passages as these we must set the idyllic description of Juan and Haidée in Canto IV, which is managed with great delicacy, and ends finely:

> No stone is there to show, no tongue to say
> What was; no dirge, except the hollow sea's,
> Mourns o'er the beauty of the Cyclades.   (IV. lxxii)

Of all the differences between *Don Juan* and *Childe Harold* perhaps the most important lies in the presentation of their heroes, and this is closely related to the style in which the two poems are written. Although some details in Don Juan's life may be paralleled in Byron's own, he is not a self-projection in the sense in which Childe Harold is: as a consequence he is presented with a detachment and irony which are not to be found in the earlier poem. The fundamental difference between the two poems is that Byron has moved from a world in which the passions are presented 'straight' to one in which the predominant spirit is that of satiric comedy. As a consequence, while it might be said that there are in *Childe Harold* no other people, apart from the hero himself, *Don Juan* is almost as full of human beings as the *Canterbury Tales*. Life is no longer portrayed as the oppression of one individual by the rest of the world working in collusion. The alternations between passages 'droll or pathetic, descriptive or sentimental, tender or satirical' which were to have been a feature of *Childe Harold* but which in fact can hardly be found in that poem, are the hallmark and glory of *Don Juan*. As we read it we are reminded that what Byron found in *Whistlecraft* was not simply a new stanza: it was a new idiom—and with it the inducement to look at life in a new way. 'It will . . . show them that I can write cheerfully, and repel the charge of monotony and mannerism', as he had written to John Murray of *Beppo*. To see what the new idiom did for Byron we have only to turn to *Don Juan* from the poems he had been writing little more than a year before, *The Lament of Tasso* and *Manfred*. It is not surprising that Shelley noticed that Byron was more cheerful as he worked at his new satire. In the new rhythm Byron found emancipation: what it brought him (with other gifts) was a sense of proportion. There are few clearer examples of the way in which the discovery of a new medium may enable a writer to discover a new aspect of his personality— or rather to express an aspect of his personality that has remained unexpressed and therefore undeveloped.

Don Juan sold very rapidly, but most of its original readers were, or pretended to be, scandalized. One of the things that particularly shocked them was Byron's satire on his wife. So great was the public disapproval that after the publication of the second part (Cantos III–V) the Countess Guiccioli prevailed on Byron to put the poem aside: when he took it up again it was on the understanding that it was to be 'more guarded and decorous and sentimental'. Even so, there was further trouble, and the last eleven Cantos were published by John Hunt. When Byron died sixteen cantos and some fragments had been written, but the poem was not in sight of completion.

Byron's last major poem was an outcome of the storm aroused by the early cantos of *Don Juan*. When Southey published his Laureate elegy on George III in 1821 he included in the preface 'a few comments on Don Juan'. Everything about Southey's *A Vision of Judgement* seemed to mark it out for ridicule. In dedicating it to George IV he asked rhetorically: 'To whom could an experiment, which, perhaps, may be considered hereafter as of some importance in English Poetry, be so fitly inscribed, as to the Royal and munificent Patron of science, art, and literature?' To whom—we may rephrase it—more fitly than to such a King

as George IV could a poem be dedicated which was fated never
to be read except as a joke, to help the reader to enjoy one of the
most unanswerable satires in all literature? Southey's whole preface is written in a strain which must have inspired a mixture
of contempt and fury in a man of Byron's political sympathies.
Southey particularly mentions the 'perfect integrity . . . mani-
fested in the whole administration of public affairs' and prophesies that 'the brightest portion of British history will be that
which records the improvements, the works, and the achievements of the Georgian Age'. In the poem itself the poet falls
into a trance in which he sees that George III's coffin is empty
and then overhears Perceval reporting to the late Monarch on
the state of the country—a report which is more favourable on
foreign affairs than on matters at home, where 'rabid fanatics'
are on the prowl, foolishly pursuing what they imagine to be
Liberty. The poet then sees the King arriving at the Gate of
Heaven, where Good Spirits assemble to support him while Evil
Spirits appear from Hell, led, rather unobtrusively, by Satan in
person. Wilkes and Junius appear to speak against the King,
but they are so overwhelmed by the presence of the Deity that
they are unable to open their mouths. The other accusers of the
King admit that what they said against him during his lifetime
was unjust. Even Washington admits that nothing but circumstances led to their opposition:

Heaven in these things fulfill'd its wise, though inscrutable purpose,
While we work'd its will, doing each in his place as became him.

After he has spoken 'with earnest humility' on his own behalf
the King receives a blessing and the ministering spirits 'clap . . .
their pennons' and burst into song. As the King is received into
Heaven the reception committee includes the most eminent of
the former monarchs of England as well as other worthies like
Bede, Friar Bacon, Chaucer, Cranmer, Cecil, Spenser, and
Shakespeare—it is all very 'snob'. The Worthies of the Georgian
Age include Wolfe, Handel, Hogarth, Wesley, Burke, Warren
Hastings, Cowper, and Nelson—but not (as Southey pointed
out delightedly in a letter) either Pitt or Fox. The fact that there
is yet another tier of Worthies—The Young Spirits—serves to
emphasize that the poem is in some sort a Hymn on the
Georgian Age.

Many even among Southey's admirers were embarrassed by

his *Vision of Judgement*, and it was parodied by more than one of
his opponents. Pursued by that Spirit of Comedy which seems
to have been keeping so remorseless a watch on his doings at
this time, he went so far as to invite Byron to attack him in verse.
'When he attacks me again', he wrote in a letter in the *Courier*,
'let it be in rhyme. For one who has so little command of
himself, it will be a great advantage that his temper should be
obliged to *keep tune*.' If Southey had only known it, Byron had
already written *The Vision of Judgment* in which he 'keeps tune'
to some purpose. Neither the tune nor the politics are Southey's.
Writing from Italy on 1 October 1821 Byron told Moore:

> I have written . . . about sixty stanzas of a poem, in octave stanzas,
> (in the Pulci style, which the fools in England think was invented by
> Whistlecraft—it is as old as the hills in Italy,)—called *The Vision of
> Judgment*, by Quevedo Redivivus, with this motto—
>
> > A Daniel come to *judgment*, yea, a Daniel:
> > I thank thee, Jew, for teaching me that word.
>
> In this it is my intent to put the said George's Apotheosis in a Whig
> point of view, not forgetting the Poet Laureate for his preface and
> his other demerits.

It is hardly surprising that John Murray refused to have anything to do with *The Vision of Judgment*. After some delay John
Hunt published it in *The Liberal*, but although he omitted the
preface he was eventually fined a hundred pounds for publishing a work 'calumniating the late king, and wounding the feelings of his present majesty'. If the preface had been published
the fine would probably have been much heavier. In it Byron
refers to 'the gross flattery, the dull impudence, the renegado
intolerance, and impious cant, of the poem by the author of
"Wat Tyler"' and says that it is 'something so stupendous as to
form the sublime of himself—containing the quintessence of his
own attributes'. The gravamen of Byron's charges is contained
in the following sentences:

> To attempt to canonise a monarch, who, whatever were his house-
> hold virtues, was neither a successful nor a patriot king,—inasmuch
> as several years of his reign passed in war with America and Ireland,
> to say nothing of the aggression upon France—like all other exag-
> geration, necessarily begets opposition. In whatever manner he

may be spoken of in this new *Vision*, his *public* career will not be more favourably transmitted by history. Of his private virtues (although a little expensive to the nation) there can be no doubt.

Since the contrast of tunes is part of the satire, it is worth recalling the opening of Southey's *Vision*:

'Twas at that sober hour when the light of day is receding,
And from surrounding things the hues wherewith day has adorned
them
Fade, like the hopes of youth, till the beauty of earth is departed.

Byron's irreverent octaves form the most marked contrast possible with these sombre hexameters:

Saint Peter sat by the celestial gate:
　His keys were rusty, and the lock was dull,
So little trouble had been given of late;
　Not that the place by any means was full,
But since the Gallic era 'eighty-eight'
　The Devils had ta'en a longer, stronger pull,
And 'a pull altogether', as they say
At sea—which drew most souls another way.

After he has set his scene on the threshold of Heaven Byron glances back to the carnage of Waterloo—so reminding us that *The Vision of Judgment* was written during the composition of *Don Juan*, and prompting the suggestion that some ideas he was thinking of utilizing if he sent the Don to Hell may have found their way (instead) into his other great satire. Then, after some satirical stanzas on the character of the late King, he returns to St. Peter, to whom the news of the King's death is reported by a cherub:

'And who *is* George the Third?' replied the apostle:
'*What George? What Third?*'

Among the host of good angels and bad who arrive in the King's train there is 'a spirit of a different aspect' who is none other than the familiar Byronic hero now playing the role of the Prince of Darkness:

His brow was like the deep when tempest-tossed;
Fierce and unfathomable thoughts engraved
Eternal wrath on his immortal face,
And *where* he gazed a gloom pervaded space.

The meeting between Satan and Michael has all the courtesy appropriate to proceedings in the Upper Chamber:

> .   . Though they did not kiss,
> Yet still between his Darkness and his Brightness
> There passed a mutual glance of great politeness.

Michael bowed low, while Satan responded

> With more hauteur, as might an old Castilian
> Poor Noble meet a mushroom rich civilian.

As Satan speaks in support of his claim to the King's soul the serious intention of Byron's satire becomes evident:

> He ever warred with freedom and the free:
>   Nations as men, home subjects, foreign foes,
> So that they uttered the word 'Liberty!'
>   Found George III their first opponent. Whose
> History was ever stained as his will be
>   With national and individual woes?

His appeal to St. Peter asking whether a King who has opposed Catholic emancipation should be allowed to enter heaven is an excellent example of *argumentum ad hominem*—or rather, in this case, *argumentum ad angelum*. When the witnesses against the King are summoned such a host appears that it is decided that Wilkes and Junius shall speak for them all. Instead of being reduced to silence by shame, as they are in Southey's poem, they speak briefly but devastatingly. Wilkes is too magnanimous to press his charges, adding:

> I don't like ripping up old stories, since
> His conduct was but natural in a prince.

Junius (mysterious in death as in life) contents himself with saying

> I loved my country, and I hated him,

and adds that he stands by what he has written. At this point, when Washington, Horne Tooke, and Franklin are about to be called to give further evidence, there is a stir, and a devil elbows his way in carrying Southey under his wing and complaining bitterly at the weight. The prospect of his speech in his own defence causes consternation, and St. Peter appeals to him (as one author to another) to confine his reply to prose. The gist of Southey's reply is that he is a professional turncoat who must sell his wares in the best market. There is a delightful touch in stanza xcix, where he turns to Satan and offers to write his Life 'In two octavo volumes, nicely bound, With notes and preface', adding that there is no need to be anxious about the reception of the book, as he can choose his own reviewers. When Satan bows without answering, Southey hastens to make the same offer to Michael. Then he begins to read his latest poem, *A Vision of Judgement*, and the effect is dramatic:

> Those grand heroics acted as a spell;
>   The Angels stopped their ears and plied their pinions;
> The Devils ran howling, deafened, down to Hell;
>   The ghosts fled, gibbering, for their own dominions—
> (For 'tis not yet decided where they dwell,
>   And I leave every man to his opinions);
> Michael took refuge in his trump—but lo!
> His teeth were set on edge, he could not blow!

St. Peter knocked Southey down with his keys. The vision faded, and all that Byron saw, in the end,

> Was, that King George slipped into Heaven for one;
>   And when the tumult dwindled to a calm,
>   I left him practising the hundredth psalm.

It is a perfect ending for a poem which is not the less lethal for the ubiquitous spirit of comedy. Byron can afford to treat the King with a contemptuous magnanimity because his main concern is with the conduct of public affairs during his reign. It is appropriate that *The Vision of Judgment* should have been written so soon after the inquiry into the affairs of Queen Caroline: it remains the perfect satiric commentary on one of the most tawdry periods in our history, a trenchant indictment of the age of reaction that followed Waterloo—the age which was beginning, even as Byron wrote, to give way to what Halévy called 'The Age of the Liberal Awakening'. It is the quintessence of Byron's satire, 'the sublime of himself', and forms a fitting climax to his poetic career.

When he died at Missolonghi Byron wrote his name in history. The handsome young poet who was also a *milord anglais* and a trenchant critic of all things English was perfectly calculated to appeal to the heart of Europe. His fame grew rapidly and to this day he remains a central figure in the European

'Romantic Movement' and one of the sources of the popular
idea of a poet. His life and personality had a remarkable influence on Goethe. His influence on the Romantic Movements
in Germany, France, Italy, Spain, and Russia was at once
obvious and profound. He is the only English poet to have a
chapter devoted to him in Bertrand Russell's *History of Western
Philosophy*.

His true stature as a poet is another matter. Although it would
have made more difference to the history of Europe if Byron had
never lived than if Keats had never lived, it would have made
more difference to the history of English poetry if Keats had
never lived. There is in fact a connexion between the limited
nature of Byron's poetic achievement and his high reputation
abroad. It is precisely because no powerful electric current
passes through the language when he uses it—as it does when
Shakespeare and Milton use it—that so much of Byron's poetry
survives the processes of export and translation. The Continental critics who insist most strongly on his greatness often turn
out to read what are (from a critical point of view) the wrong
poems, or the right poems in the wrong language. How much
of Byron's poetry had Goethe read, with full understanding, in
English? In an intelligent full-scale study, published as recently as
1955–7, M. Robert Escarpit more often offers his readers quotations from Byron's poetry in French than in English. It must
be acknowledged that Byron himself might not have objected.
'I cannot alter the Sentiments', he wrote to Murray in September
1811, when he was asked to make some revisions in the first two
Cantos of *Childe Harold*; 'but if there are any alterations in the
structure of the versification you would wish to be made, I will
tag rhymes and turn stanzas as much as you please'. But if
poetry is the best words in the best order, great poetry cannot
be altered in such a manner, and it is no accident that the
poems of Byron's which suffer most from alteration or translation—*Don Juan* and *The Vision of Judgment*—are those which are
most highly valued in England and which most often tend to
be underrated in foreign studies of his work. While Byron's life
and character will continue to provide a splendid subject for
debate, few English critics are ever likely to disagree with
Tennyson's view that of all Byron's poems it is the satires which
survive.

III

SHELLEY

IT is a paradox that Shelley is often described as a 'pure poet'.[1] In fact, as Mary Shelley pointed out, he combined two qualities of intellect that are not often associated in so high a development: 'a brilliant imagination' and 'a logical exactness of reason'. As a consequence he 'deliberated at one time whether he should dedicate himself to poetry or metaphysics', and it can only have been after anxious consideration that he decided to be a poet. Although we are told that he then began to educate himself for poetry by 'engaging . . . in the study of the poets of Greece, Italy, and England', it is possible to exaggerate the extent to which he discarded 'his philosophical pursuits'. When he was at work on *Prometheus Unbound* he could still tell Peacock that he considered poetry 'very subordinate to moral and political science', adding that he would have devoted himself to the latter study if he had been more robust. This makes it the less surprising that he is one of the most didactic of all our poets. His remark in the preface to *Prometheus Unbound*, 'Didactic poetry is my abhorrence', is the most misleading sentence he ever wrote. By 'didactic poetry' he here means primarily close

---

[1] Percy Bysshe Shelley (1792–1822) belonged to an ancient family. His father Timothy Shelley was a conservative country gentleman without intellectual sympathies. He was educated at Sion House Academy, Brentford, and at Eton, where he was intensely miserable and felt himself to be 'apart from the whole school'. Dr. Lind, a Fellow of the Royal Society who lived at Windsor, befriended Shelley and encouraged his scientific interests. While he was still at school he published *Zastrozzi*, a wild Gothic romance: *St. Irvyne; or, The Rosicrucian* appeared just after he had left. In 1810 he went to University College, Oxford, but the following year he was sent down for circulating a brief pamphlet, *The Necessity of Atheism*, to the Heads of Colleges. Soon after this he ran away with Harriet Westbrook, marrying her in Edinburgh. He met Southey and was soon corresponding with Godwin. After some comically ineffective attempts to participate in politics he printed *Queen Mab* in 1813. In 1815 he left his wife for Mary Godwin, whom he married after Harriet's suicide at the end of 1816. Earlier that year he and Mary had paid a prolonged visit to Byron in Switzerland. After a period at Marlow when he saw a good deal of Leigh Hunt and Peacock he travelled on the Continent and visited Byron again, in Venice. Shelley spent the rest of his brief life in Italy, where he wrote almost all his finest poetry. He was drowned while crossing alone in a small boat from Leghorn to Lerici. His body was cremated on the beach in the presence of Byron, Trelawny, and Hunt.

reasoning in verse, in the manner of Lucretius. As we study his longer poems we shall find him concerned with the problem of how to be didactic most tellingly, rather than with that of whether to be didactic.

His earlier work is inferior to the *juvenilia* of many less gifted poets. Poor as it is as poetry, however, *Queen Mab* is of great interest: with its mottoes from Voltaire, Lucretius, and Archimedes, this 'pamphlet in verse' (as Dowden called it) is one of the most nakedly didactic poems ever written. 'The Past, the Present, and the Future, are the grand and comprehensive topics of this poem', as he wrote in a letter. It was written to disseminate his ideas and begin the process of proselytizing the world. It is clear that he was uncertain how openly didactic a poet could dare to be. 'The notes . . . will be long and philosophical', he wrote; 'I shall take that opportunity . . . of propagating my principles, which I decline to do syllogistically in [a] poem. A poem very didactic is, I think, very stupid.' But three weeks later he tells another friend that the didactic part of the poem is in blank verse, while the descriptive parts are in an unrhymed lyrical measure. In fact the poem and its notes form a unity, and it is to the notes that a reader in search of the ideas of the young Shelley is more likely to turn. They are a strange jumble: the poet is against monarchy, against Christianity, against chastity (as it is usually understood), and against the eating of animal flesh. It is difficult to read some of the notes without reflecting that the author was a very young man: 'Since writing this note I have some reason to suspect that Jesus was an ambitious man, who aspired to the throne of Judea.' Yet the notes are not the work of a fool, and many of the criticisms of the accepted ideas of the time are extremely shrewd. The Don Quixote of English poetry is already committed to the campaign against tyranny and hypocrisy which was to end only with his death.

A man with a message is a man in search of an audience, and Shelley speculated a great deal about who would read his poems. The difficulty was that a large audience was incompatible with the nature of his views. 'As I have not abated an iota of the infidelity or cosmopolicy of it', he wrote of *Queen Mab*, 'sufficient will remain . . . to make it very unpopular. Like all egotists, I shall console myself with what I may call, if I please, the suffrages of the chosen few.' He took it for granted that these would come from the wealthier classes, ordering that only 250 copies should be printed—'a small, neat quarto, on fine paper, . . . so as to catch the aristocrats'. In the event Shelley withdrew the book after some seventy presentation copies had been distributed and before a single copy of the original edition had been sold; and yet, by a typically Shelleyan paradox, this was the only one of his books to circulate at all widely in the earlier part of the century. Soon the Radicals made it a sort of Bible, and Robert Owen never ceased to quote from it in writings which were by no stretch of the imagination addressed to 'the aristocrats'.

The preface to *The Revolt of Islam* (1818) makes it clear that Shelley was anxious to discover how far an audience existed for the sort of views that he wished to propagate and how far he had the power of propagating them. He described the poem as 'an experiment on the temper of the public mind, as to how far a thirst for a happier condition of . . . society survives, among the enlightened and refined, the tempests which have shaken the age in which we live'. But characteristically he made no concessions. The poem opens with a canto of perplexed and obscure allegory, radically different (as Shelley acknowledged) from the remaining cantos; yet he sent this canto to a publisher as a specimen of the whole. What is more, in the poem as he originally wrote it (as *Laon and Cythna*) the lovers who are the main characters are brother and sister, so that their love is incestuous. 'It was my object', he wrote in the original preface, 'to break through the crust of those outworn opinions on which established institutions depend.' His aim was to 'accustom men to that charity and toleration which the exhibition of a practice widely differing from their own has a tendency to promote'. One sometimes wonders whether Shelley ever met any ordinary men and women. The lack of human insight or common sense displayed in the whole affair is very striking. It was only with the greatest difficulty that his friends prevailed on him to make the necessary changes. Even so, they did not think that the poem was likely to sell well. 'The work cannot possibly be popular' Leigh Hunt wrote, as if in answer to a question.

There can be no doubt of the didactic intention of the poem. The sub-title of *Laon and Cythna* had been 'The Revolution of the Golden City: A Vision of the Nineteenth Century', while the preface proclaims that the poem has been written 'in the cause of a liberal and comprehensive morality' on behalf of 'liberty and justice'. The allegorical first canto describes a battle between an Eagle and a Serpent, representing (respectively) Evil and Good. Good is defeated, but not, as it turns out, killed. The poet, who is depressed at the course taken by the French Revolution, is a spectator at this battle; but he is told not to give way to despair. Like Peacock, Shelley was alarmed by the pessimism of much of the literature of the age, regarding it as the expression of an exaggerated reaction from the French Revolution. He had been seeing a good deal of Byron at this time, and *The Revolt* appears to be an anti-Byronic poem. Shelley's challenge sounds out clearly in the preface: 'Those who now live have survived an age of despair.' Despair is an enemy that must be kept at bay: as the mysterious Genius says to the poet,

> .   . to grieve is wise, but the despair
> Was weak and vain which led thee here from sleep.
>
> (I. xxi)

The message of the poem is optimistic. It describes the adventures of two reformers and all that they accomplish in a State until the forces of reaction rally and burn them to death on a great pyre. We leave them in a paradisaical condition, in the Temple of the Spirit in which the poet had first seen them. The whole thing is 'a tale', as Shelley wrote to a publisher, 'illustrative of such a Revolution as might be supposed to take place in an European nation, acted upon by the opinions of . . . the modern philosophy . . .' The inspiration is clearly what had happened in France, but the intention is to be as general as possible. It is a sort of handbook for bloodless revolutionaries; and would no doubt be useful for anyone who happened to live in a world in essential respects different from this old world of ours. As Mary Shelley pointed out, it is a work embodying 'forms defecated of all the weakness and evil which cling to real life'.

The presentation of such idealized creatures now seemed to Shelley to be the mode of didacticism most likely to succeed. In the preface to a much greater work than *The Revolt*, *Prometheus Unbound* (1820), he acknowledges 'a passion for reforming the world' but denies that he dedicates his poems 'solely to the direct enforcement of reform' or considers them 'as containing a reasoned system on the theory of human life'. He goes on: 'My purpose has . . . been . . . to familiarise the highly refined imagination of the more select classes of poetical readers with beautiful idealisms of moral excellence.' His idea, which is Platonic, is that 'reasoned principles of moral conduct' are useless until men have been taught to love that which is beautiful and virtuous. Experience has taught him how small the class of such readers is. 'If I may judge by its merits,' he wrote, 'the "Prometheus" cannot sell beyond twenty copies.' Later he claimed that it 'was never intended for more than five or six persons'. Leigh Hunt, who deeply admired it, aptly described it as an 'odi profanum sort of poem' and despaired of making it 'at all recommendable to readers in general'. It is wholly appropriate that the young Yeats should have been intoxicated by it and should have hoped that his fellow students would join him in regarding it as a sacred book—no less appropriate that they should have done no such thing.

As Mary Shelley pointed out, *Prometheus Unbound* is 'a more idealized image of the same subject' as *The Revolt of Islam*. Whereas Laon strives to bring freedom (primarily political and social freedom) to one particular State, Prometheus brings Freedom in the deepest and most comprehensive sense to the whole of mankind. Just as Laon is separated from his lover Cythna for most of the action, so Prometheus is separated from the more passive Asia. Prometheus and Asia are more ethereal than Laon and Cythna because they are not human beings but Titans, and they end (fittingly) in a more ethereal form of paradise. They are Aeschylean figures far transcending mere humanity: while Laon is concerned in the highest sense with politics, Prometheus is involved in a drama which is rather metaphysical than political. Leigh Hunt perceptively referred to the 'sublime cosmopolitics' of the work. We are now seeing the conflict between the Eagle and the Serpent, Tyranny and Freedom, 'at the highest possible level'—to use reporters' jargon. This revolution takes place in heaven, and cannot be assigned to a particular point in time.

It is not difficult to see why Prometheus is the perfect hero for Shelley, and his story the perfect subject for his poetry. As Mary Shelley tells us, 'the subject he loved best to dwell on was the image of One warring with the Evil Principle, oppressed not only by it, but by all—even the good, who were deluded into considering evil a necessary portion of humanity'. In Aeschylus

Jupiter and Prometheus are reconciled, the latter buying his
release from torment by disclosing the secret that is essential to
Jupiter's safety. Shelley 'was averse from a catastrophe so feeble
as that of reconciling the Champion with the Oppressor of Mankind'. To Shelley Prometheus meant very much what Christ
means for Christians,

> The saviour and the strength of suffering man.
>
> (i. 817)

The drama describes the last act, as it were, in the triumph
of Prometheus over Jupiter. The past history of the struggle is
narrated in retrospective speeches. Although it is often said that
the action takes place in the mind of Prometheus, in a sense his
spiritual victory occurs before the play opens, or at the very
beginning. From the first, in foretelling the final overthrow of
Jupiter, he speaks 'in grief, Not exultation'; and when he is reminded of his curse against Jupiter he revokes it, with the words:

> I wish no living thing to suffer pain.   (i. 305)

This in no way involves submission to Jupiter. One of the worst
torments that he is made to suffer is the contemplation of the
fate of Christ, whose wishes for Man had been so like his own:

> .   . Thy name I will not speak,
> It hath become a curse.   (i. 603–4)

As a climax of his suffering he witnesses in a vision the failure
of the French Revolution. Yet Act I closes with the promise that
the Hour of 'Wisdom, Justice, Love, and Peace' is on the way.
In Act II Asia awaits his coming, in a distant Eastern valley.
Her conversation with Demogorgon (who stands for Eternity:
'Demand no direr name', he warns her) fills in the metaphysical
background of the myth as Shelley interprets it. In the beginning there were the Heaven and Earth, and Light and Love.
Then Saturn came to reign. In a sense the *Saturnia regna* were
idyllically happy, but his coming brought with it Time, 'an
envious shadow', and under him men were without Knowledge,
'the birthright of their being', and without

> Self-empire, and the majesty of love;
> For thirst of which they fainted.   (II. iv. 42–43)

Saturn's child Jupiter succeeds him, to whom Prometheus
gives wisdom 'which is strength', with one law only, 'Let man

be free'. Tyrant-like, Jupiter violates this law, and man becomes the victim of tyranny. Prometheus responds by awakening 'the legioned hopes' and sending Love to mankind, and
all other good and beautiful things—thought, speech, the arts,
civilization:

> .   .   Cities then
> Were built, and through their snow-like columns flowed
> The warm winds, and the azure aether shone,
> And the blue sea and shadowy hills were seen. (II. iv. 94–97)

Jupiter then chains Prometheus to the rock in the Caucasus
where we see him.

Inevitably there is some obscurity in the metaphysics of the
poem, as in every attempt to explain the apparently inexplicable. We are told that God reigns supreme over Jupiter and all
else, but what is meant by the word 'God' is not altogether clear.
He appears to be morally neutral, the author of terror, madness,
and crime, as well as of the reason and the imagination. Jupiter
is evil, but he is not the origin of evil: that is inexpressible,
though one may use the words

> Fate, Time, Occasion, Chance, and Change. (II. iv. 119)

How God is related to these entities is obscure. Apparently
'eternal Love' is superior to all except God—if not to God
himself.

At the beginning of Act III Jupiter is rejoicing. He has gained
all that he wished, except that

> The soul of man, like unextinguished fire,
> Yet burns towards heaven with fierce reproach.
>
> (III. i. 4–5)

He is confident because he has now begotten 'a strange wonder,
That fatal child, the terror of the earth', who will somehow
'trample out the spark' of the spirit of man. At this point Jupiter
himself is overthrown. Demogorgon tells him that no tyrant like
himself will ever arise again, while a Spirit of Earth describes
the change that has come over everything in an astonishing
passage of verse:

> All things had put their evil nature off:
> I cannot tell my joy, when o'er a lake
> Upon a drooping bough with nightshade twined,
> I saw two azure halcyons clinging downward

And thinning one bright bunch of amber berries,
With quick long beaks, and in the deep there lay
Those lovely forms imaged as in a sky;
So, with my thoughts full of these happy changes,
We meet again, the happiest change of all.

(III. iv. 77–85)

The downfall of Jupiter is the downfall of tyranny of every kind.
It is true that mankind is not exempt

From chance, and death, and mutability;   (III. iv. 201)

yet in some undefined way these have now become its slaves,
instead of being its masters.

Prometheus Unbound was originally written in three Acts. Some
months later Shelley thought that a fourth Act should be added,
'a sort of hymn of rejoicing in the fulfilment of the prophecies
with regard to Prometheus'. The fourth Act, which is much the
most lyrical part of the whole work, contains some magnificent
verse; but it is more obscure than the rest of the drama, and it
is by no means evident that it forms a fitting conclusion to the
first three Acts. It has certainly discouraged many readers who
can understand the rest of *Prometheus Unbound*, and this is not
necessarily their fault. At times one feels, in reading this work
of genius, as Asia feels when she addresses Panthea in Act II:

.   .   Thou speakest, but thy words
Are as the air: I feel them not.   (II. i. 108–9)

Shelley has gone beyond the normal range of the human ear.

Shelley was aware that *Prometheus Unbound* was a masterpiece;
yet it is not surprising that he followed it with a drama designed
to reach a wide audience.[1] The contrast between *Prometheus
Unbound* and *The Cenci* (1820) is the contrast between the esoteric and the exoteric, and it seems clear that Shelley was beginning to think of many of his works as falling into one or
other of these contrasting categories. Bewildered by the problem
of reaching an audience, he was coming to the conclusion that
he must choose on each occasion between writing to please
himself—and so abjuring any possibility of being widely read—
and writing in such a way as to appeal to a considerable section
of the reading public—and laying aside most of his own parti-

[1] Although *The Cenci* was published in March 1820, and *Prometheus Unbound* did
not appear until September, the three-Act version of *Prometheus Unbound* was written
just before *The Cenci*.

cular opinions and habits of imagination to gain this object. He told Peacock that *The Cenci* was 'totally different from anything you might conjecture that I should write; of a more popular kind', and once he went so far as to describe it as 'written for the multitude'. On several occasions he explicitly contrasted it with *Prometheus Unbound*: from that work, he wrote, 'I expect and desire no great sale. "The Cenci" ought to have been popular.' It was written (or so he supposed) 'without any of the peculiar feelings and opinions which characterise my other compositions': that was the price he had to pay, if he was to make any effort at popularity. It was composed with a view to performance: he hoped that Miss O'Neill might take the part of Beatrice, while ideally he would have liked Kean to have played Count Cenci.

As so often happened with Shelley, the result was the opposite of what he intended. Perhaps no other man would have based a play which he wished to be popular on the theme of a father's incestuous passion for his daughter. Although he claimed, quite justly, that this subject is handled with great delicacy, it prevented the play from receiving a public performance for many decades after his death. All the self-discipline which had enabled him to write about real men and women, avoiding, as he said, 'dreams of what ought to be', proved to have been in vain. It is not surprising that he was profoundly discouraged. As he wrote to Peacock, nothing is 'more difficult and unwelcome' than to write 'without a confidence of finding readers; and if my play of "The Cenci" found none or few, I despair of ever producing anything that shall merit them'.

The Cenci might be described as an attempt to escape from the prison of subjectivity and intellectual abstraction, but Shelley himself saw it in rather different terms. He tells us that in writing it he 'sacrificed [his] own peculiar notions in a certain sort by treating of any subject, the basis of which is moral error': in another letter he mentions that his aim was 'to produce a delineation of passions which I had never participated in': while in a third reference he says that it was written 'rather to try my powers than to unburthen my full heart'. The play has no conscious didactic purpose: it aims solely at truth to character in a given set of circumstances. But as Mary Shelley wrote:

The bent of his mind went the other way; and, even when employed on subjects whose interest depended on character and incident, he would start off in another direction, and leave the delineations of human passion, which he could depict in so able a manner, for fantastic creations of his fancy, or the expression of those opinions and sentiments, with regard to human nature and its destiny, a desire to diffuse which was the master passion of his soul.

Both the Fourth Act of *Prometheus Unbound* and *The Witch of Atlas* (a much less important work) may be regarded as the product of Shelley's reaction from the strain of writing *The Cenci*.

It had been the opinion of Shelley himself, and that of most of his friends, that he was devoid of dramatic instinct. *The Cenci* triumphantly refutes this. Count Cenci and Beatrice are considerable creations. Part of Shelley's success must be attributed to the fact that the chain of actions on which he built his drama did in fact appeal to his own 'peculiar feelings and opinions'. We are now shown the war between Freedom and Tyranny transferred to the human stage. If Aeschylus and Sophocles were in his mind when he wrote *Prometheus Unbound*, it is of Euripides (among the Greeks) that we are now most forcibly reminded.

It is sometimes said that Shelley lacks variety of style: that whatever the demands of genre and subject-matter may be, what he writes is always just a passage of Shelley. To compare the idiom of *The Cenci* with that of *Prometheus Unbound* is to see how untrue that is. He tells us that he has 'avoided with great care . . . what is commonly called mere poetry', pointing out that 'there will scarcely be found a detached simile or a single isolated description' in the whole drama. He claims to have avoided 'an over-fastidious and learned use of words', keeping instead to 'the real language of men' (he quotes Wordsworth's phrase). His aim was clearly to forge a flexible dramatic idiom for the play. He was deliberately facing many of the charges that had been made against his verse, and trying to meet them: in this work at least it was to be evident that his imagination was his servant and not his master. And indeed the contrast between the idiom of this work and that of *Prometheus Unbound*, a 'lyrical drama', is very striking:

> The loathsome mask has fallen, the man remains
> Sceptreless, free, uncircumscribed, but man
> Equal, unclassed, tribeless, and nationless,
> Exempt from awe, worship, degree, the king
> Over himself; just, gentle, wise: but man
> Passionless?—no, yet free from guilt or pain,

Which were, for his will made or suffered them,
Nor yet exempt, though ruling them like slaves,
From chance, and death, and mutability,
The clogs of that which else might oversoar
The loftiest star of unascended heaven,
Pinnacled dim in the intense inane.   (iii. iv. 193–204)

We may compare this with a representative passage of *The
Cenci*:

        .   .   We
Are now no more, as once, parent and child,
But man to man; the oppressor to the oppressed;
The slanderer to the slandered; foe to foe:
He has cast Nature off, which was his shield,
And Nature casts him off, who is her shame;
And I spurn both.   (iii. i. 282–8)

It is the contrast between an idiom which is epic, Greek, and
Miltonic in its inspiration, and an idiom which is dramatic,
Elizabethan, and Shakespearian. Although one of the remarkable features of the contrast lies in the fact that both dramas are
written predominantly in blank verse, it is important to notice
that it is not merely the versification that differs: the whole
idiom or style is different. There have not been many poets
capable of such radically different idioms in the same metre at
the same point in their careers. It must also be stressed that no
one quotation can give a fair impression of the idiom of *The
Cenci*. It is a necessary attribute of dramatic verse that it should
be capable of a wider range of effects than is required in most
kinds of poetry. Here *The Cenci* passes with credit, as we may
see by comparing Act II, scene ii, lines 82–87—

Ask me not what I think; the unwilling brain
Feigns often what it would not; and we trust
Imagination with such phantasies
As the tongue dares not fashion into words,
Which have no words, their horror makes them dim
To the mind's eye

—with the majesty of Beatrice's addresses to the Court, or the
penetrating simplicity of her last words of all:

Give yourself no unnecessary pain,
My dear Lord Cardinal. Here, Mother, tie
My girdle for me, and bind up this hair

In any simple knot; ay, that does well.
And yours I see is coming down. How often
Have we done this for one another; now
We shall not do it any more. My Lord,
We are quite ready. Well, 'tis very well.

(v. iv. 158–165)

Prometheus Unbound demonstrates Shelley's mastery of almost every tone in blank verse except a bare simplicity: in *The Cenci* we find that as well.

Shelley actually applied the word 'esoteric' to *Epipsychidion* (1821) in a letter, saying that it was to be published 'simply for the esoteric few': he hardly expected that so 'abstruse' a poem would find a hundred readers. This is acknowledged in the preliminary lines, which are a version of Dante:

> My Song, I fear that thou wilt find but few
> Who fitly shall conceive thy reasoning.

In a letter written on 22 October 1821 we find one of the most bitter of all Shelley's comments on the question of his audience:

> The Epipsychidion is a mystery; as to real flesh and blood, you know that I do not deal in those articles; you might as well go to a gin-shop for a leg of mutton, as expect anything human or earthly from me. I desired Ollier not to circulate this piece except to the συνετοί, and even they, it seems, are inclined to approximate me to the circle of a servant girl and her sweetheart.

Shelley described the poem as an 'idealized history of my life and feelings', while Mary Shelley preferred to call it his 'Pisan Platonics'. Its origin was Shelley's meeting with the beautiful Emilia Viviani, who was confined in a convent near Pisa: its motto is a quotation from an essay she had written on the subject of love. Although Shelley pretends in the preface that the poem is the work of a writer who had died at Florence—

> as he was preparing for a voyage to one of the wildest of the Sporades, which he had bought, and where he had fitted up the ruins of an old building, and where it was his hope to have realised a scheme of life, suited perhaps to that happier and better world of which he is now an inhabitant, but hardly practicable in this

—it was his own work, and may even have begun as an invitation to Emilia to elope with him. It is clear that he had fallen out of love with her by the time the poem was published, and he describes it as 'a production of a portion of me already dead'. No doubt that is why the longer poem, to which the 600 lines of *Epipsychidion* as we have it were intended to serve as an introduction, was never completed: perhaps it would have been based on Dante's *Vita Nuova*, to which he refers in the preface. Newman Ivey White believed that the poem originally ended at line 387. That is possible: up to that point it could perhaps be divided into four parts: a description of the poet's search for love, reflections on the nature of love, his eventual meeting with Emilia, and a triumphant meditation on love. The remaining 200 lines are an appeal to Emilia to elope with him and a description of the earthly paradise which they are to inhabit together. It is tempting to suggest that the first four lines were an afterthought, but conjecture must be very uncertain, because the poem as we have it is in a sense incomplete, and the rejected passages which survive make it clear how much the original idea grew under Shelley's hands.

Although it lacks a profound unity, *Epipsychidion* is a remarkable poem which contains passages of extraordinary beauty. Lines 502–12, for example, must have appealed to Yeats:

> Parasite flowers illume with dewy gems
> The lampless halls, and when they fade, the sky
> Peeps through their winter-woof of tracery
> With moonlight patches, or star-atoms keen,
> Or fragments of the day's intense serene;—
> Working mosaic on their Parian floors.
> And, day and night, aloof, from the high towers
> And terraces, the Earth and Ocean seem
> To sleep in one another's arms, and dream
> Of waves, flowers, clouds, woods, rocks, and all that we
> Read in their smiles, and call reality.

As we read this poem we are often reminded of Crashaw. Such a phrase as 'faint with . . . delicious pain' sends us back to the earlier poet, as does the style of lines 39–40:

> Weeping, till sorrow becomes ecstasy:
> Then smile on it, so that it may not die.

Crashaw could have written lines 17–18, with their reference to 'thy panting, wounded breast' which

> Stains with dear blood its unmaternal nest.

Like Crashaw, Shelley was profoundly attracted by Italy, but while it is possible that he was influenced by some of the same Italian poets, the remarkable resemblances between the style of *Epipsychidion* and that of many of Crashaw's poems are probably due as much to psychological similarities between the two men as to common literary influences. We notice that, subjective and 'esoteric' as it is, *Epipsychidion* does not disintegrate, as do so many of Shelley's poems. The inspiration outlasts the six hundred lines, and the result is a poem as peculiarly characteristic of Shelley as the *Hymn to the Name and Honor of the Admirable S. Teresa* is of Crashaw.

Although *Adonais* (1821) is now the best-known of all Shelley's poems, he himself seems to have regarded it as belonging to the esoteric category of his work. Describing it as 'perhaps the least imperfect of my compositions', he added that it was 'little adapted for popularity'. He looked forward to reading it to the Gisbornes because they were among 'the very few persons who will be interested in it and understand it'. Perhaps the most revealing of all his remarks on the subject of his poetic audience occurs in a passage relating to this poem. 'I am glad you like "Adonais"', he wrote to Horace Smith, 'and, particularly, that you do not think it metaphysical, which I was afraid it was. . . . I wrote, as usual, with a total ignorance of the effect that I should produce.'

The elegy is a form practised by almost every poet, and nothing is more revealing than to examine what becomes of it in the hands of different writers. When Donne wrote *The Second Anniversary*, for example, he made it an occasion for contemplating 'The Incommodities of the Soul in this Life, and her Exaltation in the Next'. The death of a girl whom he had never met gave him the starting point for a sermon *de contemptu mundi*. *Adonais* is equally characteristic of its author. It does not tell us much about Keats as an individual, and what it does tell us is misleading. Shelley exaggerates the importance of the unfavourable reviews, portraying the reviewers as wolves, obscene ravens, and vultures who have hunted down a wounded deer. For Shelley Keats is a type and a symbol, 'the great genius whom envy and ingratitude scourged out of the world'. *Adonais* is essentially a passionate cry of protest against the oppressors of mankind.

It is one of the most carefully written of Shelley's poems. Since Keats had been treated with injustice during his lifetime, he was particularly anxious to do him honour after his death. The poem was printed with particular care, and at Pisa, where Shelley himself could supervise the proof-reading. The result is a handsome book, printed 'With the Types of Didot'. The poem is written in Spenserian stanzas. In the preface to *The Revolt of Islam* Shelley had described this as 'a measure inexpressibly beautiful', emphasizing the 'brilliancy and magnificence of sound which a mind that has been nourished upon musical thoughts can produce by a just and harmonious arrangement of the pauses of this measure'. As one reads *Adonais* one feels (as in reading the 'Ode to the West Wind') that Shelley has found the perfect stanza-form for what he wishes to say: it is impossible to imagine the poem transposed into another metre. Yet he uses the stanza in a highly personal way. It is only necessary to turn back to *The Faerie Queene* to be struck by the extraordinary rapidity of Shelley's stanzas. That 'want of repose' which Severn pointed out in this poem, and which is one of the most striking peculiarities of almost everything Shelley ever wrote, is not characteristic of *The Faerie Queene*, or of most other poems written in the Spenserian stanza. Shelley takes a normally slow-moving metre and makes of it something new and personal. It is possible that he associated the Spenserian stanza with Keats: according to Medwin, *The Revolt of Islam* had been written in competition with *Endymion*, to see which of the young poets could write the better long poem. It is also certainly true that the Spenserian stanza was a favourite with Keats (as with Leigh Hunt), although he did not use it often in his mature poetry. There is another possible connexion. The writers of elegies on poets sometimes imitate the style of the man whom they are lamenting. Shelley did not do this, but it is conceivable that, as he wrote *Adonais*, he remembered the advice Keats had sent him in a letter: 'Be more of an artist, and "load every rift" of your subject with ore.' Perhaps this is why Shelley described the poem as 'a highly-wrought *piece of art*', underlining the last three words and adding that it was 'perhaps better, in point of composition', than anything else he had written.

It is often said that 'Lycidas' tells us more about Milton than about Edward King, and *Adonais* certainly tells us more about Shelley than about Keats. Yet this is perfectly appropriate, for he had a strong fellow-feeling for Keats. Both in the cancelled passages of the preface and in the unsent letter to the editor of

the *Quarterly Review* Shelley explicitly links himself with Keats
as the object of persecution and libellous attacks. He feels
both 'indignation and sympathy' with him, and is moved to a
counter-attack which no merely 'personal offence' could have
prompted. In the four stanzas in which he describes himself
he acknowledges that he is a man

> Who in another's fate now wept his own.   (300)

The true subject of the poem, we might say, is neither the individual Keats nor the individual Shelley, but rather the poetic
and creative impulse itself, which used both of them as its
medium. It is appropriate that towards the end of the poem the
influence of the Greek elegists wanes, as mourning gives way to
the celebration of

> That Beauty in which all things work and move.   (479)

While indignation provided the original incentive of the poem,
indignation is left behind as the climax is reached and the
poet rises to the contemplation of the unchanging realm of
Eternity.

In 'The Triumph of Life', with its insistence on 'the contagion
of the world's slow stain', Shelley may be abandoning the idea
that happiness is possible on earth. It is not surprising that
a great deal has recently been written about this poem, for
an unfinished work always presents a challenge. The critic is
stimulated by the opportunity of proving himself more astute
than his predecessors, while the inevitable uncertainty of interpretation allows him to attribute to the developing poet views
consonant with his own. If Shakespeare's last play had been
incomplete his critics would have enjoyed a 'liberty of interpretation' beyond their wildest dreams. This is the opportunity
that is afforded by both Keats and Shelley. Accordingly we find
Dr. Leavis insisting that 'the induction to the revised *Hyperion*
... justifies the high estimate of Keats's potentialities' which he
would hesitate to advance on the evidence of the earlier poems
and Mr. Eliot discovering in 'The Triumph of Life' 'evidence
not only of better writing than in any previous long poem, but
of greater wisdom'. For less sophisticated readers there is also
the sphinx-like appeal of a poem left as a fragment at the poet's
death: they stand questioning it, as Tennyson used to question
very old men about their views on what happens after death.

The fact that Mary Shelley's text of the poem ends with the words

'Then, what is life? I cried'—

has helped to make its fortune.

As we read the five hundred lines of 'The Triumph of Life' it is at least as easy to see why Dr. Leavis finds in them what he regards as the typical 'Shelleyan confusion' as why Mr. Eliot discerns 'a precision of image and an economy . . . new to Shelley'. Many interpretations have been offered of the 'Shape all light' which must clearly be central to an understanding of the poem. Almost all that we can say for certain is that the poem is a sombre one, partly inspired by Dante, in which the poet sees in a vision a multitude of people hastening along a dusty thoroughfare, and that he is addressed by Rousseau, who delivers an admonitory speech about life which is unfinished when the poem breaks off. The verse has a hypnotic urgency, and we notice that Shelley is even more unwilling than usual to employ a full-stop: the second sentence of the poem, for example, runs on for thirty-two lines. Mr. Eliot particularly admires the Goya-like description of the gnarled root on the hillside which turns out to be Rousseau:

And that the grass, which methought hung so wide
And white, was but his thin discoloured hair,
And that the holes he vainly sought to hide,
Were or had been eyes. (185–8)

There is certainly a compelling vividness about the opening of the vision:

Methought I sate beside a public way

Thick strewn with summer dust, and a great stream
Of people there was hurrying to and fro,
Numerous as gnats upon the evening gleam,

All hastening onward, yet none seemed to know
Whither he went, or whence he came, or why
He made one of the multitude . . .

Some flying from the thing they feared, and some
Seeking the object of another's fear. (43–55)

There are also individual lines of remarkable power, such as the description of men like Gregory and John,

Who rose like shadows between man and God, (289)

or that in lines 354–5:

> And the invisible rain did ever sing
> A silver music on the mossy lawn.

Yet 'The Triumph of Life' remains an enigma, and to single it out (with Dr. Leavis) as 'among the few things one can still read and go back to in Shelley' is simply an oblique way of dismissing most of the remainder of his poems.

In containing a markedly subjective element *Adonais* and 'The Triumph of Life' are not unusual in Shelley's work. In the preface to *Frankenstein* Mary Shelley describes how the poet, confronted with the challenge to write a ghost story and being always 'more apt to embody ideas in the radiance of brilliant imagery and in the music of . . . melodious verse . . . than to invent the machinery of a story', instinctively began a tale 'founded on the experiences of his own early life'. When he wrote a poem he was just as likely to turn to his own experiences for his material: his description of *Epipsychidion* as 'an idealised history of my life and feelings' would apply to a great many of his compositions. It may now be of interest to glance back at the major poems already discussed to emphasize the personal element which they contain; but first something must be said of *Alastor* (1816), an early work which gains from being examined in relation to the two poems which have just been considered.

It is obvious that the nameless poet (Alastor is the name of the Avenging Spirit which pursues him) is in some sense a representation of Shelley himself, and the main outline of the story is evident enough. The 'child of grace and genius' leaves his 'alienated home' and travels across the world, musing on the present and the past and coming to understand

> The thrilling secrets of the birth of time.   (128)

He is a Rasselas without a sister or an Imlac, a Rasselas who has read Volney's *Ruins*. All goes well with him at first, but then 'The spirit of sweet human love' sends

> A vision to the sleep of him who spurned
> Her choicest gifts.   (204–5)

From this time onwards Death and Sleep are twins in the poet's mind. Impelled by the thought that Death will perhaps restore to him the woman he has met in sleep—she is probably Intellectual Beauty—he travels wretchedly about and finally embarks in a leaky little boat with the desire of finding death by drowning. His further travels are described, and then his death. The poem ends with a sort of elegy on this 'surpassing Spirit'. Much of the allegory of *Alastor* remains obscure, while the second paragraph of the preface has led to a good deal of debate. Yet it is not necessary to go as far as Professor Carlos Baker, who has commented that this passage 'looks very much like an ex post facto attempt by Shelley to moralize his song'. *Alastor* is a meditation on the grandeur and misery of the life of a man of genius and on the grandeur and misery of solitude. Epigraphs might readily be provided from the different parts of Zimmerman's famous treatise on Solitude, a book which Shelley is certain to have known:

> The first and most incontestable advantage of SOLITUDE is, that it accustoms the mind to think: the imagination becomes more vivid, and the memory more faithful, while the senses remain undisturbed, and no external object agitates the soul. . . . The moment that a character finds itself alone, all the energies of his soul put themselves into motion, and rise to a height incomparably greater than they could have reached under the impulse of a mind clogged and oppressed by the incumbrances of society. (*Solitude*, by J. G. Zimmerman [anon. Eng. trans., 1799–1800], i, 18, 24–25.)

> SOLITUDE, in its strict and literal acceptation, is equally unfriendly to the happiness and foreign to the nature of mankind. An inclination to exercise the faculty of speech, to interchange the sentiments of the mind, to indulge the affections of the heart, and to receive themselves, while they bestow on others, a kind assistance and support, drives men . . . from SOLITUDE to SOCIETY; and teaches them that the highest temporal felicity they are capable of enjoying, must be sought for in a suitable union of the sexes, and in a friendly intercourse with their fellow-creatures. . . . It is not to the senseless rock, or to the passing gale, that we can satisfactorily communicate our pleasures and our pains. (*Solitude*, ii (*The pernicious Influence of A total Seclusion from Society upon The Mind and the Heart*), 1–3.)

In the preface Shelley writes of two very different categories of men who 'keep aloof from sympathies with their kind': on the one hand there are 'the luminaries of the world', namely those who are 'deluded by [some] generous error, instigated by [some]

sacred thirst of doubtful knowledge, [or] duped by [some] illustrious superstition': and on the other those who are merely
'selfish, blind, and torpid'. On both Alastor, which reminds us
of the 'Shape all light' and which must stand for something like
Human Love or the need for Human Society, takes its revenge.
The selfish are doomed to 'a slow and poisonous decay', the
luminaries to 'sudden darkness and extinction' due to their
being awakened to 'too exquisite a perception' of the influence of
Alastor. The latter category, the 'pure and tender-hearted, perish
through the intensity and passion of their search' for human
sympathy, 'when the vacancy of their spirit suddenly makes
itself felt'. The ambiguity of the poem springs from the fact that
the poet is so obviously a projection of some of Shelley's own
qualities and from the fact that he insists that the life of such a man
is at once in some way mistaken and yet of the greatest value to
mankind. It is as if Don Quixote had written his autobiography.
The conclusion of the poem does not claim that the poet survives
after death, but rather that 'birth and the grave', the very conditions of human life, are affected by the fact that such a man has
lived. This is precisely what Shelley was later to assert, more
eloquently, at the end of *Adonais*. *Alastor*, then, is not an optimistic poem. It is a 'solemn song'. Set in its place in Shelley's
development it may be read as an expression of his determination to follow his own destiny, although he realizes that there
is a sense in which he is deluded and that in any event such
a course will not lead to personal happiness but to tragedy.
The world that the poem paints is not a world of justice: it is
a world in which the idealist is doomed. Shelley foresees his own
doom, and accepts it. If *Adonais* is an elegy on Shelley himself
by proxy, *Alastor* is an elegy on Shelley by anticipation.

   In *The Revolt of Islam* the autobiographical element is hardly
less evident. Mary Shelley tells us that the Hermit who cares for
Laon during his years of madness is based on Dr. Lind, Shelley's
Eton friend, and there can be no doubt that Laon is an idealized
representation of Shelley himself. Cythna is based on Mary
Shelley, but may also contain hints of her mother Mary Woll-
stonecraft and of the poet's sister Hellen. As the action progresses
autobiography shades into wish-fulfilment: we hear not of what
Shelley has done but of what he would like to do. The hero of
Prometheus Unbound is a greatly superior idealization of Shelley.
'The type of the highest perfection of moral and intellectual

nature, impelled by the purest and the truest motives to the best and noblest ends', Prometheus presented himself to Shelley as the supreme possibility of idealizing his characteristic hero, with the added dignity and solidity of thousands of years' existence in mythology. This is Laon become a Titan. Less obviously, Beatrice Cenci fulfils a role in many respects similar. In *The Cenci* the conflict between Jupiter and Prometheus is transposed to the human level. While this drama is exceptional among Shelley's longer poems in that the forces of oppression triumph over those of liberty, it is possible that we are intended to feel that Beatrice triumphs in the spirit, as the poet triumphs at the end of *Adonais*. The tyranny of Count Cenci combines most of the aspects of tyranny which Shelley detested: the tyranny of the Family, that of the Church, and that of the Law. The parallels between paternal power, political power, and the supreme authority of the Pope are emphasized at several points. It is significant that, in the story as it reached Shelley, Cenci was portrayed as an atheist: he makes him a 'good Catholic' in order to bring all the forces of tyranny into alignment. It is wholly appropriate that the play is dedicated to Leigh Hunt, with a reference to 'that patient and irreconcilable enmity with domestic and political tyranny and imposture' which both men have at heart.

A general description of a long poem by Shelley may now be attempted. Its subject is the struggle between Tyranny and Freedom, or Hate and Love: it includes a vision of a heaven and a hell: and among the main characters are found an idealized representation of the poet himself, his beloved, and (very often) a tyrant. Time and again this same general pattern may be detected. It is almost as if Shelley were writing a series of plays for a small company of actors—a company in which he himself always played the male lead. Yet this formula is offered as a help to understanding, and not as a gesture of depreciation, for amongst the works which it covers there are several masterpieces. What matters is not the formula (which also covers some of the shorter poems), but the use to which it is put. The same self-projection which is embarrassing and even absurd in *The Sensitive Plant* is triumphantly justified in *Prometheus Unbound* and *Adonais*.

The greater part of this chapter has been devoted to the longer poems of Shelley not only because they include much of

his finest work but also because they provide the clearest guidance to the nature of his poetic ambitions. When we turn to the
shorter poems we notice a striking difference of mood. Whereas
in the longer poems Shelley is often optimistic, in the lyrics he
is almost always pessimistic. These are his two moods, the two
sides of his mind and art. There is no contradiction between
them. He was optimistic about the future of the human race,
pessimistic (almost always) about his own future as an individual. Being the most directly personal of all his poems, his
short lyrics are naturally the most melancholy. Religion has
been described as what man makes of his solitude: the same
description might be applied to Shelley's lyrics. As Mary Shelley
pointed out, 'it is the nature of that poetry . . . which overflows
from the soul oftener to express sorrow and regret than joy; for
it is when oppressed by the weight of life, and away from those
he loves, that the poet has recourse to the solace of expression
in verse'. It is not surprising to find that laments and complaints
are among the commonest types of his lyrics:

> O world! O life! O time!
> On whose last steps I climb,
>   Trembling at that where I had stood before;
> When will return the glory of your prime?
>   No more—Oh, never more!

'Autumn: A Dirge' is thoroughly characteristic, as is the lament
in 'Ginevra', which has the accent of Webster or Ford with a
hint of mystery added:

> She is still, she is cold
>   On the bridal couch,
> One step to the white deathbed,
>   And one to the bier,
> And one to the charnel—and one, oh where?
>   The dark arrow fled
>   In the noon.
>   (206–12)

Shelley's lyrics are the utterance of a solitary. If we compare
them with those of George Herbert, for example, we find that
not only is there the Christian God in Herbert's universe: there
are also other people. In Shelley's lyric world there are no other
people. In his 'Invocation to Misery'—which is almost a self-

parody, the true product of Peacock's Scythrop—he addresses
Misery in these words:

> All the wide world, beside us,
> Show like multitudinous
> Puppets passing from a scene;
> What but mockery can they mean,
> Where I am—where thou hast been?   (61–65)

This is the solipsism of a melancholiac. It might be said of
Shelley, as Belisarius says over the body of Imogen-Fidele, 'Thou
diedst, a most rare boy, of melancholy'. One of the aptest
psychological descriptions of Shelley may be found in Burton's
Anatomy of Melancholy, part I, section 2, member 2, subsection 6,
in the paragraph dealing with 'Voluntary Solitariness'. Being
the work of such a man, his lyrics lack the dramatic element
which appeals to us so much in Donne's. Shelley's lyrics are
soliloquies, not dramatic monologues: they have a disembodied
quality which makes it appropriate that when they are inter-
polated in his longer works they are often the utterance of
spirits. The women addressed in his love-lyrics have seldom any
reality. He does not describe them: he hardly even addresses
them. There is none of the objectivity which sensuality often
brings with it. He usually remains at a distance from the physical
aspects of love, associating love above all with music—as in
'To Constantia, Singing', 'With a Guitar, to Jane', and in the
fine lines 'The keen stars are twinkling'. Although the well-
known lines 'Music, when soft voices die' proclaim the lasting
power of love, it is more characteristic of Shelley to lament love's
transitoriness, as he does in 'When the lamp is shattered' and
'When passion's trance is overpast':

> All things revive in field or grove,
> And sky and sea, but two, which move
> And form all others, life and love.

We notice that several of the themes most commonly found in
the love poetry of the seventeenth century are missing from
Shelley's work: celebrations of fortunate love, for example, re-
joicings in the physical beauty of his mistress, deliberate attempts
to shock and give piquancy by flaunted cynicism. His love poems
are uniformly serious, and hardly ever witty. Like Donne,
Shelley was interested in philosophy; but whereas Donne in his

erotic verse amuses himself with philosophical notions, Shelley
believes in his philosophy—which is less entertaining. 'You well
know', as he wrote to a friend, 'I am not much of a hand at *love*
songs—you see I mingle metaphysics with even this, but perhaps
in this age of Philosophy that may be excused.' What he is looking for in love (one comes to feel) is escape from the world of
flux, escape from the world of everyday reality: love is merely
the means of escape. This may be an unfashionable attitude
today, yet after all it is not peculiar to Shelley: it is one of the
universal attitudes to love throughout human history, and few
poets have described it more perfectly:

> The desire of the moth for the star,
>   Of the night for the morrow,
> The devotion to something afar
>   From the sphere of our sorrow.   ('To —'.)

As he writes in his *Letters from Italy*, 'perhaps all discontent with
the *less* (to use a Platonic sophism) supposes the sense of a just
claim to the *greater*, and that we admirers of "Faust" are on the
right road to Paradise'. In his love poems, as elsewhere, he often
speaks like an exile from some other world, a wanderer who
hopes in vain to find in love a cure for his nostalgia for the
Ithaca of his dreams.

It would not be true to say that just as there are no other
people in Shelley's lyrics, so there is no external nature. We
have only to turn to 'Evening: Ponte al Mare, Pisa' to see his
fine powers of description:

> The sun is set; the swallows are asleep;
>   The bats are flitting fast in the gray air;
> The slow soft toads out of damp corners creep,
>   And evening's breath, wandering here and there
> Over the quivering surface of the stream,
> Wakes not one ripple from its summer dream.
>
> There is no dew on the dry grass to-night,
>   Nor damp within the shadow of the trees;
> The wind is intermitting, dry, and light;
>   And in the inconstant motion of the breeze
> The dust and straws are driven up and down,
> And whirled about the pavement of the town.

Yet pure description is by no means characteristic of Shelley. Perhaps good poetry is less often descriptive than we are apt to suppose. As Mme de Staël once pointed out:

il faut, pour concevoir la vraie grandeur de la poésie lyrique . . . considérer l'univers entier comme un symbole des émotions de l'âme. . . . Le poète sait rétablir l'unité du monde physique avec le monde moral: son imagination forme un lien entre l'un et l'autre.

It is precisely true to say that Shelley considered the whole universe as a symbol, or a system of symbols, for the feelings of the human soul. To quote again from the *Letters from Italy*: 'You know I always seek in what I see the manifestation of something beyond the present and tangible object.' He looks to the external world to provide him with a language of symbolism. One reason why he is more at home with clouds and mountains and rivers than with men and women is that they lend themselves more readily to symbolism. In 'The Skylark', for example, the bird acts as a symbol and rallying-point for thoughts from his private world. The subject of the poem is at once the bird and Shelley's personal desires and ambitions. The bird is

> Like a Poet hidden
> In the light of thought,
> Singing hymns unbidden,
> Till the world is wrought
> To sympathy with hopes and fears it heeded not.
> (36–40)

It is able to do what Shelley himself would have liked to do. It knows love but not the disillusionment of love, its 'sad satiety': hence the soaring of its song. It is exempt from the human yearning for the absent and the unattainable:

> We look before and after,
> And pine for what is not:
> Our sincerest laughter
> With some pain is fraught;
> Our sweetest songs are those that tell of saddest thought
> (86–90)

By contemplating the bird the poet is carried outside the obsessive circle of his own feelings sufficiently to be able to express them with the required measure of objectivity. He remains in the world of reality—however imaginatively it is regarded—and is therefore able to give body and actuality to his thought and so communicate with his readers. The same thing happens, triumphantly, in the 'Ode to the West Wind'. One reason for the success of this poem is that the storm which overtook Shelley in the wood beside the river Arno brought together elements which already had a deep significance in his mind. Images already potent in his imagination leaped into a new and telling pattern. In *Alastor* he had mentioned 'autumn's hollow sighs in the sere wood' as one of the natural phenomena that were dear to him, referring to himself as a lyre passively awaiting the breath of the Mother of the World,

> .   .   that my strain
> May modulate with murmurs of the air,
> And motions of the forests and the sea,
> And voice of living beings, and woven hymns
> Of night and day, and the deep heart of man.
>
> (45–49)

In the 'Ode' the West Wind becomes the symbol of autumn and takes on autumn's double attribute of being the harbinger at once of death and of resurrection, of decay and regeneration. As he wrote it he probably remembered a line from *The Revolt of Islam*:

> The blasts of Autumn drive the wingèd seeds
> Over the earth.   (IX. xxi)

He invokes the wind and appeals to it to use him as its lyre, as the wind uses the forest: so it may take on his identity, and

> Drive my dead thoughts over the universe
> Like withered leaves to quicken a new birth!   (63–64)

The wind becomes the perfect symbol for a poet with the ambition of being a prophet who feels that the fire of his own life is dwindling and going out:

> Scatter, as from an unextinguished hearth
>   Ashes and sparks, my words among mankind!
> Be through my lips to unawakened earth
>
>   The trumpet of a prophecy!   O, Wind,
>   If Winter comes, can Spring be far behind?[1]
>
> (66–70)

---

[1] 'Man is an instrument over which a series of external and internal impressions are driven, like the alternations of an ever-changing wind over an Æolian lyre, which move it by their motion to ever-changing melody.' *A Defence of Poetry*, paragraph 2.

It is astonishing to compare the skill with which *terza rima* is handled in this poem with the clumsiness of 'The Woodman and the Nightingale', written only a year or so before. The measure has not often been employed in English with complete success. Here it is. The force and urgency are precisely what the poet requires.

The 'Ode to the West Wind' is an illuminating example of Shelley's finding something in the external world which acts as a focal point for certain of his own deepest intuitions. The discovery of a centre of this kind was his greatest problem. He had a strong tendency to avoid the actual world, and particularly the world of men and women, in order to construct a world of his own, a world of black and white, a world where cause and effect should be simplified, a world of heart's desire. This was due partly to the sort of man he was and partly to his disappointment at the failure of his attempts to bring the world of reality closer to the world of his visions. Some of his least successful poems, like *The Witch of Atlas*, owe their inferiority to this flight from reality: some of his most successful owe their high merit to the fact that a bridge has been built between the private world of his imaginings and the common world of shared human experience. On one memorable occasion a true episode from history—the story of Count Cenci and his daughter Beatrice—gave him a perfect medium through which to express his perennial theme of the conflict between Freedom and Tyranny, and the result is at once one of his most imaginative works and one of those in which the imagination is most perfectly embodied in specific characters and actions. On two other occasions at least actual events which moved him deeply gave him a starting-point: his love for Emilia Viviani precipitated what is perhaps the finest expression of his reflections on the subject of love, while the death of Keats moved him to eloquent meditation on the transitoriness of life, the conflict between genius and convention, and the eternal value of the creative imagination. It does not follow that these three poems are his greatest achievement: a higher claim should almost certainly be made for the first three acts of *Prometheus Unbound*. But it is no chance that these are among the longer poems of Shelley's which now make the widest appeal. Prophetic, didactic, and characteristic as they are, they reassure us by retaining contact with the reality which we experience from day to day.

The work of Shelley presents us with a paradox. The subject-matter of great poetry is human life and the human passions. Shelley, possessed in every other respect of the endowment of a very great poet, found it hard to bring himself to write directly about human life. No one saw the truth more clearly than Mary Shelley:

> The surpassing excellence of *The Cenci* had made me greatly desire that Shelley should increase his popularity by adopting subjects that would more suit the popular taste than a poem conceived in the abstract and dreamy spirit of the *Witch of Atlas*. It was not only that I wished him to acquire popularity . . . but I believed that he would obtain a greater mastery over his own powers, and greater happiness in his mind, if public applause crowned his endeavours. . . . Even now I believe that I was in the right. Shelley did not expect sympathy and approbation from the public; but the want of it took away a portion of the ardour that ought to have sustained him while writing. . . . My persuasions were vain, the mind could not be bent from its natural inclination. Shelley shrunk instinctively from portraying human passion, with its mixture of good and evil, of disappointment and disquiet. . . . He loved to shelter himself rather in the airiest flights of fancy, forgetting love and hate, and regret and lost hope, in such imaginations as borrowed their hues from sunrise or sunset . . . from the aspect of the far ocean or the shadows of the woods.   (Note on *The Witch of Atlas*.)

Next to Mary Shelley the critic who understood him best was Peacock, and his opinion is the complement of hers:

> What was, in my opinion, deficient in his poetry, was . . . the want of reality in the characters with which he peopled his splendid scenes, and to which he addressed or imparted the utterance of his impassioned feelings. He was advancing, I think, to the attainment of this reality. It would have given to his poetry the only element of truth which it wanted; though at the same time, the more clear development of what men were would have lowered his estimate of what they might be, and dimmed his enthusiastic prospect of the future destiny of the world. I can conceive him, if he had lived to the present time, passing his days like Volney, looking on the world from his windows without taking part in its turmoils; and perhaps . . . desiring that nothing should be inscribed on his tomb, but his name, the dates of his birth and death, and the single word

'DÉSILLUSIONNÉ'.

IV

KEATS

UNLIKE Shelley, Keats was in no doubt what he wanted
to do with his life.[1] As one of his fellow students tells us,
'Poetry was . . . the zenith of all his aspirations: the only
thing worthy the attention of superior minds: so he thought: all
other pursuits were mean and tame. . . . The greatest men in the
world were the poets and to rank among them was the chief
object of his ambition.' The difference between the two poets is
brought out clearly by a comparison between their first volumes.
It is impossible to imagine Keats's *Poems* of 1817 accompanied
by the notes on religion, morals, and politics which we find in
Queen Mab. No contemporary reader of the volume could have
been in any doubt where Keats's political sympathies lay; but
it is no less clear that his primary concern is not with politics
or philosophy or natural science, but with poetry. The spirit in
which the volume had been written is summed up in one of his
letters—'I find that I cannot exist without poetry—without
eternal poetry—half the day will not do—the whole of it.'
Whereas the authors referred to in the notes to *Queen Mab*
include Spinoza, Godwin, d'Holbach, Sir William Drummond,
Bacon, Laplace, Hume, Godwin and Condorcet, the writers

[1] John Keats (1795–1821) was the eldest son of the manager of a livery-stable
in London. His parents would have liked to send him to Harrow, but this was
beyond their means, so he went to Enfield Academy, where he became friendly
with Charles Cowden Clarke, the son of his schoolmaster. After leaving school he
was apprenticed to a surgeon and later studied at Guy's Hospital. In 1816 he met
Leigh Hunt, who had printed his sonnet 'O Solitude, if I must with thee dwell'
in the *Examiner* for 5 May. Through Hunt Keats later met Shelley, John Hamilton
Reynolds, and a number of painters and people interested in the arts. His *Poems*
attracted little attention. He wrote part of *Endymion* on a visit to the Isle of Wight.
Meanwhile he lived in Hampstead and resolved to devote himself to literature. In
1818 he said good-bye to his brother George (who emigrated to America), went on
a walking tour to the Lakes and Scotland with Charles Brown, and returned
to London to nurse his brother Tom, who was dying of tuberculosis. *Endymion*
was savagely reviewed, particularly in *Blackwood's*, where Keats was associated
with Hunt as one of the 'Cockney School'. In the late autumn of 1818 he had a
transitory affair with Isabella Jones. About this time he also met Fanny Brawne,
with whom he fell deeply in love. Most of his greatest poetry was written between
September 1818 and September 1819. A year later he sailed for Italy, accompanied by Severn. He died in Rome in February 1821.

named in the *Poems* of 1817 (and it is surprising how many are named) are all poets: Chaucer, Spenser, Shakespeare, Chapman, Boileau, Chatterton, William Browne, Burns, Petrarch, Leigh Hunt. As one reads the letters of the two men the same pattern reveals itself: it is almost always poetry that Keats is reading and discussing, while Shelley is at least as likely to be reading philosophy or political theory.

When Keats wrote most of the poems in his first collection he was a student of medicine, yet no line or image reveals the fact. Indeed one reason for the remarkably literary tone of the volume is that for Keats at this time poetry was above all a means of escape from the humdrum realities that surrounded him. That is why there are so many references to picturesque refuges and hiding-places. He refers to 'some pleasant lair of wavy grass', wishing to be "mongst boughs pavillion'd': he tells us that he will look for 'some flowery spot, sequester'd, wild, romantic': he describes 'a little space, with boughs all woven round', and exclaims that for him 'a bowery nook will be elysium'. In 'I stood tip-toe' we see him collecting the properties of what he calls, in an unfortunate phrase, a 'tasteful nook': flowers, laburnum, and long grass. It is appropriate that the epigraph of the poem is taken from Leigh Hunt: 'Places of nestling green for Poets made'.

Half of the poems in the volume have the air of having been written after a visit to Hunt, the man 'who keeps the keys Of Pleasure's temple'. What this means is brought out by a passage in *Lord Byron and Some of his Contemporaries*: 'No imaginative pleasure was left unnoticed by us, or unenjoyed; from the recollection of the bards and patriots of old, to the luxury of a summer rain at our window, or the clicking of the coal in winter-time.' (i. 410.) In the poems themselves we find frequent lists of delights of this kind: what Keats calls 'trains of peaceful images', posies of luxuries, or 'my world of blisses'. These are precisely the 'imaginative pleasures' which he had enjoyed in the company of Hunt, and while some of the lists consist wholly of natural objects—flowers, trees, the wind—in one or two of the others we find things juxtaposed from different aspects of experience. 'Sleep and Poetry', for example, the most ambitious poem in the volume, opens with a series of rhetorical questions in which we find 'Cordelia's countenance' and 'a high romance' listed beside a musk-rose and 'the leafiness of dales'. These lists have a double interest: they reveal a medical student constructing for himself a refuge from the world of the hospital corridor and the dissecting-room; and they also show us a young poet with a flair for description and evocation casting about for a method of building up a poem.

It is not difficult to see why Keats at this time so often refers to Poetry as a place, a territory, as he does most memorably in the one completely successful poem in the volume, the sonnet 'On First Looking into Chapman's Homer':

> Much have I travell'd in the realms of gold.

It had been reading Spenser that had made him realize that he was born to be a poet: as Charles Brown put it, 'in Spenser's fairy land he was enchanted, breathed in a new world, and became another being'. Poetry was the country he escaped to. 'In a room', as we are told, he was always at the window, 'peering into space'. It is not surprising that he was fond of casements in his poetry, using this image most memorably in the *Ode to a Nightingale*, where he says that throughout the ages the song of this bird has

> Charm'd magic casements, opening on the foam
> Of perilous seas, in faery lands forlorn.

The most ambitious of his attempts to escape from mundane reality into a fairy-land of poetry and romance was *Endymion* (1818). 'I have heard Hunt say and may be asked—why endeavour after a long Poem?', he wrote in a letter. 'To which I should answer—Do not the Lovers of Poetry like to have a little Region to wander in where they may pick and choose, and in which the images are so numerous that many are forgotten and found new in a second Reading: which may be food for a Week's stroll in the Summer.' It is easier to see the point of this comparison of *Endymion* to a sort of wild pleasure-garden in which delightful vistas meet the eye wherever one turns than to decide how seriously the poem is to be taken. The critics of Keats have given very different answers to this question, just as they have differed in their evaluation of the poem. Some have taken it as a serious philosophic work which must be expounded in detail if we are to understand Keats's thought: others have tended to dismiss it impatiently as the work of a poetic tyro.

Sidney Colvin and C. L. Finney both devote a great deal of space to *Endymion*, while Mr. E. C. Pettet, who does not deal with *Hyperion* at any length, gives nearly a quarter of his book to the earlier poem. At the other extreme, Garrod ignored *Endymion* altogether, remarking that 'if it were possible to say something about it without saying too much, it would have been done already'. One can readily understand these divergent points of view. Passages here and there seem to call out for symbolic interpretation; yet as soon as one undertakes such a task, irrelevancies and inconsistencies spring up on every side. It is as well to remember the poet's own avowal, in his draft for a preface: 'Before I began I had no inward feel of being able to finish; and as I proceeded my steps were all uncertain.' Yet *Endymion* is no mere Bottom's Dream, and to refuse to see more in it than the erotic fancies of a young man is to carry scepticism too far. We cannot brush aside all symbolic interpretation. The action describes the falling in love of Endymion with Cynthia, the moon goddess, and his pursuit of her. We know from 'I stood tip-toe' how deeply this myth appealed to Keats, and it is clear that he interpreted it as the pursuit of Beauty by the enamoured Soul. The resemblances between *Endymion* and *Alastor* are obvious, and Keats was probably influenced in some degree by Shelley. *Endymion* is 'A Poetic Romance', and like many Romances it is shot through with symbolic suggestions.

When Hunt tried to dissuade Keats from writing a long poem it was probably because he thought him too inexperienced to succeed rather than because he doubted the value of the long poem. If so, Hunt was both right and wrong. The publication of *Endymion* had a disastrous effect on the reputation of Keats: whereas his first volume was well received by his friends, and almost ignored by the reviewers, his second called forth some of the most bitter attacks in the history of periodical criticism. Yet Keats knew within himself that he must explore his own mind and his own poetic potentialities, and the way to do this was by writing a longer poem than any he had so far attempted. If he had not written *Endymion* his poetic progress would almost certainly have been less astonishingly swift. 'The whole thing must I think have appeared to you, who are a consequitive Man, as a thing almost of mere words', as he wrote to his publisher; 'but I assure you that when I wrote it, it was a regular stepping of the Imagination towards a Truth. My having

written that Argument will perhaps be of the greatest Service
to me of any thing I ever did—It set before me at once the
gradations of Happiness even like a kind of Pleasure Thermometer.' This might be applied to the whole poem, though Keats
is writing about lines 777–81 of Book I:

> Wherein lies Happiness? In that which becks
> Our ready Minds to fellowship divine;
> A fellowship with essence, till we shine
> Full alchymized and free of space. Behold
> The clear Religion of heaven!

As we read these lines we are present at the birth of his characteristic philosophy of beauty. Up to now he has been attracted
by beautiful things and moving thoughts without any conscious
aim except that of delighting in their luxury. Now he is asking
himself why he has become a collector of luxuries and trying
to account for his strong sense that there is a profounder value
in 'A thing of beauty' than might at first appear. What he is
saying is that the deepest happiness for mankind lies in the
attempt to get in touch with the highest reality—'essences'—and
that this may be achieved through the apprehension of the
beautiful. It was as he wrote *Endymion* that this belief began to
formulate itself in his mind. The letters he wrote at the same
time provide a commentary on it. Whatever the philosophical
validity of this elusive belief, it is what supported Keats as he
approached the task of writing his greatest poetry.

Almost all of this is contained in the one extraordinary
volume, *Lamia, Isabella, The Eve of St. Agnes, and Other Poems*,
which appeared in 1820. Each of the three tales tells a story of
love. Each is drawn from a different source, set in a different
period and place, and shows its lovers meeting with a different
destiny. The hero of *Lamia* discovers that he has been deceived
in the very nature of his love, and dies of sorrow: the hero of
Isabella is murdered by the brothers of the lady he loves, but is
loyally mourned by her until she dies of grief: while the hero
of *The Eve of St. Agnes* escapes with his lady from the castle in
which she has been living in the midst of his enemies. It is easy
to think of this last poem as representing Keats's hopes in love,
of *Isabella* as a sort of second best, and of *Lamia* as the portrayal
of his deepest fears; but while this sort of autobiographical interpretation is attractive, it need not be taken very seriously. These

are the hopes and fears of any one who is in love, and they form the subject of most of the love-stories ever written.

By common consent, there is hardly a transition in the history of our literature more dramatic than that from *Endymion* to the volume of 1820; yet the transition from *Endymion* to the first two tales is less dramatic than that to the other poems. Although Keats himself, or his publisher, thought well enough of the Tales to put them at the beginning of the collection, the first two of them are not on a par with the remaining poems. We are told by Brown that *Lamia*, based on *The Anatomy of Melancholy* (Keats's favourite prose reading), was written 'after much studying of Dryden's versification'. This is interesting because it shows that Keats had come to agree with his critics that in rebelling against the Augustan modes of using the pentameter couplet he had gone too far in the direction of metrical licence and erratic syntax. In the opening lines we are fleetingly reminded of the Dryden of the Tales; while in one of the most impressive passages—the description of the banqueting room— Pope's *Homer* comes to mind; yet in most of the poem the verse is handled in a way much closer to Keats's own early manner than to Dryden's 'long majestic march, and energy divine'. The handling of the metre is not wholly satisfactory, while too many of the old amorous banalities remain—Keats is still capable of describing a kiss as 'the ruddy strife of hearts and lips' and assuring us that

> There is not such a treat among them all . . .
> As a real woman.   (330–2)

The moral of the poem is as uncertain as the style: it is significant that Keats seems to have been uncertain how to bring it to an end. *Isabella or, The Pot of Basil* is based on a story in *The Decameron*, as are several of Dryden's Tales. Whereas Dryden chose stories that lent themselves to straightforward accounts of passion, however, Keats took one with potentialities for pathos, a story recommended to the attention of modern poets in one of Hazlitt's lectures. The heading of the tale in the edition which Keats probably used may also have attracted his attention:

> Wherein is plainly proved, that love cannot be rooted uppe, by any humane power or Providence; especially in such a soule, where it hath bene really apprehended.

Boccaccio tells the story for what it is worth as a tale. Keats

makes it four times as long, using *ottava rima* and embroidering
the narrative with an elaborate rhetoric of pathos. A single
line—

The quiet glooms of such a piteous theme   (152)

—sums up the atmosphere of the poem. The story unfolds in
a leisurely manner, one sombre picture slowly succeeding another. Repetition is frequently used to emphasize the effect of
pathos, as in stanza lv. Although good critics have thought
highly of *Isabella*—Lamb devoted a large part of his review to
it, and did not mention *Hyperion* at all—it now appears distasteful
in theme and in parts poorly written. It is interesting to find
that Keats himself was dissatisfied with it. 'There is too much
inexperience of life, and simplicity of knowledge in it', he wrote
in a letter. '. . . It is possible to write fine things which cannot
be laugh'd at in any way. Isabella is what I should call were
I a reviewer "A weak-sided Poem" with an amusing sober-
sadness about it.'

The superiority of *The Eve of St. Agnes* to the other Tales is
partly due to the fact that in it Keats has found the perfect
metre for his theme. The story is based on a popular superstition
and the atmosphere is vaguely medieval. It is not surprising,
therefore, that Spenser was much in Keats's mind as he wrote
it; for Spenser, like Chatterton, was always associated in his
mind with any medieval subject. What had first appealed to
Keats about Spenser, we may guess, was above all the music and
the processional quality of his stanza, with the opportunities it
gives for rich effects of vowel music and sensuous luxury. It is
surprising that this is the only serious poem of his maturity in
which he uses it. Whereas *ottava rima* does not seem the perfect
metre for *Isabella*—its potentialities for epigram in the final
couplet, which inspired Byron in *Don Juan*, are irrelevant to the
purposes of Keats—it is impossible to imagine *The Eve of St.
Agnes* in any other metre than the Spenserian stanza.

Another source of inspiration was Gothic architecture. The
poem was written at Chichester, and it reminds us even more
forcibly of Keats's love of Winchester. In the 'Specimen of an
Induction' in his first volume he had asked:

.   .   Then how shall I
Revive the dying tones of minstrelsy,
Which linger yet about lone Gothic arches?

Critics have often noticed the importance of the architectural background of the poem, and of the carving in the church described near the beginning. The description of 'the sculptur'd dead, on each side', who 'seem to freeze,

> Emprison'd in black, purgatorial rails',

contrasts brilliantly with the tale of youthful passion which is about to be told. We remember it when we come to the moment before the consummation of the lovers' desires:

> Upon his knees he sank, pale as smooth-sculptured stone.

No less brilliant is the description of 'The carved angels, ever eager-eyed' under the cornice,

> With hair blown back, and wings put cross-wise on their breasts.

We first see Porphyro 'Beside the portal doors, Buttress'd from moonlight', and when he enters he hides 'Behind a broad hall-pillar', much as Romeo must do. He follows Angela 'through a lowly arched way' into 'a little moonlight room,

> Pale, lattic'd, chill, and silent as a tomb'.

He is led to Madeline's room 'through many a dusky gallery'. No reader is likely to forget the casement[1] in the room in which she sleeps:

> A casement high and triple-arch'd there was,
> All garlanded with carven imag'ries
> Of fruits, and flowers, and bunches of knot-grass,
> And diamonded with panes of quaint device
>
> .   .   .   .
>
> Full on this casement shone the wintry moon,
> And threw warm gules on Madeline's fair breast,
> As down she knelt for heaven's grace and boon;
> Rose-bloom fell on her hands, together prest,
> And on her silver cross soft amethyst,
> And on her hair a glory, like a saint.

Just before the end of the tale one or two further touches of description of the castle give added vividness:

> The arras, rich with horseman, hawk, and hound,
> Flutter'd in the besieging wind's uproar;
> And the long carpets rose along the gusty floor.

---

[1] 'Casement' is a Gothic, Mrs. Radcliffe word: the heroine in *Northanger Abbey* is delighted to find that some of the windows are 'casements', though they are not as dark and gloomy as she could have wished.

We also hear of the wide stairs, the iron porch, and the heavy door through which the lovers escape into the night.

Colour-imagery, which is so brilliantly exemplified in this description of the casement, is less prominent than one might expect. At the beginning of the poem everything is colourless, as it is numb and cold. Colour really enters the poem with the wild thought that suddenly comes to Porphyro, 'like a full-blown rose, Flushing his brow' and making 'purple riot' in his heart. Colour, as we come to see, represents passion, and the arrival of the richest colours is heralded by the 'silver taper's light' which Madeline is carrying when she arrives at her room. Colour is used brilliantly in the description of Madeline and of the strange, rich meal which Porphyro heaps up beside her bed. But it is above all on sound that Keats depends to gain his effects. At the beginning only the muttering of the beadsman's prayer disturbs the unmoving silence. Then, with a powerful effect of contrast, we hear 'Music's golden tongue' through a door and have the incomparable image, which Browning must have envied, of music 'yearning like a God in pain'. Amidst the sounds of revelry and the whispers of the revellers (the poem is full of whispering, as it is of doors opening and closing)— Madeline is at first silent and preoccupied: we hear her sigh, and we hear her breathing. The feeble laugh of Angela, as she talks with Porphyro, is somehow macabre and shocking. When we return to Madeline silence takes over again in her room, 'silken, hush'd, and chaste'. Silence is part of the magic, and we hear nothing but the sound of her breathing and the rustling of her clothes as she prepares for sleep. For a moment a door opens and the sound of the music penetrates to the 'retired quiet' of her chamber. Silence returns, and the next thing we hear is Porphyro's whisper to Madeline, and the sudden tumult as he takes her lute and begins to play. She weeps, and begins to 'moan forth witless words with many a sigh'. As the lovers embrace 'the frost-wind blows

> Like Love's alarum pattering the sharp sleet
> Against the window-panes; St. Agnes' moon hath set'.

The lovers speak to one another, but as they make their escape silence descends once more:

> They glide, like phantoms, into the wide hall;
> Like phantoms, to the iron porch, they glide.

The bolts slide soundlessly, the chains 'lie silent on the footworn stones', and the last sound that we hear is that of the door as it groans on its hinges. Few poems are built so surely on a contrasting pattern of cold and warmth, colour and colourlessness, tumultuous sound and silence. This patterning echoes the contrast between the hostile world outside and the warmth and beauty within. The background of feud, which is reminiscent of *Romeo and Juliet*, also helps to give the tale its perfect frame and definition.

No poet is ever likely to write a finer description of young love in an unreal world of heart's desire, but some recent critics have accorded *The Eve of St. Agnes* praise which could only be appropriate to a poem of a much profounder nature. Professor Earl Wasserman, for example, considers the action symbolical: for him Porphyro's journey to Madeline's chamber represents the progress of the human soul as described in Keats's letter on life as a 'Mansion of Many Apartments'. It is impossible to believe that Keats had any such intention. Ten months after writing the poem, indeed, he wrote to John Taylor:

The little dramatic skill I may as yet have however badly it might show in a Drama would I think be sufficient for a Poem—I wish to diffuse the colouring of St. Agnes eve throughout a Poem in which Character and Sentiment would be the figures to such drapery—Two or three such Poems . . . would be a famous gradus ad Parnassum altissimum—I mean they would nerve me up to the writing of a few fine Plays—my greatest ambition.

It is perfectly true that 'Character and Sentiment' are absent from *The Eve of St. Agnes*: one has only to remember *Troilus and Criseyde* to acknowledge the fact. It is surely sufficient praise for Keats's poem that it comes near perfection in its own kind.

If we remember *Endymion* as we approach the Odes in this volume of 1820 we shall be in a good position to understand them. In that poem Keats had begun to try to explain the unique value to mankind of the beautiful things which he had so often merely listed in his earliest poems. From the first line onwards Beauty is the theme:

A thing of beauty is a joy for ever.

As he says a few lines later:

Some shape of beauty moves away the pall
From our dark spirits.

As examples, he gives a characteristically heterogeneous list of beautiful objects of contemplation: the sun and moon, trees, daffodils, 'the grandeur of the dooms We have imagined for the mighty dead' and 'all lovely tales'. He believes that 'these essences'

> Haunt us till they become a cheering light
> Unto our souls   .   .   .
> They alway must be with us, or we die.

It is easy to see that the subjects of the first three Odes (in the order in which they appear in 1820, which is not that of composition) may be considered as examples of such 'essences': the song of a nightingale, a Grecian urn, and the goddess Psyche. A passage will be quoted shortly in which autumn is explicitly mentioned by Keats as a source of delight of this kind; while the subject of the remaining Ode, melancholy, may be regarded in much the same light. If we look back to the best-known of the hymns in *Endymion* which are the predecessors of the great Odes, the hymn to Pan, we find that the god is addressed in these words:

> Be still the unimaginable lodge
> For solitary thinkings; such as dodge
> Conception to the very bourne of heaven . . .
> Be still a symbol of immensity.   (i. 293-9)

It is made clear that the poet has a special duty to such 'symbols', and the task laid on the shoulders of the enigmatic old man Glaucus in Book III represents this duty. He expounds

> The meanings of all motions, shapes, and sounds;
> .   . Explores all forms and substances
> Straight homeward to their symbol-essences. (iii. 698-700)

Only by doing so can he win immortality. This, we might say, is what Keats himself does with the nightingale's song and the subjects of the other Odes: he probes their meaning, their significance to man, and tries to discover what he here terms 'their symbol-essences'.

It is possible that the state immediately preceding the composition of the Odes was one of relaxation rather than of conscious effort. In one of his letters he describes the origin of the *Ode on Indolence*:

This morning I am in a sort of temper indolent and supremely careless: I long after a stanza or two of Thompson's Castle of indolence—My passions are all asleep. . . . In this state of effeminacy the fibres of the brain are relaxed in common with the rest of the body, and to such a happy degree that pleasure has no show of entice-ment and pain no unbearable frown. Neither Poetry, nor Ambition, nor Love have any alertness of countenance as they pass by me: they seem rather like three figures on a greek vase—a Man and two women—whom no one but myself could distinguish in their disguisement. This is the only happiness. . . .

(To George and Georgiana Keats, 19 March 1819.)

The *Ode on Indolence* seems to have been the last of the Odes to be written, except *To Autumn*, and it is so inferior to the rest that it might be the work of an imitator: Keats himself did not publish it, and probably never would have published it. Yet it may well be that the process of its gestation was similar to that of the great Odes. 'Contemplative indolence'—a phrase Keats heard Hazlitt use in relation to the letters of Gray—would prob-ably fit the mood in which the Odes were written. They are reveries in which the contemplation of 'a thing of beauty' leads the poet into a train of reflections.

Critics who insist on the profundity of the thought in the Odes of Keats are doing his memory a doubtful service. It is true that he wished to make progress in philosophy: one reason for this was that he believed that an epic poet must be a philosopher. But alongside the passages in his letters where he talks of his philosophical ambitions we find others in which he expresses his fear that he is unsuited to such studies. He often realized that the truth which it was in his power to attain was not systematic philosophical truth but truth of 'sensation', truth of impression or feeling. The form of the Ode suited him both because it required less sustained physical effort than a long poem, and because it did not demand a full development of thought. In the famous passage about 'Negative Capability' he complains that Coleridge 'would let go by a fine isolated verisimilitude caught from the Penetralium of mystery, from being incapable of re-maining content with half knowledge'. He continues: 'This pursued through Volumes would perhaps take us no further than this, that with a great poet the sense of Beauty overcomes every other consideration, or rather obliterates all considera-tion.' In some of the Odes the thought is very slight, while in others it is perplexed in a way that suggests confusion in the poet's own mind rather than philosophical profundity. The

value of these great poems lies in the fact that each of them gives
us a 'fine verisimilitude', a splinter of the truth that has presented itself to Keats, though he may be quite unable to fit it
into any coherent philosophical system.

The Odes are the sort of poetry that Hamlet might have
written. One of the first two Odes that Keats ever wrote was
addressed to Hope, and prays for relief from 'that fiend Despondence'. In 'Sleep and Poetry' and *Endymion* 'despondence' remains an enemy to be kept at bay. We know enough about the
life of Keats to realize that there is no element of affectation in
this. He once acknowledged that he had 'a horrid Morbidity
of Temperament' which he considered 'the greatest Enemy and
stumbling block I have to fear', while his brother George tells
us that he was subject to 'many a bitter fit of hypochondriasm'.
Although he says in one of his letters that he will not 'spoil [his]
love of gloom by writing an Ode to darkness' it was inevitable
that one of his Odes should be addressed to Melancholy, and
although the result is not the finest of the Odes it is in a way the
centre of the pattern. Except *To Autumn* every one of the Odes
could be annotated from the *Anatomy of Melancholy*. Above all,
the poet is obsessed by the transitoriness of love and beauty:

> She dwells with Beauty—Beauty that must die;
> And Joy, whose hand is ever at his lips
> Bidding adieu.

As Keats had said in the *Ode to a Nightingale*, this world is a place

> Where Beauty cannot keep her lustrous eyes,
> Or new Love pine at them beyond to-morrow.

It is because he is oppressed by this reflection that the poet
searches for something beyond the transitory, some 'shape of
beauty'. The attraction of the song of the nightingale and of the
Grecian urn is that they are above the flux. The song has been
heard 'In ancient days by emperor and clown': it is

> Perhaps the self-same song that found a path
> Through the sad heart of Ruth, when, sick for home,
> She stood in tears amid the alien corn;
> The same that oft-times hath
> Charm'd magic casements, opening on the foam
> Of perilous seas, in faery lands forlorn.

In the same way the love portrayed on the urn is independent
of time on account of the very nature of art:

> She cannot fade, though thou hast not thy bliss,
>   For ever wilt thou love, and she be fair!

Keats's obsession with time reaches its culmination in this poem,
which has at its centre a series of tolling repetitions: 'Nor ever
. . . Never, never . . . For ever . . . Nor ever . . . For ever . . .
For ever . . . For ever . . . For ever . . . For ever . . .'

This obsession with Time is characteristic of the three central
Odes, the Nightingale, the Grecian Urn, and Melancholy. It is
not to be found in the last and most triumphant of them all,
To Autumn. No melancholy throws its shadow over this poem of
fruition and acceptance. Autumn had always been a season that
had meant a great deal to Keats, as may be seen by tracing the
earlier allusions in his poems; and it was always the achievement of autumn that appealed to him, rather than the fact that
it heralds winter and death. Whereas Shelley, in the 'Ode to the
West Wind', regards autumn as the forerunner of death, and rises
to hope only by contemplating the resurgence of spring that
lies beyond, Keats remains wholly in the present. This suits the
characters of the two poems: Shelley's is one of the swiftest-
moving in our literature, and is aptly cast in *terza rima*: Keats's
poem is serenely poised and static, and is no less fittingly written
in the elaborate galleon-like stanza-form which he had evolved
for his Odes.

It is interesting to notice that autumn is given in a list of
delights in one of Keats's early sonnets. He is using a string of
images to illustrate the delightful way in which winter begins
to give way to spring. Characteristically, he draws them from
very different aspects of experience:

> Sweet Sappho's cheek—a sleeping infant's breath,—
>   The gradual sand that through an hour-glass runs,—
> A woodland rivulet,—a Poet's death.

But here is the beginning of the list:

> The calmest thoughts come round us—as of leaves,
>   Budding,—fruit ripening in stillness,—autumn suns
> Smiling at eve upon the quiet sheaves.

It is the most natural of transitions from this early sonnet to the letter in which Keats describes the origin of *To Autumn*:

How beautiful the season is now—How fine the air. A temperate sharpness about it. Really, without joking, chaste weather—Dian skies—I never lik'd stubble fields so much as now—Aye better than the chilly green of the spring. Somehow a stubble plain looks warm—in the same way that some pictures look warm.

One of the secrets of the remarkable success of this poem is perhaps that the poet himself makes no appearance. One would have expected him to have made some reference to the parallel between the season and the corresponding period in a man's life. He does nothing of the kind. Nor does he explicitly contrast the recurrence and therefore, in a sense, the immortality of the season and its sights and occupations with the transitoriness of human life, as he does with the song of the nightingale. Like a painter he loses himself in the contemplation of what he is describing. Borrowing a word from Hopkins, we might say that he 'inscapes' the season. When he was writing the earliest of the Odes, the *Ode to Psyche*, he said that he hoped it would be in 'a more peaceable and healthy spirit' than anything else that he had composed. It is a paradox of genius that the Ode *To Autumn*, almost the last poem that he was ever to write, is written in precisely this spirit.

As several critics have pointed out, more light is thrown on the form of these remarkable poems by considering their relation to the sonnet than by exploring the work of earlier writers of the ode. 'I have been endeavouring to discover a better sonnet stanza than we have', Keats wrote immediately after transcribing the *Ode to Psyche*. 'The legitimate [Petrarchan] does not suit the language over-well from the pouncing rhymes—the other kind [the Shakespearian] appears too elegiac—and the couplet at the end of it has seldom a pleasing effect.' There follows a sonnet on the sonnet in which the poet emphasizes that it is necessary to 'weigh the stress

> Of every chord, and see what may be gain'd
> By ear industrious, and attention meet'.

This sonnet has the experimental rhyme-scheme *abc abd cabcdede*. Of the five other sonnets in the same letter, three are Shakespearian, one combines a Shakespearian octave with a sestet rhyming *bcefef,* while the other rhymes *abab cdcd efeggf.* It is clear that the Shakespearian sonnet was one of the chief formative influences on the stanzaic form of the Odes. In an early poem— 'Woman! when I behold thee flippant, vain'—we find Keats using one type of Petrarchan sonnet as a stanza; while the single stanza of the unfinished *Ode to May,* which was written a year before the *Ode to Psyche* and which is the true forerunner of the great Odes in its beauty of rhythm, has fourteen lines (of which four are shortened) rhyming *ababccdedefgfg*: that is to say it consists of the three quatrains of a Shakespearian sonnet, with a couplet following the first quatrain instead of the last. As Garrod pointed out, in its first form the first stanza of the *Ode to Psyche* consists of a Shakespearian octave followed by one of the permissible types of Petrarchan sestet, except that the twelfth line is a trimeter. In the final form of the poem each stanza begins with a Shakespearian octave, although there are trimeters in stanza ii, while stanza iii rhymes *cddc* instead of *cdcd* in lines 5–8.

After experimenting in this way Keats based what have been termed his three central Odes, as well as the inferior *Ode on Indolence,* on a stanza of ten lines rhyming *ababcdecde.* (The *Ode to a Nightingale* has a trimeter in the eighth line, three of the five stanzas of the *Ode on a Grecian Urn* have the rhyme-scheme slightly rearranged in the last six lines, while *To Autumn* has an eleventh line and a slightly varied rhyme-scheme). Essentially, the stanza consists of half of a Shakespearian octave followed by one of the commonest forms of the Petrarchan sestet. Keats disliked the couplets which may be found in both types of sonnet, and in the central Odes he manages to avoid couplets altogether, though there are four in the *Ode to Psyche* and one in each stanza of *To Autumn* as the concomitant of the eleventh line. Other influences may be found behind the stanza of the Odes: possibly that of Chatterton, whose 'Battle of Hastings' is in stanzas of ten lines: certainly that of Spenser, the rhythm of whose lines was always in Keats's mind (it is surprising that there is not a single Alexandrine in the Odes): and probably also that of some of the imitators of Spenser, notably Thomson in *The Castle of Indolence.* But all these influences are subordinate to that of the sonnet. In particular, only a man who knew Shakespeare's sonnets intimately could have evolved this stanza and handled its complicated rhymes

and rhythms with so certain a touch, succeeding so memorably
in his search for a measure 'more interwoven and complete'
than the conventional sonnet 'To fit the naked foot of poesy'.[1]
This makes it interesting to notice the juxtaposition of the
sonnet and the ode in the epistle to Charles Cowden Clarke:

> Who read for me the sonnet swelling loudly
> Up to its climax and then dying proudly?
> Who found for me the grandeur of the ode,
> Growing, like Atlas, stronger from its load? (60–63)

This is no doubt fortuitous, yet it is suggestive. When Keats
turned to the writing of Odes he did not forget the secret of
making a poem die proudly—what better description could
there be of the end of the *Ode on Melancholy*?—

> His soul shall taste the sadness of her might,
> And be among·her cloudy trophies hung.

In the description of the ode, the words 'grandeur' and 'load'
are significant, and remind us of the advice Keats gave Shelley,
' "load every rift" of your subject with ore'. He loved richness
in poetry, and the key words in the Odes—flowers, sweet,
drowsy—are words that contribute to the effect of almost
oppressive luxury. There are no poems in the language richer
in sensuous imagery (even in imagery of taste, which is not
common in poetry). This is what Keats himself once called
'distilled poesy'. Many of the remarks about poetry in the letters

---

[1] To demonstrate the close relationship between the Odes of Keats and the
sonnet, here is the opening stanza of his *Ode to Sleep*:

> O soft embalmer of the still midnight,
>   Shutting, with careful fingers and benign,
> Our gloom-pleas'd eyes, embower'd from the light,
>   Enshaded in forgetfulness divine;
>   O soothest Sleep! if so it please thee, close,
>   In midst of this thine hymn, my willing eyes—
>   Save me from curious conscience, that still lords:
>   Or wait the amen, ere thy poppy throws
>   Around my bed its lulling charities;
>   Turn the key deftly in the oilèd wards.

This consists of the first six lines of the sonnet 'To Sleep', followed by lines 11, 7, 8,
and 13. It is interesting to notice that it is not only the rhyme-scheme of the Odes
that is close to that of many of the sonnets: the whole style is closely related. The
syntax, diction, and imagery of these lines could hardly be distinguished from those
of the Odes. This sonnet was written about the same time as the first of the major
Odes, *Psyche*, and is given in the same letter. (To George and Georgiana Keats,
14 Feb.–3 May 1819, a.f.)

take on a new meaning when we consider them in relation to the Odes. 'Poetry should surprise by a fine excess,' he once wrote, for example; while in the same letter he goes on in these words: 'The rise, the progress, the setting of imagery should like the Sun come natural to him—shine over him and set soberly although in magnificence leaving him in the Luxury of twilight.'

The sudden illumination that such a sentence throws on the nature of poetry is characteristic of the letters of Keats, and it is not surprising that the publication of the first collection in 1848 had an important influence on the development of his reputation. Although the appearance of his letters to Fanny Brawne thirty years later was regretted by Matthew Arnold and most other admirers of his poetry, we notice that in 1880 Arnold repeatedly quotes from the main body of the letters in order to support his insistence that Keats 'had flint and iron in him . . ., had character'. Lecturing in Oxford at the beginning of the present century, Bradley was equally emphatic in his appeal to his audience to 'study the letters of Keats'. Today they are among the most famous letters in the language and it is even possible to imagine an anti-intentionalist critic making an appeal of a different sort. He might insist that we should base our estimate of Keats on the poems themselves: that there is danger in paying too much attention to the letters, with their hints about the poems that Keats intended to write, or would have liked to write. He might point to the misleading use occasionally made of the letters in Middleton Murry's brilliant *Keats and Shakespeare* and to Dr. Leavis's reliance on the letters to show that Keats is more of a poet after his own heart than the poems themselves might suggest. Yet although the danger is real, only a doctrinaire critic could argue in such a way. It would be as rational to argue that paintings must always be looked at with one eye closed as that the letters of Keats should be ignored by the reader who wishes to understand his poetry.

What distinguishes them from the letters of most other poets is that they do not only contain penetrating phrases and observations about poetry in general and his own poems in particular: they give us a peculiarly vivid impression of what it is like to be a poet:

As to the poetical Character itself, (I mean that sort of which, if I am any thing, I am a Member; that sort distinguished from the

wordsworthian or egotistical sublime; which is a thing per se and
stands alone) it is not itself—it has no self—it is every thing and
nothing—It has no character—it enjoys light and shade; it lives in
gusto, be it foul or fair, high or low, rich or poor, mean or elevated
—It has as much delight in conceiving an Iago as an Imogen.
What shocks the virtuous philosopher, delights the camelion Poet...
A Poet is the most unpoetical of any thing in existence.
                    (To Richard Woodhouse, 27 October 1818.)

It is clear that the act of writing the letters must have been
of the greatest importance to Keats. Just as the composition of
The Prelude helped Wordsworth to find himself, so that of his
letters enabled Keats to discover his own poetic identity. As we
read them we are not merely listening to a poet describing his
own development: we are watching the process going on under
our eyes.

Since Keats was exceptionally sensitive to the personalities
of his correspondents—'I wish I knew always the humour my
friends would be in at opening a letter of mine, to suit it to them
[as] nearly as possible'—it is natural to inquire who they were.
Most of the letters were written to men whose characters and
abilities did not prevent him from enjoying his 'own unfettered
scope'. On 8 October 1817 we find him writing to Bailey that
he is 'quite disgusted with literary Men and will never know
another except Wordsworth—no not even Byron', while in a
later letter he complains that even with men like Wordsworth
and Hunt conversation is too often 'not a search after know-
lege, but an endeavour at effect'. He soon quarrelled with Hunt
and Haydon: that he never broke with Hazlitt may be due
to the fact that Hazlitt was usually so much more impressive
in writing than in conversation. Keats felt at ease with this
awkward man of genius as he could never have done with the
aristocratic and charming Shelley. When he wrote a letter he
wanted a good listener on paper: intelligent men of the second
rank like John Hamilton Reynolds, Richard Woodhouse, and
Benjamin Bailey provided him with the sort of sympathetic and
understanding audience that he required, and we notice that
passages of vital importance may be found in letters to any one
of his small circle of close friends.

Yet it may be that more of them occur in the letters to his
brother George than anywhere else, and one has only to glance
through them to realize the significance to Keats of his brother's

departure to America. George had always played a very important part in the poet's life. As Keats wrote to Sarah Jeffrey at the end of May 1819:

> I have been always till now almost as careless of the world as a fly—my troubles were all of the Imagination—My Brother George always stood between me and any dealings with the world—Now I find I must buffet it—I must take my stand upon some vantage ground and begin to fight.

When so much has been said of the influence on Keats of Tom's illness and death it is surprising that the importance of George's departure should have attracted so little attention; yet in part of a letter to America written on 21 September 1819 we find him stating categorically: 'From the time you left me, our friends say I have altered completely—am not the same person.' Keats was developing very rapidly at this time, and one of the things that helped him to develop was the composition of these long journal-letters to George and Georgiana. To many passages in these letters one is tempted to apply his remark about a passage in *Endymion* that has already been quoted: 'My having written that Argument will perhaps be of the greatest service to me of any thing I ever did.'

Not the least interesting of the letters are those relating to *Hyperion*, to which we must now turn. The first thing to be understood if we are to have any chance of making sense of the poem is that it was intended to be an epic. Like most of his contemporaries, Keats was brought up to think of the epic as the greatest of the poetic kinds. Cowden Clarke, as he says in a verse-epistle,

> Shew'd me that epic was of all the king,
> Round, vast, and spanning all like Saturn's ring.
>
> (66–67)

His letters make it clear that he devoted a great deal of thought to the subject of epic poetry. 'No sooner am I alone', he wrote in October 1818, 'than shapes of epic greatness are stationed around me. . . . Then "Tragedy, with scepter'd pall, comes sweeping by".' In March of the following year he complains that he is in a bad mood for writing, 'not exactly on the road to an epic poem'. There is no need to wonder, with Garrod, whether 'this passion for grand-scale effects' was caught from Haydon: Haydon's profound enthusiasm for heroic painting may well have had an influence on Keats: but there is, in any event, nothing surprising, or vulgar, in his desire to write an epic poem. This epic ambition helps to explain Keats's desire to master philosophy. He doubted whether he had the necessary powers; but he did not doubt that an epic poem required a secure philosophical foundation. It is no chance that a few weeks after the announcement that he intends to write a poem about Hyperion we find him speculating about the relation between poetry and philosophy and determining, in about a year's time, to seek Hazlitt's advice on 'the best metaphysical road'. While he had no use for directly didactic poetry—'poetry that has a palpable design upon us—and if we do not agree, seems to put its hand in its breeches pocket'—he realized that an epic poem does not merely tell a story: it embodies a whole interpretation of life. *Hyperion* was not simply to be a better-written *Endymion*: it was to belong to a different and much more important poetic kind.

It is because of this pre-occupation with the epic that Keats keeps returning to the relative merits of Milton and Wordsworth. In one letter he tells us that he has been reflecting on Wordsworth's genius, 'and as a help . . . how he differs from Milton. . . . Whether Wordsworth has in truth epic passion.' Unless we understand Keats's own ambitions this may seem rather an academic question, as may that of the precise 'difference' between Ariosto and Spenser, which we find mentioned in another letter. Spenser was important because he had gone a long way on the road to writing an epic: Milton was important because he was the one English poet who had completed a successful epic: Wordsworth was important because he was the only living poet who seemed possibly of epic calibre, as he had shown in *The Excursion*. The Italians Ariosto, Tasso, Boiardo, and above all Dante were important for ultimately the same reasons. Keats studied them for what they could teach him. His interest in epic poetry is similarly evident in his inferior *Ode to Apollo*, where Shakespeare is the only poet mentioned who did not write an epic. Keats wished to join the company of the

> Bards, that erst sublimely told
> Heroic deeds, and sang of fate.

Above all, Keats must have been interested in the philosophical standpoint of the epic poets and the nature of the high styles which they had evolved. Milton had based *Paradise Lost* on Christian doctrine which Keats could not accept. Wordsworth had attempted to work out a private philosophy of which Keats disapproved—his disapproval eliciting some of the most perceptive comments on Wordsworth ever made. The phrase 'the wordsworthian or egotistical sublime' occurs in the same letter in which Keats remarks that he may well be reflecting on the characters of Saturn and Ops. It reminds us of the earlier letter in which he had asked:

For the sake of a few fine imaginative or domestic passages, are we to be bullied into a certain Philosophy engendered in the whims of an Egotist—Every man has his speculations, but every man does not brood and peacock over them till he makes a false coinage and deceives himself—Many a man can travel to the very bourne of Heaven, and yet want confidence to put down his halfseeing.

Unable as he was to accept the Christian philosophy, and unwilling to erect a philosophical system of his own, Keats instinctively turned back to 'the beautiful mythology of Greece', with which he had already discovered an exceptional affinity. By doing so he made it inevitable that the teaching of his poem should be conveyed allegorically.

The discovery of a suitable style for epic poetry is perhaps the most difficult task that an English poet can set himself. It is made at once easier and more difficult by the fact that the man who has succeeded most brilliantly is Milton: easier, because there is the encouragement of his example: more difficult, because it is hardly possible to learn from Milton without falling into imitation. It was almost inevitable that it should have been of Milton that Keats was thinking most as he made his own bid to write an epic poem: no less inevitable that he should have been distressed by the fear of becoming a mere imitator.

The fragment called 'The Fall of Hyperion—A Dream' was first published by Monckton Milnes in 1856. At first he supposed it to be the first draft of *Hyperion*, but later he changed his mind, and although there is curiously little evidence about the relation of the two versions a close comparison of the texts makes it clear that 'The Fall' represents an attempt to rewrite the poem. It appears that Keats's reason for dissatisfaction was the feeling that he was being betrayed into insincerity by modelling himself on Milton: 'I have given up Hyperion [he wrote on

21 September 1819]—there were too many Miltonic inversions
in it—Miltonic verse cannot be written but in an artful or
rather artist's humour.' On the same day he wrote in another
letter:

I shall never become attach'd to a foreign idiom so as to put it into
my writings. The Paradise lost though so fine in itself is a corruption
of our Language—it should be kept as it is unique—a curiosity, a
beautiful and grand Curiosity. The most remarkable Production of
the world—A northern dialect accommodating itself to greek and
latin inversions and intonations.

It seems possible that his dissatisfaction with his Miltonic style
was connected with some doubts in his mind whether epic
poetry was still possible. Haydon tells us that 'one day he was
full of an epic poem; the next day epic poems were splendid
impositions on the world'. In any event the 'sort of induction'
that Keats wrote for the second version of the poem is almost
a reversion to the manner of *Endymion* (though without rhyme)
and is notable mainly for its final line—

When this warm scribe my hand is in the grave.

The other 270 lines which now precede the revised former
beginning of the poem, interesting as they are, are less splendidly
impressive than the original opening. Keats presumably wrote
them because he felt that some explanation of the action
of the poem should be given before the reader is plunged *in
medias res*. 'The Fall of Hyperion' should persuade anyone
who believes that *Hyperion* is merely a narrative poem that
such is not the intention (at least) of the revised form of the
poem. Whereas the poet himself makes no appearance in the
first *Hyperion*, so far as it goes, he is present (as the dreamer)
throughout the second version. He finds himself in a beautiful
garden and drinks a mysterious potion, as a result of which he
swoons. He then finds himself in a vast building, at the end of
which there is an immense flight of steps, with a priestess standing at the summit. A great deal of light is thrown on the interpretation of this by a letter which he had written to Reynolds
in May 1818, comparing life to a 'large Mansion of Many Apartments'. The second apartment is the 'Chamber of Maiden-
Thought': at first it is full of pleasant wonders, and we are
tempted to remain in it for ever; but after a time our vision is

sharpened and we see more deeply 'into the heart and nature of Man', becoming convinced

that the World is full of Misery and Heartbreak, Pain, Sickness and oppression—whereby This Chamber of Maiden Thought becomes gradually darken'd and at the same time on all sides of it many doors are set open—but all dark—all leading to dark passages—We see not the ballance of good and evil. We are in a Mist.

As he addresses the mysterious goddess Moneta, the dreamer is in such a mist:

> 'None can usurp this height,' returned that shade,
> 'But those to whom the miseries of the world
> Are misery, and will not let them rest.
> All else who find a haven in the world,
> Where they may thoughtless sleep away their days,
> If by a chance into this fane they come,
> Rot on the pavement where thou rotted'st half.'
>
> (i. 147–53)

Keats would not have published 'The Fall of Hyperion' as it stands: it is a draft, and a great deal is imperfectly worked out. But it seems clear that he is reverting to an old theme: the nature and value of poetry. The dreamer cries:

> Majestic shadow, tell me: sure not all
> Those melodies sung into the world's ear
> Are useless; sure a poet is a sage;
> A humanist, Physician to all men.   (i. 187–90)

Moneta replies by insisting on the difference between true poets and mere dreamers:

> The poet and the dreamer are distinct,
> Diverse, sheer opposite, antipodes.
> The one pours out a balm upon the world,
> The other vexes it.   (i. 199–202)

Although Keats intended to erase this passage, it is significant that he should be returning to one of his deepest preoccupations, the difference between romance (poetry of delight and escape) and the greatest poetry, which helps us to interpret the significance of human life itself: the difference between *The Faerie Queene* (as he read it) and *King Lear*. We are reminded of 'Sleep and Poetry', where he had prayed for ten years to devote himself to poetry. There he had taken up his favourite image of poetry as a country of the mind:

> Then will I pass the countries that I see
> In long perspective, and continually
> Taste their pure fountains. First the realm I'll pass
> Of Flora, and old Pan: sleep in the grass,
> Feed upon apples red, and strawberries,
> And choose each pleasure that my fancy sees. (99–104)

But it is his duty to bid farewell to such joys:

> Yes, I must pass them for a nobler life,
> Where I may find the agonies, the strife
> Of human hearts. (123–5)

Instead of ten years, he was to be granted little more than three further years of active life. It is foolish to press a metaphor too far, but if we keep to the image of poetry as a territory we may say that in the *Poems* of 1817 we are still predominantly in the Realm of Flora and Old Pan, and that we stay there for most of *Endymion*, though in it there are glimpses of what lies beyond. The Odes, by their very nature, stand rather aside from the scope of the metaphor. It is in *Hyperion*, above all, that we reach the more serious of poetry's domains. No other poet has gone so far in so short a time. Perhaps it is useless to ask what Keats would have done if he had lived: to such a question there can be no answer: yet when it ceases to be asked, it will be because no one is any longer interested in English poetry.

V

CLARE AND THE MINOR POETS

T HE most striking feature of this period is the contrast between the wealth of poetic talent and the shortage of satisfactory poems. Whereas in the early seventeenth century
almost any educated man seems to have been able to produce
one or two tolerable lyrics, two hundred years later we find
men of unmistakable poetic ability who failed to produce a
single good poem. It is as if the poetry were spilt between the
poet and the poem that should have contained it. What makes
Clare exceptional is that he was not merely a man with a gift
for poetry, like Darley or John Hamilton Reynolds: he was
a poet who produced one volume of poems—*The Shepherd's
Calendar*—that ranks among the most delightful in our language, and who also wrote a handful of visionary lyrics that
leave a resonance in the mind like that set up by Blake's *Songs
of Innocence and Experience*.[1]

[1] John Clare (1793–1864) was born at Helpstone, the son of a Northamptonshire
labourer. His father 'could read a little in a Bible, or testament, and was very fond
of the superstitious tales that are hawked about a street for a penny', as Clare
mentions in his memoir; but his mother was illiterate. His origins were thus more
humble than those of Burns. He was at first 'of a waukly constitution' and although
he was remarkably precocious his formal education was of the slightest. He soon
revealed a 'furious' passion for reading, however, and he tells us that the Bible,
popular ballads, chapbooks, and *Robinson Crusoe* were included in his early reading.
The discovery of Thomson's *Seasons* about the age of thirteen was a landmark in
his development. In his early years he worked at various country employments,
scribbling verses on such pieces of paper as he could lay his hands on. In 1817 he
finally succeeded in printing proposals for a volume of verse, and three years later
the interest shown by Taylor and Hessey enabled him to fulfil his ambition. In 1820
he visited London for the first time, meeting Hazlitt, Lamb, De Quincey, and a
number of the other Londoners. In the same year he married 'Patty' (Martha
Turner). In 1832 he left Helpstone for Northborough and his wife gave birth to
their seventh child. For some time he had suffered from delusions and other mental
aberrations, and in 1837 he was removed to Dr. Allen's asylum at High Beech,
Epping Forest, where he was kindly and intelligently treated and spent much of his
time working in the fields. Four years later he escaped and was allowed to remain
at home for five months, but at the end of 1841 he had to be taken to Northampton
General Lunatic Asylum, where he spent the remainder of his life. He suffered
from delusions—believing himself to be Byron or Napoleon—and longed for the
girls whom he had known as a youth. The entry in the asylum records states that
he died in 1864, 'After years addicted to Poetical prosing'.

The success of Clare's *Poems Descriptive of Rural Life and Scenery*, published in 1820, was partly due to the fact that there was an eager public for 'peasant poetry' at this time; yet it was not in the imitations of Burns that Clare revealed his promise, or in the poems influenced by Pomfret, Goldsmith, and Thomson, but in such pieces as 'Noon', 'Summer Morning', and 'Summer Evening': poems that reveal his gift for precise observation, his use of a countryman's words to gain exactness, and his skilled handling of tetrameter verse. Since several of the poems in this first volume deal with Clare's own life it is not surprising that the title-poem in his second collection, *The Village Minstrel* (1821), is autobiographical; but we notice at once that the descriptive parts of the poem are superior to the more personal passages, in which he is obviously writing for his patrons. The best things in the collection are such minor poems as 'Holywell', 'Cowper Green', 'Solitude', 'Rural Morning', and 'Rural Evening'. When Clare describes a blacksmith's shop, 'where ploughs and harrows lie', we are reminded of Crabbe, as we are when he describes sparrows leaving their nests 'In dust to flutter at the cool of eve'. Time and again he conveys the business and bustle of country life, the fact that something is always going on.

Although it was unsuccessful in its own day and its merit has even yet received scant acknowledgement, there is no doubt that *The Shepherd's Calendar* (1827) stands head and shoulders above Clare's earlier volumes. 'I hope my low station in life will not be set off as a foil against my verses', he wrote in the preface; but the only result of the fact that less attention was now paid to his origins was that less attention was paid to his poetry. The form of the principal series of poems in the volume was the result of a great deal of thought. Hessey had complained that Clare's poems contained 'too much . . . mere description' and not enough 'Sentiment and Feeling and human Interest'; and eventually his colleague John Taylor suggested that Clare should write two poems for each month of the year: a description and a narrative. Clare replied that he 'could soon daub pictures' but that he would find the narratives more difficult, and eventually he ran the descriptions together to form the title-poem and gave four Village Stories in a different section of the book. The structure of each month is simplicity itself: Clare does not even give a chronological description of the progress of

the day: he simply presents us with a series of pictures. He had
a countryman's love of the evening, and the close of his January
day is brilliantly managed:

> The shutter closed, the lamp alight,
> The faggot chopt and blazing bright—
> The shepherd now, from labour free,
> Dances his children on his knee;
> While, underneath his master's seat,
> The tired dog lies in slumbers sweet,
> Starting and whimpering in his sleep,
> Chasing still the straying sheep.

In 'February' we hear of the melting of the snow, of children
hunting for pooty-shells, and prematurely building 'Their
spring-time huts of sticks or straw', and then of the key-figures
in Clare's village: the milkmaid, the shepherd, and the shep-
herds' dogs pursuing their sheep,

> While, following fast, a misty smoke
> Reeks from the moist grass as they run.

Each month has its characteristic sounds, as well as its sights: in
July 'Scythes tinkle in each grassy dell' and the meadows are
filled with the sound 'Of laughing maids and shouting boys':
in September we hear the 'creaking noise of opening gate' and
the 'clanking pumps': while there is a brilliant description of
the strange silence that often falls about noon in midsummer,
when 'day lies still as death'. Clare seldom turns aside from
description to reflection in *The Shepherd's Calendar*, but when he
does the result often reminds us vividly of the poets of the seventeenth century. Of children playing in a churchyard he writes:

> They think not, in their jovial cry,
> The time will come, when they shall lie
> As lowly and as still as they
> While other boys above them play,
> Heedless, as they are now, to know
> The unconscious dust that lies below.

On occasion he can write lines reminiscent of Marvell:

> But woodmen still on Spring intrude,
> And thin the shadow's solitude;
> With sharpen'd axes felling down
> The oak-trees budding into brown.

If we turn to Clare's poetry from that of other descriptive
poets we are reminded of Corin's remark in *As You Like It*, 'Sir,

I am a true countryman.' It is not surprising that he was a severe critic of the pastoralizing of Shenstone or that he disliked the 'peasantry' of Darley's *Sylvia*. He also made a shrewd objection to the descriptions of natural scenery in Keats:

When he speaks of woods, Dryads and Fauns and Satyrs are sure to follow, and the brook looks alone without her naiads to his mind. . . . With other inhabitants of great cities, he often described nature as she appeared to his fancies, and not as he would have described her had he witnessed the things he describes.

This gives us a hint of Clare's own secret. Even as a boy he was astonished by other people's lack of interest in the world of the eye. He had the psychology of a painter, and one notices how often he uses painter-like language in talking of poetry. He once decided to write a hundred sonnets 'as a set of pictures on the scenes . . . that appear in the different seasons'. He had every right to claim 'images . . . not noticed before' in many of his poems. It is not surprising that he numbered de Wint, Rippingille, and Hilton among his friends. His fragmentary essay on landscape throws a great deal of light on his poetry. The men and women in his poems remind us of the figures in a landscape painting: the true subject is the seasons as they pass, and the hours of the day: men and women figure only as playing their part in this unending natural process.

Clare was an expert naturalist. Even before he began to write poetry, he tells us, he 'noticd every thing as anxious' as he did later. He collected flowers, made a list of Northamptonshire birds, and studied the reproductive processes of plants. He once thought of calling his *Natural History of Helpstone* 'Biographies of Birds and Flowers'. His love of accuracy explains his characteristic use of unusual and provincial words in his poetry. If he felt that the usual word was imprecise, he did not hesitate to turn to 'the unwritten language of England'. He uses a great many unfamiliar epithets—in his early poetry, as in that of many poets, epithets are too common—but in his mature work it is his use of unusual verbs which is most striking, verbs which have a vivid exactness, visual or auditory, which would otherwise be unobtainable:

> The crow goes flopping on from wood to wood,
> The wild duck wherries to the distant flood,
> The starnels hurry o'er in merry crowds,
> And overhead whew by like hasty clouds.

In the same poem, 'The Flight of Birds', the pigeon 'suthers by on rapid wing' while the peewit 'whizzes' over the ploughman 'with many a whew and whirl and sudden scream'. In his desire to convey the precise nature of what he is describing Clare sometimes reminds us of Hopkins; yet his approach to truth is not that of a theologian but that of a countryman of genius who knows that most people keep their eyes and ears half shut. As we read these records of actuality we notice the delight that the poet is taking in the sequence of morning and evening, of spring and summer, his undulled pleasure in the perpetual bustle and purposeful activity of the countryside. No fewer than twenty-eight of his poems begin with the word 'Now'. A great many others begin with the words 'I love', while such words as 'joy', 'delight', 'merry', 'pleasure', 'glee', and 'mirth' occur on every page. It is when Clare is driven in on himself that he becomes a prey to melancholy. Uneducated as he was, he was a highly intelligent man, and he seems to have realized that to preserve his sanity it was essential for him to maintain his almost organic sense of unity with external nature. Far more than most descriptive poets, he is himself a part of the process that he describes: he is not a visitor to the country, but a part of it. Perhaps his awareness was increased by his observation of the way in which the enclosures were killing the beauty and the rhythm of country life.

Although his discovery of *The Seasons* marked an epoch in Clare's life, *The Shepherd's Calendar* has little in common with Thomson's poem. Thomson is a philosopher who takes the whole world and the whole of history for his subject: he is concerned with the universal causes of things. Clare writes as a countryman in one place at one time. In his inland poem he has nothing to do with the sublime: he is seldom the moralist and never the philosopher. He is Bewick to Thomson's Turner. Thomson's blank verse, with its diction, as Johnson said, ' in the highest degree florid and luxuriant', is the antithesis of Clare's simple metrical patterns and his pure English idiom.

Like 'The Cross Roads' in *The Village Minstrel*, the four tales in *The Shepherd's Calendar* owe a good deal to Crabbe. As in his descriptive poems Clare shows a countryman's knowledge of trees, flowers, and animals, so in these stories he describes the lives of country people without sentiment or humbug. In his view even Crabbe saw rural life from outside: 'Whats he know of the distresses of the poor', he once wrote, 'musing over a snug coal fire in his parsonage box.' In 'The Sorrows of Love', which is a triumph in the informal style which is so difficult to manage, Clare 'keeps decorum' most skilfully, not indeed by limiting himself exclusively to such idioms as his narrator would use but by being careful to set passages in a colloquial style in key positions. At the end we are told how the old woman snuffed the candle,

> Then laid her knitting down, and shook her head,
> And stoop'd to stir the fire, and talk of bed.

The same volume includes a lyric which is, as Clare said himself, 'out of my way' ('Life, Death and Eternity') and a very remarkable poem, 'The Dream', which reveals an aspect of his genius that appears again in some of his asylum lyrics. It is a vision of the end of the universe:

> When years, in drowsy thousands counted by,
> Are hung on minutes with their destiny:
> When Time in terror drops his draining glass,
> And all things mortal, like to shadows, pass,
> As 'neath approaching tempests sinks the sun—
> When Time shall leave Eternity begun.

The combination of an apparent _naïveté_ of expression with a penetrating prophetic vision is singularly impressive: Clare never revealed more clearly his gift for the incomparable image:

> Winds urged them onward, like to restless ships;
> And Light dim faded in its last eclipse;
> And Agitation turn'd a straining eye;
> And Hope stood watching like a bird to fly.

From the destruction of the world Clare makes something of a terrifying beauty:

> The colour'd flower, the green of field and tree,
> What they had been, for ever ceased to be:
> Clouds, raining fire, scorch'd up the hissing dews;
> Grass shrivell'd brown in miserable hues;
> Leaves fell to ashes in the air's hot breath,
> And all awaited universal Death.

It is natural to Clare to remember the fate of the brute creation, the death of the cattle, the dogs that 'dropp'd, and dying lick'd their masters' feet', and the terrified birds that

> Beat through the evil air in vain for rest.

The supreme horror is the extinction of the light:

> The pallid moon hung fluttering on the sight,
> As startled bird whose wings are stretch'd for flight;
> And o'er the east a fearful light begun
> To show the sun rise—not the morning sun,
> But one in wild confusion, doom'd to rise
> And drop again in horror from the skies—
> To heaven's midway it reel'd, and changed to blood,
> Then dropp'd, and Light rush'd after like a flood.

For all its horror it is not a hysterical poem. The poignancy of the return to life in the last line is profoundly moving:

> I heard the cock crow, and I blest the sound.

It seems possible that Clare could have essayed more poems in this vein; but he shrank from the experience. 'I mustnt do no more terrible things yet', as he wrote in a letter, 'they stir me up to such a pitch that leaves a disrelish for my old accustomed wanderings after nature.'

After such a poem *The Rural Muse*, published in 1835, when Mrs. Emmerson had succeeded Taylor as Clare's adviser, comes as an anticlimax. Instead of concentrating on his true vein he seems here to be striving to show his capacity for variety and his competence in traditional poetic forms. Once again many of the poems are descriptive, but now they are too often turned to moral or personal applications of a highly conventional kind.

Literary influences are more obvious again, as in his earlier volumes: at least three of the poems had originally been written as imitations of seventeenth-century poetry, while we are often reminded of the muted music of Collins. 'Autumn' is in the unrhymed stanza of the 'Ode to Evening', as is the original version of 'Summer Images'. But adjectives in -y spring up on all sides like literary weeds:

> The pranking bat its flighty circlet makes

reads like a line from a parody of textbook 'Pre-Romanticism'. It is sickening to find a poet of Clare's stature using phrases like 'silly sheep' and 'balmy trills'. There are also occasional reminiscences of Byron, a poet who meant less to Clare than did Wordsworth, although in his madness he came to think that he was himself the author of *Childe Harold* and *Don Juan*. In spite of the metrical variety of the volume it is interesting to notice that he avoids blank verse. Half of the poems (on the other hand) are sonnets, reminding us—in spite of an outburst in a letter against 'the short winded peevishness that hovers round this 14 line article in poetry'—that Clare was throughout his life a prolific sonneteer. As Taylor pointed out, he excelled in 'little things', and as we turn over his hundreds of sonnets we become aware that he was experimenting endlessly to find a verbal equivalent for the small woodcut so brilliantly practised by Bewick. Many of Clare's sonnets, indeed, are sketches or jottings rather than completed wholes, and they all have their interest for a critic who wishes to study his genius for recreating nature in words. In none of his poems is it more evident that description is his forte. 'The cat runs races with her tail' is a brilliant little genre-piece, while 'Farm Breakfast' is surely a poem of which Swift would have approved:

> Maids shout to breakfast in a merry strife,
> And the cat runs to hear the whetted knife.

From the end of 1836 until his death in 1864 Clare was never wholly sane, and no further collection of his verse was published in his lifetime. He was, however, treated with remarkable humanity, and over the years he wrote a great many poems, a few of them of the highest merit. The best of these are lyrics of a penetrating simplicity which neither requires nor permits of analysis, such as 'Song's Eternity', first published by Edmund Blunden and Alan Porter:

> Mighty songs that miss decay,
>   What are they?
> Crowds and cities pass away
>   Like a day.
> Books are out and books are read,
>   What are they?
> Years will lay them with the dead—
>   Sigh, sigh;
> Trifles unto nothing wed,
>   They die.

'Dying Child' appeared in J. L. Cherry's *Life and Remains of John Clare* in 1873:

> He could not die when trees were green,
> For he loved the time too well.

'*Now* is past' is one of the most remarkable of all these poems:

> Wood strawberries faded from wood-sides,
>   Green leaves have all turned yellow;
> No Adelaide walks the wood-rides,
>   True love has no bed-fellow.
>   *Now* is past.

One of the characteristic themes of these last poems is the poet's search for reality—his own reality and the reality of the past. In 'I am' he complains of the shipwreck of his life:

> I AM: yet what I am none cares or knows,
> My friends forsake me like a memory lost.

Sometimes, as in reading 'I lost the love of heaven above', we feel that Blake is the only possible parallel:

> I snatched the sun's eternal ray,
> And wrote till earth was but a name.

One of the most moving of these poems is the 'Invitation to Eternity', in which Clare's love-yearning fuses with his perpetual questionings about eternity:

> Say, wilt thou go with me, sweet maid,
> Say, maiden, wilt thou go with me
> Through the valley-depths of shade,
> Of night and dark obscurity;
>
>   .   .   .
>
> Where stones will turn to flooding streams,
> Where plains will rise like ocean's waves,
> Where life will fade like visioned dreams,
> And mountains darken into caves,
> Say, maiden, wilt thou go with me
> Through this sad non-identity,
> Where parents live and are forgot,
> And sisters live and know us not?

The questioning of life and death that we find in many of Clare's lyrics is the main subject of the poetry of Beddoes; but in him it takes on a deeper and more macabre aspect. In background he was far removed from the poet of *The Shepherd's Calendar*. His father was a scientist of genius who had marked literary interests.[1] Although Dr. Beddoes died when his son was five it seems clear that the son's fascination with death was the direct result of the father's dissections and speculations about human anatomy and the human soul. The poet was a sort of Frankenstein, a sombre and impressive manifestation of the *Zeitgeist* who seems necessary to complete the literary scene in his age. He devoted many years of his own life to medicine, and claimed that 'the studies . . . of the dramatist & physician are closely, almost inseparably, allied; the application alone is different'.

The early work of Beddoes already exhibits the mixture of what his friends called 'mysticism' and grotesque humour that is one of his characteristics. We have only to read 'Alfarabi the World-Maker' to understand why Browning was so interested in Beddoes—intending to make him the subject of his first lecture, had he been elected Professor of Poetry at Oxford:

> But he was one not satisfied with man,
> As man has made himself: he thought this life
> Was something deeper than a jest, and sought
> Into its roots: himself was his best science.
> He touched the springs, the unheeded hieroglyphics
> Deciphered.

Like Shelley, whom he greatly admired, Beddoes nurtured his boyish imagination on Gothic romances, and the result of such reading is evident in the three 'tales of guilt and woe' which make up *The Improvisatore*, a work which Beddoes thought little of and later tried to suppress. It is in *The Brides' Tragedy*, so

---

[1] Thomas Lovell Beddoes (1803–49) was the son of Dr. Thomas Beddoes, the friend of Coleridge and Southey. His mother was a sister of Maria Edgeworth. He was educated at the Charterhouse and Pembroke College, Oxford. As a freshman there he published *The Improvisatore*. *The Brides' Tragedy* appeared in 1822. In 1825 he took his B.A. and began to work on *Death's Jest-Book*. Later he studied at Göttingen and Würzburg (where he took his M.D. in 1831). At Würzburg Beddoes took a prominent part in radical politics, being received into a club called the *Freie Reichsstadt*—an unusual distinction for a foreigner. Later he was obliged to flee to Berlin. There he studied at the university and continued to take a keen interest in politics. Although he paid occasional visits to England he spent the remainder of his life abroad, mainly in Switzerland, and wrote a good deal in German. His interest in German literature is discussed in Chapter XIV. In 1849 he committed suicide in Basle.

highly praised by Darley, that Beddoes first appears as a considerable writer. His subject is a murder commemorated in a popular ballad, and he handles it in a spirit that reminds us of Webster. As one reads this play it becomes difficult to agree with Professor Donner—the man who has done more than any other for the reputation of Beddoes—that the poet's obsession with death dates from the death of his mother. A passage in a letter written by his brother after the poet's death suggests that the bent of his mind had remained the same throughout his life: 'I was glad to find the Mandrake so much suppressed [in *Death's Jest-Book*]. It was a character in which my brother delighted long ago when a boy, and the idea I can imagine ever haunted his imagination.' *The Brides' Tragedy* was the work of a man who had thought a great deal about the nature of drama. Beddoes made some penetrating notes about the function of dramatic plot, as well as observations on the possibility of discriminating characters 'by appropriating to each . . . a peculiar style of versification; and metaphors drawn from certain circumstances of nature or art'. In the preface to *Death's Jest-Book* he was to follow the Schlegels and the Dutch critic Bilderdijk in maintaining that modern critics are unduly 'prejudiced . . . in favour of the literature of the South': he argues that there is an affinity 'between an old English Play and one of our ancient Cathedrals': 'it is not Shakspeare who is lawless, they are lawless who judge his British example by the precept of the Greeks'. Beddoes was more deeply read in the work of the Elizabethan dramatists than Darley or most of his other contemporaries: at one time he contemplated producing a volume of *Specimens* supplementary to Lamb's. Yet he found it difficult to decide how far the Elizabethans were eligible models. While he regretted that Shelley in *The Cenci* 'seemed to have the Greeks, instead of Shakespeare, as his model' (a surprising judgement), he wrote in another letter that 'just now the drama is a haunted ruin', concluding that 'we had better beget than revive'.

There can be no doubt that *Death's Jest-Book*, which Beddoes sometimes called *The Fool's Tragedy* and once described as an example 'of what might be called the florid Gothic in poetry', is more Elizabethan than classical in inspiration—and more German, perhaps, than either. Beddoes had little hope that it would be appreciated by reviewers 'who have learned the Odes of Horace by heart at Eton'. He was disconcerted when his friends told him that he must not publish it without comprehensive revision. It is an interesting question whether his friends were right. If Beddoes had published this 'strange conglomerate' he would certainly have been attacked by the reviewers; yet publication is the only way in which a poet can escape from a poem, and as it turned out Beddoes was never to escape from *Death's Jest-Book*. There is a possible analogy with *Endymion*. If Keats had taken Hunt's advice and revised his poem, or left it unpublished, he would have been saved from severe and painful criticism; but he might not have developed as rapidly as he did to become the poet of *Hyperion* and the Odes. Beddoes was to struggle in the toils of his extraordinary poem for the rest of his life, practically everything that he wrote being apparently related to it in some way.

It would be difficult to find a better image for *Death's Jest-Book* than the image of a Gothic cathedral which Beddoes himself uses for the non-classical drama. It is 'intricate, vast, and gloomy, [intimating] the supernatural and . . . full of indistinct thoughts of immortality'. Like a cathedral it is the work of a 'wild fancy, sometimes light and joyous, sometimes fearfully hideous—often satirical, grotesque or ludicrous'. The grotesque and the ludicrous are particularly evident in the prose passages, which are an inherent part of the work and yet seldom successful. It is extraordinary to move from the laboured prose of the opening to the brilliance of the first lines of verse:

> The turning tide; the sea's wide leafless wind,
> Wherein no birds inhabit and few traffic,
> Making his cave within your sunny sails.

Sometimes a single line compels our admiration:

> When the thin harvests shed their withered grain.

As always, it is Time, Death, and Eternity that move Beddoes to the most memorable utterance:

> Can a man die? Ay, as the sun doth set:
> It is the earth that falls away from light.   (II. ii. 39–40)

In a remarkable passage he refers to our remotest progenitors, 'who were

> Ere our grey ancestors wrote history;
> When these our ruined towers were in the rock;
> And our great forests, which do feed the sea

> With storm-souled fleets, lay in an acorn's cup:
> When all was seed that now is dust.'   (ii. iii. 532–7)

There is no difficulty in finding the 'mysticism' that distressed
his friends in such lines as these—

> . . . Deeply have I slept.
> As one who doth go down unto the springs
> Of his existence and there bathed, I come
> Regenerate up into the world again   (B text: i. ii. 64–67)

—a passage which might come from one of Shakespeare's last
plays, as might the lines that follow:

> 'Tis nearly passed, for I begin to hear
> Strange but sweet sounds, and the loud rocky dashing
> Of waves, where time into Eternity
> Falls over ruined worlds.   (iv. iii. 107–110)

If the greatness of Shakespeare lay in isolated words and images,
Beddoes too would rank as a great poet. But in fact *Death's Jest-
Book* completely fails to become a coherent whole: there are few
works which leave one in such uncertainty whether the author
was a madman or a visionary. The intention is clearly to use
'Gothic' material as a means of exploring the problem of death
and the whole significance of human life. Beddoes sets death
before us with extraordinary vividness, in a manner that recalls
both the medieval preacher and the modern dramatist:

> As I was newly dead, and sat beside
> My corpse, looking on it, as one who muses
> Gazing upon a house he was burnt out of. (v. iv. 198–200)

While Beddoes acknowledged his own deficiency in humour,
there are occasions when his characteristic *humour noir* appears
to advantage, as in Mandrake's speech: 'After all being dead's
not so uncomfortable when one's got into the knack of it.' The
other great weakness of Beddoes, his inability (in Kelsall's
words) to create 'characters quite different from his own', would
be fatal to the work as an ordinary drama but seems hardly
relevant to it as it stands. It is impossible to keep one's attention
on the plot: what we listen for are the incomparable passages of
meditation on life and death, the poet's own strivings towards
'a wished-for change of being'. It is as if one of the distempered

minds described by Burton were to step out of *The Anatomy of Melancholy* and write a play.

As a lyric poet Beddoes is seldom at his best. In reading some of his shorter poems one understands why he once described himself as 'essentially unpoetical'. 'Squats on a toad-stool under a tree' reminds one of Browning at his most uncompromising— and perhaps also of Hardy. Beddoes has a liking for rude mouthfuls of consonants and other unacceptable combinations of sounds:

> But the owl's brown eye's the sky's new blue.
> Heigho! Foolscap!

There is an element of the grotesque in him, something 'Gothic', unmelodious, unclassical. He turns as if by instinct from the classical orders of the Mediterranean to the wilder forms of the North. There is a revealing passage in one of his letters: 'I often very shrewdly suspect that I have no real poetical call. I w^d write more songs if I could, but I can't manage rhyme well or easily; I very seldom get a glimpse of the right sort of idea in the right light for a song.' It is curious that a man with such a profound understanding of blank verse should have been so uncertain with the lighter metres. Although Beddoes told a friend that he had 'a decided and clear critical theory' about song-writing, his lyrics lack inevitability: in this respect he was the antithesis of Darley, who had a fine ear for lyric metres but suffered from a paucity of material. Beddoes once commented that if he could have 'rhyme[d] well and order[ed] complicated verse harmoniously' he would have written odes, and it seems possible that the weight and seriousness of the ode might have acted as an inspiration to him.

Yet it is not any aspect of his technique that is the most remarkable feature of the poetry of Beddoes: it is the extent to which Death dominates everything that he wrote. He often confessed to being 'haunted for ever' by the problem of death: he was the Muses' Sexton: by comparison with him, neither Donne nor Webster was 'much possessed by death'. In his unfinished play, *The Second Brother*, one of the characters points out that 'death is the one condition of our life', and it is the one subject of his poetry. For him man is 'a soul and skeleton in a flesh doublet'. He looks at men and women with the speculative eye of an undresser—only it is not the clothes that he strips off,

but the skin and flesh that cover the skeleton. He made notes on
Dr. Dee, and his interest in magic and the occult occasionally
reminds us of Yeats. His thoughts could not escape from the
problems posed by the material and perishable nature of the
human body:

> Art not sewn up with veins and pegged together
> With bony sticks and hinges?

—as one of his characters asks another. It is characteristic of
him to have rewritten the story of Cupid and Psyche, turning
the winged boy into a 'gaunt anatomy'. One of the last fragments of his writing describes him as wandering 'within the
doubt-brakes of obscurest Thought'. If he had been as interested
in life as he was in death he might have been a very great poet.
As it is he remains the most tantalizing of all our writers: a man
of genius who wrote nothing that is commonly remembered.

George Darley was an Irishman belonging to a gifted family
who failed to win a Fellowship at Trinity College, Dublin, and
spent his life as a freelance writer in London.[1] As his letters
reveal, he had a good deal in common with Lamb. His very
severe stutter, together with the terrible 'tertian headaches' from
which he suffered, made him a 'Solitudinarian': much as he was
attracted by 'fireside, tea-table, chit-chat, and petticoatism' he
had the resolution to renounce the comforts of marriage. In the
writing of mathematical textbooks he found something of the
same steadying influence that Lamb found in his drudgery at
the South Sea House. Throughout his career we notice a contrast between the unusual clarity of his critical insight and his
apparent inability to profit from his own understanding. In
a comment on *The Errors of Ecstasie*, for example, he pointed out
that 'since the time of Rousseau, it has been the tendency of
imaginative writers to embody their own history in their works',
and in spite of his own disclaimer it is difficult not to identify
the Mystic in this poem with Darley himself. His habit of using
an exaggerated poetical diction is already evident when he talks

[1] George Darley (1795–1846) took his B.A. at T.C.D. in 1820. The following
year he came to London, where he published *The Errors of Ecstasie* in 1822. He also
became a contributor to the *London Magazine*. In the next few years he published
several mathematical textbooks and *Sylvia*, which appeared in 1827. In 1830 he
travelled on the Continent and studied painting and sculpture in France and Italy.
From 1834 to his death he contributed to the *Athenaeum*, most often writing on fine
art. *Nepenthe*, which he circulated among his friends in 1835, was a dismal failure.
He was an excellent critic and letter-writer.

of the 'susurring' of the wind 'Puffing amid the flow'ry-finger'd groves'. As the work of a critic who understood the need for unity in drama *Sylvia; or, The May Queen* is a curiosity. It is serious and humorous by turns and seems to hover uneasily between Elizabethan masque and modern pantomime. One can imagine Lord Curryfin in *Gryll Grange* producing such a thing, if the ladies had pleaded for something less classical than an Aristophanic comedy.

The best parts of *Sylvia* are the lyrics, and Darley is always more at home in detached lyrics than in longer poems. His merits as a lyric poet are already foreshadowed in 'Love droop'd when Beauty fled the bow'r' in his first volume. In one of his letters we find him writing that 'the secret of true poetry' is to 'set beautiful thoughts to music'. 'Every true poet has a *song in his mind*', he wrote elsewhere, 'the notes of which, little as they precede his thoughts—so little as to seem simultaneous with them—do precede, suggest and inspire many of these, modify and beautify them. . . . Rhythm . . . is the poet's latent inspirer.' His success in catching the accents of our older poets is shown by the fact that Palgrave printed 'It is not beautie I demande' in *The Golden Treasury* as the work of an unknown Cavalier. It is not surprising that Tennyson was interested in Darley's work: 'To my dead Mistress' is very like Tennyson, while several of Darley's lyrics could have helped to inspire 'The Brook'. His lyrics often open splendidly, but unfortunately he had too often little to say, while his characteristic faults of diction are never far away. Few poets have in their language so little contact with the spoken idiom of their own day. He is too apt to avoid the obvious word even when it is the right word, and has an unfortunate habit of spoiling a fine line or stanza by suddenly using a word that is quite inappropriate, like a pianist striking the wrong key. In the unfinished *Nepenthe*, which was intended to illustrate 'the folly of discontent with the natural tone of human life', there are some gloriously ridiculous lines, such as 'With her flush bridegroom on the ooze' and 'Dingling beside me, as I glid'. The author of *Hudibras* would have enjoyed this poem, which is none the less nonsense for being the nonsense of a poet. It is curious that a man with a stutter should have produced such a work, unfinished and in an exceptionally unattractive format: as if he were resigned to the perpetual impossibility of communication.

On reading *Nepenthe* Miss Mitford advised Darley to turn to a subject uniting 'the imaginative and the real'. It is ironical that Darley should have needed such advice, for twelve years before he had begun to publish a series of 'Letters to the Dramatists of the Day' which contain shrewd and penetrating counsel and in which he censured his contemporaries for using 'a mode of language which is wholly inconsistent with dramatic effect' with the result that they produced 'not tragedies, but—Amoeban Poems, in five cantos each'. Yet Darley himself was driven to the inconsistency of writing closet dramas. In *Thomas à Becket* we find him faithful to his own view that the drama flourishes on bold effects rather than nuances, and the result is a play in which excellent use is made of contrast. The swift killing of Becket, followed almost at once by the silent enactment of the ceremony of a lustration in St. Benedict's Chapel, and then the procession of mourners past the bier of the dead Archbishop, shows real dramatic flair. Unfortunately *Ethelstan; or, The Battle of Brunanburh* in no way bears out this promise. It is interesting to notice that Darley was keenly interested in Saxon history and literature: in a letter with which Beddoes would have sympathized he tells a friend that he is turning back to the ruggedness of Old English poetry in reaction against the 'eternal cud of rose-leaves' of Barry Cornwall and other of his contemporaries. But the result of his choosing the Anglo-Saxon period for his play is that he has names like Gorm, Ellisif and Egil Skillagrym on his hands: 'torquetur Apollo, Nomine percussus'. The verse of *Ethelstan* is slightly influenced by that of Old English and presents what is presumably the first Sceop in the modern English drama.

By the time when he had acclaimed the work of Byron, Shelley, and Keats, Leigh Hunt was under no illusions about his own stature as a poet. Yet his poetry remains an interesting foil to that of his major contemporaries, while his prefaces and notes provide a shrewd commentary on the poetic scene in his time. It is characteristic of him to have written an essay on the subject 'Poetry and Cheerfulness', and his 1832 preface contains a significant protest against the fashion for melancholy, the snobbery of being miserable. Perhaps it was because there was a persistent, though shallow, vein of melancholy in his own temperament that Hunt deliberately cultivated his powers of enjoyment—a habit which made him the perfect mentor for the youthful Keats. Enjoyment is the spirit of most of Hunt's own

poetry: the antithesis of Beddoes, he is the least philosophical
of poets and the furthest from tragedy. *Captain Sword and Captain
Pen* (1835) is unique in his work in being a poem in which indignation led him to hammer out lines with a primitive urgency
that is strangely compelling—

> The drums and the music say never a word.

Enjoyment, not indignation, is the usual inspiration of Hunt's
poetry.

In his prematurely published *Juvenilia* (1801) we already see
Hunt's accessibility to foreign influences (particularly that of
Italian literature) and his love of painting. Something will be
said in Chapter XIV of the important part Hunt played in
introducing Italian literature into England, but here we may
note that he turned to the Italians, as well as to Chaucer and
Dryden, in his search for 'a freer spirit of versification'. He was
particularly attracted by the double rhyming of Italian poetry.
When he set out to 'correct' *Rimini* his first intention was to
eliminate the double rhymes altogether, but he could not bring
himself to go so far, and double rhymes are prominent in many
of his poems. One reason for his love of Italy may have been
that he had, as he believed, tropical blood in his veins, and his
'southern insight into the beauties of colour' is one of the outstanding features of his poetry. Edmund Blunden has described
his poem 'To Hampstead', with its picture of 'The cold sky
whitening through the wiry trees', as 'a sonnet in water colours',
and Hunt often gives the impression of writing his poems on an
easel. He peopled Hampstead Heath with gods and goddesses
and nymphs. There are no more characteristic lines in his poetry
than those describing the nymphs tying up their hair,

> Their white backs glistening through the myrtles green.

Too often, indeed, amorous description was the fatal Cleopatra
for whom he lost the world, and was content to lose it. His
descriptions of girls are the verbal equivalent of Etty's nudes.
He had the imagination of a poet, and the fancy of a cit. At one
moment he can write of 'The laughing queen that caught the
world's great hands' and at another inform us that Francesca
'had stout notions on the marrying score' or describe

> The two divinest things this world has got,
> A lovely woman in a rural spot.

The reader of his poems may well echo the words of the Second Shepherd in *The Descent of Liberty* (1815):

> We have come, I think,
> Through nothing but sweet spots from first to last.

Hunt is fatally fond of such words as 'spot', 'gush', and 'balmy', and defends 'delicious' against Byron's view that it 'should be applied only to eatables'. He lacks the passion which can transform amorous feeling into poetry free from vulgarity. It is not surprising that Keats outgrew him, or that he was singled out to be the butt of an unscrupulous Right-wing journalistic stunt. Yet if there was an element of cheapness in his suburban epicureanism, there was an element of unmistakable nobility in the man himself.

It is remarkable that the poems of an even closer friend of Keats than Leigh Hunt, John Hamilton Reynolds, have never been collected. 'Let the man be who he will,' Clare wrote on reading *The Garden of Florence*, 'he's a poet & as far above many as white bread's before brown.'[1] His early work is of interest primarily because it reflects the main influences of the time. *Safie: An Eastern Tale* is a transparent imitation of Byron, to whom it is dedicated; while *The Eden of Imagination* is a sort of *Pleasures of the Imagination* in pentameter couplets that are more reminiscent of Campbell and Rogers than of Wordsworth. While such a phrase as 'usefulness, not luxury' marks the poem as decisively eighteenth-century, in other passages we see a new sensibility struggling to emerge from an outmoded idiom. Reynolds had a deep love of Wordsworth which survived that great poet's discouraging comments on *The Naiad*, a poem

---

[1] John Hamilton Reynolds (1794–1852) was the son of a schoolmaster who later taught at Christ's Hospital. He himself was educated at Shrewsbury and St. Paul's. For some years he worked in an insurance office, publishing *Safie* and *The Eden of Imagination* at the age of 19. In 1815 he began to contribute to the *Champion*. The following year he met Keats, with whom he became very friendly, and published *The Naiad*. At the end of 1816 Hunt hailed Shelley, Reynolds, and Keats as the coming poets of the day in an article in the *Examiner*. Reynolds published *The Fancy* in 1820 and *The Garden of Florence* in 1821, and began to contribute to the *London Magazine* in the latter year. By this time he had become a solicitor. Although he professed to bid farewell to the Muses before his marriage in 1822 he did not abandon poetry, collaborating with Hood in the *Odes and Addresses to Great People* in 1825. From this time onwards, however, he wrote mainly in prose, in the *Athenaeum* and other periodicals. In 1847 he was appointed an assistant clerk to the County Court in Newport in the Isle of Wight. During the last five years of his life he was bored and unhappy.

'founded on a beautiful Scotch ballad . . . procured from a young girl of Galloway, who delighted in preserving the romantic songs of her country' and written in the medley of metres which was fashionable at this time.

But it is by the poems contained in *The Garden of Florence* that Reynolds's reputation as a poet stands or falls. Although the volume was not published until 1821 the fact that most of the poems had been written some years before explains the valedictory air that hangs about it. As Reynolds writes to his fiancée in the dedicatory poem, he has decided to 'give up drawling verse for drawing leases'. 'The Romance of Youth' is the only canto that was completed of a projected poem in Spenserian stanzas on the poet's own development—that favourite theme of the time: it is interesting to notice that Keats refers to this poem in his letter about the Mansion of Many Apartments. Reynolds writes that 'the world of imagination is darkened by the shadow of the world of reality'. Unlike Keats he seems not to have conceived of a further world of poetry lying beyond the realm 'Of Flora and old Pan'. 'The Romance of Youth' is the work of a young poet who is still ambitious, and contains some good lines, such as the reference to the flowers of spring which

> Dance through all years in the eternal mind.

A short poem, in blank verse, 'Devon', shows higher promise than anything else that Reynolds was ever to write. It was no doubt inspired by *Tintern Abbey*, but contains some eloquent references to the sea

> That talks for ever to the quiet sands.

Reynolds reminds us of Keats in the passionate pleasure he takes in contemplating the sea in its every mood: he likes to watch it when it

> Tosses its hoar-hair on the raving wind,

but no less

> To see it gently playing on loose rocks,
> Lifting the idle sea-weed carelessly;
> Or hear it in some dreary cavern, muttering
> A solitary legend of old times.

The volume also contains a verse-epistle, three sonnets to Keats, and the sonnet in praise of dark eyes which inspired Keats to write a reply. *The Garden of Florence* itself, like 'The Ladye of Provence', is a companion-piece to *Isabella,* the outcome of the design of the two friends to produce a volume of stories from Boccaccio. Each of the tales tells a tragic love-story with an element of the macabre about it, and each attains a measure of success. Lines 87–88 of *The Garden of Florence* remain memorable—

> Passion lays desolate the fields of sleep,
> And wakes a thousand eyes to watch and weep,

while 'The Ladye of Provence' tells a story that would have appealed to Browning in a loosely moving blank verse that might easily be his.

It was the 'sombre sadness of memory' in the poetry of Reynolds that appealed to Clare, but Reynolds had also a marked flair for parody and comic verse. In 1819, hearing that Wordsworth was about to publish a poem called *Peter Bell,* he wrote his brilliant parody under that title and succeeded in publishing it before Wordsworth's own poem appeared. If the preface parodies Wordsworth's complacency a trifle heavy-handedly, the poem itself is mischievously right:

> Not a brother owneth he,
> Peter Bell he hath no brother;
> His mother had no other son,
> No other son e'er call'd her mother;
> Peter Bell hath brother none.

The following year Reynolds published a curious volume, *The Fancy: A Selection from the Poetical Remains of the late Peter Corcoran.* It is tempting to suppose that Corcoran had been Reynolds himself, and that the account of his life given in the preface is meant as a humorous warning to his fiancée of what may happen to him if they become estranged. In the preface to one of the poems Reynolds refers to 'those literary deceptions for which this age has become too infamously celebrated', and the slightly indeterminate impression left by some of the lyrics in the volume may be due to the fact that they had originally been written seriously but were now meant to be laughed at. 'The Fields of Tothill' raises an interesting critical question. If it were not for the claim in the preface that its model is *Whistlecraft* we should have supposed it a parody of *Beppo*; and as such it would be a more successful achievement than simply as a comic poem in its own right. Further evidence of Reynolds's ability as a comic poet is to be found in *Odes and Addresses to Great People*, in which he collaborated with Thomas Hood.

It is appropriate that one of the best of Reynolds's shorter pieces is a 'Farewell to the Muses'. As we read his work we have perpetually the impression of a man with a true poetic gift hesitating on the threshold of discovering his own poetic individuality. That he did not pursue his poetic career is greatly to our loss.

Reynolds's brother-in-law Thomas Hood published *The Plea of the Midsummer Fairies* in 1827.[1] His literary allegiances are indicated by the dedications to Lamb, Coleridge, and Reynolds himself. The allegorical title-poem contains some delightful description and manages to maintain contact with reality in a way in which Shelley's *Witch of Atlas*, for example, does not. Many of the conceits in 'Hero and Leander' remind us of Hood's interest in metaphor and simile, as do the 'elastic links' which in the lines 'To an Absentee' signally fail to rival Donne's compasses. Throughout the volume the influence of Keats, whose *Lamia* Hood had dramatized as a boy, is ubiquitous. Hood had the audacity to write an 'Ode: Autumn'—and the poetic skill to produce a reputable poem which is in no danger of ridicule. The other odes are less successful, but the sonnets contain some fine lines.

While these serious poems sold poorly, however, the *Odes and Addresses to Great People*, which had appeared two years before, were a resounding success. In their form the *Odes* represent the last indignity inflicted on the battered corpse of the eighteenth-century Pindaric. Coleridge praised the lack of sting in Hood's poems, and this lack of mordancy may be one reason why they do not survive as great satire survives: for all their technical expertise they remain brilliantly jocose journalism. As we read

[1] Thomas Hood (1799–1845) became a clerk about the age of thirteen, but in 1815 he was sent to Dundee on account of his delicate health. When he returned to London in 1817 he worked for some time with two firms of engravers, but in 1821 he was more suitably employed by Taylor and Hessey to help edit the *London Magazine*. He met the Londoners and collaborated with J. H. Reynolds (whose sister he had married in 1825) in *Odes and Addresses*. He was now a full-time writer and editor. At the end of 1834 he was beset by money difficulties, and he soon withdrew to the Continent so that he might earn enough to pay off his debts in full. He lived successively at Coblentz and Ostend. He returned to England in 1840 and edited Colburn's *New Monthly Magazine* for a time. Peel comforted him in his courageous last months by the award of a pension, which continued to be paid to his widow.

them we are often reminded of the eighteenth century, but more of its novelists than its poets. We are reminded how deeply Hood was influenced by Smollett by his Trunnion-like farewell to D. M. Moir. Having been apprenticed to an engraver early in his life, he remained a lifelong admirer of Hogarth; and we notice that such poems as the 'Ode to Mr. Malthus', the '*Friendly* Address to Mrs. Fry *in* Newgate', 'I'm going to Bombay', the under-ostler's 'Sonnet on Steam' and the ode to those in favour of the removal of Smithfield Market are illuminating documents on the history of his time. But although they resemble the paintings of Hogarth in this respect, they do not, like his pictures, remain works of art in their own right, so that Lamb's description of Hood as 'our half-Hogarth' is extremely apt.

Hood was a splendid human being, but we must not let our admiration for his courage blind us to the curious and unpleasant qualities that often appear in his verse. There is something sinister about his sense of humour: his pages are thronged with comic mourners and undertakers, and a corpse is always good for a horse-laugh. The nightmares of his imagination often burst out, like a skeleton falling from a cupboard. When this happens he puns his way out of the embarrassment. He began to pun as soon as he began to speak, and he died as he had lived. His puns are related to the interest in figurative language and in perceiving 'similarity in dissimilarity' that Wainewright noticed in his work. Each stanza of 'Faithless Sally Brown', for example, ends with a play on words, the last with the most famous of all:

> They went and told the sexton, and
> The sexton toll'd the bell.

One of the ways in which he uses puns may be regarded as a mode of Tieck's 'romantic irony': serious lines are followed, as Dryden said of Tassoni, by afterthoughts which 'turn them all into a pleasant ridicule'. So Hood tells us that he must 'die in harness like a Hero—or a horse'. As with Byron, we sense that the poet is on the defensive. The result is a juxtaposition of sentiment and humour rather than a fusion of passion and wit. To use Dryden's word, it is all rather 'boyish'. There is something pathological about Hood's punning: in his writings as in Cleveland's it becomes a nervous tic.

Three of his poems deserve particular mention. 'The Dream

of Eugene Aram, the Murderer' was based on an historical happening but owed its atmosphere to 'one of those unaccountable visions, which come upon us like frightful monsters . . . from the great black deeps of slumber'. 'The Last Man', a poem on a subject also attempted by Campbell, Beddoes, and (later) Mary Shelley, is even more impressive: something of the horror is due to the influence of *The Ancient Mariner*. 'The Song of the Shirt', which was inspired by a report in *The Times* and first published in *Punch* in 1843, is noteworthy for its celebrity in its own age. It 'ran through the land like wildfire . . . and . . . became the talk of the day'. The influence of such poems as 'The Lay of the Labourer' and 'The Bridge of Sighs', similarly inspired by actual cases mentioned in the Press, must have been very considerable. It is interesting to recall that Sir Robert Peel once told Hood that he had read almost everything that he had written: he praised 'the good sense and good feeling, which have taught you to infuse so much fun and merriment into writings correcting folly, and exposing absurdities'. Even so Hood sometimes felt that he had been deficient in charity, and in a remarkable letter to Peel written on his deathbed he protested against

a literary movement in which I have had some share, a one-sided humanity, opposed to that Catholic Shaksperian sympathy, which felt with King as well as Peasant, and duly estimated the mortal temptations of both stations. . . . It should be the duty of our writers to draw [the different classes] nearer by kindly attraction, not to aggravate the existing repulsion, and place a wider moral gulf between Rich and Poor, with Hate on the one side and Fear on the other.

It is curious that Hood, of all men, should have reproached himself in this way. As he had once pointed out in a poem, he loved his neighbour 'far too well' to assail him with serious satire. Although such poems as 'My Tract' and the 'Ode to Rae Wilson, Esq.' are contributions to the chorus against cant which heralded the opening of the Victorian Age, Hood was too charitable to write satire with the sting and power of *Don Juan*. And so the force that might have directed a bullet towards the heart of the abuses of the time was used, time and again, to send up a series of puns as astonishing as a firework display, and as soon over.

There is all the difference in the world between the light verse of Hood and that of W. M. Praed.[1] With his fellow-Etonians John Hookham Frere and John Moultrie (remembered here for his brilliant *Lady Godiva*), Praed is one of a small group of men whose work forms a background to *Don Juan*. Like Byron these poets were naturally aristocratic and 'eighteenth-century' in their sympathies and chose to 'wander with pedestrian Muses' for reasons very different from those which led Wordsworth to advocate 'the real language of men'. As *The Etonian* (1820–1) reminds us—an extraordinary production, and surely the most gifted school magazine ever to appear—they were members of a 'circle of wit' who had the encouragement of knowing that what they wrote would be read with understanding. Praed was so precocious at Eton that his tutor considered that his 'scholarship' was already past its best when he reached the age of eighteen. His career there had been the opposite of Shelley's a few years before. Whereas Shelley completely failed to find an audience for his poetry at school (a failure which foreshadowed his later life), Praed found that his verses made him popular with his contemporaries as well as with the masters, and the boys at Eton were the prototype of the audience for which he was to write throughout his life. He was equally successful at Cambridge, where he became (in the words of Bulwer Lytton) 'to the University what Byron was to the world'. His attitude to contemporary poetry was not unlike that of Byron: he regarded *Endymion* as a Cockney effusion suitable for conversation at a dance, respected Wordsworth, but had a more instinctive admiration for Crabbe. He himself, we notice, could handle the pentameter couplet in the traditional manner, but he was more at home in short verse. It does not need the revealing rhyme of 'shoe-ties' and 'duties' in 'The Troubadour' to tell us that he was an admirer of *Hudibras*, to which these lines, for example, might easily be attributed:

> Resemblances begin to strike
> In things exceedingly unlike,
> All nouns, like statesmen, suit all places,
> And verbs, turned lawyers, hunt for cases.

[1] Winthrop Mackworth Praed (1802–39) had a brilliant career at Eton and at Trinity College, Cambridge, where he was elected a Fellow in 1827. Soon he became a barrister and entered Parliament. In 1834 he was appointed Secretary to the Board of Control under Peel. Most of his poems appeared in periodicals and annuals.

If he seldom reminds us of Pope, he often reminds us of Swift. The opening of 'Arrivals at a Watering-Place' is modelled on the 'Lines on the Death of Dr. Swift', and it is tempting to suppose that it was partly from Swift that Praed learned how to write idiomatic English in verse, and how to use a single, perfectly placed word, in the full assurance that his audience will take the point—as when he tells us the whole truth about one aspect of young love in the line

> Some *hopes* of dying broken-hearted.

Yet to turn to Praed after reading Swift is to be struck by an absence of passion. Swift's weapon is a razor, Praed's a pair of exquisite scissors. For a parallel it is better to turn to another Augustan, Matthew Prior: 'To Elizabeth Winthrop' is precisely in Prior's manner, while 'An Everyday Character' echoes Prior's fine epitaph on 'Saunt'ring Jack and Idle Joan'. Like most of the Augustans, Praed is essentially an urban writer. He has no more than a gentlemanly feeling for the Picturesque: now that he is no longer young, he tells us—and he died at the age of 37—his imagination 'never wanders beyond Grosvenor-square'. It is fitting that he should have been an admirer of Matthew Green, for with Praed (as with his Augustan predecessors) the Spleen is an enemy to be kept at bay. His is the sober melancholy of the eighteenth-century Horatian, which has more in common with Gray's 'leucocholy' than with the ultimate depth of despair that was known to Swift. In this, as in other respects, he seems to have changed very little as he grew older, for at Eton his 'half-melancholy . . . veiled by levity' was noticed by the publisher Charles Knight. Praed comes nearest to 'speaking out' in this matter in one of his most unusual poems, 'Time's Song'.

Within his self-imposed limitations Praed has an extraordinary sureness of touch. It is remarkable how many of the English poets with the most unfailing sense of their native idiom have been sound or brilliant as classical scholars, and here Praed may be classed with men as different as George Herbert, Dryden, and Prior. It may have been his classical training that saved him from the Elizabethanizing that was the origin of so much of the worst writing in the period, as well as of some of the best. Whereas Darley is so enamoured of what he believes to be Elizabethan English that he often loses contact with English altogether, Praed never violates the genius of the language. Light-hearted as his Tales are, for example, they are in a real sense better written than those of either Scott or Byron, and as we read them we come to see that his scrupulous regard for the grain of English was made possible by his remarkable command of metrical technique. Since he never put a foot wrong, he was never obliged to put a word wrong.

Praed's entry into political life in 1830 made it natural that he should try his hand at political verse, and some of the resulting poems are models of their kind; yet none of them transcends its occasion and challenges the description of major poetry, as does *Absalom and Achitophel*. Nor does it seem likely that he would have become a considerable political satirist if he had lived longer. He could write an excellent love lyric, when he chose, as he demonstrates in 'Oh fly with me! 'tis passion's hour'; but just as he instinctively turned away when he found himself on the verge of the language of passion, so he forbore from using the lash of satire. Almost the only occasion on which he employs mordant satire occurs in a suppressed stanza of his poem on George IV:

> He was the world's first gentleman,
> And made the appellation hideous.

Perhaps Praed was too 'well adjusted' (whatever we mean by the phrase) to be a major satirist; or perhaps Eton was, after all, too much of a forcing-house. As we study Praed we are reminded of Coleridge's view that as a boy the Younger Pitt acquired 'a premature and unnatural dexterity in the combination of words, which must of necessity have diverted his attention from present objects, obscured his impressions, and deadened his genuine feelings'. Although Praed was a very generous and likeable man, it would not be wholly untrue to apply to him what Coleridge went on to say of Pitt, that he was 'a plant sown and reared in a hot-house, for whom the very air that surrounded him, had been regulated ... to whom the light of nature had penetrated only through glasses and covers'. When Praed was little more than a boy he wrote like a man of full maturity. It seems possible that some constraint of personal development was the price that he had to pay for his astonishing precocity.

From his early childhood onwards Coleridge's eldest son

Hartley was treated as a genius.[1] His father addressed him in 'Frost at Midnight' and 'The Nightingale', Wordsworth wrote a poem to him at the age of six, while Hazlitt twice painted his portrait. As we read of 'Ejuxria', the imaginary land of his childhood, and of the philosophical romance that he dictated to his mother, we are reminded of the Brontës. As a child he was a metaphysician, as a man he was to remain a child. Diminutive, brilliant in conversation, excluded from marriage and the domesticities for which he longed, he remained throughout his life a spiritual exile. He had a fine mind, as we can see in his letter to H. N. Coleridge analysing the genius of his father (8 May 1836); yet his yearnings were always for the past, and he was happy only in a household including a baby or a small girl. One of his sonnets opens aptly with the words

> Long time a child, and still a child.

A resigned sense of unworthiness, as in 'Poietes Apoietes', is the typical note in his most personal poems. Everywhere we find that combination of tenderness and sweetness that he himself singled out as characteristic of Wordsworth's later poetry. His fifth sonnet,

> What was't awaken'd first the untried ear
> Of that sole man that was all human kind?

has a quality of wondering innocence that reminds one of Edwin Muir a century later. 'Death-Bed Reflections of Michelangelo' is unusually powerful, while 'An Old Man's Wish' is in no way inferior to the better-known 'She is not fair to outward view'. It is not surprising that his second volume, to consist of poems in 'a higher strain', never appeared; yet it must be acknowledged that the fragmentary *Prometheus* shows him on the threshold of more powerful verse than one would have expected. The description of the storm is admirably done, and there are other memorable lines:

> For he shall hear us in the vocal gloom
> Of green Dodona's leafy wilderness.

[1] Hartley Coleridge (1796–1849) was the eldest son of S. T. C. He was educated at Ambleside School under the supervision of Southey, and then went to Merton College, Oxford. When a Probationer Fellow of Oriel he was dismissed for intemperance. He tried to earn a living first by journalism in London and then by teaching in Ambleside. In 1837–8 he was a master at Sedbergh School.

Yet it remains true that his characteristic occupation was writing a sonnet on his own inadequacy or addressing a lyric to a girl of eight. The poems published after his death reveal his ability to write an occasional memorable line: it would be difficult to find a more apt description of the Sublime than the line "'Tis the Eternal struggling out of Time' or to better the simile 'Like Patience slow subsiding to Despair'. But for the most part these later poems merely confirm the impression of a muted, limited accomplishment already made by his earlier work. Time, memory, and regret are the recurring notes in the resigned music of his verse, which forms a sad, ironic postscript to the work of his great father.

When he was an old man Bryan Waller Procter, who wrote under the name of 'Barry Cornwall', claimed to have known 'far more literary men than any other person' of the time.[1] He was at school with Byron, and lived to salute the mature work of Browning. Although Byron treated his poetry with unusual forbearance, Procter wrote in what might almost be regarded as the standard manner of his time: he often reminds us of Leigh Hunt, though he lacks his tendency to amorous banality and also his flashes of near-genius. He was influenced by both Wordsworth and Byron, shared in the contemporary passion for the Elizabethans, loved Greek mythology and Italian literature, and often reminds us of the interest in painting which was characteristic of so many of the poets of the age. As he acknowledges in his *Autobiographical Fragment*, he lacked both genius and ambition and wrote merely because he enjoyed writing. For him poetry represented an escape from the humdrum practicalities of the law, but one has only to contrast him with Keats to see how limited was his notion of escape. Whereas Keats adventured beyond the Realm of Flora and Old Pan, Procter remained in it, and experienced it much less fully. It is not surprising that Keats found that Procter's poems 'teased' him: 'They are composed of Amiability, the Seasons, the Leaves, the Moon &c. upon which he rings . . . triple bob majors.'

[1] Bryan Waller Procter (1787–1874) practised as a solicitor in London and eventually became a prosperous conveyancer. He began to contribute to the *Literary Gazette* in 1815 and became the friend of Leigh Hunt and Lamb and later of Dickens. He became a barrister and was from 1832 to 1861 a metropolitan commissioner in lunacy. He lived to the age of 87. The poetess Adelaide Anne Procter was his eldest child.

The greater part of Procter's first volume consisted of Dramatic Scenes of the sort that owed their popularity at this time to
the depressing condition of the theatre. Lamb thought very
highly of these scenes, but for us it is difficult not to ask what
end is achieved by writing scenes from dramas which were never
intended to be completed and which would have been singularly pointless if they had been. Procter seems to have chosen
all the wrong stories from Boccaccio: there is something rather
silly about his broken hearts and noble renunciations. He completely lacked the flair that Browning shows in his dramatic
monologues for choosing a single moment in the life of a man
by which the whole of his existence may be laid bare. The
protagonist of *Marcian Colonna* (1820) is slightly more of a character than those of most of Procter's Dramatic Scenes, yet it
remains true that this presentation of the ill-starred hero of the
period fails to seize on the reader's imagination. Something
relaxed and unimpressive about his handling of metre also
appears in *A Sicilian Story* (1820) in which, as he so often does, he
uses neither couplets nor stanzas but loosely organized verse
paragraphs which rhyme in a rather random manner. In the
title-poem he retells the story that Keats had used in *Isabella*,
but substitutes 'the heart for the head of the lover'. The main
interest of the Tales in which he uses *ottava rima* is that they
demonstrate that the idiom of *Beppo* and *Don Juan* is not as
easily attained as one might suppose. As we read these Tales
we do not get the impression that what the poet is writing falls
naturally into verse: the peculiar charm of the metre. Too often
he is forced to use an awkward turn of expression. 'The man
whose critical gall is not stirred up by such *ottava rimas* as Barry
Cornwall's', as Shelley wrote to Peacock, 'may safely be conjectured to possess no gall at all. The world is pale with the
sickness of such stuff.' Procter's one dramatic attempt, *Mirandola*, ran for sixteen nights, with Macready and Miss Foote in
the main parts; but although there is some interest in the relationship between the father and son, on the whole it is a tragedy
of situation rather than of character. The play is full of Elizabethan reminiscences, the verse being simple and Fletcherian
(very different from the bombast of Maturin), with passages
marked which are not designed for the stage. It is interesting to notice that the prologue denies that 'large Theatres
the Drama mar'. In *The Flood of Thessaly* (1823) there are

passages in which the blank verse shows considerable
power—

.   .   The great Eagle still
In his home brooded, inaccessible,
Or, when the gloomy morning seemed to break,
Floated in silence o'er the shoreless seas

—yet it is clear that Procter has chosen a theme beyond his
imaginative reach, and we can only be glad that he did not
attempt to develop it further. It is revealing to compare the
vision of felicity with which the poem closes with the serene and
towering eloquence of the comparable passage in *Prometheus
Unbound*.

There is something unfinished and inconclusive about many
of Procter's short poems, as there is about his Dramatic Scenes.
He was much given to writing fragments and sets of stanzas
that have no completeness in themselves. He can write agree-
ably and 'poetically', but he is always sounding the same note:

Like the low voice of Syrinx, when she ran
Into the forests from Arcadian Pan:
Or sad Oenone's when she pined away
For Paris.

It is not enough to be enamoured of Greek mythology: it is
necessary to do something with it, and of this Procter was incapable. His Muse is blameless and bookish, spoilt perhaps, as
Byron feared, 'by green tea, and the praises of Pentonville and
Paradise Row'. One reason for his surprising popularity in his
own day was no doubt the absence of disturbing features in his
verse. In one of his prefaces he pointed out that he had avoided
both 'politics and polemics', but with these disquieting subjects
a great deal of life seems to be excluded. In his language we
notice the absence of the nerve and sinew of English: in his
poetry as a whole we notice the absence of human life. Too often
Procter is not a poet but merely a poetical person. *English Songs
and other Smaller Poems* (1832) were an attempt to make good
what he regarded as a serious deficiency in our literature.
Unfortunately they lack the qualities that prevent a song from
ever being forgotten. Having had their day they now rest in
peace.

'Barry Cornwall' occasionally reminds us of Peacock, a man with a much more vigorous mind who was known to a small circle of readers as a poet before he wrote the satiric tales discussed in Chapter VII. Peacock's literary career falls into two parts. In the pivotal year of 1818 he ceased to be a gentleman of leisure, entered the India House, produced his last published volume of verse, and scored a decided success with *Nightmare Abbey*. He was soon to write 'The Four Ages of Poetry', in which he asserted that 'A poet in our times is a semi-barbarian in a civilized community':

He lives in the days that are past. His ideas, thoughts, feelings, associations, are all with barbarous manners, obsolete customs, and exploded superstitions. The march of his intellect is like that of a crab, backward. The brighter the light diffused around him by the progress of reason, the thicker is the darkness of antiquated barbarism, in which he buries himself like a mole, to throw up the barren hillocks of his Cimmerian labours.

His own early poetry might be the work of a respectable minor poet of the eighteenth century. *Palmyra* is a sort of Pindaric Ode in which the poet meditates on the fact that 'Time and change have absolute dominion over every thing terrestrial but virtue and the mind'. The 1806 version is explicitly Christian in its conclusion, but in the improved text of 1812 we notice that Peacock has already moved away from revealed religion. 'To a Young Lady, Netting', might be the work of Waller, and it would be easy to assign others of these early poems to writers of the previous epochs. We notice a considerable variety of stanzas and metrical forms: it is tempting to speculate that the anapaests of 'Fiolfar' may have given Browning a hint for 'How they brought the good news from Ghent to Aix'. *The Genius of the Thames*, in which Peacock mentions Denham, Pope, and Thomson, is a loco-descriptive poem which contains some agreeable passages:

> As now the purple heather blows,
> Where once impervious forests rose;
> So perish from the burthened ground
> The monuments of human toil:
> Where cities shone, where castles frowned,
> The careless ploughman turns the soil.

It is only once or twice that we feel that the poem is becoming a little ridiculous in its backward-looking:

> O'er Nuneham Courtnay's flowery glades
>> Soft breezes wave their fragrant wings,
> And still, amid the haunted shades,
>> The tragic harp of Mason rings.

It needed a retrospective ear to catch the reedy music of *Elfrida* in the year of *Childe Harold's Pilgrimage*. *The Philosophy of Melancholy*, which also appeared in 1812, is a didactic poem which occasionally and faintly reminds us of Pope or *The Vanity of Human Wishes* but which remains of interest primarily as a document of the vogue for melancholy at this time. Peacock's statement in the analysis of the second part that 'in art, as in nature, those pleasures, in which melancholy mingles, are more powerful, and more permanent, than those which have their origin in lighter sensations', is of particular interest as the assertion of the man who was soon to be telling Shelley that he was determined to 'make a stand' against 'the encroachments of black bile'. But the most ambitious of Peacock's poems is *Rhododaphne*, which Shelley described as 'the transfused essence of Lucian, Petronius and Apuleius', and which describes how Anthemion is stolen from his lover Calliroë by the enchantress Rhododaphne until the latter is killed by Uranian Love and the lovers are reunited. This poem, with its characteristically donnish preface and notes, throws light on the attraction which Greek mythology held for so many writers of the time. Like Keats in *Endymion*, Peacock wishes to touch again 'the beautiful mythology of Greece',

> And from the songs that charmed their latest ear,
> A yet ungathered wreath, with fingers bold,
> I weave, of bleeding love and magic mysteries drear.

Rhododaphne is full of the century's nostalgia for a Greek world that never existed except in the realm of poetry:

> In ocean's caves no Nereid dwells:
> No Oread walks the mountain-dells:
> The streams no sedge-crowned Genii roll
> From bounteous urn: great Pan is dead:
> The life, the intellectual soul
> Of vale, and grove, and stream, has fled
> For ever with the creed sublime
> That nursed the Muse of earlier time.

Although the poem is full of pleasant passages there is hardly one that insists on being quoted. The quality that is almost everywhere absent may be illustrated by a single quotation from near the end of Canto III:

> Till full from Athos' distant height
> The sun poured down his golden beams
> Scattering the mists like morning dreams,
> And rocks and lakes and isles and streams
> Burst, like creation, into light.

The imaginative power of the last line is extremely rare in Peacock. At first one is tempted to say that his verse is too poetical, yet on reflection we realize that it would be a more accurate account of the matter to say that it is not in fact poetical enough. What we miss is the sense of urgency that comes from a poet's having something real to say, and the imaginative vitality which (if he is a true poet) will accompany it. One has only to examine his diction to see that it is not the kind of language a man uses when he is writing imaginatively. Except for his habit of introducing an occasional learned word—'hypæthric' and 'primogenial' both occur in the first eight lines of *Rhododaphne*—we notice that the diction is highly conventional. It is too easy to guess which epithet will accompany any given noun. This combines with the lack of reality in the story to make the reader indifferent about what is to happen next. In the first note to *The Genius of the Thames* Peacock had remarked that

The tutelary spirits, that formerly animated the scenes of nature, still continue to adorn the visions of poetry; though they are now felt only as the creatures of imagination, and no longer possess that influence of real existence, which must have imparted many enviable sensations to the mind of the ancient polytheist.

The trouble with Peacock's mythological beings, as with those in most of the writers of the time, is that they have no reality even as 'creatures of the imagination'. As he was soon to point out himself, 'we know . . . that there are no Dryads in Hyde-park nor Naiads in the Regent's-canal', and since mythology was his main source of poetic inspiration he did well to turn from verse to prose, from Anthemion and Carilloë and Rhododaphne to Scythrop and Marionetta and Stella. Yet before we leave his poetry something must be said of one fine forgotten poem and of the songs which are a characteristic ingredient of

his satiric tales. Unfortunately only the first half of 'Newark
Abbey: August, 1842, with a Reminiscence of August, 1807'
can be quoted here, but that may be enough to draw attention
to a poem that seems to have escaped the attention of critics and
anthologists:

> I gaze, where Autumn's sunbeam falls
> Along these gray and lonely walls,
> Till in its light absorbed appears
> The lapse of five-and-thirty years.
>
> If change there be, I trace it not
> In all this consecrated spot:
> No new imprint of Ruin's march
> On roofless wall and frameless arch:
> The hills, the woods, the fields, the stream,
> Are basking in the self-same beam:
> The fall, that turns the unseen mill,
> As then it murmured, murmurs still:
> It seems, as if in one were cast
> The present and the imaged past,
> Spanning, as with a bridge sublime,
> That awful lapse of human time,
> That gulph, unfathomably spread
> Between the living and the dead.

Peacock drew attention to the fourteen poems in *The Misfortunes
of Elphin* by printing a list of them at the beginning of the book,
and it comes as something of a surprise to find that the tales
contain between fifty and sixty pieces of verse, apart from the
Aristophanic comedy in *Gryll Grange*. There is a remarkable
variety in these lyrics, from the defiant vigour of the drinking
songs to the meditative note of 'The Sun-Dial' in *Melincourt*,
from Clarinda's 'In the days of old' in *Crotchet Castle* to the
admirable 'Song of the Four Winds' in *The Misfortunes of Elphin*.
Yet it is inevitable that we should remember best the parody of
Byron and Byronism in *Nightmare Abbey*:

> There is a fever of the spirit,
>   The brand of Cain's unresting doom,
> Which in the lone dark souls that bear it
>   Glows like the lamp in Tullia's tomb:
> Unlike that lamp, its subtle fire
>   Burns, blasts, consumes its cell, the heart,
> Till, one by one, hope, joy, desire,
>   Like dreams of shadowy smoke depart.

'Admirable', as Mr. Glowry comments. 'Let us all be unhappy together.'

Moore once pointed out that two of his principal incentives to writing had been an instinctive 'turn for rhyme and song', encouraged by the 'gay and sociable circle' in which he had been brought up, and the profound feelings aroused in him, as an Irishman and a lover of liberty, 'by the mighty change . . . working in the political aspect of Europe' in his youth and 'the stirring influence it had begun to exercise on the spirit and hopes of Ireland'.[1] If we add to these his perpetual need of money— he was a professional writer for most of his life, and a highly successful one—we have the main motives that led him to write. His early version of the *Odes of Anacreon* (1800) was followed by *The Poetical Works of the late Thomas Little* (Moore was a diminutive man), a collection of amorous poems which vary from the tolerable to the sort of love poetry that would make a cat wring its hands. A review of *Epistles, Odes, and Other Poems* (1806) in the *Edinburgh Review* made Moore's work a centre of controversy. Jeffrey's strictures on 'the languid, loving girl of Hayti' and her companions are of the sort that a Moderator of the Church of Scotland might pass on the *Folies-Bergère*, but it must be admitted that there is something rather distasteful in the mixture of licence and sentimentality which we find in these poems: they are vulgar in a characteristically Regency way. The publication of the *Irish Melodies* between 1808 and 1834 finally established Moore's reputation. He once wrote that his poetical talent was rooted in 'a strong and inborn feeling for music' so that it was an appropriate task for him to supply words to accompany 'a collection of the best Original Irish Melodies': words 'containing, as frequently as possible, allusions to the manners and history of the country'. The music—most of

---

[1] Thomas Moore (1779–1852) studied at Trinity College, Dublin, and entered the Middle Temple in 1799. After a remarkable social and literary success on his first arrival in London, he had a short period as Admiralty Registrar in Bermuda, and then returned to England by way of the United States. His *Irish Melodies* established him as the national poet of Ireland. He also took to satirical verse and became the friend of Byron and Leigh Hunt. When his deputy in Bermuda defaulted he became liable for £6,000 and took refuge abroad, visiting Italy with Lord John Russell. At Venice Byron presented him with his Memoirs. In 1822 the debt to the Admiralty was paid, and Moore returned to England. After Byron's death Moore consented to the destruction of the Memoirs, wrote a biography of Byron, and edited his writings. He remained a celebrity for the rest of his life, receiving a literary pension in 1835 and a Civil List pension as well fifteen years later.

which he knew to belong to the eighteenth century—was the *raison d'être* of the whole design, and the songs lose immensely if they are considered in isolation. Moore apologizes, for example, for 'occasional breaches of the laws of rhythm, which the task of adapting words to airs demands of a poet', in a sentence which might serve as a reminder to critics of Sir Thomas Wyatt. His main themes are love and patriotism, and he is often at his best when he laments the passing of the old days, as in 'The harp that once through Tara's halls' and 'Weep on, weep on, your hour is past'. The mystical and other-worldly quality of the Gaelic imagination was foreign to Moore's temperament, as it was, on the whole, to that of his age. His subject is the Irish character in society. The political spirit of the songs is always liberal; yet it is hard to agree with those of Moore's enemies who believed that their tendency was 'mischievous'. Too sentimental to be mischievous, they are rather songs of the sort that a sophisticated imperialism might connive at as a harmless safety-valve for national aspirations. A note to the *Irish Melodies* oddly confirms this view by pointing out that a publication 'of this nature' could never be intended for the lower classes, 'that gross and inflammable region of society', and claiming that the book could only be found 'upon the pianofortes of the rich and the educated,—of those who can afford to have their national zeal a little stimulated, without exciting much dread of the excesses into which it may hurry them'. The most severe comment was made by Beddoes, who wrote that Moore's 'song style is the best *false* one I know and glitters like broken glass—he calls us and will show us a beautiful prospect in heav'n or earth, gives us a tube to look thro', which looks like a telescope and is a kaleidoscope'. If we deny the *Irish Melodies* and Moore's other songs any trace of greatness it is not merely because they betray the lack of true imagination but also because in them we look in vain for the economy and purity of diction characteristic of great songs.

Someone has said that literary history deals with good books that no one read when they were first published, and bad books that no one should have read. There can be no doubt into which category *Lalla Rookh* falls. As has been mentioned in Chapter I, Longmans agreed to pay £3,000 for a poem 'upon some Oriental subject, and of those Quarto dimensions which Scott . . . had rendered the regular poetical standard'. The resultant poem consists of four romances told to the beautiful Lalla Rookh as her splendid bridal procession makes its way from Delhi to Cashmere. The task of criticizing the stories may be left to Fadladeen, Great Nazir of the Haram, who comments on each story much in the manner of the *Edinburgh Review*:

> The chief personages of the story were, if he rightly understood them, an ill-favoured gentleman, with a veil over his face; —a young lady, whose reason went and came, according as it suited the poet's convenience to be sensible or otherwise; —and a youth in one of those hideous Bucharian bonnets, who took the aforesaid gentleman in a veil for a Divinity . . . From such materials . . . what can be expected? . . . With respect to the style, it was worthy of the matter.

Fortunately for Moore and his publisher the public by no means agreed with Fadladeen, and twenty editions, as well as numerous translations, had made their appearance by 1840.

Moore's feeling of buoyancy at the success of *Lalla Rookh* helped to inspire the light-hearted satire of *The Fudge Family in Paris*. His 'natural turn . . . for the lighter skirmishing of satire' had been apparent while he was still a boy in Dublin, when he became a member of a club one of whose objects 'was to burlesque, good-humouredly, the forms and pomps of royalty'. In 1808 he went on to publish *Corruption and Intolerance*, attempts (as he acknowledges) at 'the stately, Juvenalian style of satire'; but in spite of the occasional eloquence of these poems, and of the qualified success of *The Sceptic* (1809), which is more familiar and argumentative, it was in a less formal type of satire that he found his most natural expression. *Intercepted Letters* (1813) led on to *The Fudge Family in Paris* (1818), a series of letters in verse suggested by Anstey's *Bath Guide*. The serious intention behind the poem is most evident in the letters of the enthusiastic young Phelim Connor, but the best passages are the anapaestic epistles in which the young Fudges reveal their mindlessness, and the pompous letters to Castlereagh by the time-serving Mr. Fudge. In *The Fudges in England* (1835) Moore directs his satire against an unscrupulous Irish priest turned Protestant evangelist and against some of the literary absurdities of the time. The charming Miss Fanny begins by contributing poems to the Annuals and finally produces 'A Romaunt, in twelve Cantos, entitled "Woe Woe!" ' Her 'Irregular Ode' and her 'Stanzas to my Shadow; or, Why?—What?—How?' are excellent parodies of the modish poetry of the age. The lighter satirical poems of Moore are the verbal equivalents of the cartoons of Gillray and his contemporaries, and there is no better way of reminding ourselves of the atmosphere of the time than by dipping into these witty pieces of political improvisation.

There is no need to say much of the other minor and minimus poets of the period, though several of them were much more widely read than most of their betters. The most remarkable features of the *Poems* (1808) of Felicia Dorothea Browne (later Mrs. Hemans) are the precocity of the author (they were written between the ages of eight and thirteen) and the length of the list of subscribers, which begins with the Prince of Wales and includes a thousand names.[1] In 1812 she published *The Domestic Affections*, while from 1816 another volume appeared almost every year until her death in 1835. In her work we find what may be loosely termed the new sensibility chastened and rendered thoroughly respectable: 'Turning from the dark and degraded, whether in subject or sentiment,' as D. M. Moir put it in his *Lectures on Poetical Literature*, 'she seeks out those verdant oases in the desert of human life, on which the affections may most pleasantly rest.' She took the pulse of her time, and helped to prevent it from quickening. Elaborate poems on the deaths of the Princess Charlotte and of the King himself put her loyalty beyond question, while in *Modern Greece* (1817) she had succeeded in the remarkable undertaking of producing a sort of respectable *Childe Harold's Pilgrimage*. The general level of her work is high, but unfortunately it almost always stops short of memorable poetry. Many of her better things, such as the line 'Blend with the plaintive murmur of the deep', might be the work of a poetical committee. For her, we feel, poetry was a feminine accomplishment more difficult than piano-playing and embroidery but no less respectable. She has a definite affinity with Scott in her fluency, her love of the picturesque, and her refusal to affront conventional morality. To descend a little lower, she might be described as a female Campbell—or Campbell might be described as a male Mrs. Hemans. What we miss in her work is

---

[1] Mrs. Hemans (1793–1835) was born Felicia Dorothea Browne. Her marriage with Captain Alfred Hemans at the age of 19 was unhappy and she separated from him six years later. The 'Egeria' of Maria Jane Jewsbury's *Three Histories*, she lived much at Dublin and early became a well-known literary figure and an acquaintance of Scott and Wordsworth. Her writings were extremely popular, not least in America.

poetic individuality. We read her, we commend, and we forget. In her precocity Letitia Elizabeth Landon rivalled Mrs. Hemans, but in temperament she was very different, and it is impossible not to be attracted and moved by the career of this headstrong and gifted young woman, so piquant and kitten-like in what Rossetti called the 'funnily-drawn plate' by Maclise, with her talked-of exploits, her friendships with Bulwer Lytton and Lady Blessington, her flights from the amorous Maginn, and her mysterious death in Africa.[1] William Jerdan was her first sponsor, and she began to contribute to the *Literary Gazette* when she was only thirteen. Her first volume of any note was *The Improvisatrice* (1824); while from *The Golden Violet* (1827), which contains a verbal portrait of Bulwer's Rosina, she is said to have made £1,000. The 'snub-nosed Brompton Sappho', as Disraeli called her, was as impulsive in her writing as in her life, and the best of her work has the merits of brilliant improvisation—so reminding us in some respects of the work of Byron. In the preface to *The Venetian Bracelet* (1828) she provides a spirited defence of a woman's right to take love as the subject of her poetry. Some of her best lyrics are in simple measures like the ballad-stanza:

> I hear them speak of love, the deep,
>   The true, and mock the name;
> Mock at all high and early truth,
>   And I too do the same.

At times we feel that her technique is not quite adequate to the intensity of her feeling—an unusual thing with a woman poet. At her best she writes with a simplicity that reminds us, at least, of the simplicity of great poetry:

> I cannot bear to think of this,—
>   Oh, leave me to my weeping;
> A few tears for that grave my heart,
>   Where hope in death is sleeping.

[1] The first volume of poems by 'L. E. L.' (1802–38) was published when she was 19. She contributed a great deal to periodicals and popular annuals and edited *The Drawing Room Scrapbook* from 1832. One of her best novels is *Ethel Churchill*, 1837. *Traits and Trials of Early Life* includes some passages no doubt founded on her own experience. Her first engagement (possibly to John Forster, the biographer of Dickens) was suddenly broken off and in 1838 she married George Maclean, governor of Cape Coast Castle in Africa. A few weeks after her arrival there she died mysteriously, apparently from an accidental overdose of prussic acid.

In the course of a distinguished career Henry Hart Milman was Dean of St. Paul's and Professor of Poetry at Oxford.[1] While he was still at Eton he wrote excellent verse, and 'The Belvidere Apollo' is one of the few Oxford Prize Poems that bear re-reading. He wrote *Fazio* when he was an undergraduate in an 'attempt to revive our old national drama with greater simplicity of plot'. It was written 'with some view to the stage', but Milman comments that it must be a good thing for a play to be printed before it is performed because it is 'impossible, on the present scale of our Theatres, for more than a certain proportion of those present to see or hear'. In an intellectual way he seems to have understood the nature of drama; but the important scenes are almost too obvious to be moving, while the morality of the piece is pervertedly severe, involving, as it does, a wife's informing against her husband, vindicating his name after his death, and then dying herself. *Samor, Lord of the Bright City* (1818), which was begun at Eton, is a remarkable achievement for so young a man, and remains of interest because of Milman's contention that English still lacks 'the perfect model of *narrative* blank verse'. Unlike most of Milton's eighteenth-century imitators, Milman realizes that Milton's verse is not 'for common use'; nor, he argues, can the styles of Crowe's *Lewesdon Hill*, Akenside's *Pleasures of the Imagination*, or *The Excursion* provide what is required, a metre which, 'sustaining a long poem above the level of prose, adapts itself with natural and unforced numbers to the infinite variety of thought, feeling, character, situation, interest, and even style, which must animate any long narrative poem which aspires to live'. *Samor* was followed by three of the dramas on religious subjects which form an imaginative accompaniment to Milman's laborious and creditable work as a Church historian. There was a vogue at this time for heroic poems on Biblical subjects which might all have been illustrated, like Atherstone's *Fall of Nineveh*, by John Martin. Designed to support the cause of 'virtue and religion', these works may be regarded as a sort of literary equivalent of

[1] Henry Hart Milman (1791–1868) went from Eton to Brasenose College, Oxford. He won the Newdigate Prize and the Chancellor's Essay Prize, becoming a Fellow of Brasenose in 1814 and publishing *Fazio* in 1815. He became incumbent of St. Mary's, Reading, four years later. In 1827 he was Bampton Lecturer. From 1821 to 1831 he was Professor of Poetry at Oxford. In 1849 he became Dean of St. Paul's. In the later part of his life he was better known as a divine and church historian than as a poet.

the Oratorio, and it is not surprising that they failed to compete with the sonorous uplift of such a celebration as the Crystal Palace Handel Festival. Milman once confessed to 'a latitudinarian love for poetry', adding that much as he loved Hebrew poetry, Greek, Latin, Italian, Spanish, German, and English, he could yet 'reserve some admiration for the exotic and barbarous . . . but still occasionally beautiful and even sublime conceptions of the East'. He was led into such studies (as he tells us with engaging frankness) by running out of subjects for his professorial lectures, when he took the unusual course of widening his field of knowledge. In his volume of translations from the Sanskrit, *Nala and Damayanti* (1835), he carried on the work of Sir William Jones.

Although most of Keble's work belongs to the next volume, the publication of *The Christian Year* in 1827 must be recorded here. In preferring him to George Herbert, Oliver Elton does something monstrous: to read even the best of Keble after a poem like 'The Flower', 'The Collar' or 'Love' is to turn from the work of a great religious poet to that of a well-bred and talented versifier. It is instructive to compare the variety of Herbert's metrical patterns and the rich complexity of his poetic techniques with the limitations of Keble's technical range. Keble puts the Christian life, with all its complications and its struggles, into the pint-pot of his simple measures. But, of course, it is hardly fair to compare Keble's work with great poetry. His poems are religious or devotional exercises rather than poems of religious experience: their affinity is with the 'La Corona' sonnets of Donne, not with the great sonnets that succeeded them.

The name of Charles Wells should be borne in mind by those who are interested in this period, because it acts as a sobering reminder.[1] In an age when many young men of brilliant promise died young he, who was not the least promising of them, lived on into old age without in any way fulfilling the promise of his youth. A friend of Keats, who was only five years his senior, he died in 1879, the year which saw the publication of

---

[1] Charles Jeremiah Wells (1800–79) was educated at Edmonton, where he met Keats early in his life. He offended Keats by playing a practical joke on his brother Tom, but remained a friend of Hazlitt and Leigh Hunt. From 1820 to 1830 he was a solicitor in London: then he withdrew to the country. Ten years later he taught English for a while in Brittany. In 1874 he destroyed his manuscripts. He died at Marseilles.

Henry James's *Daisy Miller*. He published *Joseph and his Brethren* (1824) in his early twenties; but although he wrote a good deal more throughout his life it is only as the author of that long dramatic poem that he is ever remembered. While the praises of Rossetti and Swinburne now seem exaggerated, Wells shows considerable power in the handling of his story and in the way in which he writes blank verse. He is not only so steeped in the work of the Elizabethans that he can produce at will a passage that might come from a contemporary of Shakespeare's: he is also under the influence of the later work of Milton, and occasional lines in his strange drama have an air of austere distinction that reminds us irresistibly of *Paradise Regained*.

While there is room for disagreement about the merits of *Joseph and his Brethren*, the worthlessness of Bernard Barton's work is no longer in dispute.[1] Yet he also serves as a reminder— a reminder of the fact that the English, who have produced the greatest poetical literature in the world, have a deep instinctive preference for the third-rate. In an age in which *The Excursion*, the poems of Shelley and Keats, and Clare's *Shepherd's Calendar* lingered unsold in the booksellers' shops, Bernard Barton enjoyed a very considerable celebrity. The names of the Queen Dowager (12 copies), Prince Albert, and the Archbishop of Canterbury head the list of subscribers to his *Poems and Letters*, while the Society of Friends were so proud of their poet that they raised a large subscription to allow him more leisure. One of the paradoxes about him is that a man who had read so much good literature, and discussed it with Charles Lamb, should have caught so little by infection. The explanation seems to be that he was rather stupid, and very idle. 'How thankful I am that I have written what good-natured critics call poetry!', he once exclaimed. As a poet he always remained an 'Amateur', as the title of one of his collections acknowledged, and an amateur in the least honourable sense

---

[1] Bernard Barton (1784–1849) was the son of a Quaker manufacturer. At the age of 14 he was apprenticed to a shopkeeper and eight years later he married his employer's daughter. He worked as a tutor in Liverpool for a year, meeting the Roscoe circle, and then became a clerk in a bank at Woodridge, where he remained for the rest of his life. By 1812 he was corresponding with Southey, and ten years later his remonstrance to Lamb on the tone of his references to Quakers led to a lifelong friendship. In 1824 J. J. Gurney and other Friends raised £1,200 for his benefit. In 1845 he dedicated *Household Verses* to Queen Victoria, and soon Peel secured him a pension. Edward FitzGerald married his daughter and wrote a Memoir to accompany his literary remains.

of the word. He was far too lazy to make any determined effort to learn his art, and never completely conquered his Quaker scruples about the language of poetry: was the critic right who reproached him with using the profane word 'November' to describe the eleventh month? He scrupulously observes that the hardships of old age

> Might move the very hearts of stones,
> If stones had hearts to heed them

—a chastening qualification. He has no feeling for language, and displays a positive preference for the anti-poetical—as we see in such a phrase as 'however that may be'. In his work the worst of Wordsworth—'The Daddy', as he called him— was watered down until it could be consumed by the humblest domestic circle. Talking of a patriarch he wishes that we

> From the same hidden fount could inly quaff:
> We trust in outward aids too much by half!

It is a pity that he did not write his projected autobiography: it would have been a capital curiosity. When the Scots have made so much of McGonagall, it is curious that the English should have allowed Bernard Barton to remain unhonoured.

Like the popularity of Barton's poetry, that of the Annuals that proliferated in the 1820's and 1830's is a fact to be reckoned with by the historian of taste. The idea came from Germany, and in 1823 Rudolph Ackerman[1] produced his *Forget-me-Not*, the first of many volumes 'expressly designed to serve as tokens of remembrance, friendship, or affection'. Alaric Watts, himself a minor poet, soon followed with his *Literary Souvenir*, Samuel Carter with *The Amulet* (intended specifically for the amusement of 'serious persons'), and Messrs. Smith and Elder with *Friendship's Offering* in 1827. One of the best of the numerous other Annuals was *The Anniversary*, edited by the talented Allan Cunningham.

---

[1] Rudolph Ackerman (1764–1834) was born in Saxony and educated at Schneeberg. After a period in Paris he moved to London and in 1795 he opened a printshop in the Strand. The establishment of lithography as a fine art in this country is due to him. In 1817 he set up a press and engaged Prout and other eminent artists. He did a great deal to relieve the sufferers from the distress in Germany after the battle of Leipzig, and also employed many Spanish *émigrés*. From 1813 his Wednesday Literary Evenings were well known. He produced *The Repository of Arts, Literature, Fashions, Manufactures, etc.* from 1809 to 1828, Rowlandson supplying many of the plates.

A great deal of thought was given to the appearance of the Annuals, which were as carefully got up as boxes of chocolates. *The Literary Souvenir*, for example, was a small octavo 'bound in pale green, pink, or violet boards, ornamented by an engraved design by Corbould', and with the edges of the leaves tastefully gilded. No expense was spared to ensure that these books would form a fitting ornament to grace the boudoir or the sofa-table. Ackerman was a print-seller, and from the first engravings were an important feature of the Annuals. While some of the illustrations are of a surpassing silliness, others are the work of highly competent artists and must have played their part in introducing the visual arts to people little acquainted with them. The fact that the Annuals were intended for women— for one's wife, one's fiancée, or one's maiden aunt—dictated the nature of the literary contents, no less than their appearance. 'L. E. L. will be ready for you on Monday with some beautiful verses,' his publisher once wrote to Alaric Watts, 'but don't give us more poetry than prose. Poetry is beyond many of the purchasers of this description of book.' But on the whole there was no objection to poetry, and when one first looks into these volumes it is exciting to see the great names of the period as well as interesting minor names. While there are still discoveries to be made, however—some of Clare's poems in Annuals appear to have been overlooked—most of the contributions by considerable poets turn out to be reprints of their least important pieces. What was most in demand was poetry that exhibited that happy blend of 'sentiment purified by taste' which Bowles was thought to have introduced. The aim (to quote from *The Fudges in England*) was a volume

> Where all such ingredients—the flowery, the sweet,
> And the gently narcotic—are mix'd *per* receipt,
> With a hand so judicious, we've no hesitation
> To say that—'bove all, for the young generation—
> 'Tis an elegant, soothing, and safe preparation.

A due caution had to be exercised even with the cover. 'The design for the covers', Watts wrote to his publishers, 'instead of being naked women, should be something emblematic of the contents—Poetry, the Arts, etc; in short, polite literature.'

Whether the vogue for Annuals was a good thing for literature is most uncertain. At first sight it might seem so, since publishers often paid the contributors well. 'The world . . . seems mad about "Forget me Nots" and Christmas boxes,' Scott wrote in 1828; 'here has been Heath the artist offering me £800 per ann: to take charge of such a concern.' The publisher of *The Keepsake* claimed to have spent no less than eleven thousand guineas on a single issue. But most of the serious writers of the time looked askance at the new commodity, even if they were prepared to contribute. Southey, who knew the literary market, complained that 'these Annuals have grievously hurt the sale of all such books as used to be bought as presents. In this way'—he adds—'my poems have suffered greatly—to the diminution, I doubt not, of half their sale.' Wordsworth told Rogers that he thought that *The Pleasures of Memory* had 'suffered in the common blight', adding that 'the ornamented annuals, those greedy receptacles of trash, those Bladders upon which the Boys of Poetry try to swim, are the cause'. For the literary historian these faded volumes retain some interest: partly because the occasional exceptional volume contains a good deal of significant work (such as *The Keepsake* for 1829, which contains two of Scott's finest short stories, as well as contributions by Wordsworth, Coleridge, Southey, Lockhart, and Shelley): and partly because it is useful to see the work of major writers surrounded by the forgotten literature of their period. To glance through the Annuals, for example, is to be reminded that the 'Ode on a Grecian Urn' was the product of a period in which many poems were written on individual paintings and works of sculpture. Yet while a comprehensive index to the Annuals would be of use, an excursion among them soon becomes fatiguing. Their epitaph may be found in *Middlemarch*, whose author was not the sort of woman for whom they were intended. Lydgate laughs scornfully at a volume of *The Keepsake* and wonders which 'will turn out to be the silliest—the engraving or the writing', so disconcerting young Plymdale, who points out that 'there are a great many celebrated people writing in "The Keepsake" ' and adds that this is the first time that he has 'heard it called silly'. It was in fact by no means the first time that it had been called silly. When Allan Cunningham told Southey that he hoped to make *The Anniversary* 'reflect the Literature of the Age' Southey replied that 'the best you can make of these things, is picturebooks for grown Children'.

Satire and parody are almost wholly lacking in the Annuals, and the absence of the latter is particularly to be regretted in a period in which the prevalence of new poetic fashions gave the parodist a splendid opportunity. The fact that the major poets of the time expressed themselves so idiosyncratically made it natural that this mode of criticism by imitation should have reached a high level. Not that the best parodies were written by those hostile to the new modes of expression: most successful parodies have always been written by admirers of the writers parodied, and the parodists of this era were no exception. The authors of *Rejected Addresses,* for example, were themselves writers of some ability, and it has sometimes been maintained that one or two of the poems in the collection are imitations rather than parodies. Scott was convinced that one of the pieces was his own work, although he could not remember when he had written it. The occasion of the volume was the competition held to find an address to be spoken at the opening of the new Drury Lane Theatre. James and Horace Smith sat down and wrote a collection of bogus entries, and the fact that the volume was published within six weeks shows that they were so familiar with the styles of their contemporaries that they had no need to get them up for the occasion.[1] The rapidity of the undertaking helps to explain the unevenness of the pieces: it is surprising that writers who had parodied Wordsworth so brilliantly should have been so much less successful with Byron and Coleridge. But by confining themselves to 'writers whose style and habit of thought, being . . . marked and peculiar, was . . . capable of exaggeration and distortion' they succeeded far more often than they failed. Thomas Campbell, who felt aggrieved that he had been passed over by the Smith brothers, is also missing from James Hogg's *Poetic Mirror* (1816), a curious volume with a curious history. As Hogg tells us in his autobiography, he took it into his head to beg a poem from each of the principal English poets, collect them in a volume, and so make his fortune. For one reason or another most of the poets failed to oblige, however, and Hogg decided that he himself 'could write a better poem than any that had been sent or would be sent to me, and

[1] James and Horatio Smith (1775–1839 and 1779–1849) were the sons of a solicitor. James succeeded his father as solicitor to the Board of Ordnance in 1812. Among other things he produced farces and books of words for the comedian Charles Mathews. Horatio (who called himself 'Horace') was introduced to the literary world by Richard Cumberland the dramatist. The brothers became famous overnight on the publication of *Rejected Addresses* in 1812. Horatio produced numerous novels and assisted Campbell for a while with the *New Monthly Magazine.*

this so completely in the style of each poet, that it should not be known but for his own production'. The status of the volume is a little difficult to determine, and the reviewers were in some doubt. In a sense it is a piece of literary forgery as much as a volume of parodies: at times Hogg seems intent simply on imitating, though in other cases—such as the alleged passages from *The Recluse* and the Coleridgean 'Isabelle'—he is clearly at the satirist's work:

> Why I should dread I cannot tell;
> There is a spirit; I know it well!
> I see it in yon falling beam—
> Is it a vision, or a dream?
> It is no dream, full well I know,
> I have a woful deed to do!

Hogg himself was parodied—not to mention his own poem or parody in *The Poetic Mirror*—in a volume entitled *Warreniana*, published in 1824, the work of William Frederick Deacon. This collection of poems in praise of Warren's Patent Blacking is supposed to be edited by Gifford, the graceless pomposity of whose style is mirrored in the preface and other supplementary matter. It is a volume of considerable interest to the literary historian, and deserves better than to be neglected: some of the parodies are excellently done (those of Barry Cornwall and Moore, for example), while the Coleridge—'The Dream, A Psychological Curiosity'—is in parts quite admirable. Keats, Gessner, Spenser, Ambrose Philips, Leigh Hunt, Lamb, and Hogg are introduced as figures in a pastoral masque supposed to be the work of Charles Wells.

Although most of the poets of the period wrote at least one drama or 'dramatic poem' it was seldom with an eye to the theatre, and a brief account of the acting drama during what William Archer called its winter solstice must be sufficient. Conditions could hardly have been less propitious. The two licensed theatres, Covent Garden and Drury Lane, were of enormous size, and there can be no doubt that this made them unsuitable for the development of a serious drama. As Scott pointed out in 1819:

Show and machinery have . . . usurped the place of tragic poetry; and the author is compelled to address himself to the eyes, not to the understanding or feelings of the spectators. . . . We have enlarged our theatres [he goes on], so as to destroy the effect of acting, without carrying to any perfection that of pantomime and dumb show.

An occasional critic, such as Bulwer Lytton, suggested that 'the astonishing richness and copiousness of modern stage illusion opens to the poet a mighty field, which his predecessors could not enter', and insisted that the dramatists should take advantage of these new possibilities instead of rejecting them; but unfortunately the typical audience of the time was perfectly happy with elaborate scenic effects alone, and did not care whether they subserved a true dramatic purpose. '*Venice Preserved* will scarcely draw a decent house', as Gerald Griffin complained to his brother; 'while such a piece of unmeaning absurdity as the Cataract of the Ganges has filled Drury Lane every night those three weeks past. The scenery and decorations, field of battle, burning forest, and Cataract of real water, afforded a succession of splendour. . . . A lady on horseback riding up a cataract is quite a bold stroke, but these things are quite the rage now' (*Life of G. Griffin*, p. 94). The general level of the audiences was low. The Court gave no lead in matters of taste, while a considerable proportion of the population was inspired by religion to 'see no plays'. The theatres were noisy and full of prostitutes, and it could never have been said of the Regency theatre that 'vice itself lost half its evil, by losing all its grossness'.

Altogether the fate of the aspiring dramatist was unenviable, as Griffin pointed out in a letter written in May 1824:

Of all the walks in literature, it certainly is at present the most heart-rending. . . . The managers only seek to fill their houses, and don't care a curse for all the dramatists that ever lived. There is a rage for fire, and water, and horses got abroad. . . . Literary men see the trouble which attends [dramatic writing], the bending and cringing to performers—the chicanery of managers . . . and content themselves with the quiet fame of a 'closet writer'.

The monopoly enjoyed by the two large theatres rendered dramatic experiment almost impossible, while the growing rewards available to a successful novelist made the profits of an unlikely success in the drama seem of little account.

Another enemy of the dramatist was the censor. Although the Methodist John Larpent seems to have been guilty of larceny, or something very like it, throughout his career, while his successor George Colman had himself been the author of a number of licentious plays, each insisted on a stupid decency and piety

in the productions of others. The most vexatious and crippling
aspect of the censorship was the prohibition of any serious treatment of religious or political controversy; for these were the
crucial topics of the day, and the natural field for the dramatist.
At the beginning of the century which immediately succeeded
the French Revolution Larpent seems to have been opposed to
any play dealing with rebellion. Bulwer Lytton as usual puts his
finger on the point: with the Greeks (he insists) 'the theatre
. . . was political':

> We banish the Political from the stage, and we therefore deprive
> the stage of the most vivid of its actual sources of interest. At present
> the English, instead of finding politics on the stage, find their stage
> in politics. . . . A censor is not required to keep immorality from the
> stage, but to prevent political allusions. . . . I doubt if the drama will
> become thoroughly popular until it is permitted to embody the most
> popular emotions. In these times the public mind is absorbed in
> politics, and yet the stage, which should represent the times, especially
> banishes appeals to the most general feelings. The national theatre . . .
> is like . . . *Hamlet* 'with the part of Hamlet left out by the particular
> desire'—of the nobility! (*England and the English*, Book IV, chap. v.)

In feeling his way towards religious and political themes and
seeking inspiration from Alfieri, 'The Poet of Liberty', Byron
was guided by a sure instinct; but his drama of liberty was
destined to be played out on the stage of the world.

Byron was also unusual, though not alone, in his belief that
great drama could not be written 'by following the old English
dramatists, who are full of gross faults' and his insistence that
Shakespeare is 'the *worst* of models, though the most extraordinary of writers'. The fact that the epidemic enthusiasm
for the work of the Elizabethan and Jacobean dramatists was
essentially an enthusiasm for their plays as poetry, and not as
drama, also exerted an unfortunate influence on the dramatic
attempts of the time. Having hardly any opportunities of seeing
the plays satisfactorily performed, the lovers of the old dramatists naturally looked on their productions as books. It was a
natural step for Charles Lamb to discuss whether *King Lear*
could really be acted at all. In the theatre as he knew it, one
might well agree that it could not. But the split between the
theatre and the serious drama which is so oddly illustrated by
the remark of Landor's brother, who had written a play called
The Count Arezzi—'No one knows less of the theatre than I do'—

was profoundly unhealthy and led writers into a complete mis-understanding of the nature of a play. George Darley, writing in the *London Magazine*, made the point with admirable clarity. '*Action* is the essence of drama', he wrote, and he complained that 'our modern tragic writers are perpetually endeavouring to make drama poetical, instead of poetry dramatical.' With equal penetration he once wrote in a letter that 'Experience confirms me more and more in the opinion that a poetic whole is far greater than all its parts unconnected; to build it up well, forms the true basis of fame'. Unfortunately Darley's own plays demonstrate that it was one thing to see what had to be done, and another to do it. As we read his plays and the other un-acted dramas of the time we find almost everywhere a subordination of the whole to the part, of the thing said to the way in which it is said. The influence of Shakespeare and his contemporaries is ubiquitous; and whatever its effect on the plays as poetry, on the plays as drama it had almost everywhere a disastrous effect. The language of most of the plays of the time is neither nineteenth-century English, nor Elizabethan: the characters are neither the contemporaries of their creators, nor of Shake-speare: the ways in which they seem to think and express them-selves are uncontemporary without being historical. They are close relations of the padded and bemuffed figures of historical romance. Not that all of the dramatists followed the Eliza-bethans: the influence of the German drama is also easy to trace in this period: but unfortunately it was the influence of bad plays rather than of good, and the result was too often the sort of 'insult and defiance to Aristotle's definition of tragedy' which Hazlitt discussed in the last of his *Lectures on the Age of Elizabeth*.

That the times were unpropitious for dramatists is startlingly demonstrated by the fact that the most successful serious drama-tists, in this age of literary genius, were three forgotten Irishmen, R. L. Sheil, Robert Maturin, and Sheridan Knowles. Sheil was a Dubliner famous for his political oratory, and it was in Dublin that *Adelaide; or, the Emigrants* was first produced in 1814.[1] It is

[1] Richard Lalor Sheil (1791–1851) was educated at Stoneyhurst and Trinity College, Dublin. In 1814 he became a barrister at Lincoln's Inn. Soon he was well known as a playwright. Having protested against O'Connell's refusal of concessions to Protestants who supported Catholic emancipation he later joined him in agita-tion, and took a prominent part in political affairs. In 1827 he was indicted for libel, but Canning did not proceed with the indictment. He first became a Member

easier to see why the play failed in London than why it succeeded in Dublin. Perhaps Hazlitt was right in conjecturing
that 'it would infallibly have been damned' on its first appearance if there had been one good passage in it; 'but it was all of
a piece; one absurdity justified another'. Even its highly reactionary politics failed to carry it to success. 'Kotzebue and
Fletcher seem to struggle over its silly corpse', as Professor
Allardyce Nicoll observes with unaccustomed petulance. *The
Apostate* and *Bellamira* are a distinct improvement, but it was
with *Evadne; or, The Statue* (1819), a free adaptation of Shirley's
The Traitor, that Sheil produced his most interesting play. The
heroine is a considerable creation, 'truly feminine and noble'
(as Leigh Hunt pointed out) without being a faultless monster.

If Maturin's *Bertram* retains more interest than any of Sheil's
plays it is because it remains a document of the taste of the
Byronic period.[1] Its atmosphere may be conveyed by one of its
stage-directions:

The Rocks—the Sea—a Storm—The Convent illuminated in the
back ground—the Bell tolls at intervals—a groupe of Monks on the
rocks with torches—a Vessel in distress in the Offing.

The verse has a certain larger-than-life eloquence, verging on
bombast; but the chief feature of interest is the character of the
protagonist, a 'man of many woes'. After talking with him the
Prior soliloquizes:

> Wild admiration thrills me to behold
> An evil strength, so above earthly pitch—
> Descending angels only could reclaim thee.

Bertram exemplifies the interest in the Outlaw which is characteristic of this period, and must have been influenced in some
degree by Schiller. Salvator Rosa would have been the man to
illustrate it. Scott and Byron were instrumental in having the
play produced at Drury Lane: at first, we are told, Kean was
worried by the thought that the part of the heroine was more

of Parliament in 1831, and proved an effective speaker. In 1838–41 he was Vice-
President of the Board of Trade, and in 1844 acted as counsel for John O'Connell.
He died soon after his appointment as Minister at Florence.

[1] Charles Robert Maturin (1782–1824) became a curate after taking his degree
at Trinity College, Dublin, but soon set up a school. After six years he abandoned
teaching, but persevered with his literary work. *Bertram* was a great success when
it was produced at Drury Lane in 1816. Maturin also wrote a number of novels,
which were extremely popular. His writings had a considerable influence in France.

important than Bertram's own, but on reflecting that there was no Mrs. Siddons 'to play Imogine and eclipse me' he went ahead with the play, which held the stage for twenty-two nights and ran through seven editions within a year, so earning its author £1,000. Kean found it 'a relief' to act in *Bertram* 'after such characters as Richard and Othello' because it was 'all sound and fury signifying nothing'. According to Scott, Maturin at one time intended to have 'our old friend Satan . . . brought on the stage bodily', but was persuaded to exorcize him. It is not necessary to attribute Coleridge's onslaught on *Bertram* in *Biographia Literaria* to jealousy on the part of the author of *Remorse*. He particularly objects to the unnatural surprise produced 'by representing the qualities of liberality, refined feeling, and a nice sense of honor . . . in persons and in classes where experience teaches us least to expect them; and by rewarding with all the sympathies which are the due of virtue, those criminals whom law, reason and religion have excommunicated from our esteem'. Although *Bertram* has some merit as a stage piece, everything about it is exaggerated and overwrought. All is for effect. At bottom it is a lie about human life, so that it is easy to understand Coleridge's indignation that such a drama should be looked to for 'the redemption of the British stage'. Maturin's second tragedy, *Manuel*, was described by Byron as 'the absurd work of a clever man'. The plot is more complicated than that of its predecessor, and there are some dramatic scenes; but it failed to hit the taste of the times as *Bertram* had done. In *Fredolfo* Maturin outdid himself in violence and horror, before returning to the writing of prose romance and producing *Melmoth the Wanderer*. Romance suited him better than the drama, for none of his writings evinces any genuine interest in human life as it really is.

There could be no more forcible illustration of the insignificance of the acting drama of the time than Hazlitt's statement that *Virginius*, by Sheridan Knowles,[1] was 'the best acting tragedy that has been produced upon the modern stage'. Such merit as his plays possess seems due to the fact that he had been

[1] James Sheridan Knowles (1784–1862) was the son of a lexicographer. After trying his hand as soldier, physician, actor, and schoolmaster, he had *Caius Gracchus* produced at Belfast in 1815. He visited America in 1834 and continued to act until 1843. Apart from his plays he published poems, adaptations, novels, and lectures on oratory.

an actor himself, and so understood the taste of his audience. *Virginius* (1820) has as its background the struggle between a tyrant and the liberty-loving forces in Rome, and the title-role of a Roman who kills his daughter to save her from being ravished gave Macready an admirable opportunity. The verse is respectable, but it never rises to eloquence and seems to have little contact with the spoken idiom of the day. *The Hunchback* (1832) is a toothless satire attacking some of the milder follies of the time. It is easy to believe that Fanny Kemble was enchanting as Julia, but in print the part seems no great matter. The morality of the play is almost absurdly innocent. The verse of an earlier play, *The Beggar's Daughter* (1828), has a boyish vigour appropriate to the story, which deals with wreckers on the Cornish coast and a hero who turns up to rescue the heroine at the moment at which she is being compelled to marry the villainous Black Norris. *The Wife* (1833) is a little more serious: in the prologue we are told what to expect:

> A touch of nature's work—an awkward start
> Or ebullition of an Irish heart.

Although some of the verse is tolerable, however, the passages of 'Elizabethan' prose are not. Knowles himself played the blameless St. Pierre, but his 'principal reliance', as he tells us, was upon the part of Mariana, which was played by Ellen Tree. Knowles was always at his best in delineating the characters of virtuous women. 'The only way in which Mr. Knowles personifies our age', R. H. Horne wrote in *A New Spirit of the Age*, 'is in his truly domestic feeling':

> The age is domestic, and so is he. Comfort—not passionate imaginings,—is the aim of every body, and he seeks to aid and gratify this love of comfort. All his dramas are domestic, and strange to say, those that should be most classic . . . are the most imbued with this spirit. . . . [In *Virginius*] we have Roman tunics, but a modern English heart,—the scene is the Forum, but the sentiments those of the 'Bedford Arms'.

It is appropriate that he should have abandoned poetry to become a Methodist preacher.

So striking was the inferiority of the acting drama that critics were tempted to suppose that there was something peculiarly undramatic about the age. Darley once suggested that the drama was unlikely to revive because 'subjective composition' was the natural tendency of the time. 'Can we restrain the tendency?', he asked, 'or *should* we, if we could? Though fatal to the drama, it may be vital to something else as desirable.' Suggestive as Darley's remark is, however, we must remember that prose fiction, which is not one of the more 'subjective' modes of composition, prospered throughout our period and was soon to flourish as it had never flourished before. All that we can say is that for a variety of reasons, one of which was the bad state of the theatres, the novel was now consolidating its place as the dominant literary form. In 1844 we find R. H. Horne recognizing this and pointing out that the true drama of the age 'is to be found more living and real in the pages of . . . Dickens, Mrs. Gore, and Mrs. Trollope, than in the play-house pieces'. In the middle of the previous century Fielding had acknowledged the superior dignity of poetry by designing *Tom Jones* as 'a comic epic poem in prose'. In the heyday of the Victorian Age Browning was to turn to the novel for guidance in the composition of *The Ring and the Book*.

VI

THE WAVERLEY ROMANCES

THE last chapter of *Waverley* is called 'A Postscript, which should have been a Preface', and in fact it might have served as a preface to the whole series of the Waverley Romances, for the paragraphs in which Scott outlines the great changes which had come to Scotland in recent times describe the inspiration of the finest of these books.[1] 'There is no European nation', he remarks, 'which, within the course of half a century, or little more, has undergone so complete a change as this kingdom of Scotland. . . . The present people of Scotland [are] a class of beings as different from their grandfathers, as the existing English are from those of Queen Elizabeth's time.' He was fascinated by the contrast between the Highlands and the

---

[1] Walter Scott (1771–1832) was the son of a Writer to the Signet in Edinburgh. His father was an unworldly man of strict Calvinist views who was given to the study of theology and the history of Scots law. His mother was the daughter of a gifted Professor of Medicine. Scott liked to trace his family tree back to more adventurous forebears, to his great-grandfather, a Jacobite 'well-known in Teviotdale by the name of Beardie', and to other semi-legendary figures in the history of the Scottish Border. As a boy he was extremely lame, and he used to listen for hours to the stories of the past told him by his uncle, Thomas Scott, and a number of other elderly people with retentive memories and time on their hands. He early became a great reader and a great lover of traditional Scottish songs, particularly songs about Border raids and the Jacobite risings. When his health improved (though he never lost his limp) he became an enthusiastic walker and rider, and he used to ride about collecting traditional songs and tales. This led to the *Minstrelsy of the Scottish Border*, 1802–3, and thence naturally enough to his own poems, *The Lay of the Last Minstrel*, *Marmion*, and *The Lady of the Lake* (poems discussed in the previous volume of this *History*). The publication of *Waverley* marks Scott's turning from romance in verse to romance in prose, partly because he felt that Byron was outpacing him.

He had been educated at the Edinburgh Royal High School and at Edinburgh University, and in 1799 had been appointed sheriff-depute of Selkirkshire. In 1804 he took up residence with his wife (whom he had married in 1797) at Ashestiel on the Tweed, near Selkirk. In 1806 he became Clerk to the Court of Session. In 1820 he was created baronet. In 1811 he bought Abbotsford, which he extended and filled with antiquarian curiosities for the rest of his life. His undoing was his connexion with the printing firm of Ballantyne. The crash came in 1826, and from then until his death he worked heroically to pay off as much as possible of the immense debt. The sale of his copyrights after his death effected this object. He was a man of remarkable charm and generosity, though he hated innovation. He did not publicly acknowledge the authorship of *Waverley* and its successors until 1827.

Lowlands in his father's lifetime. 'So little was the condition of the Highlands known at that late period', he wrote of 1745, 'that the character and appearance of their population, while thus sallying forth as military adventurers, conveyed to the south-country Lowlanders as much surprise as if an invasion of African Negroes, or Esquimaux Indians, had issued forth.' Here was a rich vein to be worked. 'The ancient traditions and high spirit of a people, who, living in a civilized age and country, retained so strong a tincture of manners belonging to an early period of society, must afford a subject favourable for romance.' Scott's aim was to amuse and excite the *Aufklärung* of Edinburgh with an account of the manners and habits of the old Scotland, and particularly of the Highlands. Nor did he limit himself to Scottish readers. Emulating Maria Edgeworth, he hoped that he might write something that would introduce the natives of Scotland to English readers 'in a more favourable light than they had been placed hitherto, and [so] tend to procure sympathy for their virtues and indulgence for their foibles'.

For such a purpose Scott was born at the right time. In his boyhood it was not difficult to find men who had taken part in these events: by the time *Waverley* was published in 1814 very few of them were left. He was proud of the authenticity of his descriptions, and in the notes to the collected editions he frequently cites his authorities. The visit of Waverley to Rob Roy, for instance, is based on an adventure which befell 'the late Mr. Abercromby of Tullibody' and Scott mentions that he heard it 'many years since . . . from the mouth of the venerable gentleman who was concerned in it'. In another note he refers to his description of 'the Highland manual exercise' with pistol and dirk, insisting that he himself had seen it 'gone through by men who had learned it in their youth'. Waverley's journey into Scotland is an allegory of Scott's own imaginative development. When Rose Bradwardine told Waverley a story of Highland feuds, he 'could not help starting at a story which bore so much resemblance to one of his own day-dreams. Here was a girl . . . who had witnessed with her own eyes such a scene as he had used to conjure up in his imagination, as only occurring in ancient times. . . . He might have said with Malvolio, "I do not now fool myself, to let imagination jade me!" I am actually in the land of military and romantic adventures. . . . ' But it was no Rose Bradwardine who roused the young Scott with stories of adventure: it was men and women in their sixties and seventies. Having nourished his boyish imagination with stories of imaginary romance, he had the good fortune to fall in with those who could satisfy the yearning that remained in him for stories at once improbable and true. To Scott himself, as to Waverley, 'it seemed like a dream . . . that these deeds of violence should be familiar to men's minds . . . as falling within the common order of things . . . without his having crossed the seas, and while he was yet in the otherwise well-ordered island of Great Britain'. This true dream was his imaginative inspiration until the end of his life.

As Scott admits, everything in *Waverley* is contrived with a view to the description of the old Scottish way of life. Waverley's journeyings do not constitute an adequate plot, being contrived merely to provide an excuse for 'some descriptions of scenery and manners, to which the reality [gives] an interest'. Nothing much happens until half the book is over. Such chapter-headings as 'A Horse-Quarter in Scotland', 'A Scottish Manor-House Sixty Years Since' and 'A Creagh [cattle-raid] and its consequences' make Scott's purpose evident enough. When we are told that Waverley's curiosity has been aroused by hearing 'many curious particulars concerning the manners, customs, and habits' of the patriarchal race of the Highland clans we are not surprised that he should inquire 'whether it was possible to make with safety an excursion into the neighbouring Highlands'. Since Waverley travels on behalf of the reader, to enable us to see what he sees, things are made easy for him, and we soon find Evan Dhu inviting him to study the headquarters of his cattle-thieves at first hand. When Waverley's Tour comes to an end and he returns to the Lowlands, geography may be said to give way to history as a background for the story. Through a series of improbable events he blunders into the '45, meets the Chevalier, attends the Jacobite ball at Holyrood, sees the Gathering of the Clans and the battle of Preston, and has many other adventures before he is united to his Rose Bradwardine. Before he returns—like Waverley himself—to everyday life, the reader has learned a good deal about some of the most striking features of Scotland and Scottish history.

Scott is no more seriously concerned with characterization than with constructing a careful plot. Waverley himself, the first of a long line of essentially similar heroes, is precisely adapted to the role he has to play: an Englishman who has never been in Scotland before, he is intelligent enough to take a keen interest in what he sees, fond enough of the picturesque to go in quest of it, ingenuous enough to blunder farther than he intends, courageous enough to dislike the idea of flight, quixotic enough to be attracted by the cause of the Pretender, amorous enough to become emotionally concerned with two Scottish families. He is not impressive enough to become important in the Jacobite movement as quickly as he does—but that is one of Scott's romance conventions. We notice that most of the people whom he meets have been deliberately chosen for their typical quality. Baron Bradwardine, for example, is 'the very model of the old Scottish cavalier, with all his excellencies and peculiarities . . . a character . . . which is fast disappearing'. Davie Gellatley, the 'natural', gives Scott an opportunity for effects of pathos as well as the introduction of antiquarian lore, notably in his scraps of song. Flora's enthusiasm for 'Celtic poetry' serves the same purpose: she sings her own translation of a Gaelic song, and assures Waverley that if the ancient Highland poems 'are ever translated into any of the languages of civilized Europe' they will not fail 'to produce a deep and general sensation'.

Each of the characters in this book is the first of a long line, and Waverley's journey is the prototype of the journey in space and time which thousands of readers were to take, in the following years, at the guidance of his creator. Like Waverley, they were to gaze in awe at the picturesque scenery of the Highlands, to admire the 'rude sweetness of the Celtic minstrelsy', and to wonder at the wild loyalties of the clans. Most of the elements which may be found in the first, most powerful group of the Waverley Romances are present in this path-finding book: seldom has a writer given so clear and so attractive a sample of what was to come.

In the preface to *The Antiquary* Scott pointed out that the first three of his romances were 'intended to illustrate the manners of Scotland at three different periods. *Waverley* embraced the age of our fathers, *Guy Mannering* that of our own youth, and the *Antiquary* refers to the last ten years of the eighteenth century.' Behind this difference of period a remarkable similarity of pattern may be discerned—a similarity which extends to most aspects of *Old Mortality* and to several of the later books. The hero of each book is a young stranger, usually

of mysterious origins, who is visiting Scotland for what is
actually or virtually the first time. Sometimes he turns out to be
a long-lost son and heir. He becomes involved in a complicated
series of events, which may be connected with historical occurrences. In spite of his youth and inexperience he rapidly becomes
a person of great importance: in *Rob Roy*, for example, which
exhibits most of the characteristics of this Common Form,
it is suggested to the astonished hero that unless he pays his
father's debts the failure of his business will precipitate the 1715
rebellion. Perhaps the most explicit statement of this peculiarity
in the career of a Scott hero is to be found in a later book,
The Abbot, where a youth of no importance whatever suddenly
finds himself, as page to the imprisoned Mary Queen of Scots,
in a position of vital significance:

> Yesterday he was of neither mark nor likelihood, a vagrant boy,
> the attendant on a relative, of whose sane judgement he himself had
> not the highest opinion; but now he had become, he knew not why,
> or wherefore, or to what extent, the custodier . . . of some important
> state secret, in the safe keeping of which the Regent himself was
> concerned. . . . He felt like one who looks on a romantic landscape, of
> which he sees the features for the first time, and then obscured with
> mist and driving tempest.

Equally characteristic of his situation is the fact that throughout he is passive rather than active: he does not initiate action
but remains the sport of circumstances. 'I have been treated . . .
as one who lacked the common attributes of free-will and human
reason, or was at least deemed unfit to exercise them', complains
the hero of the same book. 'A land of enchantment have I been
led into, and spells have been cast around me—every one has met
me in disguise—every one has spoken to me in parables—I have
been like one who walks in a weary and bewildering dream.'
His characteristic situation is following a mysterious guide to
an unknown destination, as Frank Osbaldistone follows Rob
Roy. In *The Fortunes of Nigel* the hero reproaches himself with
having allowed himself to become 'a mere victim of those events,
which I have never even attempted to influence—a thing never
acting, but perpetually acted upon—protected by one friend, deceived by another'. A love story serves to lend some continuity
to the plot. The heroine is usually a blameless but colourless
girl. Often she is a loyal daughter comforting an aged and

foolish father who has fallen on evil days: in this situation union with the hero may be expected to bring an unexpected access of wealth which enables all to be set to rights. Romance elements abound: secret passages, villainous foreigners (Scott practically never portrays a foreigner in a favourable or a fair light), wicked upstarts (often attorneys), a family divided by Jacobitism or some other political difference, recognition-scenes, gipsies and smugglers and outcasts of various sorts, hidden priests, battles and chases and sieges and every possible aspect of the exciting and the picturesque. These are the same elements that may be found in *Waverley* itself, though later they are often more skilfully mixed; and it remains true of the later books, as it is of the first, that Scott was 'more solicitous to describe manners minutely, than to arrange in any case an artificial and combined narrative'.

This is manifestly true of *Guy Mannering* (1815), in which emphasis is laid throughout on the contrast between the old order in Scotland and the new: the feudal landlord is contrasted with the villainous Glossin, who is an example of the 'new men'. Scott's intention of describing Scots manners at a certain time and place is particularly clear in the passages dealing with Dandy Dinmont. 'The present store-farmers of the south of Scotland are a much more refined race than their fathers', Scott comments, 'and the manners I am now to describe have either altogether disappeared, or are greatly modified'; while in a note he refers to farmers whose hospitality he had known as a boy, 'in his rambles through that wild country, at a time when it was totally inaccessible' except to a traveller on foot or horesback. Harry Bertram's sojourn with Dandy Dinmont makes possible a description of the Scots manner of hunting and fishing, and also allows the introduction of a compliment to the 'blunt honesty, personal strength, and hardihood' of these men, and to their generosity and hospitality. While it is impossible to regret the creation of such a character, the hero's interruption of his journey to see Julia Mannering is not very credible; and while Scott is more careful than he would have been in *Waverley* to give Dandy Dinmont some part in the plot, the true reason for his introduction remains too evident. The same is true of Paulus Pleydell the advocate, introduced as he is primarily to enable Scott to describe a characteristic trait of Scottish manners.

Of the many differences between *Guy Mannering* and *Waverley* three are outstanding. First, the later book does not contain actual personages who figure in the history of Scotland, nor are important events in the political history of the country introduced: it is an 'historical' romance in a different sense from the part of *Waverley* dealing with the '45. Secondly, it is clear that Scott was determined to avoid the most glaring weakness of the earlier book, its casual plot. In this second book we are hurried into the midst of a complicated action. The fact that the hero, 'a young English gentleman' who has not been in Scotland since his early childhood, turns out to be the heir to a Scottish estate, also helps to give the story some semblance of unity. And, thirdly (which is most important), *Guy Mannering* contains characters whose interest and vitality completely transcend anything in *Waverley*. There is nothing in the earlier book to compare with Dominie Sampson, Dandy Dinmont or—finest of all—Meg Merrilies. Each of the three belongs to a humble social class, while Meg stands outside the ordinary structure of Scottish society altogether. Scott had always been fascinated by the gipsies, these 'Pariahs of Scotland', who lived 'like wild Indians among European settlers' and had therefore to be judged 'rather by their own customs, habits, and opinions, than as if they had been members of the civilized part of the community'. He was attracted by their picturesqueness, their rugged characters, and above all by their freedom from the ordinary restraints of society.

Scott seems to have resolved that the greatest character in the book should play an integral part in the plot. Right away we notice that Meg acts as an incomparably impressive chorus. In one of the greatest speeches in Scott she prophesies that disaster will overtake the house of Ellangowan:

Ride your ways . . . ride your ways, Laird of Ellangowan—ride your ways, Godfrey Bertram!—This day have ye quenched seven smoking hearths—see if the fire in your ain parlour burn the blyther for that. Ye have riven the thack of seven cottar houses—look if your ain roof-tree stand the faster.—Ye may stable your stirks in the shealings at Derncleugh—see that the hare does not couch on the hearthstane at Ellangowan.

Meg's conservatism, which is Scott's own, is peculiarly appropriate in a choric character. Harlot and thief as she is, she acknowledges loyalties to which Hatteraick, Glossin, and indeed the younger gipsies are strangers. She is a great praiser of times gone by: 'The times are sair altered since I was a kinchen-mort. Men were men then, and fought other in the open field, and there was nae milling in the darkmans. And the gentry had kind hearts, and would have given baith lap and pannel to ony puir gypsy. . . . But ye are a' altered from the gude auld rules. . . . Yes, ye are a' altered.'[1] Yet Meg is not only a chorus: she is also the linchpin of the whole action. From the first she is convinced that Harry Bertram is still alive, and she infects others with her conviction, being always 'the unknown friend working on his behalf'. At each crisis in the action she appears as mysteriously as if she were a creature from another world. She is the first to recognize Bertram, and it is her announcement that finally confirms his identity in public: this done, she dies content. Her actions have played a vital part in bringing the restoration about, while her prophecies give the book as a whole something of poetic grandeur.

The basic pattern of *The Antiquary* (1816) is similar to that of the previous books. The hero is a young man of mysterious origins who comes to Scotland for virtually the first time and is swiftly involved in a complicated intrigue. Other romance elements are prominent: there is a visitor of unknown identity, an exciting rescue from the sea, a haunted room, a duel, a guilt-ridden earl, a villainous foreigner, a scene in a church at midnight, and a final dramatic recognition scene; while a history of past violence and wrong lies behind the events of the plot. Except in isolated scenes, however, it is impossible to feel that Scott is taking these romance elements seriously; the love interest is slight; the hero disappears during a considerable part of the action; while no attempt is made to render the villain Dousterswivel credible. From the brilliant opening scene onwards it becomes evident that the dominant spirit of the book, unlike that of its predecessors, is the spirit of comedy. So it is when the greatest of the characters is introduced:

'Yes, my dear friend [the Antiquary is remarking], from this stance it is probable,—nay, it is nearly certain, that Julius Agricola beheld what our Beaumont has so admirably described!—From this very Praetorium—'

A voice from behind interrupted his ecstatic description—'Praetorian here, Praetorian there, I mind the bigging o't.'

---

[1] kinchen-mort, girl; milling in the darkmans, murder by night; lap and pannel, liquor and food.

From this point onwards Edie Ochiltree steals the book. In some respects he is comparable with Meg Merrilies in *Guy Mannering*: the Antiquary describes him as 'one of the last specimens of the old-fashioned Scottish mendicant, who kept his rounds within a particular space, and was the news-carrier, the minstrel, and sometimes the historian of the district, . . . [a] rascal [who] knows more old ballads and traditions than any other man in this and the four next parishes'. Edie advances high claims for himself:

> What wad a' the country about do for want o' auld Edie Ochiltree, that brings news and country cracks frae ae farm-steading to anither, and gingerbread to the lasses, and helps the lads to mend their fiddles, and the gudewives to clout their pans, . . . and kens mair auld sangs and tales than a' the barony besides, and gars ilka body laugh wherever he comes?—troth . . . I canna lay down my vocation; it would be a public loss.

The blend of comedy and romance that is characteristic of *The Antiquary* is suggested by the fact that Edie's second appearance is as dramatic as his first has been amusing: it is he who saves Sir Arthur and his daughter from the sea. Like Meg Merrilies he knows everything that is going on, and turns up at critical times. He knows of Lovel's feelings for Miss Wardour earlier than anyone else, and takes his part. He tries to stop Lovel's duel with Captain M'Intyre and enables him to escape afterwards. By identifying a horn that Dousterswivel claims to have discovered and making a fool of him by 'haunting' the church he carries on the process of Dousterswivel's undoing. In acting as intermediary between Elspeth of the Craigburnfoot and the Earl, Edie also plays an important part in another aspect of the plot. Throughout he is Lovel's friend and Miss Wardour's defender, and it is appropriate that he is the bearer of the 'budget of good news' which begins the happy ending of the whole book.

In *Old Mortality* Scott continued his exploration of Scottish history. The germ of the story was his desire to show Claverhouse in a favourable light. When a friend pointed out that Claverhouse—of whom Scott had a portrait in his study— would make a fine 'hero of a . . . romance' and Scott replied that this would necessitate portraying the Covenanters much less favourably than most historians had done, his friend suggested that he might employ the method of *The Lay of the Last Minstrel*: if the story were presented as being told by 'Old Mortality', then the required bias might be attributed to him. As it turned out, most of Scott's material did not come from this picturesque old man: as Lockhart remarks, Scott was now for the first time relying on written sources for his background. And in fact—very characteristically—Scott does not follow out the original dramatic idea: he forgets about 'Old Mortality' almost from the start. But he keeps stoutly to his intention of exhibiting Claverhouse as 'every inch a soldier and a gentleman'. While Claverhouse's cruelty is acknowledged, the plot is so manipulated as to throw the emphasis on his better qualities. The height of gentility is reached when (as Morton was sent into exile) 'Claverhouse shook him by the hand, and wished him good fortune, and a happy return to Scotland in quieter times'. Scott's desire to show Claverhouse in his later role as a zealous supporter of James II after the Revolution of 1688 is responsible for the clumsy structure of the book. The climax of the love plot, and the end invented for Burley, are among the weakest things he had yet done. Although he is often successful in catching the Scriptural turn of phrase of the Covenanters— Mause Headrigg's speeches are masterly, and Cuddie is excellent on a comic level—his portrayal of them is far from satisfactory: the result is not only biased history, it also detracts from the artistic value of the book. When Morton sides with the Covenanters for a while (so complicating the action and giving Scott an opportunity of describing them at close quarters) we are at a loss to understand why he should. If Scott had been more interested in the questions at issue between the two sides, *Old Mortality* might have been a major work: as it is it remains simply an admirable example of the historical romance. In spite of its many merits we notice that there is no great character in the book, and we are left with the impression that Scott has caught at some of the more picturesque aspects of a striking period without making any attempt to go deeper.

By this time an attentive reader must have felt that he knew pretty well what to expect in a new book 'By the Author of Waverley'; but in fact the greatest of the series, *The Heart of Mid-Lothian* (1818), differs greatly from its predecessors. The usual love-plot is thrown aside, and with it the usual hero. Scott had already shown his mastery in the portrayal of Scots of a humble social class: now for the first time he makes such a character central. Jeanie Deans, who differs radically from the conventional heroine of romance, is not even allowed a love story of any importance: since it is essential that she should be a lonely figure her lover is made a very subsidiary character: there is no hero to draw our attention away from the heroine. The unity of the main part of the book—and in this it has no rival in Scott's work—springs directly from the all-importance of Jeanie Deans: this is the only one of his stories which is primarily concerned with one particular human being. The theme of Scots character, or at a deeper level of the passions of mankind, is here brought to the foreground: in this serious book there is no element of the Guide to Scotland. The effect is the more powerful because the central theme—that of a Quest for Mercy—is so simple and archetypal: its fine simplicity 'carries' the complications of the Robertson–Staunton plot. Scott's remark, in the preface to *Waverley*, that he would willingly consider the inculcation of moral lessons the main aim of his work, sounds less absurd of *The Heart of Mid-Lothian* than of most of the other books: it owes its supremacy to the fact that its action turns on a serious theme, that of a moral choice.

Scott said that he wrote it to show 'the possibility of rendering a fictitious personage interesting by mere dignity of mind and rectitude of principle, assisted by unpretending good sense and temper, without any of the beauty, grace, talent, accomplishment, and wit, to which a heroine of romance is supposed to have a prescriptive right'. It is remarkable to find a writer who had seemed so incapable of differentiating his heroines creating a woman who seems as certainly not to have been 'born to be an heroine' as Catherine Morland herself. Jeanie has no exceptional beauty to make up for her lack of birth. 'Her personal attractions were of no uncommon description. She was short, and rather too stoutly made for her size, had grey eyes, light-coloured hair, a round good-humoured face, much tanned with the sun [as well as freckled], and her only peculiar charm was an air of inexpressible serenity, which a good conscience, kind feelings, and the regular discharge of all her duties, spread over her features.' She is not clever, and she has no sense of the picturesque. Integrity, loyalty, and common sense are her characteristics: Jane Austen would have approved of her. Although she is nervous when the Duke takes her off on a mysterious journey, and in the circumstances 'a romantic heroine might have suspected and dreaded the power of her own charms', Scott comments that 'Jeanie was too wise to let such a silly thought intrude on her mind'. Her imagination not being 'the most powerful of her faculties', her very dreams are sensible— 'a wild farm in Northumberland, well stocked with milk-cows, yeald beasts, and sheep'. On the other hand, since she is 'no heroine of romance', worldly affluence has its attractions for her: she looks with curiosity at the domains of Dumbiedikes, of which she might so easily have become mistress.

What happens in the course of the action is that Jeanie's 'dignity of mind and rectitude of principle' are exhibited by her behaviour in a most testing situation. She is placed in precisely the circumstances in which, for a woman with her strong family feelings, the temptation is strongest: she is tempted to commit perjury not for herself but for a sister whom she believes to be innocent of the crime with which she is charged. Since her lover is unable to come to her aid she is 'compelled to trust for guidance to her own unassisted sense of what was right or wrong'. Her determination is simple: to save her sister from execution she will sacrifice 'all but truth and conscience'. She 'can promise nothing which is unlawful for a Christian'. The temptation is pressed home again and again. First, an anonymous stranger tempts her to forswear herself, but she replies: 'I wad ware the best blood in my body to keep her skaithless . . . but I canna change right into wrang, or make that true which is false.' Secondly, and more severely, she is subjected to the 'fearfu' temptation' of what she understands her father to be suggesting: 'Can this be? Can these be his words that I have heard, or has the Enemy taken his voice and features to give weight unto the counsel which causeth to perish?—A sister's life, and a father pointing out how to save it!—O God deliver me!' Thirdly, Jeanie has to submit to the ordeal of facing her sister in prison, and listening to the reproaches of the villainous Ratcliffe, for once compassionate: 'I must needs say that it's d—d hard, when three words of your mouth would give the girl the chance . . . that you make such scrupling.' But the greatest temptation of all occurs in the court, when her sister stretches out her hand and cries 'O Jeanie, Jeanie, save me, save me!', and the advocate for the defence puts to her the leading question whether her

sister had not told her that she was with child: when Jeanie
stands firm her father falls in a faint. Throughout this lonely
battle, which is reminiscent of Bunyan in its stark simplicity,
Jeanie displays 'that superiority, which a deep and firm mind
assures to its possessor, under the most trying circumstances'. It
is a Wordsworthian theme.

If Scott had stopped with *The Heart of Mid-Lothian*, his
reputation would stand higher today than it does. Although his
historical range increases as the series progresses, the relentless
operation of the law of diminishing returns becomes more and
more evident. Driven by his need of money, and realizing that
the opinion of the best critics mattered less than the apparently
inexhaustible appetite of 'the great variety of readers', Scott
did not give himself time to reflect or take fresh bearings. Such
variations as he introduced serve only to emphasize the underlying sameness. The fact that the remaining romances must be
considered as a group, instead of individually, matters the less
because few of them have any serious claim to be regarded
as unified wholes. It is their ingredients that demand attention.

No aspect of Scott's repetitiousness is more striking than the
persistence of the Common Form already noticed in four of
the first five books. Vestiges of this may be seen in most of the
other Waverley Romances, while most of its characteristics may
be found in *Rob Roy* (1818), *The Abbot* (1820), *The Fortunes of
Nigel* (1822), *St. Ronan's Well* (1824), and *Redgauntlet* (1824).
Although variations occur, the common element in these books
is most striking. Surprisingly enough, it is in the best of Scott's
books (*The Heart of Mid-Lothian* apart) that the Common Form is
most in evidence. In *The Abbot*, where he tells us that he 'paid
attention to such principles of composition, as I conceived were
best suited to the historical novel', he reached back to it. Roland
is one of Waverley's progeny; the suddenness with which he
becomes a person of importance parallels Waverley's meteoric
rise as a soldier and foreshadows that of Nigel Olifaunt, who
hears (a few days after his arrival in London) that 'the King,
and the Prince, and the Duke, have been by the lugs' about
him. The attraction which the Common Form exercised on
Scott is curiously illustrated in *St. Ronan's Well*. In the preface to
this book we are given to expect 'a little drama of modern life'
and are particularly assured that Scott is aiming at 'avoiding

worn-out characters and positions'. As the story progresses, however, the people at the Well are reduced more and more to the status of a chorus commenting on the main action, and that centres in the adventures of a young man of the kind familiar to readers of the earlier romances.

The adventures of such a young man formed a suitable framework for a series of scenes describing the life of a given place and period, and in these later romances, as in the earlier, 'manners' were Scott's true subject. The reader is a tourist in history. Frank Osbaldistone exists to enable Scott to describe Rob Roy and give an account of events which happened—or could have happened—just before the outbreak of the '15. Roland in *The Abbot* exists to give Scott an opportunity of describing Edinburgh in the sixteenth century and the situation of Mary Queen of Scots. *The Fortunes of Nigel* actually originated in a series of letters 'giving a picture of manners in town and country during the early part of the reign of James I'. Although he accepted the advice of his friends to lay that plan aside in favour of an historical romance, Scott admits in the preface that the incidents are 'few and meagre'—a fact further acknowledged in the motto of the book, a quotation from the *Anti-Jacobin*'s Knife-grinder:

Story? Lord bless you! I have none to tell, Sir.

Like Captain Booth in Fielding's *Amelia*, Nigel is given a weak character so that the reader may visit the sanctuary of Whitefriars and learn something of 'Alsatian' cant and manners. He also sees *Richard II* at the Fortune Playhouse, while such features of the London of the time as the state of the Strand and Charing Cross are also described, as well as the nature of a Jacobean 'ordinary' and the social status of pages. As Lockhart remarks, the book is a 'commentary on the old English drama—hardly a single picturesque point of manners touched by Ben Jonson and his contemporaries but has been dovetailed into this story'. In the same way the hero of *Peveril of the Peak* (which unhealthily resembles its immediate predecessor) exists mainly to enable Scott to describe English life at the Restoration; while the fact that he spends some time in the Isle of Man gives him an opportunity of describing the interesting customs of the island and the superstitions in which it is 'perhaps richer than even Ireland, Wales, or the Highlands of Scotland'. The London scene is described with an antiquary's enthusiasm, while the Popish Plot is prominently introduced.

Adolphus[1] pointed out that each of the Waverley Romances is an essay on a period of history, and this is just as true of those in which the Common Form is less in evidence. In *The Monastery* Scott set out to describe the period of the Reformation. 'The general plan', he tells us, 'was, to conjoin two characters in that bustling and contentious age, who . . . should, with the same sincerity and purity of intention, dedicate themselves' to the two sides. This being so, the scene between Henry Warden the Reformer and Father Eustace the Sub-Prior should have been the climax of the book: in fact its weakness makes it clear that the spiritual conflict which lay behind the Reformation had little reality for Scott. To atone for this he made too much of two subordinate characters, the supernatural White Lady of Avenel and Sir Piercie Shafton the Euphuist. It is difficult to say which of them is the more resounding failure. The contrast between this, the poorest of the books before the final decline, and *Kenilworth* (1821), the most successful of those in which Scott is not on his home ground, is extremely instructive. In *Kenilworth* it is evident that Scott has set out to describe Elizabethan England: we are given an account of the struggle between Leicester and Sussex, Raleigh and Blount appear, while there are frequent references to Shakespeare and Spenser. Drawing on the tracts collected by John Nichols in *The Progresses, and Public Processions, of Queen Elizabeth*, Scott gives a detailed picture of Elizabeth's progresses and in particular of the entertainments at Kenilworth. All this might have served as the background to a tale of the Armada, as Constable had suggested; but fortunately while Scott accepted the idea of an Elizabethan tale he rejected the Armada in favour of the story of Amy Robsart and Cumnor Hall, which had seized his imagination when he read it as a boy in the ballad version of Mickle. Although there are no great characters in the book the simple

---

[1] John Leycester Adolphus (1795–1862) was the son of the historian John Adolphus. He was educated at Merchant Taylors' and St. John's College, Oxford. In 1821 he published *Letters to Richard Heber, Esq.*, in which he argued forcibly that *Waverley* and its successors were the work of the same author as *The Lay of the Last Minstrel* and Scott's other poems. Scott was impressed by the *Letters*, which contain some illuminating criticism, and Adolphus paid several visits to Abbotsford. In 1822 he was called to the bar of the Inner Temple, and later he became judge of the Marylebone County Court.

romance of Amy's plight inspired a work which is an almost unqualified success, within the severe limitations of the historical romance.

A characteristic feature of these middle books is Scott's royal portrait-gallery. The Chevalier had made a brief appearance in *Waverley*, and Queen Caroline in *The Heart of Mid-Lothian*, but it was in *The Abbot* that such a portrait first became an important part of the story. By introducing Mary Queen of Scots, Scott was playing the trump-card of romance, and although she cannot be reckoned one of his greatest characters she is the most successful of his royal personages. Elizabeth in *Kenilworth* is adequate, but hardly more, while little can be said for the portrayal of James VI and I in *The Fortunes of Nigel* or that of Charles II in *Peveril of the Peak* and *Woodstock* (1826). A more significant feature of the Waverley Romances is Scott's interest in civil wars. A great many of his stories are set in a period of civil war, and the civil war *par excellence* was of course the rebellion of 1745. It was Scott's considered opinion that 'the Jacobite enthusiasm of the eighteenth century, particularly during the rebellion of 1745, afforded a theme, perhaps the finest that could be selected, for fictitious composition, founded upon real or probable incident'. In a letter to Byron he suggested that 'any success I may have had in hitting off the Stuarts is, I am afraid, owing to a little old Jacobite leaven which I sucked in with the numerous traditionary tales that amused my infancy'. At times he himself reminds us of the old soldier he describes in the introduction to *A Legend of Montrose*, a man who 'it is true . . . had his inconsistencies. He was a steady jacobite, his father and his four uncles having been out in the forty-five; but he was a no less steady adherent of King George . . . so that you were in equal danger to displease him, in terming Prince Charles, the Pretender, or by saying any thing derogatory to the dignity of King George.' Yet only a superficial reader could suppose that Scott was really on the side of the Pretender, and he had every reason to ridicule the suggestion, as he did when he dedicated the whole series to George IV. His real feelings are indicated by the passage in which he remarks that 'the Highlanders, who formed the principal strength of Charles Edward's army, were an ancient and high-spirited race, peculiar in their habits of war and of peace, brave to romance, and exhibiting a character turning upon points more adapted to poetry than to the prose of real life'. This contrast between poetry and 'the prose of real life' is revealing, and reminds us that Scott was an admirer of Henry Mackenzie, 'The Man of Feeling' in his books but a hard-headed man of business the rest of the time. In the Jacobites Scott found the modern equivalent of the spirit of chivalry which he had admired as a boy in the pages of Froissart. It was for reasons imaginative rather than political tha. he loved to look back to those brave men 'who did nothing in hate, but all in honour'. As he explains at the end of *Waverley*, he found the Jacobites a perfect subject because 'averse [as they were] to intermingle with the English, or adopt their customs, [they] long continued to pride themselves upon maintaining ancient Scottish manners and customs'. In the introduction to *Redgauntlet* he laments their passing:

The progress of time, which has withdrawn all of them from the field, has removed . . . a peculiar and striking feature of ancient manners. Their love of past times, their tales of bloody battles fought against romantic odds, were all dear to the imagination, and their little idolatry of locks of hair, pictures, rings, ribbons, and other memorials of the time in which they still seemed to live, was an interesting enthusiasm; and although their political principles, had they existed in the relation of fathers, might have rendered them dangerous . . . yet, as we now recollect them, there could not be on the earth supposed to exist persons better qualified to sustain the capacity of innocuous and respectable grandsires.

'An interesting enthusiasm'—the last word clearly retaining its full eighteenth-century force. One is reminded a little of Addison's treatment of the old Tory, Sir Roger de Coverley. There was no real need for Scott to apologize to 'those readers who take up novels merely for amusement' for 'plaguing them so long with old-fashioned politics, and Whig and Tory, and Hanoverians and Jacobites'. It is precisely on those aspects of 'old-fashioned politics' that are calculated to appeal to such readers that he concentrates. He dwells on the picturesque aspects of things and draws contrasts in black and white which have proved a lasting source of historical misunderstanding. In dealing with the English civil war he was no less guilty of over-simplification: the romance of royalty appealed to him irre-sistibly, and in writing of the Parliamentarians he was dealing with people whom he understood far less well than he did the Covenanters. Whereas his intimate knowledge of the idiom of the Covenanters brought with it an instinctive feeling for the grain of their minds, for the style of the Parliamentarians he was content to rely on tracts and pamphlets and on such biased history as he found in the comic and satirical writers of the Restoration: he heads too many chapters with quotations from *Hudibras* for us to expect from him an impartial account of the matter.

In the *Lives of the Novelists* and elsewhere Scott wrote more about the practice of fiction than any of his predecessors. This was not because he was passionately interested in prose fiction as a form or had any high opinion of its social or moral function. On the contrary he repeatedly acknowledged that he was 'far from thinking that the novelist or romance-writer stands high in the ranks of literature'. In *Waverley* and its successors he regarded himself as writing 'for general amusement' and he often emphasized that he was 'no great believer in the moral utility to be derived from fictitious compositions'. Many of the remarks in the introductory epistle to *The Fortunes of Nigel* constitute a disclaimer of the high status recently claimed for the novel in the fifth chapter of *Northanger Abbey*. Although he is not consistent in the matter it is noticeable that he more often refers to his own books as 'romances' than 'novels'; it is because the distinction is an important one that the word 'romance' has been used throughout the present chapter.

His cavalier attitude to prose fiction helps to explain his carelessness about unity. In his anonymous review of *Tales of my Landlord* he pointed out that 'his stories are so slightly constructed as to remind us of the showman's thread with which he draws up his pictures and presents them successively to the eye of the spectator'. While he was usually prepared to admit the supremacy of the plotting of *Tom Jones* (to the deeper unity of *Emma* he does not refer), he maintained that such men as Le Sage and Smollett had emancipated fiction from such rigours: 'these great masters have been satisfied if they amused the reader upon the road; though the conclusion only arrived because the tale must have an end'. Convenience apart, the high praise which he always accords Smollett suggests that a looser form of construction than Fielding's made a strong appeal to Scott:

Believe me . . . I have repeatedly laid down my future work to scale, divided it into volumes and chapters, and endeavoured to construct a story which I meant should evolve itself gradually and strikingly, maintain suspense, and stimulate curiosity; and which, finally, should terminate in a striking catastrophe. But I think there is a demon who seats himself on the feather of my pen when I begin to write, and leads it astray from the purpose. Characters expand under my hand; incidents are multiplied; the story lingers, while the materials increase; my regular mansion turns out a Gothic anomaly.... When I light on such a character as Bailie Jarvie, or Dalgetty, my imagination brightens, and my conception becomes clearer at every step which I take in his company, although it leads me many a weary mile from the regular road, and forces me to leap hedge and ditch to get back into the route again. If I resist the temptation, as you advise me, my thoughts become prosy, flat, and dull . . . I am no more the same author I was in my better mood, than the dog in a wheel . . . is like the same dog merrily chasing his own tail. (Introductory Epistle to *The Fortunes of Nigel*.)

In his self-reviewal Scott had compared his own characterization to that of Shakespeare, and in such a passage as this the account which he gives of his own imagination at work is strikingly similar to that attributed to Shakespeare by the critics of the period. Blending with the element of apology there is an element of scepticism whether the more 'correct' procedure has as much to recommend it as its advocates imagine. There were (in fact) two reasons for Scott's writing fast: one was that he was in a hurry to make money, but the other was that he did not really believe in the importance of unity in a work of fiction. It is significant that in a passage in his Journal he refers to 'the interest of a well-contrived story' as merely 'one way to give novelty' to a book. When his interlocutor in the Introductory Epistle from which a quotation has just been given taunts him with believing that the end of a plot is merely 'to bring in fine things', he replies: 'Grant that it were so, and that I should write with sense and spirit a few scenes unlaboured and loosely put together, but which had sufficient interest in them . . . to furnish harmless amusement'—would that be so very culpable? Perhaps the truth is that when the object of a writer of fiction is merely to amuse, and not to present his readers with an interpretation or criticism of life, then the case for careful construction and unity is greatly weakened, so that Scott was largely right, on his own terms. *The Heart of Mid-Lothian* is the one great novel of the series partly because in it Scott does not merely entertain us (whatever his original intention may have

been): the book has the deep unity of theme which is the condition of its profounder effect. The last volume always excep-
ted, it is the only one of the Waverley series that passes Aristotle's
test of unity: nothing can be added or taken away without
impairing it as a whole.

There is a passage in Lockhart which makes it clear that
Scott began many of his books without more than a general
idea of how they would end. Discussing *Rob Roy*, 'Constable
said the name of the real hero would be the best possible name
for the book. "Nay", answered Scott, "never let me have
to write up to a name. You well know I have generally
adopted a title that told nothing." ' Most of his titles are more
or less misnomers, *Old Mortality* being the extreme instance.
As he wrote he often changed the whole direction of the story.
In the introduction to *Redgauntlet* he acknowledges that 'various
circumstances in the composition induced the author to alter
its purport considerably, as it passed through his hands'. In the
introduction to *The Abbot* he mentions that *The Monastery* 'was
designed, at first, to have contained some supernatural agency,
arising out of the fact, that Melrose had been the place of
deposit of the great Robert Bruce's heart', so that as the book
stands the discovery of the heart, which forms the main part of
the introductory epistle, 'is a mystery unnecessarily introduced'.
In the introduction to *The Fortunes of Nigel* the reader is given to
understand that the hero is George Heriot, while the book is
called after Nigel Olifaunt and near the end it is King James
who is called 'our principal personage'. It is tempting to suppose
that *A Legend of Montrose* (1819) was originally intended to end
tragically (as it manifestly should), and that when Scott came
to write the preface for the collected Edition he had forgotten
that in fact it does not. We know that *Peveril of the Peak* was
extended to four volumes because Scott felt that he was making
a success of the Court scenes; while any suggestion that his
habit of changing the shape of a book during its composition
was of late development is refuted by the acknowledgement
in the introduction to *Guy Mannering* that the whole plan and
theme of the book were changed 'in the course of printing', with
the result that 'the early sheets [which] retain . . . the vestiges
of the original tenor of the story . . . now hang upon it as
an unnecessary and unnatural incumbrance'—and the title
is a flagrant misnomer. Other examples could be cited, but

perhaps it will be sufficient to mention the padding-out of *The Heart of Mid-Lothian*, so strangely noticed by Scott's remark in his Journal that 'a rogue' has written to say 'that he approves of the first three volumes . . . but totally condemns the fourth. . . . However, an author should be reasonably well pleased when three fourths of his work are acceptable to the reader.'

An uncertainty of focus resulting from this method of composition may be noticed in many of Scott's books, and it is responsible for the failure of three in particular. In *The Bride of Lammermoor*, which has been highly praised by several critics, it is evident that Scott is writing with his eye on *Macbeth*: a sense of doom hangs over the action, and the conclusion is starkly tragic. But by using Caleb Balderstone not only as a choric character but also as comic relief Scott destroys the unity of the book: although Balderstone is one of his finest comic creations his presence prevents everything in the tale from being in key. A similar uncertainty of purpose is reflected in the undefined status of the witch-like old women. The same is true of *A Legend of Montrose*, which shares the faults of its predecessor but few of its virtues. In spite of the happy ending it is essentially a tragic tale; yet Scott 'endeavoured to enliven' it by the introduction of Captain Dalgetty, who, with his horse Gustavus and his chatter of Marischal College, Aberdeen, goes far to turn the book from tragedy to farce. A fatal lack of homogeneity may also be seen in *St. Ronan's Well*, which is an interesting book to the critic of Scott. Expecting a story 'upon a plan different from any other that the author has ever written', the reader finds himself presented with yet another variation on the Common Form—and then when the end comes in sight and he expects the romance elements to combine to produce the familiar happy ending, melodrama takes over and the book ends in a storm of ghosts and Mrs. Radcliffe. The reason for this is known. When Laidlaw suggested that he should write a contemporary story Scott remembered 'a tale of dark domestic guilt which had recently come under his notice as Sheriff' and decided to make use of it. 'I have thoughts of making the tale tragic, having "a humour to be cruel" ', he wrote to Ballantyne. 'It may go off.' It did not, and the result is indeed (in spite of incidental excellences, such as Meg Dods) 'a pitiful tragedy, filled with the most lamentable mirth'. A better example could hardly be found of Scott's besetting fault—the neglect of 'keeping' or consistency of atmosphere and tone.

Almost from the start the problem of ending a story irritated and bored him. In 'The Life of Mrs. Radcliffe' he refers feelingly to 'the torment of romance-writers, those necessary evils, the concluding chapters'. For the most part he remained the slave of the conventional happy ending, yet he found it more and more difficult to describe it with a good grace. As early as *Guy Mannering* he escapes by throwing a good deal of the description into the form of a dialogue between Colonel Mannering and Mr. Pleydell. At the end of *Old Mortality* he remarks that he had intended to leave the conclusion to the reader's imagination, 'a practice, which might be found convenient to both readers and compilers'; but instead he personifies the more conventional members of his 'reading public' and introduces subsequent events in the course of a dialogue between the author and Miss Martha Buskbody, whose demands are as stereotyped and as exacting as those of a modern reader of detective stories. In *Redgauntlet* we find a similar device: a letter from an imaginary antiquary gives the few facts of subsequent history which he has been able to discover. At the end of *The Fortunes of Nigel* Scott remarks with obvious relief that since 'the fashion of such narratives as the present changes like other earthly things', a circumstantial description of the final wedding is no longer necessary: 'a change which saves an author the trouble of attempting in vain to give a new colour to the commonplace description of such matters'.

Scott's boredom as he wrote the concluding chapters of his books sprang from his boredom with the conventional shape of story which he had taken over from his predecessors. For all the originality of the matter which he brought into the range of prose fiction, his view of the nature of the form itself was unoriginal and conventional. As the series progressed he often became worried and anxious for novelty, and when this happened he chose a new period or a new setting for his story. After stories mainly set in Scotland in the eighteenth century (his true field) he wrote a succession of books mainly set in the late sixteenth and early seventeenth centuries and dealing with a variety of places. Occasionally it is clear that he has set out in a given book to avoid the repetition of some particular feature of the previous books: Di Vernon differs superficially from his earlier heroines, as Jeanie Deans differs essentially. But the relative insignificance of most of the differences between his books is underlined by the fact that when he refers to a 'different method' in *The Bride of Lammermoor* and *A Legend of Montrose* he means primarily that there is less dialogue than usual in these books, and more action. It was almost wholly the possibility of a change of subject-matter that presented itself to him: except in *The Heart of Mid-Lothian* it does not seem to have occurred to him that to write a book on a serious and unifying theme would be a novelty of a more important kind. Little interested as he was in the technique of fiction, he did not explore the possibilities of varying the point of view from which the story is told. It is a pity that he did not carry further the experiment in the epistolary novel represented by the first third of *Redgauntlet*, as this might have taught him the secret of dramatizing a story. As the prefatory matter to so many of the books bears witness, he enjoyed the creation of imaginary *personae*; but he was too impatient to sustain the pretence, and the prolonged process of revision which lies behind Jane Austen's novels was for him out of the question.

In his study of Pope, Professor Geoffrey Tillotson has used Correctness as a focal point: the Picturesque might similarly be used as the central concept in a study of the Waverley Romances. We have only to glance into the writings of William Gilpin to see how closely many of the scenes which Scott describes conform to the canons of the Picturesque. His favourite terrain—the Border country and the Highlands of Scotland—provided him with a rich storehouse of picturesque scenery, and when he moved to less familiar ground his choice was always largely dictated by the picturesque potentialities of the country. 'The site was singularly picturesque', he observes at the beginning of *St. Ronan's Well*, and the remark might stand as a comment on the great majority of his settings. Wordsworth was critical about this, complaining of 'the laborious manner in which everything is placed before your eyes for the production of picturesque effect' and insisting that 'the reader, in good narration, feels that pictures rise up before his sight, and pass away from it unostentatiously, succeeding each other. But when they are fixed upon an easel for the express purpose of being admired, the judicious are apt to take offence, and even to turn sulky at the exhibitor's officiousness.' Yet there is no doubt that the exhibition of the most beautiful aspects of our scenery was one of Scott's objects, and it seems more reasonable to agree with Goethe that 'the beauty of the three British kingdoms' is one of the sources of the charm of his work.

As a boy Waverley is described sitting in a 'large and sombre library ... exercis[ing] for hours that internal sorcery, by which past or imaginary events are presented in action, as it were, to the eye of the muser'. It was by this habit that Scott's own creative imagination was nourished, and to the end it remained very much a visualizing imagination. There is a description of a painting near the end of the first chapter of *The Bride of Lammermoor* which may well have been the germ from which the whole story grew, and it seems likely that Scott often conceived of an episode or even of a whole book in visual terms. The fact that he is composing in this way is often emphasized by the mention of a painter's name. As Adolphus pointed out, Scott was particularly fond of effects of chiaroscuro, and when he uses this device Rembrandt is the painter whom he most often mentions, as in Chapter XXXII of *The Antiquary*:

> The window, which had been shut, in order that a gloomy twilight might add to the solemnity of the funeral meeting, was opened as she commanded, and threw a sudden and strong light through the smoky and misty atmosphere of the stifling cabin. Falling in a stream upon the chimney, the rays illuminated, in the way that Rembrandt would have chosen, the features of the unfortunate nobleman, and those of the old sybil.

Most frequently of all it is his friend David Wilkie whom Scott invokes, as he does in the previous chapter of the same book and in the description of the reunion of Jeanie Deans and her father in *The Heart of Mid-Lothian*. The affinity between Fielding and Hogarth has often been remarked: that between Scott and David Wilkie is no less striking and no less significant.

Scott's quest for the picturesque is as evident in his choice of characters as in his local descriptions. His finest characters are usually men and women of striking appearance. Nothing could be more picturesque than the appearance of Meg Merrilies, for example, 'a female figure, dressed in a long cloak, [who] sate on a stone by this miserable couch; her elbows . . . upon her knees, and her face, averted from the light of an iron lamp beside her . . ., bent upon that of the dying person'. Edie

Ochiltree is no less striking. There is a fine passage in *The Antiquary* in which he is contrasted with the Earl, and this reminds us of another device which is thoroughly characteristic of Scott:

> The contrast . . . was very striking. The hale cheek, firm step, erect stature and undaunted presence and bearing of the old mendicant, indicated patience and content in the extremity of age, and in the lowest condition to which humanity can sink; while the sunken eye, pallid cheek, and tottering form of the nobleman . . . showed how little wealth, power, and even the advantages of youth, have to do with that which gives repose to the mind, and firmness to the frame.

Gilpin insisted that contrast was an essential element in the Picturesque, and one has only to read Scott's prefaces to see how often he refers to contrasts of various kinds. In the preface to *Peveril of the Peak* he explicitly mentions that once he has found a suitable subject he 'invests it with such shades of character, as will best suit with each other' and there can be no doubt that the desire for striking contrasts lay very near the heart of his imagination. At the end of the first chapter of *Waverley* he points out that 'some favourable opportunities of contrast' have been afforded him 'by the state of society in the northern part of the island at the period of my history', while in the introduction to *The Fortunes of Nigel* the importance to him of contrast and the Picturesque are particularly evident:

> The most romantic region of every country is that where the mountains unite themselves with the plains or lowlands. . . . The most picturesque period of history is that when the ancient rough and wild manners of a barbarous age are just becoming innovated upon, and contrasted, by the illumination of increased or revived learning, and the instructions of renewed or reformed religion. The strong contrast produced by the opposition of ancient manners to those which are gradually subduing them, affords the lights and shadows necessary to give effect to a fictitious narrative; and while such a period entitles the author to introduce incidents of a marvellous and improbable character, as arising out of the turbulent independence and ferocity, belonging to old habits of violence, . . . yet . . . the characters and sentiments of many of the actors may . . . be described with great variety of shading and delineation, which belongs to the newer and more improved period.

It is clear why Scotland in the eighteenth century provided

so rich a field for Scott. Rob Roy was in a sense the perfect character for him, 'playing such pranks in the beginning of the 18th century, as are usually ascribed to Robin Hood in the middle ages,—and that within forty miles of Glasgow, a great commercial city, the seat of a learned university'. It delighted Scott to reflect that 'a character like his, blending the wild virtues, the subtle policy, and unrestrained license of an American Indian, was flourishing in Scotland during the Augustan age of Queen Anne and George I. . . . It is this strong contrast betwixt the civilized and cultivated mode of life on the one side of the Highland line, and the wild and lawless adventures . . . [of] one who dwelt on the opposite side . . . which creates the interest attached to his name.' It is clear that the contrast between different characters and different modes of life attracted Scott as an eligible source of interest and a convenient structural device: that is one reason for his liking for civil wars. The deliberateness with which he used it is brought out by the fact that the first chapter of *Quentin Durward* is actually entitled 'The Contrast': there are many other chapters throughout the series that might bear the same heading.

Important as the concept of the Picturesque was to Scott, however, it does not cover what seemed to him the chief technical innovation in the Waverley Romances: he considered that they were more dramatic than the work of his predecessors, and by that he meant that they made more use of dialogue. In the first chapter of *The Bride of Lammermoor* an imaginary critic complains that his characters 'make too much use of the *gob box*; they *patter* too much. . . . There is nothing in whole pages but mere chat and dialogue'—so giving Scott an opportunity of vindicating his practice. 'The ancient philosopher', he replies, 'was wont to say, "Speak, that I may know thee"; and how is it possible for an author to introduce his *personæ dramatis* to his readers in a more interesting and effectual manner, than by the dialogue in which each is represented as supporting his own appropriate character?' This claim to originality in the matter of dialogue comes as something of a surprise today, yet there is no doubt of the importance of dialogue in most of Scott's books. Not that his dialogue is always successful. The ineptitude of many of his conversations between lovers is notorious. When a girl addresses her admirer with the words: 'Rise, Master Peveril . . . Rise! If you retain this unbecoming posture any

longer, I will leave the room, and you will never see me more'
it is hardly surprising that he is 'overawed', and such language
is too common in the mouths of Scott's heroines, highly endowed
as they are 'with that exquisite delicacy which is imprinted on
the female heart, to give warning of the slightest approach to
impropriety'. It is also noticeable that in soliloquy—which
he considered more dramatic than the direct description of a
character's thoughts—Scott was often unsuccessful; perhaps
because the thoughts of his great characters are so clear from
their actions and conversations that it is mainly such characters
as his young heroes who are obliged to soliloquize. It is in
the dialogue of the Scots-speaking characters that his greatest
passages are to be found. The advertisement to *The Antiquary*,
in which he is referring particularly to that work and to *Guy
Mannering*, makes it clear that Scott was aware of this:

I have . . . sought my principal personages in the class of society
who are the last to feel the influence of that general polish which
assimilates to each other the manners of different nations. Among the
same class I have placed some of the scenes, in which I have endeavoured to illustrate the operation of the higher and more violent
passions; both because the lower orders are less restrained by the
habit of suppressing their feelings, and because I agree with my
friend Wordsworth, that they seldom fail to express them in the
strongest and most powerful language. This is, I think, peculiarly the
case with the peasantry of my own country, a class with whom I have
long been familiar. The antique force and simplicity of their language, often tinctured with the Oriental eloquence of Scripture, in
the mouths of those of an elevated understanding, give pathos to
their grief, and dignity to their resentment.

It is difficult to realize the daring of Scott's innovation. For
a long period before his time the Scots language had habitually been used in literature for the purposes of low comedy and
farce. He had to contend with 'stock responses' which were the
result of prejudice and ignorance. How clearly he knew what he
was doing is evident from his own review, in which he draws
attention to 'the singular skill and felicity with which, in conveying the genuine sentiments of the Scottish peasant in the
genuine language of his native land, the author has avoided
that appearance of grossness and vulgarity by which the success
of every similar attempt has hitherto been defeated'. In his
work, as he goes on to claim, 'the Scottish peasant speaks the

language of his native country, his *national* language, not the
patois of an individual district; and in listening to it we not
only do not experience even the slightest feeling of disgust or
aversion, but our bosoms are responsive to every sentiment of
sublimity, or awe, or terror which the author may be disposed
to excite'. It has been given to few men to effect so great a revolution of taste in the response of readers to a language. This is
the root of Scott's greatness. It is by their speeches that he creates
every one of his most successful characters. When stress is laid
on the fact that Scott is usually more concerned to describe
Scottish life and manners than to create books which are artistic
wholes the manner of his description must be remembered. It is
not in the narrative or scenic passages that he most perfectly
depicts Scots manners, but in those in which his characters are
speaking. His painting of the countryside is nothing beside his
re-creation of the men and women who inhabit the countryside
and make up the nation. It is true that in describing the mountains and lochs of Scotland he extended the scenic possibilities
of prose fiction, but in creating his greatest characters he did
something much more important. What remains in one's mind,
after the period trappings and even the natural descriptions
have faded, is the voice of Meg Merrilies prophesying the downfall of the house of Ellangowan, the voice of Jeanie Deans pleading for her sister's life before the Queen.

VII

PEACOCK

IF it is doubtful whether *Waverley* should be called a novel, it is certain that *Gryll Grange* should not. Peacock's works of prose fiction are best considered as satiric tales. In his essay on 'French Comic Romances' he distinguishes between two types of comic tale: that in which the characters are individuals and the events such as happen in real life, and that 'in which the characters are abstractions or embodied classifications, and the implied or embodied opinions [are] the main matter of the work'. As it happens the two types are illustrated by two books that appeared in the year 1818, *Northanger Abbey* and *Nightmare Abbey*. They have a good deal in common. In each an author whose attitude is conservative and 'eighteenth-century' satirizes the excesses of modern literature as exemplified in the work of Mrs. Radcliffe and the 'German' drama of the day. In each life in an Abbey turns out to be much like life anywhere else. When Mr. Glowry in *Nightmare Abbey* tells Scythrop that his behaviour might 'do very well in a German tragedy . . . but it will not do in Lincolnshire' we are reminded of Catherine Morland's discovery that it is not in the work of Mrs. Radcliffe and her followers that 'human nature, at least in the midland counties of England, was to be looked for'. In Jane Austen's book a young woman discovers the difference between life in books and life in fact: in Peacock's a young man makes the same discovery. But there is a great difference between the two. In *Northanger Abbey* the characters are individuals, whereas in *Nightmare Abbey* the characters are abstractions and it is their opinions which form 'the main matter of the work'. Unlike Jane Austen, Peacock is more interested in ideas than in people: his concern is not with what his characters do, but with what they say. He is the great satiric commentator on the age which we are considering, the Aristophanes of the period of which Hazlitt wrote, at the beginning of his essay on Coleridge: 'The present is an age of talkers, and not of doers; and the reason is, that the world is growing old'.[1]

---

[1] Thomas Love Peacock (1785–1866) was the son of a London merchant. As a young man he found business uncongenial, and worked without enthusiasm. In

The nature of Peacock's purpose accounts for the peculiar design of his books. *Headlong Hall* (1816), *Melincourt* (1817), *Crotchet Castle* (1831), and *Gryll Grange* (1860) are strikingly similar in pattern, while the other tales retain a family resemblance. The pattern may already be observed in the two farces which Peacock seems to have written about the years 1811–13, *The Dilettanti* and *The Three Doctors*. *Headlong Hall* represents Peacock's first attempt to use the formula for the purposes of prose fiction. The scene is set in a mansion in Wales, the characters being the members of Squire Headlong's Christmas house party. There is a tenuous love story, but the main interest of the book centres in the conversation of the philosophers and dilettanti. These 'humours', representing popular opinions of the day, include Mr. Foster the perfectibilian, Mr. Escot the deteriorationist, and Mr. Jenkison the statu-quo-ite, as well as Mr. Milestone the landscape-designer, Mr. Cranium the craniologist, and Miss Poppyseed the novelist. It is sometimes said that these characters are caricatures of actual people, but in fact it is only opinions that Peacock is concerned with: Mr. Foster serves as a mouthpiece for some of Shelley's youthful ideas, Mr. Escot's views are a caricature of Lord Monboddo's, while Miss Poppyseed is an intellectual caricature of Mrs. Opie. As in the later books, the other characters include a comfort-loving cleric (Dr. Gaster, a coarser figure than his successors) and a couple of eligible young ladies. *Headlong Hall* is in fact Peacock's prospectus, as *Waverley* is Scott's. The discussion of the true meaning of Progress which opens in the first chapter does not come to an end until we reach the last chapter of the last book, *Gryll Grange*; while we have to go no farther than the second chapter to find the characters seated at table and embarked on the learned and philosophical discussion of food and drink which forms the seasoning of all Peacock's work.

1812 he met Shelley. They soon became close friends, and throughout his life Peacock was to look back with an amused delight to the conversations that they had enjoyed at Marlow. In 1819 he entered the service of the East India Company, and the following year he married a Welsh girl, Jane Gryffydh. For many years Peacock was the East India Company's chief examiner. His brief essay, 'The Four Ages of Poetry', published in *Ollier's Literary Miscellany* in 1820, provoked Shelley's brilliant *Defence*. He repeatedly refused to write a biography of Shelley, but in 1858 and 1860 he published reminiscences in *Fraser's Magazine* to set right some matters unfairly represented by Trelawny, Hogg, and Charles S. Middleton. He was particularly anxious to defend the memory of Shelley's first wife, Harriet Westbrook. His comments on Shelley are both witty and understanding.

In *Melincourt* we again find a number of 'humours' representing (as Peacock acknowledged) the 'opinions and public
characters' of men of the time. Mr. Feathernest's opinions are
intended to represent Southey's, Mr. Derrydown's satirize those
of Scott, Mr. Mystic's those of Coleridge, while Mr. Fax acts as
spokesman for the Malthusians. One character, Sir Oran Haut-
ton, is a new departure. In *Headlong Hall* Peacock had contented
himself with mocking the opinions of Monboddo in the course of
the dialogue: now he presents us with an oran-outang with 'an
air of high fashion', a startling pair of whiskers, and great skill
as an accompanist on a French horn. As well as a satire on
Monboddo's interpretation of history, however, Sir Oran acts
as an 'irresistible exposure of the universality and omnipotence
of corruption', since he is bought a seat in Parliament and it is
made clear that he has all the qualifications necessary for success
in 'high life'.

In spite of the farcical element introduced by Sir Oran,
Melincourt is a more serious work than *Headlong Hall*. In one of
his letters about this time Shelley described Peacock as 'an
enemy to every shape of tyranny and superstitious imposture',
and this precisely describes the author of the book. Written in
the period of reaction that followed Waterloo, *Melincourt* is a
passionate protest against the 'loyalist' excesses and persecu-
tions of the time. We are told that when Feathernest was asked
to explain the spirit of the age of chivalry

it burst upon him like the spectre of his youthful integrity, and he
mumbled a half-intelligible reply, about truth and liberty—disinterested benevolence—self-oblivion—heroic devotion to love and
honour—protection of the feeble, and subversion of tyranny. (Chap.
viii.)

'All the ingredients of a rank Jacobin!', Lord Anophel bursts out.
The same sort of satire becomes evident when Sir Telegraph
promises to reform his own manner of life

when ecclesiastical dignitaries imitate the temperance and humility
of the founder of that religion by which they feed and flourish: when
the man in place acts on the principles which he professed while he
was out: . . . when poets are not to be hired for the maintenance of
any opinion . . . when universities are not a hundred years in knowledge behind all the rest of the world. (Chap. xxiv.)

Peacock's anti-clericalism is particularly evident in this book, where it is associated with the attacks on *The Legitimate Review* (*The Quarterly*) which reach their climax in Chapter XXXIX. In this, transparently disguised, Wordsworth and Croker join Southey, Canning, and Gifford in chanting 'The church is in danger! the church is in danger!' whenever an embarrassing question is posed. There is an admirable scene in which Mr. Forrester asks to see the learned Mr. Portpipe's library:

> The reverend gentleman hummed awhile with great gravity and deliberation: then slowly rising from his large arm-chair, he walked across the room to the further corner, where throwing open the door of a little closet, he said with extreme complacency, 'There is my library'. (Chap. xxxvi.)

It is Mr. Portpipe who defends paper money,

> 'and for this very orthodox reason, that the system of paper-money is inseparably interwoven with the present order of things, and the present order of things I have made up my mind to stick by precisely as long as it lasts'.
> '*And no longer?*' said Mr. Fax.
> 'I am no fool, Sir,' said the divine. (Chap. xxx.)

Unlike *Headlong Hall*, however, *Melincourt* contains several sympathetic characters who contrast strongly with the time-servers and hypocrites who abound at Mainchance Villa. The heroine Anthelia, who has been brought up among 'the majestic forms and wild energies of Nature', is determined to marry no man who is not imbued with 'the spirit of the age of chivalry'. With Mr. Forester—and indeed Sir Oran, who is not a sophisticated beast—she stands in piquant opposition to the scheming suitors, the mercenary Mrs. Pinmoney, and the turncoats Feathernest, Mystic, and Derrydown. An uncritical belief in progress is satirized by the remarks of an old farmer whose freehold farm has been in his family for seven hundred years, Malthusianism by the conversation of a rustic lover and his sweetheart.

Brett-Smith conjectured that *Melincourt* originally ended with the Anti-Saccharine Fête, but that the publisher had asked Peacock to lengthen it; and it is difficult not to feel that the book as it stands is too long. It is not that the later chapters are inferior, but merely that the reader has had enough. The author

is very much in earnest. A year after the publication of the book
we find Peacock writing to Hogg:

> I have been considering the question of marriage and divorce, and
> have read everything I can get on the subject . . . I shall write when
> I have leisure a dialogue on the subject, to get a clearer view of my
> own notions.

Coming from such a master of comic dialogue, this remark is of
great interest. Yet Peacock's finest dialogue does not give us the
impression that he is thinking things out as he writes: we rather
feel that he has reached his own conclusions before beginning to
write and is now making comedy from the percussion of ideas.
In *Melincourt*, on the other hand, Peacock seems to be earnestly
in pursuit of the truth, with more passion and less tolerance than
usual. The conversation is not his most entertaining, while less
is said about food and drink than in other of his books. He was
too angry at the political situation, and was seeing too much of
Shelley, to give his genius for comedy a free rein.

Nightmare Abbey has something in common with its predecessors. Once again we have a house party, an epicurean cleric
(though Mr. Larynx is not prominent), and a number of visitors
who are essentially 'humours'. The views of Mr. Flosky the
Kantian satirize those of Coleridge: the views of Mr. Toobad,
'the manichaean Millenarian', satirize those of J. F. Newton:
while those of Mr. Cypress satirize Byron. But unlike *Headlong
Hall* and *Melincourt*, *Nightmare Abbey* has a proper plot, with
unforeseen events and a reversal of fortune. This concerns
Scythrop, the son of the host. Scythrop's opinions caricature
those of Shelley at a certain point in his life; while his position,
suspended between two girls as Mahomet's coffin is suspended
between heaven and earth, reminds us of Shelley's position between Mary and Harriet. The scene in which Scythrop is confronted by them both comes straight from the world of stage
comedy, as does the dénouement, in which each of the girls
marries another man, leaving Scythrop alone and forlorn. As in
Melincourt, rather less of the satire occurs in the form of dialogue
than in most of Peacock's books: description and narrative
are more prominent than usual. But the distinguishing feature
of the book is its atmosphere of ironically described gloom.
Melancholy is in fact the subject of the book, which is more
unified in its satire than Peacock's other tales. The host is a

melancholy man, and accordingly there is little talk of food and drink (so that Mr. Larynx never gets a chance), while the action does not end with the customary Christmas revels. There are only three songs, and the best of these is the melancholy one (already quoted) which parodies Byron:

> There is a fever of the spirit,
> The brand of Cain's unresting doom.

Peacock told Hogg in a letter that he had been 'amusing myself with the darkness and misanthropy of modern literature, from the lantern jaws of which I shall endeavour to elicit a laugh'. 'I think it necessary', he wrote in another letter, 'to "make a stand" against the "encroachments" of black bile.' This satire on melancholy inspires the characterization of Scythrop and Mr. Flosky, and particularly that of Cypress: because his own affairs are in confusion the latter argues that human life 'is not in the harmony of things; it is an all-blasting upas'. Mr. Hilary acts as the author's own mouthpiece:

> I am one of those who cannot see the good that is to result from all this mystifying and blue-devilling of society. The contrast it presents to the cheerful and solid wisdom of antiquity is too forcible not to strike any one who has the least knowledge of classical literature. To represent vice and misery as the necessary accompaniments of genius, is as mischievous as it is false, and the feeling is as unclassical as the language in which it is usually expressed. (Chap. xi.)

Throughout the book *avant-garde* attitudes are satirized in conservative terms. The values of the fashionable but absurd 'German' drama are ridiculed in a mode that owes a great deal to eighteenth-century English comedy. The pretentious is satirized from the point of view of ordinary common sense. Scythrop, 'like a shuttle-cock between two battle-dores, changing its direction as rapidly as the oscillations of a pendulum, receiving many a hard knock on the cork of a sensitive heart, and flying from point to point on the feathers of a super-sublimated head', is in a situation which recalls that of a hypocritical rake in Goldsmith or Sheridan—for all his good intentions and his metaphysical theorizings. The final comic correction is administered by his father:

> 'And the next time, have but one string to your bow.'
> 'Very good advice, sir', said Scythrop.

In *Maid Marian* (1822) and *The Misfortunes of Elphin* (1829) Peacock is again searching for a satiric medium with more of a plot than his first two discussion-books: but instead of using a contemporary setting he now turns to the historical romance. The story of Robin Hood has always lent itself to modern application, and in *Maid Marian* (which is set in the twelfth century) Peacock makes it 'the vehicle of much oblique satire on all the oppressions that are done under the sun'. He was able to draw heavily on Ritson's collection of Robin Hood ballads not only for his material but also for some of his modern parallels, since Ritson was an uncompromising Jacobin. Throughout the book such phrases as 'social order' and 'distributive justice' are mischievously used, while Richard Coeur-de-Lion is presented as the complete anti-Jacobin. As the action progresses, however, Peacock's interest in his story and its idyllic background begins to get the upper hand of his satiric intention, and the result is a disconcerting juxtaposition of romance and satire. For those interested in the medieval enthusiasm of this period (a disillusioning study) the book has considerable interest; but otherwise, in spite of one or two agreeable scenes, it is far from successful. *The Misfortunes of Elphin* is liable to many of the same criticisms. It is possible that Peacock played with the idea of attempting to do for Wales something of what Scott had done for Scotland. The book is set in the sixth century, and his enthusiasm for Wales and its history is everywhere apparent. There are some fine descriptive passages, as well as fourteen songs, most of which are translations or adaptations of traditional bardic poetry. 'The Song of the Four Winds' is admirable. But once again Peacock's satiric intention conflicts with his antiquarian enthusiasm. Just as we are becoming interested in Wales and its legendary past we are pulled up by a reminder that at this happy period 'the science of political economy was sleeping in the womb of time', or by a comment that as yet mankind 'could neither poison the air with gas, nor the water with its dregs'. There are amusing things in the book, such as the celebrated curse of Seithenyn the mighty drinker, but as a whole it is unsatisfactory and reinforces the judgement that for Peacock the historical romance was a false direction.

In *Crotchet Castle* Peacock reverted to the model of his earlier books. Once again we find ourselves amongst a house party consisting of people with strong views on everything under the

sun, while a love story, set for the most part in Wales, serves as
a sub-plot. Unamiable as he is, Mr. MacCrotchet shares Squire
Headlong's passion for discussion. He hopes before he dies to
hear the outcome of such debates as those concerning 'the
sentimental against the rational, the intuitive against the in-
ductive . . . , the intense against the tranquil, the romantic
against the classical'. Dr. Folliott the cleric is a great advance
on Dr. Gaster, being learned as well as gastronomical; while
Lady Clarinda and Miss Touchandgo are more interesting than
the ladies in *Headlong Hall*. The 'humours' include Mr. Mac
Quedy the political philosopher, Mr. Skionar the Kantian,
Mr. Trillo the musician, Mr. Fitzchrome the painter, and Mr.
Chainmail, whose passion for the twelfth century anticipates
the Greek enthusiasm of Mr. Falconer in *Gryll Grange*. There is
also an unnecessarily long train of minor 'humours'.

Like most of Peacock's books, *Crotchet Castle* belongs to a particular point in time. We have only to glance into the Reviews of
the period to realize that the main discussions in the book deal
with disputes of the day. Peacock's principal theme is announced
when Dr. Folliott bursts into the breakfast room and declares
that he is 'out of all patience with this march of mind'. One of
his main targets is Brougham and the Society for the Diffusion
of Useful Knowledge. He inveighs against 'such science as the
learned friend deals in: every thing for every body, science for
all, schools for all, rhetoric for all, law for all, physic for all,
words for all, and sense for none'. (Chap. II.) While Peacock
must not be supposed to share all his views, there can be no
doubting the intention of the peroration on political economy in
Chapter X, any more than that of Mr. MacCrotchet's onslaught
on the sin of the times in Chapter VII: 'Where the Greeks had
modesty, we have cant; where they had poetry, we have cant;
where they had patriotism, we have cant; where they had any
thing that exalts, delights, or adorns humanity, we have nothing
but cant, cant, cant.' In a sense the debate between Dr. Folliott
and his host is a continuation of that between Mr. Escot and
Mr. Foster, but the tone is now more urgent and less academic.
The perplexities of the time hang heavily over this book, which
appeared in the year before the Reform Act. Mr. MacCrotchet
and his son, who has to flee to America, are examples of unscrupulous tradesmen becoming 'highly respectable gentlemen'
at the expense of those whom they have defrauded. Sir Simon

Steeltrap, Member for Crouching Curtown, and Lord of the United Manors of Spring-gun and Treadmill, is no less a sign of the times. Dr. Folliott is actually set on by a pair of (highly stylized) desperadoes, one of whom is killed—so providing his companion with a commodity to sell to the anatomists. The Christmas revels with which, as we expect, the book concludes are dramatically interrupted by a mob shouting 'Captain Swing': 'the march of mind with a witness', as Dr. Folliott comments. The 'rabble rout'—as Peacock calls it, borrowing his phrase from *Hudibras*—has to be put to flight before the celebrations can follow their proper course, 'according to good customs long departed'. Although Peacock exerts himself to provide alternatives to the diseases of the time—whether the idyllic background of the Welsh mountains and a simple country life, or the 'images of old England' recommended by Dr. Folliott: 'old hospitality, old wine, old ale'—and sees to it that the values of Old England triumph in the end, *Crotchet Castle* lacks the sense of freedom from the pressures of everyday reality which is so remarkable in its successor.

In *Gryll Grange*, Peacock's last book by almost thirty years, the familiar formula is used once again, and the result is a masterpiece. Mr. Gryll is a much more delightful host than the dubious Mr. MacCrotchet: while he shares his love of conversation and his hospitable habits he is himself the personification of Dr. Folliott's 'Old England'. Dr. Opimian has a great deal in common with Dr. Folliott, but he is more tolerant and more intelligent, and he is hardly ever ridiculous. Mr. Falconer, with his tower and his seven damsels, is an inspired variation on Scythrop; while his passion for the Greeks forms an excuse for the ubiquitous classical conversation which is characteristic of this quintessentially Peacockian book. Lord Curryfin, an amiable Zimri, is much more interesting than his predecessor Lord Bossnowl in *Crotchet Castle*. Most of the other characters stand in recognizable descent from characters in the earlier books, though one notices that many of the minor 'humours' have been dropped: superfluous mouthpieces who 'will none of 'em be missed'. The principal additions are Miss Ilex, a charming old maid who is a marked improvement on Miss Evergreen in *Melincourt*, and Harry Hedgerow and his brothers-in-love, who form (with the damsels whom they woo) a chorus from the world of light opera.

The motto of the book comes from *Hudibras*—

> Opinion governs all mankind,
> Like the blind leading of the blind

—and in it we find one of Peacock's recurrent themes, the divergence between appearance and reality, between things as they are and things as they seem to be, consummately expressed. As Mr. Gryll comments, 'we live in a world of misnomers':

A gang of swindling bankers is a respectable old firm . . . men who sell their votes to the highest bidder . . . are a free and independent constituency . . . a man who successively betrays everybody that trusts him, and abandons every principle he ever professed, is a great statesman, and a Conservative forsooth, *à nil conservando*. . . . A change for the worse is reform. (Chap. i.)

Brougham turns up again, only to be treated like Punch's wife: while we are presented with some memorable observations on lectures, as well as a fine specimen of that 'bore of all bores, an educationist': 'His subject had no beginning, middle, or end. It was education. Never was such a journey through the desert of mind: the Great Sahara of intellect. The very recollection makes me thirsty.' (Chap. XIX.) We notice that almost every feature of the contemporary scene of which Peacock disapproves is now presented as one of the hydra-heads of the monster Progress. This is particularly true of science. 'The day would fail', Dr. Opimian observes, 'if I should attempt to enumerate the evils which science has inflicted on mankind. I almost think it is the ultimate destiny of science to exterminate the human race.' Although it touches on many debates of the time, however, *Gryll Grange* dates much less than its predecessor. As we read it we are reminded of its author's alleged injunction to Trelawny: 'Don't talk to me about anything that has happened for the last two thousand years.'

The house party is now set in Wales again, and the proceedings close with a Twelfth Night ball and a number of marriages. The air of the whole book is festive. In *Crotchet Castle* we regret the fact that Peacock so often allows his characters to escape out-of-doors: here *Gryll Grange* is irreproachable. In this book 'those ornamental varieties of the human species who live to be amused for the benefit of social order'—as he describes the upper middle class in his 'Essay on Fashionable Literature'—do not waste their time. Events are untoward, because they interrupt the conversation and the dining. From the opening lines onwards the dinner-table itself is in fact the centre of the 'action' (if such a word is in order): to it everything under the sun must be brought for judgement. The conversation is better than ever: more classical, more witty, and more quotable. Peacock must have begun the book about the time when he was completing his *Memoir of Shelley*, and it is clear that as he worked at it his mind was harking back to the early days of 'The Athenians' (as he and his friends had called themselves): not least perhaps to the time which Hogg had described, forty years before, as 'that winter at Bishopsgate, which was a mere Atticism'. The talk that had then passed between Shelley, Hogg and the rest was to remain one of Peacock's sources of inspiration throughout his life: it never produced more mellow fruit than *Gryll Grange*, which is compact of conversation recollected in tranquillity.

While the dialogue reaches a pitch of excellence higher than Peacock had attained before, we also notice that the love story and the peaceful background of the tale help to give the book its unique atmosphere. As we read it we enter an imaginative world, free from the anxieties and frustrations of everyday life. Nothing is less in demand than verisimilitude. The equable loves of Mr. Falconer and Miss Gryll belong to a world of fantasy: these favourites of fortune have nothing to do but to make up their minds. This is a realm in which when two men love the same lady the result is 'rivalry . . . without animosity'. No characters in literature are safer from the dangers of the outside world: when lightning kills their horses the only result is to bring them under the roof of an eligible bachelor at whose table they are soon seated at dinner. It is an 'enchanted palace' that Mr. Falconer inhabits: with its books and its wine and the seven charming sisters who administer to him, the Tower is a gesture of defiance at mundane reality. If the book has any 'moral', it is concerned with a wisely sceptical Epicureanism. Many years before, Peacock had remarked on the singularity of the fact that 'the popular conception of the sensualist refers his parentage to precisely that philosopher who had the most temperate doctrines and practice', insisting that Epicurus recommended temperance in all things. Mr. Gryll and Mr. Falconer are both professed Epicureans, and although the philosopher might have had difficulty in recognizing them as his disciples, they are at least far removed from the adolescent philanderers of Moore's *Epicurean*. The conclusion of *Gryll Grange* is essentially that of a less deeply pessimistic *Candide*. We are explicitly assured that Lord Curryfin is now a wiser man than he had been when he thought that he could set the world to rights by waving his wand, and there is no suggestion that Mr. Falconer and his bride are going to set about reforming mankind. Tranquillity is the rational goal.

VIII

JOHN GALT AND THE MINOR WRITERS
OF PROSE FICTION

As Miss Tompkins has pointed out in her admirable study, *The Popular Novel in England, 1770–1800*, 'during the years that follow the death of Smollett . . . the two chief facts about the novel are its popularity as a form of entertainment and its inferiority as a form of art'. In the first two decades of the new century the achievements of Maria Edgeworth, Jane Austen, and Sir Walter Scott greatly increased the prestige of prose fiction. A note which Jeffrey prefixed to his reviews of novels when he reprinted them sums up what had happened:

> As I perceive I have . . . made a sort of apology for seeking to direct the attention of my readers to things so insignificant as *Novels*, it may be worth while to inform the present generation that, *in my youth*, writings of this sort were rated very low. . . . For certainly a greater mass of trash and rubbish never disgraced the press of any country, than the ordinary Novels that filled and supported our circulating libraries, down nearly to the time of Miss Edgeworth's first appearance.

By 1844, the date of Jeffrey's collected *Contributions to the Edinburgh Review*, the position was very different. Nearly twenty years earlier, indeed, Plumer Ward was able to point out, in the preface to *De Vere; or, The Man of Independence*, that 'that species of literary composition called the Novel has been carried to so consummate a pitch of perfection during the last twenty or thirty years, that, in its power of delineating, exciting, or soothing the human heart, it almost rivals the Drama itself'. The comparison with drama, or epic, was often made. Bulwer Lytton, for example, pointed out that 'many who, in a healthful condition of our stage, would be dramatists, become novelists'. The new prestige of prose fiction was accompanied by a new interest in its origins, so that the appearance of John Dunlop's *History of Fiction* in the same year as *Waverley* is singularly appropriate.

If this were a comprehensive study of prose fiction in the period it would be necessary to classify the books into their main types, including books dealing with contemporary life (particularly fashionable life), books dealing with some particular region (such as Scotland or Ireland), historical romances, tales of horror, directly didactic stories, and works of prose fiction inspired by theories and ideas. But since our concern is with what survives as literature it is possible to follow the simpler plan of beginning with books written by Scots and then passing on to a briefer consideration of books by English and Irish writers.

It is a striking fact that a number of the ablest writers of prose fiction at this time were Scots, notably John Galt, Susan Ferrier, Lockhart, and James Hogg. In different ways it is probably true to say that each of them owed something to Scott, even if it was merely the fact that books with a Scottish setting were in great demand. When Galt mentioned his *Annals of the Parish* to Constable in 1813 the latter replied that 'Scottish novels would not do'. *Waverley* changed all that. Yet none of these writers is in any important sense an imitator of Scott, and each must be considered separately.

In his *Autobiography* John Galt complains that his books 'have been all considered as novels' although the best of them are deficient in the sort of plot that is expected of a novel.[1] He describes his first work of prose fiction, the unsuccessful and unfinished *Majolo* (1816), as 'anything but a novel', and explains that it is 'a treatise, illustrated by incidents, on sympathies and antipathies, and that class of curious, undescribed feelings which all men obey, but which few are willing to acknowledge'. *The Majolo* is characteristic of Galt in that it shows him more concerned to demonstrate some truths about human life than to tell a story for its own sake. In *The Earthquake* (1820), which he described as his 'first legitimate novel', the plot is not the strong point, although we already see Galt's keen interest in national manners, and he prided himself on the truth-to-life of the behaviour of his Sicilian characters. But it was with Scottish

---

[1] John Galt (1779–1839) came to London in 1804, after working in the Customs House and in a business firm in Greenock. He went into business, and published a number of pieces in prose and verse. While on a commercial trip to the Continent, on which he visited Constantinople and Greece, he travelled from Gibraltar to Malta in the same ship as Byron. In 1826–9 he visited Canada as secretary to a company formed for the purchase of Crown land, and there he founded the town of Guelph. He was often short of money, and in 1829 he was imprisoned for debt. William IV sent him £200. Although he was paralysed in his last years he continued to compose as long as he was able to dictate.

characters that he was destined to excel, as *The Ayrshire Legatees* (1821) was at once to demonstrate. Galt tells us that he always enjoyed showing visitors to London 'the lions' (or sights), adding that 'the zest of this kind of recreation was in proportion to the eccentricity of the characters'. The result was this description of Dr. Zachariah Pringle's visit to London to see about a legacy, a book in which the humours of the Scottish character, and of the Lowland Scots tongue, are skilfully exploited. The greater part of it consists of letters home by the various members of the family, a device no doubt suggested by *Humphry Clinker* and perhaps also by Lockhart's *Peter's Letters to his Kinsfolk*. Since 1820 was an eventful year, what with the death of George III and the scandal about Queen Caroline, the Pringles have plenty to write about; but Galt is as much concerned with light-hearted satire on his travellers themselves as with London and its ways. A further element of comedy is provided by the reactions of the 'douce folks' in Garnock as they read these remarkable letters from the centre of fashionable dissipation.

Galt did not consider *The Ayrshire Legatees* a novel. In his *Autobiography* he classifies it with those of his books which are 'more properly characterised . . . as theoretical histories, than either as novels or romances'. The other books of this kind are the *Annals of the Parish* (1821), *The Provost* (1822), and probably *The Member* and *The Radical* (both 1832), and Galt's intention in such works may be gathered from his remark that 'fables are often a better way of illustrating general truths than abstract reasoning'. These are Galt's finest works, his unique contribution to prose fiction, and it is now time to give them some consideration.

The *Annals of the Parish* was the first of all these books to be conceived. When he was still very young it was his ambition to produce something 'that would be for Scotland what the Vicar of Wakefield is for England'. At one time he thought of writing the book, which he wished to be 'a kind of treatise on the history of society in the West of Scotland during the reign of George the Third', in the form of a register kept by a village schoolmaster; but when he finally began to write he reverted to his original idea of using the minister as his narrator. One of the most delightful things about the *Annals*, indeed, is the way in which the self-importance of the old minister betrays itself as he tells his story: 'In the same year, and on the same day of the same month, that his Sacred Majesty King George . . . came to his crown and kingdom, I was placed and settled as the minister of Dalmailing.' When the news of the accession of George III reached the parish 'about a week thereafter' Mr. Balwhidder's parishioners saw the hand of Providence in the coincidence—and rightly so, the old man continues, for many years later 'in the same season that his Most Excellent Majesty . . . was set by as a precious vessel which had received a crack or a flaw . . . I was obliged, by reason of age and the growing infirmities of my recollection . . . to accept of Mr. Amos to be my helper'. His enumeration of the principal events of each year throws an amusing light on the character of the minister himself as well as on local values:

> The An. Dom. one thousand seven hundred and sixty, was remarkable for three things in the parish of Dalmailing. First and foremost, there was my placing; then, the coming of Mrs. Malcolm with her five children to settle among us; and next, my marriage upon my own cousin, Miss Betty Lanshaw.

In 1763 'the king granted peace to the French, and Charlie Malcolm . . . came home to see his mother'. In 1772 Mr. Balwhidder thought of writing to *The Scots Magazine* about the arrival of the first Muscovy duck ever seen in the parish and its narrow escape from choking—just as, in his temporary depression at the death of his first wife, he was 'seized with the notion of writing a book'. Unfortunately he could not decide between 'an orthodox poem, like *Paradise Lost* by John Milton', and 'a connect treatise on the efficacy of Free Grace', which he was inclined to think might prove 'more taking'.

Although in the *Annals* Galt gives us a fine foretaste of his skill in the ironical portrayal of character it is not to this book that we look for the most concentrated example of his art. As the *Annals* progress interest tends to shift from Mr. Balwhidder to his flock, and in particular to the changes which are affecting their lives. The very word by which Dalmailing is described changes, during these years, from 'clachan' to 'town'. We notice that while some of the changes described would certainly have been noted by a real-life Mr. Balwhidder—the new popularity of tea (from November 1762 he refrains from preaching against it as a wicked luxury), the increasing consumption of jam and

jelly, the wider practice of vaccination, the advent of the first
stage coach and of the first actors in the town—others are Galt's
own observations and reflections, set down without regard for
the limitations of the narrator's understanding. During this
period 'the taciturn regularity of ancient affairs' disappears.
As a result of the American War, the French Revolution (a
leitmotiv throughout the book), and the war with France, newspapers begin to make their appearance in the parish. A bookseller's shop is opened—not in the clachan itself, but in the little
manufacturing town that has sprung up close by—by an emigrant who has returned from America with views that shock the
worthy minister. 'Mankind read more', he notes, 'and the spirit
of reflection and reasoning was more awake than at any time
within my remembrance.' Galt was a born sociologist, and
throughout the book he emphasizes the way in which political and
economic developments have changed the traditional manner of
life. Mr. Balwhidder particularly deplores 'the sad division of
my people into government-men and Jacobins', which became
complete about the year 1794. The opening of a Dissenting
meeting-house is a sad blow to the ageing minister. Society is
splitting up into different factions. Galt holds the scales between
the old and the new much more evenly than his narrator would
have done, however. He admits that 'the progress of book-
learning and education has been wonderful' during recent years
and acknowledges that this has been accompanied by 'a greater
liberality than the world knew before', even while he deplores
unwelcome 'signs of decay in the wonted simplicity of our country
ways'. 'With wealth come wants . . .', as he sums the matter up,
'and it's hard to tell wherein the benefit of improvement in
a country parish consists.'

Although the *Annals of the Parish* is the one book of Galt's that
is generally remembered it is *The Provost*, designed as a companion-study, that should be regarded as his masterpiece. Like
the *Annals*, *The Provost* is written in the first person; but whereas
the earlier book is mainly about the parish, this is about the
Provost. Social history is now less important than self-revelation.
It is an exercise in sustained irony that has few rivals in the language. The key is struck in the opening paragraph:

It must be allowed in the world that a man who has thrice
reached the highest station of life in his line has a good right to set
forth the particulars of the discretion and prudence by which he

lifted himself so far above the ordinaries of his day and generation . . .
I have, therefore, well weighed the importance it may be of to posterity
to know by what means I have thrice been made an instrument to
represent the supreme power and authority of Majesty in the royal
burgh of Gudetown, and how I deported myself in that honour and
dignity. . . .

While nothing could be more quintessentially Scots than the
self-righteousness with which Mr. Pawkie describes his triumphant progress through life—unless it be the irony with which
Galt allows his hero to describe his own career—the reader
gradually becomes aware that Mr. Pawkie has a good deal in
common with heroes on a larger stage. The way in which Galt
comments that only 'the editors . . . of the autobiographic
memoirs of other great men' will be able to appreciate his labours
reminds us for a moment of Fielding's *Jonathan Wild the Great*,
while it is with a sense of appropriateness that we discover that
Galt was a great admirer of Machiavelli. When he first read
The Prince, he tells us, he considered it merely 'an odious collection of state maxims'; but then he decided that it should be
regarded as a satire, and re-read it with great delight. As he tells
us in his *Literary Life* this 'set him a-cogitating', and the immediate result was a treatise on the Art of Rising in the World,
a piece of 'grave irony' which began to appear in the *New
Monthly Magazine*. This treatise was regarded as so mordant that
he felt obliged to cease publishing it: it is to be hoped that the
manuscript of the unpublished part may still be in existence.
The Provost is an example of this same art—an art that many
men have understood without reading 'the politic Florentine'.
Mr. Pawkie understands as well as any Prince that 'to rule
without being felt . . . is the great mystery of policy', and he also
realizes that those anxious for power must steer their course
according to the spirit of their time: 'By this time I had learnt that
there was a wakerife [vigilant] common-sense abroad among the
opinions of men; and that the secret of the new way of ruling
the world was to follow, not to control, the evident dictates of
the popular voice.' He prides himself on having 'lived to partake
of the purer spirit which the great mutations of the age' have
brought about, although we notice that he retains a marked
gift for turning everything to his personal profit. Mr. Pawkie is
indeed too great a realist to 'think it any shame to a public man
to serve his own interests by those of the community, when he

can righteously do so'. He has his own reasons for regretting that 'such an ettering [putrefying] sore and king's-evil as a newspaper' is threatened 'in our heretofore . . . truly royal and loyal burgh; especially as it was given out that the calamity, (for I can call it no less), was to be conducted on Liberal principles, meaning, of course, in the most afflicting and vexatious manner towards his majesty's ministers'. In spite of all innovations, however, Mr. Pawkie keeps the reins of power in his own hands right to the end. When he retires he not only sees to it that he is presented with a piece of silver, but also composes the speech that is to be delivered in his honour.

Three other books written in the first person deserve consideration before we pass on to Galt's other works of fiction. He insisted that *Ringan Gilhaize* (1823) is not a novel in the usual sense, although it is not a 'philosophical sketch' like the *Annals*. Galt resented the unfair treatment of the Covenanters in *Old Mortality* and wished to present a very different interpretation of the events of that time. It is interesting to notice that whereas Scott did not in fact tell his story as if from the mouth of the old man who gives his tale its name, Galt (the great master of this art of literary ventriloquism) did keep to his plan of giving events as described by 'a covenanter of the olden time relating the adventures of his grandfather, who lived during the Reformation'. There is, therefore, a technical expertise or sophistication about *Ringan Gilhaize* which is seldom to be found in Scott—what Galt calls 'a transfusion of character'. He was disappointed by the reception of the book, since some critics treated it as if it were simply true history, while others regarded it as setting forth the writer's own views, without acknowledging the art that enabled him to recreate the character of the covenanting narrator. In fact it is an impressive book, though one feels that the powers displayed in it are out of proportion to the delight afforded by the result. *The Member* succeeds admirably, although it too was misunderstood by contemporary readers. Galt tells us that in it he 'tried to embody all that could, in my opinion, be urged against the tories of my own way of thinking' and insists that 'Mr. Jobbry is not made to make any acknowledgment unbecoming an honest man of the world, nor such as a fair partizan may not avow . . . I have represented him as neither saying nor doing aught that, I think, as the world wags, he may not unblushingly have done, nor which, in my heart,

I do not approve.' It is not surprising, then, that *The Member* is often misunderstood: it must be almost unique as a satire directed against the satirist's own point of view. The fictitious dedication, which is the work of Lockhart, catches the spirit of the book admirably:

If the Reform Bill passes, which an offended Providence seems, I fear, but too likely to permit, [the result will] be a general convulsion . . . fatal to the established institutions of a once happy and contented country. If, indeed, my dear and worthy friend, the present horrid measure be carried into full effect, it is but too plain that the axe will have been laid to the root of the British Oak. . . . A melancholy vista discloses itself to all rational understandings;—a church in tatters; a peerage humbled and degraded—no doubt, soon to be entirely got rid of; that poor, deluded man, the well-meaning William IV., probably packed off to Hanover; the three per cents down to two, at the very best of it.

Mr. Jobbry, a 'nabob' who has retired from India with a comfortable fortune, thanks to his principle of always keeping his eye on 'the main chance', becomes a Member of Parliament, so giving Galt the opportunity for satire on electioneering and the parliamentary politics of the day. By a pleasing irony Mr. Jobbry, who admits that it is sometimes necessary to 'act upon . . . the double-dealing principle', becomes a member of a committee to investigate charges of 'the most abominable bribery'. He deplores the fact that 'The French Revolution has done a deal of damage to all those establishments which time and law had taken so much pains to construct' and is particularly opposed to 'the new-fangled doctrines of the Utilitarians'. The irony is very delicately managed, for all the world as if Galt were trying to discover for himself whether it is really true that ridicule is the test of truth. Sir John Bulky's son wishes to stand for Parliament, for example, but his father has no intention of encouraging him:

I am not sure he is just the man fit for them; for though he is a young man of good parts, he has got too many philosophical crotchets about the rules and principles of government, to be what in my old-fashioned notions I think a useful English legislator. He's honest and he's firm, but honesty and firmness are not enough; there is a kind of consideration that folly is entitled to, that honesty and firmness will not grant.

In *The Radical* Galt's object was 'to show that many of those institutes, which we regard as essentials in society, owe their origin to the sacrifices required to be made by man, to partake of its securities'. The result is a more straightforward book than *The Member*. As he describes his life Nathan Butt portrays himself as the constant victim of oppression. 'It has from time immemorial been the artful aim of all education to obscure the sense of natural right', he observes with the self-righteous complacency of his type. 'To education, therefore, I am inclined, with Mr. Owen, to ascribe all . . . vice and distress.' At an early age his 'innate perception of natural right' leads him to steal apples. When his father whips him he asks indignantly: 'Who ever heard that, in a state of nature, where all is beneficent and beautiful, the cruel hyæna, which so well deserves the epithet, inflicts coercive manipulations upon the young?' But it is only as he grows up that the fullness of enlightenment is granted to him. 'Although I had now turned my fifteenth year', he tells us at one point, 'I was not at all aware of the state of society'; but acquaintance with the writings of such writers as Rousseau, Owen, and Godwin soon changes this state of affairs, and Butt continues his triumphal career by becoming the leader of a local discussion society and getting a girl into trouble. At the end of the book, by a pleasing irony, he is bullied by his wife into having their child christened in church.

'We wish Mr. Galt would do nothing but write imaginary autobiographies', wrote a reviewer in the *Athenaeum*, commenting on *The Member*. The same skill is to be found in one of his least-known works, 'The Betheral; or, the Autobiography of James Howkings', which was published in his *Literary Life and Miscellanies* (1834). No earlier writer can be compared to Galt in this field: Defoe often wrote in the first person, but his books contain little of the irony which is the presiding spirit in Galt's subtle studies, and which makes a more fitful appearance in his other works of prose fiction, to which we must now turn.

Although *Sir Andrew Wylie* (1822) has often been admired, and contains some excellent scenes, as a whole it is a vulgarization of the Scottish theme so brilliantly exemplified in the *Annals* and *The Provost*. Galt tells us in his *Autobiography* that his intention had been to describe 'the rise and progress of a Scotchman in London', and the result is a success-story banal enough to be made into a bad film. When Galt is drawing on his own observation of Scots life, it is true, there are some vivid portrayals, as in the conversation between Martha and Mr. Tannyhill about Andrew's future. We are told that Andrew had 'a happy vernacular phraseology which he retained through life and which those who had a true relish of character ... enjoyed as something as rare and original as the more elegant endowment of genius', and many of Wylie's speeches are excellent. Like his hero, Galt himself was fascinated by 'the knacky conversation of old and original characters ... it signified not ... whether ... douce or daft: it was enough that their talk was cast in queer phrases, and their minds ran among the odds and ends of things'. Yet the major failure of the book is the portrayal of Wylie's character. It is essential to the story that he should be extremely attractive, but in fact this mixture of James Boswell and Andrew Carnegie is a jaunty mannikin who would have infuriated everyone he met. Nothing could be less convincing than his success with the English aristocrats—unless it be their speech, which is very badly handled. And unfortunately, though the opening suggests that the book will contain some measure of satire on the 'great genius' whose career is about to be described, irony is almost wholly absent. *The Entail* (1823), which tells the story of an obsession, is a much more interesting book. The one object of Claud Walkinshaw's life is to recover the family estates, which have been lost by imprudence. He is a potentially tragic figure, driven further and further from the ways of common sense and common kindliness by his master-passion. Several of the scenes in which his half-witted son appears—notably the one in which, prostrated by grief at the death of his infant daughter, Claud steals another child and proclaims that it has somehow turned into his own 'little Betty Bodle'— are genuinely powerful. As the book goes on, however, Galt becomes more and more interested in Claud's widow, 'the Leddy'; yet though she is a considerable creation, with her Scots malapropisms and her characteristic mixture of meanness and generosity, in making so much of her Galt is departing from the true theme of the book, a sombre satire on greed and 'interest' which ought to have a tragic conclusion. As it stands *The Entail* is not a masterpiece, yet vestiges of the masterpiece that it might have been are to be found here and there. From time to time the lucid fidelity of Galt's portrayal of an obsession and its effects reminds the reader of Thomas Hardy. It is not surprising that Byron admired this history of a family.

The Last of the Lairds (1826), which deals with a subject that had been long in Galt's mind, is intended to 'delineate a set of persons, of his own rank, that such an obsolete character as a West Country Laird was likely, about twenty years ago, to have had for acquaintance and neighbours'. It is foreshadowed at the end of *Sir Andrew Wylie*, where we are told that an old lady has found a volume in her brother's handwriting containing 'a most full account of all manner of particularities anent the decay of the ancient families of the West Country'. D. M. Moir persuaded Galt that he would gain more than he would lose by abandoning the autobiographical form, but the fact that the autobiographical splinters of the book as we have it are the best parts suggests that the change of plan was a mistake. Galt himself finally came to this conclusion, and to the end of his life he cherished the desire of producing another book to represent 'the autobiography of one of the last race of lairds'.

The Last of the Lairds is in fact a reminder of three of the outstanding facts about Galt. One is that his rare gifts were not sufficiently appreciated during his own lifetime. He did not mix very much with other literary men, those who did give him advice (such as Moir and William Blackwood) were often mistaken, and he was too often considered a mere imitator of Sir Walter Scott. The second is that he was an exceptionally perceptive observer of the changes in the pattern of society which were going on in the Lowlands of Scotland in his day. This combined with his remarkable command of the spoken Scots idiom to enable him to recreate one section of society—and so one aspect of human life—with exceptional fidelity. 'Tell our friend Mr. North not to touch one of the Scotticisms', as we find him writing on one occasion. The third fact is that the imaginary autobiography was the medium which enabled him to approach greatness. He told Blackwood that if there was any merit in any of his sketches, it was 'in the truth of the metaphysical anatomy of the characters', and it was by his curious mastery of ironic autobiography that he was able to reach this truth and convey it to his readers.

Susan Ferrier has been called the Scots Jane Austen and although the title is something of a satire on the Scots her correspondence with a friend on the subject of *Marriage* (1818) makes it clear that her attitude to the novel had a good deal in common with that of her great contemporary.[1] 'You say there are just two styles for which you have any taste', Susan Ferrier wrote to Miss Clavering, who had suggested that they should collaborate on a novel, 'viz. the horrible and the astonishing! . . . In truth it would be as easy to compound a new element out of fire and water, as that we two should jointly write a book!' It appears that Miss Clavering had had the temerity to suggest 'a Hottentot heroine and a wild man of the woods', or even a story about men in the moon, but such subjects had no attractions for her friend. 'I *will not* enter into any of your raw head and bloody bone schemes', Susan Ferrier replied in February 1810. 'I would not even *read* a Book that had a spectre in it, and as for committing a mysterious and most foul murder, I declare I'd rather take a dose of asafœtida.' It would be difficult to find anywhere a clearer confrontation of novelist and romance-writer than we find in these letters:

You may laugh at the idea of its being at all necessary for the writer of a romance to be versed in the history, natural and political, the modes, manners, customs, &c. of the country where its wild and wanton freaks are to be played, but I consider it as most essentially so, as nothing disgusts an ordinary reader more than a discovery of the ignorance of the author, who is pretending to amuse and instruct him. (*Memoir and Correspondence of Susan Ferrier*, ed. John A. Doyle, p. 86.)

As Jane Austen asked a friend to inquire whether there were hedge-rows in Northamptonshire, so Susan Ferrier instructed her publisher to find out for her whether a midshipman could become a lieutenant in less than six years. We also notice that she was as certain as Jane Austen that a novel should instruct as well as amuse:

I don't think . . . that 'tis absolutely necessary that the good boys and girls should be rewarded, and the naughty ones punished. Yet . . . where there is much tribulation, 'tis fitter it should be the *consequence*, rather than the *cause* of misconduct or frailty. . . . The only good purpose of a book is to inculcate morality. (*Memoir*, p. 75.)

[1] Susan Edmonstone Ferrier (1782–1854) was the daughter of an Edinburgh Writer to the Signet. Her father was a colleague of Sir Walter Scott, being a principal clerk of session, so that Susan Ferrier grew up in a literary society. Several of the characters in *Marriage* were associated by its readers with real people. She led a quiet life, keeping house for her father after the death of her mother in 1797. Scott described her as 'simple, full of humour, and exceedingly ready at repartee, and all this without the least affectation of the blue-stocking'.

The purpose of *Marriage* was to be 'to warn all young ladies against runaway matches' and part of the scheme was to describe 'the sudden transition of a high-bred English beauty, who thinks she can sacrifice all for love, to an uncomfortable solitary Highland dwelling among tall red-haired sisters and grim-faced aunts'. As the book developed, however, Susan Ferrier took the matter further. *Marriage* is based on the contrasting fates of a pair of twins who have been brought up in very different ways. Their mother, having herself been unhappy as the result of a runaway match, believes that a 'prudent' marriage is all that is necessary to secure a woman's happiness. The theme of the book is the harm caused by unwise marriages, prudent or imprudent, and the importance of a girl's early upbringing in helping her to make a wise choice of a husband. It was because of her own blindness that Lady Juliana

looked no farther than to her union with Henry Douglas for the foundation of all her unhappiness—it never once occurred to her, that her marriage was only the *consequence* of something previously wrong; she saw not the headstrong passions that had impelled her to please herself—no matter at what price. She . . . considered herself as having fallen a victim to love; and could she only save her daughter from a similar error, she might yet by her means retrieve her fallen fortune. (ch. xxviii.)

Adelaide, whom Lady Juliana brings up in a foolish and unfeeling manner, is forced into a worldly marriage with an elderly Duke, and within a year she elopes with a worthless lover. But the greater part of the book is concerned with the fortunes of Mary, who has been brought up in Scotland. Mary feels bound to reject the ambitious match that her mother wishes to force on her, and in the end she marries the man she loves and returns to Scotland. Mary has a good deal in common with Elinor Dashwood in *Sense and Sensibility*, and fortunately she is contrasted with her cousin Lady Emily, who is also virtuous but less invariably admirable and whose first appearance comes as something of a relief. There are some amusing scenes in the book, and some telling phrases, as when we are told of Mary's Scottish aunts that 'their walk lay amongst thread and pickles; their sphere extended from the garret to the pantry', or when a blue-stocking insists proudly that 'nothing but conversation was spoke in her house'. But pride of place must be granted to Miss Grizzy's observation that 'Reading does young people much harm. It puts things into their heads that never would have been there, but for books.' While there is a great deal of comedy and shrewd observation in the book, however, it takes the form of description and explicit comment rather than that of dramatic portrayal. Susan Ferrier has more in common with Fanny Burney than with Jane Austen, and it is significant that she was fond of the art of caricature: 'If you see any comical carikitury,' she wrote to a friend in Edinburgh, 'as a certain burring Dowager terms a caricature, will you get it franked and send me?' Artistic delicacy was a quality with which Susan Ferrier was too little concerned.

Marriage was a great success. Scott paid its author a resounding compliment at the end of *A Legend of Montrose*, and Susan Ferrier was able to secure £1,000 for her second book. The subject of *The Inheritance* (1824) is again the importance of a young woman's choosing the right husband. When Gertrude and her supposed mother have suddenly to leave the South of France for Scotland (the sudden shock of the transition is once again amusingly portrayed) two admirers of Gertrude soon make their appearance. But the contrast between the worldly Delmour and the admirable Lyndsay becomes evident far too quickly, so that the elaborate exhibition of their characters in action is quite unnecessary. It is a relief when at last Gertrude confesses that she has been 'blinded by romantic passion' for Delmour, although her marriage to Lyndsay is a little too passionless to be satisfactory. The plot is complicated and improbable, and yet only an obtuse reader could fail to realize, by the middle of the first volume, that Gertrude is not the daughter of Mrs. St. Clair, and therefore not the heiress for whom she has been taken. Gertrude's supposed father, the vulgar and villainous American, Lewiston, is stagey and unconvincing; while several of the most important events in the story, such as the death of the Earl and the scene in which Lewiston claims to be Gertrude's father, are unprepared for and curiously offhand. The most interesting characters are Gertrude's uncle, Adam Ramsay—a Scots type well observed—and Miss Pratt, the gossiping, inquisitive, self-centred and (in some degree) intelligent old maid whose arrival at Rossville Castle in a hearse during a snowstorm is the most entertaining moment in the book. And once again there are excellent snatches of dialogue, as when Major Waddell attempts to explain to the blunt old Adam Ramsay that it is 'not customary to call ladies of a certain rank *wives* now'. But the whole thing goes on far too long. One is left longing for the brevity of a de Maupassant. The same is true of *Destiny* (1831), in which evangelical earnestness has all but killed Susan Ferrier's insight into character, and in which the comic scenes—such as those dealing with M'Dow, the gluttonous and rapacious 'Moderate' minister—tend to be unnecessarily crude.

'What a disgusting mind and imagination the author of "Matthew Wald" must possess', a friend wrote to Susan Ferrier in 1824, in a letter containing high praise of *The Inheritance*. She was not the only reader to find at least two of Lockhart's works of fiction arresting and disquieting, although the first of them, *Valerius, A Roman Story* (1821), could shock no one. Written in the first person, it describes how the son of a Roman settler in Britain travels to Rome during the reign of Hadrian to see about a lawsuit. In its romance-plot and in the author's obvious intention of describing a given place at a given time the book follows the general pattern of many of the *Waverley* romances; but though the plotting is more careful than Scott's, and the style much more deliberate (partly to suggest translation from a Latin original), there is a complete absence of the great passages that we would expect at least in the earlier of Scott's books. Valerius meets a number of persecuted Christians, and himself becomes a convert, but there is little vivid characterization and nothing penetrating about the influence of Christianity on the human character. It is an agreeable, slightly donnish sort of book that one can imagine being given as a prize in a school of the most old-fashioned kind. It was when Lockhart came to deal with the life that he knew at first-hand, life in the Lowlands of Scotland, the life of the country manse and the lawyer's office, that his gifts were revealed. *Adam Blair* (1822) and *Matthew Wald* (1824) leave us with the impression of unusual power seeking an outlet. In spite of their Scottish settings they remind us hardly at all of the work of Lockhart's father-in-law: they are more sombre than most of Scott's books and deal less with action than with the workings of the human mind. The motto of *Some Passages in the Life of Mr. Adam Blair* is from St. Paul: 'Let him that thinketh he standeth take heed lest he fall.' While he is mourning the death of his wife, to whom he has been devoted, the upright Adam Blair is visited by Charlotte Campbell, whom he has known before his marriage. For some time she lives with him innocently as his house-keeper; but then her evil husband takes her away, Blair pursues them, and he and Charlotte yield to the temptation of passion. The dreams of anguish and remorse that succeed each other in Blair's mind are reminiscent of some of De Quincey's opium visions. There is a starkly powerful scene in which Blair, now recovering from his delirium, sees a boat containing Charlotte's coffin crossing a loch on its way to the graveyard. The description of the meeting of the Presbytery to consider the misconduct of their minister is equally fine. Blair confesses and is unfrocked, but at the end of the book he is reinstated. This might be considered as simply a concession to the conventional demand for a 'happy ending', but taken in conjunction with the final quotation against spiritual pride it may also be interpreted as evidence that Lockhart was concerned to emphasize the dangers of self-righteousness. Like Hogg's *Confessions of a Justified Sinner*, *Adam Blair* is an attempt to deal with a serious moral issue: as Henry James pointed out, it invites comparison with *The Scarlet Letter*. That it was bitterly attacked on its first appearance, and was said to be fit for 'the same shelf with "Faublas", and another book unmentionable', is hardly surprising. *The History of Matthew Wald* has a good deal in common with its predecessor. Written in the first person, it describes the life of a young man who loves his cousin Katherine, with whom he has been brought up. Some of the adventures that follow his running away from the home of his foster-parents are described to us: at one point he stumbles on the truth about a murder, and it is characteristic of Lockhart to emphasize the spiritual pride which lies behind the murderer's confession. Meanwhile Wald, who has been obliged to become a private tutor, falls in love with the step-daughter of the family with whom he is staying, and marries her. She becomes a Methodist, so giving Lockhart an opportunity of discussing the effects of Methodism on the mind. In a hectic scene Wald's wife dies of shock, having seen him embracing Katherine, who has reappeared. From this point onwards the action dissolves into a storm of melodrama, rather as if it were the work of a Scots Webster writing in prose. Like *Adam Blair*, *Matthew Wald* is a powerful, sombre book, the sort of thing one can imagine the Brontës reading with approval. By way of contrast, *Reginald Dalton* (1823) is a reminder of the conventional streak in Lockhart. Whereas he explored some of the darker places of the human mind in the two books just mentioned, in this he wrote a contemporary romance of the most predictable kind. The ingredients are of the usual sort: the familiar type of hero; a heroine of mysterious foreign parentage living with a kindly old priest; unmitigated villains; the hero's father—a bookish parson who has been cheated of his rightful inheritance; satirical interludes, in which Lockhart draws on his undergraduate memories of Oxford (a tutor, the head of a college, a blue-stocking); debts, a duel and jail for the hero—all serving as a prelude to a happy ending. It is an inferior book, and proved very popular.

The Private Memoirs and Confessions of a Justified Sinner (1824) is so remarkable a work that it has sometimes been suggested that Hogg must have received help from another member of the *Blackwood's* group; and while it is dangerous logic to argue that because one book by an author seems to a critic better than all his others it cannot be his own work—as Johnson suggested with Swift and *A Tale of a Tub*—it is true that the interest in the windings of human motivation that we find in *A Justified Sinner* often reminds us of Lockhart.[1] The first third of the book describes how Robert Wringhim Colwan comes under the influence of a mysterious stranger and behaves in an extraordinary manner, harassing and finally murdering his half-brother and apparently committing a number of other horrifying crimes. The remainder of the book is a memoir by Colwan himself supposed to have been discovered when his grave is opened more than a century after his suicide. This memoir, which its supposed author describes as 'a religious parable such as the *Pilgrim's Progress*', is written throughout in a tone of extreme self-righteousness but in fact describes how its writer came completely under the sway of the Devil. He believes that the supernatural powers of the mysterious stranger must derive

---

[1] James Hogg (1770–1835), the Ettrick Shepherd, attracted attention by his verse and contributed material for Scott's *Minstrelsy of the Scottish Border*. His poems are discussed in the previous volume of this *History*. He became known to Wordsworth, Byron, Southey, and others, and settled at Altrive Lake in 1817. The same year he was part-author of the notorious 'Chaldee Manuscript', and he contributed a good deal to *Blackwood's* for the remainder of his life. He figures prominently in the *Noctes Ambrosianae*.

from 'on high'; and yet the contemplation of his own life fills him with weariness and repulsion:

> Thus was I sojourning in the midst of a chaos of confusion. I looked back on my by-past life with pain, as one looks back on a perilous journey, in which he has attained his end, without gaining any advantage either to himself or others; and I looked forward, as on a darksome waste, full of repulsive and terrific shapes, pitfalls, and precipices, to which there was no definite bourn, and from which I turned with disgust. . . . My principal feeling . . . was an insatiable longing for something that I cannot describe or denominate properly, unless I say it was for *utter oblivion* that I longed.

He describes the crimes that he has committed—he has murdered his half-brother, is prepared to murder the man whom he wrongly believes to be his father, murders his supposed mother, and murders a girl whom he has seduced, as well as an innocent preacher. The author of the book has deliberately left a good deal uncertain. The 'editor' of the Memoir suggests at the end that most, if not all, of the crimes described were delusions of Colwan's mind. 'In short', as he sums up,

> we must either conceive him, not only the greatest fool, but the greatest wretch, on whom was ever stamped the form of humanity; or, that he was a religious maniac, who wrote and wrote about a deluded creature, till he arrived at that height of madness that he believed himself the very object whom he had been all along describing.

There can be no doubt that the book is to be regarded as a satire of the most sombre sort on certain of the tenets of the fanatical Covenanters, so that the late (and unauthorized) title, *Confessions of a Fanatic*, is perfectly accurate. We notice that the Devil particularly detests any questioning of two of the most cherished beliefs of the Covenanters—the belief in Predestination, and the consequent notion that God's Elect may do as they please, 'good works' being of no account—and it is by insisting on these with the remorseless logic of a crazed theologian that he drives Colwan along the road to perdition. Colwan feels no love for his own mother, usually keeps himself at a distance from women, and takes no part in the innocent pleasures of the human race. The book is a study of the perversions of conscience which can be the consequence of a twisted faith fanatically held, an unflinching investigation of the secret places of a mind turned away from the sun of ordinary human affections.

Although *The Confessions* have occasionally been over-praised, it is not surprising that André Gide should have been impressed by so disturbing an indictment of religious 'melancholy'.

One further book by a Scottish writer can only be briefly mentioned. D. M. Moir's *Life of Mansie Waugh, Tailor in Dalkeith* (1828) is an imaginary autobiography written for 'the welfare of the human race and the improvement of society' and fittingly dedicated to John Galt.[1] The narrator is a kindly man, not without shrewdness, who sees life from the point of view of a tailor in Dalkeith: that is to say, he is as observant of the details of people's dress as Richardson's Pamela herself; while it is his secret conviction that ancient Troy, 'for all that has been said and sung about it, would be found . . . not worth half a thought when compared with the New Town of Edinburgh'—and that Dalkeith is in many ways preferable to Edinburgh. The sententiousness and complacency of the narrator are in Galt's manner, though a little more crudely done.

When we turn from Scots writers to English we are at once confronted by *Frankenstein* (1818), probably the only minor work of fiction of this period which is still widely read. When Shelley and his wife were neighbours of Byron's in Switzerland during the wet summer of 1816 Byron suggested that each of them should write a ghost story. Mary Shelley realized from the first that what was required was above all a good story, a tale 'which would speak to the mysterious fears of our nature, and awaken thrilling horror—one to make the reader dread to look round, to curdle the blood, and quicken the beatings of the heart'.[2] She could not find the perfect germ for her story until one day she heard Shelley and Byron discussing an experiment in which Erasmus Darwin was supposed to have created life

---

[1] David Macbeth Moir (1798–1851) was a doctor in Musselburgh. He soon became a regular writer of prose and verse in *Blackwood's* and other periodicals, usually signing himself *Δ* or Delta. He was a friend of De Quincey, with whom he no doubt discussed the nature and effects of opium. Apart from his literary works he published *Outlines of the Ancient History of Medicine*.

[2] Mary Wollstonecraft Shelley (1797–1851) was the daughter of William Godwin and Mary Wollstonecraft, the author of the *Vindication of the Rights of Women*. She was brought up by her stepmother with her own children, the Clairmonts. She went to the Continent with Shelley in July 1814 and married him when his first wife, Harriet Westbrook, committed suicide in December 1816. She remained in Italy after Shelley's death and saw a great deal of Byron, Leigh Hunt, and Trelawny. She returned to England in 1823, travelling on the Continent again in 1840–3. Apart from her fiction, she edited Shelley's poems and published a good deal in periodicals.

from inanimate matter. *Frankenstein* was the result of their talk of galvanism and corpses, and although it is not in fact a ghost story it certainly appeals to 'the mysterious fears of our nature'. The outline of the plot is well known. By creating a monster Frankenstein makes his own life a misery. Having murdered Frankenstein's little brother (a murder for which an innocent girl is executed), the monster pursues his creator to Chamonix. It explains to Frankenstein the progress of its intellect, and its frustrated yearning for love. Its appearance is so hideous that in spite of its original amiability everyone has always fled from it in horror. 'Everywhere I see bliss from which I alone am irrevocably excluded', it complains. 'I was benevolent and good; misery made me a fiend. Make me happy, and I shall again be virtuous.' Frankenstein is on the point of creating a mate for the monster when he feels an upsurge of remorse and destroys the new creature that he has been making. In its rage the monster devotes itself to revenge, killing Frankenstein's bride on the night of his wedding. Frankenstein's father dies broken-hearted, while he himself, assailed by calamities, sinks into madness. Recovering from his insanity he pursues the monster across the world in the hope of destroying it. This the monster encourages, as a form of revenge. In the end Frankenstein dies on a ship which has picked him up from the sea in the remote North. The monster laments over the body of his creator, explains its misery to the master of the ship, and departs across the sea to seek its own annihilation.

Frankenstein is a remarkable book to have been written by a girl of nineteen. Crude as it is in many ways, and full of gross improbabilities and fustian dialogue, it has the kind of theme that holds its reader's attention and leads different critics to produce rival interpretations. For it is not only an exciting story: it is also a philosophical romance. The way in which the monster describes the progress of his mind, his reading of Plutarch, Volney, and *The Sorrows of Werther*, and the development of his views on Man, Society, and Social Love, reminds us that Mary Shelley was the daughter of the author of *Social Justice* as well as the wife of the poet of *Alastor*. There is also an explicit parallel between Frankenstein and his monster and God and Satan; while a psychological interpretation of the tale would equally be possible. Yet it would be more effective if it were shorter, and this is much more obviously true of *Valperga, or the*

Life and Adventures of Castruccio, Prince of Lucca (1823), which is of a length to defeat all patience. The story is set in medieval Italy, and traces the deterioration of the character of the central figure, who begins as a generous youth and ends as a machiavellian tyrant, with 'a majestic figure and a countenance beautiful but sad, and tarnished by the expression of pride that animated it'. In *The Last Man* (1826) Mary Shelley seems to have been anxious to find a seminal idea as 'archetypal' as that of *Frankenstein*. Taking up a theme which fascinated a number of other writers of the time—Campbell, Beddoes, and Hood among them—she sets her story in the twenty-first century. The personal and political complications of the first part of the book are confusing, but when the plague strikes Europe the narrative improves and there are some powerful imaginative scenes. The dénouement, in which Verney is left alone in the world, is admirably conceived, although the execution does not quite match the conception. All that need be said of Mary Shelley's later fictions is that *Perkin Warbeck* is an historical romance, that *Lodore* is partly based on the relations of Shelley and Harriet, and that *Falkner*, in which the hero is modelled on Trelawny, appears to be an attempt to exculpate Shelley from any blame for the suicide of his first wife.

Lack of space forbids more than a mention of Thomas Hope's *Anastasius, or Memoirs of a Greek* (1819), a book which was at first attributed to Byron and which may possibly have influenced some of the later cantos of *Don Juan*; but something must be said of an analogous work, *Hajji Baba* (1824). Its author, James Morier, was born at Smyrna. His father was Consul-General of the Levant Company at Constantinople, while several other members of the family also had connexions with the Middle East. Morier himself returned to Constantinople after his schooling at Harrow, and in 1807 he entered the diplomatic service. In 1812 he published his *Journey through Persia, Armenia, and Asia Minor*, and six years later his *Second Journey through Persia*, a much more interesting book which is obviously the work of a man who knows Persian and is unusually at home with the Persian people. By this time Morier had already retired, and in an age in which novels were so much in demand and there was so keen an interest in the East it is not surprising that he should have decided to exploit his exceptional knowledge of a little-known country. The result was *The Adventures of*

Hajji Baba of Ispahan, the first of a number of works of fiction and the only one by which Morier is now remembered. His model, as he freely acknowledges, was *Gil Blas*: his aim was simply to produce a picaresque romance set in Persia and giving an entertaining account of life in that country. The nature of the book may be further defined by comparison with two of the best-known works of English fiction with Oriental settings. Whereas in *Rasselas* Johnson is concerned with the enforcement of important truths about human life in general, and chooses an Eastern setting for his narrative merely for the sake of vagueness and generality, Morier wishes to entertain his readers by emphasizing those aspects of life in Persia which differ most remarkably from the way of life familiar to his readers. *Rasselas* could be set almost anywhere, *Hajji Baba* nowhere but in Persia. Morier's aim is equally remote from Beckford's. The inspiration of *Vathek* was the *Arabian Nights*: that of *Hajji Baba* the real people of Persia. The one is the reverie of a young voluptuary, the other the record of long and sympathetic observation by a middle-aged man of the world who has 'done the state some service'. At the end of *Vathek* we are told how the central character, 'who for the sake of empty pomp and forbidden power had sullied himself with a thousand crimes, became a prey to grief without end and remorse without mitigation'. Hajji Baba, who tells his own story, ends on a very different note:

> I will not tire the reader with a description of the numerous details of my preparatives for the expedition. He would sicken and I should blush at my vanity. It is sufficient to say that I travelled to Ispahan with all the parade of a man of consequence; and that I entered my native city with feelings that none but a Persian, bred and born in the cravings of ambition, can understand. I found myself at the summit of . . . perfect human bliss. . . . Hajji Baba, the barber's son, entered his native place, as Mirza Hajji Baba, the Shah's deputy. Need I say more?

When we turn from Beckford's book to Morier's we turn from the world of melodrama to that of everyday Persian life, from a world of ghouls, djinns, and magic carpets to one of flattery, place-seeking, quack doctors, and petty thieving. Those who knew the old Persia best have been the most emphatic in insisting on the veracity of Morier's account. One eminent

Orientalist, E. G. Browne, was so struck by Morier's book that he questioned whether anyone who had not read it could be described as a man of cultivation 'in the full meaning of the term'. While this is absurd as a literary judgement it is impressive as a testimony to Morier's faithfulness as a recorder of Persian life.

It is a sure instinct that leads a writer whose inspiration is the urge to exploit a new milieu to revert to the picaresque tradition, and Hajji Baba is a true *picaro*, vain, resourceful, and unprincipled. No one could less resemble Johnson's Prince of Abissinia. What he is after is not the truth, but money, power, and pleasure. He has the resilience of a tennis ball: the harder he is struck downwards the higher he bounces back. In Chapter XXXIII he reflects on his own character:

> The first impulse of my nature was not cruelty, that I knew: I was neither fierce nor brave, that I also knew: I therefore marvelled greatly how of a sudden I had become such an unsainted lion. The fact is, the example of others always had the strongest influence over my mind and actions; and I now lived in such an atmosphere of violence and cruelty, I heard of nothing but of slitting noses, cutting off ears, putting out eyes, blowing up in mortars, chopping men in two, and baking them in ovens, that, in truth, I am persuaded, with a proper example before me, I could almost have impaled my own father.

In fact we hear little or nothing of some of the cruelties here mentioned, and when the others occur they are not so vividly described as to make a deep impression on the reader. *Hajji Baba* is an interesting example of the adaptation of the conventions of the picaresque romance to the taste and susceptibilities of the reading public of the 1820's.

One of the most striking features of the popular literature of this period was the vogue for 'Fashionable Novels' attacked by Hazlitt in his essay on 'The Dandy School':

> It was formerly understood to be the business of literature [he wrote] to enlarge the bounds of knowledge and feeling; to direct the mind's eye beyond the present moment and the present object . . . to make books the faithful witnesses and interpreters of nature and the human heart. Of late . . . it has taken a narrower and more superficial tone. . . . Instead of transporting you to faery-land or into

the *middle ages*, you take a turn down Bond Street or go through the mazes of the dance at Almack's. . . . Far from extending your sympathies, they are narrowed to a single point, the admiration of the folly, caprice, insolence, and affectation of a certain class;—so that with the exception of people who ride in their carriages, you are taught to look down upon the rest of the species with indifference, abhorrence, or contempt.

Before we glance at Thomas Hook, however, who was an authentic specimen of the *genus* 'Fashionable Novelist', it will be convenient to consider the work of Thomas Henry Lister, a minor novelist of real ability who has too often been loosely classified with men greatly his inferiors.[1] As we read Lister's novels we do not feel that we are peering in through the conservatory window. The important thing about his books is not that they deal with fashionable life, but that they are genuine novels. 'Do tell me your favourite novels', says a foolish character in *Granby*:

'I hope you like nothing of Miss Edgeworth's or Miss Austen's. They are full of common-place people, that one recognises at once. You cannot think how I was disappointed in Northanger Abbey, and Castle Rack-rent, for the titles did really promise something. Have you a taste for romance? . . . I am glad of it. . . . Dear Mrs. Radcliffe's were lovely things—but they are so old!'

Although there are elements of the romance in each of Lister's own novels, he is concerned for the most part with real people, and his action is illuminated by the clear light of common sense. As we read *Granby* (1826) we are repeatedly reminded of Jane Austen, both in large matters and in small— as when he refuses to describe a conversation between two women when no man is present, or shows the change in the attitude of the Jermyns to Granby when they discover that he is not as wealthy a man as they have supposed. In *Herbert Lacy* (1828) we are again reminded of Jane Austen: by the terms in which a proposal of marriage is turned down, for example: by the style of a lady's letter ('she was distinguished for her emphatic and judicious system of *dashing*'): and by the description of the hero, who was 'rather proud of the sturdiness of his

---

[1] Thomas Henry Lister (1800–42) was educated at Westminster and Trinity College, Cambridge. In 1834 and 1835 he served as commissioner to inquire into the state of religious instruction in Ireland and Scotland. In 1836 he became the first Registrar-General of England and Wales.

principles, in not being dazzled by the outward charms of the grand-daughter of an iron-monger'. There are also some admirable renderings of fashionable conversation:

And as for the Lacys, they, you know, are as old as the flood, and very well connected too. Sir William Lacy's mother was Lady Mary Loftus, aunt of the mad Lord Loftus, whose wife ran away with Sir Clement Packworth, the brother of the man who shot Lord Cheadle, husband of the naughty Lady Cheadle, whose brother was that Colonel Blake, who won so much from poor George Templeton . . ., whose sister made that unhappy low connection which we were lamenting the other day. . . .

The satire is admirably managed, and we notice that Lister is not content with describing the manners and morals of his chosen section of society: he criticizes the fashionable world, though he does so without rancour. He is skilled in the art of distinguishing between appearance and reality in human affairs, and excels in tracing the complications of a man's character to their root in his early life. Yet at times we feel as if we were listening to a lecture on psychology, and we notice that Lister is not nearly as good as Jane Austen at the dramatic portrayal of a character's development. In his earlier books Lister pays homage to Jane Austen by borrowing the names of some of her characters (Morton, Bingley, and even Maria Dashwood): in his last novel, *Arlington* (1832), he uses amateur theatricals in a country house to expose the characters of some of his principal personages in a manner that recalls *Mansfield Park*: while Julia Crawford, who is prepared to fall in with Beauchamp's plan that she should become his mistress by first marrying Arlington, is like a less intelligent cousin of Mary Crawford's. As usual, there are some melodramatic incidents in the plot: indeed the book opens like a detective story, with the discovery of the body of Lord Arlington, shot by an unknown hand. But although the mystery is not cleared up until the beginning of the third volume Lister's true concern is once again with the manners and morals of upper-class society, and the book contains some finely caught conversation and some shrewd observations on human character. It is characteristic of Lister to insist that Arlington's own character 'was not one of those which accommodate themselves to the antithetical mode of description. There were no striking contrasts, no startling incongruities, no well balanced portions of good and bad qualities,

none of those improbable co-existences which make up a character so striking upon paper, and so nearly impossible to be found.'
The worldling Denbigh, the Iago of the plot, is a considerable
creation. In his criticism of the times in which he lived, both in
this book and in its predecessors, Lister reveals himself as a very
shrewd observer, avoiding equally a facile optimism and a reactionary pessimism. He is anti-Old-Boy, anti-reactionary, and
above all anti-cant. Although the third volume of this last book
contains a good deal of intelligent discussion that seems irrelevant to the plot, it remains true that Lister is a man who deserves
to be remembered: he is notable equally as one of the very few
early and intelligent imitators of Jane Austen and as one of the
most able men to turn his attention to the novel in this period.

In *Arlington* a young man who is dancing with an unsophisticated girl, 'lately out', discovers

> that one of the subjects about which she was most anxious, was the
> internal construction of that unknown world of Fashion, which she
> had contemplated from a distance, and judged of, chiefly through
> the medium of books, written by some of the Mendez Pintoes of
> modern fiction, who, like their prototype, profess to describe regions
> which they have never trodden.

The essential characteristic of the Fashionable Novelists was
that their aim was to describe fashionable life for the benefit of
readers outside it, or on the fringes; and the most typical writer
of this class was Theodore Hook.[1] The first series of his *Sayings
and Doings*, which contained four tales, appeared in 1824, and
it proved so successful that Hook produced nearly a score of
other stories in the years that followed. Hook excels in the art of
making people outside feel that at last they are learning the
truth about people inside. Although it is a favourite trick of his
to make a couple of his characters join in deploring the inaccurate account of fashionable life given by the gossip-column-
ists, the picture that he himself presents is essentially of the same

---

[1] Theodore Edward Hook (1788–1841) was the son of the organist at Vauxhall
Gardens, who was a prolific composer and song-writer. As a boy at Harrow he
wrote words for his father's comic operas and melodramas. He early became a
friend of the Prince of Wales and was celebrated for his practical jokes and his gifts
as an improviser. In 1813 he was sent to Mauritius as accountant-general, but after
four years he was dismissed (perhaps unfairly) for deficiencies in the accounts. In
1820 he had begun to edit the Tory newspaper *John Bull*. He was a talented, disreputable man who wrote a great deal and served as the model for Lucian Gay in
Disraeli's *Coningsby* and Mr. Wagg in *Pendennis*.

sort. He flatters his readers by making them feel superior to
the common herd, while in fact he plays on the most vulgar
attitudes and prejudices—as when he informs us that a true
Dandy 'is a man who, dressing exceedingly well, without anything particularly *outré* about him, is well-informed, particularly *au fait* of what is going on, accomplished, unaffected,
gay, and agreeable; whose appointments, whether of person
or equipage, are resplendently fresh'—and so on. As Myron F.
Brightfield has pointed out, the plot of Hook's *Merton* (1824)
is similar in many ways to that of *Granby*; but one has only
to make the comparison to see the difference in intention and
value between the two books. Lister is seriously concerned
with human nature and with moral values, while Hook's
aim is simply to write an entertaining tale calculated to
appeal to the socially aspiring. His claim to give a true picture
of human life cannot be taken seriously: his books are essentially romances: in spite of the ubiquitous descriptions in his
work of the material paraphernalia of upper-class life it is a
mistake to use the word 'realism' of books like *Merton* and
Fathers and Sons. His tales have little structural unity, and
while he does occasionally seem serious (in some degree) in
the morals that he preaches, they are never more than a
secondary concern. There is a curious unreality about many
parts of his books: although he did in fact move in fashionable
society himself, his upper-class dialogue is often astonishingly
stilted. On occasion, it is true, he may catch the slang of a
couple of young Regency bucks; but his real flair is for homely
comedy or farce, while we also notice that he is sometimes
excellent in his descriptions of unpleasant people. In general it
must be admitted that his books have little literary merit; but
for the social historian they remain a mine of information,
while it is at least possible that Bulwer Lytton, whose *Pelham*
will be dealt with in the next volume of this *History*, was right
in attributing an unexpected influence to the fashionable
novelists as a class: 'Few writers', he wrote in *England and the
English*,

ever produced so great an effect on the political spirit of their generation as some of these novelists, who, without any other merit, un-
consciously exposed the falsehood, the hypocrisy, the arrogant and
vulgar insolence of patrician life. Read by all classes, in every town,
in every village, these works . . . could not but engender a mingled

indignation and disgust at the parade of frivolity, the ridiculous disdain of truth, nature, and mankind, the self-consequence and absurdity, which, falsely or truly, [they] exhibited as a picture of aristocratic society. The Utilitarians railed against them, and [yet] they were effecting with unspeakable rapidity the very purposes the Utilitarians desired. (Book IV, chap. ii.)

It would be difficult to find a greater contrast to Theodore Hook than Plumer Ward, whose first work of fiction, *Tremaine, or the Man of Refinement* (1825), appeared when he was sixty.[1] Ward's idea of the novel (when he admitted to writing novels: at times he protested against the name) was that, like History, it was 'Philosophy teaching by examples'. In the preface he acknowledges that he may be asked why he has 'recorded the series of retired scenes, and sometimes abstruse conversations, which compose the following narrative', and answers that it is because he hopes to be able to do some good. He is particularly concerned about the manners and morals of the middle class, fearing that the spread of luxury 'has undermined our independence, and left our virtue defenceless':

All would be Statesmen, Philosophers, or people of fashion. All, too, run to London. The woods and fields are unpeopled; the plain mansions and plain manners of our fathers deserted and changed; every thing is swallowed up by a devouring dissipation; and the simplicities of life are only to be found in books.

Not that Ward would counsel everyone to seek refuge in the country. One of the aims of his book, indeed, was to counter 'the very dangerous mistakes about solitude' for which he blamed Zimmermann, Byron, and 'the Swiss mountebank, Rousseau'. The trouble about *Tremaine*, which is a sort of literary equivalent of a vegetable marrow, is that it is extremely dull. After the first volume it becomes simply a very slow-moving love story, the only obstacle to the hero's happiness being that he has some doubts about Christianity. Practically the whole of the last volume is devoted to theological arguments in which

---

[1] Robert Plumer Ward (1765–1846) took his middle name in 1828. He was educated at Westminster and Christ Church, Oxford, and then travelled on the Continent. In 1790 he became a member of the Inner Temple. He wrote a great deal on legal and political questions, and was a strong supporter of Pitt. He was for many years a Member of Parliament, being at various times Under-Secretary for Foreign Affairs, a commissioner of the Admiralty, and clerk of the Ordnance.

his future father-in-law refutes the heresies by which Tremaine is tempted. Near the end Ward assures the reader that he dreads another argument 'for you as well as for myself' and the reader, for his part, is likely to become as 'silent and abstracted' as the hero of the book. If one of Ward's ancestors was Henry Mackenzie, another was Polonius. Few novels contain such long and tedious arguments: there is not even the element of drama that might result from a genuine confrontation of ideas. For a Fellow of Magdalen, Tremaine is remarkably deficient in dialectic power, and we can readily understand why one of his colleagues calls him 'little more than an illustrious mope'. What began as a novel to illustrate certain truths about Solitude and Society dwindles into a sentimental love story and drags to its conclusion as an exercise in Christian apologetics. 'Variety and incident are equally wanting', as the author disarmingly confesses: 'the Editor had almost said interest, but that his own feelings forbade'. The most dramatic thing that happens throughout these three volumes of the 'history of heart' is that the heroine scalds her pretty fingers when she spills a pot of tea, so giving Tremaine a chance to display his devoted gallantry. Little need be said of Ward's other books, *De Vere, or The Man of Independence* (1827) and *De Clifford, or The Constant Man* (1841). *De Vere* is a story of ambition and independence, set in the eighteenth century. *De Clifford*, which appeared when its author was over eighty, must have seemed laughably old-fashioned to readers of *Jane Eyre* and *Wuthering Heights*. Defending the 'many didactic digressions and episodes' in the book, Ward says that he cannot see how 'a novel which has for its object something more than the mere pictures of a magic-lanthorn, and aims at a knowledge of the springs of human nature, as well as amusement, can possibly realize that object without *partaking* of the didactic character'. Its theme is 'the impressions made by men and manners on a very young and unsophisticated mind, just starting into life, beginning even from his boyish days': a theme not wholly foreign to the interests of two writers as different from each other as Jane Austen and Dickens, but in this case totally unproductive of life or drama. When he reaches Volume IV the reader may well share the astonishment of the narrator on reflecting that he has only reached his hero's twenty-fifth year, in spite of the fact that he has not experienced any 'particular adventures'. The most that can be claimed for Ward today is a certain faded charm—although it must also be acknowledged that he influenced both Bulwer Lytton and Disraeli.

When he sent a copy of *Brambletye House* (1826) to Sir Walter Scott, Horace Smith, whose talent for the imitation of poetic styles had already been evident in the *Rejected Addresses*, confessed that his new book was merely 'a humble imitation of that style which [Scott] had so successfully introduced'. In fact *Brambletye House* appeared a few weeks before *Woodstock*, in which Scott himself tells a story of the Civil Wars; but there is no need to suspect direct influence: once the idea of the historical romance has become current, history is bound to be searched for periods rich in stirring events. It is not surprising to find, therefore, that Scott was reading Harrison Ainsworth's first book, *Sir John Chiverton*, which is set in the days of chivalry, at the same time as *Brambletye House*. The similarities between Horace Smith's romance and *Woodstock* are very striking: each is an adventure story, written to entertain and without any regard for probability or truth of characterization. In each the idea of the Cavaliers and Roundheads has something of *1066 and All That* about it, although Smith is a little less unfair to the Roundheads than Scott. Each abounds in sieges, scenes of flight and pursuit, disguises, and Wardour Street dialogue. The period of the Civil Wars as it is portrayed in these two books stands to historical time as the Forest of Arden in *As You Like It* stands to geographical place. Neither book invites, or deserves, serious criticism. Scott himself was obviously puzzled by the success of his imitators. In his *Journal* he differentiates between himself and them by saying that his own knowledge of history is greater, so that he does not need to get it up for a particular book and is thereby saved from the danger of dragging in details 'by head and shoulders'. To the modern reader the curious thing is to find the man of genius and the man of talent reduced to roughly equal terms. Encouraged by the success of his first romance, which 'hit the public taste' and went through several editions in the year of publication, Horace Smith produced *The Tor Hill*, which deals with the period of the Reformation, and went on to write a dozen more historical romances. In *The New Forest* he showed himself particularly aware of the importance of picturesque scenery as an element in the Scott-ish romance. Many scenes in this book are 'tinted with the rich harmonious hues that a painter loves', and everywhere we find 'dark vistas, athwart whose distant gloom the deer [are] occasionally seen to bound'. In the history of taste Smith's romances retain an interest which they have otherwise lost, and to the admirer of Scott it is interesting to compare *Waverley* and its successors with the romances of Mrs. Radcliffe, on the one hand, and with those of Horace Smith on the other. There is no better way of bringing out the greatness, and the originality, of Scott's earlier books, and in particular of *The Heart of Mid-Lothian*.

Each of the three Irish writers with whom this survey must end was also indebted to Scott in one way or another. The help which he gave Robert Maturin in having *Bertram* brought on the stage has already been mentioned in Chapter V, and he was similarly well disposed to Maturin's prose romances. Yet in spite of Scott's commendation we cannot linger over *The Fatal Revenge*, *The Wild Irish Boy*, or *The Milesian Chief*: if Maturin is remembered at all it is as the author of *Melmoth the Wanderer* (1820), a book which was praised by Thackeray, by Rossetti, and by Baudelaire, and which Balzac paid a double-edged compliment by writing a satirical sequel, *Melmoth Réconcilié à l'Église*. In the preface Maturin tells us that the idea of the romance came from the following passage in one of his own sermons:

At this moment is there one of us present, however we may have departed from the Lord, disobeyed his will, and disregarded his word—is there one of us who would, at this moment, accept all that man could bestow, or earth afford, to resign the hope of his salvation? —No, there is not one—not such a fool on earth, were the enemy of mankind to traverse it with the offer!

It is tempting to speculate about how such a subject would have been handled by the author of *The Confessions of a Justified Sinner*: Maturin handles it in a manner that makes it clear that he is not completely in earnest, and for an impression of the result we may turn to the notice published in the *Edinburgh Review* for July 1821:

It was said . . . of Dr. Darwin's Botanic Garden—that it was the sacrifice of Genius in the Temple of False Taste; and the remark may be applied to the work before us, with the qualifying clause, that in this instance the Genius is less obvious, and the false taste more glaring. . . . The imagination of the author runs riot, even beyond the usual license of romance . . . His hero is a modern Faustus, who has bartered his soul with the powers of darkness for protracted life, and unlimited worldly enjoyment;—his heroine, a species of insular goddess, a virgin Calypso of the Indian ocean, who, amid flowers and foliage, lives upon figs and tamarinds; associates with peacocks, loxias and monkeys; is worshipped by the occasional visitants of her island; finds her way to Spain, where she is married to the aforesaid hero by the hand of a dead hermit, the ghost of a murdered domestic being the witness of their nuptials; and finally dies in the dungeons of the Inquisition at Madrid!—To complete this phantasmagoric exhibition, we are presented with sybils and misers; parricides; maniacs in abundance; monks with scourges pursuing a naked youth streaming with blood; subterranean Jews surrounded by the skeletons of their wives and children; lovers blasted by lightning; Irish hags, Spanish grandees, shipwrecks, caverns, Donna Claras and Donna Isidoras,—all opposed to each other in glaring and violent contrast, and all their adventures narrated with the same undeviating display of turgid, vehement, and painfully elaborated language.

Exaggerated as this censure is, it is all in a sense true—yet beside the point, as if Dr. Leavis were to write a critique of *Ben Hur*. As we read *Melmoth* we sense that Maturin knew he was writing nonsense—and enjoyed it. The occasions on which the Wanderer visits those of his fellow creatures who have sunk to the depths of human misery, in the hope of persuading them to take over the terrible privilege of unending life, provide some powerful melodramatic scenes. The Indian girl Immalee captured the imagination of those of Maturin's contemporaries who were less censorious than the northern reviewers. The conclusion of the third volume may serve to give those who have not read the book some idea of its atmosphere:

Through the furze that clothed this rock, almost to its summit, there was a kind of tract as if a person had dragged, or been dragged,... through it—a downtrodden track, over which no footsteps but those of one impelled by force had ever passed. Melmoth and Monçada gained at last the summit of the rock. The ocean was underneath—the wide, waste, engulphing ocean! On a crag beneath them, something hung as floating to the blast. Melmoth clambered down and caught it. It was the handkerchief which the Wanderer had worn about his neck the preceding night—that was the last trace of the Wanderer!

Melmoth and Monçada exchanged looks of silent and unutterable horror, and returned slowly home.

Melmoth contradicts the usual rule that easy writing makes hard reading: we cannot doubt that it was easily written, yet in spite of the confusing plot and the sometimes careless syntax the book is remarkably easy to read, if one abandons one's mind to it. It is the sort of reading that the young Brontës delighted in. In the preface Maturin acknowledges that he has been charged with 'too much attempt at the revivification of the horrors of Radcliffe-Romance': what can be said for him is that he galvanized the corpse in such a way as to produce something that is almost impressive. 'With all his faults', as Edith Birkhead put it, 'Maturin was the greatest as well as the last of the Goths.' In the history of literature *Melmoth* counts for little: in the history of taste it remains a landmark.

John Banim, a Catholic from Kilkenny, was a man who had little in common with Maturin. His tedious tragedy, *Damon and Pythias*, was successfully produced at Dublin in 1821, under the ægis of Sheil; but it was the appearance of the first series of his *Tales by the O'Hara Family* four years later that revealed his genuine talent. Encouraged by the example of Maria Edgeworth and of Scott, he wished to help bring about 'the formation of a good and affectionate feeling' between his native country and England. His merits and faults are well revealed in 'Crohoore', which is set in an Ireland very different from that presented by Maria Edgeworth. In this tale and elsewhere, as Thomas Flanagan has written in his pioneering study, *The Irish Novelists, 1800–1850*, Banim

was faced with the task of writing about a bloody and violent land, in which justice was measured out by hanging judges and packed juries, and exacted by the loaded whips of squireens and the brandings and mutilations of secret societies. But there no longer existed in English fiction conventions by which such a society could be represented. In default, he accepted the conventions of the shilling shocker.

The best of his tales is 'The Nowlans'. At first he intended to write a *roman à thèse* about an evangelical movement known as the New Reformation and supported by English people who were dangerously ignorant of Irish life and character, but fortunately he changed the direction of the book and the finest passages are those which have least relevance to the original theme. His study of a Catholic priest who falls in love and breaks his vows by marrying is admirably done, as is the

account of the Protestant family with whom he and his wife
find lodgings:

> No charity was in the house, nor in a heart in the house. In the
> face of all professed beggars the street door was slammed without
> a word, but with a scowl calculated to wither the heart of the wretched
> suitor; and with respect to such as strove to hide the profession under
> barrel-organs, flutes, flageolets, hurdy-gurdies, or the big drum and
> pandean pipes, their tune was, indeed, listened to but never re-
> quited. . . . But nothing irked him so much as the ostentatious
> triumph over starvation, the provoking assumption of comfort, nay,
> elegance, as it were, and the audacious independence which resulted
> from the whole economy.

The description of the girls of the household—who 'gave no
idea of flesh and blood. They never looked as if they were warm,
or soft to the touch. One would as soon think of flirting with
them, as with the old wooden effigies to be found in the niches
of cathedrals'—might have won the approval of James Joyce.
Banim's historical romances are of less account, though *The
Boyne Water* shows an intelligent application of Scott's technique of contrast and picturesque description to the different
opportunities provided by Irish history and character.

In 1823 Banim behaved with characteristic kindliness to a
young compatriot who arrived in London full of literary ambition. Gerald Griffin was the more gifted man of the two, and
he disapproved strongly of the way in which Irish life had been
presented in the *Tales by the O'Hara Family*. His aim, as he tells
us in the preface to *Holland-Tide* (1827), was to produce something true to life and 'illustrative of manners and scenery
precisely as they stand in the South of Ireland', and the book
consists of a series of tales told to that end. In the same year
Griffin published his *Tales of the Munster Festivals*, and then with
The Collegians in 1829 (which constituted the second series of the
Tales) he produced the work by which he is still remembered.
The germ of the story was a murder which had recently attracted
attention; but Griffin transformed his material by setting his
tale in the period of his father's youth, the 1770's, and using it
as a means of exploring the structure and the dilemmas of Irish
life at that time. The charming yet ultimately ruthless Hardress
Cregan seduces Eily O'Connor, deserts her, and has her murdered. Although the girl, a rope-maker's daughter, is not very

vividly drawn, her seducer becomes an admirable symbol for one of the most characteristic aspects of Irish life. As Flanagan has commented, Cregan

is invested with a kind of kingliness, but beneath his graces and powers lie the terror and the ruthlessness of a child. He has come to manhood in a society in which religion has decayed into social ritual—'the genteel religion'—and law into an extension of social privilege. What matters is *code*, that emptiest of moral patterns, which had become synonymous with honor. It had carried him successfully through balls and drinking bouts, duels and hunts. But, for the moral choice which lies at the novel's core, it has left him stripped of every weapon save the knife in the hand of Danny the Lord.

It is a revealing comment on the difficulty of writing serious fiction at this time that Griffin was persuaded to change his intended ending: instead of being hanged Cregan is sentenced to transportation, and dies on the voyage. Yet the conclusion, in which he looks for the last time at his native place, is admirably managed:

He turned, with an aching heart, from the contemplation of the landscape, and his eye encountered a spectacle more accordant to his present feelings. The row of houses which lined the quay on which the party halted, consisted for the most part of coffin-makers' shops, a gloomy trade, although, to judge by the reckless faces of the workmen, it would appear that 'custom had made it with them a property of easiness'.

Only one of those dismal houses of traffic was open at this early hour, and the light which burned in the interior showed that the proprietor was called to the exercise of his craft at this unseasonable time by some sudden and pressing call. The profession of the man was not indicated, as in more wealthy and populous cities, by a sculptured lid, or gilded and gaudy hatchment, suspended at a window-pane. A pile of the unfinished shells, formed for all ages from childhood to maturity, were thrust out at the open window, to attract the eye of the relatives of the newly-dead.

IX

HAZLITT

'ESSAY on the Principles of Human Action, sm. 8vo.—The Eloquence of the Brit. Senate, 2v. 8vo. 1808.—A new and improved Engl. Grammar, 18mo. 1810.' Such is the entry under Hazlitt's name in *A Biographical Dictionary of the Living Authors*, published in 1816, and it may serve as a reminder that the man we remember as a great critic and essayist came rather late to both these arts.[1] It was not until the year after the appearance of the *Dictionary* that he published his first volume of criticism and his first collection of essays. Before that time he was generally known only as a writer on philosophical and political topics and a contributor to the *Examiner*. If he had been less deeply interested in philosophy and politics he would have been a less penetrating critic of the writers of his time. And since his political views accompanied him everywhere—as John Scott pointed out—like a large dog, something must be said about them at the outset.

His father had supported the cause of American independence and was a friend of Dr. Price, the preacher of a celebrated sermon in praise of the French Revolution. Hazlitt's own first publication was a letter to a newspaper defending another friend of his father's, Dr. Priestley, who was the presiding genius at Hackney College until he was compelled to emigrate in 1794. While he himself was still studying there Hazlitt planned a *Project for a New Theory of Civil and Criminal Legislation*

---

[1] William Hazlitt (1778–1830) was the son of a Unitarian minister who had become an acquaintance of Benjamin Franklin's during the latter's visit to England. Although he himself was educated for the ministry he felt an aversion from such a life and left Hackney College about 1795. He heard Coleridge's last sermon, and visited him at Stowey in 1798. He was one of the earliest admirers of Wordsworth's poetry, but in 1803 Wordsworth and his circle broke with him on account of a moral lapse on Hazlitt's part. At this point he was studying painting, and in 1804 he painted his well-known portrait of Lamb as a Venetian Senator. Four years later he married Sarah Stoddart, obtaining a divorce in 1822. In 1824, after the infatuation described in *Liber Amoris*, he married a Mrs. Bridgwater, but she soon left him, probably in 1827. He lived by writing and lecturing. Throughout his life Lamb remained his constant friend.

which he took up again towards the end of his life. When he surveyed his own life in 1827 he saw clearly that the event which had done most to form it had been the French Revolution, which broke out when he was a boy of ten. 'I set out in life with the French Revolution', as he wrote in his essay 'On the Feeling of Immortality in Youth', 'a. d that event had considerable influence on my early feelings. . . . It was the dawn of a new era. . . . Little did I dream . . . that long before my eyes should close, that dawn would be overcast, and set once more in the night of despotism.' Whereas most English sympathizers with the revolutionaries lived to change their opinions, Hazlitt remained constant, by and large, to his early loyalties. He was a disapproving auditor of the lecture in which James Mackintosh, the author of *Vindiciæ Gallicæ*, made his recantation, and viewed with distrust the shifting opinions of Wordsworth, Coleridge, and Southey. He was a brilliant man, yet (as he was later to admit) he was in a sense 'no politician'. As his contributions to the *Morning Chronicle* and the *Examiner* make clear, his approach to politics was at once highly theoretical and highly emotional. He was a child of the Enlightenment, and the infamous thing that he hated was compounded of 'the Pope, the Inquisition, the Bourbons, and the doctrine of Divine Right'. For him Napoleon was simply the man who had set his foot on the neck of kings. After Waterloo, we are told, Hazlitt 'seemed prostrated in mind and body': he hated tyranny and loved freedom, and in the years that followed it seemed to him that tyranny was triumphing throughout Europe. He could not understand how a people who had executed one king and banished another could talk as Southey and the Tories were talking of the Divine Right of Kings. He once described himself as a Jacobin or Old Whig: his landmarks were Locke's *Treatise on Government* and the Glorious Revolution of 1688. The mystical Toryism of Coleridge repelled him because he felt that the clouds of eloquence concealed a lack of clarity and a lack of honesty. He wrote against Malthus, whose *Essay on the Principle of Population* was enjoying a great vogue amongst the conservatives, because he was appalled by the doctrine that it is idle to attempt to improve the condition of mankind. Intellectually, it is true, he came to believe that 'all things move, not in progress, but in a ceaseless round; our strength lies in our weakness; our virtues are built on our vices; our faculties are as limited as our being; nor can we lift man above his nature more than above the earth he treads': yet emotionally he was always to remain true to 'that bright dream of our youth'. When he collected his *Political Essays* in 1819 it was characteristic of him to dedicate them defiantly to John Hunt, 'the tried, steady, zealous, and conscientious advocate of the liberty of his country, and the rights of mankind'. Near the end of his life he was to write his *Life of Napoleon* and to rejoice in the final overthrow of the Bourbons.

The *Memoirs of the late Thomas Holcroft*, finished in 1810 though not published until 1816, represent the transition from Hazlitt's political period to that of his essays and literary criticism. Dramatist, novelist, and radical, Holcroft had associated with Thelwall and Horne Tooke and the members of the Society for Constitutional Information and had been indicted in connexion with the trial of 1794. Hazlitt was asked to build a book on the autobiography which Holcroft had left unfinished; what he did was to follow the model of Mason's *Memoirs of Gray*, piecing together letters, diaries, and the reminiscences of his subject's other friends. The result is a biography that throws a good deal of light on a critical period in our intellectual history. In 1817 it was followed by *The Round Table* and *Characters of Shakespear's Plays*, which mark the opening of Hazlitt's major period. It will be convenient to concentrate first on his critical writings, and then to consider his work as an essayist.

Although *Characters of Shakespear's Plays* remains one of Hazlitt's best-known books, it does not represent his criticism at its best. The volume is dedicated to Charles Lamb, and throughout it Hazlitt remains a follower of Lamb's. He makes little attempt to divine the principal theme of each play; nor does he write with reference to dramatic production. By concentrating on the characters rather than the plays themselves he too often ignores the whole in favour of the part. He does not, indeed, analyse any of the characters in detail—as Maurice Morgann and others had begun to do in the previous century. What he does is to quote liberally from each play and discuss it in general terms. If the result sometimes reminds us of a collection of *Beauties of Shakespeare*, we must in justice remember that Hazlitt was reacting against the eighteenth century's tendency to condemn Shakespeare for violating rules which have in fact no relevance to his plays. Hazlitt has entered Shakespeare's universe, and is content to take it on its own terms. When he was reviewing Schlegel's *Lectures on Dramatic Literature* he had suggested that German scholars are apt to write 'not because they are full of a subject, but because they think it is a subject upon which . . . something striking may be written'. Hazlitt was full of his subject, and wrote with enthusiasm. The result is a book that contains some brilliant passages, and which has helped to introduce a great many readers to the greatest of all our poets.

The treatment of Shakespeare in *Lectures on the English Poets* (1818), the first of the three series of lectures in which Hazlitt covered the central tract of our literary history, is in many ways superior to anything in the previous volume. Although he often opposes views which he believes to be mistaken, yet the *Lectures* as a whole do not show such a revolt from the criticism of the previous century as some might expect. Half of the space is devoted to the eighteenth century: Pope's poetry is nobly praised (as is Swift's), and while Hazlitt thinks more highly of Collins than did Johnson, he follows Johnson in praising Gray's *Elegy* while censuring the 'kind of methodical borrowed phrenzy' of the odes. He agrees with the common reader in a high estimation of Thomson, and opposes the fashionable 'cant . . . about genius'. Keats was one of a number among his audience who were annoyed by his treatment of Chatterton. Apart from Shakespeare, Spenser is the only Elizabethan discussed, while Donne and his followers are virtually ignored. But it is when he comes to the living poets that Hazlitt is most interesting. After conventional praise of 'the female writers of the present day' he moves in to an attack on the very popular Rogers and Campbell, in whose work 'the decomposition of prose is substituted for the composition of poetry'. Moore is let off more lightly, while Byron and Scott receive treatment which is severe but not unfair. It is when he reaches Wordsworth that we feel that Hazlitt's interest is most deeply aroused. He has delayed dealing with him as long as he can, and we sense an embarrassment that is due to the tension between his personal feelings and his critical appreciation. To survey Hazlitt's criticisms of Wordsworth, here and elsewhere, is to watch a great critic rising superior to political disagreements and personal resentment. He praises him highly, insisting that the most successful of his poems 'open a finer and deeper vein of thought and feeling than any poet in modern times has done, or attempted';

and although he believes that Wordsworth 'cannot form a whole . . . has not the constructive faculty . . . is totally deficient in all the machinery of poetry', he also insists that 'he has produced a deeper impression, and on a smaller circle, than any other of his contemporaries'. Having spoken out magnanimously in this way for a man whose 'powers have been mistaken by the age', Hazlitt permits himself to conclude the lecture with a semi-satirical account of 'that which has been denominated the Lake school of poetry', whose origins he traces to the French Revolution and the influence of translations from German literature:

> All was to be natural and new. Nothing that was established was to be tolerated. All the common-place figures of poetry, tropes, allegories, personifications, with the whole heathen mythology, were instantly discarded. . . . Rhyme was looked upon as a relic of the feudal system, and regular metre was abolished along with regular government.

As we read this critique we are reminded of Johnson on 'the metaphysical poets':

> The paradox they set out with was, that all things are by nature equally fit subjects for poetry; or that . . . the meanest and most unpromising are the best. . . . They claimed kindred only with the commonest of the people: peasants, pedlars, and village-barbers. . . . They were for bringing poetry back to its primitive simplicity and state of nature.

Although Southey and Coleridge are mentioned at the end, it is of Wordsworth that Hazlitt is thinking most of the time. The contrast between Wordsworth and Shakespeare that is implied throughout is the origin of Keats's phrase 'the egotistical sublime': we notice that when Hazlitt is discussing Wordsworth the word 'egotism' is never far away.

The contents of *The English Comic Writers* (1819) include a surprisingly wide range of authors: Elizabethan, Restoration and eighteenth-century dramatists, poets of the early seventeenth century, and essayists and novelists of the eighteenth century: while a lecture on Hogarth is thrown in for good measure. Taken together, Lectures II, IV and VIII constitute a fairly comprehensive account of English comedy from the Elizabethan period to the end of the eighteenth century. The comparison of Shakespeare and Jonson is well managed: in spite of his admission that he 'cannot much relish Ben Jonson' Hazlitt contrasts his type of comedy with Shakespeare's very justly. On Wycherley, Congreve, Vanbrugh, and Farquhar he writes perceptively and *con amore*, while his account of Jeremy Collier, 'this sour, non-juring critic', may be read as a spirited defence of comedy.

When he reaches Donne and his followers in the third lecture, Hazlitt contents himself for the most part with quoting from Johnson; but when he comes to *Hudibras*, 'the greatest single production of wit of this period, I might say of this country', his enthusiasm is kindled and the result is the most brilliant discussion of the poem in English criticism.

It is when he is dealing with prose writers, and particularly with novelists, that Hazlitt is at his best in this volume. His account of the essayists of the early eighteenth century is admirable, and has a particular interest because it is the criticism of a later master of the form. He is excellent on the *Tatler* and the *Spectator*, decidedly preferring the former, and though he is severe on the *Rambler* and its author—*Rasselas* is described as 'the most melancholy and debilitating moral speculation that ever was put forth'—there is something fine about his description of Johnson's prejudices:

His were not time-serving, heartless, hypocritical prejudices; but deep, inwoven, not to be rooted out but with life and hope, which he found from old habit necessary to his own peace of mind, and thought so to the peace of mankind. I do not hate, but love him for them.

When he reaches the novelists of the eighteenth century Hazlitt rises to his opportunity. As he himself points out, 'this is a department of criticism which deserves more attention than has been usually bestowed upon it'. Almost a century after the publication of *Pamela* there was still no authoritative discussion of the major novelists by a competent critic. It is true that Dunlop's *History of Prose Fiction* had appeared in 1814, but when he reviewed it Hazlitt pointed out its deficiency in the 'spirit of philosophic enquiry' and in 'critical acuteness'. He himself begins with a brief discussion of the nature of the novel, and says something about *Don Quixote* and other Spanish novels which may be regarded as naturalized British subjects.

Then he comes to Fielding. Although he devotes only a few
pages to the author of *Tom Jones*, no one had written so ably
about him before; and his comparison of Fielding and Smollett
may serve to show his genuine understanding of both men:

> What then is it that gives the superiority to Fielding? It is the
> superior insight into the springs of human character, and the con-
> stant developement of that character through every change of circum-
> stance. Smollett . . . seldom probes to the quick, or penetrates beyond
> the surface. . . . We read *Roderick Random* as an entertaining story . . .
> but we regard *Tom Jones* as a real history. . . . Smollett excels most as
> the lively caricaturist: Fielding as the exact painter and profound
> metaphysician.

The account of Richardson (one of the last writers one might
have expected to find in this volume) is in no way inferior to
that of Fielding. 'There is an artificial reality about his works',
Hazlitt remarks, 'which is no where else to be met with. They
have the romantic air of a pure fiction, with the literal minuteness of a common diary. The author had the strongest matter-
of-fact imagination that ever existed.' 'If the business of life
consisted in letter-writing'—Hazlitt says later in the lecture—
'and was carried on by the post (like a Spanish game at chess),
human nature would be what Richardson represents it.' Sterne
is more briefly dealt with—Uncle Toby being described as 'one
of the finest compliments ever paid to human nature'—and we
hear something of Fanny Burney, Mrs. Radcliffe, Godwin, and
Sir Walter Scott. The absence of Jane Austen from the gallery
of novelists is regrettable, though hardly surprising; but even
this gap cannot conceal the fact that Hazlitt here proves himself far and away the best critic of the English novelists up to his
time.

Having had his say on Shakespeare and most of our main
writers since the Restoration, Hazlitt chose *The Dramatic Literature of the Age of Elizabeth* for his next series of published lectures
(1820). Here he is often dealing with writers whom he knew
less well, and his primary intention is to introduce unfamiliar
books to his audience:

> What I have undertaken to do . . . is merely to read over a set
> of authors with the audience, as I would do with a friend, to point
> out a favourite passage, to explain an objection; or if a remark or

a theory occurs, to state it in illustration of the subject, but neither
to tire him nor puzzle myself with pedantic rules and pragmatical
formulas of criticism that can do no good to any body.... In a word,
I have endeavoured to feel what was good, and to 'give a reason for
the faith that was in me'.

Accordingly he takes us on a conducted tour of such writers
as Lyly, Marlowe, Heywood, Middleton, Rowley, Marston,
Chapman, Dekker, and many others, quoting liberally 'to
make these old writers . . . vouchers for their own pretensions'.
For better or for worse one finds the germs of many historical
commonplaces in this book, such as the misleading view that
'a rage for French rules and French models' did untold harm
to our literature after the Restoration. As we read these lectures we are often reminded of Charles Lamb, as we are when
Hazlitt quotes Johnson's remark that such writers 'were sought
after because they were scarce, and would not have been scarce
had they been much esteemed' and counters by saying that this is
'neither true history nor sound criticism'. Like Lamb, Hazlitt
is here in search of good passages rather than good plays; but
occasionally he breaks away from mere appreciation, as when
he differs from Lamb about a passage in Ford's *Broken Heart* or
censures the 'craving after striking effect' and the artificiality
of Beaumont and Fletcher.

In the sixth and seventh lectures Hazlitt leaves the drama
altogether and says something of the poetry of Drummond of
Hawthornden, Herrick, and Marvell—'To his Coy Mistress'
being given *in toto*. He then discusses four prose writers: Sidney,
Bacon, Sir Thomas Browne, and Jeremy Taylor. The account
of Bacon is in his best manner, and deserves to stand beside that
'perpetual model of encomiastick criticism' (as Johnson called
it), Dryden's character of Shakespeare. It is more brilliant and
pointed than the essay on Bacon's philosophy in the *Literary
Remains*, yet like it could only have been written by a critic who
took Bacon's thought seriously. In the eighth lecture Hazlitt
returns to the drama, alluding to Lamb, Sheil, and 'Barry
Cornwall' as modern writers 'who have imbibed the spirit and
imitated the language of our elder dramatists' and then attempting to distinguish four schools of tragedy: the classical, the
Gothic or romantic, 'the French or commonplace rhetorical
style', and 'the German or paradoxical style'. Hazlitt makes
some excellent points, and it is hardly his fault that his

categories sometimes proved more influential than they deserved. His account of the 'German' species of tragedy, in which the characters are 'mouth-pieces...of certain extravagant speculative opinions', is surprisingly severe. 'It embodies', he says,'. . . the extreme opinions which are floating in our time, and which have struck their roots deep and wide below the surface of the public mind.'

It is fortunate that Hazlitt did not content himself with the fragmentary treatment of his contemporaries in his earlier books. In 1825 he published *The Spirit of the Age*, which represents him at the summit of his powers as a critic. If the first condition of good criticism is that the critic must be passionately interested in the work which he is considering, then Hazlitt was ideally fitted to criticize the writers dealt with in this brilliant volume. Some, like Godwin and Coleridge, had been the masters of his youth: others had been his associates in writing: while others, like Gifford and Southey, had been and remained his enemies and detractors. In dealing with such men Hazlitt was at once writing his spiritual autobiography and holding up a mirror to the age. There is not a slack page from the beginning to the end, not a sentence which suggests boredom or indifference. Whether he is dealing with the economic theories of Malthus or the metaphysics of Coleridge, Hazlitt writes with passion and conviction. It follows that we are not to expect an academic impartiality: he is writing as the supporter of some of his subjects and the bitter opponent of others. Yet he writes also as a critic whose flair for good writing is so unfailing that he is incapable of denying it wherever he meets it. As he says in the fifth of his *Lectures on the Age of Elizabeth*: 'Anger may sharpen our insight into men's defects; but nothing should make us blind to their excellences.'

The critical method is unusual. It is not the individual book or poem that is the unit of consideration, but the writer himself. Yet we are not given a great deal of biographical information. It is true that the appearance of the writer is often described—and when this is done we notice that Hazlitt has a painter's eye for detail and picturesque effect. But we are never given description for description's sake. At times one is reminded of the Prologue to *The Canterbury Tales*: external details are used as pointers to character—and particularly to the character of an author's writings. We come to see that

Hazlitt does not concern himself with an author apart from his writings: he sees in him the man who wrote his books, and even details of personal description turn out to be relevant. 'Mr. Bentham', we are told, '. . . turns wooden utensils in a lathe for exercise, and fancies he can turn men in the same manner.'

What Hazlitt has done is to invent a new kind of 'character' writing. Drawing on his knowledge of the 'characters' which may be found in the literature of the seventeenth and eighteenth centuries he has evolved a new species of literary character in which the subject is neither the author as an individual nor his writings regarded in themselves, but the author as an author, in his works, and as a representative of the *Zeitgeist*. The enormous penultimate sentence of the chapter on Scott is an inspired variation of Pope's 'Atticus', and it was clearly from the writers of the previous century that Hazlitt learned how to use antithesis with such telling effect as he does when he says of Cobbett that 'his principle is repulsion, his nature contradiction: he is made up of mere antipathies, an Ishmaelite indeed without a fellow'. There is nothing affected about the style: it forms the fitting expression of a brilliantly analytic critic who has long reflected on the subjects about which he is writing. At times he carries conciseness to its logical limits, and the result is a strong element of wit—wit which is always used for a purpose, as when Hazlitt remarks that Bentham's writings 'have been translated into French—they ought to be translated into English'. Yet some of his most telling passages are written in a more relaxed style, like the second sentence of the chapter on Gifford:

The low-bred, self-taught man, the pedant, and the dependant on the great contribute to form the Editor of the *Quarterly Review*. He is admirably qualified for this situation, which he has held for some years, by a happy combination of defects, natural and acquired; and in the event of his death, it will be difficult to provide him a suitable successor.

That is murder committed with words—though in the case of Gifford most courts would accept a plea of manslaughter.

Perhaps the wit of *The Spirit of the Age* has led some readers to underestimate its value as criticism. If so it is they who have been the losers. It is true that in this book certain of the critic's tasks are not attempted, certain of his techniques left unemployed: the formal *critique* is avoided, while theoretical problems are set to one side. The grammar and groundwork of criticism are taken for granted, not because they are too difficult but because they have now been relegated to the background: we are being presented with findings, the conclusions of a lifetime's reflection. It is as if Hazlitt had written a book on each of these men, but presented us only with the final chapter, the summing-up of it all.

When we survey Hazlitt's criticism as a whole we are bound to be impressed by its wide range. In the drama he deals (though often very sketchily) with most of the principal landmarks from *Gammer Gurton's Needle* onwards. In the field of poetry he writes illuminatingly on Chaucer, Spenser, and most of our later poets, although he devotes comparatively little attention to Donne and his followers. In prose he not only deals excellently with the essayists and novelists of the eighteenth century: he also provides perceptive treatments, sometimes in unexpected places, of the Authorized Version (*The Age of Elizabeth*, I), Bunyan (*English Poets*, I), Sidney's *Arcadia*, Bacon, Sir Thomas Browne and Jeremy Taylor (*The Age of Elizabeth*, VI–VII). When it is remembered that there was no comprehensive History of English Literature in his day, or for more than half a century later, the twofold importance of Hazlitt's work becomes apparent. He is not only a major critic, a worthy successor to Dryden and Johnson, as surely excelling Coleridge in the practice of criticism as he is excelled by him in discussion of critical theory: he is also a key figure in literary historiography. Starting, virtually, where Warton had left off, he deals with most of the principal writers of the seventeenth and eighteenth centuries, as well as with those of his own age. The result is that his critical writings, which contain hardly a single date, have been one of the principal source-books on which literary historians have always relied.

He could scarcely have been born at a better time. As a contemporary of Wordsworth and Coleridge, he shared their early hopes for the future of mankind, so that there was no danger of his failing to understand the aspirations of his own generation. Political estrangement, on the other hand, ensured that he would not fall into uncritical enthusiasm of their work, and as a result his criticism has a sharp edge. His sympathy with the new currents in literature also put him in a favourable position for reviewing the history of English literature as a whole from the standpoint of the new age. Although he was not greatly interested in medieval literature, he shared the new enthusiasm for the Elizabethans for which the way had been prepared by scholars like Farmer and Malone. His attitude to eighteenth-century literature is particularly interesting: his emphases and judgements differ a good deal from Johnson's, yet he is free from the tendency of many of his contemporaries to make up for exaggerated praise by exaggerated censure. He complains that 'it is mortifying to hear [Wordsworth] speak of Pope and Dryden whom, because they have been supposed to have all the possible excellences of poetry, he will allow to have none'. He once accused Lamb of reading nothing after the *Spectator*: no one could make the same charge against himself. It is clear that he relished the opportunity of revaluing Augustan literature from a new vantage ground, being stimulated by the rich deposits of anecdote and historical material which were being published during his lifetime. By avoiding the merely partisan and acknowledging merit wherever he found it he became, in effect, the first critical historian of our literature, the first man to sketch out a picture of English literary history in which the rules of perspective are decently observed.

It is now time to consider his work as an essayist. Most of the essays collected in *The Round Table* were originally published in the *Examiner*. Leigh Hunt had proposed a series of papers in the manner of the *Tatler* and the *Spectator*, undertaking as his own share 'the characteristic or dramatic part of the work'; but in the event Hazlitt wrote most of the essays. Although other influences may also be noticed, the main model is undoubtedly the eighteenth-century essay. Like the essayists of the eighteenth century Hazlitt devotes a proportion of his space to literary criticism—'Lycidas', Milton's Versification, *John Buncle*—and like them he deals with such general topics as 'The Love of Life', 'Patriotism', and 'Religious Hypocrisy'. Even in these early essays, however, he is less didactic than Addison and Steele: the opening sentence of the first essay—'It is our intention ... to expose certain vulgar errors'—does not represent the general tone of the collection. And in other ways he differs from his famous predecessors: he does not concern himself with manners in the narrower sense: humour is not one of his main ingredients: while he never gives the impression of writing for 'the fair sex'.

In *The Round Table* we see Hazlitt developing his characteristic type of essay from eighteenth-century models: in *Table-
Talk* (1821–2) and *The Plain Speaker* (1826), and such uncollected essays as 'My First Acquaintance with Poets', we find
it fully evolved. Most of these essays are three or four times as
long as their predecessors. In them (to quote from the admirable discussion of essay-writing in *The English Comic Writers*) the
writer applies

the talents and resources of the mind to all that mixed mass of human
affairs, which, though not included under the head of any regular
art, science, or profession, falls under the cognizance of the writer,
and 'comes home to the business and bosoms of men'. . . . [He] makes
familiar with the world of men and women, records their actions,
assigns their motives, exhibits their whims, characterises their pursuits
in all their singular and endless variety, ridicules their absurdities,
exposes their inconsistencies.

The essay 'is in morals and manners what the experimental is
in natural philosophy, as opposed to the dogmatical method'.
Today the essay is dying, and the reason is that we have an
exaggerated faith in 'specialists': it flourishes in periods in
which there is a belief in wisdom, and in the wise man. The
task of the essayist is to collect the fruit of his experience, reflect
on it, and set it out for our consideration. 'I endeavour to
recollect all I have ever observed or thought upon a subject',
Hazlitt remarks, 'and to express it as nearly as I can.' His
grandson tells us that he would use every scrap of paper that
came to hand for 'heads of contemplated essays on "Men and
Manners"'—and sometimes resorted to writing down his ideas
'over the mantelpiece in lead-pencil'. Today we are more
likely to find the fruits of this type of reflection in a novel
than in an essay. If we turn from a psychologist's account of
jealousy or frustration with a feeling of dissatisfaction, we
may find in *A Passage to India* or *Elders and Betters* a profounder
commentary on the matter. Hazlitt's method, however, is not
dramatic: his aim is rather to combine the advantages of a set
inquiry into a given topic with those of an informal discussion
with his friends. As he wrote in the 'Advertisement' to the
Paris edition of *Table-Talk*, explaining the title:

I had remarked that when I had written or thought upon a particular topic, and afterwards had occasion to speak of it with a friend, the
conversation generally took a much wider range, and branched off

into a number of indirect and collateral questions, which were not
strictly connected with the original view of the subject, but which
often threw a curious and striking light upon it, or upon human
life in general. It therefore occurred to me as possible to combine the
advantages of . . . the *literary* and *conversational*; or after stating and
enforcing some leading idea, to follow it up by such observations and
reflections as would probably suggest themselves in discussing the
same question in company with others. This seemed to me to promise a greater variety and richness, and perhaps a greater sincerity,
than could be attained by a more precise and scholastic method. The
same consideration had an influence on the familiarity and conversational idiom of the style which I have used.

In spite of the informality of the method, the inquiries which
Hazlitt pursues are essentially serious. Although he is not
'precise and scholastic', he includes within his scope 'subtle
distinctions and trains of thought'. The underlying subject of
all his writings is the subject of the most abstruse of his books,
An Essay on the Principles of Human Action: for all their eloquence
and charm, his essays are the work of a man trained in philosophical speculation. His first course of lectures dealt with
English Philosophy, and everywhere he writes as the pupil of
Bacon, of Locke, and of Hume. Few men have better understood the tyranny that words exercise over our lives and
thoughts. 'The history of politics, of religion, of literature, of
morals, and of private life', as he once wrote, 'is too often little
more than the history of nicknames.' The essays 'On Vulgarity
and Affectation' and 'On Means and Ends' are examples of his
admirable anxiety to define with the greatest possible clarity. As
in his style he is the heir of much that is best in the prose writers
of the seventeenth and eighteenth centuries, so in his thought he
is the heir of the Age of Reason. He moves amongst abstract
ideas with an ease and familiarity that contrast oddly with
Lamb. Lamb wrote on chimney-sweeps, the South-Sea House,
weddings, and whist: Hazlitt wrote 'On Reason and Imagination', 'On Egotism', 'On the Past and Future'. His essays are
more serious than Lamb's, or serious in a different sense. Interested as he is in the essay as a form, he is more interested
in the truth which he is pursuing. He was a man of letters in
the comprehensive sense in which Johnson and Coleridge were
men of letters.

Yet Hazlitt was no friend to the 'theoretical *mania*'. Unlike the philosopher or the theoretical psychologist, the essayist limits himself to illustrating the workings of the human mind as they have fallen under his own observation. And since the only mind of which we have direct experience is our own, the essayist is bound in some degree to be personal and autobiographical. 'My object is to paint the varieties of human nature', as Hazlitt acknowledges in his essay 'On Means and Ends', 'and . . . I can have it best from myself.' It is ironical that he so often accuses Wordsworth of 'egotism', for in this respect there is an affinity between the two men. Earlier epic poets had written about the actions of mythical heroes: Wordsworth, taking 'the mind of man' as his subject, is inevitably autobiographical. Hazlitt stands to earlier essayists rather as Wordsworth stands to earlier epic poets. Rousseau is not the least important of his ancestors. Such essays as 'My First Acquaintance with Poets', 'The Conversation of Authors', and 'On the Pleasure of Painting' are in fact chapters of autobiography. In the fine essay 'On the Feeling of Immortality in Youth' Hazlitt tells us that he has 'turned for consolation to the past, gathering up the fragments of my early recollections, and putting them into a form that might live'. It is possible that he was thinking of writing an autobiography—and quite conceivable that, if he had, the result would have been the greatest in the language. It would not only have been a masterpiece in itself, but also a testament on behalf of all those who 'set out in life with the French Revolution', only to find their extravagant hopes disappearing like the morning mist.

If part of Hazlitt's autobiography had dealt with his fortunes in love, it might have contained the least successful chapters. It is strange that his most sustained piece of autobiography should be as weak a production as the *Liber Amoris* (1823). This description of his infatuation with the daughter of his landlord is a classic example of the folly of a literary man in love. It is pathetic to see a man of Hazlitt's great powers going through 'a sort of purgatory' on account of a lodging-house jilt. We are reminded of his pitiful vulnerability: as Keats realized, he thought that no one valued him. He was 'a very child in love'— and he knew it. While it is not surprising that he should have written an account of the affair to get it out of his system, it is remarkable that a man with such critical powers should have published the result. Those whom the gods wish to drive mad, they first deprive of their sense of humour. *Liber Amoris* reads like a version of *Shamela* narrated by 'the young Squire': it is astonishing to reflect that it was written at almost the same time as *Table-Talk*.

Such essays as 'The Indian Jugglers' and 'On Living to One's Self' in that collection seem so naturally written that we are in danger of overlooking the pains that Hazlitt devoted to the perfection of his style. He refers to himself as a prose-writer with the pride of a professional. To him the writing of prose was as serious a matter—as challenging a problem—as the writing of verse. This is made clear when he discusses 'The Prose-Style of Poets'. The prose of poets lacks 'momentum' and 'elasticity', since they are in the habit of relying on metre to gain such effects. It also tends to draw attention to itself. 'The poetical prose-writer stops to describe an object, if he admires it', whereas 'the genuine prose-writer only alludes to . . . it in passing, and with reference to his subject'. The prose-writer's aim should be 'truth, force of illustration, weight of argument': his tone should be that of 'lively, sensible conversation'. Hazlitt's strictures on Coleridge help to illustrate his meaning. Coleridge

has an incessant craving . . . to exalt every idea into a metaphor, to expand every sentiment into a lengthened mystery, voluminous and vast, confused and cloudy. . . . The simple truth does not satisfy him— no direct proposition fills up the moulds of his understanding. . . . To read one of his disquisitions is like hearing the variations to a piece of music without the score.

The criticism of Lamb in the essay 'On Familiar Style' is more appreciative, but it too helps to throw light on Hazlitt's own intention in his prose style:

A sprinkling of archaisms is not amiss; but a tissue of obsolete expressions is more fit *for keep than wear.* I do not say I would not use any phrase that had been brought into fashion before the middle or the end of the last century; but I should be shy of using any that had not been employed by any approved author during the whole of that time. . . . Mr. Lamb is the only imitator of old English style I can read with pleasure. . . . There is an inward unction, a marrowy vein both in the thought and feeling . . . that carries off any quaintness or awkwardness arising from an antiquated style and dress. The matter is completely his own, though the manner is assumed.

It is interesting to note that Hazlitt's favourite, among the

Essays of Elia, was 'Mrs. Battle's Opinions on Whist', which he found 'the most free from obsolete allusions and turns of expression'. His own aim is the 'familiar style' described in this way:

It is not easy to write a familiar style. Many people mistake a familiar for a vulgar style, and suppose that to write without affectation is to write at random. On the contrary, there is nothing that requires more precision, and, if I may so say, purity of expression, than the style I am speaking of. It utterly rejects not only all unmeaning pomp, but all low, cant phrases, and loose, unconnected, *slipshod* allusions. It is not to take the first word that offers, but the best word in common use; it is not to throw words together in any combinations we please, but to follow and avail ourselves of the true idiom of the language. To write a genuine familiar or truly English style, is to write as any one would speak in common conversation, who had a thorough command and choice of words, or who could discourse with ease, force, and perspicuity, setting aside all pedantic and oratorical flourishes.

Although a familiar style is Hazlitt's most usual aim, he varied his style (like any writer worth his salt) according to the demands of the subject and the occasion. As he says of Burke, he 'rises with the lofty, descends with the mean. . . . It is all the same to him, so that he loses no particle of the exact, characteristic, extreme impression of the thing he writes about. . . .' Most of 'The Fight', for example, is deliberately written in a low, almost vulgar style, as suits the subject:

Where there's a will, there's a way.—I said so to myself, as I walked down Chancery lane, about half-past six o'clock on Monday the 10th of December, to inquire at Jack Randall's where the fight the next day was to be . . . I was determined to see this fight, come what would, and see it I did, in great style.

One of the editors of the *New Monthly Magazine* thought the essay too 'vulgar', but fortunately the other had the perception to see in it a masterly 'picture of manners'. If we wish to do justice to Hazlitt's range of styles we must remember 'The Fight' as well as the essay 'On the Feeling of Immortality in Youth': we must contrast the dry, precise manner of his philosophical essays with the moving eloquence of his excursions into autobiography, the epigrammatic rhetoric of *The Spirit of the Age* with the devastating directness of the *Letter to William Gifford, Esq.*: 'Sir,—You have an ugly trick of saying what is not true of any one you do not like; and it will be the object of this letter to cure you of it.' Sometimes he reminds us of the 'character-writers' of the seventeenth century, sometimes of Locke, sometimes of Burke. Even within a single essay there may be a marked contrast of style, as there is between the matter-of-fact opening and the lyrical climax of 'On My First Acquaintance with Poets'. What we find everywhere is an absence of padding, a concern with sense. 'Every word should be a blow: every thought should instantly grapple with its fellow.' One of the marks of his style is the sparing use of conjunctions—a habit of which some of his editors disapproved. In his essay 'On Editors' he complains that some of them 'have a passion for sticking in the word *however* at every opportunity, in order to impede the march of the style. . . . An Editor abhors an ellipsis. If you fling your thoughts into continued passages, they set to work to cut them up into short paragraphs.' The editors would no doubt have replied that although Hazlitt might know more about prose, they knew more about 'the reading public'. Though he is the clearest of writers, when read with attention, a lazy reader will soon lose the thread of his argument. At times he piles up statements with an apparent lack of any evolution in the thought. Yet the absence of conjunctions in positions where we might expect them gives an immediacy to his prose that is reminiscent of good conversation—as we may verify by taking one of his essays and adding the half-dozen possible conjunctions to the opening paragraph. He did not wish the effect of his prose to be weakened by the intrusion of these officious little sign-posts.

Although Hazlitt's way of writing prose is in a sense highly personal, he is not (as has already been noted) an eccentric like Lamb. Whereas Lamb is all idiosyncrasy, dressed only for the society of his friends, Hazlitt goes with ease in any company. He learned most from the prose-writers of the eighteenth century, with whom Lamb had at best an imperfect sympathy. He is not concerned to build up a *persona*, lovable, unusual, odd. He does not go out of his way to avoid the plain, right word. Lamb is like a games-player who excels at one or two strokes: Hazlitt knows every stroke, and plays each as the situation demands. Lamb sometimes parodies himself and is the worst of models. Hazlitt is an admirable model. One of his few faults is that he makes rather too much use of quotation.

LAMB

LAMB's early letters to Coleridge reflect a personality very different from that of Elia.[1] The first of them reveals that he has recently recovered from a fit of insanity. 'I am got somewhat rational now', Lamb writes, 'and don't bite any one. But mad I was.' In Coleridge's letters Lamb finds the qualities of Rousseau's *Confessions*, 'the same frankness, the same openness of heart, the same disclosure of all the most hidden and delicate affections of the mind', and the tone of his own letters is correspondingly intimate. This 'faithful journal of all that passes within me' is highly un-Elian. It is astonishing to find Lamb, of all men, opening a letter with the words 'My brother, my Friend', and saying in another that he is 'heartily sick of the every-day scenes of life'. His literary taste at this point differs from that of his maturity as much as his manner of writing. 'Coleridge', another letter begins, 'I love you for dedicating your poetry to Bowles.' In *Rosamund Gray*, a tale of unfortunate love that borders on *simplesse*, one character lends another *Julia de Roubigné*, and this novel that so delighted Shelley is not the only sign in Lamb's early writings of the influence of Henry Mackenzie and the Sentimental Movement. When we first

---

[1] Charles Lamb (1775–1834) was the son of poor parents, his father being servant and general factotum to Samuel Salt in the Temple. He was educated at Christ's Hospital, where he became friendly with Coleridge. In 1790 he began work as a clerk: in 1791 he entered the employment of the South-Sea Company, and in the following year he transferred to the East India Company, for whom he worked until he retired. In 1795–6 he had a brief attack of insanity. After the tragedy of September 1796 he undertook to act as Mary's guardian, so preserving her from permanent confinement in an institution. From this time onwards he wrote little verse but a good deal of prose. In 1800 he and his sister moved from Pentonville to London, which he loved. Although he was of no importance in the world of affairs his friends included Wordsworth, Hazlitt, De Quincey, and other men of note. In 1806 his farce *Mr H.* was damned at Drury Lane, and he himself took part in the demonstration against it. *Tales from Shakespear*, in which he and Mary collaborated, appeared in 1807. His refusal to leave his sister prejudiced his chances of marrying: his charming and diffident proposal of marriage to the actress Fanny Kelly may be found among his letters. In 1825 he sent his last contribution to the *London Magazine* and retired from the East India House. Retirement did not suit him, although he continued to do some literary work. He was a man whom everyone loved.
Mary Lamb was born in 1764 and died in 1847.

meet Lamb he is as much a Man of Feeling as Mackenzie himself had been in his youth.

In September 1796 Lamb's sister went mad and killed their
mother. He behaved with the greatest possible fortitude and
loyalty, and made a resolution that the whole course of his life
must be changed. 'Many a vagary my imagination played with
me', he had written of his own fit of insanity, and from this time
onwards we find in him a distrust of the unbridled workings of
the imagination that recalls Samuel Johnson. Although he rejected his brother's view that Coleridge with his 'damned silly
sensibility and melancholy' was responsible for his own fit of
madness, it is clear that he associated Coleridge with an epoch
in his life to which he must put an end. He burnt many of his
poems and literary jottings, including a love-journal, and resolved to destroy Coleridge's letters. 'Mention nothing of poetry',
he wrote to him. 'I have destroyed every vestige of past vanities
of that kind.' Soon a new independence appears in his letters.
When he wrote, early in 1798, that he owed Coleridge 'much
under God', there was something valedictory about it, an anticipation of the dedication of his poems twenty years later. His
character was changing, under the pressure of circumstance.
His habit of smoking and drinking rather heavily dates from
this time, while his attitude to life and literature underwent
a profound change. 'With me "the former things are passed
away"', as he wrote to Coleridge, 'and I have something more
to do than to feel.' He no longer likes to be called 'gentle-
hearted'. 'My *sentiment* is long since vanished', as he wrote in
August 1800. 'I hope my *virtues* have done *sucking*.' We find
him remarking on another occasion that the word 'sentiment'
in this sense 'came in with Sterne, and was a child he had by
Affectation'.

To the end of Lamb's life an evening with Coleridge would
set him up for weeks. Yet he came to see that his escape from
Coleridge had been essential: otherwise he might have continued to be towed along in his wake, unable to discover his
own identity. He was in fact exceptionally sensitive to the
characters of other people, and this helps to explain his qualities
as a letter-writer. Obscure as he was in his daily life, in terms
of friendship he was an exceptionally fortunate man. Procter
tells us that Wordsworth, Coleridge, Leigh Hunt, Hazlitt, and
Haydon were among the people he met at the Lambs': Southey,

Manning, and Hood were also frequent visitors. Lamb lived with his equals: in an age of genius he corresponded with half the men of genius. He found inspiration in the variety of his friends. When he wrote to Manning, the Cambridge mathematician, for example, he was able to criticize Wordsworth's humourless egotism with a freedom which was out of the question in a letter to Coleridge. In many ways Manning was Lamb's spiritual Antipodes, and it is noticeable that the letters to him show an unusual acuteness and satirical edge. On the other hand, Lamb often reacted against the tastes of his correspondent. The praise of London which is one of the germs of 'The Londoner', and therefore one of the anticipations of Elia, occurs in a letter to Wordsworth. Bernard Barton, who was singularly lacking in wit and irony, drew from Lamb some of his most entertaining letters. Lamb came to be conscious of his own need of friends of different types. 'So many parts of me have been numbed', he wrote to Wordsworth on hearing of the death of a friend in March 1822:

> Every departure destroys a class of sympathies. . . . One never hears any thing, but the image of the particular person occurs with whom alone almost you would care to share the intelligence. . . . Common natures do not suffice me . . . I want individuals. I am made up of queer points and I want so many answering needles.

All in all, they are remarkable letters. It is true that we need not look to them for the news of the day. Lamb did not set out, as Horace Walpole had done, to be the historian of his age. He would have regarded it as a waste of time. Many of the great themes are not to be found in his letters, or figure there only slightly. After the first few letters, religion is seldom touched on. Philosophy makes no appearance: 'Nothing puzzles me more than time and space', as he wrote to Manning, 'and yet nothing puzzles me less, for I never think about them.' Politics are hardly mentioned. Instead we hear about Lamb's friends, his determination to give up smoking, his liking for roast pork, his boredom at the East India House, and above all books—his own books, his friends' books: books he has been reading, and books he has been buying: new books and old books. Most of his criticism is to be found in his letters: it takes the form of marginalia, records of reaction, brief comments delicately phrased but hardly ever argued or discussed. Like the other contents of the letters, the criticism they contain is informal. The paragraphs never have the air of being composed. They seem to consist of vivid phrases following one another almost at haphazard. There is no evolution of argument: seldom indeed an argument to evolve. They are unmethodical letters, fanciful, ironical, courageous, punning, mischievous, aptly phrased, human.

Written in snatches, as he sat on his high stool, Lamb's letters were his way of escaping from the daunting sobriety of receipt-book and ledger. 'I fancy I succeed best in epistles of mere fun', as he wrote to Fanny Kelly; 'puns & *that* nonsense.' He would amuse himself by pretending to begin in the middle of a letter, or by writing alternate lines in inks of different colours. His hoaxing letters began in 1800, and it is not surprising that the more literal-minded of his correspondents were sometimes at a loss. 'Take my trifling *as trifling*', he told Manning. Some of the most amusing of the letters were written in deep unhappiness. The postscript of one of them, 'I write in misery', might serve for many. On one occasion he tells Manning that he has been suffering from melancholia, but that the arrival of a present of brawn has done much to cheer him. The praise of this delicacy leads him into an Elian passage fifteen years before Elia made his bow. It is a letter which throws a great deal of light on Lamb's character and reminds us that it is seldom the happiest of men who take *Vive la bagatelle* for their motto.

It is a striking fact that many of our finest letter-writers have been men and women who have been frustrated, people with marked literary gifts who have seldom or never found any other literary form which perfectly suited them. It has been true of Gray and Horace Walpole and Cowper; and of many women, such as Lady Mary Wortley Montagu and Jane Welsh Carlyle. It is no less true of Lamb, who found in the letter a medium of expression that suited him as did no other form which he attempted in early life. His essays are best regarded as developments from his familiar letters. It is in the letters written a year or two after Lamb's emergence from the shadow of Coleridge that we find the first traces of Elia, although twenty years were to pass before circumstances were favourable to his coming to maturity.

It is now time to acknowledge chronology and return to the

opening of Lamb's career. Like many writers destined for excellence in other forms, he began with verse. By 1802, when he was 27, the only prose he had published was *Rosamund Gray* and a brief imitation of Burton; but he had also printed some thirty poems and a poetic tragedy. It is fitting that the poem given first in the collected editions seems to have been a joint composition with Coleridge, for he (with Bowles and Charlotte Smith) is the dominating influence in all Lamb's early verse. One of these early pieces remains Lamb's best-known poem, 'The Old Familiar Faces'. The original version began with a stanza later omitted:

> Where are they gone, the old familiar faces?
> I had a mother, but she died, and left me,
> Died prematurely in a day of horrors—
> All, all are gone, the old familiar faces.

The unusual movement of the verse reminds us of Lamb's discussions of classical metrics with Coleridge, Southey, and other friends. The basic line is a hypermetrical iambic pentameter—the nostalgic effect owing a great deal to the final falling syllable—but dactylic suggestions counterpoint the rhythm, and the fifth line ('Drinking late, sitting late, with my bosom cronies') is almost a pure Sapphic. There is a piquant contrast between a syntax which is almost that of prose and an occasional stiffness of expression. It is hard to say how far the effect of the poem is due to metrical sophistication, and how far to a felicitous awkwardness. As we read Lamb's later poems we find that the stricter metres suited him best. He was at his worst in blank verse: at his best (often) in 'short verse' (iambic tetrameters) handled in the manner of the seventeenth century. 'Angel Help' might be the work of a lesser Crashaw, while the lines 'On an Infant Dying as soon as it was Born' remain his finest poetic achievement. He always protested against the notion that wit and feeling were incompatible, pointing out how Fuller's 'conceits are oftentimes deeply steeped in human feeling and passion' and protesting against critics who supposed that Donne's wit was a sign of lack of passion; and in this poem, and in one or two others, we find a union of wit and delicacy of feeling which was unusual at this time. The lines 'In My Own Album' are admirably turned, while the translations from Vincent Bourne—a poet after his own heart, as local and urban as he was classical—show high technical accomplishment. The 'Farewell to Tobacco' is an admirable imprecation, written in a metre learnt from George Wither: since smoking helped Lamb to refrain from stuttering there is a mischievous decorum in his choice of 'stammering verse' for his valediction to tobacco. Many of his most successful poems recall our older poets. Mary 'thinks it a little too old-fashioned in the manner, too much like what they wrote a century back', he acknowledged of one of his poems. 'But I cannot write in the modern style, if I try ever so hard.'

Although the action of *John Woodvil* (1802) is supposed to take place after the Restoration, no play has ever been more obviously Elizabethan in inspiration. From Southey onwards, every critic has been provoked by the 'exquisite silliness' of the plot. In a revealing sentence Lamb wrote in a letter that he hoped to be able to 'edge in' a particular passage 'somewhere in my play', and it is clear that what he wanted was an excuse for putting together a number of speeches. Though it may be doubted whether any whole scene could be mistaken for the work of an Elizabethan, the authentic tone is often caught admirably in individual speeches and lines:

> Better the dead were gather'd to the dead,
> Than death and life in disproportion meet.

To read *John Woodvil* after *Otho the Great* shows the difference between the Elizabethanising of a major poet and that of a very minor one. Though it was written in a hurry and on a mistaken plan, *Otho* often succeeds in using the language with an Elizabethan vigour: *John Woodvil* imitates the mannerisms of the Elizabethans, not their spirit.

The fact that it was not the plays of the Elizabethans regarded as wholes that appealed to Lamb, but their poetry, is abundantly demonstrated in his *Specimens of English Dramatic Poets who Lived about the Time of Shakespear* (1808). As Lamb points out in a letter, 'Specimens' were proliferating at this time. The expanded edition of Ellis's *Early English Poets* came out in 1803 and his *Early English Metrical Romances* in 1805, to be followed by Southey's *Later English Poets* and George Burnett's *English Prose-Writers* (with which Lamb assisted) in 1807. Although Lamb remarks that 'Specimens' is a new term for what used to be called 'Beauties', he does at least try to give whole scenes rather than detached speeches. He chose 'not so much passages of wit and humour . . . as scenes of passion . . . tragic rather than . . . comic poetry', and simply reprinted from accessible texts, omitting passages at will. He did not avoid writers who were tolerably known already, like Beaumont and Fletcher; but he also included many minor dramatists who bear out his assertion that more than a third of the plays represented could only be found in exceptionally good libraries. He was proud of this book. In his laconic 'Autobiographical Sketch' one of the few claims he makes for himself is that he was 'the first to draw . . . attention to the old English Dramatists'. It is difficult to adjust this claim precisely. Throughout the eighteenth century there had been a fair number of readers whose knowledge of the Elizabethan dramatists was by no means confined to Dodsley's collection, while separate editions of several of the dramatists had appeared. Malone, who died in 1812, knew much more about the Elizabethan drama than did Lamb. But Lamb's purpose was quite different from Malone's, and it was probably a help to him that he believed himself to be more of an explorer than he was. His aim was to recommend these plays to lovers of poetry, much as one would recommend a volume of new verse. While Swinburne's statement that Lamb was wholly responsible for the 'resurrection' of these writers is absurdly exaggerated, his claim to a very important part in the movement cannot be gainsaid: it is supported by those who must have known best, his friends and fellow-workers Coleridge, Hazlitt and Southey.

Many modern readers must have turned to the *Specimens* expecting to find full critiques of the authors represented. They will have been disappointed, for this volume presents us with the same paradox as the rest of Lamb's criticism. In the sense that the *Selections* are admirably made, they show Lamb to be an excellent critic of the Elizabethan drama; but the explicit criticism which they contain would not fill more than fifteen pages. While it is true that these *aperçus* have a value out of proportion to their bulk, we do not find in them any analysis of the dramatic structure of the plays or any detailed consideration of their characters or language. What we are given is a sentence or two in which Lamb characterizes the authors who interest him most and tries to convey to the reader his own appreciation of their peculiar savour. As the *Monthly* reviewer noted disapprovingly, the style of the notes is often 'formally abrupt and elaborately quaint', and readers today may well be put off by a note beginning with the words: 'Kit Marlowe, as old Isaak Walton assures us'; yet those who reject all criticism in an idiom uncongenial to them will miss a great many penetrating remarks.

At no time did Lamb write much formal criticism. His essay 'On the Tragedies of Shakspeare' is his most elaborate piece of criticism, and it must be acknowledged that it remains an extremist document. It demonstrates that the aspects of Shakespeare which seemed most important to Lamb were those which had least to do with the drama—not merely with the drama in the conditions of Lamb's own time, but with any drama at any time. He tells us that 'the Characters of Shakspeare are . . . the objects of meditation rather than of interest or curiosity as to their actions'; and it is the characters (so regarded), and the poetry, that appeal to him. He does not object to the plays being acted, but he regards the stage as an inferior medium for them—though one which must be used for the sake of the unreading part of the population. His statement that *Hamlet* 'is made another thing by being acted' begs the whole question. Lamb's argument is not that Shakespeare's plays should be read as well as seen, but that if they are read it does not matter whether they are seen at all. They are 'essentially . . . different' from all other plays. The essay 'On the Artificial Comedy of the Last Century' is also celebrated, and also an example of special pleading: that 'On the Genius and Character of Hogarth' is admirable, and reminds us of the very high reputation this essentially eighteenth-century artist retained in the early part of the succeeding century. Unfortunately the only elaborate review that Lamb ever wrote was cut about by Gifford, but even as it stands it speaks out finely for 'the boldness and originality' of Wordsworth's genius.

It is to the letters that we must go to fill out our picture of Lamb's critical views. At first they show him as a disciple of Coleridge, almost ludicrously anxious to follow his lead. 'My second thoughts entirely coincide with your comments', he wrote on one occasion, '. . . and I can only wonder at my childish judgment. . . . Your full and satisfactory account of personifications . . . will be a guide to my future taste.' He thanked

Coleridge for introducing him to Quarles and Wither, and as his own taste developed his knowledge of seventeenth-century poetry became very extensive. He knew the more elaborate of the prose writers almost as well as the poets—particularly the work of such men as Sir Thomas Browne, Izaak Walton, Thomas Fuller and (in the sixteenth century) Richard Hooker. He found Burton highly congenial. As his own taste developed he realized that writers in close touch with the world of everyday made a special appeal to him: 'Burns was the god of my idolatry, as Bowles of yours', he once wrote to Coleridge. He was fond of the eighteenth-century novelists, and has some admirable comments on Defoe. His dislikes were the obverse of his likes: 'masques, and Arcadian pastorals, with their train of abstractions, unimpassioned deities, passionate mortals, Claius, and Medorus, and Amintas, and Amarillis'. It is not suprising that he objected to the poetry of Shelley as 'too ideal' and containing an 'efflorescence . . . not natural'. The imaginations of these two men represent the extremities of the human mind. What is perhaps more surprising is that Lamb was one of the first critics to comment perceptively on Blake, whom he termed 'one of the most extraordinary persons of the age'.

The limitations of Lamb's taste are considerable. It is not merely that he was 'a little exclusive and national in his tastes', as Hazlitt noted. Within the field of English literature he lacked the discriminating catholicity of Hazlitt himself. Reviewing for the *Athenaeum* he stipulated for 'no natural history or useful learning', and in fact his interests were limited to what used to be called the *belles lettres*. If he mentions Hooker or Sir Thomas Browne, it is for their style and their air of antiquity, not for what they say. In general it is the part that appeals to him in a work of literature, rather than the whole. 'I can vehemently applaud, or perversely stickle, at parts', he wrote to Godwin, 'but I cannot grasp at a whole.' He never discusses the structure of a play or poem. Even the plot of a novel did not greatly interest him. 'I naturally take little interest in story', he wrote to another friend, 'the manner and not the end is the interest.' In this matter he is a 'literary man' in a very limiting sense: he rarely indulges in analysis, and shrinks from argument. If one comes to him from Coleridge his lack of interest in abstract questions and in the terminology of criticism becomes very striking. That anyone should be able to 'fill 3 volumes up with an

Essay on the Drama'—no doubt he was thinking of the Schlegels —astonished him. 'I am sure a very few sheets would hold all I have to say on the subject.' These severe limitations must be mentioned because absurdly high claims have often been made for him. Bradley called him the greatest critic of his century. No one would have been more embarrassed by such a remark than Lamb himself. He prided himself on his discrimination, and his intimate knowledge of certain old books; but he had no desire for the critical *cathedra*.

The essays for which Lamb is chiefly remembered are the work of a man in his middle forties. His earlier journalism is of little account. 'The Londoner', which was published in the *Morning Post*, was intended to be the first of a number of essays by a man with 'an almost insurmountable aversion from solitude and rural scenes', and it is possible that Manning's suggestion that a volume of essays in this manner would be successful helped to inspire Elia nine years later. Meanwhile Lamb contributed to the *Reflector* and the *Examiner* and wrote a revealing essay on 'Christ's Hospital and the Character of the Christ's Hospital Boys' in the *Gentleman's Magazine*. Although this essay is intended to be an informative contribution to a public debate, it becomes more and more personal in tone as it goes on, until in the end Lamb is writing from the heart and addressing his contemporaries at the school. In the descriptions of scenes which, 'seen through the mist of distance, come sweetly softened to the memory', we are more than half-way to Elia's avowedly personal essay on the same subject.

But it was in the *London Magazine* of the 1820's that the *Essays of Elia* made their appearance. Everything about this periodical appealed to Lamb, and above all the sense that he was among friends who understood and appreciated him. For him, at least, the editorial dinners must have meant a good deal. Until the first freshness of the thing wore off, his old yearning to belong once again to a 'body corporate', as he had done at school, must in some measure have been satisfied.

The close relationship between Lamb's essays and his letters has already been mentioned. Some of the essays even derive from particular letters. The germ of 'Amicus Redivivus', for example, is a description of George Dyer walking into the river—when he writes about Dyer Lamb is always Elia: Manning gave Lamb the idea for his 'Dissertation upon Roast Pig',

which is first handled in a letter: while several letters dealing
with Coleridge's retentive habits as a borrower of books are
the inspiration of 'The Two Races of Men'. This makes the
tone of the *Essays* less surprising. If we compare Lamb with
a typical eighteenth-century essayist, we find that the latter is
primarily concerned to improve his reader's mind: if he sets out
to amuse, it is only that his instruction may be the more effective. In Lamb, on the other hand, the didactic intention of
'Modern Gallantry' is most exceptional. The subjects of his
essays—'All Fools' Day', 'Mackery End, in Hertfordshire',
'Witches, and other Night-Fears'—may be contrasted with
those of the *Rambler*: 'Happiness not Local', 'Passion not to be
Eradicated', 'The Arts by which Bad Men are Reconciled to
Themselves'. Lamb specifically abjures 'the airy stilts of abstraction' and the proud claim to a philosophic impartiality. He
is the least philosophic of essayists, as he is the most human,
'a bundle of prejudices . . . the veriest thrall to sympathies,
apathies, antipathies', in knowledge 'a whole Encyclopædia
behind the rest of the world'. The schoolmaster who tried to
talk with him about the provision for the poor in the present
and the past had to abandon the attempt, 'finding me rather
dimly impressed with some glimmering notions from old poetic
associations, than strongly fortified with any speculations re-
ducible to calculation on the subject'. In his essays, as in his
letters, Lamb deliberately avoids whatever is urgent and disturbing: religion, sex, politics, suffering. The former acolyte of
the metaphysical Coleridge and lifelong friend of the political
Hazlitt chose such subjects as 'Old China' and 'Valentine's
Day' for his own lucubrations. He dwells on the small, reassuring aspects of life. 'I wished it might have lasted for ever', he
writes of the last game of whist that he played with Bridget,
'though we gained nothing, and lost nothing, though it was
a mere shade of play: I would be content to go on in that idle
folly for ever'.

Anyone who reads the *Essays* as direct autobiography will be
seriously misled. Lamb was fond of lying, and loved to appropriate experiences which had befallen his friends. 'My biography,
parentage, place of birth, is a strange mistake', he wrote to
Moxon, after reading the proof (as it seems) of an account of his
own life, 'part founded on some nonsense I wrote about Elia,
and was true of him, the real Elia.' Defending his 'Character of

the late Elia' against the charge of egotism, Lamb emphasizes that what Elia 'tells us, as of himself, was often true only (historically) of another'. 'If it be egotism to imply and twine with his own identity the griefs and affections of another', as he goes on to say, then novelists and dramatists stand equally chargeable. In a revealing phrase he once calls the first person 'his favourite figure' of speech. Yet although Lamb was helped (as many writers have been) by the partial anonymity of a *nom de plume*, the main fact about Elia is that he stands for Lamb himself. It was a matter of dressing up, but the costume he chose—like the black clothes that he was in the habit of wearing—suited him very well. A descendant of 'The Londoner', Elia is the 'picture of my humours' that had been in Lamb's mind when he wrote that essay.

In nothing is Lamb more characteristic of his age than in the way in which he seeks inspiration in his past life, and particularly in his memories of childhood. His early surroundings must have encouraged his tendency to look backwards: the Temple, Christ's Hospital, and the East India House, as well as the old house in which his aunt lived. Few men have acknowledged more explicitly the importance of their childhood. 'Nothing that I have been engaged in since seems of any value or importance', he wrote, 'compared to the colours which imagination gave to everything then.' It was partly that he was afraid that the new world of railroad, factory, and political economists would rob the imagination of its food. 'While childhood, and while dreams, reducing childhood, shall be left', he reflects in a revealing passage, 'imagination shall not have spread her holy wings totally to fly the earth.' 'He was too much of the boy-man', he writes of himself elsewhere. 'The impressions of infancy had burnt into him, and he resented the impertinence of manhood. These were weaknesses; but such as they were, they are a key to explicate some of his writings.' They are a key—we may add—to a great deal in the literature of the nineteenth century. In the eighteenth century men wrote about the present: in the nineteenth they wrote about the past. Lamb is therefore a most significant figure. Many of the most characteristic of his essays deal with experiences that were half a lifetime away when he set out to describe them. They are personal memories 'recollected in tranquillity', and recollected in such a manner that whatever had been disturbing in the original experiences had

been alembicated off. It is appropriate that the *Essays* begin
with 'The South-Sea House', with its description of men who
were of no importance in their own day and who are now no
more substantial than dreams: 'their importance is from the
past'. Time is a felt presence throughout the *Essays*, the perpetual theme of Elia's soliloquies. What is to be—he confesses
—means nothing to him: 'I am . . . shy of novelties; new books,
new faces, new years,—from some mental twist which makes it
difficult in me to face the prospective.' His essays are vistas
revealed by an imagination playing round the experiences of
a lifetime.

Although it is often simple, and on occasion penetratingly so,
the style of Elia is never plain. His essays are much more highly
wrought than those of Addison or Steele. His concern is not
merely to say something with clarity and force: he wishes to
evoke a mood or present a paradox in a highly personal way.
His style is designed to create and sustain his *persona*, and as
Elia is wayward and old-fashioned the style in which he writes
is full of echoes and archaisms, ellipses and nuances, peri-
phrases and calculated familiarities. Sometimes the result is
close to self-parody, as in the passage beginning with the words
'This is *Saloop*—the precocious herb-woman's darling' in 'The
Praise of Chimney-Sweepers'. The archaisms are essential to
the style, yet at times they are overdone, and we sense this
particularly if we read a number of the essays one after the
other. In the same way the allusions are on occasion excessive,
as in 'All Fools' Day', while the use of periphrasis can become
tedious. But the triumphs infinitely outweigh the incomplete
successes and the very few failures. It is a frankly literary style:
Montaigne lies behind it, and Burton and Sir Thomas Browne.
It reminds us that Lamb loved the prose of the seventeenth
century more than that of the eighteenth. In particular we are
often reminded of the character-writers, as we are when we read
his descriptions of A Poor Relation, A Scotchman (in 'Imperfect
Sympathies'), or A Beggar.

Yet it was an eighteenth-century novelist that Lamb echoed
when he wrote 'The Character of the Late Elia'. His habit of
thinking of himself as a Shakespearian Fool makes it the less
surprising that Yorick lies behind this passage: no writer did
more to help Lamb to his characteristic style than the author
of *Tristram Shandy*. Parts of 'All Fools' Day' are precisely in

Sterne's manner, while nothing could be closer to *A Sentimental Journey* than the description of a poor girl tempted in 'Barbara S—': 'In these thoughts she reached the second landing-place— the second, I mean, from the top—for there was still another left to traverse. Now virtue support Barbara!' On another occasion Elia calls on 'the pen of Yorick' to describe one of his relations, saying that no other would be capable of 'those fine Shandian lights and shades, which make up his story'. Apart from a close literary kinship (if Lamb had imitated Burton, Sterne had pillaged him), there was a strong temperamental affinity between the two men. While Sterne drew perpetual inspiration from the 'association of ideas', Lamb seems to be the first writer to describe himself as 'introspective'. It is interesting to notice that Sterne begins to be mentioned in Lamb's letters just before the turn of the century, at the time when Elia's character was in the making. It is fortunate that Lamb went beyond Henry Mackenzie and the other imitators of Sterne to Yorick himself, a master of the processes of the human heart from whom he learned a great deal.

The *persona* of Elia is less prominent in the *Last Essays*, most of which are distinctly inferior to their predecessors. Lamb was beginning to run out of subjects: 'Where shall I get another subject', we find him writing soon after the beginning of the second series—'or who shall deliver me from the body of this death?' He was discouraged by the poor sale of the first series, when it appeared as a book, and depressed by Southey's attack on his religious opinions; while a third important reason for his falling-off was the decline in the *London Magazine* itself. The only masterpiece among the later of the *Last Essays* is 'The Superannuated Man', in which he was writing on a theme which his imagination had been contemplating throughout many laborious years: it stands as a fitting epilogue to an incomparable series of essays which have always, as their deepest and truest theme, the character of Elia himself.

XI

DE QUINCEY

THERE have been few stranger literary careers.[1] By the age of seventeen De Quincey had decided that his life was to be that of a thinker and a man of letters, and he had jotted down an ambitious list of works that he intended to write: by his late twenties he was even more firmly resolved to become 'the intellectual benefactor' of his species, to accomplish 'a great revolution in the intellectual condition of the world' which would include in its scope a complete reform of education, philosophy, and mathematics. But since, 'like all persons . . . in possession of *original* knowledge', he was unwilling to 'sell' his wisdom 'for money', he seems to have published virtually nothing, except a long note on Sir John Moore prefixed to Wordsworth's *Convention of Cintra*, until he was thirty-three. He then became editor of a provincial journal of small circulation and less importance, the *Westmorland Gazette*. By this time he seems also to have decided to contribute to the Reviews, for in August 1820 we find William Blackwood reproaching him with a 'long bygone engagement to the Magazine'. The following year his *Confessions of an English Opium-Eater* were published in the *London Magazine* and he became a celebrity overnight.

From the first, the structure of the *Confessions* gave him

---

[1] Thomas De Quincey (1785–1859) was the son of a Manchester merchant of literary interests. After eighteen months he ran away from Manchester Grammar School, to which he had been sent at the age of fifteen, and wandered about in Wales before going to London. There he led a Bohemian life and met the young prostitute, Ann, described in his *Confessions*. At Worcester College, Oxford, he led the life of a recluse and continued to increase his unusual stock of erudition. He left in a panic just before completing his examinations. At this time he had begun to take opium, as well as turning to the study of German literature. He was an early admirer of Wordsworth, Coleridge, and Southey, and lived for some time in the Lake District in order to be near them. Gradually he became estranged from the Wordsworths, and in 1817 he married Margaret Simpson. In 1818–19 he edited the *Westmorland Gazette*. The publication of his *Confessions* made him famous. For the remainder of his life he lived the life of a literary displaced person, moving between one set of rooms and another, in Bath, London, and Edinburgh. He never cured himself of the habit of opium-eating.

trouble. He was not aiming at autobiography: 'not the opium-eater, but the opium, is the true hero of the tale', as he tells us—though we note that 'hero' must be taken in a morally neutral sense, since the professed object of the book is to warn its readers of the dangers of opium. He also wished to describe the 'Pleasures of Opium' as well as its 'Pains'—to give an account of some of the astonishing dreams and visions that he had experienced. For this reason he tells us something about his early life, before he became an opium-eater, both to increase our interest in him as a person and to provide us with 'a key to some parts of that tremendous scenery which afterwards peopled the dreams of the opium-eater'.

Few readers can ever have been bored by the *Confessions*, in their first form. De Quincey is an Ancient Mariner who holds us captive with his eye—and we have no desire to escape. He is fascinated by his own experiences, and we are fascinated by what he tells us. The power of opium over the human mind is a profoundly interesting subject, and the interest is greatly enhanced by the fact that the opium-eater was a man of exceptional intelligence and imagination. De Quincey was deeply interested in the processes and resources of the mind, and planned to write a great work *De emendatione humani intellectus.* The introspective penetration which he displays is the less surprising. What we would not have expected is his journalistic astuteness. In a manner that reminds us for a moment of Defoe he makes it clear that we are to hear of forbidden and disreputable things, but only for our own good: it is an 'interesting record', but it should also be found 'in a considerable degree, useful and instructive'. No other motive could have led him to break through that 'delicate and honourable reserve' which distinguishes Englishmen from all Frenchmen and many Germans. He feels that it is his duty to warn us that opium-eaters have become 'very numerous': this is particularly true amongst men 'distinguished for talents, or of eminent station', as he goes on to demonstrate with a burst of dashes most of which are easy to fill in. At the other end of the social scale the work-people in the factories of Manchester are also becoming thralls to opium. As we read the *Confessions* we can therefore congratulate ourselves on taking an interest in a matter of grave public concern. All previous writers on the subject have been liars, and their readers dupes; but we are being told the truth. And just as

De Quincey refuses to accept any blame for his opium-eating, so he insists on the innocence of his association with the outcasts and prostitutes whom he met during his period adrift in London. He is an adept at flattering his readers with the sense of being liberal and broad-minded: 'Courteous, and, I hope, indulgent reader (for all *my* readers must be indulgent ones, or else, I fear, I shall shock them too much to count on their courtesy).' In fact we are not told anything that is remarkably shocking—or so one might suppose, until one studies the revisions De Quincey felt obliged to make in 1856. What is particularly reassuring about the book, for the timid reader, is its air of being the work of a retired sea-captain, let us say: an adventurous man who has seen some odd things in his time, and associated with some odd people, yet who has retired to live in respectability with his wife in the old country. 'These troubles are past', he writes, addressing his wife (whom he calls his Electra); 'and thou wilt read these records of a period so dolorous to us both as the legend of some hideous dream that can return no more.' It is all reassuringly domestic. The adventurer is home again, and in the evening he has agreed to tell us something of his experiences. The result is a story of exploration and adventure, of a search and a loss, and above all of a memorable escape.

The Third Part of the *Confessions* promised in the *London Magazine* in 1821 never appeared, and the following year De Quincey allowed the two parts to be republished as a small book, with the addition of an appendix on the medical aspects of opium in which he reveals that his cure has not been completed after all. Although this was the book which made him famous, there was from the first something tentative and unfinished about it, and he wondered for years whether he should rewrite it. The opportunity came at the end of his life, with the publication of a collected edition of his work. He decided to double the length of the *Confessions*, so that they would fill one volume. The 'crowning grace' of the book was to be a succession of the 'dreams and noonday visions' which had come to him over the years, accounts of some of which he had already written. When he began the revision, however, he found that he had mislaid most of these descriptions, with the exception of the one entitled 'The Daughter of Lebanon'. While this was set at the end of the revised *Confessions* as a specimen of the material from which the culmination of the work was to have been constructed, De Quincey was now faced with the problem of expanding his book in some other way. This he did principally by greatly lengthening the account of his early life, by adding numerous digressions, and by rewriting the whole book in a more elaborate (and frequently verbose) style of prose.

In 1856 the account of De Quincey's early life is four times as long as it had been in 1822. This has an important effect on the proportions of the book. More than two-thirds of the narrative have passed before opium makes its appearance. In 1822 the 'Preliminary Confessions' really are preliminary: in 1856 De Quincey has moved in the direction of ordinary autobiography. In self-defence he insists that his 'opium miseries' were connected with his early sufferings in London 'by natural links of affiliation':

> The early series of sufferings was the parent of the later. Otherwise, these Confessions would break up into two disconnected sections: first, a record of boyish calamities; secondly, a record (totally independent) of sufferings consequent upon excesses in opium. And the two sections would have no link whatever to connect them, except the slight one of having both happened to the same person. (iii. 412.)

Interesting as many of the new incidents are, and valuable to the biographer, the *Confessions* of 1856 form a less unified work than those of 1822. And when we consider the long digressions which are characteristic of the revised text (such as the dog-fight with Coleridge at the very beginning) it becomes impossible to accept De Quincey's claim that he did not eke out the volume 'by any wiredrawing process'. Much of the new material is padding.

Reviewing his life at the age of 70, De Quincey naturally found himself seeing many episodes in a different light from that of his *London Magazine* days. He is much less severe, for example, in his judgements of people. But what is of more immediate interest is the fact that his attitude to opium itself has changed. Even in 1822 there are inconsistencies in his remarks about opium: although he professedly sets out to warn us against it, there are passages which would bear a rather different interpretation. In 1856 the earlier reference to 'the *moral* of my narrative' is cut altogether, and De Quincey's concern is to emphasize the medical value of opium as an anodyne and,

more particularly, its mysterious powers 'over the grander and
more shadowy world of dreams':

> All passages, written at an earlier period under cloudy and un-
> corrected views of the evil agencies presumable in opium, stand
> retracted; although, shrinking from the labour of altering an error
> diffused so widely under my own early misconceptions of the truth,
> I have suffered them to remain as they were. (iii. 429.)

The superiority of the 1822 text is particularly evident when
we consider its style. Although there are some elaborate passages in 1822, they occur only where they are appropriate, and
in general the style is relatively simple and direct: in 1856 the
style is more involved, 'literary', and artificial. To take two or
three isolated examples, 'sometimes' becomes 'oftentimes', 'up'
becomes 'astir', 'to which' becomes 'whither', 'no ways' becomes
'nowise'. Words and turns of phrase which might be regarded
as colloquial or vulgar are softened or replaced by circum-
locutions: unnecessary qualifications are frequently added.
The revisions throw a great deal of light on the development
(and in some respects the deterioration) of De Quincey's mind:
they also illuminate changes in English taste during his lifetime.
When he revised his *Confessions* Queen Victoria had been on the
throne for almost twenty years: many things which had been
openly discussed in the twenties were now considered indelicate.
The influence of the new standards of propriety is particularly
evident in the passages dealing with London prostitutes—
passages which had never been at all objectionable. It must be
stressed that some of the revisions are for the better: an outstanding example is the last dream in the main part of the book,
which De Quincey revised like a master. It is clear, however,
that he had lost the ability to write plainly, and as a result the
1856 text often seems flabby and debilitated in comparison with
that of 1822. In their later form the *Confessions* remain a very
interesting book; but the *Confessions* of 1822 may be regarded as
a minor masterpiece. Perhaps the very scantiness of detail and
inadequacy of the motivation contribute to the power of the
early version. In 1856 De Quincey is relatively intelligible—
and therefore exasperating: in 1822 we accept him as a mysterious, enigmatic figure, a Werther moved by sorrows beyond
our comprehension.

For thirty-five years after the first publication of his

Confessions 'The English Opium-Eater' was one of the most prolific contributors to the periodical press. Except for a couple of prose romances (*Walladmor* and *Klosterheim* (1825, 1832), the former a professed 'translation from the German' of a supposed original by Scott) nothing that De Quincey wrote ever made its first appearance as a book. Although his original intention may have been to make money by writing articles, so earning leisure in which to concentrate on longer works, he seems soon to have realized that periodical writing was destined to be his profession. He therefore tried to put the best of himself into his articles, looking forward to the day when he could revise them and republish them in a collected form. We must now consider the contents of the edition which he collected near the end of his life. No strict chronology can be observed: it will be convenient to begin with his autobiographical writings, moving on to his literary criticism and ending with the *Suspiria de Profundis*.

As he wrote the *Autobiographic Sketches* (which Masson less accurately terms his *Autobiography*) De Quincey's capital difficulty was that the most dramatic part of his life had already been described. One of the results of this is that some of the *Sketches* appear to have little autobiographical significance. The chapter on Oxford is a defence of a University to which he himself never acknowledged any debt. The chapters on Ireland (which have been revised, unlike that on Oxford) simply deal with recent political history, and throw little light on their author. A similar charge might be brought against 'German Studies and Kant in Particular'; but in reading this last chapter we must remember the sort of autobiographical sketches he is attempting. His subject is not events in themselves but the effects of these events on his own mind and the meaning they have come to assume for him since. It is not for nothing that he keeps echoing and quoting from *The Prelude*: these *Sketches*, too, aim at tracing the development of a creative mind. What determines the space given to a topic is not its interest to readers but its importance to the writer. The persecution which he suffered at the hands of his brother is dwelt on, for example, at tedious length. We begin to feel that we are moving in a world in which the usual proportions of things have become obsolete: large objects are invisible, or can be distinguished with difficulty: small things assume a nightmare bulk. Unfortunately, for a great deal of the time De Quincey is not successful in leading the reader to share his point of view, and the result is an effect of simple distortion. In some of the most remarkable passages, however, De Quincey's secret voice becomes audible: it is as if we were overhearing the monologue of a man under an anaesthetic retracing his own life and seeing in it the type and symbol of some profounder pattern. Yet there is also much that is of interest in the more objective parts of the *Sketches*. De Quincey was a keen observer of the changes that had taken place since his youth: changes in manners, in dress, in communications, in public opinion, in reading habits, in language, and in many other aspects of 'the shifting scenery and moving forces of the age'.

The most interesting of the papers called by Masson the *London Reminiscences* describe De Quincey's association with the brilliant group of writers who contributed to the *London Magazine* in its hey-day. He had been one of the few original purchasers of *John Woodvil*, and he gives us our only picture of Lamb at his office desk, perched on a high stool. Elsewhere he is sometimes unfair to Lamb as a prose writer, but here he sums up his merits admirably, concluding that 'of the peculiar powers which he possessed he has left to the world as exquisite a specimen as this planet is likely to exhibit'. There are also some penetrating comments on Clare, of whom De Quincey remarks: 'I very much doubt if there could be found in his poems a single commonplace image, or a description made up of hackneyed elements.' We also hear of Sir Humphry Davy, Godwin, Mrs. Grant of Laggan, Allan Cunningham, Edward Irving and the remarkable traveller John Stewart, whom he describes as 'the most interesting by far of all my friends' and the most naturally eloquent man he had ever met.

In the *Lake Reminiscences* (usually called *Recollections of the Lake Poets*) De Quincey sets out to cater for the growing interest in 'three men upon whom posterity . . . will look back with interest as profound as, perhaps, belongs to any other names of our era'. While he is most unreliable on facts, he is often a penetrating commentator, as in his denial of the existence of a 'Lake School':

> The critics . . . supposed them to have assembled under common views in literature—particularly with regard to the true functions of poetry, and the true theory of poetic diction. . . . They went on to *find* in their writings all the agreements and common characteristics which their blunder had presumed.

Inaccurate as they are, the articles on Coleridge are of considerable value. As De Quincey himself admits, through the
ruin of his own mind he 'looked into and read the latter states
of Coleridge. His chaos I comprehended by the darkness of
my own [mind], and both were the work of laudanum.' He
interprets Coleridge's love of abstractions as a form of escapism,
but insists on defending him against the charge of purposeless
digression. Unfortunately his own weakness in this respect is nowhere more evident. The section on Wordsworth also contains
some penetrating criticism—De Quincey had the advantage of
knowing *The Prelude* long before most critics—although it too
suffers from unnecessary digressions, such as the long account
of 'the bad Lord Lonsdale'.

Apart from the *Confessions*, De Quincey's literary criticism
is the most important part of his work. Unlike Coleridge and
Lamb, he was not concerned to recommend forgotten writers.
His reading was wide, but in English literature at least he wrote
only on the most eminent writers. On the minor Elizabethan
dramatists he has nothing to say, while in the seventeenth
century Milton is his only important theme, in the eighteenth
Pope. On Shakespeare he wrote only once, but the result is
important. It is characteristic that it was the Ratcliffe Highway
murders which prompted the essay 'On the Knocking at the
Gate in *Macbeth*': De Quincey writes as the author of 'Murder
Considered as One of the Fine Arts'. The reasons he gives for
the profound effect made by the knocking are, first, that
Shakespeare wants to make the audience temporarily sympathize with Macbeth rather than Duncan, and, secondly, that the
knocking is a sign that 'the pulses of life are beginning to beat
again. . . . The re-establishment of the goings-on of the world
. . . first makes us profoundly sensible of the awful parenthesis
that had suspended them.' This penetrating piece of psychological criticism is introduced by a significant remark:

> My understanding could furnish no reason why the knocking at
> the gate . . . should produce any effect. . . . My understanding said
> positively that it could *not* produce any effect. But I knew better;
> I felt that it did; and I waited and clung to the problem until further
> knowledge should enable me to solve it.

No one has been more conscious of the dependence of literary
criticism on psychology than De Quincey; as he once wrote,

'literary or *aesthetic* questions [must be brought] under the light of philosophic principles . . . problems of "taste" [must be] expanded to problems of human nature'. When he wrote on Milton, whose work he knew intimately, he also had recourse to psychology; but it is with his remarks on Milton's style that we are particularly concerned. He was clearly aware of an affinity with Milton in his love of pomp and elaboration. For critics who are disposed to censure Milton rashly he has a warning: 'You might as well tax Mozart with harshness in the divinest passages of *Don Giovanni* as Milton with any . . . offence against metrical science. Be assured it is yourself that do not read with understanding.' To Milton's language he paid the minutest attention, vehemently defending his 'exotic idioms'. Influenced perhaps by Capel Lofft, he points out the importance of Milton's characteristic spelling, and relates it to the fact that italics were not used in his day for emphasis. On Pope De Quincey is less at home, although he has one or two admirable points to make. He begins well, in his review of Roscoe's edition, by denying that Pope is merely a satiric poet; and then proceeds to his famous distinction between literature of knowledge and literature of power. He opposes, admirably, the misconception that Pope 'belonged to what is idly called the *French* School of our literature' and the view that 'he was specially distinguished from preceding poets by *correctness*'. In fact, as he points out, there are occasional faults in Pope's use of language which have been condoned, but never justified, by his critics. As he develops the point elsewhere: 'Not for superior correctness, but for qualities the very same as belong to his most distinguished brethren, is Pope to be considered a great poet.' Unfortunately he does not illustrate these remarks but allows himself to be led into a fruitless discussion of the moral justification of satire.

De Quincey acknowledged that his discovery of the *Lyrical Ballads* had been 'the greatest event in the unfolding of [his] own mind', and it was on this collection that he wrote the nearest approximation to a formal critique in his work. He points out the blighting effect that Wordsworth's theory of diction has had on his reputation and emphasizes that it conflicts with the whole history of our poetry:

If the leading classics of the English literature are . . . loyal to the canons of sound taste,—then you cut away the *locus standi* for yourself

as a reformer. . . . If they also are faulty, you undertake an *onus* of
hostility so vast that you will be found fighting against [the] stars.

He shrewdly points out that Wordsworth is far from empirical,
having been content with the same 'old original illustrations,
—two, three, or perhaps three-and-a-quarter' throughout his
whole life. An affinity between his own mind and the poet's
enables him to write penetratingly on the nature of his imagination: 'He does not willingly deal with a passion in its direct
aspect, or presenting an unmodified contour, but in forms more
complex and oblique, and when passing under the shadow of
some secondary passion.' The essay ends with the suggestion
that 'meditative poetry is perhaps that province of literature
which will ultimately maintain most power amongst the generations which are coming', and the claim that Wordsworth stands
higher in this province than any other poet since Shakespeare.
    On the younger poets De Quincey has little to say. It would
have struck him as absurd to class Byron, Shelley, and Keats
with Wordsworth and Coleridge. He hardly ever refers to
Byron, indeed, though he had read him: he thought very highly
of *Hyperion*, after being appalled by 'the most shocking abuse
of [our] mother-tongue' in *Endymion*: while he was most attracted
by Shelley, whose classical learning and visionary imagination
answered to characteristics of his own. He was shocked, on the
other hand, by Shelley's hostility to Christianity, and described
him—in a phrase which Arnold may have remembered—as
'an angel touched by lunacy'. Nor did De Quincey write much
on the novel. His remarks on prose style have a particular
interest, and betray, as one might have expected, a remarkable
lack of objectivity. In Swift he finds 'not . . . a graceful artless-
ness, but . . . a coarse inartificiality': no doubt he can write
well enough on a straightforward subject (so can Dampier and
Defoe); but what would happen if more were required?—

   Suppose . . . that the Dean had been required to write a pendant
for Sir Walter Raleigh's immortal apostrophe to Death, or to many
passages . . . in . . . 'Religio Medici' and . . . 'Urn Burial', or to
Jeremy Taylor's inaugural sections of his 'Holy Living and Dying'. . . .
What would have happened? (xi. 18.)

What would have happened—we may be pardoned for asking
—if De Quincey had been required to write a 'pendant' for

Robinson Crusoe or *Gulliver's Travels*? What interested him was
'impassioned prose' of the most elaborate and musical kind:
when he is discussing writers of other types of prose he is completely unreliable. On one occasion he states that 'Lamb had
no sense of the rhythmical in prose composition', while some
of his comments on Hazlitt—such as the absurd remark that
'Hazlitt had read nothing'—can only have been inspired by
jealousy. Some of his observations are penetrating:

> No man can be eloquent whose thoughts are abrupt, insulated,
> capricious, and . . . non-sequacious. . . . The main condition [of elo-
> quence] lies in the *key* of the evolution, in the *law* of the succession. . . .
> Now Hazlitt's brilliancy is seen chiefly in separate splinterings of
> phrase or image. . . . A flash, a solitary flash, and all is gone. (v. 231.)

What De Quincey fails to notice, however, is that this style,
which is not to be found everywhere in Hazlitt's work, was
deliberately evolved to meet the demands of some of the types
of writing on which he was engaged.

De Quincey wrote several essays on general literary topics
which are interesting both for their central arguments and for
their remarks on particular writers. The essay on Rhetoric contains a roll-call of his masters, including Burton, Milton (the
only writer he ever censured for being 'too sequacious and
processional'), Sir Thomas Browne, and Burke, 'the supreme
writer of this century, the man of the largest and finest understanding'. De Quincey suggests that 'The Rhetorical Poets'
would be a better title for Donne and his followers than 'The
Metaphysical Poets', and terms Donne himself (whom he elsewhere describes as 'a man yet unappreciated') 'the first very
eminent rhetorician in the English Literature'. 'Few writers
have shown a more extraordinary compass of powers . . .; for he
combined . . . the last sublimation of dialectical subtlety and
address with the most impassioned majesty.' (x. 101.) The
essay on Style is the work of a man who has thought long and
deeply on the subject:

> The more . . . any exercise of mind is . . . *subjective* . . . the more . . .
> does the style . . . cease to be a mere separable ornament . . . [Mr
> Wordsworth once remarked] that it is in the highest degree un-
> philosophic to call language or diction 'the *dress* of thoughts'. . . . He
> would call it 'the *incarnation* of thoughts'. . . . If language were merely

a dress, then you could separate the two . . . [whereas in fact] an image . . . often enters into a thought as a constituent part. (x. 229–30.)

The *Letters to a Young Man Whose Education has been Neglected* are full of interesting things, such as the remark that 'no complex or very important truth was ever yet transferred in full development from one mind to another. . . . It must arise by an act of genesis within the [learner's] understanding itself.' The exclusive study of languages is deplored, as leading to 'the dry rot of the human mind', and De Quincey quotes with approval the advice that we should 'dare to be ignorant of many things'.

It seems likely that most of the seminal ideas from which De Quincey's criticism sprang had been planted by his twentieth year. Much his greatest debts were to Wordsworth and Coleridge, and he refers almost reverently to the time when 'Mr. Wordsworth . . . unveiled the great philosophic distinction between the powers of *fancy* and *imagination*'. In spite of his scorn for the Schlegels and his objection to the habit of 'yielding an extraordinary precedence to German critics' (to whom in fact Coleridge owed a great deal) he himself was very much one of the 'new critics' of his day. Many of the merits of his criticism —as well as many of its faults—are due to his determination to penetrate far below the surface. He objected to what seemed to him the lack of a metaphysical and psychological basis in the criticism of Dr. Johnson, and went so far as to claim that 'in the sense of absolute and philosophic criticism, we have little or none; for, before *that* can exist, we must have a good psychology, whereas, at present, we have none at all' (xi. 294). If we compare the two men we find that the criticism of Johnson is that of a man talking in society while the criticism of De Quincey is that of a philosopher speculating in solitude.

As one reads De Quincey's inferior work one concludes that he was uniquely unqualified for periodical journalism. His faults—prolixity, irrelevance, the passion for displaying his classical learning in and out of season—unfitted him for the role; while his merits—width of knowledge, subtlety of mind, and the determination to go deeply into everything—were hardly more helpful. One is equally astonished at the forbearance of his readers and the forbearance of his editors. The letters that passed between him and his publishers make extraordinary reading. On one occasion, stung by a reproachful letter from Hessey, he described himself as 'the most benignest man that perhaps has appeared since the time of St. John'. He seldom wrote what he was asked to write, and hardly ever produced his material on time. When Lockhart invited him to contribute a book on the Lake District to a series called 'The Family Library', he replied by saying that he was 'not an Ornithologist, nor an Ichthyologist . . . no Botanist, no Mineralogist', and by doubting whether anyone less than a Humboldt or a Davy would suffice. He concluded by offering, as an alternative, 'a digest, at most in three... volumes, of the "Corpus Historiæ Byzantinæ"; that is, a continuous narrative . . . of the fortunes of the Lower Empire from Constantine to its destruction'. The result, he thought, could hardly fail to be 'a readable—a popular book'. The severity of Leslie Stephen, in his able essay on De Quincey, must be attributed partly to his own experience as an editor.

While nothing can counterbalance the fact that without the necessity of contributing to periodicals De Quincey might never have written anything, many of his characteristic faults must be attributed to this mode of publication. He did not often write on subjects that completely failed to interest him, but he was often obliged to begin before he had digested his materials. His extraordinary feats of digression—aggravated by his Shandian explanations that what seem to be irrelevancies are in fact supremely logical—must in part be attributed to this; while the tasteless facetiousness which spoils so much of his work is largely due to the same cause. In a perverse way his pedantry was enhanced by the knowledge that he had 'the unlearned equally with the learned amongst [his] readers'. This fact seems to have encouraged his besetting sin of starting with the Greeks. In the essay on Style, for example, the dissertation on Greek history and literature grows out of all proportion to its true place in the logic of the subject; while there is an extraordinary postscript in which he apologizes for forgetting to mention 'the Roman Recitations in the Porticos of Baths, &c.' There is something ominous in the announcement in the third part:

Perhaps, the unlearned reader... will thank us for here giving him, in a very few words, such an account of the Grecian Literature in its periods of manifestation, and in the relations existing between these periods, that he shall not easily forget them. (x. 203.)

One is reminded of Chaucer's Eagle in *The Hous of Fame*:

> .   . Lo, so I can
> Lewedly to a lewed man
> Speke, and shewe him swyche skiles,
> That he may shake hem by the biles.

It is the authentic voice of a bore.

The clue to a great deal in De Quincey is that he was a solitary. He once claimed that he had 'passed more of [his] life in absolute and unmitigated solitude, voluntarily, and for intellectual purposes, than any person of [his] age', and in the *Autobiographic Sketches* he traces the habit back to his unhappiness in childhood. How habituated he was to solitary thinking appears in his use of the word 'reverie' where most men would use 'reflection': he tells us, for example, that he once planned to write 'some reveries' on Greek literature. So much solitude is not good for a prose writer, in his more ordinary tasks, and many of De Quincey's faults were aggravated by the solitary life he led. At times it seems as if he is living in an Einsteinian universe in which our usual measuring-rods of importance no longer hold good. When he describes his childish aspirations and fears about his imaginary state of Gombroon, for example, the reader feels as if he were looking through an immensely powerful magnifying glass. Here there is a dramatic relevance, but De Quincey's habit of portraying things in the dimensions in which they present themselves to his private vision is not confined to his autobiographical writings. His sense of proportion is not that of other men. Yet it must be remembered that his finest writing is the fruit of his solitude no less than his inferior work; and it matters a thousand times more. 'Solitude', he once wrote, '. . . is . . . the mightiest of agencies; for solitude is essential to man.' (i. 48.) It is in the *Suspiria* that the climax of his thought on this subject is to be found: 'No man ever will unfold the capacities of his own intellect who does not at least checker his life with solitude. How much solitude, so much power.' It was in solitude that the visions came to him which he strove to express in 'impassioned prose'.

It was also as a result of the introspective musings of a solitary that his lifelong interest in psychology was born. He was of necessity a hypochondriac, and his Diary opens with the statement that 'the intimate connection . . . [between the] body and

the mind, has never (to my knowledge) been sufficiently enlarged on in theory or insisted on in practice'. Observation
of the ways of his own body and mind led him to the general
interest in psychology which may be found running through
most of his work. His interest in 'pariahs', for example, was
intellectual as well as emotional, psychological as well as sympathetic. His literary criticism, as has been pointed out, aspired
to a psychological foundation. His interest in murder was not
wholly that of a sensationalist: in reading police reports, he
wrote, 'I stand aghast at the revelations . . . of human life and
the human heart—at its colossal guilt, and its colossal misery.'
Such reflections led him to the suggestion that

It is not without probability that in the world of dreams every one
of us ratifies for himself the original transgression. In dreams . . .
each several child of our mysterious race completes for himself the
treason of the aboriginal fall. (xiii. 304.)

His own sufferings and visionary dreams were the starting-point
of most of his psychological speculations. He gives a detailed description of the extraordinary effect on him of the death of
an infant daughter of Wordsworth's, for example, 'as having
a permanent interest in the psychological history of human
nature'. 'You will think this which I am going to say too near,
too holy, for recital', he wrote in a fragment intended for the
Suspiria. 'But not so. The deeper a woe touches me in heart, so
much the more am I urged to recite it.' He lived on into an age that
was hostile to most forms of confessional writing: it is possible,
though not likely, that that is why he has nothing to say about
sex. Yet he belongs, though in a lesser degree than Rousseau or
Gide, to the company of the explorers of the human mind. It is
not for nothing that Baudelaire was fascinated by him. And he
went further, and deeper, than the majority of introspective
writers; for in the *Suspiria* the attempt to trace the workings of
his own mind becomes one with the striving to fathom the whole
significance of human life.

Suspiria de Profundis was the title De Quincey gave to the
sequel to his *Confessions*, dealing principally with his dreams.
Four instalments, making up about a third of the work as he
envisaged it, appeared in *Blackwood's* in 1845. By that date, or
within a few years afterwards, he seems to have written much
more; for in a passage already quoted from the preface to the

revised *Confessions* of 1856 he tells us that the 'crowning grace' of the book was to have been 'a succession of some twenty or twenty-five dreams and noon-day visions, which had arisen under the latter stages of opium influence'—but that most of these have been lost. Of the dreams which had not been lost, 'The Daughter of Lebanon' was printed at the end of the *Confessions* because of its connexion with the story of Ann; while others were reprinted under various headings in other volumes of the collected edition. In 1891 some further material was published by Alexander H. Japp, with a key to the *Suspiria* as a whole; so that we now possess about half of the work, though not in its final form. Since even what he had completed of the *Suspiria* seemed to De Quincey 'very greatly superior' to the *Confessions* themselves, we ignore them at our peril, and it remains possible to make out at least the main lines of the design.

The theme of the *Suspiria* as a whole is that pain and grief are essential to the development of the soul. This truth becomes apparent only to exceptional people, and even to them only when the original experience has sloughed off its 'accidents' and assumed a universal and perhaps symbolical form in the mind in a reverie years afterwards. The introductory passage on dreaming makes it evident what De Quincey is trying to do, and why he regards it as of the first importance. A man with an exceptional power of dreaming, he has come to realize that dreams are of a far profounder significance than is commonly understood, being 'the one great tube through which man communicates with the shadowy'. As he explains later, his power of dreaming is selective, interpretative, and therefore creative: 'far less like a lake reflecting the heavens than like the pencil of some mighty artist—Da Vinci or Michael Angelo— that cannot copy . . . but comments in freedom, while reflecting in fidelity'. One is reminded of both Plato and Wordsworth:

> The dreaming organ, in connexion with the heart, the eye, and the ear, composes the magnificent apparatus which forces the infinite into the chambers of a human brain, and throws dark reflections from eternities below all life upon the mirrors of that mysterious *camera obscura*—the sleeping mind. (xiii. 335.)

His aim is to take the reader into the *penetralia* of his mind, so revealing truths of the greatest moment to the life and immortality of man.

In the first of the *Suspiria* we are taken back at one point to De Quincey's infancy. His earliest recollections are connected with death, and culminate in the loss of his sister when he was seven. Already the main themes of these meditations appear: the power of death, the quest for reunion with a girl who has died, the problem of the nature of time, the significance of solitude, the value of suffering. In accordance with his belief that 'experiences of deep suffering or joy first obtain their entire fulness of expression when they are reverberated from dreams', there follow two reveries on his sister's death, one dating from his Oxford years, the other occurring in old age, 'on this dovelike morning of Pentecost'. Sometimes the seminal event and its re-creation in reverie are disconcertingly juxtaposed. It is the same difficulty that had faced him in the *Confessions* themselves: although his real subject may be the effect of early experiences on his mind, without a narrative of these experiences the reader will fail to understand the reverie. 'The English Mail-Coach' illustrates the problem. A coaching accident witnessed in his youth had been 'carried, . . . raised and idealised, into my dreams', so becoming of great importance to him. The conclusion, in which we are presented with the final significance of the experience, is impressive in the highest degree. It is a 'Dream Fugue', culminating in music which celebrates a great victory:

> Then was completed the passion of the mighty fugue. The golden tubes of the organ, which as yet had but muttered at intervals— gleaming amongst clouds and surges of incense—threw up, as from fountains unfathomable, columns of heart-shattering music. Choir and anti-choir were filling fast with unknown voices. Thou also, Dying Trumpeter, with thy love that was victorious, and thy anguish that was finishing, didst enter the tumult; trumpet and echo—farewell love, and farewell anguish—rang through the dreadful *sanctus*.
> (xiii. 326.)

There is no more eloquent passage in English prose, but the success of 'The Mail-Coach' as a whole is another matter. In their length and at times their tone the opening sections are out of all keeping with what follows; while in the concluding passages, remarkable as they are, the figure of Ann associates somewhat incongruously with the Battle of Waterloo. De Quincey added a note explaining the logic of the construction: but his claim that 'the Dream is a law to itself; . . . as well quarrel with a rainbow', merely raises the question whether many passages in the *Suspiria* do not have a higher value for the psychologist than for the literary critic.

Only the more important of the remaining *Suspiria* call for notice. The theme of 'The Palimpsest of the Human Brain', where once again the introduction is too long for what follows, is that nothing is ever finally erased from the memory. In 'Vision of Life' an analogy from music explains the connexion of grief and joy: 'The rapture of life . . . does not arise, unless as perfect music arises, . . . by the confluence of the mighty and terrific discords with the subtile concords. . . .' (xiii. 350.) Suffering is 'the price of a more searching vision'. The same theme is found in 'Levana and our Ladies of Sorrow', which as De Quincey points out prefigures the course of the whole work. The Destinies that have presided at his birth hold it as their 'commission . . . from God . . . to plague his heart until [they have] unfolded the capacities of his spirit'. In 'The Dark Interpreter' the 'root of dark uses . . . in moral convulsions' is again expounded. Perhaps the most brilliant illustration of all may be found among the notes for further *Suspiria*, where De Quincey explains that under the influence of suffering 'the mighty machinery of the brain' is exalted, 'and the Infinities appear, before which the tranquillity of man unsettles, the gracious forms of life depart, and the ghostly enters'. When 'The Daughter of Lebanon' is seen as part of the *Suspiria* its significance becomes clear. In it the Christian undertones which can just be caught elsewhere become clearly audible; in the end the help of 'one learned in the afflictions of man', an 'evangelist' (presumably St. Luke), enables the Outcast to save her life by losing it, and the quest for love and mercy which is as central in the *Suspiria* as it had been throughout its author's life comes to a triumphant close.

It is in the *Suspiria*, which he himself considered 'the *ne plus ultra* . . . which I can ever hope to attain', that the explanation and justification of De Quincey's views on prose style are to be found. They are the primary example of what he calls 'impassioned prose', a category in which he stresses the almost complete barrenness of earlier literature. Perhaps he felt that prose should extend its imaginative range, as poetry had been doing. He seems to have been groping towards the idea of 'impassioned prose' all his life, as he mused on the splendour of the visions that had come to him in reverie. Music accompanied his most moving dreams, and it is always in musical terms that he thought of his problem: 'A single word in a wrong key, ruins the whole music.' Nothing could be more revealing than the title of the last section of 'The Mail-Coach': 'Dream Fugue: Founded on the Preceding Theme.' Poets have sometimes looked to music for help in the problem of organizing their material: here, in a work which has certain affinities with Eliot's *Four Quartets*, a writer of prose has attempted the same thing. Completed, the *Suspiria* might have suggested a majestic fugue: as they stand the analogy is rather with an unfinished set of themes and variations.

As we contrast De Quincey's potentialities with his achievement we are constantly reminded of Coleridge, that other 'man of infinite title-pages'. The two had a great deal in common. Each was interested in an exceptionally wide range of subjects: psychology, philology, logic, German metaphysics, theology, universal history—to name only a few. Each of them was a great reader of travel books, each depreciated French literature as if in compensation for setting so high a value on German, each was something of a John Bull, each was keenly interested in the faculty of dreaming and in the workings of the human mind, each was chronically behindhand with the world and its editors, each was the despair of his friends, each was on occasion sentimental, humourless, and sadly lacking in a sense of proportion.

No doubt De Quincey modelled himself to some extent on the older man, having the same ambition of becoming a '*Polyhistor*, or catholic student'. Yet when we read his comparison of Coleridge and Leibnitz in the *Letters to a Young Man* we realize that De Quincey had attempted rather to follow the thinker whom he regarded as Coleridge's own model. Whereas Coleridge had been 'too self-indulgent, and almost a voluptuary in his studies', Leibnitz had 'sacrificed to the austerer muses [and] submitted to . . . regular study [and] discipline of thought'. When De Quincey tells us that 'the German had been a discursive reader, —the Englishman a desultory reader' it is clear in which category he would have placed himself.

Yet De Quincey and Coleridge had something in common which differentiates them decisively from Leibnitz: they were both opium-eaters. The result of this may be seen in almost everything either of them wrote. For this reason (as has already been pointed out) De Quincey is often an excellent commentator on the greater man. What he once wrote about a piece of his own writing is equally applicable to much of the work of Coleridge: 'In parts and fractions eternal creations are carried on, but the nexus is wanting, the life and the central principle which should bind together all the parts at the centre, with all its radiations to the circumference, are wanting.' 'Opium-eaters . . . never finish anything', as he sums up in his essay on 'Coleridge and Opium-Eating'. Yet he insists that opium gives as well as taking away: 'It defeats the *steady* habit of exertion; but it creates spasms of irregular exertion. It ruins the natural power of life; but it develops preternatural paroxysms of intermitting power.' It is possible that De Quincey would have been a happier man without opium, but unlikely that he would have been a greater writer; for, as he himself pointed out, 'it is in the faculty of mental vision, it is in the increased power of dealing with the shadowy and the dark, that the characteristic virtue of opium lies'.

XII

MISCELLANEOUS PROSE

THE paradox that confronts us as we consider the literature of this period, the fact that it is so much easier to name the major writers than the major works which they produced, is in no department of literature more striking than in that of miscellaneous prose. 'It is a great literary age', as Bulwer Lytton remarked, '—we have great literary men—but where are their works?'—and he answered his own question by pointing out that 'We must seek them not in detached and avowed and standard publications, but in periodical miscellanies. It is in these journals that the most eminent of our recent men of letters have chiefly obtained their renown.' As we consider the work of the writers discussed in this chapter we shall find that the greater part of it first appeared in periodicals of different types, and that even if it was republished in book form it often retains the marks of its origin.

If the importance of a writer were to be gauged by his demonstrable influence on his contemporaries, Cobbett[1] would have no rival in our period except Jeremy Bentham. To us as we look back he seems less a man than a phenomenon. It is impossible to think of the development of England at the beginning of the nineteenth century without thinking of Cobbett. He was an astonishingly prolific writer, and since he was born into an age of autobiography his writings are full of information about himself. As the son of unpretentious parents he received little formal education and spent most of his boyhood at the usual country tasks. During these early years he not only learned all that there was to be learnt about the country and its ways, however: he was also a great reader, and so came on the new ideas that were fermenting in Europe. We hear of him joining a circulating library at Chatham and reading the 'greatest part' of its con-

---

[1] William Cobbett (?1763–1835) was the son of a farmer and innkeeper at Farnham in Surrey. In 1784 he enlisted as a soldier. Between 1785 and 1791 he served in Nova Scotia and New Brunswick, but the following year he first took refuge in France and then in Philadelphia. Between 1805 and 1820 he farmed in Hampshire. In 1820 he wrote strongly in support of Queen Caroline. In 1826 he tried to enter Parliament: in 1832 he was successful, becoming M.P. for Oldham.

tents through more than once, and he early formed an admiration for Swift that was to have its effect on his own prose style. After an unhappy period as a clerk he joined the army, and soon we find him writing an official report on the condition of Nova Scotia and New Brunswick and building up a case against a corrupt group of officers. On his discharge he instigated a court martial against these men, but fearing that he was in greater danger than the accused he fled with his wife to France and then to the United States. His literary career probably began a few months after his arrival in America, and his first writings reveal him as a strong anti-Democrat, anti-Radical, and anti-Jacobin. Having quarrelled with his publisher he set up in Philadelphia as a bookseller and publisher for himself, soon writing *The Life and Adventures of Peter Porcupine* (1796), with its characteristic motto: 'Now you lying varlets, you shall see how a plain tale shall put you down.' Defiantly adopting the nickname that he had been given he sets out to describe his own career, and does so with the complacency of a self-made man. He makes no secret of his views, and pulls no punches. Every reader may hear that Cobbett dislikes Priestley, dislikes Franklin, enjoys life in France, and is extremely critical of what he has seen in America. His *Works*, as published in 1801, exhibit 'A Faithful Picture of the United States of America; of their Governments, Laws, Politics, and Resources; of the Character of their Presidents, Governors . . . and Military Men; and of the Customs, Manners, Morals, Religion, Virtues and Vices of the People . . .'. Before the publication of these twelve volumes, however, Cobbett thought it prudent to return to England, where he was flatteringly received by Pitt and other anti-Jacobin leaders. He insisted on retaining his independence, tried to run a newspaper of his own, and then in 1802 started the weekly *Political Register*, which continued to appear until after his death and constituted his main channel of communication with the public. He began as a supporter of William Windham and the Tories, but by 1809 the tendency of the *Register* is predominantly Radical and an article on military flogging published that year led to Cobbett's imprisonment. In 1816, worried by declining circulation, he produced a cheap version of the *Register* at 2d., so raising the circulation to between 40,000 and 50,000 copies a week and appealing direct to the working classes. The first of the 'Six Acts' of 1820 drastically cut his circulation. In 1830–2 he reprinted some of the most important articles from the *Register* in his *Two-Penny Trash*.

The *Rural Rides*, which Cobbett himself reprinted as a book and which remain his best-known work, made their first appearance in the *Political Register* in 1821 and the following years. Already a celebrated person, Cobbett set out to see for himself the condition of the agricultural community in the period of distress which had followed Waterloo. He went on horseback, for a very characteristic reason:

My object was, not to see inns and turnpike-roads, but to see the *country*; to see the farmers at home, and to see the labourers in the fields; and to do this you must go either on foot or on horseback. With a gig you cannot get about amongst bye-lanes and across fields, through bridle-ways and hunting-gates.

Wherever he went he noticed the quality of the soil, the state of the crops, and all those indications of fertility or poverty to which the townsman is blind. Cobbett knows about trees and birds, and is as interested in cloud-formations as Constable himself. He notices whether the girls are handsome and neatly dressed, not only because he is of an amorous disposition, but also because he regards them as one of the fruits of the land. He is the most abstemious of travellers, preferring milk even to small ale and making a point of being in bed by 8 p.m. It is as characteristic that he should tell us about this as it is that he should give the money so saved to the deserving poor.

But Cobbett did not only wish to see for himself. He wished to persuade the farmers that they were ill-advised to support the Corn Laws and would be better occupied in trying to have the burden of taxation lightened. His love of giving advice comes out even in small matters: when he sees a woman plaiting straw he gives her instructions and wishes to send her a copy of his *Cottage Economy* with its 'Essay on Straw Plat'. If he comes on a well-kept farm, it is sure to be because the farmer has been following Cobbett's instructions. We notice that the country people were as eager to hear Cobbett as he was to be heard, and that it was to substantial farmers and not to the discontented mob that he liked to address himself. 'I made a speech last evening to from 130 to 150', he wrote on 13 April 1830, 'almost all farmers, and most men of apparent wealth to a certain extent. I have seldom been better pleased with my audience. It is not the clapping and huzzaing that I value so much as the *silent atten-tion*, the *earnest look* at me from *all eyes* at once, and then . . . the *look and nod at each other*, as if the parties were saying, "Think of that!" ' Cobbett tells us that he has adopted this 'haranguing system' (later in the *Rides* he sometimes uses the word 'lectures') because he has been kept out of Parliament. In fact he could not have been nearly as effective in Parliament as he was out of it—as he discovered when he was carried into the Commons by the mounting wave of Reform. Through his writings and his endless public speeches Cobbett became a focus for reforming opinion, receiving letters from correspondents in all quarters. 'Since my return home', he writes near the end of one of the *Rides*, '. . . I have received letters from the east, from the north, and from the west. All tell me that . . . the crops are free from blight. . . . Before Christmas, we shall have the wheat down to what will be a fair average price in future.'

In agricultural affairs Cobbett was an expert and appears to be reasonably objective. In other matters it is clear that he finds what he sets out to find. His prejudices are deep-rooted and luxuriant. It is as certain that he will not find a man with a clean shirt in a rotten borough as that he will have no good to say of a watering place. He holds to the full rigours of the view that primary producers are the sole sources of wealth and does not hesitate to draw the conclusion that everyone else is a para-site: hence the disgust with which he regards such a place as Cheltenham, 'a nasty, ill-looking place, half clown and half cockney, . . . the residence of an assemblage of tax-eaters, . . . vermin [who] shift about between London, Cheltenham, Bath, Bognor, Brighton, Tunbridge . . . and other spots in England, while some of them get over to France and Italy'. He has the self-educated man's love of generalizations and the demagogue's habit of rousing one section of the population against another. He hates Jews, Irishmen, Quakers, clergymen, and many other categories of mankind. He would like to see some ferocious Old Testament curse falling on London, 'The Great Wen', over-whelming it in a night. He hates 'Scotch FEELOSOFERS', the *Edinburgh Review*, and Scotsmen in general, whom he regards as a 'greedy band of *invaders* . . . [who] . . . never . . . work them-selves and . . . are everlastingly publishing essays, the object of which is to keep the Irish out of England!' At times he seems to approve of no one but farmers and their labourers, shoe-makers (towards whom he displays a curious tenderness), and occasional good landlords of the old-fashioned kind.

Although he had a powerful mind Cobbett was an extraordinarily simple man, and he liked to think that reality was correspondingly simple. He had the moralist's vision of a happy community in which each man should play his part and receive his due reward, and failing to find it in the present he created it in the past. With a certain naïve felicity he chooses the moment of approaching Oxford to salute the Golden Age, 'when men lived on the simple fruits of the earth and slaked their thirst at the pure and limpid brook! when the trees shed their leaves to form a couch for their repose, and cast their bark to furnish them with a canopy!' Although he himself calls this a Quixote-like speech, it was this belief in a Golden Age that sustained Cobbett throughout his life, and like many men since he chose to locate his Golden Age in the Middle Ages. He took part of the truth and made so much of it that it became a lie. His view is summed up in the title of his *History of the Protestant 'Reformation': . . . Showing how that event has impoverished and degraded the main body of the People* (1824–6). It is easy to sympathize with him in his indignation at the complacency of many of his contemporaries about Progress:

Talk of *vassals*! Talk of *villains*! Talk of *serfs*! [Were] there any of these . . . so debased, so absolutely slaves, as the poor creatures who, in the 'enlightened' north, are compelled to work fourteen hours in a day, in a heat of eighty-four degrees; and who are liable to punishment for looking out at a window of the factory!

Yet when Cobbett begins to compare contemporary Britain with 'this once happy and moral England' one need not be very learned or very cynical to sense that the contrast is overdrawn. His attitude to feudalism reminds one of that of the Webbs to the Soviet system: he is delighted by the theory, and heedless of the practice. He has nothing but contempt for the cant of those who deplore 'the *superstition* and *dark ignorance* that induced people to found monasteries', and it is true that such a system might have done a great deal of good in Cobbett's own day, if it had worked as it had been supposed to work. Cobbett saw what was wrong with contemporary Protestant England and assumed that all was well before. It is an attitude to the Reformation that was popular a decade or two ago and produced (as its strangest bloom) Mr. Eliot's remarkable hypothesis of the 'dissociation of sensibility'. Like Scott's Meg Merrilies Cobbett was an inveterate *laudator temporis acti*. He was deeply moved by the beauty of our old churches and cathedrals and impressed by the piety of the ages in which they were built: 'I could not look up at the spire and the whole of the church at Salisbury without feeling that I lived in degenerate times. Such a thing never could be made *now*. We *feel* that, as we look at the building.' After showing his little son a cathedral Cobbett told him that 'that building was made when there were no poor wretches in England called *paupers* . . .; when every labouring man was clothed in good woollen cloth'. They then arrive at an inn, where they find an Italian translation of Cobbett's *History of the Protestant 'Reformation'* awaiting them. For sheer *naïveté* it would be hard to match Cobbett's comment—'There, Doctor Black. Write *you* a book that shall be translated into *any* foreign language.'

His own attitude to religion is a little in doubt. When he talks of the clergy it is the holders of rich livings in the South that he usually has in mind, and such clergymen he regards as 'tax-eaters', the natural associates of the 'Jews and Jobbers' who throng the watering-places. He deplores the reactionary politics of the average High Churchman, as expressed by the *Quarterly Review*. Yet we also find him writing that he knows 'of no more meritorious and ill-used men than the working clergy' (a reminder that he was a man who tried to be fair), and discover him one evening taking the service himself at St. Ives 'on a carpenter's bench in a wheelwright's shop'. He always insisted that he was a Christian, giving the very characteristic reason that he liked 'any religion, that tends to make men innocent and benevolent and happy, by taking the best possible means of furnishing them with plenty to eat and drink and wear'. He shows no interest in the dogmas or the supernatural part of the Christian faith.

His other writings, or such of them as one may reasonably be expected to read, reinforce the impression made by the *Rural Rides*: they do not modify it. *A Year's Residence in America*, reprinted from the *Political Register* in 1818–19, is one of the most interesting. Cobbett's *Grammar of the English Language* (1818) has rightly been said to be 'as entertaining as a story-book': it displays his flair for popular instruction and the same care for the purity of the English language (oddly combined with a contempt for the classics) which appears in the *Rural Rides*, where he is always ready to interrupt his political argument to discuss the meaning and derivation of such a word as 'hanger' or 'Tommy'. Many thousands of people learned to write from the *Grammar*, just as thousands learned even more practical matters from Cobbett's *Cottage Economy* (1821–2), which deals with such subjects as the brewing of beer, bread-making, and the nurture of cows, pigs, ewes, goats, poultry, and rabbits. *Cobbett's Poor Man's Friend* (1826–7), for which he himself had a particular fondness, is a political pamphlet in which he contrasts the supposed prosperity of the working classes before the Reformation with their condition in his own time. *Advice to Young Men and (incidentally) to Young Women, in the Middle and Higher Ranks of Life* (1829–30) reminds us both of Defoe and of Richardson: it consists of letters 'addressed to a Youth, a Bachelor, a Lover, a Husband, a Father, and a Citizen, or Subject'. This book is egotistical, occasionally comical, but almost always sensible. Only a very wise man, or a very superior person, could read it through without coming on one or two pieces of advice that he would do well to follow.

If the definition of a good style is a manner of using words precisely suited to the writer's purpose, then Cobbett has an excellent style. As Hazlitt pointed out, he uses 'plain, broad, downright English': he is clear, forceful, and free from affectation. He makes much use of italics and exclamation-marks, and returns repeatedly to his favourite topics. His tone and manner were admirably suited to his original audience, and he had every justification for shouting. But we are not the audience for which he wrote, and as we read him we are driven to the conclusion that his purely literary merits have sometimes been exaggerated. Read in bulk, his writings become a little tedious. We admire the extraordinary machine at work, and we acknowledge how effective it proved; but after a while it is a relief to get away from the noise. There is little variety of subject or attitude. There are no nuances or half-tones. Everything is on one plane, without shading or perspective. There is no deep understanding of human nature. There are pleasant descriptions of the countryside, but they are never great prose. Although it is easy to make an agreeable volume of selections from Cobbett's work, it does not matter very much which passages one selects. He is seldom memorable: as Hazlitt pointed out, 'there is not a single *bon-mot*, a single sentence in Cobbett that has ever been quoted again'. Perhaps the most eloquent passage in his writings occurs when he is describing the sight that he hated most and that was most characteristic of his time:

It was dark before we reached Sheffield; so that we saw the iron furnaces in all the horrible splendour of their everlasting blaze. Nothing can be conceived more grand or more terrific than the yellow waves of fire that incessantly issue from the top of these furnaces, some of which are close by the way-side. (31 January 1830.)

As a rule he has little to say about the towns through which he passes: if he approves of it he will comment that a village or town is 'clean' and 'nice' (a word that he over-works), and that will be all. He sees everything, in fact, from his own meridian. Because he was not at school, he thanks God for it. When he passes through Oxford he reflects that he and his writings will have infinitely more effect than those of all the drones in the colleges. He uses Shakespeare (as G. D. H. Cole pointed out) as a stick for beating the potato crop, and has little interest in the things of the imagination. To him Dr. Johnson was simply a 'dastardly old pensioner', a judgement he would certainly have withdrawn if he had ever met him. He was a sort of portent, God's Judgement on the men who were writing Latin verses while the ricks were burning. For him Man was not 'a being darkly wise, and rudely great', but something much more simple. He was right to protest against the cant of talking about the souls of the poor when their bodies were starving, and the things which he admired—such as strength of character, honesty, and hard work—are truly admirable. But life is more complicated than Cobbett was capable of seeing. Once a man is provided for, Cobbett has no further interest in him except as a potential audience for his harangues and pamphlets.

If we wish to understand Leigh Hunt's work as an essayist and critic it will be as well to begin with a few facts about his numerous periodicals.[1] He started the *Examiner* with his brother

---

[1] James Henry Leigh Hunt (1784–1859) was educated at Christ's Hospital and was so precocious that his father published a volume of his poetry when he was only 17. Soon he was writing dramatic criticisms for the *News*, which was edited by his brother John. During his spell in prison, which permanently damaged his health, his visitors included Byron, Lamb, and Bentham. It was Hunt who brought about the meeting between Keats and Shelley. He lived on into the heart of the Victorian Age and produced a great many books and periodicals.

John in 1808 and continued to be the principal contributor
until 1821. Its contents were 'Politics, Domestic Economy and
Theatricals', while its motto proclaimed that 'Party is the madness of many for the gain of a few'. It supported the abolition of
the slave trade, Catholic emancipation and the reform of the
criminal law, had its doubts about the war with France, criticized the Prince of Wales, and soon stated with all possible
emphasis that 'A REFORM IN PARLIAMENT WILL PURIFY THE
WHOLE CONSTITUTION'. By 1812 Bentham calculated that the
Examiner was selling between 7,000 and 8,000 copies. Its promoters were frequently threatened with libel actions. In 1811
they were unsuccessfully prosecuted for an article on the subject of military flogging, and in 1813 each of the brothers
was fined £500 and sentenced to two years' imprisonment for
one of their numerous attacks on the Prince of Wales. Although
the two men were well treated in their separate prisons, and the
Examiner was able to continue publication, Leigh Hunt was
naturally regarded as a martyr to the cause of liberty, and in
his *Poems* of 1817 we find Keats addressing him as 'Libertas'.
After this the political influence of the *Examiner* declined,
while its literary importance increased. This is not surprising:
apart from the danger and difficulty of writing freely on
politics at this point, Leigh Hunt's attitude to politics was from
the first paradoxical. Although he was a passionate supporter
of certain great causes, he was not a political animal: he was
uninterested in ways and means, parties and cabals, arguments and indirect persuasions. 'Though I was a politician
(so to speak)', as he puts it in a revealing passage in his
Autobiography, 'I had scarcely a political work in my library.
Spensers and Arabian Tales filled up the shelves.' The *Examiner*'s most important work was its perceptive and untiring
advocacy of the new poets, and particularly of Shelley and
Keats.

In the prospectus of the *Reflector*, a quarterly magazine that
had appeared in 1810–11, we find Hunt speculating about the
relation between politics and literature:

Politics, in times like these, should naturally take the lead in
periodical discussion, because they have an importance and interest
almost unexampled in history, and because *they are now, in their turn,
exhibiting their re-action upon literature, as literature in the preceding age
exhibited its action upon them.*

'The Feast of the Poets', which appeared in the fourth issue, sums up Hunt's early critical views, while Lamb's essays on Hogarth and on the plays of Shakespeare 'considered with reference to their fitness for stage representation' are also to be found in the *Reflector*. A good deal of attention is devoted to painting and sculpture because (we are told) whereas the drama in England 'is in its second infancy, with all the vices of a frivolous dotage', the fine arts 'are in their first infancy and must be handled more tenderly'. In the *Indicator*, which appeared every Wednesday from 13 October 1819 to 21 March 1821, and which Edmund Blunden has aptly described as 'the literary supplement' of the *Examiner*, Leigh Hunt felt at liberty to take a holiday from politics, and the result is undoubtedly his most successful and characteristic piece of writing. 'They tell me I am at my best at this work', as he acknowledged, and from the first the *Indicator* sold well and won high praise from such judges as Hazlitt and Lamb. Once again Hunt prints and praises the work of the new poets ('La Belle Dame sans Merci' first appeared in the *Indicator*) and draws the attention of English readers to foreign literature.

The idea for the *Liberal* (1822–3), an intended quarterly of which only four issues appeared, seems to have been Byron's, and Shelley was not alone in doubting whether such an alliance between 'the wren and the eagle' would last for long. As Hazlitt tells us, 'the Tories were shocked that Lord Byron should grace the popular side' while 'the Whigs were shocked that he should share his confidence and counsels with any one who did not unite the double recommendations of birth and genius—like themselves!' The object of this work was 'not political, except inasmuch as all writing now-a-days must involve something to that effect'; the contributors intended to contribute their 'liberalities in the shape of Poetry, Essays, Tales, Translations, and other amenities'. The 'amenities' in fact opened with Byron's *Vision of Judgment*, not noticeably softened in its effect by the instruction on the Errata leaf: 'Instead of "a *worse* king never left a realm undone", read "a *weaker* king ne'er left a realm undone".' Italian literature was to be given particular prominence in these volumes of 'Verse and Prose from the South', as well as German and Spanish. In spite of the brilliance of individual contributions, however, the *Liberal* lacks unity, and the outcry which it occasioned was out of all proportion to the size of its circulation. 'Never since I have been a publisher did I ever observe such a universal outcry . . .', Murray wrote to Byron: 'It is dreadful to think of yr. association with such outcasts from society.' The publisher was fined £100 for publishing a 'gross, impious and slanderous' libel on George III.

Some of Leigh Hunt's best essays are to be found in a weekly called the *Companion* which ran for the first seven months of 1828 and consists (as he says in his *Autobiography*) 'partly of criticisms on theatres, authors, and public events, and partly of a series of essays in the manner of the *Indicator*', but the new periodical 'did not address itself to any existing influence' and so failed to pay its way. We cannot pursue Hunt through his later periodicals, such as the *Tatler* (1830–2), which came out daily, *Leigh Hunt's London Journal* (1834–5), or *Leigh Hunt's Journal; A Miscellany for the Cultivation of the Memorable, the Progressive, and the Beautiful*, which appeared in 1850–1. Nor is there time to trace his contributions to periodicals edited by other men, from the *New Monthly Magazine* to *Household Words*. It will be more to the point to attempt a brief general characterization of his work as a critic and essayist. At Christ's Hospital Boyer was never tired of recommending the *Spectator* as the 'standard of prose writing' and the essayists of the eighteenth century were Leigh Hunt's masters. Hunt tells us that his own first essays were called 'The Traveller' and were the work of 'Mr. Town, *junior*, Critic and Censor-general'. Yet he instinctively rebelled against Boyer's 'exaction of moral observations on a given subject', preferring Goldsmith to Addison and deriving 'an entirely fresh and delightful sense of the merits of essay-writing' from the *Connoisseur*, by George Colman and Bonnell Thornton, which he discovered for himself. Whereas the eighteenth-century essayist is usually concerned to point a moral, Hunt's aim is to communicate enjoyment. Capable as he is of severity when oppression is in question (when he always remembers Voltaire, for him the great 'destroyer of the strongholds of superstition'), he is not really a moralist at all, except in the sense that he advocates a sort of innocent Epicureanism. His inborn tendency 'to reap pleasure from every object in creation' is the motive force of his essays. In his *Autobiography* he explains why he called one of the shorter-lived of his periodicals the *Seer*: 'The *Seer* does not mean a prophet . . ., but an observer of ordinary things about him, gifted by his admiration of nature with the power of discerning what everybody else may discern by a cultivation of the like secret of satisfaction.' The same attitude inspired his literary criticism. Hunt wrote almost exclusively of what he enjoyed, and few men have had a more catholic capacity for enjoyment. He was the most important of Keats's early guides to 'the realms of gold' and continued to play this role for many other readers until the middle of the century. To the end of his life he retained an uncommon flair for recognizing excellence of new kinds even when it was accompanied by obvious defects. Whereas Croker lived to be as wrong about Tennyson as he had been about Keats, Hunt was as perceptive and as generous about the one as he had been about the other. It is true that he sometimes over-praised young poets who came to nothing, true also that he seldom wrote adverse criticism; yet if a critic is to be judged by the number of times he is right about his contemporaries then Hunt has no rival in the history of English criticism. Even so one hesitates to call him a great critic. He was more often right about his contemporaries than Hazlitt, far more often right than Jeffrey; yet he was a less intelligent man than either. His strength lay in his sensibility, in his accessibility to fresh literary experience, rather than in his intellect or his ability to reason about literature. Perhaps this very fact helped him to be fair to writers, like Scott and Wordsworth, whose views about politics and about life in general he was very far from sharing.

It should be mentioned that Hunt had first attracted attention as a dramatic critic. The notices that he wrote for the *News* at the beginning of his career were published as *Critical Essays on the Performers of the London Theatres* in 1807. They are a remarkable achievement for a critic of twenty, and exhibit a pugnacity for which we look in vain in his later criticism. Soon, we are told, his 'judgment was universally sought and received as infallible by all actors and lovers of the drama'. Unlike many of his contemporaries in literature Hunt was also a musical man, and his occasional criticism of music is always intelligent and sympathetic. His writings on the visual arts are of more importance, however, particularly because of the part that he played in opening Keats's eyes to the beauty of painting and sculpture. As he explained in the *Reflector*, his aim was to estimate art 'in no other way than by the general standard of poetry, music, and other works of genius; that is to say, by its invention, its harmonious agreement, and its nature'. His object was to introduce the visual arts to 'persons of cultivated minds who would easily blend a love of painting and sculpture with that of the other liberal arts'. Like Haydon he hoped that English painting was on the threshold of a great renaissance. In his unjustly neglected book, *Imagination and Fancy* (1844), he draws some particularly interesting parallels between painting and poetry.

Although Hunt sometimes collected his essays into volumes, they remain essays rather than books, and it is better to read an individual essay than one of his books as a whole. Yet neither as an essayist nor as a critic does he reach the highest class. In spite of the part that politics played in his own life it was, as has been suggested, only in a special and limited sense that he was interested in politics; while in philosophy he was hardly interested at all. Compared with those of Coleridge, Hazlitt, or De Quincey his occasional writings are apt to seem slight and 'belletristic': what he has to say about literature, for example, excellent as it is, lacks the cross-fertilization that might have sprung from a deep and informed concern with other aspects of life. He remains a dilettante, a connoisseur, with something of the superficiality that the term implies. It is interesting to find him describing Coleridge 'eternally probing the depths of his own mind, and trying what he could make of them beyond the ordinary pale of logic and philosophy', and commenting: 'It is impossible to say what new worlds may be laid open, some day or other, by this apparently hopeless process.' Such a prophetic remark underlines Hunt's own limitations. He is content to remain on the surface of consciousness. Although he was courageous in facing political oppression, in his writing he tends to turn away from the darker sides of experience. His prose, fluent and agreeable as it is, is never concise, pointed, pregnant with meaning and reflection—as Hazlitt's so often is. It is difficult not to describe his style as 'chatty', and that is a word that cannot justly be used of the work of any of the great critics and essayists. Leigh Hunt is a delightful companion, but after a while we become tired of him, as Keats did.

When we turn from Leigh Hunt to Jeffrey we turn to a man who was less concerned with 'appreciation': Jeffrey took it for granted that his function was to evaluate, and to do so with severity: 'Iudex damnatur cum nocens absolvitur.' Although the claim of Jeffrey's early biographer[1] that he was 'the greatest of British critics' now seems absurd, his criticism retains a higher value than it is usually allowed. The clue to all his work is his background: three universities and the Speculative Society produced a keen young lawyer with a quick mind and an advocate's ability to get up his brief. Although he became a judge, in literature he remained always an advocate. He was a versatile man, and he made no attempt to limit himself to subjects of which he had a detailed knowledge. The explanation of many of the articles in the *Edinburgh Review* that surprise or irritate us today is that they were the work of non-specialists writing at a time when specialization was already destined to win the day. In less than thirty years Jeffrey contributed some two hundred essays on subjects as various as philosophy, history, biography, jurisprudence, criminology, travel, and what we should now call sociology, as well as on literature itself. He was a product of the Northern *Aufklärung*, a man of the same race as David Hume and Adam Smith, though he was much less gifted; and he shared their view that literature should be regarded simply as one of the agents of human happiness. Since he was anxious 'to combine Ethical precepts with Literary Criticism' he naturally made 'the Moral tendencies of the works under consideration a leading subject of discussion'. His attitude to literature was as different as possible from that of Charles Lamb. He was no collector of books: in an age of bibliomania he was blind to the charms of a folio. After his death, as Nichol Smith pointed out, 'his cellar, which contained well over three hundred dozens . . ., was distributed by the auctioneer; but his library was divided quietly among his friends'. Unfortunately his lack of sympathy with literary antiquarianism led him to pay too little attention to the facts of literary history: he preferred wide views based on *a priori* assumptions. And, of course, he was out of sympathy with many of the ideas that stimulated the younger writers of his own day. Although his life spanned practically the

---

[1] Francis Jeffrey (1773–1850), later Lord Jeffrey, was educated at Edinburgh High School and the Universities of Glasgow, Edinburgh and Oxford. When he first became an advocate in 1794 he obtained little business, on account of his Whig opinions. At the Speculative Society he met Scott and others. In 1806 Moore challenged him to a duel, as a result of a review of his poems in the *Edinburgh Review*, but the two men were arrested before they could fight. Soon Jeffrey prospered, visited America, and took an active part in politics. He became Dean of the Faculty of Advocates, Lord Advocate, and then a Judge of the Court of Session. In 1831 he became a Member of Parliament. He knew Wordsworth and was a friend of Dickens.

same period as Wordsworth's, his critical views developed very little from first to last. One reason for this was probably that the mind grows in solitude, though it is sharpened in society; perhaps Jeffrey was too seldom alone. His essays, in any event, are interesting, vivacious, stimulating; but they are never really penetrating or seminal. They stimulate the surface of the mind but do not give us the feeling that we have been profoundly enlightened.

As a critic of his contemporaries Jeffrey was highly erratic. In 1829 he proclaimed, though with professed regret, that Southey, Keats, Shelley, Wordsworth, Crabbe, and Moore were all declining in reputation, while 'the blazing star of Byron himself is receding from its place of pride'. Who then remained? Rogers and Campbell. Even if it is conceded that Jeffrey was here concerned with the course of literary fashion rather than with absolute poetic values it is evident that he was no spotter of winners. Yet a great deal remains to be set on the other side of the account. He praised Scott's poetry eloquently, and wrote excellent reviews of *Waverley* and a number of its successors. On Crabbe he wrote with great insight and understanding. In spite of being attacked in *English Bards and Scotch Reviewers* he was one of the first and most emphatic acclaimers of *Childe Harold's Pilgrimage*, and although he disapproved of the moral tendency of much of *Don Juan* he was in no doubt about the genius there displayed. He began his review of *Endymion* and Keats's volume of 1820 by saying that he has been 'exceedingly struck with the genius they display, and the spirit of poetry which breathes through all their extravagance' and went on to speak out boldly in praise of the young poet: 'We are very much inclined . . . to add, that we do not know any book which we would sooner employ as a test to ascertain whether any one had in him a native relish for poetry, and a genuine sensibility to its intrinsic charm.' Jeffrey had the highest regard for Dickens, although unfortunately he did not write on him. But instead of illustrating the merits of Jeffrey's other criticism it may be of greater interest to devote the little space that remains to a brief consideration of his criticism of Wordsworth, both because it has been too unreservedly condemned and because it is in itself of some importance in the history of our literature.

To be fair to Jeffrey we must remember that Wordsworth's reputation as a great poet rests most securely on one long poem and a number of shorter poems which make up only a small proportion of his total writings: *The Prelude*, 'Tintern Abbey', and certain of the other poems written between 1798 and 1808. Unfortunately Jeffrey did not have *The Prelude* before him, and he did have the preface to the second edition of the *Lyrical Ballads*. As has been suggested in Chapter I, there can be little doubt that the publication of the preface was a mistake which did a great deal of harm to Wordsworth's reputation. Jeffrey himself tells us that on their first appearance the *Lyrical Ballads* were 'unquestionably popular', adding that he considered their popularity well merited. The *Edinburgh Review* was founded in 1802, and Jeffrey's first hostile criticism of the Lake poets was a review of Southey's unreadable *Thalaba* in the first number: he used this as an occasion for writing about 'a *sect* of poets, that has established itself . . . within these ten or twelve years'. It is clear that Jeffrey was remembering Johnson's onslaught on 'the metaphysical poets': Wordsworth lies behind Southey, as Donne lies behind Cowley. There was an element of the 'stunt' about the article: it was a piece of brilliant journalism written as a *tour de force* to draw attention to a provocative new periodical for which no one anticipated a long life. But Jeffrey's attack, which was carried on in later articles and which enjoyed a wider influence than it deserved, was not merely a journalistic stunt. Since there was so much that was challenging and puzzling about Wordsworth's work, it was natural that critics should have looked round for guidance about his intentions, and inevitable that they should have regarded his preface as 'a kind of manifesto'. Unfortunately the preface is a misleading introduction to Wordsworth's poetry as a whole, as well as containing many statements which are completely incompatible with the known history of English poetry. Jeffrey was aware of the inconsistencies in Wordsworth's arguments and outraged by a document which seemed to him a heresy against the true doctrine of poetry. As we read his strictures on Wordsworth's theory about the language of poetry we are reading a critic in the main stream of Renaissance and neo-classical criticism, writing at a time when the doctrine was becoming slightly too rigid, as he deals with a revolutionary theory which is both unhistorical and self-contradictory. It is natural, though regrettable, that Jeffrey should have paid too much attention to the poems in which Wordsworth seemed to him to follow his theory, and too little to those in which he gloriously departs from it.

The preface seems always to have come between Jeffrey and an open-minded reading of Wordsworth. He failed to appreciate the importance of the *Poems* of 1807. He also did less than justice to *The Excursion*, though too many readers remember only the opening words of his review—'This will never do.' If we read on we find that Jeffrey tells us that he admires some passages of the poem so much that he is 'half inclined to rescind the severe sentence' that he has passed: but he cannot. 'His former poems were intended to recommend [his] system . . . by their individual merit; —but this, we suspect, must be recommended by the system—and can only expect to succeed where it has been previously established.' Before we condemn Jeffrey we should recall that while the publication of *The Excursion* seemed an event of profound significance to Hazlitt, Keats, and a few of the other more penetrating critics of the day, the poem has never proved popular: today it may be doubted whether one reader in ten of *The Prelude* has read through *The Excursion*. It is to Jeffrey's credit that he at least gave full enough extracts to enable readers interested in Wordsworth to assess its quality for themselves.

In 1844 Jeffrey summed up his opinion of Wordsworth. He understands, he tells us, that many readers who admire the same passages as he himself does in the *Lyrical Ballads* and *The Excursion* may be more tolerant than he of the inferior passages: with such critics he is not in serious disagreement. But he is told that 'almost all those who seek to exalt Mr. Wordsworth as the founder of a new school of poetry, consider . . . as by far his best and most characteristic productions' *The White Doe of Rylstone*, *Peter Bell*, 'Martha Rae', and the 'Sonnets upon the Punishment of Death': with such a view he can never agree. This is perfectly reasonable. The real charge against Jeffrey remains that of failing to recognize the significance of Wordsworth as an intellectual and spiritual force. Yet it must be acknowledged that there are still Wordsworthians who remind one of James Joyce's claim that his readers must devote the whole of their lives to the study of his works. If fully to appreciate Wordsworth we must abandon our minds to his philosophy and forbid our normal critical responses to function, then there will be many who prefer to remain outside with Jeffrey. If Wordsworth is to be appreciated and criticized like any other poet, then we must acknowledge that Jeffrey's attitude to him was at least perfectly defensible.

It is appropriate that Jeffrey should have dedicated his essays to Sydney Smith,[1] for although it was Jeffrey who made the *Edinburgh Review* a force to be reckoned with in the history of the early nineteenth century it was Sydney Smith who had been its 'original projector'. From the moment when he entered the Church, 'in obedience to the wishes of his father', Sydney Smith had proved himself an anomaly and a challenge to those in authority, and it is not surprising that some should have denounced his assumption of Orders as an act of hypocrisy. Yet the charge was unjust, and as we read through the letters to Jeffrey which form a running commentary on the early years of the *Edinburgh Review* we are struck by Smith's anxiety about its sceptical tendency. 'I certainly . . . do protest against your increasing and unprofitable scepticism', he wrote as early as the Spring of 1804:

I exhort you to restrain the violent tendency of your nature for analysis, and to cultivate synthetical propensities. What's the use of virtue? What's the use of wealth? What's the use of honor? . . . The whole effort of your mind is to destroy. Because others build slightly and eagerly, you employ yourself in kicking down their houses, and contract a sort of aversion for the more honorable useful and difficult task of building well yourself.

Soon he is parodying Jeffrey's mode of reviewing: 'Damn the solar system! bad light—planets too distant—pestered with comets—feeble contrivance;—could make a better with great ease.' He complained with reason that Jeffrey was giving the *Review* a character 'which makes it perilous for a clergyman . . . to be concerned in it', and it is hardly surprising that his own contributions became less frequent and then stopped altogether. Yet his own mind had something in common with Jeffrey's, and it is possible to imagine him sympathizing with the spirit of

[1] Sydney Smith (1771–1845) was educated at Winchester and New College, Oxford, where he was elected Fellow in 1791. He took Orders, became tutor to Michael Hicks Beach, and helped to start the *Edinburgh Review* during his period of residence in Edinburgh. In 1803 he moved to London, where he soon became a familiar figure in the Holland House circle and a favourite lecturer on moral philosophy at the Royal Institution. In 1808 he settled down near his living of Foston, outside York. Twenty years later he was made a prebendary at Bristol and then a canon-residentiary at St. Paul's in London. He was witty, generous, and honest.

Jeffrey's gibe about 'obscure truths—if such things exist'. When he complained about the review of *The Excursion* it was not because he admired the poem but simply because 'the subject is . . . so very uninteresting'. It would hardly be an exaggeration to say that the dimension in which Wordsworth's greatest poetry has its being is one of which Sydney Smith was wholly unaware. He once described himself as a man without secrets, a man in a house made of glass. That is one reason why this most intelligent and entertaining of correspondents never quite reaches the ranks of the great letter-writers. Another reason was perhaps that he lacked the sense of frustration. He found an outlet for his talents in a crowded social life which was the more intense and the more enjoyable because it formed a series of brilliant interludes between the periods of pastoral duty. It is not from a player on the human scene so confident and so fulfilled that the half-lights and nuances of a great letter-writer are to be expected.

When we turn to his essays we find that he is most eloquent when he is protesting: when he is dealing with such subjects as Chimney Sweepers, Game Laws, Botany Bay, Poor Laws, Ireland, and Prisons. Satirists are most often conservative, but throughout his life Sydney Smith used his wit on the side of progress: not to ridicule new ideas, but rather to demonstrate the absurdity of traditional prejudices. The best-remembered of his writings are the *Letters of Peter Plymley*, published in 1807–8. By giving the imaginary author a brother Abraham who 'lives in the country' and is 'a bit of a goose' he provides himself with an ideal vantage-point from which to deploy his brilliant rhetoric:

> In the first place, my sweet Abraham, the Pope is not landed—nor are there any curates sent out after him—nor has he been hid at St. Alban's by the Dowager Lady Spencer—nor dined privately at Holland House—nor been seen near Dropmore. If these fears exist (which I do not believe), they exist only in the mind of the Chancellor of the Exchequer; they emanate from his zeal for the Protestant interest; and, though they reflect the highest honour upon the delicate irritability of his faith, must certainly be considered as more ambiguous proofs of the sanity and vigour of his understanding.

He argues vigorously that England cannot afford to alienate the Catholics of Ireland:

> You speak of danger to the Establishment: I request to know when

the Establishment was ever so much in danger as when Hoche was in Bantry Bay, and whether all the books of Bossuet, or the arts of the Jesuits, were half so terrible? Mr. Perceval and his parsons forgot all this, in their horror lest twelve or fourteen old women may be converted to holy water, and Catholic nonsense. They never see that, while they are saving these venerable ladies from perdition, Ireland may be lost, England broken down, and the Protestant Church, with all its deans, prebendaries, Percevals and Rennels, be swept into the vortex of oblivion.

Although Sydney Smith had himself no sympathy with Catholicism he had the penetration and honesty to point out that the popular feeling against Catholicism 'is not all religion; it is, in great part, the narrow and exclusive spirit which delights to keep the common blessings of sun, and air, and freedom from other human beings'. The spirit which informs *The Letters of Peter Plymley* is not the *saeva indignatio* of the Juvenalian satirist but rather the *indignatio liberalis* of a clear head and a generous heart.

William Gifford, the editor of the *Quarterly*, was a very different kind of person from the clever young men who had started the *Edinburgh Review*.[1] Whereas Jeffrey was still in his twenties when the *Edinburgh* first appeared, Gifford was in his fifties when the *Quarterly* began publication. In capacity he was greatly Jeffrey's inferior. Whereas Jeffrey was a critic with a touch of the satirist about him, Gifford was a satirist with a touch of the critic. He was much less intelligent than Jeffrey, and had much less sense of responsibility. In the brief autobiography prefixed to his translation of Juvenal and Persius he describes his humble beginnings: how he was orphaned at the age of eleven, then befriended by a series of patrons and so enabled to study at Oxford and to see something of Europe as tutor to Lord Grosvenor's son. His translations and *The Baviad* and *Maeviad*, two satires on the 'Della Cruscan' poetasters, have little merit and do not concern us here. What does concern us is to notice that his early struggles seem to have left him with a permanent desire for revenge against the world. In 1797 he became editor

---

[1] William Gifford (1756–1826) was born at Ashburton in Devonshire. Generous patrons sent him to Exeter College, Oxford, and later he attracted the attention of Lord Grosvenor. He was one of Murray's circle of trusted advisers, and read *Emma* before it was accepted for publication. Byron professed to have a high opinion of his judgement. Like many ungenerous men he was capable of great loyalty towards those who had befriended him.

of the *Anti-Jacobin*, supplying much of the abuse while Canning and Hookham Frere supplied the wit. When Scott refused the editorship of the *Quarterly* and Gifford was appointed instead, he may be said to have resumed his Anti-Jacobin role. He seems only to have written eight complete papers himself, but he revised and rewrote the papers of his contributors, and the letters of the time are loud with complaints about the activities of 'the prose-gelder'. Lamb was furious about Gifford's treatment of his review of *The Excursion*: 'More than a third of the substance is cut away', he wrote to Wordsworth, 'and that not all from one place . . ., so as to make utter nonsense. Every warm expression is changed for a nasty cold one.' Gifford regarded it as his duty to abbreviate the work of his contributors and to enliven and season it with political and personal abuse. He clearly enjoyed the unrivalled power which his position gave him and demonstrated conclusively that anonymous reviewing, conducted on his plan, is an intolerable imposition on the public. In private life he appears to have been an amiable man, passionately grateful to those who had helped him on his way; but he was an important figure in public life, and those who knew him only in that capacity had every reason for detesting him. The truth is that he rose to a position of authority for which he was intellectually and morally quite unsuited. In his most forbearing *Autobiography* Leigh Hunt tells us that Gifford was the only man he had ever attacked without subsequent regret. Hazlitt's 'character' of Gifford in *The Spirit of the Age* is as severe as Pope, and Gifford deserved it.

While Gifford was editor of the *Quarterly* a much abler man, John Wilson Croker, was one of his most constant contributors.[1] Although Croker's political career does not concern us it is important to remember that he was (as Gifford pointed out) 'the only link' joining the *Quarterly* with 'the Ministers', and it is on account of this link that the *Review* is so often a reliable guide to Government policy. Although he wrote in 1834 that he 'never was a friend to making the *Review* a political engine' most of his

---

[1] John Wilson Croker (1780–1857) studied at Trinity College, Dublin, and at Lincoln's Inn. In 1807 he became Member of Parliament for Downpatrick. As Secretary to the Admiralty he exposed defalcations. He was a friend of Canning and of Peel, but he offended the future William IV while the latter was Duke of Clarence. In 1830 he introduced the term 'Conservative'. He resigned from Parliament in 1832 but continued to support Peel until Peel adhered to Cobden's policy in 1845.

reviews have at least political undertones, while after 1832 we
are told that 'practically *every* political article' was from his pen.
He understood very clearly the value of official propaganda and
saw no reason for keeping politics out of anything. He was an
expert on French affairs, and it is a misfortune that he did not
write a full study of the French Revolution, a task for which he
was fitted both by the number of survivors that he knew personally and by his extensive collection of revolutionary pamphlets.
Although he was far from impartial, his approach to the Revolution was more empirical than that of many of his contemporaries.
So far from regarding revolutions as 'systematic and salutary
movements, uniformly accomplishing the ends of justice with
great fairness' he believed them to be terrible cataclysms in
which the worst part of mankind gained the upper hand and
tore down all that was civilized and valuable. His attitude to
'the mob' was similar to that of Samuel Butler and Dryden
a century and a half before. He regarded France and America
as England's natural enemies, Russia as her predestined ally.
In home affairs he was equally uncompromising: if Reform
became a reality, he prophesied, 'Anarchy, with all its horrors
and miseries will ensue'. Although he was an Anglo-Irish
Protestant he was theoretically in favour of Catholic emancipation; but when it came to a vote he was against it. He had
a profound admiration for Burke but never learned the lesson
of so much of Burke's greatest writing, that circumstances are
the heart of every political problem. Like that of many of
Burke's admirers, Croker's attitude to him reminds us of Rymer's
attitude to Aristotle: he erected into dogma a body of observation and reasoning which was meant to be taken in quite a
different spirit.

Few men of his day knew so much about the eighteenth century as Croker. He did a great deal of work on the *Grenville
Papers* and wrote more than fifty reviews of biographies and
memoirs covering the period 1775–1825. As we glance at his
work for a projected edition of Pope we are reminded that most
of the men of this period who were prepared to study the eighteenth century in a scholarly way were essentially conservatives:
as were many of those who were prepared to study the Victorian
period before about 1930. Croker's aim was to have been to
'endeavour to put the reader of 1831 back into the place of the
reader of 1731', and the truth is that he would have been well

pleased to be put back to 1731 himself. A great deal of Croker's material went to enrich the Elwin-Courthope edition of Pope half a century later. His edition of Boswell's *Johnson* will be mentioned in Chapter XIV. His scholarly tenacity, like that of an academic bloodhound, may be seen at its best in his demonstration that Fanny Burney was twenty-five when *Evelina* appeared, and not seventeen. Annotation and the more limited tasks of scholarship were those at which he excelled. In a revealing passage he once envied Scott 'the *bold facility* with which he seized a subject and by the first glance determined all its properties'. As Croker pointed out, Scott 'was perpetually wrong in his details, but always right, luminous, and I had almost said exact, in his general view—but I am not of that power. I do nothing at all approaching to well but what I understand *in its details*. Would I could.' Croker could not have written Scott's *Lives* of Dryden and Swift, although he could have pointed out the errors they contain. If Scott had been a Whig Croker would not have praised him so generously; yet his enormous review of Macaulay's *History*, severe as it is, is much fairer than Macaulay's review of Croker's *Boswell*. Croker was a born scholar, and like many born scholars he lacked imagination.

As a critic he was much less respectable than as a scholar. As he himself pointed out, 'Party is much the strongest passion of an Englishman's mind. Friendship, love, even avarice give way before it'—and he was thoroughly at home in a *Review* where it was taken for granted that a writer's known or supposed political sympathies should help to determine the critic's attitude to his work. An article on the French novel, published in 1836, amusingly illustrates his inability to keep politics out of literary criticism. Than Rousseau (he tells us) 'a baser, meaner, filthier, scoundrel never polluted society', and he had no hesitation in finding evidence of the same pollution in the work of Dumas, Hugo, Balzac, and George Sand. Croker's criticism of the new poets of his own day has always been notorious for its political bias. His attitude to Leigh Hunt was bitterly hostile, though the fact that Leigh Hunt revised *The Story of Rimini* in the light of his review shows that many of Croker's strictures were just. Croker similarly regarded Shelley as a man with a 'disgraceful and flagitious history'. His, again, is the unenviable notoriety of having attacked *Endymion*, although he did refrain from attacking Keats personally. He was in the habit of asking Murray to send him 'fools' for review. 'The public', he once wrote, 'is so fastidious and indeed so *blasé* that its appetite requires a great deal of the *piquant*.' So Keats was fricassee'd to enliven a dull number. It is not, unfortunately, surprising that Croker should have picked on a young and unknown writer: on the contrary it was characteristic—although he was also prepared to attack the old and celebrated. He was a confirmed snob, and his attitude to a 'gentleman' like Byron, even when he disapproved strongly of the tendency of his work, was always different from his attitude to a Cockney like Keats.

While Myron F. Brightfield's biography is a useful contribution to literary history, it is difficult to go as far as he does in rehabilitating Croker's character. Croker's political views were undoubtedly sincere, but he supported them with a violence which it is impossible to admire. Very few men put themselves in a position to be admonished by Lockhart on this point, but it was he who advised Croker, in 1849, that 'violence nowadays does not answer as well as it did thirty years ago'. Bagehot once said that Sydney Smith lacked 'fangs' for detailed historical research: Croker had fangs, but unfortunately he did not reserve them for that purpose. Like many unimaginative men, he was cruel: the evidence of the portrait painted by William Owen confirms that of his writings. He was a Churchman rather than a Christian: he would not have understood Christian charity unless a gentleman was in question, while it is easy to imagine what his attitude would have been to the Founder of Christianity. It is not surprising that he was much hated. 'Rigby' in *Coningsby* is a caricature, but a caricature of Croker.

John Wilson, who wrote as 'Christopher North', was the most extraordinary product of the anonymous journalism of the time.[1] The strikingly handsome son of a wealthy Paisley family, he spent several years at Glasgow University and Magdalen College, Oxford, and then lived for some time at Elleray and became an associate of the Wordsworth circle. Wordsworth rightly pointed out that Wilson's poems were merely 'an attenuation' of his own, and today they are devoid of interest; but the

[1] John Wilson (1785–1854) was an outstanding athlete, and made a famous leap over the Cherwell. He contributed to Coleridge's *Friend*. In 1815 he was called to the Scottish Bar. He became a Professor at Edinburgh University in 1820. He was a vain man with something unreal at his heart.

remarkable thing about Wilson was that he was storing up materials with which to attack the Lakists at the very time during which he was their sentimental disciple. The foundation of *Blackwood's Magazine* gave him his opportunity: he was the most important single contributor, and practically all his prose writings first made their appearance anonymously in the pages of 'Maga'. The systematic mystification in which the contributors indulged and their habit of collaboration make it difficult to identify individual contributions, but it is clear that Wilson collaborated with Hogg and Lockhart in writing the 'Translation from an Ancient Chaldee Manuscript' and wrote some of the attacks on the 'Cockney School' (of which Lockhart was the principal author), while he seems also to have been the writer of the deplorable attack on *Biographia Literaria*, which even Lockhart regarded with distaste. One of Wilson's oddest and most un-amiable habits was his practice of praising and censuring the same writer at the same time. At one moment he stands out as one of the first reviewers to appreciate the genius of Wordsworth, at the next he rounds on him for 'ludicrously' over-rating his own powers, and calls *The Excursion* 'the worst poem of any character in the English language'. At times it is difficult to believe that Wilson was wholly sane. After attacking him on numerous occasions he had the assurance to ask Wordsworth for a testimonial; and although Wordsworth complied with this re-quest we again find Wilson planning to attack him in the *Quarterly*, after his death, as 'a fat ugly cur'. His motives are hard to under-stand, but much must be laid to the account of vanity and envy. He was pathologically touchy, incapable of tolerating any criti-cism of his own writings or character; and for all his physical prowess he was an abject moral coward. Although he was capable of generosity, as we see in his treatment of De Quincey, he had an innate love of hurting people, even if they had been kind to him. 'Though averse to being cut up myself', he once wrote, without a trace of irony, 'I like to abuse my friends.' But the thought that he himself might be exposed filled him with horror. In the words of one of the characters in his *City of the Plague* (1816),

> The violent
> Are weaker than the mild, and abject fear
> Dwells in the heart of passion.

Nowhere can Scottish sentimentality of the most objectionable kind be studied so remorselessly as in Wilson's *Lights and Shadows of Scottish Life* (1822), which contains stories supposed to describe the simple realities in the life of the Scottish peasantry. To describe the book as the work of 'a female Wordsworth', as one critic has done, is equally unfair to Wordsworth and to women. Wilson was outraged when Henry Mackenzie (who was an expert on sentiment and sentimentality) compared the book with the work of Gessner, but Mackenzie was right. The same sentimental falseness is to be found in *The Trials of Margaret Lyndsay* (1823) and *The Foresters* (1825). Wordsworth said that he had never come on 'more mawkish stuff' than the latter book. Yet in the history of taste it is a significant document.

But it was as the main author of *Noctes Ambrosianae* that 'Christopher North' was principally celebrated. Lockhart inaugurated the series in *Blackwood's* in 1822; but its origin may be found in the imaginary dialogues which began to appear three years earlier and which contain a mixture of fact and fiction that reminds us of Lockhart's *Peter's Letters*. Although only one of the characters, James Hogg, retains his real name, most of the speakers are based to a considerable extent on real individuals, while 'Ambrose's Tavern' had a real existence under another name. The subjects of the first dialogue give an idea of the whole: 'Apparitions—Miss Foote—The Shepherd on pastoral plays—Scott's poetry—Buchanan Lodge—The Shepherd on poultry... Tickler reappears.' The popularity of the series, which ran until 1835, reminds us of the popularity of some inferior radio or television serial today: the quality of the material is low, and it is difficult now to read more than a few pages with any enjoyment. The popularity of the *Noctes* in America is not difficult to explain: they appealed to the nostalgia of exiled Scots. The series is an example of that coarsening and cheapening of Scotland and its way of life which still proves so popular with tourists. It is easy to see why this sort of dialogue suited Wilson: he was able to attribute some sentimental outburst to the Shepherd and then make Christopher North interrupt with a sarcastic comment: rather as Byron so often turns on himself with a witty couplet at the end of an octave stanza. Throughout the series Wilson was in the position that he relished: that of the man to whom all the credit is due, but who stands safe from censure or imputed responsibility. It is interesting to notice that after his election to the Chair of Moral Philosophy in the University of Edinburgh (one of the most discreditable academic appointments ever made) Wilson wrote more, not less, in *Blackwood's*; and this in spite of the fact that he found himself pitifully unfitted to write the lectures which were required of him. In the history of literature there are few more abject spectacles than that of Professor John Wilson begging his obscure friend Alexander Blair to write his lectures for him, and so save him from ignominy: for years the letters went on, and Blair, Wilson's Jamesian phantom, seems hardly ever to have let him down. At times Wilson (as Professor) seems to have been little more than a ventriloquist's dummy; but he had a fine appearance, and his students were deeply impressed. So long as he could not be brought to book for what he wrote, on the other hand, his pen moved rapidly and with pleasure, and many of his articles bear signs of the talent that his contemporaries attributed to him—though none gives any hint of the genius that they believed him to possess. There is an unreality about 'Christopher North' that makes him uninteresting in one way and fascinating in another. Carlyle saw through him better than most, as one would expect. He remains a tempting subject for psycho-analytical inquiry.

It is refreshing to turn from a man as unreal as 'Christopher North' to a woman as real as Mary Russell Mitford.[1] When the sketches which make up *Our Village* began to appear in the *Lady's Magazine* Miss Mitford was already known as an authoress: she had published several volumes of verse, in which Coleridge had taken an interest, and she was on the point of pro-

[1] Mary Russell Mitford (1787–1855) was born at Alresford in Hampshire. She was the only child of George Mitford, a man with a mania for speculation, gambling, and the game of whist. Although he was described by someone who knew him well as 'a detestable old humbug' he never lost the affection of his wife and daughter. At the age of ten Mary Mitford chose him a ticket in a lottery which won him £20,000, and with the proceeds he built a house in Reading. Her first publication, *Poems*, appeared in 1810. By 1820 her father's extravagance made it necessary for her to turn to literature as a source of income. The family removed to a cottage at Three Mile Cross, a village between Reading and Basingstoke, where they lived for the next thirty years. Her tragedy, *Julian*, was performed at Covent Garden in 1823 with Macready in the title-role: *Foscari* and *Rienzi* were even more successful. Meanwhile *Our Village* made its author a celebrity. Her mother died in 1830, but her father lived on until 1842, and in spite of her very considerable earnings Miss Mitford knew no respite from financial troubles. Although *Belford Regis* (1835) contains some agreeable sketches, the effects of strain are beginning to be apparent. After her father's death his remaining debts were paid off by a public subscription. In 1851 Miss Mitford removed to the village of Swallowfield, where she died.

ducing three or four poetic tragedies. Yet posterity has agreed with Elizabeth Barrett in holding that Miss Mitford 'stands higher as the authoress of *Our Village* than of *Rienzi*, and writes prose better than poetry, and transcends rather in Dutch minuteness and high finishing, than in Italian ideality and passion'. Her aim was to write a collection of 'essays and characters and stories, chiefly of country life, in the manner of the "Sketch Book", but without sentimentality or pathos—two things which I abhor'. While Washington Irving's book no doubt helped to give her the idea it is to her own delightful letters that a modern reader is likely to turn when he is searching for a background to *Our Village*. She describes the pleasure which letter-writing gave her in an article 'On Letters and Letter-Writers' in the *New Monthly Magazine* for 1821:

How delightful it is to sit down and prattle to a dear friend just as carelessly as if we were seated in real talk, with our feet on the fender, by that glimmering fire-light when talk comes freest; sure that every half-word will be understood, that every trifle will interest, and every story amuse. . . . How delightful it is to pour out all one's thoughts and fancies with such a certainty of indulgence and sympathy.

The fact that she mentions Walpole, Voltaire, Shaftesbury, Hume, Johnson, Richardson, and half a dozen others within four pages makes it clear that she was a great reader of the collections of letters which had become numerous since the later eighteenth century. It is interesting to notice her objection to Gray's letters: 'Gray's letters are very clever, very poetical, very picturesque, but they want the good-nature, the constitutional kindliness: respect and admire him we must, and we do; but to love a man dead or alive it is necessary that he should know how to love too.' In the letters of Mme de Sévigné and of Cowper she found that 'tenderness and sweetness', that 'spirit of indulgence and of love to [our] kind' which she missed in Gray, and these are qualities everywhere apparent in her own letters.

As she herself pointed out, a great many of the poems in her first collection were 'addresses to private friends', and throughout her life the fact that she had friends with whom she could share her experiences meant a great deal to her. Before *Our Village* began to appear she corresponded with Sir William Elford, Haydon, and Talfourd (who acted as her literary adviser), and soon she was also exchanging letters with Lamb, R. H. Horne, Ruskin, Elizabeth Barrett, and Landor. Although her life was one long battle to keep her impossible father from bankruptcy we notice that her letters contain remarkably few complaints. It was simply that writing about her own life and the daily events of the village helped her to find a point of stability in the perpetual uncertainty and insecurity caused by her father's extravagance. She was far from a self-regarding correspondent: on the contrary she was a woman who delighted in giving pleasure, and her letters were written with that object in view. In many ways she reminds us of Lamb, whose *Essays* were also the product of his talent as a correspondent; yet unlike him she was not concerned to create a *persona*, to project a literary personality. Her style is much simpler than his. It is without the archaisms and mannerisms that are so evident in Lamb, a good, fluent, unselfconscious epistolary style, always her servant and never her master. It is so unobtrusive that we tend to underestimate the skill with which it is deployed, and it is as well to remember her remark to Talfourd, 'what looks like ease in my style is labour'.

In her very first sketch Miss Mitford gives us an admirable account of her own scope and interests, a reminder—if reminder is needed—that she was completely aware of what she was doing. 'Even in books', she wrote,

> I like a confined locality, and so do the critics when they talk of the unities. . . . Nothing is so delightful as to sit down in a country village in one of Miss Austen's delicious novels, quite sure before we leave it to become intimate with every spot and every person it contains; or to ramble with Mr. White over his own parish of Selborne, and form a friendship with the fields and coppices, as well as with the birds, mice, and squirrels, who inhabit them.

So she gives us her double theme, 'country scenery and country manners' (as she puts it in the preface), 'as they exist in a small village in the south of England'. It seems an obvious subject to choose, yet a moment's reflection reminds one that it would have been inconceivable a century before; and in spite of all the imitations since the thing has hardly been so well done again.

As we read these sketches we notice that Miss Mitford writes as a countrywoman. If she is concerned with outdoor life or scenery she begins by describing the season of the year and the state of the weather: 'April 18th.—Sad wintery weather; a north-east wind; a sun that puts out one's eyes, without affording the slightest warmth; dryness that chaps lips and hands like a frost in December; rain that comes chilling and arrowy like hail in January; nature at a dead pause.' The third essay gives an admirable description of the effects of frost on the land-scape:

There had been just snow enough to cover the earth and all its colours with one sheet of pure and uniform white, and just time enough since the snow had fallen to allow the hedges to be freed of their fleecy load, and clothed with a delicate coating of rime. The atmosphere was deliciously calm; soft, even mild, in spite of the thermometer; no perceptible air, but a stillness that might almost be felt: the sky, rather grey than blue, throwing out in bold relief the snow-covered roofs of our village, and the rimy trees that rise above them, and the sun shining dimly as through a veil, giving a pale fair light, like the moon, only brighter. There was a silence, too, that might become the moon, as we stood at our little gate looking up the quiet street; a sabbath-like pause of work and play, rare on a work-day; nothing was audible but the pleasant hum of frost, that low monotonous sound, which is perhaps the nearest approach that life and nature can make to absolute silence.

At times her descriptions of landscape remind us vividly of painting. 'What a pretty picture they would make', she remarks of a child and a dog in the first essay:

What a pretty foreground they do make to the real landscape! The road winding down the hill with a slight bend, like that in the High-street at Oxford; a waggon slowly ascending, and a horseman passing it at a full trot; . . . half-way down, just at the turn, the red cottage of the lieutenant, covered with vines, the very image of comfort and content; farther down, on the opposite side, the small white building of the little mason; then the limes and the rope-walk; then the village street, peeping through the trees, whose clustering tops hide all but the chimneys, and various roofs of the houses, and here and there some angle of a wall: farther on, the elegant town of B—, with its fine old church-towers and spires; the whole view shut in by a range of chalky hills; and over every part of the picture, trees so profusely scattered, that it appears like a woodland scene, with glades and villages intermixed.

In another early essay she describes 'a deep, woody, green lane such as Hobbema or Ruysdael might have painted' and it is clear that her power of visualizing had been strengthened by a characteristic enjoyment of prints and paintings. In her own sketches the Village—as she puts it—sits for its picture, and she often refers to herself in similar terms, as when she replies to Sir William Elford's question about the authenticity of her descriptions:

'Are the characters and descriptions true?' Yes! yes! yes! As true as is well possible. You, as a great landscape painter, know that in painting a favourite scene you do a little embellish, and can't help it; you avail yourself of happy accidents of atmosphere, and if anything be ugly you strike it out, or if anything be wanting, you put it in. But still the picture is a likeness.

Some of her descriptions of people are strongly reminiscent of portraiture and caricature. Her description of 'the insides' in the coach, for example, in 'Walks in the Country: The Hard Summer':

How well I remember the fat gentleman without his coat, who was wiping his forehead, heaving up his wig, and certainly uttering that English ejaculation, which, to our national reproach, is the phrase of our language best known on the continent. And that poor boy, red-hot, all in a flame, whose mamma, having divested her own person of all superfluous apparel, was trying to relieve his sufferings by the removal of his neck-kerchief—an operation which he resisted with all his might. How perfectly I remember him, as well as the pale girl who sate opposite, fanning herself with her bonnet into an absolute fever! They vanished after a while in their own dust; but I have them all before my eyes at this moment, a companion-picture to Hogarth's Afternoon, a standing lesson to the grumblers at cold summers.

As such a passage demonstrates, Miss Mitford was as good with 'country manners' as with 'country scenery'. Yet her longest narrative, *Atherton*, bears out her own opinion that she had not been born to write novels. 'I have begun two', she once wrote, 'and got on very well as long as I stuck to landscape and portrait painting; but when I was obliged to make my pictures walk out of their frames and speak for themselves, when I came to the action, I was foundered.' In *Our Village* she gives us little dialogue, but she excels at describing characters in a manner that sometimes reminds us of the essayists of the eighteenth century:

Of these the most notable was my friend Tom Cordery, who presented in his own person no unfit emblem of the district in which he lived—the gentlest of savages, the wildest of civilised men. He was by calling rat-catcher, hare-finder, and broom-maker; a triad of trades which he had substituted for the one grand profession of poaching, which he followed in his younger days with unrivalled talent and success, and would, undoubtedly, have pursued till his death, had not the bursting of an overloaded gun unluckily shot off his left hand. As it was, he still contrived to mingle a little of his old unlawful occupation with his honest callings; was a reference of high authority amongst the young aspirants, an adviser of undoubted honour and secrecy—suspected, and more than suspected, of being one 'who, though he played no more, o'erlooked the cards'.

Equally fine is 'The Talking Lady':

The manner of her speech has little remarkable. It is rather old-fashioned and provincial, but perfectly lady-like, low and gentle, and not seeming so fast as it is; like the great pedestrians she clears her ground easily, and never seems to use any exertion; yet 'I would my horse had the speed of her tongue, and so good a continuer'. She will talk you sixteen hours a day for twenty days together, and not deduct one poor five minutes for halts and baiting time. Talking, sheer talking, is meat and drink and sleep to her. She likes nothing else.

She is capable of a damaging wit, as when she observes of 'An Old Bachelor' who has been a Fellow of a College in his day that he 'spoke so little, that people really fell into the mistake of imagining that he thought'. But understanding and enjoyment are her native element, not censure: she takes a delight in the human scene that recalls Charles Lamb, as when she describes the curate's landlord and landlady:

Never were better or kinder people than his host and hostess: and there is a reflection of clerical importance about them, since their connection with the Church, which is quite edifying—a decorum, a gravity, a solemn politeness. Oh, to see the worthy wheeler carry the gown after his lodger on a Sunday, nicely pinned up in his wife's best handkerchief—or to hear him rebuke a squalling child or a squabbling woman! The curate is nothing to him. He is fit to be perpetual churchwarden.

What she says of 'Lucy' is equally true of herself: 'She was

a very charitable reporter too; threw her own sunshine into
the shady places, and would hope and doubt as long as either
was possible.' In her steady and deliberate emphasis on the
agreeable aspects of life she reminds us above all of Leigh
Hunt. She shared his genius for enjoyment, and was determined to set her face against the vogue of melancholy. It is not
surprising that she knew and relished Matthew Green's delightful
poem, *The Spleen,* which she quotes from in 'The Cowslip-Ball'.

Landor's long life[1]—he was born nine years before the death
of Dr. Johnson and died in the year that saw the publication of
Browning's *Dramatis Personæ*—makes it necessary for his work
to be divided between this and the previous volume, and our
concern is exclusively with his prose, and particularly the *Imaginary Conversations.* He seems first to have experimented with the
dialogue form about 1802, when he appears to have written
a dialogue between Burke and Lord Grenville and another
between Henry IV and Arnold Savage. Both of these early
dialogues must have dealt with politics. Some twenty years later
we find Landor discussing the use of dialogue in his letters to
Southey, who was at work on *Sir Thomas More: or, Colloquies on
the Progress and Prospects of Society.* Southey acknowledges that his
model has been Boethius and that his dialogues are 'consecutive'
—merely a formal device to enable him to express his views on
the condition of England—but takes it for granted that Landor
will aim at a 'dramatic variety' foreign to his own intentions.
At times there is no doubt that Landor took the view that his
own dialogues were essentially dramatic. On one occasion he
told Browning that he was 'more of a dramatist in prose than in
poetry'. *Count Julian* had failed to reach the stage. Would it then
be a true account of what happened to say that Landor was a
man with a natural bent for the drama who found the times

---

[1] Walter Savage Landor (1775–1864) was educated at Rugby and at Trinity
College, Oxford, from which he was rusticated in 1794. After three years at Tenby
and Swansea he visited Paris, moved about between Bath, Bristol, and Wells, and
fought as a volunteer in Spain. In 1808 he had bought Llanthony Abbey in Mon-
mouthshire, and three years later he married Julia Thuillier. After a quarrel with the
authorities at Llanthony he travelled abroad. In 1818 he was ordered to leave
Como on account of an insult in one of his Latin poems. He spent most of the next
17 years in Italy. In 1835 he quarrelled with his wife and left Italy. From 1837 to
1858 he lived at Bath: then he returned to Florence. Browning admired him greatly.
He was a passionate man of an abnormally irritable temper: it would be difficult
to find any writer whose works had to be published by so many different publishers.

unpropitious and therefore took to writing 'imaginary conversations' instead of plays?

Some of the *Conversations* do reveal a certain dramatic sense. In 'Lord Bacon and Richard Hooker', in which the latter consoles the former for his fall from power, the way in which Bacon's supposed lack of wisdom and self-knowledge peeps out on every page is extremely dramatic—not least the exclamation with which he curses his servant for offering Hooker 'the beverage I reserve for myself'. The same is true of 'Leofric and Godiva'. In 'Leonora di Este and Father Panigarola' Leonora's passionate desire to hear that she is still the beloved of Tasso, although she is under sentence of death, is conveyed with an extraordinary economy of means and with a psychological insight that sets us speculating about Browning's debt to Landor. Yet these are three of the shortest of the *Conversations*, and they are hardly representative. Wordsworth criticized the dialogue between Landor himself and the Abbé Delille shrewdly when he said that 'the observations are invariably just . . .; but they are fitter for illustrative notes than the body of a Dialogue, which ought always to have some little spice of dramatic effect'. In the end there were some hundred and fifty *Imaginary Conversations*, and it is natural that some of them should be more dramatic than others; but as we read through them we find more and more often that dramatic effect is far to seek because Landor is less concerned with creating vivid men and women than with expressing his own views on human affairs. In his dialogue with Middleton Landor makes Magliabechi suggest 'that Cicero had asserted things incredible to himself, merely for the sake of argument, and had probably written them before he had fixed in his mind the personages to whom they should be attributed in his dialogues'; and this was no doubt true of Landor's own practice. R. H. Super has pointed out (for example) that 'Washington and Franklin' began life as an essay on the Irish problem; when he revised it Landor broke it up into speeches which he had no hesitation in shifting from one speaker to another. From boyhood onwards he had a strong desire to comment on life, often in the most passionate terms; yet he found any kind of systematic exposition, or sustained logical argument, extremely difficult to present. The dialogue therefore offered itself as a mode of expression well suited to his unusual temperament.

From the first politics are the most constant subject of the

Conversations. He set out most of his political views in 1812, in his *Commentary on Memoirs of Mr. Fox.* It was a characteristic production. 'From the manner, from the force, from the vehemence, I concluded it must be yours', Southey wrote, 'even before I fell upon the passage respecting Spain which proves that it was yours.' The book was so controversial that Landor was obliged to suppress it, but it remains of interest because it sums up so many of the views that are to be found throughout the *Imaginary Conversations.* Landor believed that if Fox's policy were pursued it would prove 'most fatal to our interests and glory': the book is dedicated to the President of the United States and deplores the war towards which Canning's policy seemed to Landor to be leading. The arrangement of the *Commentary* is characteristically unsystematic: Landor simply takes one passage after another from Trotter's *Memoirs* and uses it as a text for the expression of his own views. One of the more convincing and eloquent passages is that in which he contrasts the sentence of death that may be passed on a poor woman for a trivial theft with the lenient treatment of Viscount Melville. Once or twice Landor digresses to discuss literary matters: 'it is soothing to take the last view of politics from among the works of the imagination', as he comments towards the end of the text, '. . . [and] escape in this manner from the mazes of politics and the discord of party'; but in the postscript he is back in the thick of the political battle. The whole work makes it clear that passion was the main motive behind Landor's political views. If politics is the art of the practicable, he was as unfitted for politics as any man has ever been. He can be eloquent and moving on generalities, but he is incapable of consistency and has a fatal tendency to see complicated issues in terms of black and white. His insistence on the importance to statesmen of a knowledge of history contrasts markedly with his own lack of political understanding. He read history in an oddly Plutarchian way, as the lives of great men, and had no interest in the functioning of political institutions. At one time he intended to collaborate with Southey on a large-scale historical work. Later he thought of writing a History of England since 1775, the year of his own birth and of the outbreak of the War of American Independence. Undramatic as it is, the conversation between Washington and Franklin is one of the clearest statements of his own political views. In the years following Waterloo he was a passionate opponent of the Holy

Alliance and a passionate supporter of the nations that were striving for independence. He regarded Canning's attitude to the freedom-seeking nations as culpably half-hearted and returned his own Spanish title and decoration in protest against the behaviour of the King of Spain. England's treatment of Ireland was a subject to which he reverted time and time again. He supported Catholic emancipation, while frequently satirizing the superstitious element in the religious practices of the Catholic Church. We notice that a number of his *Conversations* include confessors, notably the highly satiric dialogue between Louis XIV and Father La Chaise. Landor hated all wielders of power: it is appropriate that one of the first of all the *Imaginary Conversations* should have portrayed Arnold Savage, whom he liked to regard as an ancestor of his own, warning Henry IV of the limits of kingly power. The dialogue between Cromwell and Walter Noble is of interest because it is at once a study of character and a serious discussion of the ethics of regicide. Here and elsewhere we notice that Landor's classical education made him a republican, though we may suspect that it was the idea of a republic that appealed to him, rather than the reality. He loved liberty, and despised the people.

As Wordsworth pointed out, the classical dialogues are among the best of the *Imaginary Conversations*. In one of them Cicero and his brother, who have for many years supported different sides in the civil war, meet on the day before the orator's death and talk of the fate of Rome and of the great issues of human existence. It is a dialogue at once sombre and serene, slow-moving yet impressive in an unusual way. The conversation between Aeschines and Phocion is less impressive, although in Phocion (the just man who despises the fickle mob) Landor found an excellent *persona* for his own character as he liked to imagine it. Nothing could be more maladroit than the way in which Aeschines suddenly asks: 'What is your opinion on the right and expediency of making wills?', so providing Phocion with an opportunity of delivering a discourse on the subject. Landor liked to regard Epicurus as his master, and his own favourite *Conversation* was the one in which he portrays the philosopher talking with two girl-disciples, Leontion and Ternissa. In it he touches on a number of his favourite topics: the praise of solitude, the fact that death is not to be feared, and in general the art of living a serene and happy life. It is charmingly done, and

just a trifle absurd: Peacock, one feels, would have handled the
ending with more tact. In general it is difficult to believe in
Landor's Greeks and Romans. He was a passionate admirer of
the classics, and he reflected a good deal on the characters of the
great men and women who were for him the makers of history;
yet it is evident that his Epicurus and Aristotle are monuments
of nineteenth-century classicism rather than convincing recreations of the men who lived so many centuries ago. It may
be doubted whether Landor possessed a truly historical imagination. Although what they teach is not always what is taught by
schoolmasters, his Greeks and Romans remind us constantly of
the classroom and the school debating club. It is ink that circu-
lates in their veins, not blood. At times it is as if an image in
Madame Tussaud's were to raise its arm and begin an oration to
its neighbour. 'In such a profusion of viands, and so savoury,'
Caesar remarks to Lucullus, 'I perceive no odour.' Lucullus
replies: 'A flue conducts heat through the compartments of the
obelisks; and if you look up, you may observe that those gilt
roses, between the astragals in the cornice, are prominent from
it half a span.' This is the Roman House for Sixth Forms.

  Pericles and Aspasia (1836) began as an *Imaginary Conversation*
but grew to the length of an independent book. It opens with
a description of Aspasia's first meeting with Pericles at a performance of the *Prometheus Bound* of Aeschylus and ends with the
death of Pericles during the plague at Athens. It is difficult to
know how to classify the book: although it consists of letters it
has few of the characteristics of an epistolary novel (or indeed
of a novel of any kind), and in spite of eloquent passages it
remains as a whole remarkably uninteresting. The *Citation and
Examination of William Shakspeare* (1834) was an earlier dialogue
that similarly grew to the dimensions of an independent book.
In this curious work Landor has Shakespeare brought before
Sir Thomas Lucy on a charge of stealing a deer. Sir Thomas
condescends to the unlettered young man, not least on the subject of poetry, on which he regards himself as an authority. The
humour is distinctly laboured: it is the sort of funny book that
one might order with a clear conscience in the British Museum.
If we compare Landor's dialogues with those in Peacock's satiric
tales we notice how Peacock's wit acts as a preservative. Landor
can be witty, but only sporadically: the comic view of life was
not natural to him. He was too passionate, and too deficient in

a sense of proportion, to take naturally to comic writing. The nature of the third of his long conversation-books, *The Penta-meron* (1837), is best indicated by its sub-title: 'Interviews of Messer Giovanni Boccaccio and Messer Francesco Petrarca, when said Messer Giovanni lay infirm at Viletta . . . after which they saw not each other on our side of Paradise: shewing how they discoursed upon that famous Theologian Messer Dante Alighieri, and sundry other matters.' By choosing Petrarch as his main speaker Landor gives himself dramatic justification for some severe judgements on Dante, whom he considered a great poet only in his finest passages. Written towards the end of Landor's prolonged sojourn at Fiesole, *The Pentameron* may be regarded as an appropriate thank-offering for one of the calmer periods in a stormy life.

Landor has often been acclaimed as a master of English prose style. In a limited sense he is. Almost everything that he ever wrote is either a copy of verses or a prose composition. His prose demands high marks from the examiner; but unfortunately it refuses to come alive. A dozen critics have noticed that it has the air of a distinguished translation from some great classical origi-nal. He was the kind of classicist who lacks the instinctive feeling for conversational and colloquial English that is so evident in the verse of the equally classical Praed. It is not just that his dialogue is mannered and stylized: so is Peacock's, which has a vivacity that is not to be found in Landor. Landor would have been the better for the discipline of writing for the theatre or for broad-casting. But he was a wealthy man with few responsibilities, and this emphasized his natural disregard of his audience. He admired Pindar for his 'proud complacency and scornful strength'. 'If I could resemble him in nothing else', he once wrote, 'I was resolved to be as compendious and as exclusive.' There is truth in Byron's gibe that he was 'a gentleman who cultivated the private celebrity of writing Latin verses'. His life was one long angry monologue. Unfortunately he lacked the intellectual power to be a profound commentator on human life. It would be a solecism to compare him with Plato, whom he wilfully underestimated; but if one thinks for a moment of John-son or of Burke, Landor's limitations become almost embar-rassingly evident. He had a gift for stating his own convictions with eloquence and passion, but he shrank from close argument and seldom condescended to examine the premisses on which his opinions were based. He is the King Lear of English literary history, and in nothing does he resemble Lear more markedly than in his profound lack of self-knowledge. There is a startling lack of a sense of reality about a man who could talk, as Landor did, of chastising an attorney in a forthcoming Latin poem. There is more wisdom in any one of Hazlitt's essays than in a dozen of the *Imaginary Conversations.*

XIII

HISTORY, BIOGRAPHY, AND
AUTOBIOGRAPHY

ALTHOUGH no historical work comparable with Gibbon's *Decline and Fall of the Roman Empire* or Macaulay's *History of England from the Accession of James II* was published in this period, the work of Hallam and his contemporaries deserves attention both because it illustrates some of the motives that led men to study history in the earlier part of the century and because the books they wrote, combining with the immense influence of the romances of Sir Walter Scott, provided the great Victorians with the material from which they derived their sense of the past. Henry Hallam, the father of Tennyson's friend, tells us that the aim of his *View of the State of Europe during the Middle Ages* (1818) is to give 'a comprehensive survey of the chief circumstances that can interest a philosophical enquirer'.[1] His intention is to avoid mere annals and to concentrate on events 'essentially concatenated with others, or illustrative of important conclusions'. He is more concerned with 'modes of government and constitutional laws' than with battles and the minutiae of political history, and has no hesitation in passing rapidly over periods which seem to him of little importance: 'Many considerable portions of time, especially before the twelfth century, may justly be deemed so barren of events . . . that a single sentence or paragraph is often sufficient.' The book consists of a series of dissertations, instead of a narrative, and is noteworthy for such chapters as those 'On the State of Society in Europe' and 'On the Feudal System, especially in France'. Hallam insists on the importance of understanding feudalism because of its bearing on the English constitution, and because 'one of the parties which at present divide [France] professes to appeal to the original principles of its monarchy, as they subsisted before the subversion of that polity'. It is characteristic of Hallam that

[1] Henry Hallam (1777–1859) was educated at Eton and Christ Church. He became a barrister, and was appointed a commissioner of stamps. He was an occasional contributor to the *Edinburgh Review*.

when he published a *Supplemental Volume* thirty years later he refused to make it necessary for readers to buy a revision of the work as a whole: no less characteristic that he had not in many instances 'seen ground for materially altering [his] views'. Once a phrenologist said that Hallam was a musician, Macaulay 'a landscape painter or historical painter'. It was an apt mistake. Although the two men shared many of their political views, their attitude to history is quite different. Hallam is not concerned with the trappings of history, nor does he attempt to put himself in the place of the men of the past: he is interested in attitudes and themes rather than in human beings: his view of historical truth is essentially abstract. His work lacks the extraordinary vividness of Macaulay's. As Mignet put it, 'il a plutôt l'intelligence que le sentiment du passé'. His legal training fitted him admirably for his *Constitutional History of England* (1827). He begins in the reign of Henry VII and stops at the end of that of George II, but in spite of his 'unwillingness to excite the prejudices of modern politics' his political views colour his whole reading of history and greatly increase its interest for us today. He is excellent on the terms Whig and Tory in the early eighteenth century, insisting that they 'have become equivocal, and do by no means, at all periods and on all occasions, present the same sense'. It is magnificent, though it is not Namier. Appearing as it did four years before the Reform Bill, his book ended, suitably enough, with a discussion of the 'extraordinary traffic' in seats in the House of Commons in the later eighteenth century. Unlike his first book, his *Constitutional History* was carefully revised, and it long remained a work of the first importance. 'It became and has remained a text-book in the Universities,' as Gooch wrote half a century ago, 'was quoted as an oracle in Parliament, and was studied as a guide by the youthful Victoria and her Consort. . . . It was inwardly digested by the friends of constitutional liberty all over the world.' Southey described it as 'Hallam's essence of Whig vinegar'. Like his second book, Hallam's third derives from his first. His *Introduction to the Literature of Europe in the Fifteenth, Sixteenth, and Seventeenth Centuries* (1837–9) deals with literature in the widest sense. On imaginative literature he is often illuminating, but frequently ill-informed and perverse. He is commonly much more interesting on poets and men of letters who are of importance in the history of ideas —men like Hooker and Milton. In dealing with the history of philosophy he is lucid and persuasive, though hardly incisive. One can only admire the learning and the courage that carry him on through the literature of theology, mathematics, classical scholarship, physical science, and the rest. Whereas his previous book had been adversely reviewed in the *Quarterly*, his last work was praised to excess. As Hallam himself noted, such praise is apt to set one against him, but his *Introduction to the Literature of Europe* remains a remarkable achievement, as well as a remarkable attempt.

The views of John Lingard were as different from those of Hallam as one man's can be from another's.[1] His first important publication had been *The Antiquities of the Anglo-Saxon Church* (1806), and throughout his *History of England* (of which the first three volumes deal with the period before Henry VIII) his main aim is to show that the Reformation had been the fundamental disaster in English history. Lingard was a priest, and seems to be the first Roman Catholic to have written a full-scale History of England. His learning was very considerable, for his day, and the *Edinburgh Review* conceded that 'the fabric he has raised against the Reformation is reared by no vulgar hand'. His treatment of the early medieval period is superior to anything in preceding writers, and justifies his claim to have gone to the fountain-head of original sources. The attacks of the fanatical Catholic Bishop Milner show that Lingard was far from an extremist. Perhaps it would be fair to say that he is as impartial as any man can be whose general interpretation of history is determined before he begins his research. His religious bias becomes more obvious in his later volumes. He is opposed to 'the philosophy of history': as far as he is concerned what the Church proclaims as right, is right: what happened, happened. As a reviewer complained, 'he has no generous sympathy in the cause of freedom'. To the caricatures which had so long passed for likenesses of the leaders of the Roman Catholic Church he opposes caricatures of their opponents. His indignation is reserved for the wrongs done to his Church: the wrongs done by it are first minimized and then dispassionately chronicled. He is concerned to identify the Anglo-Saxon Church with the Roman Catholic,

---

[1] John Lingard (1771–1851) studied at the English College at Douay and was ordained and appointed vice-president of Crookhall College, near Durham, at the age of 24. He visited Rome in 1817 and 1825. He played a considerable part in the jurisdiction of the Roman Catholic Church in this country. In 1821 he was honoured by the Pope. His *History of England* went through five editions by the middle of the century.

and exaggerates the civilizing influence of the introduction of Christianity into Britain. His attitude to Calvinism is quite unfair, while his portrayal of the Puritans is reminiscent of *Hudibras*. Lessons learned from Hume and Gibbon are used to the disparagement of Protestantism. He has a strong bias against the Scots and the Welsh. 'Candour', in the fine eighteenth-century sense, is completely lacking. Yet he revised his work with care, and defended himself vigorously—though without ever giving the impression of having an open mind. He remains important for his genuine interest in medieval England, for his early and strong opposition to the Whig interpretation of history which dominated his century, and for the influence which his idealization of the Middle Ages exerted on many writers of his own time and the subsequent age. It is curious what an important part one exaggerated view of the Middle Ages and another have played in the history of later thought and feeling. Myth is more powerful than truth and does more to shape the course of human history. The influence of Lingard may be detected in the Oxford Movement and in many other currents of thought in the nineteenth century. His interpretation of the Middle Ages supplied nourishment to men whose views differed from his own as widely as did those of Cobbett and William Morris. The inspiration which the men of the eighteenth century had derived from the Noble Savage was often to be found by their successors in an idealized portrayal of the Middle Ages.

There is no room for more than a reference to Napier's *History of the War in the Peninsula* or Milman's *History of the Jews*, *History of Christianity*, and *History of Latin Christianity*. Patrick Fraser Tytler's *History of Scotland* is not without merit, yet one can only regret that Scott did not undertake the task himself, instead of suggesting it to one of his younger friends. James Mill's *History of British India* (1817) shows a much greater stretch of mind than Fraser Tytler was capable of, whether or not the result is better history.[1] Mill's aim was to give India 'a good sys-

---

[1] James Mill (1773–1836) was educated at the University of Edinburgh and licensed to preach in 1798. Four years later he moved to London and engaged in journalism, meeting Bentham in 1808 and soon losing his interest in theology. He was prominent in the movement that led to the foundation of University College, London. In 1819 he entered the India House. He was a friend of Ricardo's, encouraging him to publish his revolutionary views on political economy. Although he was not the editor of the *Westminster Review*, he was one of the principal contributors. The manner in which he educated his son is described in the *Autobiography of John Stuart Mill*.

tem of judicial procedure' and a judicial establishment capable of carrying it out, and this was to be done on Benthamite lines: as Bentham said, 'Mill will be the living executive—I shall be the dead legislative of British India'. Mill's immense volumes are an example of History harnessed for the purposes of practical reform. It is characteristic of Mill that he should have been able to argue that his never having been in India was in some ways an advantage: it is not merely that he is determined to avoid stirring narrative and picturesque description: it does not occur to him that the atmosphere of a country can be relevant to an historian or even to a reformer. This is history 'seraphically free From taint of personality'. The historian must understand 'the laws of human nature', but these are rather abstractly considered: he must also study 'the principles of human society' and 'the practical play of the machinery of government'. Mill seems to set himself deliberately to damp the kind of interest in Hindu civilization that the writings of Sir William Jones and others had encouraged, and the result is a sort of intellectual steam-roller which crushes flat the whole complex structure of traditional Indian society, as well as the flagrant abuses of the Company and its agents. The book is written entirely without charm and sometimes without clarity, and greatly as one is impressed by the vigour of Mill's intellect, one becomes more and more convinced, as one reads on, that human nature and human history are too subtle and complex to be treated in this manner. Macaulay's exaggerated praise of the book as the greatest historical work since Gibbon prompted Maine's no less exaggerated censure when he claimed that Mill's inaccuracy was equalled only by his bad faith.

On the whole it was not a period of distinguished historical writing; nor was it a period in which historical works sold very widely. Except for the work of Sir Francis Palgrave, whose style is intolerable but who advanced some important hypotheses about Anglo-Saxon England, the Record Commission had accomplished little, and Harris Nicolas was justified in the aggressive tone of the *Observations on the State of Historical Literature* which he addressed to the Home Secretary in 1830. 'The History of England', he wrote at the beginning of his book,

is not merely imperfect and erroneous, but . . . discreditable to a country which boasts of intellectual pre-eminence over surrounding nations. . . . If proof be demanded, it will be found in this incontrovertible fact, that whenever a contemporary document is discovered, and its contents are compared with our best historians, their narratives either receive elucidation which gives a new colouring to the transaction, or, as frequently happens, their representations are proved to be false.

One reason for this, as he goes on to explain in a chapter on the 'Want of Encouragement of Science and Literature', was that 'no remuneration whatever is to be derived from the publication of a standard Historical book, by which is meant works containing letters or other historical evidence, or treating of any particular event in English History'. It is difficult even to find a publisher for a work embodying original research. Perhaps Nicolas is looking on the gloomy side of things, but he is a witness of verity, and it is curious to realize that this was the position when Macaulay was on the threshold of his life's work—a History for which he succeeded in securing as large a circulation as that of a best-selling novel.

When we turn from history to biography we are at once confronted by Lockhart's *Memoirs of the Life of Sir Walter Scott, Bart.*, one of the few biographies that deserve the compliment of comparison with Boswell's *Life of Samuel Johnson*.[1] There are obvious parallels between the two men. Like Boswell, Lockhart was an aspiring Scots advocate whose father was unsympathetic to his literary ambitions. Like Boswell, he had already made something of a name for himself in literature before he met the most famous writer of his day, a man a generation older than himself. Scott took an immediate liking to the younger man, as Johnson did to Boswell, and hoped to draw out the best in him and save him from his own bad habits—in Lockhart's case, a marked tendency to cruel personal satire. Like Johnson, Scott came to rely on the younger man to a considerable extent—and perhaps it would have been better if he had relied on him more. In marrying the great man's daughter Lockhart may seem merely to have done the one thing that was impossible for Bos-

---

[1] John Gibson Lockhart (1794-1854) was educated at the University of Glasgow and at Balliol College, Oxford. He became an advocate in 1816 and began to play a leading part in *Blackwood's Magazine* the following year. In 1818 he met Scott, and two years later married his daughter Sophia. He was editor of the *Quarterly Review* from 1825 to 1853.

well, but which would logically have completed the pattern of his devotion. The great difference was that Lockhart was no hero-worshipper and seems to have had no intention of becoming Scott's biographer. He lacked the warm enthusiasm of Boswell's temperament—he regarded Boswell as a fool who happened to write a great book—and there is nothing to suggest that he intended to write Scott's life until he received the request contained in his will. The first definite reference to the *Life* in Lang's biography of Lockhart occurs in a letter to Robert Cadell written in 1835, while Lockhart was editing Scott's writings. 'Perhaps I may promise a volume of my own reminiscences of our intercourse and fireside talk', he remarks. 'I never thought of being a Boswell, but I have a fair memory, and to me he no doubt spoke more freely and fully on various affairs than to any other who now survives.' This is very different from Boswell, who tells us that he had a biography 'constantly in view' during the whole of the twenty years that he knew Johnson, and who was certainly collecting materials at intervals throughout the greater part of that period with a 'labour and anxious attention' which has been the admiration of his readers ever since.

Yet Lockhart produced a very remarkable book, and the first of its merits is its fullness. He distinguishes the different stages of Scott's career and shows how one evolved from another. He quotes the critic who said that the *Border Minstrelsy* contained 'the elements of a hundred historical romances' and emphasizes that the poems and prose romances which followed them owe a great deal to the researches lying behind these early volumes. Throughout his *Life*, indeed, we see the lame child becoming a boy, the boy becoming a young man with a passion for riding and picturesque excursions, the young man becoming a ballad-collector, the ballad-collector becoming an original writer, and so on to the end. He knew from Scott's own conversation that his imaginative inspiration was essentially local, springing from particular scenes and places and their history in the past, and he keeps reminding us of this essential part of the story. Lockhart was admirably qualified to be Scott's biographer by his close understanding of the milieu in which he grew up. He understands the bleak asceticism of the religion of Scott's father, and the influence that this had on his son's development. He understands the important difference in social status between an advocate and a Writer to the Signet. He understands the amount of work involved in being a Principal Clerk of Session, so saving us from the sort of misconception into which Wordsworthian students have often fallen through supposing his Distributorship of Stamps a mere sinecure. Lockhart knew more than most people about the way in which Scott organized his daily life, and so made time to undertake such a prodigious amount of writing. He is most illuminating on Scott's passionate Toryism. Although Scott had been drawn to the younger man partly because there were not many thorough-going Tories among the men of letters in Edinburgh, Lockhart soon found that Scott tended to the 'purple' in a way with which he had not much sympathy; and he most interestingly relates this to Scott's resentment at 'the implied suspicion of his having accepted something like a personal obligation at the hands of adverse politicians' when his appointment as Clerk was ratified by a Whig Ministry. Having lived for considerable periods in London, Lockhart knew that Scott had always breathed 'the hot atmosphere of a very narrow scene' as far as politics were concerned. One of the most interesting things in the book is his exposition of the difference between the type of conversation admired in Edinburgh—'the talk of a society to which lawyers and lecturers had, for at least a hundred years, given the tone'—and the less combative form of conversation admired and practised in the south (the latter being much more congenial to Scott himself). Everywhere Lockhart provides illuminating details, such as the information that Scott had little ear for music, little sense of smell, and no delicacy of taste in matters of food and wine.

Lockhart makes it clear that he does not wish 'to Boswellize Scott' and says that his aim is to make him, as far as possible, 'his own historiographer'. There was no shortage of materials: Scott was a highly autobiographical writer, and although Lockhart seems not to have come on his fragmentary Autobiography until the *Life* was nearly completed, he had at his disposal the prefaces to the collected edition of *The Waverley Novels*, as well as thousands of Scott's letters, his unpublished Journal, and such things as the 'Essay on Imitations of the Ballad'. To this we must add the letter-books in which Scott kept the letters which he received, the earlier biographical accounts of Scott, and the reminiscences and memoranda sent to Lockhart by a great many of Scott's friends. When we come to consider the use Lock-

hart made of his materials, however, we find him not very scrupulous. In dealing with Scott's letters, for example, he does not
hesitate to improve the English, omit passages without notice,
conflate two different letters, or misdate. While this exasperated
Grierson, it may be argued that few biographers scrupled to
behave in this way until very recently. But Lockhart's inaccuracy
goes farther. He did not have Boswell's passionate belief in the
importance of every fact connected with his subject. He would
not have run half across London to verify a date—or even half
across Edinburgh. It is difficult to imagine Boswell writing the
words: 'To this excursion he probably devoted the few weeks of
an autumnal vacation—whether in 1786 or 1787, it is of no
great consequence to ascertain': in fact it was an excursion which
was of some importance to Scott's imaginative development.
Lockhart's attitude may be that of common sense, but Boswell's
is that of the dedicated biographer. Boswell would not have
misdated the publication of *The Vanity of Human Wishes* by a
month, as Lockhart does with *The Heart of Mid-Lothian*. Lockhart's unfairness to the Ballantynes may be regarded as more
serious, at least from a moral point of view. As the author of a
Refutation of Lockhart's 'Mistatements and Calumnies' pointed
out in 1838, we find in his 'sketch of John Ballantyne's early
history . . . a laboured particularity, and seeming accuracy of
specification, calculated to impose upon the reader, and to in-
duce a belief that it must have been drawn up from detailed, as
well as authentic information. But a more erroneous notion
could not possibly be entertained.' It is not for nothing that
Lockhart admired Defoe, with his talent for 'lying like truth'.
The biographer of Scott has no right over the reputations of
lesser men with whom he was associated, but in his handling of
the Ballantyne episode Lockhart shows himself an advocate of
the unscrupulous sort—and an advocate with as little respect
for his judges as for his opponents. As a young contributor to
Blackwood's he had been famous for his stunts and his lies, and
the habit of disrespect for the truth never left him, as may
be seen in *Peter's Letters*. It is impossible to read his reply to
the pamphlet just quoted, which he called *The Ballantyne-Humbug
Handled*, without noticing that the tone is as far from impartiality as the title, with its reminiscence of the polemics of
the seventeenth century. He shows a contemptuous disdain for
the low fellows who were in fact among Scott's close associates.

Cadell congratulated him on the 'Rembrandt portraits' of the Ballantynes, which made him weep for joy (and also, perhaps, with relief); but in fact they bear less resemblance to Rembrandt portraits than to the highly coloured caricatures that Lockhart loved to produce. His natural turn was for satire, and he was quite capable of satirizing where he also admired. Yet he holds himself in check: only very seldom indeed does he allow himself such a remark as the one that Scott's days with the militia 'must have been more nobly spirit-stirring than even the best specimens of the fox-chase'. The difference between his view of things and Scott's is nowhere more evident than in his description of George IV's extraordinary visit to Edinburgh. We often catch him regarding Scott with the detached amusement of an adult watching a child at play, and are reminded of a phrase which he once used of some blue-stocking ladies, 'their great romance, *alias* absurd innocence'. Scott once told Lockhart that it was the writings of Cervantes which had inspired him to write tales, but it must have been of the creation rather than the creator that Lockhart was most often reminded as he studied the Great Unknown. Don Quixote, as he once wrote, 'is the symbol of Imagination, continually struggling and contrasted with Reality—he represents... the eternal discrepancy between the aspirations and the occupations of man, the omnipotence and the vanity of human dreams'.

The satire deployed against some of the minor characters in the *Life* may be regarded as compensation for the obligation to refrain from satirizing Scott himself. When the author of the *Refutation* described the *Life* as '*a romance of real life*—a picture of which the principal figure must be considerably flattered, and EVERY THING ELSE SACRIFICED TO ITS PROMINENCE AND EFFECT' he was exaggerating, yet his statement contains a part of the truth. Lockhart does not always gloss over what he calls 'the few darker points in his life and character'. The publishing troubles that brought about Scott's downfall may be compared (in a fine expression which Scott himself applied to Melville) to what we see 'when Providence . . . industriously turns the tapestry, to let us see the ragged ends of the worsted which compose its most beautiful figures'—the pattern *behind* the carpet. Yet we do sometimes detect some degree of romance or make-believe in the *Life*. One reason for this is that Lockhart was naturally eager to make use of the element of autobiography in Scott's fiction; but Alan Fairford in *Redgauntlet* (for example) is a portrait of the young Scott as he thought of himself in later life, and it is hazardous to lean on romances for biographical information. Another reason is Lockhart's love of a set piece: his descriptions of picturesque scenes, or of Scott entertaining his friends at Abbotsford, sometimes give a definite impression of stage management. It is clear that the details are being composed with an eye rather to their general effect than to their exact accuracy. Lockhart also likes to make things as dramatic as possible. The year 1814 was indeed one of phenomenal activity, yet one is bound to share Grierson's doubts whether Scott could have done quite so much in it as Lockhart claims. What may be the culminating example of Lockhart's story-telling remains regrettably uncertain: the description of Scott on his death-bed telling Lockhart to 'be a good man—be virtuous—be religious'. It is just possible that this is true, but the probabilities seem to be against it.

Lockhart's merits stand out clearly when his biography is contrasted with Moore's *Life of Byron*. Behind this *Life* we catch sight of the tantalizing shadow of the Memoirs which Byron wrote between 1818 and 1821, and which contained (as he told Murray) 'many opinions, and some fun, with a detailed account of my marriage and its consequences, as true as a party concerned can make such accounts'. Byron gave the Memoirs to Moore and he (with Byron's full approval) allowed many friends to read them before selling them to Murray; but when the news arrived from Missolonghi there was an anxious meeting in Murray's parlour and those who wished to destroy the Memoirs (including the publisher himself) prevailed over Moore, and the manuscript was burnt in the grate. Later Murray commissioned Moore to write a *Life of Byron* as a counterblast to Leigh Hunt's *Lord Byron and Some of his Contemporaries*.

There is little in Moore's *Letters and Journals of Lord Byron: with Notices of his Life* (to give the work its full title) which obviously derives from the Memoirs, and such merit as the book has is largely due to Byron's own brilliance as a correspondent. It is clear that Byron intended his letters to be published: as Moore remarks, in the letters to John Murray Byron 'was shooting his shafts far beyond Albemarle Street'. Moore deserves credit for checking his own tendency to 'Asiatico-Hibernian eloquence' in favour of Byron's 'simple English diction', and parts of his book are still of interest. Lockhart, who was soon to be describing the early life of another lame boy, commented that 'never was anything so drearily satisfactory to the imagination as the whole picture of the lame boy's start in life'. Occasionally Moore makes a shrewd comment, as when he remarks that Byron 'makes so boyishly much' of his Venetian *amourettes*. The fact that a great deal had to be omitted makes the picture a little misleading as a whole, however: as Croker pointed out, if the full story had been told it would have been clear that Byron 'sneered at all man and womankind in turn', and his sneers at his wife and mother would have been put into some sort of perspective. In general it may be said that Moore understands the poet of the Tales and of *Childe Harold* better than the man who wrote *Don Juan*. His tendency is to show Byron (in a prophetic phrase of the poet's own) as 'an *amiable*, ill-used gentleman'.

The phrase comes from the *Conversations of Lord Byron with the Countess of Blessington*, first published in the *New Monthly Magazine*, a record which remains of capital importance for anyone interested in the poet. Of the early biographies the only one which deserves attention, apart from Moore's, is Galt's *Life*. When the two men met at Gibraltar Byron came under the scrutiny of a man nine years his senior with a novelist's understanding of character. Galt considered Moore's picture 'too radiant and conciliatory', and he himself gives us a more critical study of the poet's character. He is particularly interesting on 'the Aberdonian epoch', and emphasizes that 'the dark colouring of his mind was plainly imbibed in a mountainous region, from sombre heaths, and in the midst of rudeness and grandeur'. As a consequence Byron 'had no taste for more cheerful images . . . only loneness and the solemnity of mountains'. He concentrates on Byron's 'intellectual features' rather than on the material suitable for a gossip-column. He regards the importance which Byron attached to his lameness as 'unmanly and excessive', but is under no misapprehensions about the influence it exerted on his character. Galt understood the working of a poet's imagination: he is excellent on the qualities that make a poet, and holds to the Johnsonian view that poets 'differ in no respect from other men of high endowment, but in the single circumstance of the objects to which their taste is attracted'. He cannot always restrain his satirical bent, and refers to Byron on shipboard as 'a mystery in a winding-sheet, crowned with a halo'. He considered Byron's character as a complex structure built on a base that was not very hard to understand.

The early accounts of Shelley show little biographical skill. The most illuminating part of Hogg's *Life*, published in 1858, consists of the articles that he had contributed to the *New Monthly Magazine* a quarter of a century earlier. His book is rambling and egotistical and his attempts at wit do not always succeed. Medwin's *Memoir of Shelley* had first appeared in 1833, to be followed by a fuller biography fourteen years later. Medwin was a dishonest man, and he is unreliable with facts and dates; yet his book has the merit of preserving, in however inaccurate a form, a good deal of which we should otherwise have been ignorant. The element of romancing and inaccuracy in these accounts of Shelley, so characteristic of this period and so perplexing to those who wish to discover the truth about its great men, is even more pronounced in Edward John Trelawny's *Recollections of the Last Days of Shelley and Byron*, which was published in 1858. Something will be said of this later in the chapter: meanwhile we notice that it shared with the biographies of Shelley by Hogg and C. S. Middleton the distinction of calling forth Peacock's *Memoirs of Shelley*, printed in *Fraser's Magazine* between 1858 and 1862. Peacock did not like literary gossip: his aim in writing was to correct the inaccuracies of the earlier writers and to do justice to Harriet Westbrook. He had known Shelley intimately, and makes it clear both that he regards him as a man of genius, in many ways morally admirable, and also that he realizes that Shelley was unreliable in matters of fact, subject to delusions, and on occasion extremely comic. Peacock had always been Shelley's temperamental antithesis. He managed to convert Shelley to Italian opera, but not to comedy: he tells us that Shelley often talked of 'the withering and perverting spirit of comedy'. After the untruths, half-truths, idolatry, and salacity of so much that had been written on Shelley, Peacock comes like a breath of honest air: he is obviously reliable and fair minded, and his satiric genius does not seriously distort the picture. There have been few saner summings-up.

No feature of the literature of the early nineteenth century is more striking than the prominence of the element of autobiography. At no earlier time would a poet have written a poem as long as *The Prelude* on the growth of his own mind. In a very different way, Byron is even more 'egotistical' than Wordsworth: every reviewer noticed that each of his heroes was just a new presentation of himself, and a hostile critic might be pardoned for quoting Boileau:

> Souvent, sans y penser, un écrivain qui s'aime
> Forme tous ses héros semblables à soi-même.

In many of the poems of Shelley (as has been suggested earlier) autobiography and 'wish-fulfilment' lie equally near the surface. Similar tendencies are no less obvious in the prose of the time. Lamb's letters and essays may well be regarded as so many chapters of autobiography, while Hazlitt is never better than when he is writing of his own experiences—whether or not he actually played with the idea of composing an autobiography. When we turn from a consideration of the autobiographical element in poetry and the essay to the subject of autobiography itself, we find that Scott was the first of our considerable poets (with the solitary exception of Lord Herbert of Cherbury, who did not consider his poetry an important claim to notice) to embark on an autobiography. In 1808, six years before *Waverley*, he wrote a most interesting account of his own early life, giving as his excuse the fact that 'the present age has discovered a desire, or rather a rage, for literary anecdote and private history'. This evidence is the more impressive because it comes from a man whom no one has ever considered self-centred. A decade later Byron wrote his Memoirs. The tendency to autobiography was ubiquitous. In this period we no longer feel tempted to conjecture that writers with the desire to write about themselves belong to some particular psychological category—as we are with Pepys and Boswell, for example, in the seventeenth and eighteenth centuries. It is clear that there has been a great shift in man's way of looking at himself. A new importance was now attached to the uniqueness of each man, as the product of heredity and environment.

While it is disappointing that no autobiography was written of the stature of Rousseau's *Confessions*, Coleridge's *Biographia Literaria* and De Quincey's *Confessions of an English Opium-Eater* are only the most remarkable among a host of autobiographies of the most varied kinds. Men as varied as Clare, Galt, Hogg,

Gifford, Moore, Hood, Brydges, Hobhouse, and Leigh Hunt wrote autobiographies. For those of the writers of our period who lived well into the Victorian Age, particularly, it was to become very much of a 'financial sacrifice' to refrain from some form of autobiography. And there were soon to appear other names which are only remembered because their owners wrote accounts of their own lives—men like Samuel Bamford the Radical and Alexander Somerville the Working Man, whose autobiographies are invaluable quarries for the social historian. D. M. Moir satirized the fashion admirably when at the beginning of *The Life of Mansie Wauch, Tailor in Dalkeith*, he made his narrator observe that 'of late years . . . all notable characters, whatsoever line of life they may have pursued . . . have made a trade of committing to paper all the surprising occurrences and remarkable events that chanced to happen to them . . . during their journey through life—that such as come after them might take warning and be benefited'. People were beginning to realize that they might be interesting because they were 'typical' of something or other, even if they were not famous or exceptionally gifted. John Galt's finest works of fiction were inspired by the new vogue. There was an urge to explore the social structure, to survey mankind not only from China to Peru, but also from Windsor and Holland House to Pimlico and Manchester. It is interesting to notice that it was at this time that the word 'autobiography' first became current. It seems first to be used in English in the *Monthly Review* for December 1797 (xxiv. 375).[1] Reviewing Isaac D'Israeli's *Miscellanies* the writer uses the word '*Self-biography*', commenting: 'We are doubtful whether the . . . word be legitimate: it is not very usual in English to employ hybrid words partly Saxon and partly Greek: yet *autobiography* would have seemed pedantic.' In his *Specimens of English Prose-Writers* (1807) George Burnett claims that in English '*Auto-biography* was begun by lord Herbert of Cherbury; and continued by various religious enthusiasts, who commenced the practice of keeping diaries'; while in his edition of Spence's *Anecdotes* in 1820 S. W. Singer points out that 'a complete though brief Auto-Biography of Pope may be collected' from the book. Evidence of the growing interest in autobiography as a form is provided by the series of the best autobiographies of the past published by Leigh Hunt and Cowden Clarke in the 1820's.

[1] I am indebted to Mr. James Ogden for this reference.

One of the first memoirs to be called an *Autobiography* was John Galt's, published in 1833; but the word had already been used in the titles of a number of novels, including Galt's own *Member* and *Radical* and Benjamin Disraeli's *Contarini Fleming: A Psychological Autobiography*. Galt concedes that 'it is certainly not a very gentlemanly occupation to write one's own life', yet in 1835 we find Sir Samuel Egerton Brydges publishing his *Autobiography*— and he was a man who was no more likely to doubt whether his actions were gentlemanly than whether they were of interest to the world. Of course there were opponents of the new fashion: one of them, at least at first, appears to have been Isaac D'Israeli, for in the *Quarterly Review* for May 1809 we find him expressing the fear that 'an epidemical rage for auto-biography' may break out, 'more wide in its influence and more pernicious in its tendency than the strange madness of the Abderites, so accurately described by Lucian'. 'England expects every driveller to do his Memorabilia', as another writer in the same *Review* complained in January 1827: 'thanks to "the march of intellect" we are already rich in the autobiography of pickpockets'. But the *Quarterly* was, as so often, protesting in vain: the literature of the century was to be profoundly influenced by what Colley Cibber had called 'the great pleasure of writing about one's self all day'. One aspect of the influence of this fact on literary criticism may be noticed in the title of a book published by Charles Armitage Brown, the friend of Keats, in 1838: *Shakespeare's Autobiographical Poems. Being his Sonnets clearly Developed: with his Character drawn chiefly from his Works*.

Leigh Hunt's own *Autobiography* was not published until 1850, but much of it had already appeared in 1828 in *Lord Byron and Some of his Contemporaries; with Recollections of the Author's Life*. Wishing to extricate himself from debt, Hunt seems to have planned a book of memoirs, but to have been persuaded by Colburn to feature Byron on his title-page. The whole of the first volume and part of the second are devoted to Byron, Shelley, Keats, Lamb, Coleridge, and other friends and acquaintances of Hunt's, and it was the long essay on Byron that sold the book and did the damage. Although Hunt is not wholly fair, there is little need to be indignant on Byron's behalf at this time of day. The contemporary press had changed its tone dramatically after Byron's death, and had begun to make much of him, to such a degree that Hunt felt moved to expostulate.

Having been the beneficiary of both men, he could not forbear from contrasting the instinctive gentleness and gentlemanliness of Shelley with the histrionic virtues and vices of Byron. Hunt was always at his best defending the under-dog, and his essay on Shelley is greatly superior to that on Byron. He is stimulated by the need to oppose the pious libels of established prejudice:

> For his Christianity, in the proper sense of the word, he went to the gospel of St. James, and to the sermon on the Mount by Christ himself, for whose truly divine spirit he entertained the greatest reverence. There was nothing which embittered his reviewers against him more than the knowledge of this fact, and his refusal to identify their superstitions and worldly use of the Christian doctrines with the just idea of a great Reformer and advocate of the many; one, whom they would have been the first to cry out against, had he appeared now. (2nd ed., 1828, i. 323–4.)

Nothing could be finer than the passage in which he contrasts the behaviour of the 'licentious' Shelley with the conduct of the conventional man of pleasure tolerated by Regency society. He is equally illuminating on his poetry, the work, as he understands, of a reformer who failed to find an audience. There is a paradoxical truth in his remark that 'a great deal of Mr. Shelley's poetry ought to have been written in prose', while he admirably points out that some of his poems 'look rather like store-houses of imagery, than imagery put into proper action', adding that his images 'are too much in their elementary state, as if just about to be used, and moving in their first chaos'. On the poetry of Keats, which he understood intimately, Hunt is even better. A particular merit of these essays is to be found in the brief flashes of description which remind us that Hunt had a painter's eye. 'His forehead is prodigious', he remarks of Coleridge,'—a great piece of placid marble; and his fine eyes, in which all the activity of his mind seems to concentrate, move under it with a sprightly ease, as if it were pastime to them to carry all that thought.'

The *Autobiography* of 1850 is a better book. A man in his middle sixties, Hunt now looks back on the men of genius whom it has been his fate to outlive, and comments on the improvements which he has lived to see in the general state of the country and of mankind. It would be false as well as cheap to attribute his serener view to his pension and his relative prosperity.

He had always been a natural optimist. He can now analyse his own character more dispassionately, and tells us that he is 'quick to enjoy every object in creation, everything in nature and in art, every sight, every sound, every book, picture, and flower, and at the same time really qualified to do nothing, but either to preach the enjoyment of those objects . . . or to suffer with mingled cheerfulness and poverty the consequences of advocating some theory on the side of human progress'. He writes interestingly on Carlyle, his own antithesis: both were men of ardent and generous minds, but the one turned everything to gall, the other to honey. No less interesting is the contrast that Hunt draws between his own temperament and that of another greater man when he says that 'Scott saw the good of mankind in a Tory or retrospective point of view. I saw it from a Whig, a Radical, or prospective one.' He is excellent on the changes that he has lived to see. Railroads are changing the face of Britain. The Court has become 'at once correct and unbigoted . . ., and all classes are now beginning to permit the wisdom of every species of abuse to be doubted'. He is not shy about using the word 'progress' (or 'progression'). He makes no bones about his desire for Christianity (or 'Christianism') without Hell and without what he regards as superstitious accretions. It is the love in Christianity that seems to him its essence: he has no place for complete condemnation. He has not 'a single enemy' among the living or the dead. He does not withdraw all that he had said about Byron's faults, but he concentrates on the reasons for them. Perhaps the only man whom he can hardly pardon is Gifford, the man without genius but with the power 'to trample on Keats and Shelley'. In general the book has an elegiac glow, just melting into sentimentality. Dickens, whose Skimpole has done so much to perpetuate a caricature of Hunt, but who had helped him in other ways, is referred to generously. Yet unfortunately the book is not the masterpiece that it might have been, so raising Hunt from the rank of those whom we remember for their association with greater men to that of the men we remember for one great book. It is loosely put together, and lacks unity of purpose and direction rather as do De Quincey's *Autobiographic Sketches*. The reminiscences of the theatre are interesting in themselves, but they have little to do with autobiography.

Another friend of Byron and Shelley who published an

autobiography was Edward Trelawny, whose *Adventures of a Younger Son* appeared in 1831. If he had had his way he would have called the book *The Life of a Man*, and Thackeray might have had less reason to complain that no one had dared to tell the truth since Fielding. Yet 'truth' is perhaps hardly the word: whether the book as it stands is more of an autobiography or a romance is an open question. What would a writer of historical romance do, if he wished to write a book about this period? He would take for his hero a man belonging to an old and famous family, a man interested in poets and poetry and passionately in favour of liberal political views. He would be irresistible to women, and might be described by one of his lovers in some such terms as these: 'A kind of half Arab Englishman—whose life has been as changeful as that of Anastatius & who recounts the adventures of his youth as eloquently and well as the imagined Greek—he is clever'—she might go on '—for his moral qualities I am yet in the dark [:] he is a strange web which I am endeavouring to unravel. . . . He is six feet high—raven black hair which curls thickly & shortly like a Moors. . . . He excites me to think and if any evil shade the intercourse that time will unveil. . . .' Our hero would run away to sea as a boy: serve for a time on a privateer: become the friend of Shelley and reach Viareggio in time to light his funeral pyre: swim with Byron in the waters of the Mediterranean, and arrive quickly at Missolonghi on receiving the news of his death. Not being wholly a gentleman (no picaresque hero can afford to be that), he would raise the covering of the body to examine the crippled foot which had been responsible for so much in the poet's life. He would throw himself passionately into the fight for Greek independence, survive an attempt at murder in the Cave of Odysseus, marry the beautiful young daughter of an Arab pirate, and become the passionate admirer of Mary Shelley. He would appear as a speaker in one of Landor's *Imaginary Conversations*, and survive to a great age, picturesque and formidable to the end, the subject of a painting by Millais and of a poem by Swinburne. All of this—or practically all—is in fact true of Trelawny. Although we now know that certain of the adventures described in his book are fictitious—he did not desert from the Navy, for example, to serve on a French privateer—and while it is likely that he often exaggerates the importance of his own role in incidents at which he may have been merely a spectator, a great deal of the book is essentially true. Trelawny is a reminder of the fact that nature sometimes imitates art. It is of a piece with the rest of his extraordinary life that he should have 'followed the fortunes of those invincible spirits who wandered, exiled outcasts, over the world, and lent [his] feeble aid to unveil the frauds contained in worn-out legends which have so long deluded mankind'. All Dumas had to do to increase his reputation as a writer of romance was to put Trelawny's autobiography into French.

The question of the reliability of *Recollections of the last Days of Shelley and Byron* is more important. Unfortunately Trelawny was incapable of telling the unadorned truth : instead he rushed about, Quixote-like, trying to adjust the balance of opinion so that it should be fair to both his former friends. His protective instincts were aroused by Shelley, and the attacks which followed his death brought Trelawny out strongly in his favour. The remaining two-thirds of his book, which deal with Byron, are less successful. They are just as inaccurate in detail, while the tendency of others to romanticize Byron after his death seems to have confirmed Trelawny in his early reaction against him. It is partly that Trelawny and Byron had too much in common; and partly that, while it was a privilege to have been befriended by Shelley, to have been befriended by Byron was apt to be felt as an irksome obligation. When he revised his *Recollections* near the end of his life Trelawny further shifted the balance in favour of Shelley and against Byron—while his attitude to Mary Shelley became less friendly. He was not born to be a reliable witness, but his books remain of value for their vividness and for the picturesque details which they provide.

Benjamin Robert Haydon was another remarkable man much associated with the writers of his time who wrote an account of his own life.[1] His *Autobiography* proper covers the years 1786–1820, while his Journals continue until his death in 1846. It has been common to laugh at Haydon, and there is something absurd about a man who seriously contemplated putting up

---

[1] Benjamin Robert Haydon (1786–1846) came to London in 1804 to study painting. His great aim in life was the revival of 'historical painting' in England and he was profoundly influenced by the Elgin Marbles. He had a number of distinguished pupils, and mixed much with literary men: Wordsworth and Keats both addressed sonnets to him. *The Judgement of Solomon* and *The Raising of Lazarus* were among his most celebrated paintings. He committed suicide in despair after the failure of an exhibition.

a brass plate in his own honour and was capable of the reflection—'What a race the young Haydons would have been with
the blood of Michael Angelo mingled with mine!' Yet he was
a painter of real talent—not least in comic draughtsmanship—
and if his talent had amounted to genius his absurdity might
have passed unnoticed. He was highly intelligent, full of ideas,
and had an infinite capacity for taking pains. When Keats met him
in 1816 Haydon seemed well on the way to fame: it would have
taken a shrewd prophet to have foretold that it was the painter
who was destined to be remembered as the friend of the poet.
Like many good judges, Keats deeply admired Haydon's paintings, as may be seen in the fragment called the 'Castle Builder',
where he describes his ideal study:

> My pictures all Salvator's, save a few
> Of Titian's portraiture, and one, tho' new,
> Of Haydon's in its fresh magnificence.

It was in his studio that there took place the dinner at which
Wordsworth, Keats, and Lamb were all present. Haydon describes it admirably:

On December 28th the immortal dinner came off in my painting-
room, with Jerusalem towering up behind us as a background. Wordsworth was in fine cue, and we had a glorious set-to—on Homer,
Shakespeare, Milton and Virgil. Lamb got exceedingly merry and
exquisitely witty; and his fun in the midst of Wordsworth's solemn
intonations of oratory was like the sarcasm and wit of the fool in the
intervals of Lear's passion.

This was the occasion on which Lamb and Keats agreed that
Newton 'had destroyed all the poetry of the rainbow by reducing
it to the prismatic colours' and proposed the surprising toast—
'Newton's health, and confusion to mathematics'—the night on
which Lamb addressed Wordsworth as 'you old lake poet, you
rascally poet' and upbraided him for calling Voltaire dull.
Haydon was keenly interested in literature. His taste, which
typifies the enlightened opinion of his time, is summed up in his
wish to be buried with Shakespeare placed on his heart, Homer
in his right hand, Ariosto in his left, Dante under his head,
Tasso at his feet, Keats also in a position of honour, and
Corneille, that 'heartless tirade maker', in the reverse. It was
he who gave Keats the best possible advice: 'Go on, dont

despair, collect incidents, study characters, read Shakespeare and trust in Providence.' His long campaign to have the Elgin Marbles purchased for the nation was successful, though its success may have owed more to others than to him. His passionate desire to revive English painting cannot be laughed at. Three months before his twenty-first birthday he had knelt down, brush in hand, and prayed that he might be permitted 'to create a new era in art, and to rouse the people and patrons to a just estimate of the moral value of historical painting'. 'My great object', he wrote to Keats, 'is the public encouragement of historical painting and the glory of England, in high Art, to ensure these I would lay my head on the block this instant.' Though he was not a genius, he thought he was, and his unquestioning adoption of the Life of Genius helped Keats to aim at the heights. His journals are full of vivid descriptions which (unlike so many of Trelawny's) carry instant conviction, such as his description of Wordsworth looking at a group of Cupid and Psyche kissing and exclaiming 'The Dev-ils!' He describes the Duke of Sussex's voice as 'loud, royal and asthmatic'. He was not a mere Gulley Jimson, but a true genius *manqué*. Everything about him was on a huge scale, appropriate to his conceptions of 'heroic painting'. His ambition was limitless, his paintings so large that it is now hardly possible to find them hanging in any gallery, while he wrote his own life in twenty-seven volumes in Folio. There is a sad appropriateness in the self-dramatization of his suicide, with the final quotation from *King Lear*.

It would be pleasant to say something of many other autobiographies of the time, such as Clare's *Sketches* of his own life or Thomas Bewick's *Memoir*, which contrasts as markedly with Haydon's as does his art as an engraver; but we must be content with a final glance at the autobiography of Sir Samuel Egerton Brydges, or to give it its full title, *The Autobiography, Times, Opinions, and Contemporaries of Sir Egerton Brydges, Bart., K.J. (Per legem terrae) Baron Chandos of Sudeley, etc.*[1] The title-page is further adorned with a device representing a medieval knight on his

---

[1] Sir Samuel Egerton Brydges (1762–1837) sacrificed his chances of a degree at Cambridge by 'giving himself up to English poetry'. He was called to the Bar, but never practised. In 1792 he bought Denton Court in Kent, where he did a great deal of literary work. About 1789 he persuaded his elder brother to put forward his claim to the barony of Chandos: the failure of the claim in 1803, after no fewer than 26 hearings, helped to sour the remainder of his life. Meanwhile he had moved

charger in full cry after the Infidel and by a characteristically inaccurate quotation from Shelley, while facing it we find a portrait of the author with his eyes 'in a fine frenzy rolling'. Much
is to be expected of a man who tells us at the beginning that
circumstances have conspired to 'torpify' his faculties. Wordsworth once pointed out that Brydges 'thinks laxly, and uses
words inconsiderately'; and this is as true of his prose as of his
verse. He had no feeling for words at all, and remains of interest
as a fine specimen of certain of the critical views of the time
carried to the point of absurdity. He believed that 'genuine and
undisguised opinions... are often more valuable than arguments',
and is as rich in the former as he is deficient in the latter. All
that was necessary (he thought) was to be a genius, and write.
Jane Austen read his novel, *Arthur Fitz-Albini*, and commented
that 'there is very little story, and what there is told in a strange,
unconnected way': it is pleasant to reflect that Sir Egerton may
have been one of the models for Sir Walter Elliot of Kellynch-
hall. Chronological arrangement is far to seek in his *Autobiography*, certain obsessive themes recurring everywhere—such
as his insane pride of family. 'The peerage I claim', he remarks
at one point,

> only mounts up to the year 1554, but historic evidence will establish
> that my male stock is baronial from the Conquest; ascending, as I
> will satisfy any general jurist and European genealogist, to Johannes
> de Burgo (Monoculus) founder also of the House of De Burgh, and
> ten other branches of ancient peerage ... from all the chief of which
> I am also descended in the female line. This John De Burgo is said ...
> to have been of the House of Charlemagne. . . . (ii. 422.)

While Sir Egerton Brydges had the satisfaction of seeing his
Autobiography handsomely published (at his own expense) during
his lifetime, many other writers of memoirs (like Haydon) left
their work to be published by their literary executors. One of
these, Henry Crabb Robinson, who lived until 1867, left diaries
and reading-lists which are invaluable for the student of the
literary history of this period. The *Recollections* of Byron's friend,
Hobhouse, are also of some interest, though less relevant to
literary history. Like Scott, Thomas Moore began an *Auto-*

to Lee Priory, near Canterbury. A compositor and a pressman had started a new
press there, and Brydges supplied them with scarce old books which they reprinted
for collectors in limited editions. From 1818 until his death he lived mainly abroad,
particularly in Geneva, continuing his work as a littérateur and bibliographer.

biography, but he only reached his nineteenth year: after his death, however, eight volumes of his journals and other personal writings were published by Lord John Russell. The impulse to record one's own life was now widespread, though few men had the bravado or the honesty to begin their Memoirs, like the Ettrick Shepherd, with the words 'I like to write about myself: in fact, there are few things which I like better'.

XIV

INTEREST IN FOREIGN LITERATURE AND IN EARLIER ENGLISH LITERATURE

DE QUINCEY once suggested that all literatures 'tend to superannuation' unless they are 'crossed by some other of different breed', and it seems likely that one of the reasons for the variety and vigour of English literature at the beginning of the nineteenth century was the exceptional amount of cross-fertilization at that time between our literature and the literatures of other countries. But before we turn to the relations between England and Italy and Germany we must first acknowledge the continuing influence of classical literature. It is true that some observers believed that knowledge of the classics was declining. In his 'Essay on Fashionable Literature' (1818), for example, Peacock complained that 'classical literature seems sinking into . . . repose'. It is his contention that while a few years before 'the favorite journals of the day . . . were seldom without a classical . . . article for the grace of keeping up appearances . . . now we have volume after volume . . . almost without any thing to remind us that such things were'. Yet although the influence of Latin literature was much less strong than it had been a century before, it remains true that most writers and readers were far more familiar with Virgil and Horace than we are today, thanks to the educational conservatism of the schools at which a high proportion of the future writers were still educated. 'Lily's' Latin Grammar, which had first appeared before Spenser was born, was to remain in use at Eton (with only slight modifications) until past the middle of the century. In the 1840's a master at Eton unwittingly produced a fine *reductio ad absurdum* of the argument for a classical education. 'If you do not take more pains, how can you ever expect to write good longs and shorts? If you do not write good longs and shorts, how can you ever be a man of taste? If you are not a man of taste, how can you ever be of use in the world?' Yet without embarking on the endless controversy about the best form of education, it may confidently be asserted that there are worse trainings for a man of letters than a classical education, and it is worth noticing that most of the poets of our period were prepared to turn a passage of Latin into English verse, as Hobhouse did in his *Imitations and Translations from the Ancient and Modern Classics* (1809), a volume that is remembered because it contains some of Byron's early pieces. Although it was unusual by this time to produce an 'Imitation' of a Latin poet like Byron's *Hints from Horace*, the less direct influence of Latin poetry is not hard to discover. Shelley was influenced by Lucretius, while a recent scholar has reminded us of the influence exerted on Wordsworth by the Latin prose writers.

Yet it is clear that Latin literature no longer provided the imaginative stimulus to poets that it had provided in the age of Pope. Although Keats is said to have made a complete prose translation of the *Aeneid* while he was still a boy, it is evident from his letters that he was far more interested in Homer than in Virgil. The important new fact is the increasing influence of Greek literature in this period. In their decided preference of Greek literature over Latin the Schlegels were men of the new era. We are told that in his old age Dr. Samuel Parr, who died in 1825, would often remark 'with exulting pleasure' on the improvement in Greek scholarship since his youth, and it cannot be doubted that by influencing the pattern of education the work of Porson and his disciples helped to form the imagination of the new generation. Coleridge, De Quincey, Shelley, Landor and Praed were all widely read in Greek literature, while Peacock's passion for the Greeks was that of a man educationally 'under-privileged' living at a time when the more intellectual members of society believed wholeheartedly in Greek. And, of course, politics lent immediacy and urgency to a study that might otherwise have confined its influence to universities and schools. 'We are all Greeks', as Shelley wrote in the preface to *Hellas*. 'Our laws, our literature, our religion, our arts have their root in Greece.'

Neither the continuing interest in Latin nor the growing interest in Greek produced many translations of the highest quality. Admirable versions of most of the major classical writers had appeared during the previous century, and although these now seemed old-fashioned, classical literature did not challenge the translator as did more recent poetry and prose from the Continent which had yet to make its first appearance in English. One has only to mention Gifford's translations of Juvenal and Persius, Wrangham's *Bucolics* and his *Lyrics of Horace*, Symmons's *Aeneid*, and Hawkins's *Claudian*, to make it clear that there is not much that is of literary interest. Moore's versions of Anacreon have at best an historical importance: Cary's *Pindar* and his *Birds* of Aristophanes have some value, though they cannot stand comparison with his *Dante*: while Hookham Frere's translations from Aristophanes still retain considerable merit. It is hardly surprising that those who were most deeply interested in literature began to turn back to the translators of the Elizabethan age and the early seventeenth century, so participating in that exploration of the English literary heritage which is one of the most striking features of the period. To remember Keats's sonnet 'On first looking into Chapman's Homer' is at once to be reminded of these fine old translations, and to be set on one's guard against the donnish fallacy that only those who can read the classics in the original can derive inspiration from them. Few critics have ever written anything more foolish than Lockhart wrote about Keats. Looking back with complacency on his own Balliol education he makes one of the speakers in *Peter's Letters to his Kinsfolk* utter the dangerous half-truth that there is 'no such thing as a translation', and in the same spirit we find him demanding, in *Blackwood's Magazine*, why Keats chose to write on the legends of Greece when he was ignorant of the language of the Greeks.

Yet it was not only to translations that Keats was indebted. He probably owed more to the visual arts than to any translations whatsoever, and if we wish to understand the imaginative interest in Greek mythology at this point we must remember the increased interest that men were taking in sculpture and in the paintings of Titian, Poussin, and Claude. It will be sufficient to quote from Hazlitt's description of his first visit to the Louvre:

There [Art] had gathered together all her pomp, and there was her shrine, and there her votaries came and worshipped as in a temple .... Where the triumphs of human liberty had been, there were the triumphs of human genius. For there, in the Louvre, were the precious monuments of art;—There 'stood the statue that enchants the world'; there was the *Apollo*, the *Laocoon*, the *Dying Gladiator*, the

Head of the Antinous, Diana with her *Fawn*, the *Muses* and the *Graces* in a ring, and all the glories of the antique world:—

> There was old Proteus coming from the sea,
> And wreathed Triton blew his winding horn.

And apart from the Louvre and the growing vogue of Italian travel, great paintings were finding their way to England in increasing numbers, as we are reminded by W. Buchanan's *Memoirs of Painting, with a Chronological History of The Importation of Pictures by the Great Masters into England since the French Revolution* (1824). The arrival of the Elgin Marbles in England stimulated the imaginations of men like Keats and Haydon, while a great many fine paintings on classical subjects were available to interested members of the public even before the Angerstein Collection became the nucleus of the National Gallery in 1824.

It is not surprising that admirers of the paintings of Titian should have been keenly interested in Italy and its literature, and it may fairly be claimed that the 1820's represent the climax of English interest in Italian literature. The desire to visit Italy was stimulated by the fact that the country had been inaccessible to most travellers since the outbreak of the war with France. 'The opening of the long-cherished interior of Europe has produced a vast exportation of English tourists', as a writer in the *Annual Register* for 1814 commented rather sourly, 'who, whatever returns they may bring of amusement or instruction, will certainly not improve the balance of trade.' Whatever happened to the balance of trade, we may reply, the English imagination was greatly enriched. As Leigh Hunt pointed out in his Epistle to Byron 'on his departure for Italy and Greece',

> . . . All the four great Masters of our Song,
> Stars that shine out amidst a starry throng,
> Have turned to Italy for added light,
> As earth is kissed by the sweet moon at night.

This is certainly true of three of the 'great Masters of our Song' in the early nineteenth century, and as well as Byron, Shelley, and Keats there were a host of minor writers who owed a heavy debt to Italy. Nothing could be more characteristic of the period than the longing of Keats for 'skies Italian'. England is a beautiful country, he writes in his sonnet 'Happy is England', and England's 'artless daughters' are beautiful girls,

> Yet do I often warmly burn to see
> Beauties of deeper glance, and hear their singing,
> And float with them about the summer waters.

Although Keats was to be a dying man when he reached the shores of Italy, much of the finest poetry of Byron and Shelley was written there.

English enthusiasm for Italy and Italian was encouraged by the fact that the language is so much easier to learn than German. Men who had been well grounded in Latin at school found it easy to pick up a reading knowledge of Italian, while for young ladies Italian came to be regarded as an eligible substitute for the classical languages. In *Gryll Grange* Morgana is delighted to be complimented on her Italian, but when she has to confess that she also knows Latin she adds that this may be the reason why she is still a spinster.

When we glance at the translations of Dante and other Italian writers which appeared in the early part of the century we find that they are often designed for readers who know a little Italian but cannot get far without assistance. When Cary published his translation of the *Inferno* in 1805–6 he gave the Italian on one page and the English opposite, and it is remarkable that this was the first time that the Italian text of Dante had been printed in England. At first Cary's work attracted little notice, and in 1814 he was obliged to publish his complete translation at his own expense. It was due to Coleridge, who praised the 'severity and *learned Simplicity*' of Cary's diction and the manner in which he had achieved 'the variety of Milton without any mere Miltonisms', that Taylor and Hessey published the edition that made Cary famous. The influence of Dante on English poets of the period is easy to trace. The 'minute volumes' of Cary's *Dante* were the only books that Keats took with him on his Northern tour: he seems to have read them closely, since in one of his letters he describes a dream inspired by the fifth canto of the *Inferno*, and it is clear that Dante sometimes presented himself to him as an alternative model to Milton. Like Keats, Byron was particularly delighted by the episode of Paolo and Francesca, though his translation of the passage has little to commend it. There were times when Byron reacted against Dante's theology, but numerous references in his letters make it clear how much the Italian poet meant to him and it is hardly surprising that he should have used him in *The Prophecy of Dante* to lend authority to his vision of 'liberty and the resurrection of Italy'. Yet Shelley understood Dante far better. Whereas the *terza rima* of *The Prophecy of Dante* is at best a curiosity, in the 'Ode to the West Wind' Shelley adapted the metre more brilliantly than any other English poet has ever done: the versification is very different from Dante's own, yet the poem as a whole is truly Dantesque in its speed and in the sombre urgency of its prophecy. It is not surprising that Shelley preferred the *Paradiso* to the other parts of the *Divina Commedia*: this 'perpetual hymn of everlasting love' (as he described it) is an analogue to the vision of paradise which is a recurrent element in his own longer poems. *Epipsychidion* is prefaced by a translation of two lines from the *Vita Nuova*—

> My Song, I fear that thou wilt find but few
> Who fitly shall conceive thy reasoning

—and it is in this poem, and in *Prometheus Unbound* and 'The Triumph of Life', that the influence of Dante on Shelley is to be seen at its profoundest. When we turn from Shelley to Wordsworth we find a poet who owed far less to Italian models. Although Wordsworth praised Cary's translation as 'a great national work' he seems at times to have had difficulty in making up his mind about Dante's stature as a poet. In 1824 we find him wondering whether the fashion has not gone too far:

Let me know what you think of Dante [he wrote to Landor]— it has become lately—owing a good deal, I believe, to the example of Schlegel—the fashion to extol him above measure. I have not read him for many years; his style I used to think admirable for conciseness and vigour, without abruptness; but I own that his fictions often struck me as offensively grotesque and fantastic, and I felt the Poem tedious from various causes.

Wherever we turn at this time we find Dante's merits under discussion. Hazlitt, who refers to him as often as he does to any foreign writer, writes admirably about him in his review of Sismondi and tells us that Dante is the only one of the Italian poets that he would greatly like to have seen. As one might expect, Leigh Hunt was less at home with Dante than with many other Italian writers—perhaps he was not a big enough man to see him from a suitable elevation—yet he took from him the subject of his most un-Dantesque *Story of Rimini*. Landor was a passionate admirer of Dante, while Hallam wrote eloquently on him in his *Europe during the Middle Ages*.

Little can be said of the fortunes of Petrarch, Ariosto, and

Tasso at this time. Interest in Petrarch was stimulated by the work of Mrs. Dobson, Alexander Fraser Tytler, and Ugo Foscolo, but in general his influence is more obvious in the work of minor and minimus poets than in that of their betters— though it seems certain that a passage in the *Trionfi* gave Shelley a hint for the Platonic symbolism of light and shadow at the end of *Adonais*. Ariosto was readily available in Hoole's translation, the form in which he first became known to Southey and Scott. It is clear that Southey owed a good deal to Ariosto, while Scott told Edward Cheney that he himself 'had formerly made it a practice to read through the "Orlando" of Boiardo, and the "Orlando" of Ariosto, once every year'. It is as characteristic of Scott to have found Dante 'too obscure and difficult' as to have written an essay as a student in which he 'weighed Homer against Ariosto, and pronounced him wanting'. It was Hoole's notes that first revealed to Scott that 'the Italian language contained a fund of romantic lore'. It must be counted a misfortune that W. S. Rose's version of the *Orlando Furioso* in *ottava rima*, which appeared between 1823 and 1831 and won deserved praise from Foscolo, failed to supplant Hoole's less lively version. Tasso was also well known. Hoole's translation of the *Gerusalemme Liberata* reached its eighth edition in 1802, while a more spirited version became available with the reprinting of Fairfax's translation in 1817. John Black's *Life of Tasso* had appeared in 1810. Byron and Shelley were both keenly interested in Tasso. Byron went out of his way to visit Ferrara rather than Mantua, commenting (in a way that would have shocked the Augustans) that he 'would rather see the cell where they caged Tasso' than the birthplace of 'that harmonious plagiary and miserable flatterer whose cursed hexameters' had been drilled into him at Harrow: a not uncommon reaction to a sound classical education. Shelley similarly regarded Tasso as a brother in persecution, and we find him visiting his prison and sending Peacock a piece of wood from the door. Finding in him one of the *personae* that he was always looking for, Shelley read Tasso eagerly, investigated the merits of the various biographies, and planned to write a tragedy on his madness. By 1825, when J. H. Wiffen's translation of the *Gerusalemme* into Spenserian stanzas gave Foscolo an excuse for a long essay in the *Westminster Review*, Tasso's reputation was very firmly established.

It is an odd fact that the Italian poet whose influence on the

style of English poetry at this time is most readily demonstrable
is Luigi Pulci. Hookham Frere told Foscolo in a letter that when
he chanced on some stanzas by Pulci in Ginguené's *History of
Literature* it occurred to him that Pulci's 'ingenious and humorous assumption of the vulgar character and vernacular phrase
[of] rude popular attempts at poetry among his countrymen
[was] capable of being transferred, *mutatis mutandis*, to the
English nation and the present times'. Although he soon looked
into Pulci for himself, Byron seldom made any secret of the fact
that *Beppo* was inspired by Frere's *Whistlecraft*, and it has been
argued in Chapter II that in discovering the new idiom Byron
discovered a new aspect of his own personality and so became
a great satiric poet. There can be no doubt that *Whistlecraft*
did a good deal to draw the attention of English readers to
Italian informal satire. Ugo Foscolo, whose arrival in England
in 1816 is a fact of importance in the literary relations between
the two countries, reviewed *Whistlecraft* in the *Quarterly Review*
for April 1819, along with W. S. Rose's free translation of
Casti's *Animali Parlanti*, *The Court and Parliament of Beasts*. His
review, which was headed 'Narrative and Romantic Poems of
the Italians', helped further to disseminate knowledge of Italian
poetry in England. J. H. Merivale's *Orlando in Roncesvalles*, a
poem in five cantos based on Pulci's *Morgante Maggiore*, had appeared in 1814, while in 1822 Lord Glenbervie published his
inert translation of the first canto of Forteguerri's *Ricciardetto*. It
is a striking fact that this interest in the Italian medley poets was
almost exclusively an aristocratic affair: the easy transition from
sentiment to cynicism characteristic of Pulci and Casti made a
direct appeal to the temperament of the sophisticated Regency
upper class.

As a sort of postscript to this section we may glance at Leigh
Hunt, whose influence on Keats and on many others lends importance to his lifelong passion for Italian literature. For him
Italy was 'the soil in which every species of modern poetry
seems to have originally sprung up'. When he was in prison he
bought a set of the *Parnaso Italiano*, and for the rest of his life
Italian poetry was never to be out of his thoughts for long. While
his feelings about Dante were mixed—he once called him a
'great semi-barbarian' who produced 'a kind of sublime nightmare'—he was very much at home with Ariosto, 'whose fine ear
and animal spirits gave so exquisite a tone to all he said'. In

his 'Book of Beginnings' he quotes and then translates passages from Ariosto, Berni, and Forteguerri. These and other poets are again laid under tribute in his *Stories from the Italian Poets*. Hunt's attempt to restore to the pentameter couplet a freedom of movement which it had often been denied in the previous century owed a great deal to the inspiration of these and other Italian models. Although Keats soon outgrew Hunt, including 'Italian tales' with the other things that Hunt had spoilt by making too much of them, it was probably from Hunt that he had first caught his interest in Italian poetry and his desire to use the couplet with an un-Augustan freedom. When Hazlitt, who succeeded Hunt as Keats's guide in all matters of taste, recommended that a modern writer should translate some of the more serious tales of Boccaccio, Keats and his friend John Hamilton Reynolds soon set their hands to the task. The results were *Isabella*, 'The Garden of Florence', and 'The Ladye of Provence'.

We may note in passing that the *Decamerone* was not the only prose work in Italian to attract attention at this time. Dunlop's pioneering *History of Prose Fiction* emphasized the importance of the Italian story-tellers, while Thomas Roscoe's *Italian Novelists* (1825) contains translations from Boccaccio, Sacchetti, Ser Giovanni Fiorentino, Massuccio Salernitano, Cinthio, Bandello, and many others. Roscoe produced a translation of Benvenuto Cellini's *Memoirs* in 1822, while Manzoni's *The Betrothed* was added to Bentley's 'Standard Novels' twelve years later. It is the less surprising that the periodicals paid a good deal of attention to Italian prose literature, as well as to Italian poetry: Stendhal was among the writers in the *London Magazine* who wrote on Italian literature in the later 1820's.

If Italy was the Land of the Imagination at this time, Germany was the Land of the Intellect. In his *Autobiographic Sketches* De Quincey devotes a chapter to 'German Studies and Kant in particular' and compares his own discovery of German literature to the first appearance of America 'to an ardent and sympathising spirit': he describes it as

rising, at once, like an exhalation, with all its shadowy forests, its endless savannas, and its pomp of solitary waters. . . . As a past literature [he goes on], as a literature of inheritance and tradition, the German was nothing. . . . But . . . its prospects, and the scale of its present development, were in the amplest style of American grandeur. . . . Not the tropics, not the ocean, not life itself, is such a type of

variety, of infinite forms, or of creative power, as the German literature in its recent motions (say for the last twenty years), gathering,
like the Danube, a fresh volume of power at every stage of its
advance. . . . It seemed, in those days, an El Dorado as true and
undeceiving as it was evidently inexhaustible.

Edinburgh was the centre from which interest spread. It was
as a result of Henry Mackenzie's lecture on the German Drama
in 1788 that Scott and a few of his friends began to study
German under a Dr. Willich, who played a humble part in
introducing Kant to English readers. But Scott never mastered
the grammar of the language, so that his German remained
a hit-and-miss affair. Very few people knew German well—
a fact worth remembering when sweeping assertions are made
about the influence of German literature in England at this
time. An amusing anthology might be compiled about the
unsuccessful and often half-hearted attempts which men of
letters made to learn German. When Wordsworth and Coleridge
met Klopstock in Hamburg in September 1798 Wordsworth
could converse with 'the German Milton' only in French, while
Coleridge (for once in his life) was reduced to silence. Although
Coleridge later acquired what might be described as a fluent
cribbing knowledge of German, he was never able to speak the
language correctly. Wordsworth regretted his own lack of German when he was a young man, but later in life he seems to have
thought little about the matter. Although Shelley was a fine
linguist his knowledge of German was comparatively slight.
Keats did not even mention German as one of the languages
that he hoped to learn. Landor knew no German. Byron could
swear in it. Only a minority of writers—including Beddoes,
Darley, De Quincey, Lockhart, and, of course, Carlyle—knew
German at all well.

At the time of Waterloo very few people in England knew
much about German literature. To the average reader, indeed, 'German' literature suggested only two things: sensational
Gothic romances and wildly unclassical dramas. Of the former
some were translations, while others—such as most of the 'horrid
novels' which Catherine Morland borrows from the circulating
library in *Northanger Abbey*—were the work of English hacks.
Their aim was simply to produce a delicious *frisson* or thrill.
As literature they were worthless; yet it was not only feather-
headed young women who took pleasure in them, and their

interest for us is due to the fact that they provided imaginative stimulus to such major writers as Byron, Shelley and the Brontës. The 'German' plays which vied with these books in popularity and shared with them the attentions of innumerable satirists were more often of genuinely Teutonic origin. At the end of his *Lectures on the Age of Elizabeth* Hazlitt gives an amusing account of these plays, and emphasizes that it was as a concomitant or aftermath of the French Revolution that 'the loud trampling of the German Pegasus' was first heard on the English stage. Such dramas embody 'the extreme opinions which are floating in our time, and which have struck their roots deep and wide below the surface of the public mind'. Their writers are interested above all in gaining effect, and they seek this 'by going all the lengths not only of instinctive feeling, but of speculative opinion, and startling the hearer by overturning all the established maxims of society, and setting at nought all the received rules of composition':

> The poets and philosophers of Germany ... the Goethes, the Lessings, the Schillers, the Kotzebues, felt a sudden and irresistible impulse by a convulsive effort to tear aside this factitious drapery of society.... These Titans of our days ... have made the only incorrigible Jacobins, and their school of poetry is the only real school of Radical Reform.

Schiller's *Robbers* was the first German play that Hazlitt ever read, and it made an ineffaceable impression on him. It is interesting to notice that he thought more highly of *Don Carlos* than of *Wallenstein* (in Coleridge's translation) and retained a marked interest in Kotzebue, while finding little to appeal to him in the plays of Goethe (whose name was still usually pronounced 'Go-eth'). In general we notice that anyone interested in literature at this time was likely to own a few plays translated from the German—perhaps even the six volumes of *The German Theatre, translated by Benjamin Thompson*. By the beginning of the century, when Thompson's collection appeared, all Schiller's available plays seem to have been translated into English. Other books accessible in translation included Gessner's tearful *Death of Abel*, of which no fewer than twenty English editions had appeared by the end of the eighteenth century, Klopstock's *Messiah*, Wieland's *Agathon* and *Oberon*, Lessing's *Nathan*, and that strange but influential book, 'Zimmerman on

Solitude', which even the most predatory of Lamb's friends were content to leave unmolested on his shelves. *The Sorrows of Werther* had first been translated, through French, in 1779, and throughout the following century Werther was to remain one of the most famous characters in literature. Apart from the unsatisfactory rendering of Leveson Gower, on the other hand, the first complete translation of Part I of *Faust* did not make its appearance until 1833: it was the work of A. Hayward, who tells us that he was encouraged to produce this prose version by hearing that Lamb 'had derived more pleasure from the meagre Latin versions of the Greek tragedians, than from any other versions of them he was acquainted with'. John Anster's verse translation followed two years later. The fact that most of the English critics who referred to *Faust* before the thirties were basing their comments on scraps of translation and fragments of knowledge makes it the less surprising that a critic as gifted as Hazlitt should have preferred *Werther*.

'Whatever may be thought of the Germans as Poets', Wordsworth wrote in 1822, 'there is no doubt of their being the best Critics in Europe.' One of the books that did most to introduce German criticism into England was August Wilhelm Schlegel's *Lectures on Dramatic Art and Literature*, translated by John Black in 1815 with a preface drawing attention to 'the boldness of his attacks on rules which are considered as sacred by the French critics' and suggesting that 'it will be no disadvantage to him, in our eyes, that he has been unsparing in his attack on the literature of our enemies'. In spite of his denials, Coleridge owed a good deal to Schlegel, who was soon thought by many to be the greatest critic that Shakespeare had yet found. Hazlitt's long review is a fine tribute to a critic whose method differed radically from his own. But perhaps the most influential book of all, in stimulating English interest in Germany, was *De L'Allemagne*, by Mme de Staël, which appeared in French in 1810 and in English in 1813. This study, which must have been one of the models for Bulwer Lytton's *England and the English*, deals in turn with 'Germany, and the Manners of the Germans', 'Literature and the Arts' (the longest section), 'Philosophy and Morals', and 'Religion and Enthusiasm'. The importance of Mme de Staël's book may serve as a reminder that most knowledge of German literature and thought at this time was still second-hand. Even translations 'From the German' were more often in fact from the French, as was to be the case with translations 'From the Russian' a century later.

Of the men who interpreted Germany to Englishmen at this time three deserve particular mention. First in time and importance was William Taylor of Norwich, whose *Historic Survey of German Poetry* appeared near the end of his life in 1830.[1] He had become interested in German literature during his travels there in 1781–2. Eight years later he made his famous translation of Bürger's *Lenore*, which circulated in manuscript before its publication in the *Monthly Magazine* in 1796 and which was destined to play an important part in guiding the development of Walter Scott. Taylor's translations of *Nathan the Wise* and Goethe's *Iphigenia* were privately printed in 1791 and 1793. In the latter year he became a contributor to the *Monthly Review*, to which (and to other periodicals) he contributed nearly 2,000 articles on German literature during the next thirty years. The books that he reviewed included Goethe's *Dichtung und Wahrheit* and Schlegel's *Lectures on Dramatic Art and Literature*. George Borrow was one of the many young men who became interested in German as a result of Taylor's advocacy. Unfortunately the *Historic Survey*, which is largely patched together from his articles and which contains a great many errors, was already out of date when it appeared, and Carlyle treated it with great severity. ' "The fine literature of Germany", no doubt, he has "imported" ', he commented in his review, 'yet only with the eyes of 1780 does he read it.' Following Bouterwek, Taylor regarded Novalis, Tieck, and Fouqué as 'shooting stars' and made no mention of H. von Kleist, Friedrich Schlegel, or E. T. A. Hoffmann. By this time it was a patent absurdity that so large a proportion of a general work should be devoted to Klopstock. Yet it was in no small degree due to Taylor himself that a more critical attitude to German literature existed in England by 1830, and the fact that his *Survey* contains a great many

---

[1] William Taylor (1765–1836) was the son of a well-to-do manufacturer who sent him abroad to study languages and the ways of commerce. In 1790 he visited France and attended the debates in the National Assembly. The following year he persuaded his father to retire and wind up the firm, and he himself was enabled to devote the remainder of his life to literature. He was a friend of Southey's. In his articles he made a number of suggestions for projects which were later to be realized, forecasting steam navigation, pointing out the feasibility of a Panama Canal, and recommending that Britain should establish colonies in Africa, 'the only quarter of the world' where British commerce had 'struck no root'.

translations, competently done, helps to give it a value greater than Carlyle was disposed to acknowledge.

Henry Crabb Robinson, the friend of Wordsworth, Coleridge, Lamb, and Carlyle, whose *Diaries* throw so much light on the literary history of the period, also did a good deal to make German literature better known.[1] In 1800 he went to Germany for the first time because, as he told his brother, he 'understood it to be a country in which there was a rising literature' and he was 'surfeited' but not 'nourished' by 'the cream of English literature'. He met Goethe, Schiller, Herder, Schelling, and Wieland, and spent two or three years studying at Jena, then one of the most active intellectual centres in Europe. Although he published translations and numerous articles on German literature it was above all by his enthusiastic conversation that he promoted the cause of German culture in England. Not the least of his services was his insistence on the supremacy of Goethe. 'It has been my rare good fortune to have seen a large proportion of the greatest minds of our age', he once wrote, 'in the fields of poetry and speculative philosophy . . ., but none that I have ever known came near him.' Another minor writer excited by the 'inexhaustible mine of the richest ore' to be found in German was R. P. Gillies, the friend of Scott, whose *Memoirs of a Literary Veteran* (1851) contain an amusing account of his 'vain quest after German books and German professors' in Edinburgh about the year 1817, and his eventual discovery of a Frenchman called Pierard who told him that he had '*von* German book—le voilà! mais il faut avouer,—dere are some sentences vich I do *not* understand!'[2] Gillies tells us that De Quincey was 'the first friend . . . who could profess to have a command over the German language and who consequently was able (*ex cathedrâ*) to corroborate my notions of the great stores that were contained therein'. When another friend put at his disposal a good collection of modern German literature he com-

[1] Henry Crabb Robinson (1775–1867) was articled as an attorney at Colchester and became a clerk in London in 1796. In 1813 he became a barrister at the Middle Temple. He was one of the earliest members of the Athenæum and an active supporter of London University. He wrote for *The Times* on foreign affairs.

[2] Robert Pearce Gillies (1788–1858) studied under Dugald Stewart and Playfair at the University of Edinburgh and was admitted advocate in 1813. He lost most of his money by a rash speculation and supported himself by his writing. In middle life he moved to London, where he was constantly being arrested for debt. For seven years he was obliged to live in Boulogne. His *Memoirs* contain reminiscences of Sir Walter Scott, Jeffrey, De Quincey, and John Galt.

ments that 'the discovery of Aladdin's lamp could not have been more elating'. Of his numerous translations perhaps the most important were those published in *Blackwood's* between 1819 and 1827 under the title 'Horæ Germanicæ' ('Horæ Danicæ' were also the work of Gillies). These consisted of translations of the most striking passages of many German plays, and Gillies tells us that he had often made a complete translation, although he did not print it. Later he looked back and wondered why he had not made a more determined effort to publish complete translations, commenting:

> Feeling that when I translated any one of them, fifty more equally interesting were awaiting the same process, I looked upon the printed fragments only as stepping-stones into the deeper mines of German literature. Or to improve the metaphor, they were like a bridge across the dark waters hitherto thought impassable, leading a way into the stupendous cavern, with its glittering stalactites, and its various treasures guarded by Teutonic genii, who would be propitiated by one who came before them humbly, but courageously. However, I set most store, as I do now, by the prose works [of] Germany, of which I had once a valuable collection to be used, when time served; but which . . . have drifted out of my grasp for ever.   (*Memoirs*, ii. 265–6.)

It is unnecessary to provide further evidence of the fact that many writers of the time were convinced that German literature contained unexplored wealth, or to insist further on the important part played by such periodicals as *Blackwood's*, the *London Magazine*, the *Athenaeum*, and the *Foreign Quarterly Review* in introducing German literature to English readers. It will be more useful to consider very briefly how far certain of the authors of the day were influenced in their own work by the contemporary excitement about Germany.

Scott was interested above all by the ballads and the popular element in German literature, which presented itself to him as an alternative to Latin, for which he had little feeling. In his twenties he once sat up late into the night to translate Bürger's *Lenore*, while he also 'balladized one or two other poems of Bürger'. The result was *The Chase, and William and Helen: two ballads from the German*, a pamphlet the excessive rarity of which demonstrates its lack of success, in spite of favourable notice from one reviewer. Scott's translation of *Götz von Berlichingen*,

Goethe's 'knights-in-armour' drama, is an inaccurate piece of work. M. G. Lewis published Scott's imitation of Goethe's 'Der Untreue Knabe' in his *Tales of Wonder* in 1801, while Scott's version of *The Erl-King* dates from the same period. The harper's song in *Wilhelm Meister* may well have influenced the opening of *The Lay of the Last Minstrel*, while two of the least successful of Scott's characters were avowedly the result of his German reading: the White Lady in *The Monastery* is an adaptation of de la Motte Fouqué's Undine, and Fenella in *Peveril of the Peak* owes something to the fine sketch of Mignon in *Wilhelm Meister*. In general the German influence on Scott is most evident in the poems and in the least successful of his prose romances. In spite of his veneration for Goethe, whom he once rather oddly described to Lockhart as 'my old master', he was more at home with writers who innovated less. It is not surprising that most of the 300 German books in his library dealt with antiquities and folk-lore. As he had discovered when he became a member of the Speculative Society, Scott was no more a metaphysician than he was a revolutionary. He had no sympathy with the Jacobinism of the intellect: he turned away from the dark places of the human mind, and while the supernatural attracted him he felt obliged to explain it away. His interest in German literature declined as he grew older, though he wrote an essay on Hoffmann and sometimes talked about German writers with Lockhart.

Byron was younger than Scott had been when he suffered from Gessner's *Death of Abel*, but it seems to have been *De L'Allemagne* that really aroused his interest in German literature. As a boy he had been very much struck by *Der Geisterseher*, while in 1814 he fell under the spell of Schiller's *Robbers*. Of all German books it was *Faust* that was destined to influence Byron's own work most obviously. In 1816 he heard Lewis translating longish passages, and the result may be seen in *Manfred* and in *Cain*. Byron himself described *The Deformed Transformed* as 'a Faustish kind of drama', and Shelley rightly replied that it was a bad imitation. When Goethe reviewed *Manfred* enthusiastically in *Kunst und Alterthum* in 1820, so helping to establish Byron's European reputation, Byron responded by dedicating *Werner* to him. In one of two earlier but unpublished dedications to Goethe he had already described him as 'the first of existing writers, who has created the literature of his own country, and illustrated that of Europe'. Yet while Byron was greatly impressed by German literature we must remember that knowledge of it came to him almost entirely at second hand. 'I have read . . . much less of Goethe, and Schiller, and Wieland, than I could wish', as he once confessed. 'I only know them through the medium of English, French, and Italian translations.' As one considers the influence of German literature on Byron's own writings one finds, as with Scott, that it is least evident in his finest work.

Unlike Keats, who knew next to nothing of German literature, Shelley frequently refers to German poets and philosophers, though he never fulfilled his intention of reading Kant. At first it was the most sensational type of German—and 'German'—literature that appealed to him, as may be seen from his absurd prose fictions, *Zastrozzi* and *St. Irvyne*. In 1815 he began to study the language, though he never came to know it well. As one would have expected, he was keenly interested in *Werther*: indeed he began to sketch out a different version of the story. Peacock tells us that *The Robbers* and *Faust* were among the works which 'took deepest root in his mind, and had the strongest influence on the formation of his character'. Shelley himself tells us that he read *Faust* 'over and over again . . . always with sensations which no other composition excites', and comments:

> The pleasure of sympathising with emotions known only to few, although they derive their sole charm from despair, and the scorn of the narrow good we can attain in our present state, seems more than to ease the pain which belongs to them. . . . Perhaps . . . we admirers of *Faust* are on the right road to Paradise. (Letter to John Osborn, 10. iv. 22.)

Of his translations from *Faust* the opening choruses of the Prologue in Heaven are particularly fine. Shelley once asked the Gisbornes whether they could detect the influence of *Faust* on his own poetry, and in fact several of his poems seem to owe something to Goethe's masterpiece: the influence of *Faust* can probably be detected in both *Alastor* and *Adonais*, while it is beyond doubt in *Hellas*.

Yet of all the poets of the time it was Beddoes who had the deepest affinity with Germany. He spent a considerable part of his life in Germany and wrote a good deal in German, both in verse and in prose. His remark that modern critics of the

drama are by education 'prejudiced . . . in favour of the literature of the South' has already been quoted. He himself had
little interest in Italian literature, displayed 'an aversion to the
manner and the character of the French', and turned instinctively for inspiration to 'Britain-grafted, flourishing Germany'.
Believing as he did that German literature 'touches the heaven
of the Greek in many places' he could never understand why his
contemporaries would not study the German language. 'What
an idle generation you are,' as he wrote to 'Barry Cornwall',
'why don't you learn German?' His letters are full of perceptive
criticisms of German literature. He said that he had learned
more from Wieland and Tieck than from any other German
writers, and it was his view that Tieck—whose concept of
'romantic irony' particularly appealed to him and whose
works he once thought of trying to introduce to English readers
—deserved to be 'much more relished than Goethe'. He also
thought very highly of Schiller, maintaining that 'most of our
. . . dramatic writers would gain much by the study of the
historic conduct of Schiller, & some of his predecessors . . . &
a modified imitation of it'. Towards the end of his life he translated part of the *Philosophic Letters*. It is thoroughly appropriate
that he seems to have written part of *Death's Jest-Book* while he
was studying at Göttingen— a fact that would have delighted
the authors of the *Anti-Jacobin*. His deep affinity with Germany
may be seen in the genuinely metaphysical temper of his mind,
in the remarkable masculine power of his blank verse, and perhaps also in a certain lack of psychological balance and in the
strange harshness of many of his lyrics. Professor Donner has
admirably illustrated his life and work with a number of wood-
cuts by John Stephan of Calcar: there are paintings and engravings by Dürer that would be hardly less appropriate.

Yet it is when one turns from poetry to philosophy and criticism that one finds the clearest evidence of German influence at
this time. Coleridge belongs to the preceding volume in this
series, and Carlyle to the volume that follows; but something
must be said here of De Quincey's lifelong interest in German
literature, since he was one of the principal channels by which
knowledge of German philosophy reached England. As early as
1803 his diary records the purchase of a copy of *The Ghost Seer*
for 4*d.*, but it was from his friend De Haren that he obtained his
'first lessons in German' and his 'first acquaintance with German

literature'. It was on account of De Haren and the 'small portable library which filled one of his trunks' that De Quincey
arrived in Oxford with a keen interest in German literature—
an interest which was confirmed by his reading as an undergraduate and no doubt by conversation with Schwartzburg,
who was almost the only friend he made during his period at the
University. Soon we find him studying 'German metaphysics
in the writings of Kant, Fichte, Schelling, etc.' He must also
have made some translations about this time, since in his first
published essay on German literature, which appeared in the
London Magazine for December 1821, he makes use of a version
of his own. Some of De Quincey's comments on Richter (the
subject of the article) remind us of the author himself, and this
is even more noticeable when De Quincey writes on Herder two
years later. He describes Herder as 'the German Coleridge',

having the same all-grasping erudition, the same spirit of universal
research, the same disfiguring superficiality and inaccuracy, the same
indeterminateness of object, the same obscure and fanatical mysticism
(*schwärmerey*), the same plethoric fulness of thought, the same fine
sense of the beautiful, and (I think) the same incapacity for dealing
with simple and austere grandeur.

De Quincey also began a series of articles in *Blackwood's* entitled
'A Gallery of the German Prose Classics', the first author he
dealt with being Lessing, and the second Kant. Although he
wrote elsewhere on Schiller and on *Wilhelm Meister* De Quincey
was more deeply interested in the German thinkers than in the
poets, and when Carlyle described him as 'a man of very considerable genius, and . . . a German, a Kantist', he laid his finger on
the deepest and most constant of his German preoccupations.
Throughout his life it was his ambition to make known the
name of Kant 'in a country where the structure and tendency of
society impress upon the whole activities of the nation a direction almost exclusively practical'. When he talked to his friends
in that 'most musical and impressive of voices', it was very often
of Kant. 'In a few minutes'—R. P. Gillies tells us—'he could
escape at will . . . to the soul's immortality, to Plato, and Kant,
and Schelling, and Fichte.' In the important chapter on 'German Studies' in his *Autobiographic Sketches*, from which a quotation has already been given, De Quincey describes the newly
discovered literature of Germany as an El Dorado and 'the

new or transcendental philosophy of Immanuel Kant' as 'the very tree of knowledge' standing in the centre. When De Quincey was most doubtful about the validity of Kant's philosophy (we are told) he was apt to become melancholy, assailed by a 'gloom of something like misanthropy'.

Although De Quincey always intended to try his hand as a writer of fiction, in the event he wrote only one long work of fiction, though he translated another. He translated *Walladmor*, a book by a German hack-writer which purported to be a German version of a book by Scott: as De Quincey became aware of the book's absurdities he handled his original with a great deal of freedom. *Klosterheim* appears to be original, though it would not be surprising if a German prototype were one day to turn up. It is a Gothic romance set in a town in Swabia during the Thirty Years' War. De Quincey also wrote a handful of short stories, several of them German in origin or by natural affinity. 'The Love Charm' is a translation from Tieck, while 'Mr. Snackenberger' and 'The King of Hayti' are free adaptations of German originals. Their ingredients are mystery, terror, a grotesque sense of humour, and a strong vein of sentiment verging on sentimentality. In general De Quincey's fictitious writings show little of the true novelist's interest in human character. Writing rather as the author of 'Murder considered as one of the Fine Arts', he reminds us often of Edgar Allan Poe. If he had been alive today he would have been a great reader of the more macabre and intellectual type of detective story.

Hazlitt was far from sharing De Quincey's enthusiasm for the Germans. 'He has not read Plato in his youth', De Quincey wrote in a footnote to the 1822 version of the *Confessions*, '(which most likely was only his misfortune); but neither has he read Kant in his manhood (which is his fault).' As a young man Hazlitt admired the Jacobin German drama of the time, and as early as 1796 we find him discussing German literature with his friend Joseph Fawcett; but although he wrote about German authors here and there we miss the spontaneous enthusiasm with which he wrote about Boccaccio and Ariosto. Kant must have reminded him too forcibly of the rigidity of his own upbringing, while his innate preference for lucidity of expression led him to look with distrust on the work of so abstruse a thinker (known to him only, it is probable, through Willich and Mme de Staël).

'As for the great German oracle Kant', he wrote in his review of *Biographia Literaria*, 'we must take the liberty to say, that his system appears to us the most wilful and monstrous absurdity that ever was invented.' He seems hardly ever to refer to Herder or to Schelling except when he describes Coleridge as a man 'who wandered into Germany and lost himself in the labyrinths of the Hartz Forest and of the Kantean philosophy, and amongst the cabalistic names of Fichtè and Schelling and Lessing, and God knows who'. The names of Kotzebue (an early weakness), Schiller, A. W. Schlegel and Goethe almost exhaust the list of the German writers of whom Hazlitt approved.

With Carlyle we reach a new chapter in the history of German literature in England. For us it will be sufficient to recall that three of his first four books were his translation of *Wilhelm Meister's Apprenticeship* (1824), his *Life of Schiller* (1825), and his four volumes of translations from *German Romance* (1827). It is wholly appropriate that Goethe should have served as a referee when Carlyle applied for the Chair of Moral Philosophy at St. Andrews, writing that he had 'observed with pleasure Mr. Carlyle's profound study of [German] literature'. It is no less appropriate that Goethe's testimonial should have arrived too late. Carlyle was not elected. We may remember the warning voice of Jeffrey: 'England *never will* admire your German divinities.'

While the influence of German literature in England at this time has frequently been discussed, that of French has received little attention. Yet in spite of the exaggerated contempt for the writers of France expressed by De Quincey and a few of his contemporaries, French influence was more important than might at first appear. In his *Passages of a Working Life* Charles Knight tells us that when he set up as a publisher in 1824 'translations from the French were in far greater demand than at present [1864], when an acquaintance with modern languages is much more general'. Although knowledge of French was shaky, many readers were prepared to take an interest in the literature of France, and particularly in the work of French prose writers. The same love of 'romantic research' that led Scott to study Italian as a young man induced him to improve his French, in order that he might explore the older French literature and extend his acquaintance with 'Tressan's romances, the Bibliothèque Bleue, and Bibliothèque des Romans'; while a man as different from Scott as Hazlitt more than once echoed Gray's exclamation—'Be mine to read eternal new romances of Marivaux and Crébillon!' As one might expect, the poets of the seventeenth century were not generally popular—to put in a word for Boileau was usually just a back-handed way of attacking the Lakers and the Cockneys—while not the least agreeable thing about Schlegel's lectures was that they seemed to justify the innate British tendency to be bored by Racine and the classical dramatists. The first signs of an interest in the older French poets and the first English reactions to the moderns are of greater historical interest. In the *London Magazine* Cary published a series of articles on 'The Early French Poets', illustrated by quotations, which included such men as Marot, du Bellay, Ronsard, and Villon: poets not greatly regarded in France itself at the time. Cary also wrote on two recent poets, Béranger and Lamartine, though his praise was tepid. Stendhal (also in the *London Magazine*) was even less enthusiastic, dismissing Victor Hugo as the writer of odes which 'positively do not contain the smallest particle of an idea'. It was a few years later that informed interest in the new French literature began to manifest itself, as may be seen from a letter from Letitia Elizabeth Landon to William Jerdan in 1834:

> A most delightful series of articles might be written on French literature. *We* know nothing of it; and it would require an immense deal of softening and adaptation to suit it to English taste. . . . It is full of novelty, vivid conceptions, and . . . genius, but what we should call blasphemous and indelicate to the last degree.

It must have been of the recent novelists and poets that L. E. L. was thinking, for the work of Rousseau and the writers of the *Encyclopédie*, which many Englishmen did find 'blasphemous and indelicate to the last degree', was already well known. Rousseau's writings had proved influential in England by the end of the eighteenth century: *La Nouvelle Héloïse* and *Émile* were widely read, though few readers were as clear as Hazlitt about the superiority of the *Confessions* to Rousseau's other writings. 'The best of all his works is the *Confessions*', he wrote in the *Round Table*, 'though it is that which has been least read, because it contains the fewest set paradoxes or general opinions.' In general we notice that the writers of the French Enlightenment are frequently referred to in the literature of this period, and that the tone of the references serves as a convenient index to the political sympathies of the writer. When Mr. Crotchet mentions the name of Diderot in chapter vii of *Crotchet Castle*, for example, the Rev. Dr. Folliott asks him who Diderot was:

'Who was he, sir?' [Mr. Crotchet echoes.] 'The sublime philosopher, the father of the encyclopædia, of all the encyclopædias that have ever been printed.'

The Rev. Dr. Folliott. 'Bless me, sir, a terrible progeny! they belong to the tribe of *Incubi*.'

Mr. Crotchet. 'The great philosopher, Diderot—'

The Rev. Dr. Folliott. 'Sir, Diderot is not a man after my heart. Keep to the Greeks, if you please.'

It is not surprising that the notes to *Queen Mab*, a poem which owes a considerable debt to Volney's *Ruins*, contain quotations from Rousseau, Laplace, Cabanis, Bailly, d'Holbach, Condorcet, and Cuvier. Nor is it surprising that the Reviews devote a good deal of attention to these French writers. In *Peter's Letters to his Kinsfolk* Lockhart describes 'the Scotch philosophers of the present day' as 'the legitimate offspring of the sceptical philosophers of the last age', and he would certainly have included Rousseau and Diderot among their ancestors. While *Blackwood's* attacked Playfair as 'the d'Alembert of the Northern Encyclopaedists', one notices that the *philosophes* were usually treated with respect by writers in the *Edinburgh Review*. Altogether a surprising number of books from France or about France received attention in the Reviews, and the discussions that resulted became part of the great political and constitutional debate that went on throughout the nineteenth century.

A number of Englishmen were also becoming interested in Spanish history and literature at this time. When the political situation in South America drew attention to Spain in 1809 an anonymous writer expressed the hope that the time had come when Spanish would obtain 'as many readers and admirers... as French or German'. Between 1810 and 1814 there was apparently a sufficient number of exiles and other readers of Spanish in London to justify Southey's friend Blanco White in producing a periodical called *El Español*. The growing interest in Spanish literature, which was the subject of an article in the *London Magazine* in 1820, was further stimulated by the arrival of a large number of émigrés in 1823. In August of that year

J. H. Wiffen tells us that he has 'had much conversation on the Spanish muses' with a number of the deputies of the late Cortes at a party at Sir John Bowring's. Southey had a fine collection of Spanish and Portuguese books, while his letters make it clear that he was keenly interested in many Spanish and Portuguese authors, notably Camoens (whose sonnets he at one time considered superior to *The Lusiad*). When he set out to write a description of English life and manners in 1807 he chose the pseudonym of a supposed Spanish visitor, Don Manuel Alvarez Espriella. Hookham Frere was another man who knew a good deal about Spanish literature: he had served as ambassador in both Lisbon and Madrid, and his translations from *El Cid* were described by Coleridge as 'incomparable'. Scott also took an interest in Spanish literature, while Lockhart made translations of a number of ballads for a new edition of Motteux's *Don Quixote* which appeared in 1822 and then went on to produce his volume of translations, *Ancient Spanish Ballads: Historical and Romantic* (1823). In the preface Lockhart complains of the neglect of these poems in Spain itself: while attention has been paid to very minor writers no critic of ability has studied 'those older and simpler poets who were contented with the native inspirations of Castilian pride. No Spanish Percy, or Ellis, or Ritson, has arisen.' He refers to Bouterwek's *History of Spanish and Portuguese Literature*, which was translated into English in the same year, and to the collection of Spanish ballads made by an Englishman called Depping and published at Leipzig in 1817. In 1840 Lockhart gave Borrow's *Bible in Spain* his blessing. Mrs. Hemans produced numerous translations from Camoens and other Portuguese and Spanish poets, while Thomas Campbell was also interested in the literature of Spain. Heber collected Spanish books. Richard Chenevix Trench, who contributed a number of papers on Spanish literature to the *Athenaeum* in 1828–9, had been one of 'The Apostles' at Cambridge, and it is worth remembering that Torrijos was connected with the Apostles, who made a point of supporting the cause of the Spanish exiles and studying the literature of their country. When Ferdinand VII, 'the tyrant of literature', died in 1836 and the exiles returned to Spain to launch a 'Romantic Movement' they left England a little less ignorant of their country and its literature than it had been, and took with them a considerable debt to Byron and his English contemporaries.

In 1820 there had appeared *Observations on the State of Religion and Literature in Spain*, by John (later Sir John) Bowring, and it seems appropriate to end this section with a salute to this extra-ordinary man.[1] A disciple of Jeremy Bentham's, he was the first editor of the *Westminster Review*, edited Bentham's *Works*, and left brief *Autobiographical Recollections* which contain glimpses of eminent contemporaries. Between 1820 and 1843 he favoured the world with translations from the poetry of Russia, Batavia, Spain, Servia, Poland, Hungary, and Bohemia.

Important as was the influence of foreign literature at this period, however, it was as nothing compared with the influence of earlier English literature. As Scott remarked in his preface to the poems of Patrick Carey, it was an age 'distinguished for research into poetical antiquities'. *Beowulf*, it is true, was first published abroad, by Thorkelin at Copenhagen in 1815, and until the publication of J. M. Kemble's edition in 1833 the event went almost unnoticed in England; yet a notable band of enthusiasts were now exploring the rich heritage of our older literature. The appearance of the first series of the *Retrospective Review* between 1820 and 1826 is not the least significant of the signs of the times. In the introduction Henry Southern makes his point of view clear:

The British public are almost solely occupied by the productions which daily issue from the press; newspapers, reviews, pamphlets, magazines, the popular poetry, the fashionable romances, together with new voyages and travels, occupy the reading time, and fix the attention of the people.—The old and venerable literature of the country, which has . . . tended to make us what we are, is treated with distant reverence. . . . Their authors are apotheosized, but seldom worshipped.

Southern goes on to claim that 'no study is more interesting, and few more useful, than the history of literature,—which is, in fact, the history of the mind of man', and to explain that 'the design of this Review of past literature . . . is . . . to recal the public from an exclusive attention to new books, by making

[1] Sir John Bowring (1792–1872) belonged to an ancient Devonshire family. He early revealed a remarkable gift for languages which he developed as a result of extensive travels on commercial business. In 1831 he worked with Sir H. Parnell on a report which led to a radical change in the accounting methods of the Exchequer. He became a Member of Parliament in 1835 and helped to form the Anti-Corn-Law League. Later in his life he occupied important diplomatic posts in the Far East.

the merit of old ones the subject of critical discussion'. It is characteristic of the age that he should have wished to preserve 'the interesting form and manner of the present Reviews', though without their political bias and personal invective. Deploring 'the dearth of works on the history of literature in our own language'—a deficiency that was not to be remedied until near the end of the century—he emphasized that the reviewers would 'by a careful selection of particular extracts, not only endeavour to give an idea of the mode of thought and style of individual authors, but to furnish a collection of specimens of the greatest part of our writers, so as to exhibit a bird's-eye view of the rise and progress of our literature'. Roughly three-quarters of the articles in the first four volumes deal with English literature, while the others deal with foreign books available in translation (usually in old translations). Southern particularly mentions the lack of accounts of the English prose writers, and we notice that the *Review* contains rather more articles on prose than on poetry and the drama together. There are essays on Sir Thomas Browne, Bacon's *Novum Organum*, *Mandeville's Travels*, the *Arcadia*, Ascham's *Toxophilus*, the criticism of Rymer and Dennis (the latter, by T. N. Talfourd, containing an important digression on severity in contemporary criticism), Defoe's *Memoirs of a Cavalier*, Stubbes's *Anatomy of Abuses*, and a number of memoirs and historical works. Among the poets dealt with we notice George Herbert, Vaughan, Browne the pastoralist, Southwell, Davenant, Chamberlayne, and the forgotten Leonard Lawrence, author of *Arnalte and Lucenda*. There is a series of articles on the early English drama, while attention is also paid to Ben Jonson, Chapman, Davenport, and Lee. Some of the writers dealt with remain obscure to this day: occasionally there is still no other place in which extracts may be found. But unfortunately the critical level is very uneven, and we look in vain for the incisiveness of a Hazlitt. Obvious opportunities are missed, as when Herbert is briefly and condescendingly disposed of. Other articles are the work of able men, although their titles are sometimes unhelpful: Talfourd's essay on Robert Wallace's *Various Prospects of Mankind*, for example, contains an intelligent and spirited rebuttal of the pessimistic view that literature was declining which may be read as a reply to Peacock's 'Four Ages of Poetry': Byron, Moore, Campbell, and Crabbe are played down, while generous praise is given to Wordsworth, Coleridge,

Lamb, 'Barry Cornwall', and Leigh Hunt. Such an excursion into modern literature was exceptional, however, and we notice that the sixteenth and seventeenth centuries were the favourite hunting-ground of most of the reviewers.

While the more obscure of the books discussed in the *Retrospective Review* go unmentioned in the *Edinburgh* and the *Quarterly*, reprints of others drew them to the attention of the less antiquarian reviewers. In his autobiography Charles Knight tells us that early in the century 'no publisher had . . . thought it worth while to reprint Drayton, or Wither, or Herrick, or Herbert': between 1815 and 1836—it is interesting to notice—complete or selected editions of the last three poets all made their appearance. A single publisher, C. Whittingham of Chiswick, produced reprints of Bartholomew Griffin's *Fidessa*, *Hero and Leander*, the poems of Thomas Lodge, and Chalkhill's *Thealma and Clearchus*, in attractive little volumes that may well have caught the eye of Keats on the table of one of his friends. Soon Pickering was issuing the first volumes of his Aldine Poets. A number of meritorious editions of the older prose writers also appeared, such as Reginald Heber's edition of Jeremy Taylor in 1822. But of course we remember particularly the editions of the Elizabethan and Jacobean dramatists for which Lamb's *Specimens* helped to prepare the way. 'What news in the republic of letters?' we find Peacock asking a friend in 1809. 'Has Gifford undertaken to edit Beaumont and Fletcher? Or is any new edition of those dramatists in contemplation?' As Jeffrey wrote in the *Edinburgh Review* two years later, 'All true lovers of English poetry have been long in love with the dramatists of the time of Elizabeth and James; and must have been sensibly comforted by their late restoration to some degree of favour and notoriety.' It was not only critics of progressive tastes who shared in this enthusiasm for the Elizabethans. Gifford produced editions of Massinger, Jonson and Ford between 1805 and 1827. Weber, whose edition of Ford had preceded Gifford's, brought out an inaccurate edition of Beaumont and Fletcher in 1812. In 1830 a much better scholar, Alexander Dyce, edited Webster, while in 1833 he completed an edition of Shirley which Gifford had begun. Seven years later he edited Middleton. The unreliability of the texts of many of these editions was not important: what mattered was that they made available the works of our older dramatists and so provided inspiration for many of the new poets. It is worth remembering that while no Englishman (perhaps) has ever been as passionately interested in Shakespeare as John Keats, he never refers to Malone's epoch-making edition, which had appeared in 1790 and was revised in 1821.

Collections and anthologies of our older literature continued to appear in this period: mention may be made of Campbell's *Specimens of the British Poets* (1819), in seven volumes, with its long but disappointing preface, and Allan Cunningham's *Songs of Scotland* (1825). But the most important work of this kind had been done earlier by such men as Percy, Ritson, Ellis, Scott, and Southey. As has already been mentioned, more attention was now paid to prose: George Burnett's *Specimens of English Prose-Writers* had appeared in 1807: the first edition of Dunlop's *History of Fiction* was published in 1814: while Scott's *Lives of the Novelists* (originally prefaces to the volumes of Ballantyne's *Novelists' Library*) came out between 1821 and 1824. Francis Cary had the excellent idea of continuing Johnson's *Lives of the Poets* in the *London Magazine*, but unfortunately he lacked the critical vigour to make a success of the undertaking. John Payne Collier produced his *Poetical Decameron* in 1820 and his *History of English Dramatic Poetry* eleven years later, while Allan Cunningham's *Biographical and Critical History of the British Literature of the last Fifty Years* made its appearance at Paris in 1824.

In this age of old books and new books, of antiquarian enthusiasm and fresh literary genius, Isaac D'Israeli stands in the background making notes. Like most men with literary aspirations, he set out with the ambition of becoming a creative writer; but finding that he was deficient in imaginative power he had the humility and the good sense to devote himself to the study of the lives and writings of men greater than himself. The result was a series of studies which include *Curiosities of Literature, Calamities of Authors, Quarrels of Authors*, and *Amenities of Literature*. Byron described him as 'the Bayle of literary speculation, who puts together more amusing information than anybody'. But he did not only collect and digest the materials of our literary history: he also produced one work, *The Literary Character*, which was something quite new in English. The best way to give an impression of the book will be to quote a few phrases from D'Israeli's own chapter-summaries:

Youth of genius.—Its first impulses may be illustrated by its subsequent actions. . . . Its melancholy.—Its reveries. Its love of solitude. An unsettled impulse, querulous till it finds its true occupation. . . . Of the irritability of genius.—Genius in society often in a state of suffering. . . . The habitudes of the man of genius distinct from those of the man of society. . . . The meditations of genius.—A work on the art of meditation not yet produced.

'I have a great respect for *Israeli* and his talents', Byron wrote to John Murray in 1819, 'and have read his works over and over and over repeatedly, and have been amused by them greatly, and instructed often.' As Byron read *The Literary Character*, he must have felt that he was looking into a mirror. His annotations, which encouraged D'Israeli to undertake an expanded version of the book, remain as evidence of the fact that the self-effacing recorder of the ways of genius helped the most celebrated man of genius of the age to know himself. As Byron was the perfect reader of *The Literary Character*, so D'Israeli would have been the perfect reader of Byron's Memoirs, and in 1822 we find Byron writing that he would be 'gratified' if D'Israeli had seen his manuscript, 'as you are curious in such things as relate to the human mind'. D'Israeli replied that Byron's 'Book of Life' had been 'locked up by Murray in an iron chest', but it is to be hoped that it did not always elude the eye of so penetrating a historian of the mind. In any event the friendship between these two men, the admirer of Pope who wrote *Childe Harold* and *Manfred*, and the scholar whose frustrated genius revealed itself in his brilliant and flamboyant son, remains one of the 'curiosities of literature' at this time.

D'Israeli once remarked that 'we have become a nation of book collectors', but little can be said here of the bibliophiles and bibliomaniacs who were so much a part of the literary scene. The Roxburghe sale was an event of real literary importance. 'At the death of this accomplished person', Scott wrote of the third Duke in the *Quarterly Review* for February 1831,

his noble collection . . . was at length brought to auction, attracting the greatest attention, and bringing the highest prices of any book sale that had ever been heard of in Britain. The number of noblemen and gentlemen . . . who assembled there from day to day, recorded the proceedings of each morning's sale, and lamented or boasted the event of the competition, was unexampled; and, in short, the concourse of attendants terminated in the formation of a society of about thirty amateurs . . ., who agreed to constitute a club, which should have for its object of union the common love of rare and curious volumes.

The Roxburghe Club began its series of editions and reprints of rare and curious books and manuscripts in 1812, to be followed by the Bannatyne Club a decade later. Men like Richard Heber, Thomas Park and Sir Thomas Phillipps were a feature of the age: of any of them it might have been said (as was in fact said of Heber) that 'the cutting blast of Siberia or the fainting heat of a Maltese sirocco would not make him halt or divert his course in the pursuit of a favourite volume'. A number of bibliographical works gathered in the harvest of such accumulations. Sir Samuel Egerton Brydges published his *Censura Literaria*, *British Bibliographer*, *Restituta*, and other interesting though inaccurate volumes, as well as producing editions or reprints of a great many old books. Robert Watt's *Bibliotheca Britannica* (1824) and Lowndes's *Bibliographer's Manual* (1834, and subsequently revised) are still important reference books.

The analogous works of John Nichols and his son J. B. Nichols, *Literary Anecdotes of the Eighteenth Century* (1812–15) and *Illustrations of the Literary History of the Eighteenth Century* (1817–58), may serve as a reminder of a fact often forgotten: that a great number of books relating to that century, and to the later seventeenth century, first appeared in our period. The first edition of Aubrey's *Lives* appeared in 1813, while the diaries of Evelyn and Pepys were published in 1818 and 1825. The appearance of two editions of Spence's *Anecdotes of Pope* on the same day in 1820 is one of the oddities of literary history. Six volumes of Richardson's letters came out in 1804, while various volumes containing the incomparable letters of Cowper and Horace Walpole continued to make their appearance throughout the first part of the century. When Macaulay began work on his *History of England*, therefore, he had the stimulus of newly published authorities of the greatest interest—an advantage equally enjoyed by the numerous writers of historical romance during this period. It must also be remembered that important new editions of the work of eighteenth-century writers came out during the same years. Bowles's edition of Pope, which gave rise to so bitter and so inconclusive a controversy, had been published in 1806. Scott's editions of Dryden and Swift appeared in 1808 and 1814, each accompanied by a notable biography.

Croker's edition of Boswell's *Life of Johnson*, so savagely attacked by Macaulay yet so valuable that Birkbeck Hill was to be deeply indebted to it half a century later, came out in 1831. John Wilson's admirable biography of Defoe had appeared the previous year. The principal novels of the eighteenth century were frequently reprinted and familiar to most members of 'the reading public'. The importance of all these books cannot be overlooked by anyone who consults the Reviews. The average reader in the year 1820 was as likely to be reading a book written in the eighteenth century as a book by one of his contemporaries. While this often made things difficult for the newer writers, they benefited in a great many ways from the rich deposits of earlier literature which were available to them.

XV

THE LITERARY SCENE IN 1832

In France, the good people still divert themselves with disputing the several merits of the Classical School, and the Romantic. They have the two schools—*that* is certain—let us be permitted to question the excellence of the scholars in either. The English have not disputed on the matter, and the consequence is, that their writers have contrived to amalgamate the chief qualities of *both* schools. Thus, the style of Byron is at once classical and romantic. . . . And even a Shelley, whom some would style emphatically of the Romantic School, has formed himself on the model of the Classic. His genius is eminently Greek: he has become romantic, by being peculiarly classical. Thus while the two schools abroad have been declaring an union incompatible, we have united them quietly, without saying a word on the matter. Heaven only knows to what extremes of absurdity we should have gone in the spirit of emulation, if we had thought fit to set up a couple of parties, to prove which was best!

England and the English, Book IV, chap. iv.

In the year 1819 an Italian spy reported that Byron belonged to a secret society called the 'Società Romantica', that he was in the habit of writing 'poetry of this new school', and that he had composed 'certain rules, entitled "Statutes of the Joyous Company"'. Like the spy, foreign historians of our literature have long taken it for granted that Byron belonged to the Romantic Movement; and some of them have even attempted to formulate the 'certain rules' of the Company—though none of them seems to have called it Joyous. English literary historians have usually followed their lead, though with greater caution. Since the word 'romantic' has not been used in this book—except in one or two quotations—something must now be said to explain this abstention. I do not wish to argue that the word is useless, but merely that the idea that there was a Romantic Movement in England at this time is accompanied by certain dangers—above all the danger that it tempts us to over-simplify the complicated literary landscape of the age.

The idea of a Romantic School of poetry was born in Germany. As Byron pointed out in 1821, 'Schlegel and Madame de

Staël have endeavoured . . . to reduce poetry to *two* systems, classical and romantic'—adding prophetically, 'the effect is only beginning'. Later Goethe claimed that the idea originated in an argument between Schiller and himself:

> The idea of the distinction between classical and romantic poetry [he told Eckermann], which is now spread over the whole world, . . . came originally from Schiller and myself. I laid down the maxim of objective treatment in poetry, and would allow no other; but Schiller, who worked quite in the subjective way . . ., wrote the treatise upon *Naïve and Sentimental Poetry* [in defence of his view]. He proved to me that I myself, against my will, was romantic. . . . The Schlegels took up this idea, and carried it further, so that it has now been diffused over the whole world; and every one talks about classicism and romanticism—of which nobody thought fifty years ago.

But since, as Professor Wellek has pointed out, Schiller's terminology differs in intention from that of A. W. Schlegel (Shakespeare is 'naïve' to Schiller but 'romantic' to Schlegel), it is primarily with Schlegel and Mme de Staël that we are concerned.

In the lectures which he delivered in Berlin between 1801 and 1804 August Wilhelm Schlegel makes a good deal of the contrast between romantic and classical literature. He asserts that 'romantic poetry is indisputably much nearer to our mind and heart than classical' and attempts to sketch the rise of romantic literature, which he associates with Christian chivalry. Dante, Petrarch, and Boccaccio are the writers whom he regards as the founders of romantic literature. In the Vienna lectures of 1809–11, of which an English translation appeared in 1815, Schlegel had a good deal more to say about romantic literature. He associates the antithesis between romantic and classical with the antitheses between organic and mechanical and picturesque and plastic. He contrasts the literature of classical antiquity and of the French seventeenth century with the romantic drama of Shakespeare and Calderón, the poetry of finished perfection with that of *Sehnsucht* or yearning and desire.

Mme de Staël did a great deal to popularize the concept in her influential book *De L'Allemagne*. 'If we do not admit that the empire of literature has been divided between paganism and Christianity', she wrote, 'the north and the south, antiquity and the middle ages, chivalry and the institutions of Greece and

Rome, we shall never succeed in forming a philosophical judgment of ancient and modern taste.'

In Germany, Italy, and France there was a great deal of discussion about the terms 'classical' and 'romantic', and in each of these countries it came to be the accepted view that the early nineteenth century had seen the birth of some sort of Romantic Movement:

> I perceive that in Germany, as well as in Italy, there is a great struggle about what they call *'Classical'* and *'Romantic'*, [Byron wrote from Ravenna on 14 October 1820]—terms which were not subjects of classification in England, at least when I left it four or five years ago. Some of the English Scribblers, it is true, abused Pope and Swift, but the reason was that they themselves did not know how to write either prose or verse; but nobody thought them worth making a sect of. Perhaps there may be something of the kind sprung up lately, but I have not heard much about it, and it would be such bad taste that I shall be very sorry to believe it.

Since the English are notoriously lazy about general ideas and problems of historiography it is perhaps the less surprising that there was an increasing tendency, as the century wore on, to assent to the view that English literature too had had its Romantic Movement. The idea was given currency partly by foreign scholars and *comparatistes* struck by the similarities between the English literature of the early nineteenth century and the literature of Germany (in particular), and partly by Englishmen impressed by the usefulness of the terms when they were applied to foreign literature.

The question remains whether there was really a Romantic Movement in England, or rather (to put it in a more realistic form) whether it is useful to think of the major English writers of the age as forming a Romantic Movement.

It may be as well to begin with a reminder that the commonest meaning of the word 'romantic' at this time was not the same as its commonest meaning today. In his well-known essay 'On the Application of the Epithet Romantic', published in 1805, John Foster complains that the word is most often used as a vague term of abuse and recommends that it should be used only in passages describing the dangerous ascendancy of the imagination over the judgement. Although Foster was not a major writer, this testimony that to him the word 'romantic' was still essentially pejorative is of great interest. A survey of the uses of the word in a number of representative writers of the time is badly needed. Meanwhile it may be worth while to outline the ways in which it is used in Leigh Hunt's *Lord Byron and Some of his Contemporaries* (1828)—the first version of the autobiography of the critic who did more than any other to win recognition for the new poets.

The centre from which the different shades of meaning radiate is of course 'like something in a story'. On at least one occasion the modern reader is likely to hesitate over Hunt's meaning—when he describes an eccentric friend some of whose stories 'were a little romantic, and no less authentic'. When he insists that 'some of the most romantic sorrows' with which men are afflicted are really due to faulty diet, he reminds us of Johnson's remark that he has no sympathy with 'metaphysical' distresses. In the reference to the chivalrous Lord Dillon, who 'ought to have been eternally at the head of his brigade, charging on his war-horse, and meditating romantic stories', the word is more definitely favourable, as it is when Hunt describes Byron listening to music 'with an air of romantic regret' which was in fact largely affectation. The meaning is similar when we are told that when Byron had discovered 'that the romantic character was not necessary to fame' he shocked Shelley by asking him 'whether he did not feel . . . a greater respect for the rich man of the company, than for any other?' Similarly Hunt tells us that his jailers 'were more like the romantic jailers drawn in some of our modern plays, than real Horsemonger-lane palpabilities'. Approaching the shores of Spain, Hunt felt that he was 'crossing a real line, over which knights and lovers had passed. And so they have, both real and fabulous; the former not less romantic, the latter scarcely less real.' The sight of the flag of an unfriendly country is 'less romantic' than that of 'the coast of Provence . . ., the land of the Troubadours'. It is important to notice that when Hunt, more than once, refers to the 'classical and romantic' associations of Italy and the Mediterranean, he has no idea of any opposition between the two: he simply means that these parts of the world remind us of books and of ancient times. His use of the word 'romance' corresponds to his use of 'romantic'. On one occasion he finds 'a greater degree of romance' in Gibbon than he would have expected: on another he remarks that Don Quixote might have attacked a mysterious statue that he saw near Lyons, 'and not been thought mad: so much has romance done for us'. We notice that most or all of these passages could have been written a century before; and when we turn to the *Autobiography* of 1850 we find that practically all of them are retained, while on the few occasions on which the word 'romantic' makes a new appearance its meaning remains unchanged. The only omission of interest occurs in the sentence 'Here commences the (classical) ground of Italian romance', where Hunt must have realized that some readers might feel an incompatibility between the two words. The most striking fact is that in neither form of a book which is so largely concerned with the men who are now termed the 'Romantic Poets' does Hunt ever use the word 'romantic' with reference to the poetry that they wrote.

A careful study of the meanings of the word 'romantic' in the poetry and prose of a number of the major writers of the period might produce some interesting results. Hazlitt, for example, seems less often to use the word pejoratively than most of his contemporaries. But it is quite clear that most writers of the time commonly used the word in what we regard as being its eighteenth-century sense and did not usually think of it as denoting a particular kind of literature. It is equally clear that Wordsworth, Byron, Shelley, and Keats did not regard themselves as writing 'romantic' poems and would not—in fact— have been particularly flattered if they had been told that that was what they were doing. They did not regard themselves as constituting a Romantic Movement. Did they regard themselves as part of a Movement at all?

In the strict sense a Movement consists of a number of writers who share certain views on literature (views which may be expressed in some sort of manifesto) and who are conscious of moving in roughly the same direction. To determine whether these writers conceived of themselves as forming a Movement it will therefore be necessary to summarize their views on the poetry of each other.

Except for Coleridge, for whose powers he had the highest admiration, Wordsworth was a severe and unsympathetic critic of his contemporaries. Since he had a high sense of the didactic function of poetry it is not surprising that he was shocked by Byron: 'Though cordially admitting his lordship's extraordinary power, and his claims as a man of genius'—R. P. Gillies tells us—Wordsworth 'firmly believed that his application of that power was reprehensible, perverted, and vicious.' Wordsworth noticed that a good deal in *Childe Harold* III was inspired by his own poetry but had no doubt that it was 'spoiled in the transmission'. In general he 'admitted the power of Byron in describing the workings of human passion, but denied that he knew anything of the beauties of Nature'. He considered *Don Juan* 'infamous' and told John Scott that Byron would probably end his career in a madhouse. Although he disapproved of Shelley's opinions on many subjects, Wordsworth thought him superior to Byron in poetic genius. According to Trelawny (an unreliable witness), Wordsworth said in 1819 that he thought nothing of Shelley as a poet, but later admitted that he was 'the greatest master of harmonious verse in our modern literature'. He also expressed the view that he was a poet who appealed mainly to the young because his work was too remote from 'the humanities'. Wordsworth regarded Keats as another poet who had not lived to fulfil his promise, complaining that he tended —like the young Tennyson—to be 'overluscious'. It is very clear that he had no sense of being the leader of a Movement of which these other poets were members. He was conscious of a great debt to Coleridge, but otherwise—in spite of the fame which came to him as he grew older—his creative career was essentially a lonely one.

If Wordsworth was coldly detached about contemporary poetry, Byron was positively hostile. Although his opinions fluctuated to some extent he never wavered in his passionate admiration for Pope or in his pessimistic view of the condition of poetry in his own lifetime:

That this is the age of the decline of English poetry will be doubted by few who have calmly considered the subject. That there are men of genius among the present poets makes little against the fact, because it has been well said, that 'next to him who forms the taste of his country, the greatest genius is he who corrupts it'. (*Letters and Journals*, iv. 485.)

He had no doubt that the conservative writers of the age would outlive the revolutionaries. In the dedication to *Don Juan* he attacks Southey, Wordsworth, and Coleridge and assures them that

Scott, Rogers, Campbell, Moore, and Crabbe, will try
'Gainst you the question with posterity

Although his early hostility to Wordsworth was modified later, in 1820 we still find him describing Wordsworth as 'essentially a bad writer'. He had no patience with what he regarded as Wordsworth's perverse views about the subjects and diction appropriate to poetry. Byron also disagreed 'essentially' with Shelley on the merits of Keats, whom he regarded at first simply as a follower of Leigh Hunt's. Some of the cruellest and most uncomprehending remarks about Keats ever made are to be found in Byron's letters, though he later revised his opinion to some extent, acknowledging that *Hyperion* was 'as sublime as Æschylus' and that Keats's genius, 'malgré all the fantastic fopperies of his style, was undoubtedly of great promise'. One reason for his improved opinion of Keats may have been the report that Keats had been 'persuaded to reform . . . his style upon the more classical models of the language'. Of Shelley Byron thought more highly. He had an uncritically high opinion of *Queen Mab*, which Medwin described as one of his 'favourite *cribbing* books', considered that *The Revolt of Islam* 'had much poetry', and gave high praise to *Prometheus Unbound*. His most interesting remark about Shelley occurs in a letter written on 26 April 1821: 'You . . . know my high opinion of your own poetry,—because it is of *no* school. I read *Cenci*—but, besides that I think the *subject* essentially *un*dramatic, I am not an admirer of our old dramatists *as models*. . . . Your *Cenci*, however, was a work of power, and poetry.' It is interesting that Byron should have said that Shelley belonged to '*no* school', because he believed that many of his contemporaries did belong to a school. He was infuriated by the 'attorneys' clerks' and others who were 'smitten by being told that the new school were to revive the language of Queen Elizabeth, the true English; as every body in the reign of Queen Anne wrote no better than French, by a species of literary treason'. He himself had been by no means guiltless:

I am convinced, the more I think of it, that . . . *all* of us—Scott, Southey, Wordsworth, Moore, Campbell I,—are . . . in the wrong, one as much as another; that we are upon a wrong revolutionary poetical system, or systems, not worth a damn in itself, and from which none but Rogers and Crabbe are free . . . I am the more confirmed in this by having lately gone over some of our classics, particularly *Pope*. . . . (*Letters and Journals*, iv. 169.)

It is not surprising that this passage delighted Gifford, but it is a great pity that Byron did not explain what he meant by the 'wrong revolutionary poetical system, or systems', particularly in view of his earlier decided rejection of the terms 'classical' and 'romantic'. It is clear in any event that Byron believed that there was something wrong with most contemporary poetry and felt that he had contributed to this by writing too heedlessly and allowing himself to be too much influenced by his contemporaries.

Shelley was an abler critic than Byron and it is not surprising that the two men failed to agree about poetry:

> We talked a great deal of poetry and such matters last night [Shelley wrote on 7 August 1821]; and as usual differed, and I think more than ever. He affects to patronise a system of criticism fit for the production of mediocrity, and although all his fine poems and passages have been produced in defiance of this system, yet I recognise the pernicious effects of it in the 'Doge of Venice'; and it will cramp and limit his future efforts however great they may be, unless he gets rid of it.

Whereas Byron was hostile to the new poetry, Shelley admired it and regarded it as natural that the poets of the age should have something in common:

> I have avoided [he wrote in the preface to *The Revolt of Islam*] . . . the imitation of any contemporary style. But there must be a resemblance, which does not depend upon their own will, between all the writers of any particular age. They cannot escape from subjection to a common influence which arises out of an infinite combination of circumstances belonging to the times in which they live.

As examples Shelley cites the tragic poets of the age of Pericles, 'the Italian revivers of ancient learning', and Shakespeare and his contemporaries. He was exasperated by the charge that he himself was an imitator of Wordsworth: 'It may as well be said that Lord Byron imitates Wordsworth, or that Wordsworth imitates Lord Byron, both being great poets, and deriving from the new springs of thought and feeling, which the great events of our age have exposed to view, a similar tone of sentiment, imagery, and expression.' It is most unfortunate that Shelley never wrote the second and third parts of his *Defence of Poetry*, in which he proposed to apply his general principles 'to the present state of the cultivation of poetry' and to provide 'a defence of the attempt to idealise the modern forms of manners and opinions, and compel them into a subordination to the imaginative and creative faculty'. Even as it stands, however, the *Defence of Poetry* makes it clear that Shelley's sense of a unity in the poetry of the day was largely due to his passionate interest in political reform. He argues that 'the literature of England, an energetic development of which has ever preceded or accompanied a great and free development of the national will, has arisen as it were from a new birth', and goes on to claim that he and his contemporaries 'live among such philosophers and poets as surpass beyond comparison any who have appeared since the last national struggle for civil and religious liberty', adding that 'it is impossible to read the compositions of the most celebrated writers of the present day without being startled by the electric life which burns within their words'. His opinion of individual writers of the time corresponded with this general view. He venerated Wordsworth's genius as a poet, though he distrusted his views on the language of poetry and detested his politics. He thought very highly of much of the poetry of Byron, going so far as to claim that one of his volumes contained 'finer poetry than had appeared in England since the publication of *Paradise Regained*'. As one would expect, however, he disapproved of Byron's determination to 'follow the French tragedians and Alfieri, rather than those of England and Spain'. It is easier to sympathize with his low opinion of *The Doge of Venice* than with his high admiration for *Cain*, which he described as 'apocalyptic . . . a revelation not before communicated to man'. It is remarkable how justly he appreciated the genius displayed in *Don Juan*, a poem remote from his own poetic scope and aims. 'He has read to me one of the unpublished cantos of Don Juan', he wrote in August 1821, 'which is astonishingly fine. It sets him not only above, but far above, all the poets of the day—every word is stamped with immortality. . . . It fulfils, in a certain degree, what I have long preached of producing—something wholly new and relative to the age, and yet surpassingly beautiful.' The poetry of Keats he knew much less well: he realized that the early poems revealed promise rather than achievement, but he was profoundly impressed by *Hyperion*, 'an astonishing piece of writing, [which] gives me a conception of Keats which I confess I had not before'. It is disappointing to find that he makes no reference to the Odes.

As we are reminded by his famous advice to Shelley to 'be more of an artist', Keats lacked Shelley's ability to appreciate the work of poets working on quite different lines from himself. He had no sense of common purpose with Shelley, whom he regarded as being too much preoccupied with causes other than that of poetry itself, and once told Bailey that he had 'refused to visit' him in order that he might retain his 'own unfetterd scope'. In many ways the brief and astonishing career of Keats may be regarded as a study in increasing, though voluntary, loneliness. When he wrote the early sonnet 'Great spirits now on earth are sojourning' he felt himself to be the ally of Wordsworth, Leigh Hunt, and Haydon; but he was soon to become estranged from both Hunt and Haydon, and while his admiration for Wordsworth persisted (in spite of his hatred of his political views) it became increasingly clear to him that his own genius had little in common with that of the older poet and his 'egotistical sublime'. Coleridge does not seem to have attracted him deeply, if we may judge from his passage about Coleridge's lack of 'negative capability' and by the fact that he never made any attempt to go to any of his lectures. Byron was a poet for whom Keats had little admiration. 'Lord Byron cuts a figure'— he once wrote—'but he is not figurative': unlike Shakespeare and the truly great poets. 'There is this great difference between us', he wrote on another occasion. 'He describes what he sees —I describe what I imagine.—Mine is the hardest task.' He detested *Don Juan*, 'Lord Byron's last flash poem': he read it on his way to Italy, and exclaimed that it was 'a paltry originality, which consists in making solemn things gay, and gay things solemn'. When he wrote his greatest work, Keats was on his own as a writer.

It is clear, therefore, that these four 'romantic' poets were very much inclined to be individualists. Only one of them seems to have regarded himself as in any sense a part of a Movement of which he approved, and even he (Shelley) thought of this Movement as something vague and impersonal. Byron, who explicitly rejected the terms 'classical' and 'romantic', sometimes regarded himself as part of a Movement; but in his case it was a Movement of which he strongly disapproved, while his greatest work—*Don Juan* and *The Vision of Judgment*—has little in common with the poetry of Wordsworth, Shelley, and Keats. Neither Wordsworth nor Keats appears to have regarded himself as belonging to a Movement. It is consistent with this that Shelley was the only one of the four who warmly admired the poetry of all three of the others—although even he highly admired only one of Keats's poems, *Hyperion*.

There is certainly nothing that can be regarded as a manifesto of the new poets. There has, indeed, only been one candidate for this position, the preface to the second edition of *Lyrical Ballads*. To the end of his life Wordsworth maintained that he wrote the preface 'solely to gratify Coleridge', and he soon had reason to regret it. In *Biographia Literaria* Coleridge himself had no difficulty in demonstrating that some of Wordsworth's tenets were historically untenable, others logically inconsistent. As has already been suggested, eloquent as many passages are, the preface is a most misleading introduction to Wordsworth's poems and there can be no doubt that it did his reputation a great deal of harm. It is hardly surprising that the other poets of the day made no attempt to follow its precepts. The effect of the preface was in fact to provide Coleridge with a perfect subject for dissection, to prejudice Byron against the greatest poet of the day, and to furnish the journalistic critics of the time with a big stick with which to belabour 'The Lake School'. There are few references to the preface in the writings of Shelley, hardly any in those of Keats. The only poet who appears to have tried to carry out Wordsworth's precepts on the language of poetry seems, ironically enough, to have been Leigh Hunt, and by common consent *The Story of Rimini* is neither a successful poem nor the sort of thing that Wordsworth had in mind when he wrote that the poet should use a selection of 'the real language of men'.

But of course historians often discover movements of which contemporaries were partly or wholly unaware. Granted that 'The Romantic Movement' is an historian's term, someone may ask, can it be denied that it stands very well for something that happened to English literature in the early nineteenth century? The answer to this question depends on the standpoint of the observer and the degree of precision in definition that he considers desirable.

It depends on the standpoint of the observer. The question whether Keats is a poet of the Romantic Movement is a little like the question whether an Englishman is a European: of course he is, if you look at him from far enough away. An observer in any particular European country will be more aware of the differences between Englishmen, Frenchmen, and Greeks, for example, than of anything that they have in common. If he then moves to Australia he is more likely to notice that Englishmen share certain characteristics with other Europeans which are not necessarily to be found in Australians. It is the same with literary history. A man who has been reading the literature of the early nineteenth century for a period of years becomes more conscious of the differences between the writers of the time than of any qualities that they have in common. If he were then to concentrate on some other period—let us say the fourteenth century—he might soon find himself contrasting the poets he was reading with 'the romantics'. Although this would in a sense be inexact—it would still be more useful to compare Chaucer with Wordsworth, on the one hand, or with Keats, on the other, than to compare him with 'the romantics' in general—it would not be altogether wrong. It depends on the degree of generalization to which one aspires, or which one is prepared to tolerate. 'The Romantics' will always serve as a sort of accommodation address.

The trouble is that several bad companions tend to accompany the idea of a Romantic Movement in England. One of them is the tendency to value any given poet rather as he is 'romantic'—or characteristic of the European Romantic Movement as a whole—than according to the merit of his poetry. Byron is the obvious instance. Continental critics have always taken him more seriously than his compatriots, and it is not always his best poems that they consider most important. *Childe Harold* and *Manfred* often receive more attention than *Don Juan* and *The Vision of Judgment*. As has been argued in Chapter II, if Byron had not discovered his characteristic satiric mode he would not be considered a great poet at all by English critics today; yet continental critics would still have regarded him (like Ossian) as one of the central figures in the European Romantic Movement. There are far more references to Byron than to Keats in most French and German studies of 'English Romanticism'; yet Keats was the greater poet.

Another and greater danger is that 'romantic' is a word that always brings another with it for company. It is unavoidably linked with 'classical', and 'classical' is a term that cannot without ambiguity be applied to any period of English literature. In

France we may call the seventeenth century the 'classical' period without fear of misunderstanding: it was not only the period in which Greek and Latin models were kept most constantly in view, but also the greatest period of French literature. In England the epoch in which Greek and Latin models were most important was probably the century following the Restoration; but this was by no means the greatest period of our literature and if we call it 'classical' we are in danger not only of underestimating the importance of classical influence in other periods but also of encouraging the old fallacy that this was a time at which English poetry was somehow diverted from its true course and dominated by the influence of the French. As soon as we begin to talk about 'the classical' and 'the romantic' ages we are in danger of over-emphasizing the differences between the Augustans and their predecessors (for in many ways the Augustan age is best regarded as the last wave of the Renaissance) and of exaggerating the (very great) differences between the Augustans and the writers of the early nineteenth century until we create a false antithesis. There was, after all, some continuity. No one has ever admired Pope more passionately than did Byron: Boswell's *Life of Johnson* was the only book about which Byron and Leigh Hunt were in agreement: *The Vanity of Human Wishes* was one of Scott's favourite poems: Keats studied Dryden in order to learn how to improve on the verse of *Endymion*: *Rasselas* was the source of Shelley's description of poets as 'the unacknowledged legislators of the world'. Every one of the great writers of the early nineteenth century owed something to the literature of the previous century, and several of them—like Scott and Wordsworth himself—owed a great deal.

A further danger of this schematization is that critics are tempted to suppose that 'the romantics' had a definite and largely shared aesthetic which distinguishes them sharply from 'the classicists' and other earlier writers. Like the inventors of the term 'The Lake School', such critics are in danger of supposing that the writers in question had 'common views in literature— particularly with regard to the true functions of poetry, and the true theory of poetic diction. Under this original blunder'—to repeat the quotation from De Quincey—'laughable it is to mention that they [go on] to *find* in their writings all the agreements and common characteristics which their blunder [has] presumed' (*Collected Writings*, ed. Masson, ii. 172–3). Even Sir Maurice Bowra is not beyond reproach in this matter. 'If we wish to distinguish a single characteristic which differentiates the English Romantics from the poets of the eighteenth century,' he writes in *The Romantic Imagination*, 'it is to be found in the importance which they attached to the imagination and in the special view which they held of it.' But is it really true to say that 'on this, despite significant differences on points of detail, Blake, Coleridge, Wordsworth, Shelley, and Keats agree, and for each it sustains a deeply considered theory of poetry'? One notices that Byron, inevitably, is excluded; and one begins to wonder whether it is the case that a poet writes a certain kind of poetry because he possesses 'a deeply considered theory of poetry'. Did Keats write his great Odes because he had a certain theory of the imagination? Did he, for that matter, have a completely different kind of imagination from Shakespeare?

While *The Romantic Imagination* may raise these questions in our minds, *The Romantic Theory of Poetry* by Mrs. Dodds (A. E. Powell) illustrates the dangers of such reasoning far more vividly. Mrs. Dodds assures us that from the work of Blake, Coleridge, Wordsworth, De Quincey, Shelley, and Keats 'there emerges, in spite of individual differences, a coherent theory of the poet's function'. Following Croce she argues that 'the romantic artist . . . is one who values content more than form', whereas 'the classic cares first for form and scarcely knows what he forms until it emerges in the completed work'. We have only to try to apply such remarks to the Odes of Keats, on the one hand, and to the *Epistle to Arbuthnot*, on the other, to see how profoundly unhelpful they are. When the words 'classical' and 'romantic' are contrasted in this way they make nonsense of the true complexity of literary history and have a fatal tendency to drift semantically towards creative–positive–good and critical–negative–bad respectively. In *The Romantic Movement in English Poetry* Arthur Symons makes the revealing claim that 'the great poets of every age but the eighteenth have been romantic: what are Chaucer [and] Shakespeare . . . if not romantic?'

A critic who believes that all great poets are 'romantic' may at least be saved from one other danger that often accompanies too unquestioning a belief in the English Romantic Movement: the belief that there is a 'typically romantic' style in poetry or in prose. It is true that in this period, as in others, a critic who is widely read can usually date a passage with more or less accuracy; but it is easy to deceive such a critic, and most writers who refer to a 'typically romantic style' appear to be claiming more than they would if they were to claim that they could usually date a passage of verse written in the early nineteenth century. Some believe that there is a 'characteristically romantic' use of versification, diction, imagery, or personification. Others seek to demonstrate an affinity between the style of the poetry or prose written at this time in different countries. This is as dangerous as it is attractive. As Chateaubriand once pointed out, 'ideas can be and are cosmopolitan, but not style, which has a soil, a sky, and a sun all its own'. That is why the idea of a Romantic Movement is so much more attractive to the historian of ideas than to the critic who is primarily interested in literature itself.

The truth is perhaps that the writing of literary history follows a dialectic course, and we have reached a point at which it may be useful for one critic to have written about the literature of the early nineteenth century in England without using the word 'romantic'. The task of the first literary historians was to draw large outline maps: that of their successors is to point out the faults of their maps as a preliminary to improving them. There is no harm in talking about a Romantic Movement in European literature as a whole, and not much in talking about a Romantic Movement in English literature itself, so long as we realize that we are using very general terms and that as soon as we say that something is 'typically romantic', discuss whether one poem is 'more romantic' than another, or give way to the temptation of using the term 'Romanticism' to explain everything that happened, the risk that we are saying less than we think is increasing alarmingly. The historians who have written most confidently of a Romantic Movement in England have always been men whose primary training has been in German or French literature, and they have shown a marked tendency to make Romanticism a bed of Procrustes on which to stretch the English literature of the time. Since their knowledge is horizontal rather than vertical, such scholars are always more keenly aware of the qualities that the English literature of the period shares with the literature of Germany or France than of the qualities in it that may be found in English literature of quite different periods. The reasons why something in any literature is as it is are more often to be found in earlier literature, after all, than in contemporary literature from another country. And to me at least sources have always been more interesting than analogues.

But it is time to turn back from hypothesis to fact, from historiography to history; and it is a matter of history that there occurred in the mid-1820's a severe slump in publishing, and particularly in the publishing of poetry. As a result of the financial crisis of 1825–6 the whole structure of Ballantyne and Constable collapsed, and they were not the only publishers to go under in the storm. The entire book-trade was affected. It is symptomatic of the change in the spirit of the age that T. F. Dibdin, who had published *The Bibliomania or Book-Madness* in 1809, turned in 1832 to write *Bibliophobia. Remarks on the Present Languid and Depressed State of Literature and the Book Trade*, a curious work in which he looks back nostalgically to the happy days of publishing and book-collecting and reports John Murray's decided opinion that 'the taste for literature [is] ebbing'. Old books were no longer in demand as they had been fifteen or twenty years before, while publishing had become a hazardous and unrewarding profession. In February 1832 Carlyle told Macvey Napier that he had 'given up the notion' of hawking his *History of the French Revolution* round any further publishers. 'The bookselling trade', he wrote, 'seems on the edge of dissolution; the force of puffing can go no farther, yet bankruptcy clamours at every door: sad fate! to serve the Devil, and get no wages even from *him*!' While all imaginative literature was hit in some degree—Murray went so far as to sell the copyright in Jane Austen's novels—poetry suffered most of all. The boom which had once led Murray to 'wade through seven hundred . . . poems in a year' and Wordsworth to complain that 'poetry . . . overruns the country in all the shapes of the Plagues of Egypt' was now a thing of the past.

There is no lack of evidence of the waning interest in poetry at this time. Within a few weeks of Byron's death we find a writer in *Blackwood's* remarking that nowadays 'few write poetry . . . and nobody at all reads it. Our poets . . . have over-dosed us.' Although Wordsworth's reputation continued to rise among people seriously interested in poetry, it took Longmans four years to exhaust the five hundred copies of the collected edition which they published in 1820. There was a reaction even against Byron, while new poetry was not in demand. Publishers did not dare to meddle with poetry: it is startling to find John Taylor, the friend and publisher of Keats, describing himself in 1830 as 'no publisher of poetry now'. As a writer commented in the *Edinburgh Review* on the appearance of Henry Taylor's *Philip van Artevelde* in 1834, it was 'a period of marked indifference to poetical productions'. In the same year a writer in the *New Monthly Magazine* complained that 'in the department of poetry we have had nothing for several years worth mentioning. A desultory effusion now and then finds its way into the periodical journals, as if to show that the fire of genius is not as yet wholly extinct amongst us. But no poem of any length or character has lately seen the light in this country.' The letters of the time are full of the complaints of unpublished poets: in 1837 Beddoes told an aspiring poet that his own poems remained in his desk, 'there being no vent for such things in a *market* more than glutted'.

It is appropriate that the most successful volume of verse to be published at this time should have been the *Corn-Law Rhymes* of Ebenezer Elliott. 'Strange as it may seem', Carlyle wrote in the *Edinburgh Review* for July 1832, '. . . here we have once more got sight of a Book calling itself Poetry, yet which actually is a kind of Book, and no empty pasteboard Case.' He emphasizes that the Corn-Law Rhymer is a self-taught man, and comments that 'for a generation that reads Cobbett's Prose, and Burns's Poetry, it need be no miracle that here also is a man who can handle both pen and hammer like a man'. The review throws a great deal of light on the condition of England in a memorable year:

Most persons, who have had eyes to look with, may have verified, in their own circle, the statement of this Sheffield Eye-witness, and 'from their own knowledge and observation fearlessly declare that the little master-manufacturer', that the working man generally, 'is in a much worse condition than he was in twenty-five years ago'. Unhappily, the fact is too plain. . . . In this state of things, every new man is a new misfortune. . . . It is as if from that Gehenna of Manufacturing Radicalism, from amid its loud roaring and cursing, whereby nothing became feasible, nothing knowable, except this only, that misery and malady existed there, we heard now some manful tone of reason and determination, wherein alone can there be profit, or promise of deliverance. In this Corn-Law Rhymer we seem to trace something of the antique spirit; a spirit which had long become invisible among our working as among other classes;

which here, perhaps almost for the first time, reveals itself in an altogether modern political vesture. . . . It appears to us as if in this humble chant of the *Village Patriarch* might be traced rudiments of a truly great idea. . . . Rudiments of an Epic, we say; and of the true Epic of our Time,—were the genius but arrived that could sing it! Not 'Arms and the Man'; 'Tools and the Man', that were now our Epic.

Yet while the work of the Corn-Law Rhymer is of great interest to the social historian it is of little account as poetry, and Carlyle acknowledged this when he urged Elliott (as he was soon to be urging Tennyson) to leave verse and rhyme for prose and work. England was entering an age of prose, and Thomas Hood was only one of a number of promising poets who did in fact turn away from serious poetry to other forms of composition in order to make a living. A few years later R. H. Horne was to sell the first edition of his epic, *Orion*, at a farthing; and about the same time we find an adaptable authoress, Eliza Acton, being told by Longman that there is no point in sending him poetry. 'Nobody wants poetry now', he wrote. 'Bring me a cookery book, and we might come to terms.' Such was the origin of a highly successful volume entitled *Modern Cookery*.

Nothing could better epitomize the practical temper of the new age than a laconic remark in Knight's *Passages of a Working Life*. 'Coleridge died in 1834. I went to live at Highgate the year after.' This was the age of Harriet Martineau, with her hearing-aid and her *Illustrations of Political Economy*. 'Every time has its genius,' as Bulwer Lytton observed, 'the genius of this time is wholly anti-poetic':

When Byron passed away, the feeling he had represented craved utterance no more. With a sigh we turned to the actual and practical career of life: we awoke from the morbid, the passionate, the dream-ing. . . . And this with the more intenseness, because, the death of a great poet invariably produces an indifference to the art itself. . . . Hence that strong attachment to the Practical, which became so visible a little time after the death of Byron, and which continues . . . to characterize the temper of the time. Insensibly acted upon by the doctrine of the Utilitarians, we desired to see Utility in every branch of intellectual labour. (*England and the English,* Book IV, chap. ii.)

There were many reasons for the waning interest in imaginative literature, but probably the most important was the political crisis. As Dibdin put it in *Bibliophobia,* 'the wished for *Reform in*

Parliament, like Aaron's serpent, has swallowed up every other interest and pursuit'.

Nowhere are such signs of the time to be seen more clearly than in the *Westminster Review*, founded in 1824 and already mentioned in Chapter I. Before a little more is said of this most important periodical a brief account must be given of Jeremy Bentham himself, since he was a man who exerted a profound influence on his own age and the age that was to follow.[1] By 1815 he was already 67, but he lived on in robust health until the year of the Reform Act. Although his first book, the *Fragment on Government*, had appeared as early as 1776, and by 1792 he was so highly thought of in France that the National Assembly made him an honorary 'French Citizen', his fame in England grew much more slowly. By our period, however, he had gathered round himself a small but brilliant circle who were destined to carry his influence into almost every department of the national life.

Bentham was by training a lawyer and the *Fragment on Government* is a closely reasoned attack on Blackstone's eulogy of the British Constitution. The book was characteristic of Bentham: as John Stuart Mill pointed out in an admirable essay, Bentham's 'peculiar province' was 'the field of practical abuses'. It was his task 'to carry the warfare against absurdity into things practical'. From the law he moved to government itself, always with the same purpose. In Mill's words, 'he has swept away the accumulated cobwebs of centuries—he has untied knots which the efforts of the ablest thinkers, age after age, had only drawn tighter; and it is no exaggeration to say of him that over a great part of the field he was the first to shed the light of reason'.

Although Bentham's initial stimulus was usually the illogicality or absurdity of the existing state of affairs, he was by no means a purely destructive thinker. He always tried to propose a sound alternative to the unsound principle that he rejected. In order to do this he would begin by surveying the particular problem as comprehensively as he could—in relation, that is, to the whole problem of the right conduct of human life. And this

[1] Jeremy Bentham (1748–1832) was educated at Westminster and Queen's College, Oxford. He took his B.A. at the age of 16, and summed up the effects of an English university education as 'Mendacity and insincerity'. He went on to study the law, but made little attempt to succeed as a barrister, turning his mind to the physical sciences and to speculations on politics and jurisprudence. His principal writings are listed in the Bibliography.

great problem he regarded, characteristically, as essentially a practical problem. His primary aim was clarity: he hated the vague, the general, the indefinite. His object was to introduce some sort of scientific method into the study of man's behaviour in society, though in pursuing it he may be said to have paid too little attention both to history and to psychology. It is characteristic of him to have drawn up a 'Table of the Springs of Action': no less characteristic that (as Mill pointed out) the table 'overlooks the existence of about half of the whole number of mental feelings which human beings are capable of, including all those of which the direct objects are states of their own mind'. By Bentham 'Man is conceived . . . as a being susceptible of pleasures and pains, and governed in all his conduct partly by the different modifications of self-interest, and the passions commonly classed as selfish, partly by sympathies, or occasionally antipathies, towards other beings'. And here Bentham's conception of human nature stops. If ethics or psychology had been his main concern such limitations would have been fatal; but fortunately he concerned himself primarily with the practical aspects of human life. He is an outstanding example of the fact that those who have influenced human affairs most decisively have often been men who have seen one side of the truth with unusual clarity, while remaining unusually blind to the other. Through his disciples James Mill, John Stuart Mill, Ricardo, Sir Samuel Romilly, Henry Brougham, and John Bowring, Bentham exerted a great and beneficial influence on the development of English society and its institutions throughout the nineteenth century. That is why John Stuart Mill bracketed him with Coleridge as one of 'the two great seminal minds of England in their age'. These two men, he wrote,

have never been read by the multitude. . . . Their readers have been few: but they have been the teachers of the teachers; there is hardly to be found in England an individual of any importance in the world of mind, who (whatever opinions he may have afterwards adopted) did not first learn to think from one of these two. . . . There is already scarcely a publication of any consequence addressed to the educated classes, which, if these persons had not existed, would not have been different from what it is.[1]

---

[1] Bentham was also responsible for some additions to the English vocabulary. Apart from 'utilitarian' itself, he seems to have been the first man to use the words 'international', 'codify', and 'minimize'.

It was largely through the *Westminster Review* that Bentham's opinions were drawn to the attention of those outside the circle of his immediate disciples and so made available to help meet the problems of the Victorian Age. The classic account of the establishment of the *Review* is to be found in John Stuart Mill's *Autobiography*. As he there points out,

the need of a Radical organ to make head against the Edinburgh and Quarterly (then in the period of their greatest reputation and influence), had been a topic of conversation between [James Mill] and Mr. Bentham many years earlier...; but the idea had never assumed any practical shape. In 1823, however, Mr. Bentham determined to establish the Review at his own cost.

The prospectus made it clear that it was the intention of the proprietors to make the *Review* 'the representative of the true interests of the majority, and the firm and invariable advocate of those principles which tend to increase the sum of human happiness, and to ameliorate the condition of mankind'. The contributors to the *Review* did not speak with one voice, but they taught one lesson: they were all believers in the doctrine of 'the greatest happiness of the greatest number'. James Mill had recently provided an admirable summary of Bentham's views in a supplement to the *Encyclopaedia Britannica*: the *Review* carried on the work of dissemination. Like the early contributors to the *Edinburgh*, we notice, most of the writers in the *Westminster* were young men. Bentham himself seldom contributed, and while James Mill and Francis Place were both in their fifties Bowring was in his early thirties and most of his contributors were younger—John Stuart Mill being only seventeen.

For so serious a periodical the *Westminster* sold remarkably well. Of the first number, which contained nearly 300 pages and cost 6*s.*, some three thousand copies were sold; and since (as Bowring pointed out) most of its readers were to be found 'among the non-opulent and democratic classes, whose access to books is principally by associations of various sorts, the number of its readers was very great'. It was therefore a large and receptive audience that attended to the *Westminster*'s exposure of prejudice and its warfare against the 'Establishment' of the day: the aristocracy, the clergy, the law, and the Tory and Whig parties as represented by the *Quarterly* and the *Edinburgh*. Among the most characteristic contributions to the first number they found an attack on aristocratic education, a severe criticism of fashionable poetry (as exemplified by Tom Moore), two defences of the democratic system of the United States (the *Westminster* was highly favourable to most things American, except slavery), and the trenchant article on the two official Reviews already referred to in Chapter I. As G. L. Nesbitt has pointed out in his book *Benthamite Reviewing*, during its first few years the *Westminster* concentrated on weakening the power of the two main political factions and strengthening that of the educated middle class, while insisting on the need for a number of specific reforms in government and society.

As might be expected, the diminishing prestige of imaginative literature at this time is particularly evident in the pages of the *Westminster*. Bentham allowed his dislike of things which cannot be precisely defined to prejudice him against poetry, so betraying a misunderstanding of the true nature of language which is not uncommon among philosophers. We are even told that he 'could not bear to hear pronounced in his presence' the phrases '*good* and *bad taste*'. He explained the difference between poetry and prose by saying that '*prose* is where all the lines but the last go on to the margin—*poetry* is where some of them fall short of it'—and while this was a joke it was the joke of a man who once stated that 'All poetry is misrepresentation.' When he decided that half the space in the *Review* was to be 'consecrated to politics and morals, the other half left to literary insignificancies' the latter provision was simply designed as a sop to those who did not understand, as he did himself, that, 'quantity of pleasure being equal, push-pin is as good as poetry'. He disliked the very word 'literature': as a reviewer wrote in an early issue, literature 'is a cant word of the age; and to be literary, to be a littérateur, . . . a bel esprit, or a blue stocking is the disease of the age. The world is to be stormed by poetry and to be occupied by reviews and albums.' It is as if Peacock's prophecy in 'The Four Ages of Poetry' had now come to pass:

Mathematicians, astronomers, chemists, moralists, metaphysicians, historians, politicians, and political economists . . . have built into the upper air of intelligence a pyramid, from the summit of which they see the modern Parnassus far beneath them, and, knowing how small a place it occupies in the comprehensiveness of their prospect, smile at the little ambition and the circumscribed perceptions with which the drivellers and mountebanks upon it are contending for the poetical palm and the critical chair.

About the same time Peacock had written to Shelley that 'there is no longer a poetical audience among the higher class of minds; . . . moral, political, and physical science have entirely withdrawn from poetry the attention of all whose attention is worth having; . . . the poetical reading public [is] composed of the mere dregs of the intellectual community'. In 1820 that had been a pessimistic view: by the late 1820's it approximated to the simple truth. England was entering on what one survivor from an earlier age, Leigh Hunt, described as 'this formidable mechanical epoch, that was to take all the *dulce* out of the *utile*', an age in which there was much to do and in which many of the leading minds felt for literature that impatience with theory and disinterested speculation that is characteristic of such periods. Bentham and his followers often failed to remember how much visionaries and poets had done to prepare the public to desire a better order of society. Poetic justice is a conception with which Bentham would have had little patience, yet there is poetic justice in the fact that it was in the poetry of Wordsworth that his brilliant disciple John Stuart Mill was to find relief from his dejection in the autumn of 1828:

I now began to find meaning in the things which I had read or heard about the importance of poetry and art as instruments of human culture [he wrote in his *Autobiography*]. . . . What made Wordsworth's poems a medicine for my state of mind, was that they expressed, not mere outward beauty, but states of feeling, and of thought coloured by feeling, under the excitement of beauty. They seemed to be the very culture of the feelings, which I was in quest of. . . . From them I seemed to learn what would be the perennial sources of happiness, when all the greater evils of life shall have been removed.

The effects of the practical temper of the new age and of the crisis in the book trade may be seen in the fashion for cheaper books. About the year 1831 John Murray complained to Dibdin that nowadays 'men wished to get for *five*, what they knew they could not formerly obtain for *fifteen*, shillings. The love of quartos was well nigh extinct. . . . There was no resisting the tide of fashion. . . . The dwarf had vanquished the giant.' In this revolu-

tion Cobbett and other left-wing writers had led the way. In
1819 Charles Knight had pointed out that as a result of the
increase of literacy there had been an 'excessive spread of cheap
publications almost exclusively directed to the united object of
inspiring hatred of the Government and contempt of the Religious Institutions of the country'. Such works were often published in parts 'at a price accessible even to the unhappy
mechanics who labour sixteen hours a-day for less than a shilling'.
The promoters of the Christian Knowledge Society were timid
and ineffectual opponents of such publications: they 'meddled
not with dangerous Science or more dangerous History', while
'Poetry and all works of Imagination they eschewed'. And so
Knight himself began his long campaign to bring knowledge
within the reach of the working classes with his periodical *The
Plain Englishman*.[1] At first, as he acknowledges, 'the very notion
of cheap books stank in the nostrils' of publishers:

> For a new work which involved the purchase of copyright, it was
> the established rule that the wealthy few, to whom price was not
> a consideration, were alone to be depended upon for the remunera-
> tion of the author and the first profit of the publisher. The proud
> quarto, with a rivulet of text meandering through a wide plain of
> margin, was the 'decus et tutamen' of the Row and of Albemarle
> Street. (*Passages of a Working Life*, i. 276.)

Soon other publishers were obliged to compete in this new field.
Lockhart describes a conversation between Scott and Constable
in 1825 in which the publisher complained that even middle-
class families were too apt to be 'contented with a review or
a magazine, or at best with a paltry subscription to some circulating library' and announced his new idea of producing 'a
three-shilling or half-crown volume every month' which should
sell in unprecedented numbers. The preface to the resulting
series, *Constable's Miscellany*, is an interesting document:

> The change that has gradually taken place during the last thirty
> or forty years in the numbers and circumstances of the reading public,

---

[1] Charles Knight (1791–1873) was the son and for a time the apprentice of a
bookseller at Windsor. Having gained experience as a newspaper reporter for the
Globe and the *British Press*, he started the *Windsor and Eton Express* with his father
in 1812. He was a friend of Praed and of many other men of letters of the time.
His main publications are listed in the Bibliography.

and the unlimited desire of knowledge that now pervades every class of society, have suggested the present undertaking. Previously to the commencement of the late war, the buyers of books consisted principally of the richer classes—of those who were brought up to some of the learned professions, or who had received a liberal education. The saving of a few shillings on the price of a volume was not an object of much importance. . . . But now . . . a change in the mode of publishing seems to be called for. The strong desire entertained by most of those who are engaged in the various details of agriculture, manufactures, and commerce, for the acquisition of useful knowledge, and the culture of their minds, is strikingly evinced by the establishment of subscription libraries and scientific institutions, even in the most inconsiderable towns and villages.

The intention was to intersperse original books among reprints of standard works, always avoiding both 'party politics' and anything contrary to 'the principles of religion and morality'. Although the progress of the series was soon interrupted by Constable's financial ruin it performed a notable service and led the way, as Lockhart remarked, 'in one of the greatest revolutions that literary history will ever have to record'. Publishers began to vie with one another in cheap books, as they were already doing in Reviews and Magazines. The same day in April 1829 saw the appearance of the first volume of Murray's *Family Library* and Knight's *Library of Entertaining Knowledge*; but Knight hastened to assure his formidable competitor that they had 'plenty of sea-room and need never run foul of each other', adding that it was his belief that 'in a very few years, scarcely any other description of books will be published'. Another venture of Murray's, the *Cabinet Cyclopædia*, also deserves mention. In his *Bibliomania* Dibdin describes his discovery that 'a whole army of Lilliputians, headed by Dr. Lardner, was making glorious progress in the Republic of Literature. *Science, History,* and *Art,* each and all contributed to render such progress instrumental to the best interests of the body politic.' In 1830 the newly formed firm of Colburn and Bentley projected no fewer than four series of inexpensive books: the *National Library of General Knowledge*, the *Novelist's Library*, the *Library of Voyages and Travels*, and the *Juvenile Library*. 'Many are the hands which are feeding and stuffing that great lubberly brat, the Public', as the *Athenaeum* complained. Some publishers, like Constable and Murray, concentrated on middle-class readers, while others were more concerned with working men. The *Library of Useful Knowledge*, published by Knight for the Society for the Diffusion of Useful Knowledge, was intended above all for working-class readers. It consisted of fortnightly parts of thirty-two pages and cost sixpence a part. The subjects of the books in this series were almost exclusively practical and at first the scheme worked well, nearly 30,000 copies of some of the early parts being sold. Christopher Thomson, who published his *Autobiography of an Artisan* in 1847, was the sort of person Knight had in mind: Thomson tells us how he went without sugar in his tea in order to buy Knight's *Penny Magazine*, which began to appear in 1832. Chambers's *Edinburgh Journal* started earlier in the same year. As Knight rightly claimed, such publications 'were making readers. They were raising up a new class, and a much larger class than previously existed, to be the purchasers of books, [and so] changing the whole form of social life.' Booksellers had to become reconciled to 'the terrible era of cheapness which commenced in 1827'. In Knight's words, 'Books, which at the beginning of the century had been a luxury, had now become a necessity.'

Yet an important reservation must be made. Although the vogue for cheap books is a major fact to be reckoned with in the history of the nineteenth century, it does not follow that they made their publishers' fortunes. Knight and his fellow-enthusiasts took a sanguine view of the reading public, and in particular of the working man. As Professor Royal A. Gettmann has recently pointed out, while 'a significant number of them did read the serious factual books prepared for them by publishers and educational organisations . . . there were some who refused to be marshalled and who preferred inflammatory political pamphlets'. And apart from these there were others, more numerous, 'who craved even more amusement than they found, for example, in *Insect Architecture*, one of the titles in the Library of Entertaining Knowledge which Charles Knight founded when the series on Useful Knowledge failed to capture as many readers as was hoped. In the late 1830's this last group had a decided preference for faded imitations of the novel of fashionable life.' Although it was a utilitarian age the imagination of the public continued to demand some sustenance, so that Bentley's *Standard Novels* were a great success while his *National* and *Juvenile Libraries* were hopeless failures.

Henry Brougham, who played an important part in the

Society for the Diffusion of Useful Knowledge, was no less active in promoting the Mechanics' Institutes which were to be so much a part of the Victorian scene.[1] The idea was provided by Dr. George Birkbeck, who organized science classes for Glasgow artisans at the beginning of the century. The London Mechanics' Institution was founded in 1824, and within twenty-five years there were more than seven hundred similar institutions with more than a hundred thousand members between them. Although the main emphasis was intended to be on the teaching of the more practical aspects of science it was also hoped that the institutes, with their libraries, would serve as general centres of knowledge and enlightenment. As an enthusiastic pamphleteer put it in 1825, 'the spectacle of hundreds of industrious individuals, who have finished the labours of the day, congregating together in a spacious apartment, listening with mute admiration to the sublime truths of philosophy, is worthy of a great and enlightened people'. Yet by no means everyone shared the feelings of the pamphleteer. 'God bless my soul, sir!', exclaims the Reverend Doctor Folliott at the beginning of the second chapter of *Crotchet Castle*, 'I am out of all patience with this march of mind. Here has my house been nearly burned down, by my cook taking it into her head to study hydrostatics, in a sixpenny tract, published by the Steam Intellect Society, and written by a learned friend who is for doing all the world's business as well as his own, and is equally well qualified to handle every branch of human knowledge.' The 'learned friend' is

---

[1] Henry Peter Brougham, Baron Brougham and Vaux (1778–1868), was educated at the High School and the University of Edinburgh. As a young advocate he was one of the original contributors to the *Edinburgh Review*. He then moved to London, was called to the Bar, and in 1810 became a Member of Parliament. He quickly attracted attention by his eloquent and untiring advocacy of the abolition of slavery and by his speeches and writings on popular education, a sound commercial policy, and the question of the abuse of charitable funds by the public schools and universities. Queen Caroline appointed him her Attorney General: at her trial in 1820 it fell to him to defend her. In 1826 he formed the Society for the Diffusion of Useful Knowledge, and soon he was playing a leading part in establishing the University of London. Having urged the Government to resist the dictation of the Holy Alliance in Europe, and done a great deal to reform the common law procedure, he was elevated to the peerage on becoming Lord Chancellor in 1830. In 1831 he made a celebrated speech on the second reading of the Reform Bill. Three years later he lost office on the dismissal of Melbourne's government. He sat constantly in the supreme Court of Appeal and on the Judicial Committee of the Privy Council. He was a man of extraordinary energy. He was often attacked and satirized, but it is easier to laugh at a man like Brougham than to be a man like Brougham.

Brougham, the Steam Intellect Society is the Useful Knowledge Society, and the objections of Doctor Folliott are those of the majority of the Tories and the orthodox churchmen of the time. They did not believe that a smattering of scientific knowledge would make the working classes more pious, and they did not see what good it could do to encourage them to meddle with matters above their station. Nor did they like the idea that the institutes should branch out and deal with subjects other than science. In 1825 a clergyman told the members of the newly formed Mechanics' Institution in Aberdeen that 'Belles Lettres, Political Economy, and even History, were dangerous studies'. It was not only the Tories who were critical: there are many sarcastic passages in Cobbett's *Political Register* about the 'brilliant enterprise to make us '*a*' *enlightened*' and fill us with '*antellect*', brought, ready bottled up, from the north of the Tweed'. 'The "*expansion* of the *mind*" is very well', Cobbett wrote on another occasion, 'but, really, the thing which presses most, at this time, is the getting of something to *expand the body* a little more: a little more *bread, bacon,* and *beer*.' Another reason for Cobbett's hostility to the institutes was his realization that they would inevitably fall under the domination of the middle classes. This happened almost from the first. Most working men were too deficient in elementary education to make much of the books and lectures— you cannot study engineering if you have never been taught to count—and they were far too tired to start learning at the end of the day. It is not surprising that they were mainly interested in matters bearing directly on their own standard of living. 'Take at random any score of working-men', as one contemporary wrote, 'and it will almost invariably be found that they would sooner attend a political meeting, to demand what they consider their 'rights', than a scientific lecture; that they would rather read a party newspaper than a calm historical narrative; and that they would sooner invest money in a benefit club or building society than in a mechanics' institute.' As the Victorian Age wore on, however, the influence of the Mechanics' Institutes did begin to make itself felt fairly widely, encouraging the habit of reading and debating and so lending weight to the growing demand for public libraries.

'There have been periods when the country heard with dismay that the soldier was abroad', Brougham told the Commons in 1828. 'That is not the case now. . . . There is another person abroad—a less important person, in the eyes of some an insignificant person, whose labours have tended to produce this state of things—the schoolmaster is abroad, and I trust to the schoolmaster armed with his primer more than I do to the soldier in full military array for upholding and extending the liberties of the country.' The schoolmaster was one of the influences that helped to bring about the Reform Act and determine the way in which England was to develop as the nineteenth century went on. Another was the invention of a cheaper method of printing, which greatly increased the power of the press. In *Arlington* in 1832 T. H. Lister comments that 'the activity of the press' at the beginning of the century had been 'but as that of the dray-horse to the racer' compared with its activity and 'unexampled expedition' in more recent years. The increasing speed of travel, inconsiderable as it must seem to us today, also played its part in modifying the pattern of English life. It is curious to find Lister remarking elsewhere on the 'macadamization' of the roads and complaining that road travel is no longer adventurous enough to provide a novelist with rich materials:

> Farewell those golden days when an hundred miles' journey was an era in the life of him who undertook it; when the making of a will was the proper preface to a journey to London. . . . Then, it was chiefly at the outset of a journey that [the novelist] plunged with [his hero] into the thickest medley of conflicting events—an inn became the hot-bed of incident—and fear and laughter dogged the wheels. . . . Witness the rambles of a Jones; the slow, but varied and eventful progress of a Roderick Random in the stage-waggon; and the fortunes of the day that exposed an Andrews to the tender mercies of a couple of footpads. . . . But the age of highwaymen is past . . . and the glories of the road are extinguished for ever. (*Granby*, 1826, i. 231–2.)

Within a decade Dickens was to demonstrate that the imaginative possibilities of the English Road were by no means exhausted. Yet it was railways that were the true portent of the new era, and as it approached England itself was beginning to gather speed, ready to thunder into the Victorian Age, with its shining rails, its dark cuttings, its smoke-filled tunnels, and its ugly, sprawling cities—with tantalizing glimpses from the windows of an old England that was rapidly being destroyed.

Everything was changing. As we move into the Railway Age we are bound to notice the growing addiction to an exaggerated propriety of language. Lockhart tells us that a great-aunt of Scott's once asked him to lend her a copy of Aphra Behn, whose novels she had greatly enjoyed as a girl. When next they met she gave him back the book and advised him to burn it, adding: 'Is it not a very odd thing that I, an old woman of eighty and upwards, sitting alone, feel myself ashamed to read a book which, sixty years ago, I have heard read aloud for the amusement of large circles, consisting of the first and most creditable society in London?' This appears to have taken place about the turn of the century, and Lockhart comments that it 'was owing to the gradual improvement of the national taste and delicacy'. A later example is mentioned in Leigh Hunt's *Autobiography*, when he explains why one of the poems in his *Poetical Works* of 1832 bears a curious title, 'The Gentle Armour':

It originated in curious notions of delicacy. The poem is founded on one of the French *fabliaux*, *Les Trois Chevaliers et la Chemise*. . . . The late Mr. Way, who first introduced the story to the British public, and who was as respectable and conventional a gentleman . . . as could be desired, had no hesitation, some years ago, in rendering the French title of the poem by its (then) corresponding English words, *The Three Knights and the Smock*; but so rapid are the changes that take place in people's notions of what is decorous, that not only has the word 'smock' (of which it was impossible to see the indelicacy, till people were determined to find it) been displaced since that time by the word 'shift'; but even that harmless expression for the act of changing one garment for another, has been set aside in favour of the French word 'chemise'; and at length not even this word, it seems, is to be mentioned, nor the garment itself alluded to, by any decent writer! . . . The title was [therefore] altered . . .; and in a subsequent edition of the Works, the poem itself was withdrawn.

Particularly revealing examples of this shift of sensibility may be found in books written early in the century and later revised. In the 1822 version of *Confessions of an English Opium-Eater*, for example, De Quincey refers straightforwardly to women who 'subsist upon the wages of prostitution', whereas in 1856 he refers to them as 'the outcasts and pariahs of our female population'. If we compare the passages in detail we are likely to be struck by the shrillness of the one written at the middle of the century: De Quincey is by now thoroughly embarrassed by the necessity of mentioning prostitutes at all. The reasons for the change were complex, but from one point of view what happened was that standards of gentility originally associated with the middle or lower-middle classes came to be shared by the upper classes themselves. This development had some curious results. Paradoxically enough, as Humphry House pointed out, the new standards of 'delicacy' were often a hindrance to the very men who were most set on reform, so that the more distressing consequences of Nancy's occupation in *Oliver Twist* could not be referred to, while a writer in *The Times* rebuked a Parliamentary committee for its 'indecency' in asking a woman factory worker how often she had had a miscarriage.

It is not surprising that the approach of the Victorian Age was greeted by an outburst of satire on cant. 'The cant which is the crying sin of this double-dealing and false-speaking time' is one of the most constant objects of Byron's satire, and it has been argued in Chapter II that *Don Juan* may be read as a sustained satire on cant. 'The truth is', Byron wrote in his letter to Murray 'On the Rev. W. L. Bowles' Strictures on Pope', 'that in these days the grand "*primum mobile*" of England is *cant*; cant political, cant poetical, cant religious, cant moral; but always *cant*, multiplied through all the varieties of life.' 'Luz is an excellent joke', Beddoes wrote from Germany in 1829, 'but tell me if I do not write too irreligiously for Cantland.' Lamb and Hood were never tired of attacking cant, the latter using his gifts as an etcher to this end as well as his gifts as a writer. In Hood's 'Progress of Cant', as Lamb pointed out in the *New Monthly Magazine*, 'all the projected improvements of the age' are depicted as so many different species of cant, as 'priests, anti-priests, architects, politicians, reformers, flaming loyalty men, high and low, rich and poor, one with another, all go on "progressing"'. Peacock's tales are full of satire on the characteristic failing of the time. As Mr. Crotchet points out in a passage already quoted, 'where the Greeks had modesty, we have cant; where they had poetry, we have cant; where they had patriotism, we have cant; where they had any thing that exalts, delights, or adorns humanity, we have nothing but cant, cant, cant'. In 1831 England stood on the threshold of what Grote was to call 'The Age of Steam and Cant'.

The following year, that of the Reform Act, is as good a terminal date as any for a volume of literary history. Keats,

Shelley, and Byron were dead, as was Hazlitt. Coleridge and Lamb had only two more years to live. And while Wordsworth lived on, with Southey, De Quincey, Peacock, and Leigh Hunt, they were by now unmistakably figures from a former age. In 1832, as Scott lay on his deathbed, we find Lockhart wondering whether to produce a special, 'entirely biographical' issue of the *Quarterly Review*. So many men had died: 'we have just lost Cuvier, Goethe, Mackintosh, Crabbe and Bentham', as Lockhart wrote to Milman. One age had ended, and another was beginning—for several of the men whom we think of as the great Victorians were now hard at work. Carlyle, Macaulay, and Disraeli were already well known. Dickens was working as a journalist. Lyell's *Principles of Geology* began to appear in 1830, while at the end of the following year Darwin set out in the *Beagle* on the voyage that was to have such memorable results. In 1832 Tennyson was 23, Browning 20. In five years a young Queen would mount the throne, and the Victorian Age would have begun.

CHRONOLOGICAL TABLES

NOTE: In compiling the list of plays I have leaned heavily on Professor Allardyce Nicoll's *History of Early Nineteenth Century Drama, 1800–1850*, rev. ed. 1955. I have given a few examples of the dramatizations of Scott's romances as a reminder of their great popularity at this time.

No indication of anonymity is given in these lists.

Date	Public Events	Literary History (including translations)	Verse
1815	Napoleon's return from Elba. Battle of Waterloo. Restoration of Louis XVIII. Napoleon exiled to St. Helena.	Anthony Trollope b. Byron marries. Ackermann's *University of Cambridge.* Béranger, *Chansons.* F. Schlegel, *Geschichte der alten und neuen Literatur. Beowulf* pub. at Copenhagen, ed. Thorkelin. A. W. Schlegel's *Lectures on Dramatic Art and Literature,* trans. J. Black. Cowper, *Poems,* ed. J. Johnson. Charles Lloyd trans. *The Tragedies of Alfieri.*	Byron, *Hebrew Melodies.* Hogg, *The Pilgrims of the Sun.* Hunt, *The Descent of Liberty.* Milman, *Fazio.* Scott, *The Lord of the Isles; The Field of Waterloo.* Wordsworth, *The White Doe of Rylstone; Poems,* 2 vols.
1816	Depression and discontent. Spa Fields Riot. Prosecution of Hone.	R. B. Sheridan d. Harriet Westbrook commits suicide. Shelley marries Mary Godwin. Charlotte Brontë b. Byron leaves England for the last time. Coleridge settles at Highgate. Elgin Marbles become accessible to the general public. Benjamin Constant, *Adolphe.* Goethe, *Italienische Reise* (1816–17). Jacob and Wilhelm Grimm, *Deutsche Sagen* (concl. 1818). Goethe, ed. *Über Kunst und Alterthum* (1816–32). Cowper, *Memoir of Early Life, Written by Himself.* Gifford, ed. Ben Jonson. Gray, *The Works,* ed. J. Mitford. Johnson, *A Diary of a Journey into North Wales in 1774,* ed. R. Duppa. W. S. Rose, *The Court and Parliament of Beasts freely translated from Casti.* Ugo Foscolo arrives in England.	Byron, *The Siege of Corinth* [with] *Parisina; The Prisoner of Chillon; Childe Harold's Pilgrimage,* Canto III. Coleridge, *Christabel* [with] *Kubla Khan, a Vision* [and] *The Pains of Sleep.* Hogg, *The Poetic Mirror; Mador of the Moor.* Mrs. Hemans, *The Restoration of the Works of Art to Italy.* Hunt, *The Story of Rimini.* Moore, *Sacred Songs,* i. J. H. Reynolds, *The Naiad.* Shelley, *Alastor.* Southey, *The Poet's Pilgrimage to Waterloo; The Lay of the Laureate.* J. Wilson ('Christopher North'), *The City of the Plague.* Wordsworth, *Thanksgiving Ode, January 18, 1816.*
1817	Death of the Princess Charlotte. Monroe President of U.S.A.	Jane Austen d. Mme de Staël d. Thoreau b. G. H. Lewes b.	Byron, *The Lament of Tasso; Manfred.* Coleridge, *Sibylline Leaves; Zapolya.*

Prose	*Drama (date of acting)*
Sir John Malcolm, *The History of Persia.* Malthus, *An Inquiry into Rent.* Jane Porter, *The Pastor's Fire-Side.* Scott, *Guy Mannering.* Dugald Stewart, *A General View of the Progress of Philosophy* (Supplement to *Encyclopaedia Britannica*, pt. i, 1815; pt. ii, 1821.)	Sheridan Knowles, *Caius Gracchus.* Isaac Pocock, *The Magpie, or the Maid?*
Jane Austen, *Emma.* Bentham, *Chrestomathia.* Coleridge, *The Statesman's Manual.* Galt, *The Majolo*; *Life and Studies of Benjamin West*, i (ii, 1820). Hazlitt, *Memoirs of Thomas Holcroft.* Hunt, 'Young Poets', in the *Examiner.* Lady Caroline Lamb, *Glenarvon.* Peacock, *Headlong Hall.* Scott, *The Antiquary*; *Tales of my Landlord* (*The Black Dwarf* and *Old Mortality*); *Paul's Letters to his Kinsfolk.* Wordsworth, *A Letter to A Friend of Robert Burns.*	Maturin, *Bertram.* Milman, *Fazio* (as *The Italian Wife*). Benjamin Thompson, *Oberon's Oath.* John Tobin, *The Faro Table.* T. J. Dibdin, *What Next?* Scott and D. Terry, *Guy Mannering* (adaptation).
E. S. Barrett, *Six Weeks at Long's.* Coleridge, *Biographia Literaria.* T. F. Dibdin, *The Bibliographical Decameron.* N. Drake, *Shakespeare and his Times.* Maria Edgeworth, *Harrington*	Joanna Baillie, *The Election.* George Colman the younger, *The Actor of All Work.* Maturin, *Manuel.*

Date	Public Events	Literary History (including translations)	Verse
1817 (cont.)		Tom Taylor b. Branwell Brontë b. Benjamin Jowett b. *Blackwood's Edinburgh Magazine* started. The *Literary Gazette* started by William Jerdan. *The Scotsman* started. Grillparzer, *Die Ahnfrau*. Chesterfield, *Letters to Arthur Charles Stanhope*. *Theological and Miscellaneous Works of Joseph Priestley*, ed. J. T. Rutt (1817–32.) *Letters from Mrs. Carter to Mrs. Montagu*, ed. M. Pennington.	Frere, *The Monks and the Giants*, i–ii (iii–iv, 1818). Mrs. Hemans, *Modern Greece*. Keats, *Poems*. Moore, *Lalla Rookh*. Scott, *Harold the Dauntless*. Southey, *Wat Tyler* (maliciously pub. by his enemies). Wolcot ('Peter Pindar'), *Epistle to the Emperor of China*. C. Wolfe, 'The Burial of Sir John Moore' (first pub. in *The Newry Telegraph*, 19 April 1817).
1818	General Election. Conference of Aix-la-Chapelle. European Alliance. Karl Marx b.	M. G. Lewis d. Emily Brontë b. J. A. Froude b. J. M. Neale b. Shelley's final departure from England. Attacks on Keats. Evelyn, *Memoirs*, ed. W. Bray. Horace Walpole, *Letters to George Montagu, William Cole and Others*. Grillparzer, *Sappho*.	Barton, *Poems by an Amateur*. Byron, *Childe Harold's Pilgrimage*, Canto iv; *Beppo*. T. Doubleday, *Sixty-five Sonnets*. Mrs. Hemans, *Translations from Camoens*. Hunt, *Foliage*. Keats, *Endymion*. Milman, *Samor*. Moore, *National Airs*, i (compl. 1827); *The Fudge Family in Paris*. Peacock, *Rhododaphne*. Shelley, *The Revolt of Islam*. Sotheby, *Farewell to Italy*.
1819	The Peterloo 'Massacre'. The Six Acts. Murder of Kotzebue. Birth of Queen Victoria.	John Wolcot ('Peter Pindar') d. Charles Kingsley b. John Ruskin b. J. R. Lowell b. A. H. Clough b. Mary Ann Evans ('George Eliot') b. Herman Melville b. Walt Whitman b. Campbell, *Specimens of the British Poets*. Hogg, ed. *The Jacobite Relics of Scotland*, i (ii, 1821). Hugo and his brother found *Le Conservateur littéraire*.	Byron, *Mazeppa*; *Don Juan*, i–ii. Crabbe, *Tales of the Hall*. Barron Field, *The First Fruits of Australian Poetry*. (priv. prtd.) Mrs. Hemans, *Tales and Historic Scenes*; *Wallace's Invocation to Bruce*. Hunt, *Hero and Leander, and Bacchus and Ariadne*; *Poetical Works*. Charles Lloyd, *Nugae Canorae*. H. Luttrell, *Lines Written at Ampthill Park*. Macaulay, *Pompeii*.

Prose Drama (*date of acting*)

[with] *Ormond*. Godwin, *Mandeville*. Hazlitt, *Characters of Shakespear's Plays*; *The Round Table*. Hogg, *Dramatic Tales*. James Mill, *The History of British India*. John Nichols, *Illustrations of the Literary History of the Eighteenth Century* (concl. 1858). Robert Owen, *Report to the Committee on the Poor Law*. Peacock, *Melincourt*. Ricardo, *Principles of Political Economy and Taxation*. Shelley, *A Proposal for Putting Reform to the Vote*; *History of a Six Weeks' Tour* (with Mary Shelley). Southey, *A Letter to William Smith, Esq., M.P.*; ed. Malory, *The Byrth, Lyf, and Actes of Kyng Arthur*.

Pocock, *Robinson Crusoe*.
R. L. Sheil, *The Apostate*.

Lucy Aikin, *Memoirs of the Court of Queen Elizabeth*. Jane Austen, *Northanger Abbey and Persuasion* (with memoir). Cobbett, *A Year's Residence in the United States of America*; *A Grammar of the English Language*. Coleridge, *On Method* (in *Encyclopaedia Metropolitana*). Pierce Egan, *Boxiana* (1818–24). Susan Ferrier, *Marriage*. Hallam, *View of the State of Europe during the Middle Ages*. Hazlitt, *Lectures on the English Poets*; *A View of the English Stage*. Hogg, *The Brownie of Bodsbeck*. Hunt, *The Literary Pocket-Book* (1818–22). Lamb, *The Works*. Maturin, *Women, or Pour et Contre*. Lady Morgan, *Florence Macarthy*. Mrs. Opie, *New Tales*. Peacock, *Nightmare Abbey*. Scott, *Rob Roy*; *Tales of my Landlord, Second Series* (*The Heart of Mid-Lothian*). Mary Shelley, *Frankenstein*. Mary Sherwood, *The History of the Fairchild Family* (1818–47).

T. J. Dibdin, *The Invisible Witness* (based on Pixérécourt's *La chapelle du bois, ou le témoin invisible*).
W. T. Moncrieff, *Rochester, or King Charles the Second's Merry Days*.
J. R. Planché, *Amoroso, King of Little Britain*.
Pocock, *The Antiquary* (based on Scott).
R. L. Sheil, *Bellamira*.
[Scott] *Rob Roy*: numerous stage-adaptations from this year onwards.

Bentham, *Radical Reform Bill*. Mary Brunton, *Emmeline*, with Memoir by A. Brunton. Hazlitt, *Lectures on the English Comic Writers*; *Political Essays*; *A Letter to William Gifford, Esq.* Hunt, *The Indicator* (1819–21); Hone, *The Political House that Jack Built*. Thomas Hope, *Anastasius*. Washington Irving, *The Sketch Book* (New York, 1819–20). Lingard, *A History of England* (concl. 1830). Lockhart *Peter's Letters to his Kinsfolk*. H. Matthews, *The Diary of an Invalid*. J. W. Polidori, *The Vampire*. Scott, *Tales of my Landlord, Third Series* (*The Bride of Lammermoor* and *A Legend of Montrose*).

Charles Bucke, *The Italians*.
Holcroft, *The Marriage of Figaro*.
Maturin, *Fredolfo*.
T. Morton, *A Roland for an Oliver*.
[Scott], *The Heart of Mid-Lothian* (at least five versions).
Sheil, *Evadne, or the Statue* (based on *The Traitor*, by Shirley).
Horace Twiss, *The Carib Chief*.

Date	Public Events	Literary History (including translations)	Verse
1819 (cont.)		Chénier, *Œuvres choisies*, ed. H. de Latouche. Goethe, *West-östlicher Divan*. Hoffmann, *Die Serapionsbrüder* (1819–21). Schopenhauer, *Die Welt als Wille und Vorstellung*. *The Poems of Allan Ramsay*, ed. W. Tennant. *Poetical Remains of John Leyden*, ed. J. Morton.	James Montgomery, *The Poetical Works; Greenland*. B. W. Procter ('Barry Cornwall'), *Dramatic Scenes*. J. H. Reynolds, *Peter Bell; Benjamin, the Waggoner*. Rogers, *Human Life*. Shelley, *Rosalind and Helen*. Wordsworth, *Peter Bell; The Waggoner*.
1820	Death of George III. Accession of George IV. Trial of Queen Caroline. Dissolution of Parliament. Cato Street Conspiracy. Royalist reaction in Europe. Revolution in Spain and Portugal.	William Hayley d. Anne Brontë b. Herbert Spencer b. Jean Ingelow b. *London Magazine* started. *Retrospective Review* started. *John Bull* started. *The Etonian* (1820–1). Lamartine, *Méditations poétiques*. Joseph Spence, *Anecdotes*, ed. Malone and ed. S. W. Singer (two separate eds.) *Private Correspondence of Horace Walpole*. Tasso's *Amyntas*, trans. by Hunt. Hegel, *Grundlegung einer Philosophie des Rechts*. Grillparzer, *Das goldene Vliess*.	Robert Anderson, *Poetical Works*. Sir J. Bowring, *Specimens of the Russian Poets*. Elizabeth Barrett [Browning], *The Battle of Marathon*. B. Barton, *Poems*. Clare, *Poems Descriptive of Rural Life and Scenery*. Combe, *The Second Tour of Dr. Syntax*. George Croly, *The Angel of the World*. Mrs. Hemans, *The Sceptic; Stanzas to the Memory of the late King*. J. A. Heraud, *The Legend of St. Loy*. Keats, *Lamia, Isabella, The Eve of St. Agnes, and Other Poems*. Landor, *Idyllia Heroica Decem*. Henry Luttrell, *Advice to Julia*. E. G. E. Lytton (Bulwer Lytton), *Ismael*. Milman, *The Fall of Jerusalem*. B. W. Procter ('Barry Cornwall'), *A Sicilian Story; Marcian Colonna*. J. H. Reynolds, *The Fancy*. Scott, *Miscellaneous Poems*. Shelley, *The Cenci; Prometheus Unbound; Oedipus Tyrannus*. J. H. Wiffen, *Julia Alpinula*. Wordsworth, *The River Duddon; Memorials of a Tour on the Continent*.

Prose *Drama (date of acting)*

R. H. Barham, *Baldwin, or a Miser's Heir.*
Thomas Brown, *Lectures on the Philosophy of
the Human Mind.* J. P. Collier, *The Poetical
Decameron.* M. Edgeworth, *Memoirs of R. L.
Edgeworth.* John Foster, *An Essay on the Evils
of Popular Ignorance.* Galt, *The Earthquake.*
Godwin, *Of Population, An Answer to Mr.
Malthus.* Hazlitt, *Lectures on the Dramatic
Literature of the Age of Elizabeth.* Hogg, *Win-
ter Evening Tales.* Lamb, *Essays of Elia* (in
London Magazine, 1820–2). Lloyd, *Isabel.*
Malthus, *Principles of Political Economy.*
Maturin, *Melmoth the Wanderer.* Mrs. Opie,
Tales of the Heart. Peacock, *The Four Ages of
Poetry* (in *Ollier's Literary Miscellany*). Scott,
Ivanhoe; The Monastery; The Abbot. Southey,
*The Life of Wesley, and the Rise and Progress of
Methodism.*

Charles Dibdin, Jr., *Shakespeare Versus Harle-
quin.*
C. Farley, *The Battle of Bothwell Brig* (based
on *Old Mortality*).
T. E. Hook, *Oil and Vinegar; Exchange no
Robbery.*
Sheridan Knowles, *Virginius.*
W. T. Moncrieff, *The Lear of Private Life.*
Pocock and D. Terry, *The Antiquary* (based
on Scott).
[Scott], *Ivanhoe* (at least seven versions for the
stage).
R. L. Sheil, *Montoni, or The Phantom.*

Date	Public Events	Literary History (including translations)	Verse
1821	Death of Napoleon. Death of Queen Caroline. Measures for Catholic relief. *Cordon sanitaire.* Greek War of Liberation begins. Monroe President of U.S.A., second term.	Keats d. Hester Lynch Piozzi (Mrs. Thrale) d. John Scott killed in duel by John Christie, deputizing for Lockhart. H. T. Buckle b. G. J. Whyte-Melville b. Malone's ed. of Shakespeare, ed. J. Boswell, Jr. *Memoirs* of James, Earl of Waldegrave, pub. *Manchester Guardian* started. Flaubert b. Baudelaire b. Goethe, *Wilhelm Meisters Wanderjahre* (1821–9). H. von Kleist, *Der Prinz von Homburg.* Hogg, *Jacobite Relics*, ii. *The Lyrics of Horace*, trans. F. Wrangham.	Joanna Baillie, *Metrical Legends.* Beddoes, *The Improvisatore.* Byron, *Marino Faliero; The Prophecy of Dante; Sardanapalus; The Two Foscari; Cain; Don Juan,* iii–v. Clare, *The Village Minstrel.* Combe, *The Third Tour of Dr. Syntax.* Mrs. Hemans, *Dartmoor.* L. E. Landon, *The Fate of Adelaide.* Charles Lloyd, *Desultory Thoughts in London; Poetical Essays.* Moore, *Irish Melodies* (first authorized ed. of words alone). Newman, *St. Bartholomew's Eve* (with J. W. Bowden). B. W. Procter ('Barry Cornwall'), *Mirandola, A Tragedy.* J. H. Reynolds, *The Garden of Florence.* Shelley, *Epipsychidion; Adonais.* H. Smith, *Amarynthus, the Nympholept.* Southey, *A Vision of Judgement.*
1822	Suicide of Castlereagh. Canning Foreign Secretary. Peel Home Secretary. Independence of Brazil.	Shelley d. E. T. A. Hoffmann d Matthew Arnold b. Sir Henry Maine b. Thomas Hughes b. Sir Francis Galton b. ? Boucicault b. Hunt starts *The Liberal* (1822–3). The *Sunday Times* starts. Walpole, *Memoires of the Last Ten Years of George II*, ed. Lord Holland. Edmond Goncourt b. Hugo, *Odes et poésies diverses.* Stendhal, *De l'amour.* *Memoirs of Benvenuto Cellini*, trans. T. Roscoe. Bannatyne Club founded. Heine, *Gedichte.* Jeremy Taylor, *The Whole*	Beddoes, *The Brides' Tragedy.* Bloomfield, *May Day with the Muses.* Bowles, *The Grave of the Last Saxon.* Byron, *The Vision of Judgment* (in *The Liberal*). Allan Cunningham, *Sir Marmaduke Maxwell.* Darley, *The Errors of Ecstasie.* Sir Aubrey De Vere, *Julian the Apostate.* Mrs. Hemans, *Welsh Melodies.* Charles Lloyd, *The Duke D'Ormond.* Henry Luttrell, *Letters to Julia* (3rd ed., rev. and enlarged). Milman, *The Martyr of*

Prose   *Drama (date of acting)*

J. L. Adolphus, *Letters to Richard Heber* (on the *Waverley Novels*). Byron, *A Letter on W. L. Bowles' Strictures on Pope*. Cobbett, *The American Gardener*; *Cottage Economy*. J. Fenimore Cooper, *The Spy*. De Quincey, *Confessions of an English Opium-Eater* (in the *London Magazine*). T. F. Dibdin, *A Bibliographical Tour in France and Germany*. Pierce Egan, *Life in London*. Galt, *The Ayrshire Legatees* (in book form); *The Annals of the Parish*. Hazlitt, *Table Talk* (1821–2). Hunt, *The Months*. Lockhart, *Valerius, A Roman Story*. James Mill, *Elements of Political Economy*. Sir W. E. Parry, *Journal of a Voyage for the Discovery of a N.-W. Passage* (1821–4). Scott, *Kenilworth*; *Lives of the Novelists* (prefaces to Ballantyne's *Novelist's Library*, 1821–4).

J. Banim, *Damon and Pythias* (altered for the stage by R. L. Sheil).
Alfred Bunn, *Kenilworth* (a rehandling of T. J. Dibdin's dramatization).
Byron, *Marino Faliero, Doge of Venice*.
B. W. Procter ('Barry Cornwall'), *Mirandola*.
W. T. Moncrieff, *Tom and Jerry* (adapted from P. Egan's *Life in London*).
James Haynes, *Conscience, or The Bridal Night*.
Douglas Jerrold, *More Frightened than Hurt* (originally called *The Duellists*); *The Chieftain's Oath*; *The Gipsy of Derncleuch* (partly based on *Guy Mannering*).
[Scott], *Kenilworth* (at least six versions).

Lucy Aikin, *Memoirs of the Court of James I*. Bentham, *The Influence of Natural Religion upon Temporal Happiness*. Allan Cunningham, *Traditional Tales of the English and Scottish Peasantry*. Kenelm Digby, *The Broad Stone of Honour*. De Quincey, *Confessions of an English Opium-Eater* (as a book). Galt, *Sir Andrew Wylie*; *The Provost*; *The Gathering of the West*. Hogg, *The Three Perils of Man*. Washington Irving, *Bracebridge Hall*. Lady Caroline Lamb, *Graham Hamilton*. Lockhart, *Adam Blair*. Nares, *Glossary*. Peacock, *Maid Marian*. Francis Place, *Illustrations and Proofs of the Principle of Population*. Scott, *The Pirate*; *The Fortunes of Nigel*; *Peveril of the Peak*. C. J. Wells, *Stories after Nature*. John Wilson ('Christopher North'), *Lights and Shadows of Scottish Life*. Wilson, Hogg, Lockhart, and Maginn, *Noctes Ambrosianae* (in *Blackwood's Magazine*, 1822–35). Wordsworth, *A Description of the Scenery of the Lakes* (3rd ed., first separate ed.)

George Colman the younger, *The Law of Java*.
E. Fitzball, *The Fortunes of Nigel* (from Scott).
[Scott], *Waverley* (anon. dramatization); *The Pirate* (at least three dramatic versions).
R. L. Sheil, *The Huguenot*.

Date	Public Events	Literary History (including translations)	Verse
1822 (cont.)		Works, ed. Reginald Heber.	Antioch; Belshazzar. Procter, The Poetical Works of Barry Cornwall. Rogers, Italy, i. Scott, Halidon Hill. Shelley, Hellas, A Lyrical Drama. A. Watts, Poetical Sketches. Wordsworth, Ecclesiastical Sketches. Crabbe, The Poetical Works.
1823	Agricultural discontent. War between France and Spain. Monroe Doctrine.	Ann Radcliffe d. Coventry Patmore b. E. A. Freeman b. Charlotte Mary Yonge b. Spanish émigrés arrive in London. Max Müller b. Renan b. Stendhal, Racine et Shakspeare. La Muse française, 1823–4. Knight's Quarterly Magazine begun. The Lancet begins. Lamartine, Nouvelles Méditations. W. S. Rose, trans. Ariosto's Orlando furioso, 1823–31. Bouterwek's History of Spanish and Portugese Literature, trans. Thomasina Ross. Lockhart, trans. Ancient Spanish Ballads. Tales of J. L. C. and W. C. Grimm, trans. E. Taylor, 1823, 1826.	Bowles, Ellen Gray. Sir John Bowring, Matins and Vespers. Byron, The Age of Bronze; The Island; Werner; Don Juan, vi–xiv. Joseph Cottle, Dartmoor. Sir Aubrey De Vere, The Duke of Mercia. Mrs. Hemans, The Siege of Valencia [with] The Last Constantine. Hunt, Ultra-Crepidarius. Charles Lloyd, Poems. Bulwer Lytton, Delmour and other Poems. Moore, The Loves of the Angels; Fables for the Holy Alliance. Praed, Australasia. B. W. Procter ('Barry Cornwall'), The Flood of Thessaly [with] The Girl of Provence. Shelley, Poetical Pieces.
1824	Conference at St. Petersburg, 1824–5.	Byron d. Wilkie Collins b. George Macdonald b. Sydney Dobell b. F. T. Palgrave b. William Allingham b. Opening of National Gallery. Westminster Review started. Foundation of London Mechanics' Institution. A. Watts, first volume of The Literary Souvenir.	Barton, Poetic Vigils. Robert Bloomfield, The Remains. Byron, Don Juan, xv–xvi; The Deformed Transformed. Campbell, Theodric and Other Poems; Miscellaneous Poems. Josiah Conder, The Star in the East. L. E. Landon, The Improvisatrice. R. E. Landor, The Count

Prose   *Drama (date of acting)*

Joseph Bosworth, *The Elements of Anglo-Saxon Grammar*. Fenimore Cooper, *The Pioneers*; *The Pirate*. De Quincey, *Letters to a Young Man whose Education has been Neglected* (in *London Magazine*). I. d'Israeli, *Curiosities of Literature* (expanded ed.). Sir John Franklin, *Narrative of a Journey to the Polar Sea*. Galt, *The Entail*; *Ringan Gilhaize*; *The Spaewife*. Hazlitt, *Liber Amoris*; *Characteristics*. Hogg, *The Three Perils of Woman*. Lady Caroline Lamb, *Ada Reis, A Tale*. Lamb, *Essays of Elia* (as a book). Lockhart, *Reginald Dalton*. Scott, *Quentin Durward*. Mary Shelley, *Valperga*. Southey, *History of the Peninsular War* (concl. 1832). John Wilson ('Christopher North'), *The Trials of Margaret Lyndsay*.

E. Fitzball, *Peveril of the Peak* (from Scott). Mrs. Hemans, *The Vespers of Palermo*. T. E. Hook, *A Day at an Inn* (based on his own *Killing No Murder*). Douglas Jerrold, *The Island* (based on Byron's poem); *Dolly and the Rat*; *The Smoked Miser*. H. M. Milner, *Frankenstein* (based on Mary Shelley's romance: several other stage versions). M. R. Mitford, *Julian*.

Bentham, *Book of Fallacies*. Cobbett, *A History of the Protestant 'Reformation'* (1824–6). R. C. Dallas, *Recollections of Lord Byron*. Susan Ferrier, *The Inheritance*. Galt, *Rothelan*. Godwin, *History of the Commonwealth of England*. Hazlitt, *Sketches of the Principal Picture-Galleries*. Hogg, *The Private Memoirs and Confessions of a Justified Sinner*. Landor, *Imaginary Conversations*, i–ii. Lockhart, *The History of Matthew Wald*. Medwin, *Journal of the Conversations of Lord Byron at Pisa*. M. R. Mitford, *Our Village* (1824–32). James Morier, *The Adventures of Hajji Baba of Ispahan*. W. E. Parry, *Journal of a Second*

George Croly, *Pride shall have a Fall*. J. F. Kind, *Der Freischütz* (at least five adaptations this year). W. T. Moncrieff, *Zoroaster*. Planché, *A Woman never Vext*. [Scott], *Redgauntlet* (adaptation). Sir Martin Archer Shee, *Alasco*.

Date	Public Events	Literary History (including translations)	Verse
1824 (cont.)		Robert Watt, *Bibliotheca Britannica*. J. H. Wiffen, trans. Tasso's *Jerusalem Delivered*, 1824–5. W. Roscoe's ed. of *The Works of Pope*. Carlyle, trans. Goethe's *Wilhelm Meister's Apprenticeship*. H. F. Cary, trans. *The Birds of Aristophanes*. Heyday of 'The Apostles' at Cambridge begins.	*Arezzi.* J. Montgomery, ed. *The Chimney-sweeper's Friend.* Moore, *Sacred Songs*, ii. Shelley, *Posthumous Poems*. Charles Wells, *Joseph and his Brethren*.
1825	Speculative frenzy. Financial panic. George IV opposes further measures for Catholic Emancipation. Death of Tsar Alexander I. John Quincy Adams President of U.S.A.	Anna Barbauld d. Samuel Parr d. H. Fuseli d. T. H. Huxley b. William Stubbs b. R. D. Blackmore b. Richter d. Lamartine, *Le Dernier Chant du pèlerinage d'Harold*. Grillparzer, *König Ottokar*. A. Cunningham ed. *The Songs of Scotland, Ancient and Modern*. Milton, *De Doctrina Christiana*. *Memoirs of Samuel Pepys*, ed. Braybrooke. Manzoni, *I Promessi Sposi*, 1825–6. Walpole, *Letters to Lord Hertford and Henry Zouch*, ed. Croker.	Mrs. Hemans, *The Forest Sanctuary*; *Lays of Many Lands*. Hogg, *Queen Hynde*. Hood and J. H. Reynolds, *Odes and Addresses to Great People*. L. E. Landon, *The Troubadour*. Bulwer Lytton, *Sculpture*. William Sotheby, *Poems* (enlarged ed.) Southey, *A Tale of Paraguay*. Charles Wolfe, *The Burial of Sir John Moore, with Other Poems*. Thomas Wade, *Tasso, and the Sisters*.
1826	End of Liverpool's ministry. England sends troops to Portugal. Election brings Catholic Emancipation and Corn Laws into prominence.	William Gifford d. Reginald Heber d. Walter Bagehot b. Hone's *Every-Day Book* (1826–7). Hugo, *Odes et ballades*. de Vigny, *Poèmes antiques et modernes*; *Cinq-Mars*. Chateaubriand, *Les Aventures du dernier Abencérage*. Eichendorff, *Aus dem Leben eines Taugenichts*. Heine, *Die Harzreise*. John Burke's *Dictionary of the Peerage and Baronetage* first appears.	Barton, *Devotional Verses*. Elizabeth Barrett [Browning], *An Essay on Mind; with Other Poems*. Hood, *Whims and Oddities*, i (ii, 1827: verse and prose). Milman, *Anne Boleyn*. J. Montgomery, *The Pelican Island*. Wordsworth, *The Poetical Works*, Paris ed. Moore, *Evenings in Greece, First Evening* (ii, 1832).

Prose   *Drama (date of acting)*

Voyage, 1821–3. Scott, *St. Ronan's Well*; *Redgauntlet*. Southey, *The Book of the Church*. William Thompson, *An Inquiry into the Principles of the Distribution of Wealth*.

Banim, *Tales by the O'Hara Family*, i (ii, 1826). Bentham, *The Rationale of Reward* (first English ed.). Brougham, *Practical Observations upon the Education of the People*. Carlyle, *The Life of Schiller*. Coleridge, *Aids to Reflection*. T. C. Croker, *Fairy Legends and Traditions of the South of Ireland*, 1825–8. De Quincey, *Walladmor*. Galt, *The Omen*. R. G. Gleig, *The Subaltern*. Hazlitt, *Table-Talk*; *The Spirit of the Age*. Macaulay, essay on Milton (in *Edinburgh Review*). J. R. McCulloch, *Principles of Political Economy*. James Mill, *Essays on Government, etc.* (privately printed). Moore, *Memoirs of Sheridan*. Mrs. Opie, *Tales of the Pemberton Family*. W. S. Rose, *Thoughts and Recollections*. Scott, *Tales of the Crusaders* (*The Betrothed* and *The Talisman*). H. Smith, *Gaieties and Gravities*. Plumer Ward, *Tremaine*. Charles Waterton, *Wanderings in South America*. John Wilson, *The Foresters*.

Fitzball, *The Pilot* (from Fenimore Cooper). Douglas Jerrold, *The Living Skeleton*; *London Characters: Puff! Puff! Puff!* Sheridan Knowles, *The Fatal Dowry* (adapted from Massinger); *William Tell*. Harriet Lee, *The Three Strangers*. J. R. Planché, *Success, or A Hit if you like it*. J. Poole, *Tribulation* (from *Un moment d'imprudence*). George Soane and Daniel Terry, *Faustus*.

Anna Bray, *De Foix*. A. Cunningham, *Paul Jones*. Fenimore Cooper, *The Last of the Mohicans*. Darley, *The Labours of Idleness*. Disraeli, *Vivian Grey*, i–ii (iii–v, 1827). Galt, *The Last of the Lairds*. Hazlitt, *The Plain Speaker*; *Notes of a Journey through France and Italy*. Anna Jameson, *Diary of an Ennuyée*. Lister, *Granby*. W. E. Parry, *Journal of a Third Voyage*. P. G. Patmore, *Rejected Articles*. Jane and Anna Porter, *Tales round a Winter Hearth*. Scott, *Woodstock*. Mary Shelley, *The Last Man*. H. Smith, *Brambletye House*; *The Tor Hill*. Southey, *Vindiciae Ecclesiae Anglicanae*. Whately, *Elements of Logic*.

J. B. Buckstone, *Luke the Labourer*. George Macfarren, *Malvina*. M. R. Mitford, *Foscari*. Douglas Jerrold, *Popular Felons*. Pocock, *Woodstock* (from Scott).

Date	Public Events	Literary History (including translations)	Verse
1827	Death of Canning. Battle of Navarino. University of London (University College) founded. Thomas Arnold becomes Headmaster of Rugby.	Blake d. Helen Maria Williams d. Ugo Foscolo d. 'Cuthbert Bede' (Edward Bradley) b. Scott acknowledges authorship of the *Waverley Novels*. *Constable's Miscellany* started. W. J. Thoms, *Early Prose Romances* (1827–8). Gifford's ed. of Ford. Burke, *Epistolary Correspondence with Dr. French Laurence*. Sir Kenelm Digby (d. 1665), *Private Memoirs*, ed. Sir N. H. Nicolas. Hone's *Table Book* (1827–8). Hugo, preface to *Cromwell*. Heine, *Das Buch der Lieder*. Carlyle, *German Romance: Specimens of its chief Authors*.	Barton, *A Widow's Tale*. R. Bloomfield, *The Poems*. Clare, *The Shepherd's Calendar*. Darley, *Sylvia*. Reginald Heber, *Hymns*. Hood, *The Plea of the Midsummer Fairies*. Keble, *The Christian Year*. L. E. Landon, *The Golden Violet*. H. Luttrell, *Crockford-House*. Bulwer Lytton, *O'Neill, or the Rebel*. Mitford, *Dramatic Scenes*. Poe, *Tamerlane*. Pollok, *The Course of Time*. Tennyson (with C. Tennyson), *Poems by Two Brothers*. Wordsworth, *The Poetical Works*, 5 vols.
1828	Wellington Premier. Repeal of the Test and Corporation Acts. George IV opposed to Catholic Relief. Russia goes to war with Turkey. The Greek Question.	Dugald Stewart d. Meredith b. D. G. Rossetti b. Mrs. Oliphant b. Taine b. The *Athenaeum* started. The *Spectator* started. A. Watts, *The Poetical Album* (2nd series, 1829). Balzac, *Physiologie du mariage*. de Musset, *L'Anglais mangeur d'opium* (a very free trans.). Sainte-Beuve, *Tableau historique et critique de la poésie française et du théâtre français au XVIe siècle*. Manzoni, *I Promessi Sposi*, trans. English by C. Swan.	Barton, *A New Year's Eve*. S. L. Blanchard, *Lyric Offerings*. Bowles, *Days Departed*. Mrs. Hemans, *Records of Woman*. L. E. Landon, *The Venetian Bracelet*. R. E. Landor, *The Impious Feast*. Robert Montgomery, *The Omnipresence of the Deity*. Moore, *Odes upon Cash, Corn, Catholics, and other Matters*. Rogers, *Italy*, ii. Coleridge, *The Poetical Works*, 3 vols. J. H. Merivale, *Poems Original and Translated*, i (ii, 1838).

Prose

Bentham, *The Rationale of Evidence*, ed. J. S. Mill. Fenimore Cooper, *The Prairie*. W. Crowe, *A Treatise on English Versification*. De Quincey, 'On Murder considered as One of the Fine Arts' (in *Blackwood's Magazine*). Pierce Egan, *Anecdotes of the Turf*. Hallam, *Constitutional History*. J. C. and A. W. Hare, *Guesses at Truth*, i. Hood, *National Tales*. Bulwer Lytton, *Falkland*. Sir John Malcolm, *Sketches of Persia*. Moore, *The Epicurean*. Scott, *Chronicles of the Canongate* (*The Highland Widow, The Two Drovers, The Surgeon's Daughter*); *Life of Napoleon*; *Miscellaneous Prose Works*; ed. *The Bannatyne Miscellany*. H. Smith, *Reuben Apsley*. Plumer Ward, *De Vere*. Lady Charlotte Bury, *Flirtation*.

Drama (date of acting)

E. Fitzball, *The Flying Dutchman, or The Phantom Ship*.
Douglas Jerrold, *Paul Pry*.
Pocock, *Alfred the Great*.
Charles de Vœux, *William Tell* (from Schiller).

Carlyle, essay on Burns (in *Edinburgh Review*). George Combe, *The Constitution of Man*. Fenimore Cooper, *The Red Rover*. Croly, *Salathiel, A Story of the Past, the Present, and the Future*. A. Cunningham, *Sir Michael Scott*. B. Disraeli, *The Voyage of Captain Popanilla*. I. d'Israeli, *The Life and Reign of Charles I*, (1828–31). N. Drake, *Memorials of Shakespeare*. Pierce Egan, *Finish to the Adventures of Tom, Jerry and Logic*. Sir John Franklin, *Narrative of a Second Expedition to the Polar Sea*. Hazlitt, *Life of Napoleon*, i–ii (iii–iv, 1830). Reginald Heber, *A Journey through India*. Hunt, *Lord Byron and Some of his Contemporaries*; *The Companion*. Landor, *Imaginary Conversations*, iii. Washington Irving, *History of Christopher Columbus*. T. H. Lister, *Herbert Lacy*. Lockhart, *Life of Robert Burns*. Bulwer Lytton, *Pelham*. D. M. Moir, *Mansie Wauch*. Morier, *Hajji Baba in England*. Napier, *History of the War in the Peninsula* (concl. 1840). Sir W. E. Parry, *Narrative of an Attempt to reach the North Pole*. Scott, *Tales of a Grandfather*, i; *Chronicles of the Canongate, Second Series* (*The Fair Maid of Perth*); 'My Aunt Margaret's Mirror', 'The Tapestried Chamber', 'Death of the Laird's Jock' (all in *The Keepsake*); *Religious Discourses. By a Layman*. J. T. Smith, *Nollekens and his Times*. D. Stewart, *The Philosophy*

Douglas Jerrold, *The Statue Lover*; *Descart, the French Buccaneer*; *The Tower of Lochlain*; *Wives by Advertisement, or Courting in the Newspapers*; *Ambrose Gwinett*; *Two Eyes between Two*; *Fifteen Years of a Drunkard's Life!*
Sheridan Knowles, *The Beggar's Daughter of Bethnal Green*.
M. R. Lacy, *The Two Friends* (adapted from Scribe's *Rodolphe*).
M. R. Mitford, *Rienzi*.
Planché, *Paris and London*.
Thomas Wade, *Woman's Love*.

Date	Public Events	Literary History (including translations)	Verse
1829	Wellington and Peel support Catholic Relief. Catholic Emancipation. Duel between Wellington and Winchilsea. Huskisson killed by a railway train. Exclusion of O'Connell from Parliament. Jackson President of U.S.A.	Alexander Smith b. S. R. Gardiner b. T. W. Robertson b. Knight's *Library of Entertaining Knowledge* started. Murray's *Family Library* started. Lady Anne Fanshawe, *Memoirs*, ed. Sir N. H. Nicolas. Balzac, *Les Chouans*. Hugo, *Les Orientales*. Dumas père, *Henri III et sa cour*. de Vigny, *Othello* (adaptation). Mérimée, *Chronique du règne de Charles IX*. Sainte-Beuve, *Vie de Joseph Delorme*. *La Revue des Deux Mondes* founded.	*The Poetical Works of Coleridge, Shelley and Keats*, unauthorized Paris ed. E. Elliott, *The Village Patriarch*. Hood, 'The Dream of Eugene Aram' (in *The Gem*); *The Epping Hunt*. Poe, *Al Aaraaf, Tamerlane and other Poems*. Southey, *All for Love*, and *The Pilgrim to Compostella*. Tennyson, *Timbuctoo*.
1830	Reform agitation. Death of George IV and accession of William IV. Fall of Wellington's Ministry. Grey accepts office. Regency Bill. Manchester and Liverpool Railway. July Revolution in France. Louis Philippe recognized. Greece independent. France conquers Algiers.	Hazlitt d. Christina Rossetti b. Henry Kingsley b. J. Goncourt b. *Fraser's Magazine* started. Lardner's *Cabinet Cyclopaedia* and *Cabinet Library* started. Hood's *Comic Annual*, 1830–42. T. Forster ed. *Letters of Locke, Algernon Sidney and Shaftesbury*. Southey ed. *The Pilgrim's Progress*. Gautier, *Poésies*. Comte, *Cours de philosophie positive* (1830–42). Hugo, *Hernani*. Lamartine, *Les harmonies poétiques et religieuses*.	Coleridge, *The Devil's Walk* (with Southey: first pub. 1799). Croly, *Poetical Works*. Mrs. Hemans, *Songs of the Affections*. Heraud, *The Descent into Hell*. Lamb, *Album Verses*. Robert Montgomery, *Satan*. Rogers, *Italy*, illustrated by J. M. W. Turner and T. Stothard. Tennyson, *Poems, chiefly Lyrical*.
	First Reform Bill. Dissolution of Parliament. General Election. Second Reform Bill rejected	H. Mackenzie d. W. Roscoe d. Hegel d. 'Mark Rutherford' (W.	E. Elliott, *Corn-Law Rhymes*. Hogg, *Songs*. Campbell, *Poland*.

Prose

Drama (*date of acting*)

of the Active and Moral Powers of Man. Patrick Fraser Tytler, *History of Scotland* (concl. 1843). William Taylor, *Historic Survey of German Poetry* (concl. 1830). Whateley, *Elements of Rhetoric.*

T. Arnold, *Sermons*, i. Carlyle, 'Signs of the Times' (in *Edinburgh Review*). A. Cunningham, *Lives of British Painters* (concl. 1833). Darley, *The New Sketch Book.* Reginald Heber, *Sermons.* Hogg, *The Shepherd's Calendar.* Hood, *The Epping Hunt.* Washington Irving, *The Conquest of Granada.* Jefferson, *Autobiography.* Landor, *Imaginary Conversations*, iv–v. Bulwer Lytton, *The Disowned*; *Devereux.* Marryat, *The Naval Officer, or Frank Mildmay.* James Mill, *Analysis of the Human Mind.* Milman, *History of the Jews.* Peacock, *The Misfortunes of Elphin.* Michael Scott, *Tom Cringle's Log* (in *Blackwood's Magazine*, 1829–33). Scott, *Anne of Geierstein*; *Tales of a Grandfather, Second Series.* Southey, *Sir Thomas More: The Progress and Prospects of Society.* Isaac Taylor, *The Natural History of Enthusiasm.*

A. V. Campbell, *The Forest Oracle.* Douglas Jerrold, *Vidocq! The French Police Spy*; *Bampfylde Moore Carew*; *John Overy, the Miser*; *Law and Lions!*; *Black Eyed Susan, or All in the Downs*; *The Flying Dutchman*; *The Lonely Man of Shiraz*; *Thomas à Becket*; *The Witch-Finder.*
T. H. Lister, *Epicharis.*
Scott, *The House of Aspen.*
C. A. Somerset, *Shakespeare's Early Days.*

Bentham, *The Rationale of Punishment*; *Constitutional Code for all Nations.* Byron, *Letters and Journals*, with *Life* by Moore. Carleton, *Traits and Stories of the Irish Peasantry, First Series.* Cobbett, *Rural Rides*, i; *Advice to Young Men.* Coleridge, *On the Constitution of the Church and State.* Frere, *Fables for Five-Years-Old.* Galt, *Lawrie Todd*; *Life of Lord Byron.* Godwin, *Cloudesley.* Hazlitt, *Conversations of James Northcote.* Hook, *Maxwell.* Hunt, *The Tatler*, 1830–2. G. P. R. James, *De L'Orme.* Keightley, *History of the War of Independence in Greece.* Lyell, *Principles of Geology* (concl. 1833). Bulwer Lytton, *Paul Clifford.* Macaulay, essay on Robert Montgomery (in *Edinburgh Review*). Mackintosh, *History of England*, i. Maginn, *Gallery of Illustrious Literary Characters* (in *Fraser's Magazine*, 1830–8). Marryat, *The King's Own.* Moore, *Life of Byron* (as above). Nicolas, *Observations on the State of Historical Literature.* Scott, *Letters on Demonology and Witchcraft*; *Essays on Ballad Poetry*; *Tales of a Grandfather, Third Series.* Mary Shelley, *Perkin Warbeck.* W. Wilson, *Memoirs of Daniel De Foe.*

T. H. Bayly, *Perfection or The Lady of Munster.*
Byron, *Werner.*
Douglas Jerrold, *Sally in our Alley*; *Gervaise Skinner*; *The Mutiny at the Nore*; *The Press-Gang*; *The Devil's Ducat.*
J. Kerr, *The Wandering Boys* (adapted from Pixérécourt's *Le Pèlerin blanc*).
W. T. Moncrieff, *Shakespeare's Festival.*
Scott, *Auchindrane, or The Ayrshire Tragedy.*
Thomas Wade, *The Phrenologists*; *The Jew of Aragon.*

Sir D. Brewster, *Treatise on Optics.* J. P. Collier, *The History of English Dramatic Poetry and Annals of the Stage.* B. Disraeli, *The Young Duke.* S. Ferrier, *Destiny.* Galt,

Mrs. Gore, *The School for Coquettes*; *Lords and Commons.*
Douglas Jerrold, *Martha Willis, the Servant Maid, or Service in London*; *The Bride of*

Date	Public Events	Literary History (including translations)	Verse
1831 (cont.)	by the Lords. Riots. Final Reform Bill introduced. Leopold becomes King of the Belgians. War between Belgium and Holland. Faraday's electromagnetic current.	Hale White) b. E. R. Bulwer Lytton, Earl Lytton ('Owen Meredith') b. C. S. Calverley b. First meeting of the British Association. Croker ed. Boswell's *Life of Johnson*. J. Boaden ed. *Private Correspondence of David Garrick*, 1831–2. Hugo, *Les Feuilles d'automne*. Dumas père, *Antony*. Grillparzer, *Des Meeres und der Liebe Wellen*. Sotheby trans. *The Iliad*. Balzac, *La Peau de chagrin*. Stendhal, *Le Rouge et le Noir*. Bentley's Standard Novels started.	Moore, *The Summer Fête*. Poe, *Poems*. C. Whitehead, *The Solitary*. Whittier, *Legends of New England*.
1832	Grey resigns. Wellington fails to form a ministry. Grey recalled. Reform Act becomes law. Cholera epidemic. General election. Jackson's second term as President of U.S.A.	Goethe d. Sir Walter Scott d. Crabbe d. Jeremy Bentham d. Sir James Mackintosh d. C. L. Dodgson ('Lewis Carroll') b. Sir Leslie Stephen b. T. Watts-Dunton b. Sir Edwin Arnold b. Chambers's *Edinburgh Journal* started. *Tait's Edinburgh Magazine* started. *The British Magazine* started. Caedmon ed. and trans. by Benjamin Thorpe. de Vigny, *Stello* (as a book). Dumas père, *La Tour de Nesle*. Gautier, *Albertus ou l'âme et le péché*. Goethe, *Faust*, ii. Knight's *Penny Magazine* started. Sainte-Beuve, *Critiques et portraits littéraires*, i.	Byron, *Works*, ed. Moore, 1832–5. Hunt, *Poetical Works*. R. Montgomery, *The Messiah*. B. W. Procter ('Barry Cornwall'), *English Songs*. Shelley, *The Masque of Anarchy*. Tennyson, *Poems* ('1833').

Prose	Drama (date of acting)
Bogle Corbet; Lives of the Players. Godwin, Thoughts on Man. Mrs. Gore, Mothers and Daughters. Grote, Parliamentary Reform. Charles Knight, The Working Man's Companion. L. E. Landon, Romance and Reality. Lover, Legends and Stories of Ireland, 1831–4. Macaulay, essay on Boswell (rev. of Croker's ed. in Edinburgh Review). Moore, Life of Lord Edward Fitzgerald. Peacock, Crotchet Castle. Jane Porter, Sir Edward Seaward's Narrative of his Shipwreck. Trelawny, The Adventures of a Younger Son. Watts, Scenes of Life and Shades of Character.	Ludgate. Sheridan Knowles, Alfred the Great, or The Patriot King. M. R. Mitford, Inez de Castro. J. R. Planché, Olympic Revels. C. M. Westmacott, Nettlewig Hall. Lord Francis Leveson-Gower, Hernani, or The Honour of a Castilian (adapted from Hugo.)

John Austin, *The Province of Jurisprudence determined.* Frances Burney, *Memoirs of Dr. Burney.* R. Chambers, *Biographical Dictionary of Eminent Scotsmen.* (concl. 1835). De Quincey, *Klosterheim.* Dibdin, *Bibliophobia.* Disraeli, *Contarini Fleming.* Genest, *Account of the English Stage.* Hogg, *Altrive Tales; A Queer Book.* Hunt, *Sir Ralph Esher; Christianism* (privately printed). Galt, *The Member; The Radical.* Washington Irving, *The Alhambra.* G. P. R. James, *Henry Masterton.* Anna Jameson, *Characteristics of Women.* T. H. Lister, *Arlington.* Bulwer Lytton, *Eugene Aram.* Harriet Martineau, *Illustrations of Political Economy* (concl. 1834). Marryat, *Newton Forster.* Scott, *Tales of my Landlord, Fourth Series (Count Robert of Paris, Castle Dangerous).* Earl Stanhope, *History of the War of the Succession in Spain.* Frances Trollope, *The Refugee in America; Domestic Manners of the Americans.* S. Warren, *Passages from the Diary of a late Physician* (pirated American edition the previous year: concl. 1838: originally pub. in *Blackwood's Magazine,* 1830–7). Southey, *Essays, Moral and Political.*

T. H. Bayly, *My Eleventh Day; Der Alchymist; Cupid.* Lord Francis Leveson-Gower, *Catherine of Cleves* (adapted from *Henri III,* by Dumas). Douglas Jerrold, *The Broken Heart; The Rent Day; The Golden Calf; The Factory Girl.* Frances Anne Kemble (Mrs. Butler), *Francis the First.* Sheridan Knowles, *The Hunchback; The Vision of the Bard* (in honour of Scott). T. E. Wilks, *The Wolf and the Lamb.* Eugene Aram (several stage versions).

BIBLIOGRAPHY

THIS bibliography is arranged in six sections:

    I. General Bibliographies and Works of Reference.

    II. General Collections and Anthologies.

    III. General Literary History and Criticism (Early Studies; Histories and Surveys; Studies of Romanticism).

    IV. Special Literary Studies and Literary Forms (The Language; Newspapers, Reviews, and Magazines; Prose Fiction; Literary Criticism; The Drama; History, Biography, and Autobiography; Interest in Foreign Literature and in Earlier English Literature; Travel; Annuals, and the Reading Public; The Profession of Letters and the Publishing Trade).

    V. The Background of Literature (Political and Social History, and Political Thought; Contemporary Autobiographies, Memoirs, and Letters; Religion and Moral Attitudes; Science and Technology; Education; Architecture, Painting, and Music).

    VI. Individual Authors.

Since this bibliography is selective a good deal that is of interest has had to be omitted. Those seeking further guidance are referred to Section I below.

A great many of the novels and other books of the time first appeared anonymously: as a rule no mention is made of this in the Bibliography. Short titles are usually given—the words 'and Other Poems' (for example) being often omitted.

ABBREVIATIONS:

CBEL   *Cambridge Bibliography of English Literature.*
DNB   *Dictionary of National Biography.*
EC   *Essays in Criticism.*
EHR   *English Historical Review.*
ELH   *English Literary History.*

ERP   *The English Romantic Poets: A Review of Research,* ed.
T. M. Raysor, rev. ed., New York, 1956.

ERPE   *The English Romantic Poets and Essayists: A Review of
Research and Criticism,* ed. C. W. and L. H. Houtchens,
New York, 1957.

ESEA   *Essays and Studies by Members of the English Association*
(entitled *English Studies* in 1948 and 1949).

HLB   *Huntington Library Bulletin.*

HLQ   *Huntington Library Quarterly.*

JEGP   *Journal of English and Germanic Philology.*

JHI   *Journal of the History of Ideas.*

K.-Sh.B.   *Bulletin of the Keats–Shelley Memorial Association.*

K.-Sh.J.   *The Keats–Shelley Journal* (New York).

MLN   *Modern Language Notes.*

MLQ   *Modern Language Quarterly.*

MLR   *Modern Language Review.*

MP   *Modern Philology.*

NQ   *Notes and Queries.*

PMLA   *Publications of the Modern Language Association of America.*

PQ   *Philological Quarterly.*

RES   *Review of English Studies.*

SP   *Studies in Philology.*

SR   *Studies in Romanticism* (Boston).

TLS   *Times Literary Supplement.*

UTQ   *University of Toronto Quarterly.*

The place of publication is usually given if it is other than
London, Edinburgh, Oxford, Cambridge, or (for French books)
Paris.

I. GENERAL BIBLIOGRAPHIES AND
WORKS OF REFERENCE

The best guide is, of course, the *Cambridge Bibliography of English Literature*, ed. F. W. Bateson, of which vol. iii (1940) covers the nineteenth century. This is supplemented in vol. v, ed. G. Watson (1957). The *Concise Cambridge Bibliography*, 1958, gives some later books. The Oxford *Annals of English Literature, 1475–1950*, 2nd ed., 1961, list the main books published each year. The *Oxford Companion to English Literature*, ed. Sir Paul Harvey, 3rd ed., 1946, gives brief details of some of the principal writers and their books.

Valuable lists of new books throughout the period may be found in a book-trade periodical, Bent's *Monthly Literary Advertiser*. From 1826 this attempted a complete list of new books once a year. The *Monthly Review* also published lists of new books, while the *Quarterly* similarly gave the titles of many new publications. Reference may also be made to *The English Catalogue of Books . . . 1801–36*, ed. R. A. Peddie and Q. Waddington, 1914, although it is not wholly reliable and the fact that it is one huge consolidated list detracts from its usefulness.

Help may also be found in the *British Museum General Catalogue of Printed Books* (in progress) and *The Bibliographer's Manual*, by W. T. Lowndes, rev. ed., 6 vols. in eleven, 1857–64.

Halkett and Laing's *Dictionary of Anonymous and Pseudonymous English Literature*, rev. by J. Kennedy and others, 7 vols., 1926–34, suppl. vols. 1956 and 1962, is a valuable guide, though inevitably very incomplete.

There is a useful *Guide to Archives and Manuscripts in the United States*, ed. P. M. Hamer, New Haven, 1961, the first attempt at a really comprehensive survey of MS. material in the United States. It is inevitably incomplete: no details are given of the papers in the Berg collection at the New York Public Library, for example, while the Byron material in the Pierpont Morgan Library is not mentioned.

The *Dictionary of National Biography* is particularly valuable for writers of the nineteenth century, although there are of course errors and natural reticences.

The best bibliographies of recent work on this period are to be found in two books published at New York by the Modern

Language Association of America: *The English Romantic Poets: A Review of Research*, ed. T. M. Raysor, 1950 (2nd ed., 1956), covers the Romantic Movement, Wordsworth, Coleridge, Byron, Shelley, and Keats: while *The English Romantic Poets and Essayists: A Review of Research and Criticism*, ed. Carolyn W. and L. H. Houtchens, 1957, deals with Blake, Lamb, Hazlitt, Scott, Southey, Campbell, Moore, Landor, Hunt, and De Quincey. Each book consists of signed articles in which the relevant scholarship is discussed and evaluated. 'The Romantic Movement: A Selective and Critical Bibliography' appeared in *ELH* from 1937 to 1949 and now appears in *PQ*. *The Year's Work in English Studies* is an annual volume published by the English Association; while there is also an *Annual Bibliography of English Language and Literature* which is published by the Modern Humanities Research Association. *PMLA* publishes a list of books and articles on this period once a year, though its list of 'Research in Progress' has been abandoned.

A critical bibliography of writings on the Romantic Movement may be found in the 2nd ed. of E. Bernbaum's *Guide through the Romantic Movement*, 1949. L. Leary's *Contemporary Literary Scholarship: A Critical Review*, New York, 1958, has 30 pp. on the Romantic Movement, with brief discussions of the work listed.

For bibliographies of the novel and other literary forms see Section IV below.

II. GENERAL COLLECTIONS AND ANTHOLOGIES

1. Prose

There are innumerable anthologies which give selections from Hazlitt and Lamb and the other essayists. Among the fullest are W. Peacock, *English Prose*, vols. iii–iv (World's Classics, 1921), and E. Bernbaum, *Anthology of Romanticism and Guide through the Romantic Movement*, 5 vols., New York, 1929–30. See also H. Craik, *English Prose Selections*, vol. v, 1896; F. W. Roe, *Nineteenth Century English Prose*, New York, 1923; C. H. Grabo, *Romantic Prose of the Early Nineteenth Century*, New York, 1927; R. W. King, *England from Wordsworth to Dickens*, [1929]; G. Sampson, *Nineteenth Century Essays*, Cambridge, 1929; E. H. Lacon Watson, *Contemporary Comments: Writers of the Early*

Nineteenth Century as they appeared to each other, 1931; O. J. Camp-
bell, J. F. A. Pyre, and B. Weaver, *Poetry and Criticism of the
Romantic Movement*, New York, 1932; C. F. Macintyre and M.
Ewing, *English Prose of the Romantic Period*, 1938; G. Grigson,
The Romantics, 1943; and *Prose of the Romantic Period, 1780–1830*,
ed. R. Wright, 1956 (*The Pelican Book of English Prose*, ed. K.
Allott, vol. iv).

F. A. Mumby's *Letters of Literary Men: The Nineteenth Century*,
1906, is a useful collection. *A Cabinet of Gems*, ed. B. A. Booth,
Berkeley, 1938, is a collection of short stories from the *Annuals*.
For collections of critical essays see IV. 4 below.

2. POETRY

There is an interesting early anthology, published in Paris:
The Living Poets of England, 2 vols., 1827, which in fact includes selections from Byron, Shelley, and Keats, as well as
many minor poets of the period, and contains biographical and
critical introductions, including an essay on 'Wordsworth and
the Lake-School of Poetry'. *The Poetical Album*, ed. A. A. Watts,
2 vols., 1828–9, contains much interesting minor verse.

The fullest selections are those in A. H. Miles and others, *The
Poets and the Poetry of the Century*, which first appeared in 10
vols. in 1891–7 and was revised in 12 vols. in 1905–7. Selections
may also be found in Bernbaum and in Campbell, Pyre, and
Weaver, as above; in T. H. Ward and others, *The English
Poets*, vol. iv, 1880; in the *Oxford Book of English Verse of the
Romantic Period, 1798–1837*, ed. H. S. Milford, 1935 (first issued
as the *Oxford Book of Regency Verse*, 1928); in *Blake to Poe* (vol. iv
of *Poets of the English Language*, ed. W. H. Auden and N. H.
Pearson), 1951; and in *English Romantic Poetry*, ed. H. Bloom,
New York, 1961.

Palgrave's *Golden Treasury*, which first appeared in 1861 and
has frequently been revised, occupies a special place in the
history of taste. His *Treasury of Sacred Song*, 1889, and *The
Golden Treasury, Second Series*, 1897, may also be consulted. Other
anthologies include *The English Parnassus*, ed. W. Macneile
Dixon and H. J. C. Grierson, 1909, which contains longer
poems by Byron, Shelley, and Keats; J. D[over] Wilson, *The
Poetry of the Age of Wordsworth*, 1927; O. J. Campbell, J. F. A.
Pyre, and B. Weaver, *Poetry and Criticism of the Romantic Move-*

ment, 1932 (as above); J. Hayward, *Nineteenth-Century Poetry: An Anthology,* 1932; S. Spender, *A Choice of English Romantic Poetry,* New York, 1947; *Pope to Keats* and *Hood to Hardy,* both ed. D. K. Roberts, 1949 (vols. iii–iv of *The Centuries' Poetry,* Penguin Books); and J. Heath-Stubbs and D. Wright, *The Forsaken Garden: An Anthology of Poetry, 1824–1909,* 1950. *Fifteen Poets,* by H. S. Bennett, C. S. Lewis, and others, 1941, contains selections from Byron, Shelley, and Keats, with brief prefaces.

For Scottish poetry see *The Scottish Songs,* ed. R. Chambers, 2 vols., 1829–32; *The Modern Scottish Minstrel,* ed. C. Rogers, 6 vols., 1856–7; and *Modern Scottish Poets,* ed. D. H. Edwards, 16 vols., Brechin, 1880–97.

III. GENERAL LITERARY HISTORY AND CRITICISM

So much has been written on this period, in England and America and elsewhere, that it seems necessary to be exceptionally selective in this section. This list is accordingly confined to (*a*) a few Early Studies; (*b*) Histories and Surveys; and (*c*) Studies of Romanticism which are of particular relevance to the period.

(*a*) Book IV of Bulwer Lytton's *England and the English,* 2 vols., 1833, gives a 'View of the Intellectual Spirit of the Time' which includes penetrating remarks on the state of literature. A good deal of biographical and other information may be found in *The Living Poets,* mentioned above on p. 462. Two early surveys are Allan Cunningham's *Biographical and Critical History of the British Literature of the Last Fifty Years,* Paris, 1834, and D. M. Moir's *Sketches of the Poetical Literature of the Past Half-Century, in Six Lectures,* Edinburgh, 1851. Mrs. [Margaret] Oliphant's *The Literary History of England in the End of the Eighteenth and Beginning of the Nineteenth Century,* 3 vols., 1882 (new issue), remains of real interest.

The Poets and their Critics, vol. ii, ed. H. Sykes Davies, 1962, gives outstanding passages of criticism of the poets from Blake to Browning.

(*b*) Two of the best surveys are those by Oliver Elton in *A Survey of English Literature, 1780–1830,* 2 vols., 1912, and by S. C. Chew in *The Nineteenth Century and After, 1789–1939,* part iv of *A Literary History of England*, ed. A. C. Baugh, New York, 1948 (Eng. ed., 1950). The period is also intelligently treated in *A History of English Literature*, by P. Legouis and L. Cazamian, rev. ed. (Eng. trans.) 1948, and in D. Daiches's *Critical History of English Literature*, vol. ii, 1960. Vol. iv of George Brandes's *Main Currents in Nineteenth Century Literature, Naturalism in England* (Eng. trans. 1905), is still worth consulting, as is vol. vi (1910) of W. J. Courthope's *History of English Poetry*. Helene Richter's *Geschichte der englischen Romantik*, 2 vols., Halle, 1911–16, is now of less interest. Vol. xii is the relevant volume of the *Cambridge History of English Literature* (*The Nineteenth Century I*, 1914, 2nd ed., 1932). *The Age of Wordsworth*, by C. H. Herford, 1897, is a sensible old-fashioned survey. *Currents and Eddies in the English Romantic Generation*, by F. E. Pierce, New Haven, 1918, deals interestingly with minor writers and the literary *milieux* of Bristol, Edinburgh, London, and the Lakes. (On Bristol see also C. A. Weber, *Bristols Bedeutung für die englische Romantik und die deutsch-englischen Beziehungen*, Halle, 1935.)

Mention must also be made of *Literary Anecdotes of the Nineteenth Century: Contributions towards a Literary History of the Period*, ed. W. Robertson Nicoll and Thomas J[ames] Wise (*verb. sap.*), 2 vols., 1895–6, which contains information about Shelley, Keats, Charles Wells, the Landor–Blessington papers, and other topics; and *Little Memoirs of the Nineteenth Century*, by 'George Paston', 1902, which contains essays on Haydon, Lady Morgan, N. P. Willis, Lady Hester Stanhope, William and Mary Howitt, and Prince Pückler-Muskau in England.

Vol. iii of G. Saintsbury's *History of English Prosody, From Blake to Mr. Swinburne*, 1910, includes this period, as do chapters ix and x of his *History of English Prose Rhythm*, 1912.

Good brief surveys include *Augustans and Romantics, 1689–1830*, by H. V. D. Dyson and J. Butt, rev. ed. 1950 (*Introductions to English Literature*, ed. B. Dobrée, vol. iii: with useful brief bibliographies); and *The Romantic Poets*, by G. Hough, 1953. Vol. 5 of the *Pelican Guide to English Literature*, ed. B. Ford (*From Blake to Byron*, 1957), can only be described as disappointing.

(*c*) In his *Guide through the Romantic Movement*, 2nd ed., 1948, Bernbaum discusses twenty-eight of the hundreds of meanings of the words 'romanticism'. For the earlier period there is an elaborate and admirable study by F. Baldensperger, ' "Romantique", ses analogues et ses équivalents: tableau synoptique de

1650 à 1810' in *Harvard Studies and Notes in Philology and Literature*, xix (1937). One of the most learned and patient discussions is the two-part article by R. Wellek in *Comparative Literature*, vol. i, nos. 1–2, 1949: Part i of 'The Concept of "Romanticism" in Literary History' is entitled 'The Term "Romantic" and its Derivatives', and Part ii 'The Unity of European Romanticism'. In vol. ii of his *History of Modern Criticism, 1750–1950* (*The Romantic Age*, 1955) Wellek gives it as his view that 'In England, as opposed to the Continent, there was no "romantic" movement, if we limit the meaning of such a term to a conscious program and consider the precise name as crucial' (p. 110). A. O. Lovejoy's well-known essay, 'On the Discrimination of Romanticisms' is reprinted from *PMLA* xxxix (1924) in his *Essays in the History of Ideas*, New York, 1948 (a volume which also contains several other essays relevant to the concept 'romanticism'), and in *English Romantic Poets: Modern Essays in Criticism*, ed. M. H. Abrams, New York, 1960. For a criticism of Lovejoy's approach see B. Phillips, 'Logical Positivism and the Function of Reason', in *Philosophy*, 1948. Praz discusses the word as 'an approximate term' in *The Romantic Agony* (mentioned below). H. J. C. Grierson's 'Classical and Romantic', reprinted in his *The Background of English Literature*, 1925, is still of some interest, while L. P. Smith's *Four Words* (1924, as a pamphlet: reprinted as 'Four Romantic Words' in *Words and Idioms: Studies in the English Language*, 1925) remains one of the most suggestive approaches to the whole period: the words are 'romantic', 'originality', 'creative', and 'genius'. The meaning of 'romantic' and 'romanticism' are also intelligently discussed in M. H. Abrams, *The Mirror and the Lamp: Romantic Theory and the Critical Tradition*, New York, 1953, and W. K. Wimsatt, Jr., and Cleanth Brooks, *Literary Criticism: A Short History*, 1957. Other discussions are mentioned in *ERP*, pp. 24–27, and in articles listed by R. Wellek and A. Warren on pp. 381–2 of their *Theory of Literature*, 1949.

The so-called 'pre-romantic movement' is outside our scope.

Le mouvement romantique, by P. van Tieghem, 2nd ed., Paris, 1923, is an annotated collection of statements about literature by the leading writers of England, Germany, Italy, and France. The same writer's *Le romantisme dans la littérature européenne*, 1948, is a wide survey. See also his articles, 'La place du romantisme anglais dans le romantisme européen', *Lettres* v–vi, 1946. The very brief treatment of English literature by H. N. Fairchild in 'Romanticism: A Symposium' (*PMLA*, vol. lv, No. 1, March 1940) is of little value.

One of the most stimulating books on the romantic period is still Irving Babbitt's *Rousseau and Romanticism*, 1919: Babbitt has, of course, far more references to Byron and Shelley than to Keats. The value of his book lies in his learning, wit, and detachment. *The Romantic Comedy*, by D. G. James, 1948, throws a great deal of light on Shelley and Keats. Sir Maurice Bowra's *The Romantic Imagination*, 1950, is a notably lucid exposition from a point of view different from that adopted in this study. A. Gérard's *L'Idée romantique de la poésie en Angleterre*, 1955, is another intelligent study.

Mario Praz is the author of two stimulating books. *The Romantic Agony*, Eng. trans. 1933 (Italian ed., *La carne, la morte, e il diavolo nella letteratura romantica*, Milan and Rome, 1930), is a study of the erotic sensibility of the nineteenth century, demonstrating how the decadents may be regarded as the descendants of the writers of the earlier part of the century. In *The Hero in Eclipse in Victorian Fiction* (Eng. trans. 1956), Praz argues that in the work of Coleridge, Wordsworth, Scott, Lamb, De Quincey, Peacock and later writers 'romanticism turns bourgeois'. F. Brie's *Exotismus der Sinne, eine Studie zur Psychologie der Romantik*, Heidelberg, 1920, is a briefer study on lines partly similar to those of *The Romantic Agony*.

The Romantic Movement in English Poetry, by Arthur Symons, 1909, has the merit of dealing individually and often perceptively with a great many major and minor writers. *A History of English Romanticism in the Nineteenth Century*, by H. A. Beers, 1902, is mainly concerned with the revival of medievalism and is now of little value. *Nature in English Literature*, by E. Blunden, 1929, and *The Concept of Nature in Nineteenth-Century English Poetry*, by J. W. Beach, New York, 1936, may also be consulted. *The Visionary Company*, by H. Bloom, New York, 1961, gives a highly individual reading of certain of the principal poems.

Three stimulating books are *The Poet's Defence*, by J. Bronowski, 1939, which deals with attitudes to the imagination in our period and in the present century; *Romanticism and the Modern Ego*, by J. Barzun, Boston, 1943 (rev. as *Classic, Romantic, and Modern*, 1962); and *The Misinterpretation of Man*, 1949, by P. Roubiczek, an attack on European romanticism. *The Decline and*

Fall of the Romantic Ideal, by F. L. Lucas, 1936, is a series of related essays. *Le Romantisme anglais*, 1946, is a special issue of *Les Lettres* containing essays by L. Cazamian, Middleton Murry, P. van Tieghem, and others; *JHI* ii, 1941, contains a symposium on Romanticism by A. O. Lovejoy and others. *Romanticism: Points of View*, ed. R. F. Gleckner and G. E. Enscoe, New Jersey, 1963, is a collection of essays from Pater onwards.

There are several collections of essays on the period mainly by American scholars. *The Major English Romantic Poets: A Symposium in Reappraisal*, was edited by C. D. Thorpe and others and published in Southern Illinois in 1957. *English Romantic Poets: Modern Essays in Criticism*, ed. M. H. Abrams, 1960 (Galaxy paperback), contains Lovejoy's essay mentioned on p. 465 above, 'The Structure of Romantic Nature Imagery', by W. K. Wimsatt, and 'The Correspondent Breeze: A Romantic Metaphor', by Abrams himself, as well as essays on individual authors mentioned elsewhere (some of them reprinted from the previously mentioned collection). A forthcoming volume, ed. J. E. Jordan, Northrop Frye, and J. V. Logan, will contain essays on many of the major writers of the period.

D. Bush's *Mythology and the Romantic Tradition in English Poetry*, Cambridge, Mass., 1937, is a learned and valuable survey which devotes more than a hundred pages to our period. A. C. Bradley's 'The Long Poem in the Age of Wordsworth', in his *Oxford Lectures on Poetry*, 1909, is still illuminating. K. Kroeber's *Romantic Narrative Art*, Madison, Wisconsin, 1960, discusses the poetry of Byron and others. The scope of D. Perkins, *The Quest for Permanence: The Symbolism of Wordsworth, Shelley and Keats*, Cambridge, Mass., 1959, is sufficiently indicated by its title. Ilse Gugler's study, *Das Problem der fragmentarischen Dichtung in der englischen Romantik (Schweizer Anglistische Arbeiten*, xv, Bern, 1944), should also be mentioned. In *The Romantic Assertion*, 1958, R. A. Foakes discusses modern approaches to nineteenth-century poetry and offers his readings of *The Eve of St. Agnes* and *Adonais*. *The Lost Travellers*, by B. Blackstone, 1962, is a study of Blake, Byron, and other major writers of the period in relation to the common theme of travel which he finds running through their work.

T. S. Eliot has not written much about the writers of this period, although there is a brief discussion of Shelley and Keats in *The Use of Poetry and the Use of Criticism*, 1933. In *The Star-Lit*

Dome: Studies in the Poetry of Vision, 1941, G. Wilson Knight has written characteristically and often penetratingly on Keats and Shelley.

Two articles by R. H. Fogle discuss critical approaches: 'Romantic Bards and Metaphysical Reviewers', *ELH* xii, 1945, and 'A Recent Attack upon Romanticism', *College English*, ix, 1948.

IV. SPECIAL LITERARY STUDIES AND LITERARY FORMS

This section comprises: (1) The Language; (2) Newspapers, Reviews, and Magazines; (3) Prose Fiction; (4) Literary Criticism; (5) The Drama; (6) History, Biography, and Autobiography; (7) Interest in Foreign Literature and in Earlier English Literature; (8) Travel; (9) Annuals, and the Reading Public; and (10) The Profession of Letters and the Publishing Trade.

1. THE LANGUAGE

The development of the English language in the eighteenth and nineteenth centuries has been very much neglected. The best general *History of the English Language*, that by A. C. Baugh, New York, 1935, 2nd edn. 1959, has naturally little to say about our period. A number of brief studies of eighteenth-century usage are of background relevance: see (for example) two notes by R. W. Babcock, 'Benevolence, Sensibility and Sentiment in Some Eighteenth-Century Periodicals', *MLN* lxii, 1947, and 'A Note on Genius, Imagination and Enthusiasm in Some Late Eighteenth-Century Periodicals', *NQ* cxcii, 1947; and Caroline Thompson's 'Sensibility', *Psyche*, xv, 1935. An example of one of the kinds of study that is wanted is R. W. Chapman's appendix on 'Miss Austen's English' in his edition of *Sense and Sensibility*, 1923 (3rd edn. 1933). Also see Index VII to his edition of *Jane Austen's Letters*, 2nd ed., 1932. Cobbett's *Grammar* and other writings provide a great deal of information. Reference may also be made to the essay by L. P. Smith mentioned above on p. 465, and to Baldensperger's study of the meanings of the word 'romantique' up to 1810 (pp. 464–5 above). Uno Philipson's *Political Slang, 1750–1850* (Lund Studies in English,

9, 1941), should also be mentioned. The language of Dickens, which lies beyond our limits, has recently been studied by Professor Randolph Quirk in *Charles Dickens and Appropriate Language* (Durham, 1959), and in 'Some Observations on the Language of Dickens', *A Review of English Literature*, ii, 1961.

The emergence of key terms in political and social thinking deserves further study, as does the development of the terminology of literary criticism. Changes in linguistic habits also throw light on the increasing squeamishness of the time, and on changes in people's feelings about social class. The Reviews are full of material, while revisions in books republished many years after their first appearance sometimes provide unusually precise evidence. See (for example) 'De Quincey Revises his *Confessions*', by I. Jack, *PMLA* lxxii, 1957.

2. NEWSPAPERS, REVIEWS, AND MAGAZINES

For guidance on where to find runs of periodicals and other general information see the American *Union List of Serials in Libraries of the United States and Canada*, ed. W. Gregory, 2nd ed., New York, 1943 (Supplements 1945 and 1953), the *British Union-Catalogue of Periodicals: A Record of the Periodicals of the World, from the Seventeenth Century to the Present Day in British Libraries*, ed. J. D. Stewart, M. E. Hammond, and E. Saenger, 4 vols., 1955–8 (and *Supplement to 1960*, ed. J. D. Stewart and others, 1962); and the *Index and Finding List of Serials published in the British Isles, 1789–1832*, ed. W. S. Ward, Lexington, 1953.

'*The Times*' *Centenary Handlist of English and Welsh Newspapers, Magazines and Reviews* [by J. G. Muddiman], 1920, is still of use, though not invariably accurate.

(a) Newspapers

The scope of Stanley Morison's *The English Newspaper: Some Account of the Physical Development of Journals Printed in London between 1622 & the Present Day*, 1932, is accurately defined by the sub-title. The book includes numerous illustrations of newspapers. There is no good up-to-date history of English journalism. H. R. Fox Bourne's *English Newspapers*, 2 vols., 1887, is still the best general book; but see also F. Knight Hunt, *The*

Fourth Estate: Contributions towards A History of Newspapers, and of the Liberty of the Press, 2 vols., 1850, and W. H. Wickwar, *The Struggle for the Freedom of the Press, 1819–1832*, 1928. A. Aspinall is the author of an important book, *Politics and the Press, c. 1780–1850*, 1949, and of a number of articles, notably 'Statistical Accounts of the London Newspapers, 1800–36', *EHR* lxv, 1950 (on advertisement duty returns); 'The Circulation of Newspapers in the Early Nineteenth Century', *RES* xxii, 1946; and 'The Social Status of Journalists at the Beginning of the Nineteenth Century', *RES* xxi, 1945. E. E. Kellett's chapter in *Early Victorian England, 1830–1865*, ed. G. M. Young, 2 vols., 1934, touches on the end of our period. D. Read's *Press and People, 1790–1850*, 1961, gives information about the circulation of newspapers in Leeds, Manchester and Sheffield.

Vol. i of *The History of The Times*, '*The Thunderer' in the Making, 1785–1841*, 1935 (anonymous), throws important light on the period, as does D. Hudson's briefer *Thomas Barnes of 'The Times'*, 1943.

For further books and articles see *CBEL* iii, 779, and v, 678. Reference should also be made to Barnes, Hone, Jerdan, Hook, Knight, and others in the individual entries below. See also *Babylon the Great*, referred to on p. 485 below.

(b) Reviews and Magazines

The Wellesley Index to Victorian Periodicals, ed. W. E. Houghton and others, will list all known authors in some thirty quarterlies and monthlies from 1824 to 1900. It will also include the *Edinburgh Review* from its foundation, but not the early years of *Blackwood's* or the *Quarterly*, as indexes for these already exist (see below).

W. A. Copinger's *On the Authorship of the First Hundred Numbers of the 'Edinburgh Review'*, privately printed, Manchester, 1895, goes up to January 1830. More recent information may be found in important articles by E. Schneider and others in *MP* xlii–xliii, 1945–6, and *MLN* lxi, 1946; by L. G. Johnson and C. Blagden in *The Library*, 5th series, vii, 1952; by F. W. Fetter in the *Journal of Political Economy*, lxi, 1953; and by P. L. Carver, *RES* iv, 1928. *The Quarterly Review under Gifford: Identification of Contributors, 1809–1824*, by H. and H. C. Shine, Chapel Hill, 1949, is authoritative and contains a list of memoirs, &c., throwing light on problems of authorship. For the contributors on

literary subjects under Lockhart's editorship see M. F. Brightfield in *PMLA* lix, 1944. For the contributors to *Blackwood's* see
A. L. Strout, *A Bibliography of Articles in Blackwood's Magazine,
1817–1825*, 1959.

A great deal of information will be found in volumes of letters,
memoirs, &c., listed under individual authors below. Scott's
letters are particularly important, as are Southey's (see particularly *The Life and Correspondence*, ed. C. C. Southey, 6 vols.,
1849–50, and *Selections from the Letters*, ed. J. W. Warter, 4 vols.,
1856).

The best survey of Reviews and Magazines in the period
is Walter Graham's valuable study, *English Literary Periodicals*,
New York, 1930.

Of the mass of contemporary comment one may refer to
Edward Copleston's brilliant parody, *Advice to a Young Re-
viewer, with a Specimen of the Art*, 1807, and the comments in
Bulwer Lytton's *England and the English*, 2 vols., 1833, and in
Lockhart's anonymous *John Bull's Letter to Lord Byron*, 1821.
Peacock refers to the Reviews in his 'Essay on Fashionable
Literature' (in vol. viii of the Halliford Edition) and elsewhere
in his writings.

A great deal of information about the *Edinburgh*, the *Quarterly*,
and *Blackwood's* may be found in (respectively) T. Constable,
Archibald Constable and his Literary Correspondents, 3 vols., 1873;
S. Smiles, *A Publisher and his Friends: Memoir and Correspondence
of the late John Murray*, 2 vols., 1891; and Mrs. [Margaret]
Oliphant, *Annals of a Publishing House: William Blackwood and
his Sons*, 2 vols., 1897 (vol. iii, by Mrs. Gerald Porter, 1898,
deals with a later period). See also under the names of individual contributors below.

The *Memoirs and Correspondence of Francis Horner, M.P.*, ed.
L. Horner, 2 vols., 1843, throw light on the early years of the
Edinburgh Review, while *Selections from the Correspondence of Macvey
Napier*, ed. M. Napier, 1877 (privately printed), are important
for the slightly later period. For the *Monthly Review* see J. W.
Robberds, *A Memoir of William Taylor*, 2 vols., 1843. For the
Westminster see the *Autobiography* of John Stuart Mill, 1873 (*The
Early Draft* . . . was ed. by J. Stillinger, Urbana, Illinois, 1961),
as well as entries under Bentham, Bowring, and James Mill,
below. Colburn's *New Monthly Magazine* has received little
attention from scholars: information may, however, be found

in many contemporary memoirs, notably the *Life and Letters of Thomas Campbell*, by W. Beattie, 3 vols., 1849.

The following monographs are of importance: J. Clive, *Scotch Reviewers*, 1957; W. Graham, *Tory Criticism in the Quarterly Review, 1809–1853*, Columbia, 1921; *Leigh Hunt's 'Examiner' Examined*, by E. Blunden, 1928; *The London Magazine, 1820–29*, by Josephine Bauer, Copenhagen, 1953 (*Anglistica*, ed. T. Dahl and others, vol. i: see also E. Blunden, *Keats's Publisher: A Memoir of John Taylor (1781–1864)*, 1936); and *Rebellious Fraser's*, by Miriam M. H. Thrall, New York, 1934. *Benthamite Reviewing*, by G. L. Nesbitt, New York, 1934, deals with the *Westminster Review* from 1824 to 1836. *The Dissidence of Dissent*, by F. E. Mineka, North Carolina, 1944, deals with *The Monthly Repository* from 1806 to 1838 and includes a chapter on religious periodicals between 1700 and 1825. *The Athenaeum: A Mirror of Victorian Culture*, by L. A. Marchand, Chapel Hill, North Carolina, 1941, is an admirable study. (See also the Memoir of C. W. Dilke prefixed to *The Papers of a Critic*, 2 vols., 1875.)

Special mention should be made of *Selected Journalism from the English Reviews by Stendhal*, ed. G. Strickland, 1959. In the 1820's Stendhal contributed (from Paris) to the *London Magazine*, the *New Monthly Magazine*, and the *Athenaeum*. *Shelley–Leigh Hunt: How Friendship Made History*, ed. R. Brimley Johnson, 1928, is a valuable collection of reviews and leaders from the *Examiner*, with letters between the Shelleys and Leigh Hunt.

Two important essays with the same title, 'The First Edinburgh Reviewers', by Leslie Stephen and Walter Bagehot, respectively, may be found in *Hours in a Library*, 3rd series, 1879, and *Literary Studies*, ed. R. H. Hutton, vol. i, 1895. See also 'Memorials of a Man of Letters' in J. Morley's *Studies in Literature*, 1891. *Cobwebs of Criticism*, by T. Hall Caine, 1883, is an indignant 'Review of the First Reviewers of the "Lake", "Satanic", and "Cockney" Schools'.

The Criticism of Poetry in British Periodicals, 1798–1820, by W. S. Ward (Duke University dissertation, 1943: microcards, University of Kentucky, 1955), is a statistical survey based on 831 periodicals. R. D. Mayo's *The English Novel in the Magazines, 1740–1815*, Illinois, 1962, stops on the threshold of our period. Recent articles include R. G. Cox, 'The Great Reviews', *Scrutiny*, vi, 1937; J. J. Welker, 'The Position of the Quarterlies on Some Classical Dogmas', *SP* xxxvii, 1940; V. Lloréns, 'Colaboraciones de emigrados españoles en revistas inglesas (1824–34)', *Hispanic Review*, xix, 1951; W. Graham, 'Robert Southey as Tory Reviewer', *PQ* ii, 1923, and 'Some Infamous Tory Reviews', *SP* xxii, 1925; W. S. Ward, 'Some Aspects of the Conservative Attitude toward Poetry: 1798–1820', *PMLA*, lx, 1945; and G. Carnall, 'The *Monthly Magazine*', *RES*, new series, v, 1954. '*The Edinburgh Review' and Romantic Poetry (1802–29)*, by T. Crawford, Auckland, New Zealand, 1955, is a brief treatment in the compass of 42 pages.

Selections from the Edinburgh Review, ed. M. Cross, 4 vols., 1833, is a collection of 'the best articles' with a preliminary dissertation and explanatory notes. For other books containing selections from the Reviews see p. 475 below. See also Jeffrey, Brougham, Croker and others under Individual Authors.

3. PROSE FICTION

XIX Century Fiction: A Bibliographical Record, by Michael Sadleir, 2 vols., 1951, is a mine of accurate information, although it is limited to books in his own collection. *The Minerva Press, 1790–1820*, by Dorothy Blakey, published by the Bibliographical Society in 1939, is also of value for our period. The chapters on 'Printing and Publishing at the Minerva, 1773–1859', 'Forgotten Favourites, 1790–1820', and (particularly) 'The Circulating Library' are of interest and importance. A. Block's *The English Novel, 1740–1850. A Catalogue including Prose Romances, Short Stories, and Translations of Foreign Fiction*, 1939 (2nd ed., 1961), is also of use, though it is not invariably reliable. There is also *A General Analytical Bibliography of the Regional Novelists of the British Isles, 1800–1950*, by L. Leclaire, Clermont-Ferrand, 1953. *A Gothic Bibliography*, by Montague Summers [1941], includes some novels of the nineteenth century.

Some account of the fiction of the period is given in histories of the novel. The fullest, that by E. A. Baker, 10 vols., 1924–1939, is in many ways unsatisfactory. *The Popular Novel in England, 1770–1800*, by J. M. S. Tompkins, 1932, provides an amusing and reliable background. *The Tale of Terror: A Study of the Gothic Romance*, by Edith Birkhead, 1921, is a dependable survey which includes the early nineteenth century. See also *The Gothic Flame*, by D. P. Varma, 1957. *The Gothic Quest: A History of the Gothic Novel*, by Montague Summers [1938], is unreliable but full of curious information. Eino Railo, *The Haunted Castle*, English trans. 1927, deals with certain 'elements of English Romanticism' mainly in eighteenth-century fiction. P. Yvon, *Le Gothique et la Renaissance Gothique en Angleterre, 1750–1880*, Caen & Paris, 1931, covers the period 1750–1880. *Le Roman Social en Angleterre (1830–1850)*, by L. Cazamian, 2 vols., 1903 (2nd ed., 1934) deals very briefly with 'le roman à thèse avant 1830'. Kathleen Tillotson's learned and illuminating *Novels of the Eighteen-Forties*, 1954, contains a great deal of relevant information. G. Lukács's important study was translated into English in 1961 as *The Historical Novel*. For *The Hero in Eclipse in Victorian Fiction*, by M. Praz, see p. 466 above. We may also consult *Horace Walpole and the English Novel: A Study of the Influence of 'The Castle of Otranto', 1764–1820*, by K. K. Mehrotra, 1934, and *The English Novel in the Magazines* (p. 472 above).

On the fashionable novelists see M. W. Rosa, *The Silver-Fork School: Novels of Fashion preceding 'Vanity Fair'*, New York, 1936, and M. F. Brightfield, *Theodore Hook and his Novels*, Cambridge, Mass., 1928. T. Flanagan's *The Irish Novelists, 1800–1850*, New York 1959, is cited in the text.

Although Bulwer Lytton falls outside our scope reference must be made to two books relating to him by a scholar who knew this period as few have ever known it: Michael Sadleir's *Edward and Rosina*, 1931 (reissued as *Bulwer and his Wife: a Panorama, 1803–1836*, 1933), and *Blessington–d'Orsay: A Masquerade*, 1933 (revised ed., 1947). Both studies throw a great deal of light on the literary and social scene.

There are important articles on Gothic fiction by R. D. Mayo in *MLR* xxxvii, 1942, *MLN* lviii, 1943, and *PMLA* lxv, 1950. See also W. F. Gallaway, 'The Conservative Attitude toward Fiction, 1770–1830', *PMLA* lv, 1940; *Early Opposition to the English Novel: The Popular Reaction from 1760 to 1830*, by T. T. Taylor, New York, 1943; and B. A. Booth, 'Form and Technique in the Novel', in *The Reinterpretation of Victorian Literature*, ed. J. E. Baker, Princeton, 1950.

4. LITERARY CRITICISM

There is no collection of critical essays of this period comparable with those of Gregory Smith, Spingarn, and Elledge. A good collection with a wide scope is *Literary Criticism: Pope to Croce*, ed. G. W. Allen and H. H. Clark, New York, 1941 (reprinted 1962). See also *Critical Essays of the Early Nineteenth Century*, ed. R. M. Alden, New York, 1921. Some criticism of the period is to be found in other collections, such as *Criticism: The Major Texts*, ed. W. J. Bate, New York, 1952. There is also a volume of *English Critical Essays: Nineteenth Century*, ed. E. D. Jones, in the World's Classics series (1916). For *The Poets and Their Critics*, ii, see p. 463 above.

There are several collections of reviews of the period. As one would expect, they tend to overlap. These include *Early Reviews of Great Writers (1786–1832)*, ed. E. Stevenson (The Scott Library [1890]); *Early Reviews of English Poets*, ed. J. L. Haney, Philadelphia, 1904; *Famous Reviews*, ed. R. Brimley Johnson, 1914 (the fullest selection); and *Contemporary Reviews of Romantic Poetry*, ed. J. Wain, 1953. Jeffrey and many other reviewers collected much of their work. See under Individual Authors.

The criticism of the time is discussed in vol. iii of G. Saintsbury's *A History of Criticism and Literary Taste in Europe*, 1904. For our period this is now largely superseded by vol. ii of R. Wellek's *A History of Modern Criticism: 1750–1950 (The Romantic Age*, 1955). W. J. Bate's *From Classic to Romantic: Premises of Taste in Eighteenth-Century England*, Harvard, 1946, is a penetrating examination of critical development in the previous century. W. K. Wimsatt and Cleanth Brooks, *Literary Criticism: A Short History*, 1957, has intelligent discussions, while *The Mirror and the Lamp: Romantic Theory and the Critical Tradition*, by M. H. Abrams, New York, 1953, is outstanding. See also A. E. Powell's *The Romantic Theory of Poetry: An examination in the light of Croce's Æsthetic*, 1926; and *English Poetic Theory, 1825–65*, by A. H. Warren, Princeton, 1950. There are brief considerations of some of the critics of the period in W. J. Bate's *Prefaces to Criticism* (paperback 1959, reprinted from *Criticism: The Major Texts*, above) and G. Watson, *The Literary Critics*, 1962 (Penguin). *Dryden & Pope in the Early Nineteenth Century*, by U. Amarasinghe, 1962 is a study in the history of taste.

5. THE DRAMA

The best general account of the drama of the time is *A History of Early Nineteenth Century Drama, 1800–1850*, by Allardyce Nicoll, 2 vols., 1930, rev. ed., one vol., 1955. The second section consists of a Hand-List of Plays. John Genest's *Some Account of the English Stage from 1660 to 1830*, 10 vols., Bath, 1832 (anon.), includes our period. R. W. Lowe's *A Bibliographical Account of English Theatrical Literature*, 1888, is also useful. Background is supplied by *The Reminiscences of Thomas Dibdin*, 2 vols., 1827. For *The Life of Edmund Kean*, by 'Barry Cornwall', 2 vols., 1835, and other biographies of actors the reader is referred to Nicoll. Quotations from the *Life of Gerald Griffin*, 1843, have been given in the text of this *History*. The first chapter of *Thomas Lovell Beddoes*, by H. W. Donner, 1935, gives a clear account of 'Tragedy in the Early Nineteenth Century'. A little information may be gleaned from *Early Victorian Drama (1830–1870)*, by E. Reynolds, 1936, and *The Burlesque Tradition in the English Theatre after 1660*, by V. C. Clinton-Baddeley, 1952. *The Old Drama and the New. An Essay in Re-Valuation*, by William Archer, 1923, is brief and devastating on the early nineteenth century. W. M. Merchant's *Shakespeare and the Artist*, 1959, throws a great deal of light on stage production. In 'English Tragedy: 1819–1823', *PQ* xli (1962) C. J. Stratman discusses some of the bibliographical problems connected with tragedy in this period. For the most intelligent comments on the state of the drama see the letters of Byron and Beddoes and Darley's 'Letters to the Dramatists of the Day'. Hazlitt and Hunt were the best dramatic critics of the time. Also see below under Knowles, Maturin, Sheil, and Horace and James Smith.

6. History, Biography, and Autobiography

Such general Histories of History as H. E. Barnes, *A History of Historical Writing*, Oklahoma, 1937, and J. W. Thompson and B. J. Holm, *A History of Historical Writing*, 2 vols., New York, 1942, have naturally little to say about the (comparatively minor) historians of our period. G. P. Gooch's *History and Historians in the Nineteenth Century*, 1913, has brief treatments of one or two of our men, while T. P. Peardon's *The Transition in English Historical Writing, 1760–1830*, New York, 1933, is of obvious relevance. The reviews of historical works in the *Edinburgh* and *Quarterly* often throw a great deal of light on the interrelations between historical attitudes and the political actualities of the time.

See also under the names of individual historians.

This is not the place to list general studies of biography, though reference may be made to W. H. Dunn, *English Biography*, New York, 1916; A. Maurois, *Aspects of Biography* (Eng. trans. 1929); E. Johnson, *One Mighty Torrent: The Drama of Biography*, New York, 1937 (new ed., New York, 1957); H. Nicolson, *The Development of English Biography*, 1927; and J. A. Garraty, *The Nature of Biography*, New York, 1957. In *Biography as an Art: Selected Criticism, 1560–1960*, 1962, James L. Clifford includes extracts from several writers of this period, including the author of 'the first full-scale book on biography', James Field Stanfield, who published *An Essay on the Study and Composition of Biography* at Sunderland in 1813. Clifford gives a useful list of twentieth-century writings on biography. As he mentions, J. L. Adolphus published a prize essay, on biography, at Oxford in 1818. There is an illuminating article by F. R. Hart, 'Boswell and the Romantics: A Chapter in the History of Biographical Theory', in *ELH* xxvii, 1960.

I. D'Israeli discusses 'self-biography' at several points in his writings, while the Reviews frequently complain about the spate of memoirs and autobiographies. There is a useful list by W. Matthews, *British Autobiographies. An Annotated Bibliography*, Berkeley, *c.* 1957, which comes up to 1950. Most of the general books, such as W. Shumaker's *English Autobiography: Its Emergence, Materials, and Form*, Berkeley, 1954, and R. Pascal's *Design and Truth in Autobiography*, 1960, have no special bearing on our period. Leslie Stephen's essay in *Hours in a Library*, 3rd series, 1879, remains of interest. The present writer has not seen Zaidée Eudora Greene's privately printed *Nineteenth Century Autobiography*, Ithaca, New York, 1933, an abstract of a dissertation.

7. INTEREST IN FOREIGN LITERATURE AND IN EARLIER ENGLISH LITERATURE

The first place to look is in the Reviews and Magazines. Of particular importance are the *Foreign Quarterly Review* (1827–46) and the *Retrospective Review* (1820–8). The list of modern writings below is confined mainly to book-length studies.

For classical literature there is a bibliography of *English Translations from the Greek*, by F. M. K. Foster, New York, 1918. M. L. Clarke's *Greek Studies in England, 1700–1830*, 1945, contains a list of translations in an appendix. J. E. Sandys deals with this period in vol. iii of his *History of Classical Scholarship*, 1908.

See also the section on Education on pp. 494–5 below.

For Philhellenism in this period one may refer to T. Spencer's *Fair Greece Sad Relic: Literary Philhellenism from Shakespeare to Byron*, 1954 (with bibliography); to *The Broken Column: A Study in Romantic Hellenism*, by H. Levin, Cambridge, Mass., 1932; and to *British and American Philhellenes during the War of Greek Independence, 1821–1833*, by D. Dakin, Thessalonika, 1955. See also an article by Virginia Penn, 'Philhellenism in England (1821–1827)', in the *Slavonic Review*, xiv, 1935–6.

A good deal has been written on the Italian influence on English literature at this time. R. Marshall's *Italy in English Literature, 1755–1815*, New York, 1934, leads up to our period. C. P. Brand's *Italy and the English Romantics: The Italianate Fashion in Early Nineteenth-Century England*, 1957, deals fully with the years covered in the present volume. H. W. Rudman's *Italian Nationalism and English Letters: Figures of the Risorgimento and Victorian Men of Letters*, 1940, begins *c.* 1830. All three books have useful bibliographies. P. Toynbee's *Dante in English Literature from Chaucer to Cary*, 2 vols., 1909, is a useful collection of passages with an introduction and notes. H. G. Wright's *Boccaccio in England from Chaucer to Tennyson*, 1957, also contains a great deal that is relevant to our period. There is an important article by R. W. King, 'Italian Influence in English Scholarship', *MLR* xxi, 1926. Reference may also be made to M. C. W. Wicks, *The Italian Exiles in London 1816–1848*, Manchester 1937.

On Foscolo, a central figure, see F. Viglione, *Ugo Foscolo in Inghilterra*, Catania, 1910; and E. R. Vincent, *Ugo Foscolo: An Italian in Regency England*, 1953, and *Byron, Hobhouse and Foscolo: New Documents in the History of a Collaboration*, 1949. Foscolo's *Essays on Petrarch* were privately printed in 1820 and 1821 and finally published in 1823. F. May has written a number of studies of the history and publication of these *Essays*, notably in the *University of Leeds Review*, viii, 1962, in *The Library* (forthcoming), and in *Italian Studies presented to E. R. Vincent*, 1962. See also his 'Milman and Foscolo', *TLS*, 29 June 1962.

Material relevant to Italian influence may be found under many of the Individual Authors below.

Early works worth mentioning, in addition to those named in the text, include the edition of Boiardo's *Orlando Innamorato* and Ariosto's *Orlando Furioso*, by A. Panizzi, 9 vols., 1830–4 (including an essay on the romantic narrative poetry of the Italians); H. Stebbing's *Lives of the Italian Poets*, 3 vols., 1831; C. Herbert's *Italy and Italian Literature*, 1835; and *Lives of the Most Eminent Literary and Scientific Men of Italy, Spain and Portugal*, 2 vols., 1835.

So much has been written on German influence at this time that only a few of the principal contributions can be mentioned. B. Q. Morgan's *Critical Bibliography of German Literature in English Translation*, 2nd ed., Stanford, 1938, is still of use, though inevitably incomplete; F. W. Stokoe's *German Influence in the English Romantic Period, 1788–1818*, 1926, concentrates on Henry Mackenzie, William Taylor, Crabb Robinson, Scott, Coleridge, Shelley, and Byron and makes virtually no reference to Beddoes. V. Stockley's *German Literature as Known in England, 1750–1830*, 1929, is pedestrian but occasionally useful. H. Shine's introduction to *Carlyle's Unfinished History of German Literature*, Kentucky, 1953, describes the impact of German literature in England up to 1830. There are several important German studies, notably W. F. Schirmer's *Der Einfluß der deutschen Literatur auf die englische im 19. Jahrhundert*, Halle, 1947. See also E. Margraf, *Der Einfluß der deutschen Literatur auf die englische am Ende des 18. und im ersten Drittel des 19. Jahrhunderts*, Leipzig, 1901; and H. Oppel, 'Englische und deutsche Romantik: Gemeinsamkeit und Unterschiede', *Die Neueren Sprachen*, 1956.

R. Wellek deals interestingly with English–German relations in his *History of Modern Criticism*, mentioned above on p. 475. See also his important *Immanuel Kant in England (1793–1838)*, Princeton, 1931. There is a useful book by B. Q. Morgan and A. R. Hohlfeld, *German Literature in British Magazines, 1750–1860*, Madison, Wisconsin, 1949. The influence of English literature on German is outside our scope, but reference may be made to L. M. Price's *English > German Literary Influences: Bibliography and Survey*, Berkeley, 1919–20, 1953.

On Goethe see E. Oswald's bibliography, *Goethe in England and America*, 2nd ed., 1909; J.-M. Carré, *Goethe en Angleterre*, 2 parts, 1920; F. Strich and others, *Goethe and World Literature*, trans. C. A. M. Sym, 1949; W. H. Bruford, 'Goethe's Reputation in England', in *Essays on Goethe*, ed. W. Rose, 1949; L. Baumann, *Die englischen Übersetzungen von Goethes Faust*, Halle, 1907; S. P. Atkins, *The Testament of Werther in Poetry and*

Drama, Cambridge, Mass., 1949; W. F. Hauhart, *The Reception of Goethe's Faust in England in the first half of the Nineteenth Century*, New York, 1909; and E. M. Butler, *The Fortunes of Faust*, 1952. For E. M. Butler's *Byron and Goethe*, see p. 514 below.

R. Pick's *Schiller in England* (Institute of Germanic Languages and Literatures) is a bibliography of publications 'by, of or about Schiller in English books and periodicals from 1787 to 1960'. It has a useful introduction.

See also C. A. Weber, *Bristols Bedeutung für die englische Romantik und die deutsch-englischen Beziehungen*, Halle, 1935; Sir Leslie Stephen, 'The Importation of German', in *Studies of a Biographer*, vol. ii, 1898; and A. C. Bradley, *English Poetry and German Philosophy in the Age of Wordsworth*, 1909, reprinted in *A Miscellany*, 1929.

Information in the text of this *History*, pp. 383–95, is not repeated here. Coleridge belongs to the previous volume, Carlyle to vol. xi. A good deal of information bearing on German influence may also be found under Individual Authors below.

French influence at this time has received little attention. F. Baldensperger, *Le mouvement des idées dans l'émigration française*, 2 vols., 1924, may be consulted. M. E. Elkington, *Les relations de société entre l'Angleterre et la France, 1814–30*, 1929, is also of interest. Books on the influence of the French Revolution in England are mentioned below on p. 488. There is a study by E. Partridge, *The French Romantics' Knowledge of English Literature*, Paris, 1924. M. Moraud's *Le Romantisme français en Angleterre*, 1933, is mainly concerned with the Victorian period. For Stendhal's contributions to English periodicals see p. 472 above. See also *Stendhal et l'Angleterre*, by D. Gunnell, 1909.

Southey is one of the central figures in the story of English interest in Spain and its literature. Reference may be made here to his correspondence, and to his *Letters Written During a Short Residence in Spain and Portugal*, Bristol 1797. Other material is mentioned under Individual Authors: see particularly Bowring, Mrs. Hemans, Lockhart, and Wiffen. See also *Lives of the Most Eminent Literary and Scientific Men of Italy, Spain and Portugal*, 2 vols., 1835. *The Life of the Rev. Joseph Blanco White written by Himself*, ed. J. H. Thom, 3 vols., 1845, is an important document. See also Blanco White's *Letters from Spain*, by 'Don

Leucadio Boblado, 1822; and A. Anaya, *An Essay on Spanish Literature*, 1818.

More detailed information may be found in V. L. Castillo's *Liberales y Románticos*, Mexico, 1954, and an important article by N. Glendinning, 'Spanish Books in England: 1800–1850', in *Transactions of the Cambridge Bibliographical Society*, III. i, 1960. V. Lloréns has an article on 'Colaboraciones de emigrados españoles en revistas inglesas (1824–34)', *Hispanic Review*, xix, 1951.

For Scandinavia see F. E. Farley's *Scandinavian Influence on the English Romantic Movement*, 1903.

For interest in earlier English literature in the period the *Retrospective Review* is of primary importance, as are the letters of Coleridge, Southey, and Lamb. See below under Brydges, Cary, Dibdin, D'Israeli, Dunlop, Gifford, Hazlitt, and Jeffrey. Vol. 3 (1954) of *Phillipps Studies*, by A. N. L. Munby, describes the growth of the library of Sir Thomas Phillipps up to the year 1840. *The Heber Letters, 1783–1832*, ed. R. H. Cholmondeley, 1950, throw light on the activities of another great book-collector. J. P. Collier edited *A Catalogue of Heber's Collection of Early English Poetry* in 1834.

8. Travel

A list of some of the principal travel books of the nineteenth century may be found in *CBEL* iii. 988–93. J. N. L. Baker's *History of Geographical Discovery and Exploration*, 1931, includes this period. J. R. Hale discusses some aspects of Italian travel in his introduction to *The Italian Journal of Samuel Rogers*, 1956; while T. Spencer considers English travellers in Greece in *Fair Greece Sad Relic*, 1954. See also Wallace C. Brown, 'The Popularity of English Travel Books about the Near East, 1775–1825', *PQ*, xv, 1936; 'Byron and English Interest in the Near East', *SP* xxxiv, 1937; and 'English Travel Books, 1775–1825', *PQ* xvi, 1937.

Some descriptions of the English scene by foreign visitors are mentioned below on p. 485.

9. Annuals, and the Reading Public

On the Annuals see *Literary Annuals and Gift Books: A Bibliography with a Descriptive Introduction*, by F. W. Faxon, Boston, 1912. Unfortunately the Index to the Annuals by Andrew

Boyle remained unpublished at his death. A. Bose wrote on 'The Verse of the English "Annuals"' in *RES*, n.s., iv, 1953 (repr. in his *Chroniclers of Life*, Orient Longmans, 1962). Information may also be found in Knight's *Passages of a Working Life*, vol. ii (1864), pp. 53–54, and in many memoirs and collections of letters: see (for example) *Alaric Watts: A Narrative of his Life*, by A. A. Watts, 2 vols., 1884, and *The Literary Life and Correspondence of the Countess of Blessington*, ed. R. R. Madden, 3 vols., 1855. Numerous references to the Annuals may be found in the two books by Sadleir mentioned on p. 474. There are two modern volumes of selections: *The Annual: Being a Selection from the Forget-Me-Nots, Keepsakes, and Other Annuals*, ed. Dorothy Wellesley, with an introduction by V. Sackville-West, London, n.d.; and *A Cabinet of Gems*, ed. B. A. Booth, Berkeley, 1938, a collection of short stories from *The Keepsake* and its competitors.

On the Reading Public R. D. Altick's excellent study, *The English Common Reader: A Social History of the Mass Reading Public, 1800–1900*, Chicago, 1957, may be supplemented by R. K. Webb's *The British Working Class Reader, 1790–1848: Literacy and Social Tension*, 1955. On the 'dainty delicacy' of the time one may consult M. J. Quinlan, *Victorian Prelude*, New York, 1941, and *Pamela's Daughters*, by R. P. Utter and Gwendolyn B. Needham, 1937. O. Maurer's article, 'My Squeamish Public', in *Studies in Bibliography*, Charlottesville, Virginia, 1958, like other articles on the subject elsewhere, is concerned with the Victorian period. The development of squeamishness earlier in the century calls for further investigation.

10. THE PROFESSION OF LETTERS AND THE PUBLISHING TRADE

There is no need to repeat the names of the primary sources referred to in the first and last chapters of this book. The only account of writing as a career at this time, *The Profession of Letters: A Study of the Relation of Author to Patron, Publisher, and Public, 1780–1832*, 1928, by A. S. Collins, needs to be revised or superseded.

A standard work on the book trade is F. A. Mumby's *Publishing and Bookselling: A History from the Earliest Times to the Present Day*, 4th ed., 1956, which contains a useful bibliography. G. Pollard dealt briefly with this period in his unpublished Sandars Lectures for 1959, 'The English Market for Printed

Books'. I am indebted to Dr. A. N. L. Munby for an opportunity of reading these lectures in typescript. It is to be hoped
that Mr. Pollard will soon produce a book on the subject.

A great deal of information is to be found in the histories of
the publishing houses of Constable, Murray, and Blackwood
listed above on p. 471. To these we may add E. Blunden's
admirable study, *Keats's Publisher: A Memoir of John Taylor
(1781–1864)*, 1936; R. A. Gettmann's *A Victorian Publisher: A
Study of the Bentley Papers*, 1960; *The Publishing Firm of Cadell &
Davies: Select Correspondence and Accounts, 1793–1836*, ed. T. Bester-
man, 1938, a valuable collection of material with a helpful
introduction; *Edward Moxon, Publisher of Poets*, by H. G. Merriam, New York, 1939; *The House of Collins*, by D. Keir, 1952,
which is sketchy on our period; and a very brief study, *The
House of Longman, 1724–1924*, 1925, by H. Cox and J. E. Chandler
(privately printed).

An important book, frequently cited in the text, is *Passages
of a Working Life*, by Charles Knight, 3 vols., 1864–5. See also
Reminiscences of Literary London, by T. Rees and J. Britton, 1853
(privately printed, rev. ed., New York, 1896), 1896. The bibliographies by Sadleir and Dorothy Blakey listed above on p. 473
contain a great deal of information. There is also an interesting
article by G. Barber, 'Galignani's and the Publication of English
Books in France from 1800 to 1852', in *The Library*, 1961.

V. The Background of Literature

This section comprises: (1) Political and Social History, and
Political Thought; (2) Contemporary Autobiographies, Memoirs, and Letters; (3) Religion and Moral Attitudes; (4) Science
and Technology; (5) Education; and (6) Architecture, Painting,
and Music.

1. Political and Social History, and Political Thought

Useful bibliographical guidance may be found in *Reaction
and Revolution 1814–1832*, by F. B. Artz, New York, 1934, rev.
ed. 1945 (a vol. in the series *The Rise of Modern Europe*, ed.
W. L. Langer). Artz's book may be supplemented by G. Weill,
L'éveil des nationalités et le mouvement libéral, 1815–48, 1930 (in the
series *Peuples et civilisations*, vol. xv). Another valuable work is

A. Stern's *Geschichte Europas seit den Verträgen von 1815 bis zum Frankfurter Frieden von 1871*, new ed., 10 vols., Stuttgart, 1913–28. E. J. Hobsbawm's study, *The Age of Revolution: Europe 1789–1848*, 1962, covers this period, as will vol. ix of the *New Cambridge Modern History*.

The *Annual Register* gives an account of the main events of each year. Documents may be found in *English Historical Documents, 1783–1832*, ed. A. Aspinall and E. A. Smith, 1959, and in two smaller collections: *Britain and Europe: Pitt to Churchill, 1793–1940*, ed. J. Joll, 1950, and *The English Radical Tradition, 1763–1914*, ed. S. MacCoby, 1952 (both in *The British Political Tradition Series*, ed. A. Bullock and F. W. Deakin).

Much the best account of English history at this time is still Élie Halévy's *Histoire du peuple anglais au XIXᵉ siècle*, which appeared in French between 1912 and 1932. The relevant volumes of the English translation are *England in 1815*, 1924, *The Liberal Awakening 1815–1830*, 1926, and *The Triumph of Reform 1830–1841*, 1927 (revised editions, 1949–50).

The History of England (1801–1837), by G. C. Brodrick and J. K. Fotheringham, new impression, 1911 (vol. xi of *The Political History of England*, ed. W. Hunt and R. L. Poole), is still useful on account of its lucid narrative and the annalistic arrangement of the Table of Contents. An authoritative and up-to-date book is *The Age of Reform, 1815–1870*, by Sir Llewellyn Woodward, 2nd ed., 1962 (vol. xiii of the *Oxford History of England*).

Other books of interest to the student of literature include: *British History in the Nineteenth Century (1782–1901)*, by G. M. Trevelyan, 1922; the same author's *English Social History . . . Chaucer to Queen Victoria*, 1942 (in the illustrated edition our period is covered in vol. iv, 1952); *The Age of Improvement*, by A. Briggs, 1959 (vol. viii in *A History of England*, ed. W. N. Medlicott: covers the years 1780–1867); *The First Four Georges*, by J. H. Plumb, 1956; *The Age of Elegance, 1812–1822*, by Sir Arthur Bryant, 1950; R. J. White, *From Waterloo to Peterloo*, 1957, an agreeable sketch of social transition; O. MacDonagh, *A Pattern of Government Growth*, 1961; F. O. Darvall, *Popular Disturbances and Public Order in Regency England*, 1934; and G. Kitson Clark, *The Making of Victorian England*, 1962.

A small but interesting category of writings includes real and supposed travel books by visitors to England about this time.

Southey's *Letters from England* ('By Don Manuel Alvarez Espriella') were published in 1807; while in *Peter's Letters to his Kinsfolk*, 3 vols., 1819, Lockhart mixed fiction with fact to give a striking picture of Edinburgh. Genuine travel-books include Louis Simond's anonymous *Journal of a Tour and Residence in Great Britain, during the Years 1810 and 1811, by a French Traveller*, 2 vols., 1815; A. Pichot's anonymous *Voyage historique et littéraire en Angleterre et en Écosse*, 3 vols., 1825 (Eng. trans., 2 vols., the same year); *Erik Gustaf Geijer: Impressions of England, 1809–1810: Compiled from his Letters and Diaries* by Anton Blanck, translated from the Swedish, 1932; and Prince Pückler-Muskau's *Tour in England*, 4 vols., 1832 (selections ed. E. M. Butler as *A Regency Visitor*, 1957).

Satirical accounts of Edinburgh and London are given in two books published anonymously by Robert Mudie in 1825: *The Modern Athens: A Dissection and Demonstration of Men and Things in the Scotch Capital. By a Modern Greek*; and *Babylon the Great: A Dissection and Demonstration of Men and Things in the British Capital*, 2 vols. (vol. ii contains seven chapters on the Press).

Of particular importance are the studies by J. L. and Barbara Hammond: *The Skilled Labourer, 1760–1832*, 1919; *The Town Labourer, 1760–1832*, 1917; *The Village Labourer, 1760–1832*, 1911; and *The Rise of Modern Industry*, 1925. Their *The Age of the Chartists, 1832–1854*, 1930, like other books on Chartism, also throws light on our period, as does *The Bleak Age*, 2nd ed., 1947, which is based on it. See also *A History of the English Agricultural Labourer*, by W. Hasbach, 2nd impr., 1909 (German ed., 1894), and two shorter studies by J. L. Hammond, 'The Industrial Revolution and Discontent', *Economic History*, ii, no. 2, and *The Growth of Common Enjoyment*, 1933.

Dorothy George's *England in Transition*, 1931 (rev. ed., Penguin Books, 1953), helps to explain how England in 1815 came to be what it was. *Early Victorian England, 1830–1865*, ed. G. M. Young, 2 vols., 1934, throws a great deal of light on what had happened by 1832, as does his *Victorian England: Portrait of an Age*, 1936. *Culture and Society 1780–1950*, by Raymond Williams, 1958, is 'an account and an interpretation of our responses in thought and feeling to changes in English Society'. On the Reform Bill one may consult G. M. Trevelyan, *Lord Grey of the Reform Bill*, 2nd ed., 1929; H. W. C. Davis, *The Age of Grey and Peel*, 1929; J. R. M. Butler, *The Passing of the Great*

Reform Bill, 1914; and G. Milner, *The Threshold of the Victorian Age*, 1934.

Of the numerous modern studies of the statesmen of the period very few can be mentioned here: *William Huskisson and Liberal Reform*, by A. Brady, 1928; *The Patriot King* (William IV), by G. E. Thompson, 1932; *The Divorce Case of Queen Caroline*, by W. D. Bowman, 1930 (a popular account); *The Rise of Castlereagh*, by H. M. Hyde, 1933; *The Foreign Policy of Castlereagh, 1815–1822*, by C. K. Webster, 2nd ed., 1934; *The Foreign Policy of Canning, 1822–1827*, by H. W. V. Temperley, 1925; *The Monroe Doctrine, 1823–6*, by D. Perkins, Cambridge, Mass., 1927; *Mr. Secretary Peel*, by N. Gash (1961); *Lord Liverpool and Liberal Toryism, 1820–7*, by W. R. Brock, 1941; *Lord Brougham and the Whig Party*, by A. Aspinall, Manchester, 1927; and *Radical Jack: The Life of John George Lambton, first Earl of Durham*, by L. Cooper, 1959. In *Sketches in Nineteenth Century Biography*, 1930, K. Feiling deals incisively and wittily with Pitt, Liverpool, Canning, Croker, Southey and Wordsworth, Coleridge, Newman, Bulwer Lytton, and others.

Apart from the work of the Hammonds, already mentioned, there are the following important studies of the working classes, trade unionism, and allied subjects: *Some Working Class Movements of the Nineteenth Century*, by R. F. Wearmouth, 1948; *The Early English Trade Unions: Documents*, ed. A. Aspinall, 1949; *Agricultural Depression and Farm Relief in England, 1813–52*, by L. P. Adams, 1932; Sidney and Beatrice Webb, *The History of Trade Unionism*, rev. ed., 1920; *A Short History of the British Working Class Movement, 1789–1947*, by G. D. H. Cole, rev. ed., 1948; the same author's *Attempts at General Union . . ., 1818–1834*, 1953; *A History of Factory Legislation*, by B. L. Hutchins and A. Harrison, 3rd ed., 1926; and 'The Combination Laws Reconsidered', by M. D. George, *Economic Journal* (Economic Series i, 1927).

The Life of Francis Place, 1771–1854, by G. Wallas, rev. ed., 1918, throws a great deal of light on the first half of the nineteenth century.

The first volume of J. H. Clapham's *Economic History of Modern Britain: The Early Railway Age, 1820–1850*, 1926, 2nd ed., 1930, is an authoritative work. There is an excellent survey of writings on the Industrial Revolution by T. S. Ashton in the *Economic History Review* for Oct. 1934 (vol. v, no. 1), which may be supplemented by J. U. Nef's article in the *Journal of Economic History* for 1943 and by 'Progress and Poverty in Britain, 1750–1850: A Reappraisal', by A. J. Taylor, in *History*, vol. xlv, no. 153 (February 1960). *The Industrial Revolution in the Eighteenth Century*, by P. Mantoux (Fr. ed., 1906), rev. ed. trans. into English 1928, remains an admirable study. T. S. Ashton's *The Industrial Revolution, 1760–1830*, 1948 (Home University Library) is a good brief survey. See also *The Industrial Revolution and the World of To-day*, by L. W. White and E. W. Shanahan, 1932; *English Apprenticeship and Child Labour*, by O. J. Dunlop, 1912; *Health, Wealth, and Population in the Early Days of the Industrial Revolution*, by M. C. Buer, 1926; 'The Population Problem during the Industrial Revolution', by T. H. Marshall, in *Economic History*, vol. i, no. 4 (a powerful criticism of G. Talbot Griffith's *Population Problems of the Age of Malthus*, 1926); W. W. Rostow, *British Economy of the Nineteenth Century*, 1948; *The Malthusian Controversy*, by K. Smith, 1951; E. C. K. Gonner, *Common Land and Inclosure*, 1912; L. C. A. Knowles, *The Industrial and Commercial Revolutions in Great Britain during the Nineteenth Century*, rev. ed., 1924; C. R. Fay, *Life and Labour in the Nineteenth Century*, 1920; and Sir John Clapham, *The Bank of England*, 1944. A great deal of information may be found in the recent histories of Birmingham, Brighton, and Manchester by C. Gill, E. W. Gilbert, and A. Redford respectively.

Special mention must be made of *The Works and Correspondence of David Ricardo*, ed. P. Sraffa with M. H. Dobb, 10 vols., 1951–5, an important collection admirably edited.

A further group of books on particular topics sufficiently indicated by their titles may be listed here: D. G. Barnes, *A History of the English Corn Laws, 1660–1846*, 1930; C. R. Fay, *The Corn Laws and Social England*, 1932; D. R. Gwynn, *The Struggle for Catholic Emancipation, 1750–1829*, 1928; R. Coupland, *The British Anti-Slavery Movement*, 1933; C. W. Crawley, *The Question of Greek Independence: A Study of British Policy in the Near East, 1821–1833*, 1930; C. H. Philips, *The East India Company, 1784–1834*, Manchester, 1940; K. Feiling, *The Second Tory Party: 1714–1832*, 1938; *Britain and the Independence of Latin America, 1812–30: Select Documents*, ed. C. K. Webster, 2 vols., 1938; F. A. Bruton, *Three Accounts of Peterloo by Eyewitnesses*, Manchester, 1921; W. W. Kaufmann, *British Policy and the Independence of Latin America, 1804–28*, New Haven, 1951; D. M. Young, *The Colonial Office in the Early*

Nineteenth Century, 1961; A. S. Turberville, *The House of Lords in the Age of Reform, 1784–1837*, 1958; *Lectures on the Relation between Law & Public Opinion in England during the Nineteenth Century*, by A. V. Dicey, 1905 (rev. ed., 1962); and the *History of the Athenæum* [Club], *1824–1925*, by Humphry Ward, 1926. C. W. Cunnington's *English Women's Clothing in the Nineteenth Century*, 1956, also throws light on the period, as does a study he has written with Phillis Cunnington, *Handbook of English Costume in the Nineteenth Century*, 1959. *English Political Caricature, 1793–1832: A Study of Opinion and Propaganda*, by M. Dorothy George, 1959, throws an amusing light on the social life of the time, and includes a useful Index of Artists. Vols. vii–xi of the same author's *Catalogue of Political and Personal Satires*, 1942–54, cover the corresponding period. The studies by Michael Sadleir mentioned on p. 474 above are of interest to the social historian.

Two books by E. W. Bovill, *The England of Nimrod and Surtees, 1815–1854* (1959), and *English Country Life, 1780–1830* (1962), give an agreeable picture of life outside the towns.

A great deal has been written on the influence of the French Revolution on English literature. Mention may be made of *The French Revolution and English Literature*, by E. Dowden, 1897; *The French Revolution and the English Poets*, by A. E. Hancock, New York, 1899; *La révolution française et les poètes anglais (1789–1809)*, by C. Cestre, 1906; *The French Revolution and the English Novel*, by Allene Gregory, New York 1915.

C. E. Vaughan's *Studies in the History of Political Philosophy*, ed. A. G. Little, 2 vols., Manchester, 1925, contains material relevant to the early nineteenth century. C. C. Brinton's *English Political Thought in the Nineteenth Century*, 1933, suffers from over-simplification, as does his earlier *The Political Ideas of the English Romanticists*, 1926. On Socialist thought see H. L. Beales, *The Early English Socialists*, 1933; H. W. Laidler, *A History of Socialist Thought*, 1927; S. MacCoby, *English Radicalism, 1786–1832*, 1955; and G. D. H. Cole's *History of Socialist Thought*, i, 1953.

A whole library of books has been devoted to the Utilitarians. The *Autobiography* of John Stuart Mill, 1873, remains of primary importance: there have been various editions, while J. Stillinger published *The Early Draft of John Stuart Mill's 'Autobiography'* in 1961 (Urbana, Illinois). The outstanding secondary books are *The English Utilitarians*, by Leslie Stephen, 3 vols., 1900; and *La formation du radicalisme philosophique*, by Élie Halévy, Paris, 1901–4,

Eng. trans. as *The Growth of Philosophic Radicalism*, 1928. See also *Mill's Utilitarianism reprinted with a study of the English Utilitarians*, by J. Plamenatz, 1949. A briefer account is that of W. L. Davidson: *Political Thought in England: The Utilitarians from Bentham to Mill*, 1915 (Home University Library). E. Stokes, *The English Utilitarians and India*, 1959, is of great interest.

The importance of writers dealt with in other volumes hardly needs to be stressed, but one or two secondary books should perhaps be mentioned here: A. V. Dicey, *The Statesmanship of Wordsworth*, 1917; *Robert Southey and his Age: The Development of a Conservative Mind*, by G. Carnall, 1960; R. K. Webb, *Harriet Martineau: A Radical Victorian*, 1960; *Political Thought of S. T. Coleridge*, ed. R. J. White, 1938; and *Coleridge: Critic of Society*, by J. Colmer, 1959.

There are several collections of political pamphlets which include this period: see, for example, *From the French Revolution to the Nineteen-Thirties*, ed. R. Reynolds, 1951 (*British Pamphleteers*, ii), and *Political Tracts of Wordsworth, Coleridge and Shelley*, ed. R. J. White, Cambridge, 1953.

For Scottish history see G. S. Pryde, *Scotland from 1603 to the Present Day*, 1962; Agnes Mure Mackenzie, *Scotland in Modern Times, 1720–1939*, 1941; L. J. Saunders, *Scottish Democracy, 1815–40: the Social and Intellectual Background*, 1950; and G. E. Davie, *The Democratic Intellect* (p. 495 below).

Three interesting books on Ireland are D. Gwynn, *Daniel O'Connell, the Irish Liberator*, rev. ed., Cork, 1947; J. E. Pomfret, *The Struggle for Land in Ireland, 1800–1923*, Princeton, 1930; and W. F. Adams, *Ireland and Irish Emigration to the New World, from 1815 to the Famine*, New Haven, 1932.

For Welsh history see D. Williams, *A History of Modern Wales, 1485–1939*, 1950.

2. CONTEMPORARY AUTOBIOGRAPHIES, MEMOIRS, AND LETTERS

Material relating to Wordsworth, Coleridge, Southey, Jane Austen, Campbell, and Rogers, on the one hand, and to Harriet Martineau, Macaulay, Carlyle, Dickens, and Bulwer Lytton on the other, must be sought in other volumes. Fuller lists of letters, diaries, and autobiographies may be found in *CBEL* iii. 14–17 and 149–55, and v. 522 and 546–7.

For the details of 'who's in, who's out' at Court we may consult *The Greville Memoirs*, by Charles Greville, Clerk to the Privy Council. The first part, which covers our period, appeared in 3 vols., ed. H. Reeve, in 1874. The most recent edition of the *Memoirs* as a whole is that of Lytton Strachey and R. Fulford, 8 vols., 1938. There is a volume of selections edited by C. Lloyd, 1948. Other memoirs throwing light on the life of the Court and aristocracy include the third series of the *Despatches, Correspondence, and Memoranda of the Duke of Wellington*, ed. by his son, 8 vols., 1867–80. The *Memoirs and Correspondence* of Castlereagh were edited by C. W. Stewart in 12 vols. in 1848–53. *The Early Correspondence of Lord John Russell*, ed. R. Russell, 2 vols., 1913, covers the years 1805–40. See also Lady Charlotte Bury's *Diary Illustrative of the Times of George IV*, 2 vols., 1838 (ed. A. F. Steuart, 2 vols., 1908); *The Public and Private Life of John Scott (Earl of Eldon)*, by H. Twiss, 3 vols., 1844 (but also the anonymous *Life, political and official, of John, Earl of Eldon*, 1827, which is sometimes more illuminating); *Life and Correspondence of Henry Addington (Lord Sidmouth)*, ed. G. Pellew, 3 vols., 1847; *Memoirs of the Life of Sir Samuel Romilly, Written by Himself*, ed. by his sons, 3 vols., 1840; *The Creevey Papers*, ed. Sir H. Maxwell, 2 vols., 1903, and *Creevey's Life and Times*, ed. J. Gore, 1934; *The Jerningham Letters (1780–1843)*, ed. E. Castle, 2 vols., 1896; and *The Life of Henry John Temple, Viscount Palmerston*, ed. Sir H. Lytton Bulwer and A. E. M. Ashley, 5 vols., 1871–6 (revised and abridged, 2 vols., 1879).

For the Holland House circle, which was of great importance to literature at this time, see Sydney Smith under Individual Authors and also *The Holland House Circle*, by L. Sanders, 1908; *Holland House*, by Princess Marie Liechtenstein, 2 vols., 1874 (a Victorian conducted tour, with anecdotes); *The 'Pope' of Holland House*, ed. Lady Seymour, 1906; *The Home of the Hollands 1605–1820* and *Chronicles of Holland House 1820–1900*, both by the Earl of Ilchester and both published in 1937; *Lord Melbourne's Papers*, ed. L. C. Sanders, 1889; *Lady Bessborough and her Family Circle*, ed. Earl of Bessborough and A. Aspinall, 1940; *The Journal of the Hon. Henry Edward Fox* [later Lord Holland] *1818–1830*, ed. the Earl of Ilchester, 1923; *Elizabeth, Lady Holland to her Son* (letters, 1821–45), ed. the Earl of Ilchester, 1946; C. and F. Brookfield, *Mrs. Brookfield and her Circle*, 1905; and two books by Lord David Cecil, *The Young Melbourne*, 1939, and *Lord M.*, 1954.

Other contemporary records include *Three Early Nineteenth Century Diaries* (by Sir D. Le Marchant, E. J. Littleton, and Lord Ellenborough), ed. A. Aspinall, 1952; *The Correspondence of Charles Arbuthnot*, ed. A. Aspinall (Camden Society, 3rd series, lxv, 1941); *The Journal of Harriet Arbuthnot* [*née* Fane], *1820–1832*, ed. F. Bamford and the Duke of Wellington, 2 vols., 1950; *The Heber Letters, 1783–1832*, ed. R. H. Cholmondeley, 1950; *The Remains of Henry Angelo*, 2 vols., 1830 (reprinted, 2 vols., 1904); *Reminiscences of the University, Town and County of Cambridge from the Year 1780*, by Henry Gunning, 2 vols., 1854–5; the auto-biographies of Samuel Roberts (1849), Ann Taylor (later Gilbert, 1874), and Eliza Fletcher (1875); and the scandalous *Memoirs* of Harriette Wilson, 1825 (ed. J. Laver, 1929).

Books by men near the bottom of the social scale include *Passages in the Life of a Radical*, by S. Bamford, 2 vols., 1844 (ed. H. Dunckley, 2 vols., 1893); *The Autobiography of an Artisan*, by Christopher Thomson, 1847; *The Autobiography of a Working Man* [by Alexander Somerville], 1848 (abridged ed. by J. Carswell, 1951); *The Life of Robert Owen, Written by Himself*, 1857; *The Life and Struggles of William Lovett*, 1876 (ed. R. H. Tawney, 2 vols., 1920); and *Memoirs of a Working Man* [by T. Carter], ed. C. Knight, 1845 (followed by a *Continuation* in 1850).

Charles Knight's *Passages of a Working Life*, 3 vols., 1864–5, has already been mentioned elsewhere. Other memoirs by people more or less closely connected with literature include P. G. Patmore's important book, *My Friends and Acquaintances*, 3 vols., 1855; Lady Morgan's *Memoirs: Autobiography, Diaries and Correspondence*, ed. W. H. Dixon, 2 vols., 1862; *The Life and Correspondence of John Foster*, ed. J. E. Ryland, 2 vols., 1846; *Recollections of Literary Characters and Celebrated Places*, by Mrs. Thomson ('Grace Wharton'), 2 vols., 1854; *Fifty Years' Recollections, Literary and Personal*, 3 vols., 1858, and *Past Celebrities Whom I Have Known*, 2 vols., 1866, by C. Redding; *Letters of Sir James Stephen*, ed. by his daughter, 1906 (Gloucester, priv. prtd.); *Autobiographical Recollections*, by C. R. Leslie, ed. T. Taylor, Boston, 1860; *A Book of Memories*, 1871, and *Retrospect of a Long Life*, 2 vols., 1883, by S. C. Hall; *Memoir of the Rev. Francis Hodgson* (the friend of Byron), ed. J. T. Hodgson, 2 vols., 1878; *Reminiscences of Thomas John Dibdin*, 2 vols., 1827; *Records of my Life*, by John Taylor (1757–1832), 2 vols., 1832; *Memoirs of Lady Hester Lucy Stanhope*, ed. C. L. Meryon, 1845; *Remains of Richard Hurrell Froude*, 4 vols., ed. J. Keble, J. H. Newman, and J. B. Mozley, 1838–9; *Diary of Henry Hobhouse, 1820–1827*, ed. A. Aspinall, 1947; *Harriet Martineau's Autobiography*, ed. Maria Weston Chapman, 3 vols., 1877; *The Life of Joseph Blanco White, Written by Himself*, ed. J. H. Thom, 3 vols., 1845; *Extracts of the Journals and Correspondence of Miss* [Mary] *Berry*, . . . *1783–1852*, ed. Lady T. Lewis, 3 vols., 1865; and, of course, the *Diary and Letters of Madame d'Arblay* (*née* Burney), ed. C. Barrett, rev. A. Dobson, 6 vols., 1904–5.

Memoirs from Scotland include *Memorials of his Time*, by Henry Thomas, Lord Cockburn, Edinburgh, 1856; *Memoir and Correspondence of Mrs. Grant of Laggan*, ed. J. P. Grant, 3 vols., 1844; *Letters from and to Charles Kirkpatrick Sharpe*, ed. A. Allardyce, with a Memoir by W. K. R. Bedford, 2 vols., 1888; *Reminiscences of Scottish Life and Character*, by E. B. Ramsay, 1858; and *Parties and Pleasures: The Diaries of Helen Graham, 1823–26*, ed. J. Irvine, 1957.

Three of the Americans who left a record of their impressions of England at this time were Washington Irving, whose *Life and Letters* was ed. by P. M. Irving in 4 vols. in 1862–4 (New York); G. Ticknor, whose *Life, Letters, and Journals*, 2 vols., 1876 (2nd ed.), contain useful information about publishing and other matters; and N. P. Willis, whose *Pencillings by the Way*, 3 vols., 1836 (rev. ed. 1852) and *Famous Persons and Famous Places*, New York, 1854, are also of interest (on Willis see 'G. Paston', *Little Memoirs of the Nineteenth Century*, 1902).

3. Religion and Moral Attitudes

The standard history of the Church at this time is F. Warre Cornish's *The English Church in the Nineteenth Century*, two parts, 1910; J. H. Overton's *The English Church in the Nineteenth Century, 1800–1833*, 1894, is important for the old High Church party; S. C. Carpenter's *Church and People, 1789–1889*, 1933, is a good popular outline. We may also consult *The Church in an Age of Revolution, 1789 to the Present Day*, by A. R. Vidler, 1961, and *The Development of English Theology in the Nineteenth Century, 1800–1860*, by V. F. Storr. Vol. iii of *Worship and Theology in England*, by Horton Davies, 1962, covers the period 'From Watts and Wesley to Maurice, 1690–1850'. G. S. R. Kitson Clark's *The English Inheritance*, 1950, considers the general influence of religion in nineteenth-century England. W. L. Mathieson's *English Church*

Reform, 1815–1840, 1923, covers an important topic (see also the same writer's *Church and Reform in Scotland, 1797–1843*). Thomas Arnold's *Principles of Church Reform,* 1833 (reprinted in his *Miscellaneous Works,* 1845), has recently been reprinted again (1962). Book III of Bulwer Lytton's *England and the English,* 1833, considers 'the general influences of morality and religion in England'. In 'The Whigs and the Church Establishment in the Age of Grey and Holland', *History,* vol. xlv, no. 154 (June 1960), G. F. A. Best discusses the Tory claim that the Whigs were hostile to the Church of England. There is a useful bibliographical article by Canon C. Smyth in the *Cambridge Historical Journal,* vol. vii, 1943 ('The Evangelical Movement in Perspective'). J. P. Whitney's *Bibliography of Church History* (Historical Association Leaflet lv, 1923) is useful so far as it goes. Father Hugh's *Nineteenth Century Pamphlets at Pusey House* (Faith Press, Oxford), lists 18,500 pamphlets of religious interest.

On Methodism we may consult R. F. Wearmouth, *Methodism and the History of Working Class Movements of England, 1800–1850,* 1937; M. L. Edwards, *After Wesley: A Study of the Influence of Methodism, 1791–1849,* 1943; J. F. Hurst, *The History of Methodism,* 3 vols., 1901; W. J. Townsend and others, *A New History of Methodism,* 2 vols., 1909; W. J. Warner, *The Wesleyan Movement in the Industrial Revolution,* 1930; and F. C. Gill, *The Romantic Movement and Methodism,* 1937.

Ford K. Brown's *Fathers of the Victorians: The Age of Wilberforce,* 1961, deals interestingly with the Evangelicals; see also L. E. Binns [Elliott-Binns], *The Evangelical Movement in the English Church,* 1928; J. Venn, *Annals of a Clerical Family,* 1904; E. Stock, *A History of the Church Missionary Society,* 3 vols., 1899; R. G. Cowherd, *The Politics of English Dissent,* 1959; and F. E. Mineka, *The Dissidence of Dissent: 'The Monthly Repository', 1806–1838,* Chapel Hill, 1944 (a useful study). Olive Brose's *Church and Parliament,* 1959, should also be mentioned.

There is no need to emphasize the historical importance of *The Letters and Diaries of John Henry Newman,* ed. by C. S. Dessain (in progress), of which the first volumes will be relevant to our period.

Many books bear on the history of the Quakers at this time. See, for example, *Mary Howitt: An Autobiography,* ed. Margaret Howitt, 2 vols., 1889; Amice Lee, *Laurels and Rosemary: The Life of William and Mary Howitt,* 1955; *Memoir of Elizabeth Fry, ed. by two of her daughters*, 2 vols., 1847; *A Quaker Journal* (by William Lucas), ed. G. E. Bryant and G. P. Baker, 2 vols., 1834; and Bernard Barton under Individual Authors.

Basil Willey's *Nineteenth Century Studies*, 1949, concentrates on the thought of the Victorian Age, but also throws light on the earlier age. The most ambitious attempt to deal with the religious views of the poets of the period is vol. iii of Hoxie N. Fairchild's *Religious Trends in English Poetry (Romantic Faith)*, New York, 1949.

4. SCIENCE AND TECHNOLOGY

There is a good general *History of Science*, by J. D. Dampier, 3rd ed., New York, 1942. One may also consult F. Albèrgamo, *La critica della scienza nel novecento*, Florence, 1941, and *A Short History of Science in the Nineteenth Century*, by C. Singer, 1941. *The Edge of Objectivity*, by C. C. Gillispie, Princeton 1960, is an outstanding history of scientific thought which throws light on our period. There are two useful books on chemistry: *The Chemical Industry during the Nineteenth Century*, by L. F. Haber, 1958, and *The Chemical Revolution*, by A. and N. L. Clow, 1952.

There is a *History of Technology*, ed. C. Singer, E. J. Holmyard, A. R. Hall, and T. I. Williams. Vol. 4 covers the early nineteenth century. A. P. Usher's *History of Mechanical Inventions*, 1929, may also be consulted, as may *Kulturgeschichte der Technik*, by F. Feldhaus, 2 vols., Berlin, 1928–30. H. J. Habakkuk's *American and British Technology in the Nineteenth Century*, 1962, deals with difficult economic and historical problems and rewards the reader who is prepared to follow rigorous reasoning. Two studies by Samuel Smiles are still of interest: *Lives of the Engineers*, 3 vols., 1861–2, and *Industrial Biography: Iron Workers and Tool Makers*, 1863. Other writings on technology are listed in the article by T. S. Ashton referred to on p. 486 above.

E. Nordenskiöld's *History of Biology*, New York 1928, is still the best general account of the subject. A good deal has recently been written on the history of the concept of evolution. L. Eiseley's book, *Darwin's Century: Evolution and the Men Who Discovered It*, 1960, is an excellent survey of evolutionary biology in the nineteenth century. *Forerunners of Darwin, 1745–1859*, ed. B. Glass and others, 1959, contains essays by members of the Johns Hopkins History of Ideas Club.

5. EDUCATION

J. W. Adamson's *English Education, 1789–1902*, 1930, is sound in itself and useful for its bibliography. See also S. J. Curtis, *History of Education in Great Britain*, rev. ed. 1957; E. H. Reisner, *Nationalism and Education since 1789*, New York, 1922; and R. L. Archer, *Secondary Education in the Nineteenth Century*, 1921 (useful bibliographies). In general, histories of universities and schools cannot be included here, but exception must be made for A. P. Stanley's *Life and Correspondence of Thomas Arnold*, 2 vols., 1844; G. A. T. Allen, *Christ's Hospital*, 1937; E. Blunden, *Christ's Hospital: A Retrospect* [1923]; Sir C. E. Mallet, *A History of the University of Oxford*, vol. 3, 1927; D. A. Winstanley, *Early Victorian Cambridge*, 1940; Sir G. C. Faber, *Jowett*, 1957; and H. H. Bellot, *University College, London, 1826–1926*, 1929. T. Kelly's *History of Adult Education in Great Britain*, Liverpool, 1962, may also be consulted.

For classical studies see J. E. Sandys, *A History of Classical Scholarship*, vol. iii, 1908, and M. L. Clarke, *Greek Studies in England 1700–1830*, Cambridge, 1945. *The Democratic Intellect*, by G. E. Davie, 1961, throws light on the different educational traditions of Scotland and England.

6. ARCHITECTURE, PAINTING, AND MUSIC

On the architecture of the period one may consult *Architecture in Britain, 1530 to 1830*, by (Sir) John Summerson, 1953 (a volume in the *Pelican History of Art*, ed. N. Pevsner). It has a brief bibliography of books relevant to our period. See also *The Regency Style, 1800 to 1830*, by D. Pilcher, 1947; *The Romantic Theories of Architecture of the Nineteenth Century in Germany, England and France*, by R. Bradbury, New York, 1934; *British Architects and Craftsmen: A Survey of Taste, Design, and Style . . . 1600–1830*, by S. Sitwell, 1945.

Modern books on the history of painting include *English Art, 1800–1870*, by T. S. R. Boase, 1959 (vol. x of the *Oxford History of English Art*), with its useful bibliography, and two books by W. T. Whitley, *Art in England 1800–1820*, 1928, and *Art in England 1821–1837*, 1930. *The Gothic Revival*, by (Sir) Kenneth Clark, 1923 (2nd ed., 1950), and *The Picturesque*, by C. Hussey, 1927, are also of some relevance. For M. Dorothy George's *English Political Caricature, 1793–1832* see p. 488 above.

On literature and the visual arts see S. A. Larrabee, *English Bards and Grecian Marbles: The Relationship between Sculpture and Poetry, Especially in the Romantic Period*, New York, 1943; C. B. Tinker, *Painter and Poet*, Princeton, 1939 (Blake, Wilson, Turner, Constable, and others); and E. Blunden, *Romantic Poetry and the Fine Arts* (British Academy Lecture, 1942). *Shakespeare and the Artist*, by W. M. Merchant, 1959, is of particular interest.

The following biographies are outstanding: *Nollekens and his Times: Comprehending Memoirs of Several Artists*, by J. T. Smith, 2 vols., 1828 (ed. Sir E. Gosse, 1894; ed. W. Whitten, 2 vols., 1920; ed. G. W. Stonier, 1949; abridged ed. in World's Classics, 1929); C. R. Leslie, *Memoirs of the Life of John Constable, R.A.*, 1843 (ed. and enlarged by A. Shirley, 1937; ed. J. Mayne, 1951); *Autobiographical Recollections of the Life of C. R. Leslie*, ed. T. Taylor, 1860; *Samuel Palmer's Valley of Vision*, by G. Grigson, 1960. And see below under Ackermann, Bewick, Haydon, Hazlitt, Hunt, Wainewright, and others.

Haydon's *Journals* (listed under Individual Authors) are of particular importance to the student of literature. *The Farington Diary*, ed. J. Greig, 8 vols., 1922–8, throws a great deal of light on the history of art during these years. Fifteen typed volumes of the *Correspondence and Other Memorials of John Constable, R.A.*, compiled by Mr. R. B. Beckett, may be consulted in the Reference Library of the Victoria and Albert Museum. Each volume has a separate index. Mr. Beckett has published *John Constable and the Fishers*, 1952, and *John Constable's Correspondence*, 1962 (mainly family letters to Constable).

E. Walker's *History of Music in England*, 2nd ed., 1924, gives an account of music at this time. The chapter on music in vol. ii of *Early Victorian England*, by E. Dent, begins at 1830. For reference we have the *Oxford Companion to Music*, ed. P. A. Scholes, 9th ed., 1955, and Grove's *Dictionary of Music and Musicians*, 5th ed., ed. E. Blom, 1954.

VI. INDIVIDUAL AUTHORS

RUDOLPH ACKERMAN(N), 1764–1834.

As a publisher Ackermann was responsible for the appearance of a great many works, most of them illustrated, highly characteristic of the period. *The Microcosm of London* came out in 3 vols. in 1808–11. The most interesting of all his publications, *Ackermann's Repositary of Arts, Literature, Commerce, Manufactures, Fashions and Politics*, was published in three series from January 1809 to December 1828. The work contains 1,500 colour plates and is without a rival as a guide to the external appearance of Regency life. Many contributions were afterwards reprinted in other forms. Ackermann's *Poetical Magazine*, in which Combe's 'Dr. Syntax's Tour in search of the Picturesque' first appeared, came out between 1809 and 1811. Ackermann's other publications include *The History of ... Westminster* [Abbey], 2 vols., 1812; *A History of the University of Oxford*, 2 vols., 1814; *A History of the University of Cambridge*, 2 vols., 1815; and *The Colleges of Winchester, Eton, Westminster, &c.*, 1816. From 1823 onwards he published *The Forget-Me-Not* and so set the fashion for Annuals. He also produced a number of notable 'Picturesque Tours'. Rowlandson and Pugin were two of his principal collaborators.

A brief account of Ackermann's career may be found in the *DNB*. See also *NQ*, fourth series, iv, pp. 109, 129; fifth series, vol. ix, p. 346 and vol. x, p. 18; *Didaskalia* (Frankfurt-am-Main), no. 103, 13 April 1864; *Gentleman's Magazine*, 1834, i. 560; and the *Annual Biography* for 1835.

JOHN LEYCESTER ADOLPHUS, 1795–1862.

Adolphus is remembered for his *Letters to Richard Heber, Esq. containing Critical Remarks on the Series of Novels beginning with 'Waverley', and an Attempt to ascertain their Author*, which he published anonymously in 1821. There was a second edition the following year. In 1814 he published an Oxford Prize Poem on 'Niobe', and in 1818 a prize essay on *Biography*. In later life his principal publication was a work entitled *Letters from Spain in 1856 and 1857*, 1858.

Scott admired Adolphus's detective work, and the two men became friends. Adolphus contributed reminiscences to Lockhart's *Memoirs of ... Scott*. Information about Adolphus may be found in contemporary memoirs, in the *DNB*, and in an article by W. F. Gray, 'An Early Critic of Scott', in the *Sir Walter Scott Quarterly*, 1927.

JOHN BANIM, 1798–1842, AND MICHAEL BANIM, 1796–1874.

The following works by the Banim brothers are listed by Sadleir: *The Celt's Paradise: in four Duans*, by John Banim, 1821; *Damon and Pythias: a Tragedy*, 1821; *A Letter to the Committee ...*

[concerning a] *National Testimonial*, by John Banim, 1822; *Revelations of the Dead-Alive*, 1824 (a satirical tale reissued in 1845 as *London and its Eccentricities in the Year 2023: or Revelations of the Dead Alive*); *Tales by the O'Hara Family*, 3 vols., 1825; *Tales by the O'Hara Family: Second Series*, 3 vols., 1826; *The Boyne Water: a Tale*, 3 vols., 1826; *The Anglo-Irish of the Nineteenth Century: a Novel*, 3 vols., 1828; *The Croppy: a Tale of 1798*, 3 vols., 1828; *The Denounced*, 3 vols., 1830; *The Chaunt of the Cholera: Songs for Ireland*, 1831; *The Smuggler: a Tale*, 3 vols., 1831; *The Ghost Hunter and his Family*, 1833; *The Mayor of Wind-Gap and Canvassing*, 3 vols., 1835; *The Bit o' Writin' and other Tales*, 3 vols., 1838; *Father Connell*, 3 vols., 1842; *The Town of the Cascades*, by Michael Banim, 2 vols., 1864.

The pseudonym 'The O'Hara Family' was sometimes used by one or other of the brothers and sometimes by the two when collaborating.

See D. Griffin, *The Life of Gerald Griffin*, 1843; R. H. Horne, *A New Spirit of the Age*, vol. ii, 1844; 'John Banim', *Irish Quarterly Review*, iv–vi, 1854–6; P. J. Murray, *The Life of John Banim*, 1857; A. Steger, *John Banim, ein Nachahmer Walter Scotts*, Erlangen, 1935; and T. Flanagan, *The Irish Novelists, 1800–1850*, New York, 1959.

BERNARD BARTON, 1784–1849.

Barton's principal publications were *Metrical Effusions* (1812); *The Triumph of the Orwell*, Woodbridge [1817]; *The Convict's Appeal* (1818); *Poems by an Amateur* (1818); *A Day in Autumn, A Poem* (1820); *Poems* (1820: reprinted with additions, 1821, 1822, 1825); *Napoleon, and other Poems* (1822); *Verses on the Death of P. B. Shelley* (1822); *Minor Poems* (1824); *Poetic Vigils* (1824); *Devotional Verses* (1826); *A Missionary's Memorial* (1826); *A Widow's Tale* (1827); *A New Year's Eve* (1828); *Household Verses* (1845); *A Memorial of J. J. Gurney*, 1847; and 4 vols. published at Woodbridge: *Sea-Weeds, gathered at Aldborough* [1846] (privately printed); *Birthday Verses at Sixty-Four* (1848); *Ichabod!* (1848); and *On the Signs of the Times* (1848). He also contributed material to *Bible Letters for Children* [by Lucy Barton], 1831, and other collections.

Selections from the Poems and Letters of Bernard Barton were edited by his daughter L. Barton in 1849 and 1853 (with a memoir by E. FitzGerald).

E. V. Lucas published *Bernard Barton and his Friends* in 1893.

See also 'Unpublished Letters from Edward FitzGerald to Bernard Barton', *Scribner's Magazine*, lxxii, 1922; A. M. Terhune, *The Life of Edward FitzGerald* (New Haven, 1947); and C. R. Woodring, 'Letters from Bernard Barton to Robert Southey', *Harvard Library Bulletin*, iv, 1950.

THOMAS LOVELL BEDDOES, 1803–49.

Beddoes published two volumes of verse: *The Improvisatore* (1821), and *The Brides' Tragedy* (1822). *Death's Jest-Book or The Fool's Tragedy* was published anonymously after his death, in 1850. Vol. ii of *The Poems posthumous and collected*, 2 vols., 1851, includes *Death's Jest-Book*, 1850: there was also a 1-vol. edition without *Death's Jest-Book*, but with a Memoir by T. F. Kelsall, in 1851. The *Poetical Works* were edited by Sir E. Gosse in 2 vols. in 1890. This and the original Muses' Library edition (by R. Colles, 1907), and Sir E. Gosse's *Complete Works* (2 vols., 1928), were rendered obsolete by *The Works*, ed. H. W. Donner, 1935 (which also includes the letters and supersedes Gosse's edition of *The Letters*, 1894). Donner has also produced a new Muses' Library edition (*Plays and Poems*, 1950), which includes the first version of *Death's Jest-Book*: written the standard biography, *Thomas Lovell Beddoes: The Making of a Poet* (1935): and collected letters relating to Beddoes in *The Browning Box* (1935). F. L. Lucas's *Thomas Lovell Beddoes: An Anthology* (1932) has an introduction reprinted in *Studies French and English* (1934). See also R. H. Snow, *Thomas Lovell Beddoes. Eccentric and Poet* (New York, 1928), and C. A. Weber (p. 464 above). There are articles by C. C. Abbott ('The Parents of Beddoes', *Durham University Journal*, xxxiv, 1941–2); H. K. Johnson ('Beddoes: a Psychiatric Study', *Psychiatric Quarterly*, 1943); H. Gregory ('On the Gothic Imagination . . . and the Survival of Beddoes', in *The Shield of Achilles*, New York, 1944); J. Heath-Stubbs (in *The Darkling Plain*, 1950); L. Forster ('Beddoes's Views on German Literature', *English Studies*, xxx, 1949); and A. C. Todd ('Beddoes and his Guardian', *TLS*, 10 Oct. 1952). Donner's 'Echoes of Beddoesian Rambles', *Studia Neophilologica*, vol. xxxiii, no. 2, 1961, is an important article which contains more letters and fresh information. See also A. C. Todd's article on the poet's mother, in *Studia Neophilologica*, vol. xxix, 1957.

JEREMY BENTHAM, 1748–1832.

Bentham's principal individual works include: *A Fragment on*

Government, 1776 (ed. F. C. Montague, 1891: ed. W. Harrison (with *An Introduction to the Principles of Morals and Legislation*), 1948); *A View of the Hard-Labour-Bill*, 1778; *Defence of Usury*, 1787; *An Introduction to the Principles of Morals and Legislation*, 1789, 2 vols., 'corrected', 1823 (reprinted, Oxford, 1879); *Panopticon; or, The Inspection House*, 1791; *A Protest against Law Taxes*, 1795; 'Poor Laws and Pauper Management' (in Arthur Young's *Annals*, Sept. 1797 and later); *A Plea for the Constitution*, 1803; *Scotch Reform*, 1808; *Panopticon versus New South Wales*, 1812; *Chrestomathia*, 1816; '*Swear not at all*', 1817; *A Table of the Springs of Action* (printed 1815, first published 1817); 'Catechism of Parliamentary Reform', *The Pamphleteer*, January 1817; *Papers upon Codification and Public Instruction*, 1817; *Church of Englandism and its Catechism examined*, 1818; 'Radical Reform Bill, with Explanations', *The Pamphleteer*, December 1819; *Elements of the Art of Packing as applied to Special Juries*, 1821; *Three Tracts relating to Spanish and Portuguese Affairs*, 1821; *On the Liberty of the Press*, 1821; *Analysis of the Influence of Natural Religion on the Temporal Happiness of Mankind*, by 'Philip Beauchamp', 1822; *Not Paul, but Jesus*, by 'Gamaliel Smith', 1823; *Codification Proposals*, 1822; *Book of Fallacies*, 1824; *The Rationale of Reward*, 1825; *The Rationale of Evidence* [ed. J. S. Mill], 5 vols., 1827; *The Rationale of Punishment*, 1830 (this and the *Rationale of Reward* were translated from the French version of E. Dumont, with some reference to Bentham's early MSS.); *Constitutional Code for the use of all Nations*, vol. i, 1830 (no more published separately); *Official Aptitude maximised—Expense minimised*, 1830 (a collection of papers); and *Deontology; or, the Science of Morality*, ed. Sir J. Bowring, 2 vols., 1834. *The Theory of Legislation* (first published in English in the translation by R. Hildreth in 1876) was edited by C. K. Ogden in 1931. C. W. Everett, ed. *A Comment on the Commentaries* in 1928 and *The Limits of Jurisprudence Defined* in 1945 (New York). The *Handbook of Political Fallacies* was ed. by H. A. Larrabee, Baltimore, 1952. Like several other works, this latter had appeared in French, compiled by E. Dumont from Bentham's manuscripts.

    Bentham's *Works* were edited by Sir John Bowring in 11 vols. in 1838–43, the last 2 vols. containing a Life and Index. W. Stark edited *Bentham's Economic Writings: [A] Critical Edition Based on his Printed Works and Unprinted Manuscripts*, in 3 vols. in 1952–4. A complete edition of his writings, making use of the voluminous manuscripts, is under way at University College, London.

Jeremy Bentham 1748–1792, by Mary Mack, is the first part of a comprehensive new study (1962). The best guide to Bentham's thought is in many ways E. Halévy's *The Growth of Philosophic Radicalism*, English translation, 1928 (French ed., 3 vols., 1901–4). Earlier books partly or wholly on Bentham include *Dissertations and Discussions*, i, by J. S. Mill, 1859; *Geschichte und Litteratur der Staatswissenschaften*, iii, by R. von Mohl, Erlangen, 1858; *The English Utilitarians*, by Leslie Stephen, 3 vols., 1900; *Études de Droit international*, by E. Nys, 1901; *Miscellaneous Essays and Addresses*, by H. Sidgwick, 1904; *Jeremy Bentham*, by C. M. Atkinson, 1905; *Lectures on the Relation between Law & Public Opinion in England . . .*, by A. V. Dicey, 1905 (rev. ed., 1962); *The Philosophical Radicals*, by A. S. Pringle Pattison, 1907; *Political Thought in England: The Utilitarians from Bentham to Mill*, by W. C. Davidson, 1915; *Bentham's Theory of Fictions*, by C. K. Ogden, 1932; *Jeremy Bentham*, by J. L. Stocks, Manchester, 1933 (a lecture); *The Education of Bentham*, by C. W. Everett, New York, 1931; *Bentham and the Ethics of Today, with Bentham Manuscripts Hitherto Unpublished*, by D. Baumgardt, Princeton, 1952; *Machiavelli to Bentham*, by W. T. Jones (*Masters of Political Thought*, ed. E. M. Sait, vol. ii, 1947); *Bentham and the Law: A Symposium*, ed. G. W. Keeton and G. Schwartzenberger, 1948; and *The Province and Function of Law*, by J. Stone, Sydney, 1950. For one example of Bentham's tremendous influence abroad one may consult V. A. Belaunde's *Bolivar and the Political Thought of the Spanish American Revolution*, Baltimore, 1938.

Of the many articles on Bentham very few can be mentioned: see, for example, C. S. Kenny in the *Law Quarterly Review*, xi, 1895; G. Wallas in the *Political Science Quarterly*, March 1923, and the *Contemporary Review*, March 1926; 'Bentham's Place in English Legal History', by Sir W. Holdsworth, *California Law Review*, xxviii, 1940; 'Benthamism in England and America', by P. A. Palmer, *American Political Science Review*, xxxv, 1941; 'Bentham as an Economist', by W. Stark, *Economic Journal*, li and lvi, 1941 and 1946; 'Bentham's "Censorial" Method', by D. Baumgardt, *JHI* vi, 1945; 'A Bentham Collection', by A. Muirhead, *The Library*, 5th series, i, 1946; 'The "Proof" of Utility in Bentham and Mill', by E. W. Hall, *Ethics*, lx, 1949; 'Bentham's Ideal Republic', by P. T. Peardon, *Canadian Journal of Economics*, xvii, 1951; and 'Utilitarianism: A System of Political Tolerance', by S. R. Letwin, *Cambridge Journal*, vi, 1953.

Mill on Bentham and Coleridge, ed. F. R. Leavis, 1950, reprints these two important essays from the *Dissertations and Discussions*.

C. W. Everett contributed a useful bibliography of books by and about Bentham (now, inevitably, somewhat out of date) to the English translation of Halévy's *Growth of Philosophic Radicalism*.

Also see above, pp. 488–9.

THOMAS BEWICK, 1753–1828.

A Memoir of Thomas Bewick, Written by Himself, appeared in 1862. There are subsequent editions by A. Dobson, Newcastle, 1887; Selwyn Image, 1924; M. Weekley, 1961 (with omissions, but a valuable introduction); and E. Blunden, 1961 (a photo-lithographic reproduction of the 1924 edition with a new introduction). There is no full edition from the manuscript in the British Museum, Add. MSS. 41481. In 1885–7 A. Dobson edited the Memorial Edition of the *Works*, in 5 vols.

T. Landseer's *Life and Letters of William Bewick* appeared in 2 vols. in 1871, to be followed by D. C. Thomson's *Life and Works* in 1882, A. Dobson's *Thomas Bewick and his Pupils* in 1884 (revised edition, 1889) and R. Robinson's *Life and Times* in 1887 (Newcastle). M. Weekley published his *Thomas Bewick* in 1953. As early as 1866 T. Hugo published *The Bewick Collector: A Descriptive Catalogue of the Works of Thomas and John Bewick* (Supplement, 1868). We now have *Thomas Bewick. A Bibliography Raisonné*, by S. Roscoe, 1953.

SAMUEL LAMAN BLANCHARD, 1804–45.

Blanchard published *Lyric Offerings* in 1828 and edited the *Life and Literary Remains* of L. E. L[andon] in 2 vols. in 1841. His essays were collected as *Sketches from Life* and edited with a memoir by Sir E. Bulwer Lytton in 3 vols. in 1846. His prose sketches, *Corporation Characters*, came out in 1855. His *Poetical Works* were edited, with a memoir, by B. Jerrold in 1876. His Memoir of Harrison Ainsworth is to be found in the 14-vol. edition of the latter's *Works* published in 1850–1. He contributed to *The Examiner* and many other periodicals. Among periodicals which he edited at one time or another were the *Monthly Magazine*, *The True Sun*, *The Constitutional and Public Ledger*, *The Court Journal*, *The Courier*, and *George Cruickshank's Omnibus*. See W. M. Thackeray, 'A Brother of the Press . . . the Chances of the

Literary Profession', *Fraser's Magazine*, xxxiii, 1846 (reprinted in Thackeray's *Works*, ed. A. T. Ritchie, xiii, 1899). Selections are given in Miles, iii, with an essay by A. H. Japp.

BLESSINGTON, MARGUERITE, COUNTESS OF (*née* POWER), 1789–1849.

She wrote a number of novels: *The Repealers*, 3 vols., 1833 (as *Grace Cassidy*, 3 vols., 1834); *The Confessions of an Elderly Gentleman*, 1836; *The Victims of Society*, 3 vols., 1837; *The Confessions of an Elderly Lady*, 1838; *The Governess*, 2 vols., 1839; *The Lottery of Life*, 3 vols., 1842; *Meredith*, 3 vols., 1843; *Strathern; or Life at Home and Abroad*, 4 vols., 1845; *Memoirs of a Femme de Chambre*, 3 vols., 1846; *Marmaduke Herbert, or the Fatal Error*, 3 vols., 1847; and *Country Quarters*, 3 vols., 1850 (with a Memoir by Miss Power).

As well as editing and contributing largely to *The Book of Beauty*, *The Keepsake* and other gift-books, the Countess also published *The Magic Lantern, or Sketches of Scenes in the Metropolis*, 1822; *Sketches and Fragments*, 1822 [a doubtful attribution]; *Conversations of Lord Byron with the Countess of Blessington*, 1834 (first published in the *New Monthly Magazine*, July 1832–December 1833); *The Honeymoon, and Other Tales*, 2 vols., Philadelphia, 1837; *The Idler in Italy*, 2 vols., 1839 (2nd ed., with new third volume, also 1839); *Desultory Thoughts and Reflections*, 1839; *The Belle of a Season* (a poem), 1840; and *The Idler in France*, 2 vols., 1841. *The Works of Lady Blessington*, published in 2 vols. at Philadelphia in 1838, contain some material which Lady Blessington did not herself collect, and some which is probably not her work.

The second of the two editions of *The Literary Life and Correspondence of the Countess of Blessington*, edited by R. R. Madden in 3 vols. in 1855, is the less inaccurate, but A. Morrison's *The Blessington Papers*, 1895, is much more reliable. See also W. Maginn, *A Gallery of Illustrious Literary Characters*, ed. W. Bates [1873]; M. Sadleir, *Blessington–D'Orsay*, rev. ed., 1947 (valuable); and M. W. Rosa, *The Silver-Fork School: Novels of Fashion preceding Vanity Fair*, New York, 1936. On her *Conversations* with Byron see (among others) Doris Langley Moore, *The Late Lord Byron*, 1961.

SIR JOHN BOWRING, 1792–1872.

Bowring's voluminous writings include a number of volumes of translations: *Specimens of the Russian Poets*, 1820 (enlarged into two parts, 1821–3); *Batavian Anthology; or, Specimens of the Dutch Poets* (1824, with H. S. Van Dyk); *Ancient Poetry and Romances of Spain* (1824); *Servian Popular Poetry* (1827); *Specimens of the Polish Poets* (1827); *Poetry of the Magyars* (1830); *Cheskian* [Czech] *Anthology* (1832); *Manuscript of the Queen's Court. A Collection of Old Bohemian Lyrico-Epic Songs* (Prague, 1843); *Ode to the Deity: Translated from the Russian of Derzhavin* [Brighton, 1861]; and *Translations from A. Petöfi, the Magyar Poet* (1866).

In original verse Bowring also published *Matins and Vespers* (1823, revised and enlarged 1824 and 1841); and *Hymns* (1825). A *Memorial Volume of Sacred Poetry*, with a Memoir, was edited by Lady Bowring in 1873.

In prose Bowring published *Observations on the State of Religion and Literature in Spain*, 1820; *Peter Schlemihl: from the German* (1824); a *Sketch of the Language and Literature of Holland* (Amsterdam, 1829); and *Minor Morals for Young People*, 3 parts, 1834–9. His *Autobiographical Recollections* were edited by L. B. Bowring in 1877.

Bowring was editor of the *Westminster Review* from 1824 to 1836 and edited Bentham's *Collected Works*, 1838–43.

On Bowring see 'The Oratory of Sir John Bowring', *Fraser's Magazine*, xxxiv, 1846; L. Moor, *Bowring, Cobden and China: A Memoir*, 1857; G. L. Nesbitt, *Benthamite Reviewing*, New York, 1934; A. C. Wardle, *Benjamin Bowring and his Descendants*, 1938; M. Sova, 'Sir John Bowring and the Slavs', *Slavonic Review*, xxi, 1943; and D. F. S. Scott, *Some English Correspondents of Goethe*, 1949.

HENRY PETER BROUGHAM (BARON BROUGHAM AND VAUX), 1778–1868.

His main publications include *An Inquiry into the Colonial Policy of the European Powers*, 2 vols., 1803; *An Inquiry into the State of the Nation*, 1806; *A Letter to Sir Samuel Romilly upon the Abuse of Charities*, 1818 (first published in *The Pamphleteer*); *Practical Observations upon the Education of the People*, 1825; *Thoughts upon the Aristocracy of England. By Isaac Tomkins, Gent.*, 1835; '*We Can't Afford It!*' (Part 2 of the preceding), 1835; *A Discourse of Natural Theology*, Brussels, 1835; *Select Cases decided by Lord Brougham in the Court of Chancery, 1833 and 1834*, vol. i, ed. C. P. Cooper, 1835; *Speeches upon Questions relating to Public Rights, etc.*, 4 vols., 1838 (several had been published separately); *Historical Sketches of Statesmen in the Time of George III*, 3 series, 1839–43, 6 vols., 1845;

Political Philosophy (Society for the Diffusion of Useful Knowledge), 3 vols., 1842–3; *Albert Lunel: or the Château of Languedoc*, 3 vols., 1844 (a novel); *Lives of Men of Letters and Science, in the Time of George III*, 2 vols., 1845–6; *A Letter to Lord Denman* . . ., 1850; *History of England and France under the House of Lancaster*, 1852; *Contributions to the Edinburgh Review*, 3 vols., 1856; and *Tracts, Mathematical and Physical*, 1860. His *Works* were collected in 11 vols. in 1855–61, 2nd ed., 1872–3. New's biography lists his very numerous and important contributions to the *Edinburgh Review*.

As New pointed out, a complete bibliography of writings relating to Brougham would be 'gigantic, hopeless, and useless'. There are two important modern studies, *Lord Brougham and the Whig Party*, by A. Aspinall, Manchester, 1927, and C. W. New's *Life of Henry Brougham to 1830*, 1961. *The Life and Times of Henry, Lord Brougham, Written by Himself* had appeared in 3 vols. in 1871 (see A. Aspinall, *English Historical Review*, lix, 1944). We may also consult *Lord Brougham's Law Reforms*, by Sir J. E. Eardley-Wilmot, 1860; *The Work of Lord Brougham for Education in England*, by A. M. Gilbert, Chambersburg, 1922; and 'Wordsworth versus Brougham (1818, 1820, 1826)' and 'Thomas Clarkson as Champion of Brougham in 1818', by A. L. Strout, *NQ*, 4 and 28 May 1938. G. T. Garratt's *Lord Brougham*, 1935, is of no scholarly value. Mrs. Hawes's biography, published in 1957, is brief but accurate.

CHARLES BROWN, 1787–1842.

Charles Brown, who changed his name to Charles Armitage Brown long after the death of Keats, had a comic opera, *Narensky; or, The Road to Yaroslaf*, produced at Drury Lane in January 1814, and published the same year. His book, *Shakespeare's Autobiographical Poems*, a study of the sonnets, appeared in 1838. He contributed to *The Examiner*, *The Liberal*, the *New Monthly Magazine*, and other periodicals. M. Buxton Forman collected *Some Letters & Miscellanea of Charles Brown* in 1937. Brown's unpublished *Life of John Keats* was edited by D. H. Bodurtha and W. B. Pope in 1937. Up-to-date information about him may be found in *The Keats Circle: Letters and Papers*, ed. H. E. Rollins, 2 vols., Harvard, 1948 (which includes a brief Memoir by his son); an article by H. E. Rollins in the *Harvard Library Bulletin*, iv, 1950; and *The Letters of John Keats*, ed. H. E. Rollins, 2 vols., 1958.

THOMAS BROWN, 1778–1820.

Professor Thomas Brown, M.D., a philosopher of importance in his day, published *Observations on the Zoonomia of Erasmus Darwin*, 1798; *Observations on . . . the Doctrine of Mr. Hume . . .*, 1805 (enlarged in third edition in 1818 as *Inquiry into the Relation of Cause and Effect*); and *Lectures on the Philosophy of the Human Mind*, 4 vols., 1820.

Brown also published a well-known satirical poem, *The Paradise of Coquettes* (with an interesting preface), in 1814. His *Collected Poems*, 1820, includes poems from several volumes, published between 1814 and 1819.

There is an *Account of the Life and Writings*, by the Rev. D. Welsh, 1825, of which an abridged version is prefixed to later editions of Brown's *Lectures*. See also A. L. Jones, 'A Note on Dr. Thomas Brown's Contribution to Aesthetics', *Studies in the History of Ideas*, vol. i, New York, 1918.

SIR SAMUEL EGERTON BRYDGES, 1762–1837.

Books published by Brydges include *Sonnets and Other Poems*, 1785 (expanded in later editions); *Mary de Clifford: a Story*, 1792; *Verses on the Late Unanimous Resolutions to Support the Constitution*, 1794; *Arthur Fitz Albini: A Novel*, 2 vols., 1798; *Le Forester, A Novel*, 3 vols., 1802; *The Sylvan Wanderer . . . Essays*, 4 parts, Lee Priory, 1813–21 (privately printed); *The Ruminator: . . . A Series of . . . Essays*, 2 vols., 1813; *Occasional Poems, written in the year MDCCCXI*, Lee Priory, 1814 (privately printed); *Select Poems*, Lee Priory, 1814 (privately printed); *Bertram, a Poetical Tale*, Lee Priory, 1814 (privately printed); *Desultoria: or Comments . . . on Books and Men*, Lee Priory, 1815 (privately printed); *Lord Brokenhurst*, Geneva, 1819 (reprinted, like the next entry, in *Tragic Tales*, 1820); *Coningsby*, Paris, 1819; *Sir Ralph Willoughby*, Florence, 1820; *The Hall of Hellingsby*, 3 vols., 1821; *Odo, Count of Lingen: a poetical tale in six cantos*, Geneva, 1824; *Gnomica, Detached Thoughts . . .*, Geneva, 1824; *Letters on the Character and Poetical Genius of Lord Byron*, 1824; *An Impartial Portrait of Lord Byron*, Paris, 1825; *Recollections of Foreign Travel on Life, Literature, and Self-knowledge*, 2 vols., 1825; *Modern Aristocracy or the Bard's Reception*, Geneva, 1831 (a poem on Byron); *The Lake of Geneva, A Poem*, 2 vols., Geneva, 1832; *Imaginative Biography*, 2 vols., 1834; *The Autobiography, Times, Opinions, and*

Contemporaries of Sir Egerton Brydges, 2 vols., 1834; *Moral Axioms in Single Couplets: for the use of the young*, 1837; *Human Fate, and An Address to the Poets Wordsworth & Southey: Poems*, Great Totham, 1846 (privately printed).

His bibliographical and antiquarian publications include *The Topographer*, 4 vols., 1789–91 (with L. S. Shaw); *Topographical Miscellanies*, 1792; *Censura Literaria*, 10 vols., 1805–9, 10 vols., 1815 (articles rearranged according to chronology); *The British Bibliographer*, 4 vols., 1810–14; *Restituta; or Titles, Extracts, and Characters of Old Books*, 4 vols., 1814–16; *Excerpta Tudoriana*, 2 vols., Lee Priory, 1814–18 (privately printed); *Archaica: Containing A Reprint of Scarce Old English Tracts*, 2 vols., 1815 (privately printed); *Res Literariae: Bibliographical and Critical*, 3 nos., Naples, Rome, Geneva, 1821–2.

A much fuller list of Brydges's publications may be found in *The Literary Career of Sir Samuel Egerton Brydges*, by Mary Katherine Woodworth, 1935. A few *addenda* are noted in *TLS*, 16 November 1935, p. 744.

GEORGE GORDON BYRON, BARON BYRON, 1788–1824.

Fugitive Pieces were privately printed at Newark in [1806]. Like a number of Byron's later volumes, this was anonymous. A facsimile was edited by H. Buxton Forman in 1886, another by M. Kessel in 1933 (New York). There are twelve new pieces in *Poems on Various Occasions*, Newark, 1807, also anonymous and privately printed; *Hours of Idleness* was published at Newark in 1807, and contained twelve further new pieces.

Poems Original and Translated. Second Edition, Newark, 1808, contains only five new pieces. Nine poems by Byron were published in *Imitations and Translations from the Ancient and Modern Classics*, by J. C. Hobhouse, 1809. *English Bards, and Scotch Reviewers, A Satire*, came out in [1809], incorporating a good deal of an unpublished poem, *The British Bards* [Newark, 1808], of which there is a proof copy in the British Museum: there were considerable additions and revisions in the 2nd and 5th editions of *English Bards*, 1809 and 1816; (there is a facsimile edition of a copy with Byron's MS. notes, ed. J. Murray for the Roxburghe Club, 1936); *Hints from Horace* was not published in full during Byron's lifetime, but an 1811 proof exists in the British Museum.

The first two cantos of *Childe Harold's Pilgrimage, A Romaunt*, came out in 1812: Canto III in 1816: and Canto IV in 1818. The four cantos were published together in 2 vols. in 1819. *Euthanasia* was first published in the 2nd edition of *Childe Harold*, I–II, 1812.

The following volumes appeared in the next few years: *The Curse of Minerva*, 1812 (privately printed), 'Philadelphia', 1815, and later editions; *Waltz: An Apostrophic Hymn*, 'By Horace Hornem, Esq.', 1813; *The Giaour, A Fragment of a Turkish Tale*, 1813 (later editions had various additions); *The Bride of Abydos, A Turkish Tale*, 1813; *The Corsair, A Tale*, 1814; *Ode to Napoleon Buonaparte*, 1814; *Lara, A Tale* (with *Jacqueline, A Tale* [by Samuel Rogers]), 1814, 4th ed., 1814 (first separate and acknowledged edition); *Hebrew Melodies*, 2 parts, 1815; *The Siege of Corinth, A Poem* [with] *Parisina, A Poem*, 1816; *Poems*, 1816; *The Prisoner of Chillon, and other Poems*, 1816; *Monody on the Death of the Right Honourable R. B. Sheridan*, 1816; *The Lament of Tasso*, 1817; *Manfred. A Dramatic Poem*, 1817; *Beppo. A Venetian Story*, 1818 (4th ed. with additional stanzas, 1818); *Mazeppa. A Poem*, 1819.

The first two cantos of *Don Juan* appeared in 1819; Cantos III–V in 1821; Cantos VI–VIII, Cantos IX–XI, and Cantos XII–XIV all in 1823; Cantos XV–XVI in 1824; and the Dedication in 1833. There were editions of Cantos I–V in 1822, V–XI in 1823, and I–XVI in 1826, in two volumes.

Marino Faliero, Doge of Venice was published with *The Prophecy of Dante. A Poem* in 1821; *Sardanapalus, A Tragedy, The Two Foscari, A Tragedy*, [and] *Cain, A Mystery* in 1821; there is an 1821 proof of *Heaven and Earth*, but it was first published in *The Liberal*, no. 2, 1823; *The Vision of Judgment* first appeared in *The Liberal*, no. 1, 1822; *The Age of Bronze; or, Carmen Seculare et Annus haud Mirabilis* appeared in 1823, as did *The Island, or, Christian and his Comrades* and *Werner: A Tragedy*. *The Deformed Transformed* was published in 1824.

Several minor pieces are omitted from this list, but mention should also be made of the so-called 'Poems on his Domestic Circumstances', two poems first printed at Bristol by Barry and Son in 1816.

The standard collected edition of the poems is still vols. i–vii of *The Works*, ed. E. H. Coleridge, 1898–1904. The basis of his text is the 6-vol. *Works* published by Murray in 1831. Murray had published earlier editions in 1815 (4 vols.), 1818–20 (8 vols.), 1825 (8 vols.), and at other times, and there were numerous un-authorized collections. The fullest edition of *Don Juan* is now that edited by T. G. Steffan and W. W. Pratt, 4 vols., 1957: vol. i contains a detailed study of the composition of the poem.

There is a 3-vol. edition of Byron's *Poems* in Everyman's Lib-rary, ed. G. Pocock, 1949. There are innumerable volumes of selections, including those with the prefaces of Swinburne and Matthew Arnold, 1866 and 1881. Mention may also be made of *Poems*, ed. H. J. C. Grierson, 1923; *The Best of Byron*, ed. R. A. Rice, New York, 1933; *Selected Poems*, ed. L. A. Marchand ('Modern Library'); *Don Juan and Other Satiric Poems*, ed. L. I. Bredvold, New York, 1935; *Childe Harold's Pilgrimage and Other Romantic Poems*, ed. S. C. Chew, 1936; *Satirical and Critical Poems*, ed. Joan Bennett, 1937; and *Selections* (poetry and prose), ed. P. Quennell, 1950 (Nonesuch edition).

In prose Byron published a 'Letter to the Editor of "My Grandmother's Review" ', in the *Liberal*, no. 1, 1822; and *A Letter to* [John Murray] *on the Rev. W. L. Bowles' Strictures on . . . Pope*, 1821. Several other prose pieces were printed after his death, some of them existing in earlier 'proofs'.

Unpublished verse has been printed by T. G. Steffan in 'An Early Byron MS. in the Pierpont Morgan Library', *Texas Studies in English*, xxvii, 1948, and by W. Pafford in 'An Un-published Poem', *K.-Sh.J.* i, 1952.

The *Correspondence of Lord Byron with a Friend* was edited by A. R. C. Dallas in [1824], but suppressed before publication. It appeared in 3 vols. in Paris in 1825. His *Letters and Journals* first appeared in Moore's biography in 2 vols. in 1830. Other letters were published at various times. At the moment the standard edition of the letters remains that by R. E. Prothero, 6 vols., 1898–1901 (which complements E. H. Coleridge's ed. of the poems); but see also *Astarte* (mentioned below); *Poems and Letters of Lord Byron*, ed. W. N. C. Carlton, Chicago, 1912 (privately printed); and (more important) *Lord Byron's Correspondence, chiefly with Lady Melbourne, Mr. Hobhouse, the Hon. Douglas Kinnaird, and P. B. Shelley*, ed. John Murray, 2 vols., 1922. Other letters may be found in *The Last Attachment*, by Iris Origo, 1949; *Byron: A Self-Portrait. Letters and Diaries, 1798 to 1824*, ed. P. Quennell, 2 vols., 1950; and 'Byron and Count Alborghetti', by L. A. Marchand, *PMLA* lxiv, 1949. Readers of Russian may refer to

'Avtografy Bayrona v SSSR', by M. P. Alekseev, in *Literaturnoe Nasledstvo*, lviii, 1952.

There are several volumes of selected letters, including one in Everyman's Library, ed. R. G. Howarth, 1936.

For the writings of J. C. Hobhouse relevant to Byron see under Hobhouse. Only a few of the other early biographical accounts can be mentioned here: *Journal of the Conversations of Lord Byron at Pisa*, by Thomas Medwin, 1824; *Recollections of the Life of Lord Byron* (1808–1814), by R. C. Dallas, 1824; Leigh Hunt, *Lord Byron and Some of his Contemporaries*, 1828 (2-vol. ed. same year) and *Autobiography*, 3 vols., 1850; *Letters and Journals of Lord Byron, with Notices of his Life*, by Thomas Moore, 2 vols., 1830; *The Life of Lord Byron*, by John Galt, 1830; *Conversations of Lord Byron with the Countess of Blessington*, 1834 (first published in *New Monthly Magazine*, July 1832–December 1833); E. J. Trelawny, *Recollections of the Last Days of Shelley and Byron*, 1858, revised as *Records of Shelley, Byron, and the Author* (see Trelawny); and *My Recollections of Lord Byron and those of Eye-witnesses of his Life*, by the Countess Guiccioli, translated by H. E. H. Jerningham, 2 vols., 1869. Much information is to be found in the *Memoirs* of Thomas Moore, in *A Publisher and his Friends* (see p. 471 above), and in many other memoirs and accounts of the period. There are discussions of these and other early biographical accounts in S. C. Chew's *Byron in England: His Fame and After-Fame*, 1924, L. A. Marchand's *Byron*, 3 vols., 1957, and Doris Langley Moore's *The Late Lord Byron*, 1961.

Of later biographies, Karl Elze's *Lord Byron*, Berlin, 1870 (English translation, with additions, 1872), John Nichol's volume in the English Men of Letters series, 1880, and J. C. Jeaffreson's *The Real Lord Byron*, 1883, are now of slight importance. *Astarte, A Fragment of Truth concerning . . . Lord Byron*, by the Earl of Lovelace (privately printed, 1905: better edition by Lady Lovelace, 1921), which concerns Byron's relations with Augusta Leigh, is still of interest. See further Harold Nicolson, *Byron: The Last Journey*, 1924 (rev. ed., 1940); *Byron*, by Ethel Colburn Mayne, 2 vols., 1912 (rev. ed., 1 vol., 1924), for many years the main biography (see also her *Life and Letters of . . . Lady Noel Byron*, 1929); J. Drinkwater, *The Pilgrim of Eternity: Byron —A Conflict*, 1925; Helene Richter, *Lord Byron: Persönlichkeit und Werk*, Halle, 1929; and Charles du Bos, *Byron et le besoin de la fatalité*, 1929 (translated by Ethel Colburn Mayne [1932]), a

speculative psychological study which is of greater value than
A. Maurois's biography, as is M. Castelain's *Byron*, Paris, 1931.
Peter Quennell has produced *Byron. The Years of Fame*, 1935,
and *Byron in Italy*, 1941, as well as editing some letters to Byron
(with 'George Paston') in '*To Lord Byron': Feminine Profiles*, 1939.
W. A. Borst's *Lord Byron's First Pilgrimage*, New Haven, 1948,
provides a useful background for *Childe Harold*, I–II. *Byron,
Shelley, Hunt, and 'The Liberal'*, by W. H. Marshall, Philadelphia,
1960, is also of interest. C. L. Cline's *Byron, Shelley and their
Pisan Circle*, 1952, provided a little new information, as did
F. L. Jones by editing the *Journal of Edward E. Williams* in 1951.
The Last Attachment (Byron and Teresa Guiccioli), by Iris Origo,
1949, is an important study. In general the truth is the last
thing that one looks for in the work of Byron's biographers, but
a remarkable amount of it is to be found in L. A. Marchand's
Byron: A Biography, 3 vols., 1957, which should long remain the
standard Life. See also *Lord Byron's Wife*, by M. Elwin, 1962.

A most useful book is *His Very Self and Voice*, ed. E. J. Lovell,
1954, a collection of Byron's conversation. His conversations
with Medwin and the Countess of Blessington are reserved for
a second volume. Some new light on Byron's early poetic career
is contained in W. W. Pratt's *Byron at Southwell: The Making of a
Poet*, Austin, Texas, 1948. Some letters may be found in *Shelley
and his Circle* (p. 615 below).

G. Wilson Knight has written at length on Byron in *The Burning
Oracle*, 1939, where he is also concerned with Spenser, Milton, and
Pope; in 'Byron's Dramatic Prose' (Byron Foundation Lecture,
Nottingham, 1953); in *Lord Byron: Christian Virtues*, 1952, a
work on 'a man in whom poetry has become incarnate . . . our
greatest poet in the widest sense of the term since Shakespeare'
(reviewed by R. W. King in *RES*, new series, v, 1954); and in the
highly conjectural *Lord Byron's Marriage: The Evidence of Asterisks*,
1957 (on which see A. Rutherford's review in *EC* viii, 1958).
See also Wilson Knight's *Byron and Hamlet*, Manchester, 1963.

The Reviews of Byron's own day contained much intelligent
comment, as did certain of the early biographical studies. A
few early reviews are reprinted in the volumes of selections
mentioned on p. 475 above. Lockhart's anonymous *John Bull's
Letter to Lord Byron*, 1821, was reprinted by A. L. Strout in 1947.
S. C. Chew's *Byron in England: His Fame and After-Fame*, 1924,
deals with early reactions to Byron.

Sir Egerton Brydges's *Letters on the Character and Poetical Genius of Lord Byron*, 1824, remain a curiosity. Macaulay's essay on Byron is reprinted from the *Edinburgh Review*, June 1831, in *Critical and Miscellaneous Essays*, vol. i, 1843. Ruskin's interesting remarks on Byron are most readily found in *Ruskin as Literary Critic, Selections*, ed. A. H. R. Ball, 1928, or by means of the index to the Cook–Wedderburn edition. Swinburne's 'Wordsworth and Byron', *Nineteenth Century*, April–May 1884, is reprinted in his *Miscellanies*, 1886. Arnold's important essay may be found in *Essays in Criticism*, 2nd series, 1888 (it first appeared in 1881 as a preface to his volume of selections).

Turning to recent criticism, we find a balanced and intelligent treatment in *Byron: A Critical Study*, by A. Rutherford, 1961. W. W. Robson's *Byron as Poet* (British Academy, 1957) is a penetrating critique stimulated by the essays of F. R. Leavis and T. S. Eliot mentioned below. *Lord Byron: un tempérament littéraire*, by R. Escarpit, 2 vols., 1955–7, is a valuable and thorough study in which biography is subordinated to criticism. Most modern critics, including those just mentioned, pay particular attention to Byron's satires. Their work is usefully supplemented by the important study of the composition of the poem in vol. i of the 1957 Variorum edition of *Don Juan* mentioned above (1957); by *Byron's Don Juan: A Critical Study*, by Elizabeth French Boyd, 1945 (reprinted 1958); by *The Style of Don Juan*, by G. M. Ridenour, New Haven, 1960; and by the introduction to R. D. Waller's edition of Hookham Frere's *The Monks and the Giants*, Manchester, 1926. Important sidelights on Byron may also be found in *The Romantic Agony*, by M. Praz, translated by A. Davidson, 1933 (Italian edition, *La carne, la morte ed il diavolo nella letteratura romantica*, Milan, 1930); and in *Rousseau and Romanticism*, by Irving Babbitt, Boston and New York, 1919. See also *Byron the Poet*, by M. K. Joseph, 1964.

Other books which deserve attention include *Lord Byron as a Satirist in Verse*, by C. M. Fuess, New York, 1912; *The Dramas of Lord Byron*, by S. C. Chew, Göttingen, 1915; *Byron the Poet* (essays by Haldane, Grierson, and others), ed. W. A. Briscoe, 1924; *Byron: Romantic Paradox*, by W. J. Calvert, North Carolina, 1935 (reprinted, New York, 1962); *Byron as Skeptic and Believer*, by E. M. Marjarum, Princeton, 1938 (reprinted 1962); *Byron: The Record of a Quest: Studies in a Poet's Concept and Treatment of Nature*, by E. J. Lovell, Austin, Texas, 1949; *The Byronic*

Hero: *Types and Prototypes*, by P. L. Thorslev, Minnesota, 1962; and *The Structure of Byron's Major Poems*, by W. H. Marshall, Philadelphia, 1963. Bertrand Russell devotes a chapter of his *History of Western Philosophy* to Byron (1946: see also Russell's article in *JHI* i, 1940). *Fair Greece Sad Relic: Literary Philhellenism from Shakespeare to Byron*, by T. Spencer, 1954, throws a good deal of light on Byron. *Byron and the Spoiler's Art*, by P. West, 1960, is fitfully illuminating. *The Death of Tragedy*, by G. Steiner, 1961, has a brief discussion of Byron's tragedies in their European setting. One of the best of the various discussions of the Don Juan story is *La Légende de Don Juan*, by G. Gendarme de Bevotte, Paris, 1906.

A number of essays first published separately were included by their authors in collections of essays. These include 'Byron, 1824–1924', by H. W. Garrod (in *The Profession of Poetry and other Lectures*, 1929); 'Byron and the Comic Spirit', by G. R. Elliott (in *The Cycle of Modern Poetry*, Princeton, 1929: reprinted from *PMLA* xxxix, 1924); 'Byron', by W. P. Ker (in *Collected Essays*, ed. C. Whibley, i, 1925); 'Byron and English Society', by H. J. C. Grierson (in *The Background of English Literature*, 1925: see also his British Academy lecture, 'Lord Byron: Arnold and Swinburne', 1921); and 'Byron', by E. de Selincourt (in *Wordsworthian and other Studies*, 1947). 'Byron's Satire' in *Revaluation*, by F. R. Leavis, 1936, has been influential, as has 'Byron', by T. S. Eliot, in *From Anne to Victoria*, ed. B. Dobrée, 1937 (reprinted in Eliot's *On Poetry and Poets*, 1957, and in *English Romantic Poets*, ed. M. H. Abrams, mentioned on p. 467 above).

Lectures and articles of importance include *Ruskin (and others) on Byron*, by R. W. Chambers (English Association, 1925); 'Coleridge and Byron', by E. L. Griggs, *PMLA* xlv, 1930; 'Byron and English Interest in the Near East', by W. C. Brown, *SP* xxxiv, 1937 (cf. 'Byron and the East: Literary Sources of the Turkish Tales', by H. S. L. Wiener, in *Nineteenth-Century Studies in Honor of C. S. Northup*, ed. H. Davis and others, Ithaca, New York, 1940); 'Byron and the Colloquial Tradition in English Poetry', by R. Bottrall, *The Criterion*, xviii, 1939 (reprinted in Abrams's collection, as above); five articles by D. V. Erdman— 'Byron's Stage Fright: the History of his Ambition and Fear of Writing for the Stage', *ELH* vi, 1939; 'Lord Byron and the Genteel Reformers', *PMLA* lvi, 1941; 'Lord Byron as Rinaldo',

PMLA lvii, 1942; 'Byron and Revolt in England', *Science and Society*, xi, 1947; and 'Byron and "the New Force of the People"', *K.-Sh.J.* xi, 1962; two articles by E. D. H. Johnson—'Don Juan in England', *ELH* xi, 1944, and 'A Political Interpretation of Byron's *Marino Faliero*', *MLQ* 1942; 'The Poetry of Byron', by Sir Harold Nicolson (English Association, 1943); 'Byron's "Hours of Idleness" and other than Scotch Reviewers', by W. S. Ward, *MLN* lix, 1944; 'Byron and the Ballad', by A. P. Hudson, *SP* xlii, 1945; 'Manfred's Remorse and Dramatic Tradition', by B. Evans, *PMLA* lxii, 1947; 'Byron's "Observations on an Article in *Blackwood's Magazine*"', by P. B. Daghlian, *RES* xxiii, 1947; 'The Colloquial Mode of Byron', by M. Bewley, *Scrutiny*, xvi, 1949; 'Byron's *Hebrew Melodies*', by J. Slater, *SP* xlix, 1952; 'Lord Byron's Fiery Convert of Revenge', by C. Lefevre, *SP* xlix, 1952; 'The Devil a Bit of Our Beppo', by T. G. Steffan, *PQ* xxxii, 1953; 'Traduzioni e citazioni di Byron dai classici italiani', by A. Guidi, *Annali Triestini*, xxiii, Trieste, 1953; and two articles by A. Rutherford—'An Early MS. of *English Bards and Scotch Reviewers*', *K.-Sh.B.* vii, 1956, and 'The Influence of Hobhouse on *Childe Harold's Pilgrimage*, Canto IV', *RES*, N.S., xii, 1961.

The following are among the best of the Nottingham Byron Foundation lectures: *Byron's Lyrics*, by L. C. Martin (1948); *Byron and Switzerland*, by H. Straumann (1948–9); *Byron and Shelley*, by D. G. James (1951); *Byron's Dramatic Prose*, by G. Wilson Knight (1953: already mentioned); *Two Exiles: Lord Byron and D. H. Lawrence*, by G. Hough (1956: reprinted in *Image and Experience*, 1960); *Byron and Italy*, by G. Melchiori (1958); *Byron and the Greek Tradition*, by T. J. B. Spencer (1959); and *Byron's Dramas*, by B. Dobrée (1962).

Although the best considerations of Byron's criticism are usually to be found in studies of his poetry, mention may also be made of two old-fashioned studies, H. Hartmann, *Lord Byrons Stellung zu den Klassizisten seiner Zeit*, 1932, and J. J. Van Rennes, *Bowles, Byron, and the Pope-Controversy*, 1927. U. Amarasinghe's book is also relevant (p. 475, above).

So much has been written on Byron's influence in Europe and elsewhere that only very few titles can be mentioned here: *Byron and Goethe: Analysis of a Passion*, by E. M. Butler, 1956, is primarily concerned with 'the extraordinary effect of Byron's personality and life on the mind and heart of Goethe'. It was inspired by J. G. Robertson's *Goethe and Byron* (English Goethe Society, 1925), which superseded Brandl's earlier study. Two studies with a more general scope are *Die Aufnahme Lord Byrons in Deutschland und sein Einfluß auf den jungen Heine*, Berne, 1905, by W. Ochsenbein, and *Lord Byron in Deutschland*, by G. Dobosal, Zwickau, 1911. His influence on Italy has often been studied: there were two pioneering studies by G. Muoni, *La Fama del Byron e il Byronismo in Italia*, Milan, 1903, and *La Leggenda del Byron in Italia*, Milan, 1907. M. Praz's *La Fortuna di Byron in Inghilterra*, Florence, 1925, has some useful illustrations. For France, E. Estève's *Byron et le romantisme français: Essai sur la fortune et l'influence de l'œuvre de Byron en France de 1812 à 1850*, 1907, remains of great value. Studies of his influence in other countries are listed in the standard bibliographies. Escarpit's bibliography is particularly helpful.

Further bibliographical aid may be sought in *CBEL*; in E. H. Coleridge's edition; in *ERP*; in *The Roe–Byron Collection, Newstead Abbey*, Nottingham, 1937; in *A Descriptive Catalogue of . . . Manuscripts and First Editions . . . at the University of Texas*, ed. R. H. Griffith and H. M. Jones, Austin, Texas, 1924; and in *Byron and his Circle: A Catalogue of Manuscripts in the University of Texas Library*, by W. W. Pratt, Austin, Texas, 1948. (See also T. G. Steffan's contribution to *Texas Studies in English*, 1946, and comments in *SP* xliii, 1946, and *MLQ* viii, 1947.)

HENRY FRANCIS CARY, 1772–1844.

Cary published *An Irregular Ode to General Elliott*, Birmingham [1788]; *Sonnets and Odes* (1788); and an *Ode to General Kosciusko* (1797). *The Inferno of Dante Alighieri . . ., With a Translation in English Blank Verse, Notes, and a Life of the Author*, appeared in 2 vols. in 1805–6. His complete translation, *The Vision; or Hell, Purgatory, and Paradise, of Dante Alighieri* was published at his own expense in 3 vols. in 1814 and republished in a much superior format by Taylor and Hessey in 3 vols. in 1819. It was illustrated by Gustave Doré in 1866, and has been often reprinted. Cary's other productions were *The Birds of Aristophanes. Translated*, 1824; *Pindar in English Verse*, 1833; *Lives of English Poets, from Johnson to Kirke White*, 1846 (reprinted from *The London Magazine*, August 1821–December 1824); and *The Early French Poets: Notices and Translations*, 1846 (also reprinted from

The London Magazine, November 1821–April 1824: ed. T. E. Welby, without the French texts, 1923).

Cary's son, Henry, published his *Memoir of the Rev. Henry Francis Cary . . . with his Literary Journal and Letters* in 2 vols. in 1847. In 1925 R. W. King produced *The Translator of Dante,* an interesting and reliable study. See also articles in the *Edinburgh Review,* xxix, February 1818 (by Ugo Foscolo and others), and the *Quarterly Review,* li, March 1834 (by H. N. Coleridge); P. Toynbee, *Dante in English Literature from Chaucer to Cary,* 2 vols., 1909; P. Toynbee, 'The Centenary of Cary's Dante', *MLR* vii, 1912; A. Farinelli, 'Dante in Inghilterra', in *Dante in Spagna, Francia, &c.,* Turin, 1922; V. Cenami, *La Divina Commedia nelle traduzioni di Longfellow e di Cary,* Lucca, 1933; and S. Roscoe, 'Cary: "Dante"', *Book Collector,* ii, 1953. In the *TLS* for 3 May 1934 J. L. Lowes wrote briefly on '"La Belle Dame sans Merci" and Dante', and on 19 August 1944 W. M. Parker wrote on the centenary of Cary's death.

JOHN CLARE, 1793–1864.

Clare published four collections of poetry: *Poems Descriptive of Rural Life and Scenery* (1820, 4th ed., 1821); *The Village Minstrel and other Poems,* 2 vols. (1821); *The Shepherd's Calendar; with Village Stories, and other Poems* (1827); and *The Rural Muse, Poems* (1835). Throughout his life he contributed numerous poems to periodicals and annuals, some of them still uncollected. The *Life and Remains,* by J. L. Cherry, appeared in 1873. N. Gale published *Poems by John Clare* at Rugby in 1901, and another volume of selections was produced by Arthur Symons in 1908. More important were *John Clare: Poems Chiefly from Manuscript,* ed. E. Blunden and A. Porter, 1920, and *Madrigals and Chronicles,* ed. E. Blunden, 1924. In 1935 J. W. Tibble produced much the fullest edition of Clare, *The Poems,* in 2 vols., although even this omits many of the poems which Clare himself published and is unsatisfactory in other respects. Geoffrey Grigson's *Poems of John Clare's Madness* (1949) prints some poems from the manuscript for the first time and has a notable introduction. Grigson also edited *Selected Poems* (Muses' Library, 1950). J. Reeves edited a volume of selections in 1954. *Sketches in the Life of John Clare Written by Himself,* ed. E. Blunden, appeared in 1931. J. W. and Anne Tibble edited *The Prose of John Clare* (1951) and *The Letters* (1951).

The first biography was F. Martin's *Life of John Clare* (1865). In 1932 J. W. and Anne Tibble produced *John Clare: A Life*, superseded by their own briefer *John Clare: His Life and Poetry* (1956). J. Wilson's *Green Shadows: The Life of Clare* (1951) is of little independent value. There is still no satisfactory biography.

See also *Four Letters from the Rev. W. Allen, to the Rt. Hon. Lord Radstock . . . on the Poems of John Clare* (1824); De Quincey, *London Reminiscences* (*Collected Writings*, ed. Masson, vol. iii, 1890); *The John Clare Centenary Exhibition Catalogue* [ed. C. Dack and J. W. Bodger], Peterborough, 1893; J. Middleton Murry, 'The Poetry of John Clare', in *Countries of the Mind*, first series, 1922 (revised edition, 1931); J. Heath-Stubbs, 'Clare and the Peasant Tradition', in *The Darkling Plain*, 1950; 'Some Unpublished Poetical Manuscripts of John Clare', by A. J. V. Chapple, *Yale University Library Gazette*, vol. 31 (July 1956); E. Robinson and G. Summerfield, 'John Clare: An Interpretation of Certain Asylum Letters', *RES*, new series, vol. xiii, May 1962; and I. Jack, 'The Sanity of John Clare', in a collection of essays on this period to be edited by J. E. Jordan, Northrop Frye, and J. V. Logan.

WILLIAM COBBETT, ? 1763–1835.

Cobbett wrote, translated, edited, and published so much, often anonymously, that the bibliography of his writings is extremely complicated. Much guidance is provided by M. L. Pearl's *William Cobbett: A Bibliographical Account of his Life and Times*, 1953, although Pearl is not invariably to be relied on. Here only a few of Cobbett's principal writings can be listed, with drastically abbreviated titles: *Observations on the Emigration of Dr. Joseph Priestley*, Philadelphia, 1794; *A Bone to Gnaw for the Democrats*, 2 parts, Philadelphia, 1795; *A Kick for a Bite*, Philadelphia, 1795; *Le Tuteur Anglais, ou Grammaire . . . de la Langue Anglaise*, Philadelphia, 1795; *A Little Plain English addressed to the People of the United States*, Philadelphia, 1795; *A New Year's Gift to the Democrats*, Philadelphia, 1796; *The Bloody Buoy* (an account of atrocities in France), Philadelphia, 1796; *The Political Censor or Monthly Review of . . . Political Occurrences, Relative to the United States of America*, Philadelphia, 1796–7 (the first number was entitled *A Prospect from the Congress Gallery*: several articles were reprinted separately); *The Life and Adventures of*

Peter Porcupine, Philadelphia, 1796; *Porcupine's Gazette*, 4 March 1797–13 January 1800 (edited by Cobbett and mainly published in Philadelphia: much material was reprinted in pamphlet form); *The Democratic Judge*, Philadelphia, 1798 (London, 1798, as *The Republican Judge*: this work is Cobbett's account of his trial for an alleged libel against the King of Spain); *Detection of a Conspiracy* . . . [against] . . . *the United States of America*, Philadelphia, 1798; *The Trial of Republicanism*, Philadelphia, 1799; *The Rush-Light*, 6 numbers, 1800 (the first 5 published at New York, and the 6th at London: the London edition was entitled *The American Rush-Light*); *The Porcupine*, 1800–1 (a daily newspaper); *A Collection of Facts and Observations, relative to the Peace with Bonaparte*, 1801 (mostly reprinted from *The Porcupine*); *Letters to the Right Honourable Lord Hawkesbury, and . . . Henry Addington . . .*, 1802; *Cobbett's Political Register*, 1802–35 (a weekly periodical, after the first two numbers, of which the title varied slightly from time to time. From 12 September 1810 to 22 June 1811 it appeared twice a week). Cobbett and others reprinted a great deal from this work, including most of the following titles: *Letters on the Late War between the United States and Great Britain*, 1815; *Paper against Gold*, 2 vols., 1815; *To the Journeymen and Labourers of England, Wales, Scotland and Ireland*, 1816; *Cobbett's New Year's Gift to Old George Rose*, Nottingham, 1817; *A Year's Residence in the United States of America*, 3 parts, New York, 1818–19; *A Grammar of the English Language*, New York, 1818; *Cobbett's Evening Post*, 29 January–1 April 1820 (a daily paper edited by Cobbett); *Cobbett's Parliamentary Register* (a periodical edited by Cobbett from 6 May to December 1820); *Cobbett's Sermons*, 12 monthly parts, 1821–2 (the first 3 were entitled *Cobbett's Monthly Religious Tracts*); *The American Gardener*, 1821; *Cottage Economy*, 1822 (first published in seven monthly parts, 1821–2); *A French Grammar*, 1824; *A History of the Protestant 'Reformation', in England and Ireland* (first published in parts 1824–6: another part was published in 1827); *Big O. and Sir Glory; or, 'Leisure to Laugh'. A Comedy*, 1825; *Cobbett's Poor Man's Friend*, 1826 (first published in parts, some additional parts appearing after 1826); *The Woodlands; or, A Treatise On the preparing of ground for planting*, '1825' (actually 1828: first published in parts); *The English Gardener*, 1828 (a revised form of *The American Gardener*); *A Treatise on Cobbett's Corn*, 1828; and *The Emigrant's Guide*, 1829.

The first collection of *Rural Rides*, reprinted from the *Political Register*, 1821–6, appeared in 1830. Later editions contained further *Rides*. Later publications included: *Advice to Young Men and (incidentally) to Young Women*, '1829' (actually 1830: first issued in parts); *Eleven Lectures on the French and Belgian Revolutions, and English Boroughmongering*, 1830 (first published in parts); *History of the Regency and Reign of King George the Fourth*, 1830 (first published in parts); *Cobbett's Two-Penny Trash; or, Politics for the Poor*, 2 vols., 1831–2 (partly reprinted from the *Political Register*, and first published in parts); *A Spelling Book*, 1831; *Cobbett's Manchester Lectures, in Support of . . . Reform*, 1832; *A Geographical Dictionary of England and Wales*, 1832; *Cobbett's Tour in Scotland: and in the Four Northern Counties of England: in the Autumn of the Year 1832*, '1832' (actually 1833); *Cobbett's Legacy to Labourers*, '1834' (actually 1835); and *Cobbett's Legacy to Parsons*, 1835. Mention must also be made of *Cobbett's Parliamentary Debates*, 1804–12, which Cobbett sold to the printer, T. C. Hansard, in the latter year, and which became known as *Hansard's Parliamentary Debates* from 1818. A companion series, *Cobbett's Parliamentary History*, also passed out of Cobbett's hands in 1812, having begun in 1806.

The first collection calling itself *The Works of Peter Porcupine* appeared as early as 1795, in Philadelphia. There were other collections, of which the most notable was *Porcupine's Works*, collected by Cobbett himself, 12 vols., 1801. *Selections from Cobbett's Political Works* were edited with notes by J. M. Cobbett and J. P. Cobbett, in 4 vols. in 1835. *The Last of the Saxons*, ed. E. P. Hood, 1854, is a volume of selections.

There are several later editions of the *Rural Rides*, including those edited by J. P. Cobbett (1853), P. Cobbett (2 vols., 1885), and J. H. Lobban, 1908. The 1957 reprint of the Everyman Edition, in 2 vols., has a brief preface by A. Briggs. The best edition, that of G. D. H. and M. Cole, 3 vols., 1930, includes the *Tour in Scotland* and *Letters from Ireland*. S. E. Buckley edited an abridged version of the *Rural Rides* in 1948. G. D. H. Cole edited *The Life . . . of Peter Porcupine* in 1927, and other works have been reprinted as follows: *A Year's Residence in the United States . . .*, ed. J. Freeman, 1923; *A Grammar of the English Language*, ed. J. P. Cobbett, 1866, ed. A. Ayres, New York, 1888, ed. H. L. Stephen, 1906; *Cobbett's Cottage Economy*, reprinted 1916, ed. G. K. Chesterton, 1926; *A History of the Protestant 'Reformation'*, ed. F. A. Gasquet, 1896; *Advice to Young Men*, ed. H. Morley, 1887, ed. P. Snowden, 1926, ed. E. E. Fisk, 1930; *Cobbett's Legacy to Labourers*, ed. J. M. Cobbett, 1872; *Cobbett's Legacy to Parsons*, ed. W. Cobbett, jun., 1869; and *A History of the Last Hundred Days of English Freedom*, ed. J. L. Hammond, 1921 (extracted from the *Political Register*, 1817). In 1937 G. D. H. Cole edited *Letters from William Cobbett to Edward Thornton . . . 1797 to 1800. The Progress of a Plough-Boy to a Seat in Parliament*, ed. W. Reitzel, 1933, is a useful collection of autobiographical passages from Cobbett's writings, revised in 1947 as *The Autobiography of Cobbett*. See also *Cobbett: Selections*, ed A. M. D. Hughes, 1923, and *The Opinions of Cobbett*, by G. D. H. and M. Cole, 1944.

Throughout his life Cobbett was a centre of controversy: many of the resulting pamphlets are mentioned in Pearl's bibliography. J. M. Cobbett wrote an obituary in the *Political Register*, lxxxviii, 1835. The best modern *Life* is that by G. D. H. Cole, 1927. There were earlier biographies by R. Huish (2 vols., 1836: inaccurate), E. Smith (2 vols., 1879), E. I. Carlyle (1904), T. Smith (1906), and 'Lewis Melville' (L. S. Benjamin, 2 vols., 1913). There are later books by G. K. Chesterton (1925), M. Bowen (*Peter Porcupine*, 1935), and W. B. Pemberton (1949, Penguin). On the date of his birth see A. Booth, *TLS*, 16 February, 1962.

Hazlitt wrote on Cobbett in *Table-Talk*, i, 1821, the essay being transferred to the 2nd ed. of *The Spirit of the Age*. There are also essays or chapters in the following books: *Galleries of Literary Portraits*, ii, by G. Gilfillan, 1857; *Political Characters*, ii, by Sir H. L. Bulwer, 1868; *Historical Gleanings*, by J. E. T. Rogers, 1869; *Horae Sabbaticae*, iii, by Sir J. F. Stephen, 1892; *English Portraits and Essays*, by J. Freeman, 1924; *Pioneers of Reform. Cobbett, Owen, Place*, by D. C. Johnson, 1925; *Collected Essays*, i, by G. Saintsbury, 1925; and *Votive Tablets*, by E. Blunden, 1931. The comparative scarcity of articles in learned periodicals emphasizes the need for a more scholarly approach to Cobbett's life and work. L. Woolf wrote on 'An Englishman' in the *Nation*, 25 August, 1923; E. Sellers on 'Cobbett on Choosing a Wife' in the *Contemporary Review*, cxxxiii, 1928; J. Beresford on 'Cobbett and the Reverend Beresford' in the *TLS*, 29 January 1931; H. H. Bellot on the sources of the *Parliamentary History* in the *Bulletin of the Institute of Historical Research*, x, 1932–3; and W. Reitzel on 'Cobbett and Philadelphia Journalism, 1794–1800', in the *Pennsylvania Magazine*, lix, 1935. Also see Raymond

Williams, *Culture and Society 1780&1950*, 1958. On the date of Cobbett's birth see a letter by A. Booth, *TLS*, 16 February 1962.

HARTLEY COLERIDGE, 1796–1849.

Hartley Coleridge published *Poems. Vol. i* (all published) in Leeds in 1833 (a book reissued as *Poems, Songs and Sonnets*); *Biographia Borealis; or Lives of Distinguished Northerns*, Leeds, 1833 (3 vols., 1852, as *Lives of Northern Worthies; Lives of Illustrious Worthies of Yorkshire* is part of the same work re-issued at Hull in 1835 with a new title-page); and *The Dramatic Works of Massinger and Ford, with an Introduction by Hartley Coleridge*, 1840.

His brother, Derwent Coleridge, edited his *Poems*, with a Memoir in 2 vols. in 1851 and his *Essays and Marginalia*, also in 2 vols., in the same year. R. Colles produced *The Complete Poetical Works* in 1908 (n.d., Muses' Library). J. Drinkwater edited his *Essays on Parties in Poetry and on the Character of Hamlet* (from the *Essays and Marginalia*) in 1925. G. E. and E. L. Griggs edited his *Letters* in 1937, while E. L. Griggs also produced *New Poems, including a Selection from his Published Poetry* in 1942. The standard books are those by E. L. Griggs (*Hartley Coleridge: His Life and Work*, 1929) and H. Hartman (*Hartley Coleridge, Poet's Son and Poet*, 1931). There are useful studies of Hartley Coleridge in R. H. Horne, *A New Spirit of the Age*, vol. i, 1844; W. Bagehot, *Literary Studies*, vol. i. 1879; A. M. Turner, 'Wordsworth and Hartley Coleridge', *JEGP* xxii, 1923; M. J. Pomeroy, *The Poetry of Hartley Coleridge*, Washington, 1927; S. T. Williams, 'Hartley Coleridge as a Critic of Literature', *Southern Atlantic Quarterly*, xxiii, 1924; four articles by E. L. Griggs, 'Coleridge and his Son', *SP* xxvii, 1930; 'Hartley Coleridge on his Father', *PMLA* xlvi, 1931; 'Hartley Coleridge's Unpublished Correspondence', *London Mercury*, xxiv, 1931; and 'Four Letters of Hartley Coleridge', *HLQ* ix, 1946; E. Blunden, 'Coleridge the Less' (in *Votive Tablets*, 1931); and J. D. Rea, 'Hartley Coleridge and Wordsworth's Lucy', *SP* xxviii, 1931. One of his numerous unprinted poems was published in the *TLS* by A. S. Whitefield, 15 March 1947.

WILLIAM COMBE, 1741–1823.

A great many of Combe's volumes of verse belong to the later eighteenth century. Here we are concerned only with *Dr. Syntax* and his later publications. *The Tour of Dr. Syntax in Search of the Picturesque* was first published in Ackermann's

Poetical Magazine in 1809 as 'The Schoolmaster's Tour'. It appeared as a volume in 1812 and other editions followed quickly. *The Second Tour of Dr. Syntax. In Search of Consolation* came out in 1820 (having first been issued in monthly parts). *The Third Tour of Dr. Syntax in Search of a Wife* appeared in 1821. Each of the three had coloured plates by Rowlandson. *The Three Tours of Dr. Syntax* were collected in 3 vols. in 1826, and there were several later editions.

In verse Combe also published *Six Poems. Illustrative of Engravings by H.R.H. the Princess Elizabeth*, 1813; *Poetical Sketches of Scarborough*, 1813; *The English Dance of Death from the Designs of Thomas Rowlandson with Metrical Illustrations*, 2 vols., 1815; *The Dance of Life*, 1816–17; and *The History of Johnny Quae Genus the Little Foundling of the late Dr. Syntax*, 1822 (first issued in monthly parts). The verse-portions of *The Forget-me-not* for 1823 are by Combe, who also published numerous books in prose, most of them in the eighteenth century.

On Combe see H. W. Hamilton, *William Combe*, Ithaca, 1935; H. Fluchère, 'Sterne et Combe', *Revue Anglo-américaine*, viii, 1931; L. P. Curtis, 'Forged Letters of Laurence Sterne', *PMLA* l (50), 1935; F. Montgomery, 'Alexander Mackenzie's Literary Assistant', *Canadian Historical Review*, xviii, 1937; and the same writer's note on 'The Birth and Parentage of Combe', *NQ*, 12 April 1941; and 'William Combe', *TLS*, 19 July 1941. The article in the *DNB* is still helpful. A great deal of Combe's work was done for Rudolph Ackermann.

JOHN WILSON CROKER, 1780–1857.

Croker's poems include: *Familiar Epistles . . . on the Present State of the Irish Stage*, Dublin, 1804; *An Intercepted Letter from J— T—, . . . at Canton*, Dublin, 1804; and *The Battles of Talavera*, Dublin, 1809 (often reprinted, in 1812 with *Other Poems*).

Croker's most important writings were in the *Quarterly Review*. M. F. Brightfield's biography lists more than 250 contributions. Several of his articles were reprinted, often in revised form: for example, his *Robespierre*, 1835, his *History of the Guillotine*, 1853, and his *Essays on the Early Period of the French Revolution*, 1857. He also published two children's books and a number of important speeches and writings on political questions. More relevant to us is his editing of Boswell's *Life of Samuel Johnson*, 5 vols., 1831, a labour of love to which subsequent editors have been indebted. He also edited a number of historical memoirs. His *Correspondence with the Rt. Hon. Lord John Russell on Some Passages of Moore's Diary* appeared in 1854. *An Essay towards a new edition of Pope's works* was privately printed in 1871, the year that the first volume of the Elwin–Courthope edition appeared, with its acknowledgement on the title-page that the 'new materials' had been 'collected in part by the late Rt. Hon. John Wilson Croker'.

The Croker Papers: The Correspondence and Diaries were edited with a memoir by L. J. Jennings in 3 vols. in 1884 (revised edition, 1885). Macaulay's severe (and unfair) review of the *Boswell* was reprinted in his *Critical and Historical Essays*, 3 vols., 1843. There is an article on Croker in the *Quarterly Review* for October 1884, and an incisive little portrait by K. Feiling in *Sketches in Nineteenth Century Biography*, 1930. The standard modern study is M. F. Brightfield's *John Wilson Croker*, 1940. Notes on Croker and Tennyson appeared in the *TLS* for 30 November 1946, 14 and 21 December 1946, and 18 January 1947, and a communication on 'Croker's Pettifoggery' on 25 August 1950.

ALLAN CUNNINGHAM, 1784–1842.

Cunningham wrote romances and poems as well as editing Burns and collecting Scottish songs and stories. The date of *The Magic Bridle* may be *c.* 1812; *Songs, chiefly in the Rural Language of Scotland* appeared in 1813; *Sir Marmaduke Maxwell, A Dramatic Poem* (with other poems and songs) in 1822; *Traditional Tales of the English and Scottish Peasantry* in 2 vols. in 1822 (all but one Tale had previously appeared in the *London Magazine*: the book was edited by H. Morley, without the interesting preface, 1887); and *The Songs of Scotland, Ancient and Modern* in 4 vols. in 1825. Cunningham also wrote two romances, *Paul Jones* and *Sir Michael Scott*, each in 3 vols., in 1826 and 1828; *Lives of the Most Emiment British Painters, Sculptors and Architects*, 6 vols., 1829–33 (selections were edited by W. Sharp in 1886); *The Maid of Elvar, A Poem in Twelve Parts*, 1833; *The Cabinet Gallery of Pictures . . . with Biographical and Critical Descriptions*, 2 vols., 1833–4; *Biographical and Critical History of the British Literature of the Last Fifty Years* (Paris, 1834: first published in the *Athenaeum*); *Lord Roldan, A Romance*, 3 vols., 1836; and *The Life of Sir David Wilkie* [ed. P. Cunningham], 3 vols., 1843. In 1841

Cunningham edited Thomson's *Seasons* and *Castle of Indolence*. *Poems and Songs*, ed. P. Cunningham, appeared in 1847.

Mention should also be made of Cunningham's work on Burns. In 1826 he contributed 'Last Moments of Robert Burns' to *The Curious Book* (Edinburgh). In 1834 there appeared *The Works of Robert Burns* with a biography by Cunningham in the first of the eight volumes.

Cunningham was one of the *London Magazine* group: many of his contributions were subsequently reprinted in his separate publications. He also edited *The Anniversary* for some years and contributed to *The Club Book*, edited by Andrew Picken, 3 vols., 1831, and many other periodicals.

A *Life of Allan Cunningham, with Selections from his Works and Correspondence* was published by David Hogg at Dumfries in 1875. Reminiscences of him may be found in De Quincey's *London Reminiscences* (*Collected Writings*, ed. Masson, vol. iii, 1890), and in the work of other members of the London group. See also G. Gilfillan, *Galleries of Literary Portraits*, vol. i, 1856; S. C. Hall, 'Allan Cunningham', *Art Journal*, xviii, 1866; *TLS*, 31 October 1942; and L. A. Marchand, *The Athenaeum: A Mirror of Victorian Culture*, Chapel Hill, 1941.

GEORGE DARLEY, 1795–1846.

Darley published two volumes of verse and two verse-plays: *The Errors of Ecstasie* (1822); *Sylvia; or, The May Queen* (1827); *Thomas à Becket* (1840) and *Ethelstan; or, The Battle of Brunanburh* (1841). *Nepenthe* was privately printed in 1835. He also published *The Labours of Idleness, or, Seven Nights' Entertainments* ('By Guy Penseval'), 1826; a number of mathematical textbooks; *The New Sketch Book* ('by G. Crayon, Jun.', 2 vols., 1829); and *The Works of Beaumont and Fletcher*, with an introduction, 2 vols., 1840. A volume of selections, *Poems*, was published at Liverpool in [1889] for private circulation and contains the first printing of 'Lenimina Laborum'. R. A. Streatfeild produced *Selections* in 1904, and R. Colles, *The Complete Poetical Works* in 1908 (n.d. Muses' Library edition). Professor C. C. Abbott is preparing a new edition for the Muses' Library. There is a reprint of *Sylvia*, ed. J. H. Ingram, 1892, and one of *Nepenthe*, ed. R. A. Streatfeild, 1897.

Darley contributed to a number of annuals and periodicals, including the *London Magazine* (which contains his 'Letters to the Dramatists of the Day', by 'John Lacy'), the *Athenaeum*, and

Bentley's Miscellany (1844). The standard biography is *The Life and Letters*, by C. C. Abbott, 1928, which contains a fuller bibliography. See also E. Blunden (in *Votive Tablets*, 1931); R. Bridges (in *Collected Essays*, v, 1931 (written 1906)); L. Wolff ('George Darley, poète et critique d'art', *Revue Anglo-américaine*, Feb. 1931); C. C. Abbott ('The Letters of Darley', *Durham University Journal*, xxxiii, 1940); J. Heath-Stubbs in *The Darkling Plain*, 1950; and 'Uncollected Authors, No. 28' by C. Woolf, in *The Book Collector*, Summer 1961. For the dating of the memorial *Poems* as [1889] instead of [1890] see the notice of Woolf's article in the *TLS*.

THOMAS DE QUINCEY, 1785–1859.

The greater part of De Quincey's writings first appeared in periodicals. The only books that he published were *Confessions of an English Opium-Eater*, 1822 (reprinted from the *London Magazine*, September and October 1821, with an appendix added: for the 1856 text see below); *Walladmor. A Novel. Freely translated from the English of Sir Walter Scott, and now freely translated from the German into English*, 2 vols., 1825 (De Quincey made a very free rendering indeed of this German forgery); *Klosterheim, or the Masque*, 1832; and *The Logic of Political Economy*, 1844.

He also contributed to the following books: *Juvenile Library*, i, 1800 (trans. of Horace, Ode 22, Lib. 1); *Concerning the Relations of Great Britain, Spain and Portugal . . .*, 1809 (Wordsworth's 'Tract on the Convention of Cintra': contains an appendix by De Quincey on the letters of Sir J. Moore); *Popular Tales and Romances of the Northern Nations*, 3 vols., 1823 (De Quincey contributed 'The Fatal Marksman', trans. from the German of J. A. Apel); *The Gallery of Portraits*, ed. A. T. Malkin, 7 vols., 1832–7 (De Quincey contributed a Life of Milton to vol. i); *Encyclopaedia Britannica*, 7th ed., 1827–42 (De Quincey wrote on Goethe, Pope, Schiller, and Shakespeare).

There is no absolutely complete edition of De Quincey's writings, and there may never be. But numerous attempts have been made to collect his contributions to the *London Magazine*, *Blackwood's Magazine*, *Tait's Magazine*, *Hogg's Instructor*, and the numerous other periodicals for which he wrote. The American publishers Ticknor and Fields published *De Quincey's Writings* in 24 vols. at Boston in 1851–9. *Selections Grave and Gay from . . . Thomas De Quincey*, published by James Hogg (not the Ettrick

Shepherd) in 14 vols. in 1853–60 is a collected edition of his writings revised by De Quincey himself. The later and much longer text of the *Confessions* first appeared as vol. v of this edition. Of later attempts at collected editions much the most important is that edited by David Masson in 14 vols. (1889–90). Although it is unsatisfactory in many ways, this is still regarded as the standard edition. It contains prefaces, notes, and an index.

Other writings of De Quincey's have been reprinted in *The Uncollected Writings*, ed. James Hogg, 2 vols., 1890; *The Posthumous Works*, ed. A. H. Japp, 2 vols., 1891–3; *A Diary of Thomas De Quincey, 1803*, edited, with manuscript facsimile, by H. A. Eaton, [1927]; and *Niels Klim, being an Incomplete Translation, by Thomas De Quincey, from the Danish*, ed. S. Musgrove (Auckland, N.Z., 1953).

Many letters may be found in Japp's biography (below), in *De Quincey Memorials. Being Letters and other Records*, ed. A. H. Japp, 2 vols., 1891; in *De Quincey at Work: As Seen in One Hundred and Thirty . . . Letters*, ed. W. H. Bonner, Buffalo, 1936; in 'Some Unpublished Letters of Thomas De Quincey', by E. H. Moore, *RES* ix, 1933; and in *De Quincey to Wordsworth: A Biography of a Relationship*, by J. E. Jordan, Berkeley and Los Angeles, 1962, which contains De Quincey's letters to the Wordsworth family.

The bibliography by J. E. Jordan in *ERPE* gives further information about De Quincey manuscripts and scattered writings reprinted in various places.

The original text of the *Confessions* has been reprinted on several occasions: ed. R. Garnett, 1885 (with 'Notes of Conversations with Thomas De Quincey', by R. Woodhouse); ed. G. Saintsbury, 1928; ed. E. Sackville-West, 1950; and ed. M. Elwin, 1956 (both versions, with a useful introduction and the *Blackwood's* text of the *Suspiria*). The 1856 text has been frequently reprinted. The Everyman's Library edition has an Introduction by J. E. Jordan.

There are various volumes of selections. *De Quincey's Literary Criticism*, ed. H[elen] Darbishire, 1909, is of particular interest. *Recollections of the Lake Poets* were edited by E. Sackville-West in 1948 and by J. E. Jordan in 1961 (Everyman's Library, as *Reminiscences of the English Lake Poets*).

It is impossible to mention all the books of the period which contain information about De Quincey: they include books by, and about, Wordsworth, Carlyle, John Wilson, Crabb

Robinson, R. P. Gillies, and Charles Knight. James Hogg's *De Quincey and his Friends: Personal Recollections, Souvenirs and Anecdotes*, 1895, is a useful collection. The first full biography, which is still of interest, is *Thomas De Quincey: His Life and Writings. With Unpublished Correspondence*, by A. H. Japp, 2 vols., 1877 (rev. ed., 1 vol., 1890). D. Masson's volume in the English Men of Letters series, 1881, leans heavily on Japp. Of more recent biographies and book-length studies the best are: *A Flame in Sunlight*, by E. Sackville West, 1936; *Thomas De Quincey*, by H. A. Eaton, 1936; and *De Quincey to Wordsworth*, by J. E. Jordan, as mentioned above.

Other books wholly or partly about De Quincey include *De Quincey*, by H. S. Salt, 1904 (see also his *Literary Sketches*, 1888); *De Quincey's Editorship of the Westmorland Gazette, with Selections* . . ., by C. Pollitt, 1890; *Thomas De Quincey. A Study*, by R. Hitchcock, 1899; *Thomas De Quincey's Relation to German Literature and Philosophy*, by W. A. Dunn, Strasburg, 1900; *The Prose Poetry of Thomas De Quincey*, by L. Cooper, Leipzig, 1902; *Étude médico-psychologique sur Thomas De Quincey*, by P. Guerrier, Lyons, 1907 (a book which contains information about French translations, and about nineteenth-century studies of opium); *Rydal*, by M. L. Armitt, 1916; *Immanuel Kant in England (1793–1838)*, by R. Wellek, Princeton, 1931; *Baudelaire and De Quincey*, by G. T. Clapton, 1931; *The Milk of Paradise. The Effect of Opium Visions on* . . . *De Quincey, Crabbe, Francis Thompson, and Coleridge*, by M. H. Abrams, Cambridge, Mass., 1934; *Grands névropathes*, by A. Cabanès, 1935; *Geschichtliches und religiöses Denken bei De Quincey*, by E. T. Sehrt (*Neue Deutsche Forschungen* CIII, Berlin, 1936); *Thomas De Quincey's Theory of Literature*, by S. K. Proctor, Ann Arbor, 1943 (with an appendix on De Quincey scholarship by C. D. Thorpe); *Thomas De Quincey, Literary Critic*, by J. E. Jordan, Berkeley, 1952; and *Rhythm in the Prose of Thomas De Quincey*, by S. Kobayashi, 1956.

The French have always been interested in De Quincey. In 1828 de Musset produced a fictionalized version of the *Confessions, L'anglais mangeur d'opium*, while in 1860 Baudelaire wrote penetratingly about De Quincey in *Les paradis artificiels, opium et haschisch*, including passages of translation.

The following include some of the more important essays and articles: 'Life and Writings of Thomas De Quincey', by H. W. S., *Fraser's Magazine*, 1860–1; review of *Selections, Grave and Gay*, [by T. E. Kebbel], *Quarterly Review*, cx, 1861; 'De Quincey', by Sir Leslie Stephen, in *Hours in a Library*, i, 1874; *Studies in Prose and Verse*, by A. Symons, 1904; 'De Quincey's Love of Music', by H. A. Eaton, *JEGP*, 1914; 'De Quincey as Literary Critic', by J. H. Fowler, 1922 (Eng. Assoc.); 'The Syntax of De Quincey', by 'Vernon Lee' (Violet Page), in *The Handling of Words*, 1923; *The Romantic Theory of Poetry*, by A. E. Powell, 1926; 'Impassioned Prose', *TLS*, 16 September 1926; 'De Quincey's Autobiography', in *The Common Reader*, 2nd series, by Virginia Woolf, 1932; 'The Musical Structure of De Quincey's *Dream-Fugue*', by C. S. Brown, *Musical Quarterly*, 1938; ' "Libellous Attack" on De Quincey', by K. Forward, *PMLA* lii, 1937, and 'De Quincey's "Cessio Bonorum" ', by the same scholar, *PMLA* liv, 1939; 'De Quincey's Status in the History of Ideas', by R. Wellek, *PQ* xxiii, 1944; 'De Quincey's Use of Americanisms', by R. E. Hollinger, *American Speech*, 1948; '*Walladmor*: A Pseudo-Translation of Scott', by L. H. C. Thomas, *MLR*, xlvi, 1951; 'De Quincey on Wordsworth's Theory of Diction', by J. E. Jordan, *PMLA* lxviii, 1953; the same writer's earlier 'De Quincey's Dramaturgic Criticisms', *ELH* xviii, 1951; 'De Quincey and the Ending of *Moby-Dick*', by F. S. Rockwell, *Nineteenth-Century Fiction*, 1954; 'Some Unpublished Works of De Quincey', by R. H. Byrns, *PMLA* lxxi, 1956; and 'De Quincey Revises his *Confessions*', by I. Jack, *PMLA* lxxii, 1957.

See also 'How De Quincey Worked', by E. Dowden, *Saturday Review*, lxxix, 1895; 'The Letters of De Quincey to Wordsworth, 1803–7', by H. A. Eaton, *ELH* iii, 1936; 'The Depreciation of De Quincey', by H. S. Salt, *National Review*, cxliii, 1928; 'Coleridge, De Quincey, and Nineteenth-Century Editing', by E. L. Griggs, *MLN* xlvii, 1932; 'The Woes of Thomas De Quincey', by C. O. Parsons, *RES* x, 1934; 'Thomas De Quincey, mystique et symboliste', by G.-A. Astre, *La revue hebdomadaire*, 23 October 1937, and the same writer's essay on Balzac and De Quincey, *Revue de la littérature comparée*, December 1935; 'Is Thomas De Quincey Author of *The Love-Charm?*', by H. K. Galinsky, *MLN* lii, 1937; 'Wordsworth and De Quincey in Westmorland Politics, 1818', by J. E. Wells, *PMLA* lv, 1940, and 'De Quincey and *The Prelude* in 1839', by the same writer, *PQ* xx, 1941; 'Some De Quincey Manuscripts', by C. E. Jones, *ELH* viii, 1941; 'De Quincey, Symptomatologist', *PMLA* lx, 1945, by C. H. Hendricks; and 'Berlioz, Musset and De Quincey', by J.-G. Prud'homme, *Musical Quarterly*, xxxii, 1946.

Bibliographical information may be found in an appendix to Masson's edition, in *Thomas De Quincey: A Bibliography based upon the De Quincey Collection in the Moss Side Library*, by J. A. Green, 1908 (supplemented by W. E. A. Axon in 'The Canon of De Quincey's Writings . . .', *Transactions of the Royal Society of Literature*, 1914), in the *CBEL*, and in J. E. Jordan's excellent contribution to *ERPE*.

THOMAS FROGNALL DIBDIN, 1776–1847.

Dibdin's main publications include: *Poems*, 1797; *An Introduction to the Knowledge of Rare and Valuable Editions of the Greek and Latin Classics*, Gloucester, 1802 (revised and enlarged editions, 1804, 1808 (2 vols.) and 1827 (2 vols., 'greatly enlarged')); *The Director. A Weekly Literary Journal*, 2 vols., 1807; *Specimen Bibliothecae Britannicae*, 1808; *The Bibliomania; or Book-Madness*, 1809, 1811 (enlarged edition), 1842 (fuller edition), 1876; *Typographical Antiquities; or the History of Printing in England*, 4 vols., 1810–19 (based on the work of Ames and Herbert); *Bibliotheca Spenceriana: A Descriptive Catalogue of* [rare and early books] *in the Library of Earl Spencer*, 4 vols., 1814–15 (supplemented in *Ædes Althorpianæ* [with a] *Supplement to the Bibliotheca Spenceriana*, 1822, and the *Catalogue of the Books . . . of the Duke de Cassano Serra*, 1823); *The Bibliographical Decameron*, 3 vols., 1817; *Sermons Doctrinal and Practical*, 2 vols., 1820; *A Bibliographical, Antiquarian and Picturesque Tour in France and Germany*, 3 vols., 1821 (another edition, with omissions and additions, 3 vols., 1829); *The Museum*, 27 April 1822–14 February 1824 (from 1823, *The Literary Museum*); *The Library Companion: or, The Young Man's Guide, and The Old Man's Comfort, in the Choice of a Library, Vol. I* (all published), 1824 (2nd ed., 1825); *The Sunday Library: A Selection of Sermons from Eminent Divines*, 6 vols., 1831; *Bibliophobia: Remarks on the Present Languid . . . State of Literature and the Book Trade*, 1832; *Reminiscences of a Literary Life*, 2 vols., 1836; *Roxburghe Revels . . . including Answers to the Attack on the Memory of Joseph Haslewood*, privately printed, 1837; *A Bibliographical Antiquarian and Picturesque Tour in the Northern Counties of England and in Scotland*, 2 vols., 1838 (also in 3 vols., another format); and *Cranmer* (a novel), 3 vols., 1839. *Bibliography, A Poem*, 1812, was privately printed. Dibdin also edited numerous books and pamphlets for the Roxburghe Club. Information about him may be found in the *DNB* and in *The Bibliographer's Manual*, by W. T. Lowndes, rev. ed., vol. ii, part i, 1858.

Isaac D'Israeli, 1766–1848.

His main publications were *A Defence of Poetry* [and] *Specimens of a New Version of Telemachus*, 1790; *Curiosities of Literature*, 3 vols., 1791, 1793, 1817 (a Second Series, in 3 vols., appeared in 1823: the 9th edition, in 6 vols., included both Series); *Eighty-Nine Fugitive Fables*, 1792; *A Dissertation on Anecdotes*, 1793; *Domestic Anecdotes of the French Nation*, 1794; *An Essay on the Literary Character*, 1795 (enlarged and revised editions in 1818, 1822, and 1828); *Miscellanies; Or, Literary Recreations*, 1796 (*Literary Miscellanies*, 2nd edition, with 2nd edition of *A Dissertation on Anecdotes*, 1801); *Vaurien*, 2 vols., 1797 (a novel); *Romances*, 1799 (revised editions, 1801 and 1807); *Narrative Poems*, 1803; *Flim-Flams!*, 3 vols., 1805 (a novel); *An Apology for Flim-Flams*, 1806; *Despotism*, 2 vols., 1811 (a novel); *Calamities of Authors*, 2 vols., 1812; *Quarrels of Authors*, 3 vols., 1814; *An Inquiry into the Character of James I*, 1816; *Psyche*, [? 1823]; *Commentaries on the Life and Reign of Charles I*, 5 vols., 1828–31 (revised edition, 2 vols., 1851); *Eliot, Hampden, and Pym*, 1832; *The Genius of Judaism*, 1833; *The Illustrator Illustrated*, 1838; and *Amenities of Literature*, 2 vols., 1841. *A Letter from I. D'Israeli to C. P. Cooper* was privately printed in 1857.

A partial collection of his writings on literary history appeared as *Miscellanies of Literature* in one huge volume in 1840. *The Works*, edited by his son, first appeared in 7 vols. in 1859, including *Curiosities*, *Amenities*, *The Literary Character*, *Literary Miscellanies*, *James I*, *Calamities*, and *Quarrels*. His 'Unpublished Notes on the Romantic Poets' were published by C. L. Cline in *Texas Studies in English* in 1941.

There are numerous references to Isaac D'Israeli in the literature of his age. Benjamin Disraeli wrote a memoir of his father for the 1849 edition of the *Curiosities* which was also prefixed to *The Works*. Information may also be found in the *DNB*, in Monypenny and Buckle's *Life of Benjamin Disraeli*, 2 vols., 1929 (rev. ed.), and in other works on the statesman. Sarah Kopstein's German study, *Isaac D'Israeli*, Jerusalem, 1939, does not add very much. There is a good unpublished thesis by James Ogden (Oxford, 1961), now being rewritten as a book.

Recent information has been provided by C. L. Cline in 'The Correspondence of Robert Southey and D'Israeli', *RES* xvii, 1941; by G. K. Anderson in 'D'Israeli's "Amenities of Literature": A Centennial Review', *PQ* xxii, 1943; and by W. S. Samuel in 'D'Israeli: First Published Writings', *NQ*, 30 April 1949.

JOHN COLIN DUNLOP, d. 1842.

Dunlop published *The History of Fiction . . . from the Earliest Greek Romances to the Novels of the Present Age* in 3 vols. in 1814. There was a revised edition, also in 3 vols., two years later, and the work was translated into German in 1851. There is also an edition revised and edited by H. Wilson, 2 vols., 1888. Dunlop's *History of Roman Literature from its Earliest Period to the Augustan Age* appeared in 3 vols. in 1823–8: his *Memoirs of Spain . . . from 1621 to 1700* in 2 vols. in 1834: and his *Selections from the Latin Anthology, Translated into English Verse* in 1838.

EBENEZER ELLIOTT, 1781–1849.

Elliott's (mostly indifferent) earlier poetry includes *The Vernal Walk*, 1801; *Night*, 1818; *Love*, 1823; and *The Village Patriarch*, 1829. His *Corn-Law Rhymes* appeared in 1831 and went through several editions. *The Splendid Village; Corn-Law Rhymes; and Other Poems* appeared in 3 vols. in 1833–5, and his *Poetical Works* in 1840 and then in 3 vols. in 1844. In 1876 they were edited by E. Elliott, in 2 vols. *More Verse and Prose by the Corn-Law Rhymer* was published in 2 vols. in 1850.

The Life, Poetry, and Letters of Ebenezer Elliott, ed. John Watkins, 1850, includes a brief autobiographical sketch. See also the *Edinburgh Review*, lv, 1832 (reprinted in *Critical and Miscellaneous Essays of Thomas Carlyle*, 1839); *Blackwood's Magazine*, xxxv, 1834 (repr. in *The Works of John Wilson*, vi, 1856); 'J. Searle' (G. S. Phillips), *The Life of Ebenezer Elliott*, 1850; J. W. King, *Ebenezer Elliott, A Sketch*, Sheffield, 1854; W. Odom, *Two Sheffield Poets: James Montgomery and Ebenezer Elliott*, [1929]; G. L. Phillips, 'Elliott's "The Giaour" ', *RES* xv, 1939; E. R. Seary, 'Robert Southey and Ebenezer Elliott', *RES* xv, 1939; A. A. Eaglestone, E. R. Seary, and G. L. Phillips, *Ebenezer Elliott: A Commemorative Brochure with Bibliography*, Sheffield, 1949; J. B. Hobman, 'Ebenezer Elliott, Corn Law Rhymer', *Contemporary Review*, clxxvi, 1949; 'Corn-law Rhymer', *TLS*, 2 December 1949; and

A. Briggs, 'Ebenezer Elliott, the Corn Law Rhymer', *Cambridge Journal*, iii, 1950.

SUSAN EDMONSTONE FERRIER, 1782–1854.

She published three novels, *Marriage*, 3 vols., 1818; *The Inheritance*, 3 vols., 1824; and *Destiny, or, The Chief's Daughter*, 3 vols., 1831. Her novels were republished in 6 vols. in 1882 and in 6 vols. in 1894, ed. R. B. Johnson. They were edited with an introduction by Lady Margaret Sackville in 4 vols. in 1928 as *The Works*, vol. iv being a reissue of the Ferrier–Doyle *Memoir*. There are editions of *Marriage* and *The Inheritance* with biographical prefaces by A. Goodrich-Freer and critical notices by Walter, Earl of Iddesleigh (each in 2 vols.), 1902, 1903.

The *Memoir and Correspondence of Susan Ferrier . . . by her Grandnephew John Ferrier*, ed. J. A. Doyle, 1898, is the only book. See also 'Noctes Ambrosianae', lviii [by J. G. Lockhart], in *Blackwood's Magazine*, xxx, 1831; *Edinburgh Review*, lxxiv, 1842; 'Miss Ferrier's Novels', *Temple Bar*, liv, 1878; C. J. Hamilton, *Women Writers, their Works and Ways*, Series 1, 1892; Sir G. Douglas, *The Blackwood Group* [1897]; R. B. Johnson, *The Women Novelists* [1918]; and A. Birrell, *More Obiter Dicta*, 1924.

JOHN HOOKHAM FRERE, 1769–1846.

Frere contributed to *The Microcosm*, Eton, 1786–7, and *The Anti-Jacobin*, 1797–8. He also produced the following books: *Prospectus and Specimen of an Intended National Work, by William and Robert Whistlecraft . . . relating to King Arthur and his Round Table*, cantos i–ii, 1817, cantos iii–iv, 1818: as *The Monks and the Giants*, 1818 (ed. R. D. Waller, with a useful introduction on Frere's Italian models, Manchester, 1926); *Fables for Five-Years-Old*, Malta, 1830; *The Frogs*, 1839 (privately printed); *A Metrical Version of the Acharnians, the Knights and the Birds*, 1840 (each play having been privately printed for Frere in Malta the previous year); *Theognis restitutus*, Malta, 1842 (privately printed); and *Psalms, &c.*, [? 1848]—verse paraphrases. His Etonian metrical version of the 'Ode on Athelstan's Victory' was printed in the 2nd edition of Ellis's *Specimens of the Early English Poets*, vol. i, 1801, and three of his passages of translation from the 'Poem of the Cid' were printed as an appendix to Southey's *Chronicle of the Cid*, 1808. Although he was one of the original projectors of the *Quarterly Review* his only certain

contribution was the review of Mitchell's translation of Aristophanes in July 1820.

His *Works . . . in Verse and Prose*, with a Memoir by Sir Bartle
Frere, appeared in 2 vols. in 1872 and in a revised 3-vol.
edition in 1874. See also G. Festing, *John Hookham Frere and
his Friends*, 1899, and A. von Eichler, *John Hookham Frere: Sein
Leben und seine Werke . . .*, Vienna, 1905.

JOHN GALT, 1779–1839.

Galt published the following principal books: *The Battle of
Largs. A Gothic Poem*, 1804; *Voyages and Travels in the Years 1809,
1810 and 1811*, 1812; *The Life and Administration of Cardinal
Wolsey*, 1812; *The Tragedies of Maddalen, Agamemnon, Lady
Macbeth, Antonia and Clytemnestra*, 1812; *Letters from the Levant*,
1813; *The Majolo*, 2 vols., 1816; *The Crusade* (a poem), 1816;
The Life and Studies of Benjamin West, Part i, 1816; *The Appeal:
A Tragedy*, 1818 (with a prologue by Lockhart and an epilogue
by Scott); *The Wandering Jew*, 1820 ('By the Rev. T. Clark');
The Life, Studies and Works of Benjamin West, Parts i–ii, 1820; *All
the Voyages round the World* ('By Samuel Prior', 1820); *A Tour of
Europe and Asia*, 2 vols., 1820 ('By the Rev. T. Clark'); *The
Earthquake*, 3 vols., 1820; *George the Third, his Court and Family*,
2 vols., 1820; *Glenfell, or Macdonalds and Campbells*, 1820; *Pictures, Historical and Biographical, drawn from . . . History*, 2 vols.,
1821; *The Ayrshire Legatees*, 1821 (*Blackwood's*, Oct. 1820–March
1821); *Annals of the Parish*, 1821; *Sir Andrew Wylie, of That Ilk*,
3 vols., 1822; *The Provost*, 1822; *The Steam-Boat* (*Blackwood's*,
1821), 1822; *The Gathering of the West*, 1823; *The Entail*, 3 vols.,
1823; *Ringan Gilhaize*, 3 vols., 1823; *The Spaewife*, 3 vols., 1823;
Rothelan, 3 vols., 1824 (with three other tales appended in vol.
iii); *The Bachelor's Wife . . ., Extracts, with Cursory Observations*,
1824 (an anthology, with dramatized comments); *The Omen*,
'1825' (probably 1826); *The Last of the Lairds*, 1826; *Lawrie Todd*,
3 vols., 1830; *Southennan*, 3 vols., 1830; *The Life of Lord Byron*,
1830; *The Lives of the Players*, 2 vols., 1831; *Bogle Corbet*, 3 vols.,
[1831]; *The Member*, 1832; *The Radical*, 1832 (the two books
were also published together the next year as *The Reform*);
Stanley Buxton, 3 vols., 1832; *The Canadas as they . . . commend
themselves to . . . Emigrants . . . from . . . Documents furnished by John
Galt* (by Andrew Picken), 1832; *Eben Erskine*, 3 vols., 1833;
Poems, 1833; *The Stolen Child*, 1833 ('The Library of Romance',

published by Smith, Elder, vol. iv); *The Autobiography of John Galt*, 2 vols., 1833; *Stories of the Study*, 3 vols., 1833; *The Ourano-logos, or the Celestial Volume*, 1833 (illustrated by John Martin); *The Literary Life, and Miscellanies, of John Galt*, 3 vols., 1834; *Efforts, By an Invalid*, Greenock, 1835; *A Contribution to the Green-ock Calamity Fund*, Greenock, 1835 (poems); and *The Demon of Destiny and Other Poems*, Greenock, 1839. In 1831 he had con-tributed five tales to *The Club Book*, ed. Andrew Picken (3 vols.)

A fuller list of his writings, including those in periodicals and other collections, may be found in *John Galt*, by Jennie W. Aber-dein, 1936. See also the list in the *Autobiography*, and H. Lums-den, 'The Bibliography of John Galt', *Records of Glasgow Bib-liographical Society*, ix, 1931, and B. A. Booth, 'A Bibliography of John Galt', *Bulletin of Bibliography*, xvi, 1936.

For discussions of the authorship of 'The Canadian Boat Song' see Lockhart below.

The Works, ed. D. S. Meldrum and W. Roughead, 10 vols., 1936, include only the principal novels. Several of the novels have been reprinted more than once, particularly the *Annals of the Parish* (the 1908 reprint has a preface by G. Gordon reprinted in *The Lives of Authors*, 1950). W. Roughead edited *The Howdie and Other Tales* in 1923 and *A Rich Man and Other Stories* in 1925. There are recent editions of *The Life of Benjamin West*, ed. N. Wright, Gainesville, Florida, 1960, and of *The Gathering of the West*, ed. B. A. Booth, Baltimore, 1939.

For early criticism see *Edinburgh Review*, xxxix, Oct. 1823, (reprinted in Jeffrey's *Contributions*, 4 vols., 1844); and A. Cun-ningham, *Biographical and Critical History of the British Literature of the Last Fifty Years*, Paris, 1834.

There is a valuable Memoir by '*Δ*' (D. M. Moir) in *The Annals of the Parish and The Ayrshire Legatees*, n.d. [1841] ('Blackwood's Standard Novels'). There are modern studies by R. K. Gordon (*John Galt*, Toronto, 1920); Jennie W. Aberdein (as above); and E. Frykman (*John Galt's Scottish Stories, 1820–1823*, Uppsala, 1959). F. H. Lyell's *Study of the Novels of John Galt* is an unpub-lished Princeton dissertation (1942): there is a mimeographed copy in Edinburgh University Library.

John Galt's Dramas: A Brief Review, by G. H. Needler, Toronto, 1945, is a pamphlet containing an expanded form of an article first published in *UTQ*, January 1942. See also 'John Galt', by G. Kitchin, in *Edinburgh Essays on Scots Literature*, ed. H. J. C.

Grierson, 1933; W. M. Parker, 'New Galt Letters', *TLS*, 6
June 1942; B. A. Booth, 'Galt's Lives of the Admirals', *NQ*, 29
October 1938; M. Q. Innis, 'A Galt Centenary', *Dalhousie
Review*, xix, 1940; and V. S. Pritchett, 'A Scottish Documentary',
in *The Living Novel*, 1946.

WILLIAM GIFFORD, 1756–1826.

Gifford's main claim to remembrance is that he was editor of
the *Quarterly Review* from 1809 to 1824 (having edited the *Anti-
Jacobin* in 1797–8). But he also wrote the following: *The Baviad.
A Paraphrastic Imitation of . . . Persius*, 1791; *The Mæviad*, 1795
(the two were printed together in 1797 and frequently reprinted); *An Epistle to Peter Pindar*, 1800 (revised in subsequent
printings and later reprinted with the preceding satires); *The
Satires of Decimus Junius Juvenalis Translated*, 1802 (preceded by
a brief autobiography, reprinted separately in 1827); *An Examination of the Strictures of the Critical Reviewers on the translation of
Juvenal*, 1803 (Supplement, 1804); and *The Satires of . . . Persius
Translated*, 1821 (first published in *The Satires of D. J. Juvenalis, and
of A. Persius Flaccus, Translated into English Verse*, 2 vols., 1817).

Gifford edited *The Plays of Philip Massinger*, 4 vols., 1805;
The Works of Ben Jonson, 9 vols., 1816; and *The Dramatic Works
of John Ford*, 2 vols., 1827. Alexander Dyce completed his edition of *The . . . Works . . . of James Shirley* in 6 vols. in 1833.

Much information about Gifford is to be found in the works
relating to the *Quarterly Review* mentioned above on pp. 470–3.

Outstanding early attacks on Gifford are Hazlitt's *A Letter
to William Gifford*, 1819, and the essay in *The Spirit of the Age*,
1825. Leigh Hunt published *Ultra-Crepidarius; a Satire on William
Gifford*, in 1823. There are two books about Gifford: J. Long-
aker's *The Della Cruscans and William Gifford*, Philadelphia, 1924,
and R. B. Clark's *William Gifford: Tory Satirist, Critic, and Editor*,
New York, 1930.

ROBERT PEARCE GILLIES, 1788–1858.

Gillies's writings include *Wallace, a Fragment*, 1813; *Childe
Alarique: A Poet's Reverie*, 1814; *Confessions of Sir H. Longueville* (a
novel), 1814; *Oswald; A Metrical Tale: Illustrative of a Poetical
Character: In Four Cantos*, 1814 (privately printed; not published),
1817; *Rinaldo the Visionary, a Desultory Poem*, 1816; *Illustrations of*

a Poetical Character, in six tales, with other Poems, 2nd ed., 1816; *Müllners's Guilt, or the Anniversary*, 1819 (privately printed); *German Stories, selected . . . by R. P. Gillies*, 3 vols., 1826; *The Seventh Day*, 1826; *Tales of a Voyager to the Arctic Ocean*, 6 vols., 2 series, 1826 and 1829; *Thurlston Tales*, 3 vols., 1835; *Recollections of Sir Walter Scott, Bart.*, 1837; *Palmario*, 1839; and *Memoirs of a Literary Veteran*, 3 vols., 1851. In 1814 he edited the *Essayes of a Prentise in the Divine Art of Poesie* by King James VI and I. He was associated with the founding of the *Foreign Quarterly Review* in 1827, contributed voluminously to *Blackwood's* and other periodicals, and is a figure of importance in the introduction of German literature into England. In 1876 R. H. Stoddard edited selections from his Memoirs, with a biography, for the 'Bric à Brac' series, New York. There are numerous references to Gillies in Lockhart and other writers of the period. See in particular J. G. Robertson, 'Gillies and Goethe', *MLR* iv, 1908, and R. Girardin, *R. P. Gillies and the Propagation of German Literature in England*, Berlin, 1916. A little information is to be found in the books by F. W. Stokoe and V. Stockley mentioned above on pp. 479–80.

GEORGE ROBERT GLEIG, 1796–1888.

Gleig published the following works of fiction: *The Subaltern*, 1825 (first published in *Blackwood's*: revised and corrected edition, 1872); *Tales of a Voyage to the Arctic Ocean*, 3 vols., 1826; *The Chelsea Pensioners*, 3 vols., 1829; *The Country Curate*, 2 vols., 1830; *Allan Breck*, 3 vols., 1834; *The Chronicles of Waltham*, 3 vols., 1835; *The Hussar*, 2 vols., 1837; *The Light Dragoon*, 2 vols., 1844; and *With the Harrises Seventy Years Ago*, 1889. He also edited *Katherine Randolph, or Self-Devotion*, 1847.

His historical, religious, and miscellaneous writings, most of which appeared in the Victorian Age, are listed in *CBEL* and *DNB*. He published *Essays, Biographical, Historical and Miscellaneous: Contributed chiefly to the Edinburgh and Quarterly Reviews* in 2 vols. in 1858. He had also contributed to *Fraser's Magazine* and other periodicals.

The fullest account of Gleig is that in the *DNB*.

GERALD GRIFFIN, 1803–40.

In fiction Griffin published *Holland Tide, or Munster Popular Tales*, 1827; *Tales of the Munster Festivals*, 3 vols., 1827; *The*

Collegians, 3 vols., 1829 (ed. P. Colum, 1918); *The Rivals* [with] *Tracy's Ambition*, 3 vols., 1829; *The Christian Physiologist: Tales Illustrative of the Five Senses*, 1830 (Dublin, 1854, as *The Offering of Friendship*); *The Invasion*, 4 vols., 1832; *Tales of my Neighbourhood*, 3 vols., 1835; and *The Duke of Monmouth*, 3 vols., 1836. After his death there appeared *Talis Qualis, or Tales of the Jury Room*, 3 vols., 1842. He also wrote *Gisippus . . . A Play*, published in 1842. There is an 8-vol. edition of *The Life and Works*, 1842–3, vol. i being a *Life* by his brother. This contains the best of his prose fiction and his poems. His *Poetical Works* appeared separately in 1851 and were reprinted with *Gisippus* at Dublin in 1926.

See Ethel Mannin, *Two Studies in Integrity: Gerald Griffin and the Rev. Francis Mahony*, 1954, and the more scholarly treatment in T. Flanagan, *The Irish Novelists, 1800–1850*, New York, 1959.

HENRY HALLAM, 1777–1859.

Hallam published his *View of the State of Europe during the Middle Ages* in 2 vols. in 1818. *Supplemental Notes* appeared in 1848 and were incorporated in the edition of 1853 and later editions. *The Constitutional History of England from . . . Henry VII to . . . George II* came out in 2 vols. in 1827. In 1833 Sir R. H. Inglis and Hallam published their *Survey of the Principal Repositories of the Public Records*. The *Introduction to the Literature of Europe, in the Fifteenth, Sixteenth, and Seventeenth Centuries* appeared in 4 vols. between 1837 and 1839. There were numerous editions of Hallam's three main books. In 1834 he edited the privately printed *Remains In Verse and Prose of Arthur Henry Hallam*, with a Memoir. He also contributed to the *Edinburgh Review*, and wrote a brief account of his friend Lord Webb Seymour, published in an Appendix to the first volume of the *Memoirs . . . of Francis Horner*, 1843.

There is still no full biography or historiographical study of Hallam. Southey reviewed his *Constitutional History* in the *Quarterly Review*, xxxvii, 1828, Macaulay in the *Edinburgh Review*, xlviii, 1828. C. Wordsworth published *King Charles the First, the Author of Icôn Basilikè, in Reply to Mr. Hallam*, in 1828. See also J. C. Hare's 'Reply to Mr Hallam's Remarks on Luther' in his *In Vindication of Luther*, 1855 (2nd ed.), and F.-A. 'Hallam', in *Éloges historiques*, 1864. See also the books on historiography mentioned on p. 476 above.

Benjamin Robert Haydon, 1786–1846.

Among other things Haydon published *The Judgment of Connoisseurs upon Works of Art compared with that of Professional Men, in Reference more particularly to the Elgin Marbles*, 1816; *New Churches* . . . [and] *the Encouragement of Painting*, 1818; *Some Enquiry into the Causes which have obstructed . . . Historical Painting . . . in England*, 1829; *On Academies of Art (more particularly the Royal Academy), and their Pernicious Effect on the Genius of Europe: Lecture xiii*, 1839; *Thoughts on . . . Fresco and Oil Painting . . . [for] the Houses of Parliament*, 1842; and *Lectures on Painting and Design*, 2 vols., 1844–6. Haydon was for some time virtual editor of James Elmes's *Annals of the Fine Arts*, 1817–20. His *Correspondence and Table-Talk* were edited by F. W. Haydon in 2 vols. in 1876.

The Life of Benjamin Robert Haydon, from his Autobiography and Journals, ed. Tom Taylor, appeared in 3 vols. in 1853: the same year there was another 3-vol. edition with an additional appendix and an index. There is also an edition with an introduction by Aldous Huxley (2 vols., 1926): an edition by A. P. D. Penrose, 1927: and one by E. Blunden (World's Classics, 1927). W. B. Pope's edition of *The Diary*, 5 vols., Cambridge, Massachusetts, 1960–3, is definitive.

The only books about Haydon are 'G. Paston', *B. R. Haydon and his Friends*, 1905; E. George, *The Life and Death of Benjamin Robert Haydon*, 1948; and C. Olney, *Benjamin Robert Haydon*, Georgia, 1952. Four early articles are to be found in *Fraser's Magazine*, xxxvi, 1847 and xlviii, 1853, the *Edinburgh Review*, xcviii, 1853, and the *Quarterly Review*, xciii, 1853 (the last three all dealing with his *Autobiography*). See also *Temple Bar*, xciv, 1891; H. B. Forman, 'Keats and Haydon', *Athenaeum*, 21 May 1904; F. W. Sargant, 'Benjamin Haydon, Fore-runner', *Nineteenth Century*, xciii, 1923; Virginia Woolf, 'Genius: Haydon', in *The Moment and Other Essays*, 1947 (reprinted from the *New Republic*, xlix, 1926); F. R. Walker, 'The Diary of a Defeated Painter', *The Independent*, cxviii, 1927; E. Blunden, 'Haydon outside his Autobiography', *Nation*, 7 April 1928; and 'Haydon's Tragedy', *TLS*, 22 June and 6 July 1946. *Letters from Elizabeth Barrett to B. R. Haydon* were edited by M. H. Shackford at New York in 1939.

William Hazlitt, 1778–1830.

Hazlitt's principal publications were: *An Essay on the Prin-*

ciples of Human Action, 1805; *Free Thoughts on Public Affairs: or Advice to a Patriot*, 1806; *An Abridgment of The Light of Nature Pursued*, by Abraham Tucker, 1807; *The Eloquence of the British Senate . . . With Notes*, 2 vols., 1807; *A Reply to the Essay on Population, by the Rev. T. R. Malthus*, 1807 (Letters i–iii first published in Cobbett's *Political Register*, 14 March–23 May, 1807); *A New and Improved Grammar of the English Tongue*, 1810; *Memoirs of the late Thomas Holcroft*, 3 vols., 1816 (ed. E. Colby, 2 vols., 1925); *The Round Table: A Collection of Essays*, 2 vols., 1817 (includes 12 essays by Leigh Hunt: most of Hazlitt's essays had first appeared in the *Examiner*); *Characters of Shakespear's Plays*, 1817; *A View of the English Stage*, 1818 (originally published in various periodicals); *Lectures on the English Poets*, 1818; *A Letter to William Gifford, Esq.*, 1819 (first draft in the *Examiner*, 15 June 1818); *Lectures on the English Comic Writers*, 1819; *Political Essays, with Sketches of Public Characters*, 1819 (mainly reprinted from periodicals); *Lectures chiefly on the Dramatic Literature of the Age of Elizabeth*, 1820; *Table Talk; or, Original Essays*, 2 vols., 1821–2 (some of these essays were reprinted from the *London Magazine* and the *New Monthly Magazine*), ed. W. Hazlitt, jun., 2 vols., 1845–6 (includes two other essays); *Liber Amoris; or, the New Pygmalion*, 1823 (ed. R. Le Gallienne and W. C. Hazlitt, 1894); privately printed: contains additional matter: ed. C. Morgan, with Hazlitt's *Dramatic Criticisms*, 1948); *Characteristics: in the Manner of Rochefoucault's Maxims*, 1823; *Sketches of the Principal Picture Galleries in England*, 1824 (originally published in the *London Magazine*, 1822–3, and in *The Round Table*); *Select British Poets . . . with critical remarks*, 1824 (1825, omitting copyright material, as *Select Poets of Great Britain*); *The Spirit of the Age: or Contemporary Portraits*, 1825 (the second edition, which appeared in the same year, contains some additional material, while the 2-vol. Paris edition of 1825 omits Moore and adds Canning and Knowles. Parts of the volume were reprinted from the *London Magazine* and the *New Monthly Magazine*); *Table-Talk: or, Original Essays*, 2 vols., Paris, 1825 (a selection from *Table Talk*, 1821–2, and from the next book mentioned, made by Hazlitt himself); *The Plain Speaker: Opinions on Books, Men, and Things*, 2 vols., 1826 (mainly reprinted from the *London Magazine* and the *New Monthly Magazine*); *Notes of a Journey through France and Italy*, 1826; *The Life of Napoleon Buonaparte*, 4 vols., 1828–30; *Conversations of James Northcote, Esq., R.A.,*

1830 (reprinted from *New Monthly Magazine* and other periodicals: ed. F. Swinnerton, 1949).

After his death there appeared *Literary Remains of the late William Hazlitt. With a notice of his life, by his son, and thoughts on his genius and writings, by E. L. Bulwer . . . and Mr. Sergeant Talfourd*, 2 vols., 1836 (the *Remains* being mainly reprinted from periodicals); *Painting* [by B. R. Haydon] *and the Fine Arts* [by Hazlitt], 1838 (reprinted from the *Encyclopaedia Britannica*, 7th ed., Supplement, vol. i, 1816); *Sketches and Essays. Now first collected by his son*, 1839 (reprinted from various periodicals: reprinted in 1852 as *Men and Manners*); *Criticisms on Art: and Sketches of the Picture Galleries of England*, edited by his son, 2 series, 1843–4; *Winterslow*, 1850; *Memoirs of William Hazlitt. With Portions of his Correspondence*, ed. W. C. Hazlitt, 2 vols., 1867; *Lamb and Hazlitt. Further Letters*, ed. W. C. Hazlitt, 1900; *A Reply to Z.*, ed. C. Whibley, 1923 (an unpublished retort to an article in *Blackwood's Magazine*, August 1818); *New Writings of William Hazlitt*, ed. P. P. Howe, 2 series, 1925 and 1927 (reprinted from various periodicals); and *Hazlitt in the Workshop: The Manuscript of 'The Fight'*, ed. S. C. Wilcox, Baltimore, 1943.

There are two collected editions: *The Collected Works*, ed. A. R. Waller and A. Glover with an introduction by W. E. Henley, 12 vols. and index, 1902–6: and the standard edition, *The Complete Works*, ed. P. P. Howe, 20 vols. and index, 1930–4 (a reissue of the previous edition with additional notes, *The Life of Napoleon*, and other new material). Between 1838 and 1851 Hazlitt's son edited 12 vols., which were part of a projected complete edition; and between 1869 and 1886 W. C. Hazlitt produced 7 vols. that were part of another projected collection.

There is a *Bibliography of William Hazlitt* by G. Keynes, 1931, which confines itself to books and leaves aside questions of attribution. Recent additions to the canon have been made by G. Carnall, *TLS*, 19 June 1953, and E. L. Brooks, *NQ*, 1954.

Of many volumes of selections one of the best and most comprehensive is *Selected Essays*, ed. G. Keynes, 1930. Others include *Hazlitt: Essays on Poetry*, ed. D. Nichol Smith, 1901; *Essays*, ed. C. Whibley, [1906]; *Hazlitt on English Literature*, ed. J. Zeitlin, New York, 1913 (with comprehensive introduction); *Hazlitt: Selected Essays*, ed. G. Sampson, 1917; *The Best of Hazlitt*, ed. P. P. Howe, 1923; and *The Essays: A Selection*, ed. C. M. Maclean, 1949. *Hazlitt Painted by Himself and Presented by Catherine*

Macdonald Maclean, 1948, is a first-person retelling of his life 'as closely as possible in his own words'. Unfortunately the editor has done a good deal of rewriting, so that the result is neither pure Hazlitt nor pure Miss Maclean. Additional letters were published by P. P. Howe in the *Athenaeum*, 8 and 15 August 1919, in the *London Mercury*, March 1923, May 1924, and August 1925, in the *TLS*, 21 March 1936, and in *PMLA* lxxvii (1962).

A great deal of biographical information is to be found in three works edited by W. C. Hazlitt: *Memoirs of William Hazlitt. With Portions of his Correspondence*, 2 vols., 1867 (already mentioned); *Four Generations of a Literary Family*, 2 vols., 1897; and *The Hazlitts: an Account of their Origin and Descent. With Autobiographical Particulars of William Hazlitt*, 2 vols., 1911–12 (privately printed). The standard biography is still *The Life of William Hazlitt*, by P. P. Howe, 1922, revised 1928, revised 1947.

Other studies are A. Birrell, *William Hazlitt*, 1902 ('English Men of Letters' series: badly dated); J. Douady, *Vie de William Hazlitt, l'Essayiste*, 1907; H. W. Stephenson, *William Hazlitt and Hackney College*, 1930 (a useful pamphlet); M. F. Brightfield, 'Scott, Hazlitt and Napoleon', *University of California Publications in English*, xiv, 1943; Catherine M. Maclean, *Born Under Saturn: A Biography of Hazlitt*, 1943; W. P. Albrecht, *William Halitt and the Malthusian Controversy*, Albuquerque, 1950; *William Hazlitt's Life of Napoleon: Its Sources and Characteristics*, by R. E. Robinson, Geneva and Paris, 1959 (a concise study of limited interest); and *William Hazlitt*, by H. Baker, Cambridge, Mass., 1962 (an important book on Hazlitt's life, his ideas, and his age).

A list of some of the early reviews and criticisms of Hazlitt may be found in *CBEL* iii, 643. P. G. Patmore's *My Friends and Acquaintances*, 3 vols., 1854, includes important reminiscences of Hazlitt. Briefer accounts may be found in B. W. Procter ('Barry Cornwall'), 'My Recollections of the late William Hazlitt', in the *New Monthly Magazine*, November 1830; G. Gilfillan, 'William Hazlitt' and 'Hazlitt and Hallam' *in Galleries of Literary Portraits*, vol. ii, 1850; the *Collected Writings of Thomas De Quincey*, ed. D. Masson, vols. ix and xi, 1890; and R. H. Stoddard, *Personal Recollections of Lamb, Hazlitt and Others*, 1903. There is an excellent critique of Hazlitt by Leslie Stephen in *Hours in a Library*, series 2, 1876.

Of the many articles and chapters in books devoted to Hazlitt mention may be made of: O. Elton, *A Survey of English Literature, 1780–1830*, vol. ii, 1912; G. Saintsbury, *Essays in English Literature (1780–1860)*, 1890; P. E. More, *Shelburne Essays*, series 2, New York, 1905; S. T. Irwin, 'Hazlitt and Lamb', *Quarterly Review*, cciv, 1906; three articles by P. P. Howe: 'Hazlitt and *Liber Amoris*', *Fortnightly Review*, cv, 1916: 'Hazlitt's Second Marriage', *Fortnightly Review*, cvi, 1916: and 'Hazlitt and *Blackwood's Magazine*', *Fortnightly Review*, cxii, 1919; R. S. Newdick, 'Coleridge on Hazlitt', *Texas Review*, ix, 1924; P. L. Carver, 'Hazlitt's Contributions to the *Edinburgh Review*', *RES* iv, 1928; C. Olney, 'William Hazlitt and Benjamin Robert Haydon', *NQ* 5 and 12 October 1935; A. L. Strout, 'Hunt, Hazlitt and *Maga.*', *ELH* iv, 1937; R. Vigneron, 'Stendhal et Hazlitt', *MP* xxxv, 1938; four articles by S. C. Wilcox: 'Hazlitt and Northcote', *ELH* vii, 1940: 'A Manuscript Addition to Hazlitt's Essay "On the Fear of Death" ', *MLN* lv, 1940: 'Hazlitt on Systematic in Contrast to Familiar Composition', *MLQ*, ii, 1941; and 'Hazlitt's Aphorisms', *MLQ* ix, 1948; R. M. Wardle, 'Outwitting Hazlitt', *MLN* lvii, 1942; R. Withington, 'Old Books and New', *South Atlantic Quarterly*, xliii, 1944; M. Goodwin, 'The Childhood of Hazlitt', *Nineteenth Century*, cxxxix, 1946; W. J. Sykes, 'Hazlitt's Place in Literature', *Queen's Quarterly*, liii, 1946; P. G. Gates, 'Bacon, Keats and Hazlitt', *South Atlantic Quarterly*, xlvi, 1947; C. D. Thorpe, 'Keats and Hazlitt: A Record of Personal Relationship and Critical Estimate', *PMLA* lxii, 1947; W. P. Albrecht, 'Hazlitt's Principles of Human Action and the Improvement of Society' in *If by your Art: Testament to Percival Hunt*, Pittsburgh, 1948; R. K. Gordon, 'Hazlitt on some of his Contemporaries', *Transactions of the Royal Society of Canada*, xlii, 1948; B. B. Cohen, 'Hazlitt: Bonapartist Critic of "The Excursion"', *MLQ* x, 1949; J. C. Maxwell, 'Some Hazlitt Quotations', *NQ* 15 September 1951 (and see subsequently S. C. Wilcox, 10 May 1952 and D. S. Bland, 19 July 1952); and L. Haddakin, 'Keats's "Ode on a Grecian Urn" and Hazlitt's Lecture "On Poetry in General"', *NQ* 29 March 1952. Letters in the *TLS* between February and June 1953 discussed the persons alluded to in the essay 'Of Persons One Would Wish to have Seen', H. Tyler and R. W. King being the principal correspondents.

Many of these books and articles deal in part with Hazlitt as a critic, but this is the particular theme of a number of other writers. In *The Aesthetics of William Hazlitt*, Philadelphia, 1933 (2nd impr., 1952), Elisabeth W. Schneider is concerned with the theoretical basis of his criticism. The preface to J. Zeitlin's *Hazlitt on English Literature*, 1913 (already mentioned), contains a conscientious survey of Hazlitt's criticism. 'The Place of Hazlitt in English Criticism', by H. W. Garrod, in *The Profession of Poetry and Other Lectures*, 1929, is brief but intelligent. R. Wellek considers Hazlitt in vol. ii of his *History of Modern Criticism, 1750–1950*, 1955. See also R. W. Babcock, 'The Direct Influence of Late Eighteenth-Century Criticism on Hazlitt and Coleridge', *MLN* xlv, 1930; G. Schnöckelborg, *August Wilhelm Schlegels Einfluß auf William Hazlitt als Shakespeare-Kritiker*, 1931; J. M. Bullitt, 'Hazlitt and the Romantic Conception of the Imagination', *PQ* xxiv, 1945; C. I. Patterson, 'William Hazlitt as a Critic of Prose Fiction', *PMLA* lxviii, 1953; and G. D. Klingopulos, 'Hazlitt as Critic', *EC*, vi, 1956. A. Whitley has considered his theatrical criticism in 'Hazlitt and the Theatre', *University of Texas Studies in English*, 1955. Few writers have done justice to Hazlitt as a critic of the visual arts, though one may consult 'Hazlitt as a Critic of Art', by S. P. Chase, *PMLA* xxxix, 1924; 'Hazlitt as a Critic of Painting', by G. M. Sargeaunt, in *The Classical Spirit*, 1936; and 'Hazlitt's Criticism of Greek Sculpture', by S. A. Larrabee, *JHI* ii, 1941.

For work on other aspects of Hazlitt's life, such as the break with Wordsworth and the disputed authorship of the review of *Christabel* (almost certainly not by Hazlitt), the reader is referred to the relevant article in *ERPE*, as listed on p. 459 above. For the question of Hazlitt's influence on Keats, see under Keats.

REGINALD HEBER, 1783–1826.

Heber's *Hymns, written and adapted to the Weekly Church Service of the Year* were published in 1827 [ed. A. Heber], and reached a tenth edition by 1834. Some of them had first been published in *The Christian Observer*, 1811–16. His Prize Poem, *Palestine*, had been published at Oxford in 1807 and had gone through several editions, being translated into Welsh and Latin. He also published (in verse) *Europe; Lines on the Present War*, 1809; and *Poems and Translations*, 1812. *Select Portions of Psalms and Hymns: With Some Compositions of a late Distinguished Prelate* appeared in 1827. His *Poetical Works* were published in 1841; and *Blue-Beard. A Serio-Comic Oriental Romance in One Act* in 1868.

His prose writings include *A Sense of Honour, a Prize Essay*, 1805; *Narrative of a Journey through . . . India, 1824–5* [ed. A. Heber], 2 vols., 1828 (and several later editions); *Sermons Preached in England* [ed. A. Heber], 1829; and *Sermons Preached in India* [ed. A. Heber], 1829. *The Personality and Office of the Christian Comforter* were Bampton Lectures published in 1816. He also published a number of other sermons, and edited the *Whole Works* of Jeremy Taylor, 15 vols., 1822 (revised edition by C. P. Eden, 10 vols., 1847–54). His *Life of . . . Jeremy Taylor, D.D., with a Critical Examination of his Writings*, was published separately in 2 vols. in 1824 and in 1 vol. in 1828. Taylor also contributed to the *Quarterly Review*. In 1830 his widow published *The Life and Unpublished Works*, in 2 vols.

On Heber see articles in the *Quarterly Review*, xxxv, 1827, xxxviii, 1828, and lxx, 1842, and in the *Edinburgh Review*, xlviii, 1828. Reference may also be made to *Some Account of the Life of Reginald Heber* (anon.), 1829; T. S. Smyth, *The Character and Religious Doctrines of Bishop Heber*, 1831; G. Bonner, *Memoir of Heber*, Cheltenham, 1833; T. Taylor, *Memoirs of Heber*, 3rd ed., 1836; and G. Smith, *Bishop Heber: Poet and Missionary*, 1895. His hymns are discussed in J. Julian's *Dictionary of Hymnology*, 1892. A number of his letters are printed in *The Heber Letters, 1783–1832*, ed. R. H. Cholmondeley, 1950.

FELICIA DOROTHEA HEMANS (*NÉE* BROWNE), 1793–1835.

Poems by Felicia Dorothea Browne were published at Liverpool in 1808. Her other publications were as follows: *England and Spain* (a poem), 1808; *The Domestic Affections, and Other Poems*, 1812; *The Restoration of the Works of Art to Italy, A Poem*, 1816; *Modern Greece*, 1817; *Translations from Camoens and Other Poets*, 1818; *Tales and Historic Scenes*, 1819; *Wallace's Invocation to Bruce, a Poem*, 1819; *The Sceptic*, 1820; *Stanzas to the Memory of the late King*, 1820; *Dartmoor, A Poem*, 1821; *Welsh Melodies*, 1822; *Vespers of Palermo*, 1823 (a tragedy in verse); *The Siege of Valencia, a Dramatic Poem* [and] *The Last Constantine, with Other Poems*, 1823; *The Forest Sanctuary, and Other Poems*, 1825 (2nd ed., including 'Casabianca', 1829); *Lays of Many Lands*, 1825; *Records of Woman, with Other Poems*, 1828; *Songs of the Affections, with Other Poems*, 1830; *Hymns on the Works of Nature for the Use of Children*, 1833; *Hymns for Childhood*, Dublin, 1834 (American ed., 1827); *National Lyrics and Songs for Music*, Dublin, 1834; and *Scenes and Hymns of Life, with Other Religious Poems*, 1834.

Her *Poetical Remains*, with a Memoir by '*Δ*' (D. M. Moir), were published in 1836. (There had been an American edition, edited by Professor Norton, in 1825.) Juvenile poems, *Early Blossoms*, appeared with a *Life* in 1840. Mrs. Hemans contributed to numerous periodicals, including *Blackwood's Magazine*, Colburn's *New Monthly Magazine*, and the *Edinburgh Monthly Magazine*. In 1839 her sister Mrs. Hughes edited *The Works*, in 7 vols., with a Memoir. There were various subsequent editions.

A Short Sketch of the Life of Mrs. Hemans appeared in 1835. H. F. Chorley's *Memorials of Mrs. Hemans*, 2 vols., 1836, is a fuller biography. W. Ledderbogen published *Felicia Hemans Lyrik* at Heidelberg in 1913, and E. Duméril, *Une femme poète au déclin du romantisme anglais: Felicia Hemans* at Toulouse in 1929.

See also Jeffrey's article in the *Edinburgh Review*, l (50), 1829; D. M. Moir, *Sketches of the Poetical Literature of the Past Half-Century*, 1851; Lady A. T. Ritchie, 'Felicia Felix', in *Blackstick Papers*, 1908; I. A. Williams, 'Wordsworth, Mrs. Hemans, and R. P. Graves', *London Mercury*, vi, 1922; W. K. Rupprecht, 'Felicia Hemans und die englischen Beziehungen zur deutschen Literatur', *Anglia*, xlviii, 1924; and W. R. Cunningham, 'Mrs. Hemans at Mount Rydal', *TLS*, 23 October 1943.

JOHN CAM HOBHOUSE (BARON BROUGHTON), 1786–1869.

Hobhouse began and ended his literary career in association with Byron. His *Imitations and Translations from the Ancient and Modern Classics*, 1809, contains nine poems by Byron. *A Journey through Albania and Other Provinces of Turkey*, 2 vols., 1813 (see Borst, below: rewritten as *Travels in Albania*, 2 vols., 1855), describes the journey that also produced *Childe Harold's Pilgrimage*. *The Substance of Some Letters Written by an Englishman Resident at Paris during the Last Reign of the Emperor Napoleon* was published in 2 vols. in 1816, the proofs having been submitted to Benjamin Constant. 'Voilà les libelles finis', Napoleon is said to have commented on reading the book, 'les bons livres vont commencer'. The *Quarterly* reviewer, on the other hand, read the volumes 'with equal displeasure and disgust'. In 1818 Hobhouse produced *Historical Illustrations of the Fourth Canto of Childe Harold*. He then wrote two articles in the *Westminster Review* worth mentioning: 'Lord Byron's Residence in Greece', July 1824, and a review of 'Dallas's Recollections and Medwin's Conversations', January 1825. In 1859 he published *Italy; Remarks Made in Several Visits from 1816 to 1854*, 2 vols.; and in 1865 he printed privately *Recollections of a long Life*, in 5 vols. This was published in 6 vols. in 1909–11, vol. ii then including his 'Contemporary Account of the Separation of Lord and Lady Byron, also of the Destruction of Lord Byron's Memoirs', which had been privately printed in 1870.

There is a biography of Hobhouse, *My Friend H*, by M. Joyce, 1948. Contemporary reviews of his books provide a useful background. Much information about his early career is to be found in books on Byron, including *Lord Byron's First Pilgrimage*, by W. A. Borst, New Haven, 1948. See also E. R. Vincent's *Byron, Hobhouse and Foscolo*, 1949, and A. Rutherford's 'The Influence of Hobhouse on *Childe Harold's Pilgrimage*, Canto IV', *RES*, N.S., xii, 1961. Joyce's biography contains some information about the numerous manuscripts and about Hobhouse's other writings on politics, &c. According to the *New English Dictionary* Hobhouse invented the phrase 'His Majesty's Opposition', in 1826.

JAMES HOGG, 'THE ETTRICK SHEPHERD', 1770–1835.

His principal volumes of verse may be mentioned here, although most of them fall outside the scope of this study: *Scottish Pastorals, Poems, Songs*, &c., 1801; *The Mountain Bard; consisting of Ballads and Songs*, 1807 (enlarged in later editions); *The Forest Minstrel; a Selection of Songs* (by Hogg and others), 1810; *The Queen's Wake: a Legendary Poem*, 1813; *The Hunting of Badlewe, a Dramatic Tale*, 1814; *The Pilgrims of the Sun; a Poem*, 1815; *The Ettricke Garland; being Two Excellent New Songs*, 1815 (one of the songs is by Hogg, the other by Scott); *The Poetic Mirror, or The Living Bards of Britain*, 1816 (ed. T. E. Welby, 1929); *Mador of the Moor; a Poem*, 1816; *Dramatic Tales*, 2 vols., 1817; *The Royal Jubilee: A Scottish Mask*, 1822; *Queen Hynde*, 1825; *Select and Rare Scottish Melodies*, 1829; *Songs, Now First Collected*, 1831; *A Queer Book*, 1832.

His other principal writings include *The Shepherd's Guide: being a Practical Treatise on the Diseases of Sheep*, 1807; *The Spy: A Periodical Paper, of Literary Amusement and Instruction*, 1811 (mainly by Hogg); *The Long Pack: A Northumbrian Tale*, Newcastle, 1817; *The Brownie of Bodsbeck, and other Tales*, 2 vols.,

1818; *The Jacobite Relics of Scotland . . . Collected and illustrated by James Hogg*, 2 series, 1819, 1821; *Winter Evening Tales*, 2 vols., 1820; *The Three Perils of Man; or War, Women and Witchcraft: A Border Romance*, 3 vols., 1822; *The Three Perils of Woman, or Love, Leasing, and Jealousy: A Series of Domestic Scottish Tales*, 3 vols., 1823; *The Private Memoirs and Confessions of a Justified Sinner: written by himself*, 1824 (1828, as *The Suicide's Grave;* 1837, with omissions and alterations, as *The Confessions of a Fanatic*; ed. T. E. Welby, 1924; with an introduction by André Gide, 1947); *The Shepherd's Calendar*, 2 vols., 1829; *Altrive Tales*, 1832 (only 1 vol. published); *A Series of Lay Sermons*, 1834; *The Domestic Manners and Private Life of Sir Walter Scott*, Glasgow, 1834; *Tales of the Wars of Montrose*, 3 vols., 1835 (ed. J. E. H. Thomson, Stirling, 1909); *The Works of Robert Burns: Edited by the Ettrick Shepherd, and William Motherwell*, 5 vols., Glasgow, '1840' (1838–41: vol. v contains a Memoir of Burns by Hogg); *A Tour in the Highlands in 1803: A Series of Letters by James Hogg . . . to Sir Walter Scott*, Paisley, 1888. Hogg contributed to *The Club Book*, edited by Andrew Picken, 3 vols., 1831.

It should be mentioned that a great deal that was later reprinted in the books just mentioned had first appeared in *Blackwood's Magazine* and other periodicals. A complete edition of Hogg's writings would hardly be possible. The *Poetical Works* appeared in 4 vols. in 1822, and in 5 vols. in [1838–40] (published at Glasgow: with his Memoir or Autobiography in vol. v). *Tales and Sketches . . . Including . . . several Pieces not before printed* were published in 6 vols. in 1837, while *The Works*, ed. T. Thomson, 2 vols., 1865, includes both poems and tales and is the most complete edition, though the text is not always reliable. There are two selected eds. of his *Poems*, ed. Mrs. Garden, 1887, and ed. W. Wallace, 1903. See also *Works, Letters and Manuscripts*, ed. R. B. Adam, priv. prtd., Buffalo, 1930.

Bibliographical information is to be found in the books by Edith C. Batho and A. L. Strout mentioned below, and in 'Notes on the Bibliography of James Hogg', *The Library*, xvi, 1935, by Edith C. Batho, as well as F. E. Pierce's 'James Hogg', *Yale University Library Gazette*, v, 1931.

There are a number of books on Hogg: *Memorials of James Hogg*, edited by his daughter Mrs. Garden, published at Paisley in [1884] and twice reprinted; H. T. Stephenson's *The Ettrick Shepherd: a Biography*, Bloomington, 1922; *The Ettrick Shepherd*, by

Edith C. Batho, 1927 (an excellent study); *The Life and Letters of James Hogg, vol. i, 1770–1825*, by A. L. Strout, Lubbock, Texas, 1946; and *James Hogg: A Critical Study*, by L. Simpson, 1962. The Memoir in T. Thomson's edition of *The Works* is also of use.

Further information may be found in a series of notes and articles by A. L. Strout listed in *CBEL* and largely incorporated into his book ('Hogg's "Chaldee Manuscript"', *PMLA* lxv, 1950, is later, and deserves separate mention). D. Carswell, *Sir Walter: a Four-Part Study in Biography*, 1930, deals with Scott, Hogg, Lockhart, and Joanna Baillie. There are also two notes in the *TLS*: 'The Ettrick Shepherd: a Centenary Exhibition', 30 November 1935, and 'The Ettrick Shepherd', by D. Cook, 8 May 1937; as well as 'The Ettrick Shepherd: two Unnoted Articles', *NQ*, 2 September 1950.

WILLIAM HONE, 1780–1842.

A complete bibliography of Hone is never likely to be compiled, since he published on a large scale and many of his publications were necessarily anonymous. Bibliographical help may be found in the *DNB* and *CBEL*, F. W. Hackwood's *William Hone: His Life and Times*, 1912, in F. G. Stephens's *Memoir of G. Cruikshank*, 1891, in B. Jerrold's *Life of G. Cruikshank*, 1891, and in some of the articles mentioned below.

The Every-Day Book: or Everlasting Calendar of Popular Amusements appeared in 2 vols. in 1826–7; *The Table Book* in 1827–8; and *The Year Book of Daily Recreation and Information* in 1832. Mention may also be made here of *Ancient Mysteries Described*, 1823, and of *The Early Life and Conversion of William Hone by Himself: Edited by his Son*, 1841 (see also *Some Account of the Conversion of the late W. Hone, with . . . Extracts from his Correspondence*, 1853). A dozen of his most successful political pamphlets were reprinted as *Facetiae and Miscellanies with One Hundred and Twenty Engravings drawn by George Cruikshank* in 1827 (2nd ed.) Further information may be found in *The Three Trials of William Hone*, 1818 (ed. W. Tegg, 1876); and in H. M. Sikes, 'William Hone: Regency Patriot, Parodist, and *Pamphleteer*', *Newberry Library Bulletin*, vol. v, no. 8 (Chicago: The Library). A background to Hone is provided by *English Political Caricature, 1793–1832*, by M. Dorothy George, 1959.

THOMAS HOOD, 1799–1845.

Odes and Addresses to Great People appeared anonymously in

1825, the joint work of Hood and J. H. Reynolds. The two series of *Whims and Oddities: in Prose and Verse* were published in 1826–7. Hood then published *The Plea of the Midsummer Fairies, Hero and Leander, Lycus the Centaur, and other Poems,* 1827; *National Tales* (in prose), 2 vols., 1827; *The Epping Hunt* (illustrated by Cruikshank), 1829; *The Dream of Eugene Aram* (with designs by W. Harvey), 1831 (first published in *The Gem,* 1829); *Tylney Hall: A Novel,* 3 vols., 1834; *Hood's Own, or Laughter from Year to Year* (containing the *Literary Reminiscences*), 1839, 2nd series, with preface by his son, 1861; *Up the Rhine,* Frankfort, 1840 (mainly prose); *The Loves of Sally Brown and Ben the Carpenter* ([1840?]: a single quarto sheet); *Whimsicalities: A Periodical Gathering: With Illustrations by Leech,* 2 vols., 1844, 1870 (enlarged: verse and prose). *Fairy Land: By the late Thomas and Jane Hood, their Son and Daughter,* appeared in 1861. 'The Song of the Shirt' first appeared in the Christmas Number of *Punch,* 1843. 'Lamia; A Romance' was printed in vol. i of *The Autobiography of William Jerdan,* 4 vols., 1852–3.

Hood edited *The Gem,* vol. i, 1829; *The Comic Annual,* 11 vols., 1830–42 (he himself wrote most of the literary contributions: no volumes were issued for 1840–1); the *New Monthly Magazine and Humorist,* lxiii–lxviii, 1841–3; and *Hood's Magazine and Comic Miscellany,* i–iii, 1844–5. He assisted John Taylor to edit the *London Magazine,* iv–viii, July 1821–July 1823, and contributed a good deal. He also contributed to *Sporting,* ed. 'Nimrod' (C. J. Apperley), 1838.

Poems, 2 vols., 1846, and *Poems of Wit and Humour,* 1847, constitute the first collected edition of his poems. *The Poetical Works, with Some Account of the Author* appeared at Boston in 4 vols. in 1856. There have been numerous other editions of his poems, including *The Poetical Works,* ed. W. M. Rossetti, illustrated by G. Doré, 2 series [1871–5]; and a selection in the World's Classics series. The fullest edition is that published at Oxford in 1920, ed. W. Jerrold. There have been various volumes of selections, including one edited by C. Dyment, 1948.

The Works . . . Comic and Serious, in Prose and Verse, were edited with notes by his son, T. Hood, Jr., in 7 vols. in 1862. There is also a 10-vol. edition with illustrations, 1869–73 (11 vols., 1882–4).

Memorials of Thomas Hood: Collected by his Daughter [F. F. Broderip]*: With a Preface and Notes by his Son* appeared in 2 vols.

in 1860. In 1945 L. A. Marchand edited at New Brunswick a small volume of *Letters of Thomas Hood from the Dilke Papers in the British Museum*. There are also books by A. Elliot (*Hood in Scotland*, Dundee, 1885), E. Oswald (*Thomas Hood und die soziale Tendenzdichtung seiner Zeit*, Vienna and Leipzig, 1904), and W. Jerrold (*Thomas Hood: His Life and Times*, 1907, and *Thomas Hood & Charles Lamb, The Story of a Friendship*—with a reprint of the *Literary Reminiscences*, 1930). J. C. Reid published a new study in 1963.

See also R. H. Horne, *A New Spirit of the Age*, vol. ii, 1844; G. Gilfillan, *A Gallery of Literary Portraits*, vol. i, 1845; D. Masson, 'Thomas Hood', in *Macmillan's Magazine*, August 1860; W. M. Thackeray, 'On a Joke I once heard from the late Thomas Hood', in *Roundabout Papers*, 1863; J. Ashton, 'The True Story of Eugene Aram', in *Eighteenth Century Waifs*, 1887; W. E. Henley, *Views and Reviews*, 1890; H. C. Shelley, 'Thomas Hood's Homes and Friends', in *Literary By-paths in Old England*, 1909; P. E. More, 'The Wit of Thomas Hood', in *Shelburne Essays*, vii, New York, 1910; W. H. Hudson, 'Thomas Hood: the Man, the Wit, and the Poet', in *A Quiet Corner in a Library*, Chicago, 1915; 'The Exhibition of Hood MSS. at Bristol Reference Library', *Bookman*, lxiv, 1923; J. H. Swann, 'The Serious Poems of Thomas Hood', *Manchester Quarterly*, li, 1925; and E. Blunden, 'Hood's Literary Reminiscences', in *Votive Tablets*, 1931.

There have been notes and articles in the last thirty years as follows: T. O. Mabbott, 'Letters of Leigh Hunt, Thomas Hood, and Allan Cunningham', *NQ*, 23 May 1931; J. M. Turnbull, 'Reynolds, the Hoods, and Mary Lamb', *TLS*, 5 November 1931; J. Heath-Stubbs, 'Hood', *Time and Tide*, 28 April 1945; 'Hood: The Poet Behind the Jester's Mask', *TLS*, 5 May 1945; 'L.B.', 'Thomas Hood: A Centenary Note', *NQ*, 19 May 1945; D. Hudson, 'Hood and Praed', *TLS*, 19 May 1945; V. S. Pritchett, 'Our Half-Hogarth', in *The Living Novel*, 1946; A. Voss, 'Lowell, Hood and the Pun', *MLN* lxiii, 1948; A. Whitley, 'Hood and Dickens: Some New Letters', *HLQ* xiv, 1951, and 'Hood as a Dramatist', *SE* xxx, 1951; J. Hennig, 'The Literary Relations between Goethe and Hood', *MLQ* xii, 1951; and 'Hood: The Language of Poetry', *TLS*, 19 September 1952.

THEODORE EDWARD HOOK, 1788–1841.

Hook published a number of farces and other slight dramatic

pieces, including: *The Soldier's Return*, 1805; *Catch Him Who Can*, 1806; *The Invisible Girl*, 1806; *Tekeli; or, The Siege of Montgatz*, 1806; *The Fortress . . . from the French*, 1807; *Music Mad*, 1808; *Killing No Murder*, 1809 (2nd ed. the same year, with a preface and the scene censored by the Lord Chamberlain); *Safe and Sound*, 1809; *Darkness Visible*, 1811; *Trial by Jury*, 1811; and *Exchange No Robbery*, 1820.

He also wrote the following prose fictions: *The Man of Sorrow*, by 'Alfred Allendale', 3 vols., 1808 (reprinted as *Ned Musgrave*, 1842); *Sayings and Doings: A Series of Sketches from Life*, three series, 9 vols., 1824–8; *Maxwell*, 3 vols., 1830; *Love and Pride*, 3 vols., 1833 (1842, as *The Widow and the Marquess, or Love and Pride*); *The Parson's Daughter*, 3 vols., 1833, 1835 (revised and corrected); *Gilbert Gurney*, 3 vols., 1836; *Jack Brag*, 3 vols., 1837; *Gurney Married*, 3 vols., 1838; *Births, Deaths, and Marriages*, 3 vols., 1839 (1842, as *All in the Wrong; or, Births, Deaths, and Marriages*); *Precepts and Practice*, 3 vols., 1840; *Fathers and Sons*, 3 vols., 1842; and *Peregrine Bunce*, 3 vols., 1842. There have been various reprints and partial collections of his novels.

A fuller list of Hook's writings may be found in *CBEL* iii, 399–400, and in Myron F. Brightfield's useful study, *Theodore Hook and his Novels*, Cambridge, Mass., 1928. Hook wrote and edited a large number of books and did a great deal of journalism, editing and contributing to *John Bull* from 1820 to his death and the *New Monthly Magazine and Humorist*, vols. xlix–lxii. Some of his journalism was reprinted in *The Ramsbottom Letters*, 1872, and *The Choice Humorous Works . . . with a New Life of the Author . . .* [1873].

Lockhart produced *Theodore Hook: A Sketch* in 1852. Earlier accounts of Hook had appeared in the *New Monthly Magazine*, lxiii, 1841, and the *Quarterly Review*, May 1843 (by Lockhart). Other accounts may be found in R. H. Horne's *A New Spirit of the Age*, vol. ii, 1844; *Chambers's Journal*, v, 1846; the *New Monthly Magazine*, lxxx, 1847 ('A Graybeard's Gossip, no. 6'); and A. M. and S. C. Hall's 'Memories of Authors', in the *Atlantic Monthly*, xv, 1865. R. H. D. Barham produced a fuller account in *The Life and Remains*, 2 vols., 1849 (revised and corrected in 1853 and 1877).

See also W. Maginn's *A Gallery of Illustrious Literary Characters*, ed. W. Bates [1873]; F. G. Waugh, 'Unpublished Letters of Theodore Hook', *Gentleman's Magazine*, lvi, 1896; S. H. N.

St. Cyres, 'Theodore Hook', *Cornhill Magazine*, lxxxix, 1904;
A. Repplier, 'The Laugh that Failed', *Atlantic Monthly*, clviii,
1936; and 'Hoaxer and Wit: Theodore Hook, 1788–1841',
TLS, 23 August 1941.

LEIGH HUNT, 1784–1859.

Hunt published the following volumes of verse: *Juvenilia*,
1801; *The Feast of the Poets*, 1814 (first published in *The Reflector* for December 1811: significantly revised in this and later
editions); *The Descent of Liberty, a Mask*, 1815; *The Story of
Rimini*, 1816; *Foliage, or Poems Original and Translated*, 1818;
Hero and Leander, and, Bacchus and Ariadne, 1819; *Amyntas . . .
from the Italian of . . . Tasso*, 1820; *Ultra-Crepidarius; a Satire on
William Gifford*, 1823; *Bacchus in Tuscany, a Dithyrambic Poem,
from . . . Redi*, 1825; *Captain Sword and Captain Pen*, 1835, 1849
(with new preface); *A Legend of Florence: A Play*, 1840; *The
Palfrey; A Love-Story of Old Times*, 1842; and *Stories in Verse: Now
first collected*, 1855. He contributed the tales of the Squire and
the Friar to *The Poems of Geoffrey Chaucer Modernized*, 1841 (ed.
R. H. Horne).

The most nearly complete edition of Hunt's poems is H. S.
Milford's *The Poetical Works*, 1923. His own editions of his
Poetical Works in 1819 (3 vols.), 1832, and 1844, are in fact
selected editions. His son, Thornton Hunt, produced a revised
edition in 1860. In 1922 L. A. Brewer edited Hunt's *Ballads of
Robin Hood*, Cedar Rapids, Iowa.

His main volumes in prose include *Critical Essays on the Performers of the London Theatres*, 1807; *An Attempt to Shew the Folly
and Danger of Methodism*, 1809; *The Prince of Wales v. the Examiner*,
1813; *The Round Table: A Collection of Essays*, 2 vols., 1817 (a
number of the essays are by Hunt); *The Months*, 1821; *Lord
Byron and Some of his Contemporaries*, 1828 (two eds., one in 2 vols.);
Sir Ralph Esher, 3 vols., 1832 (a novel); *Christianism, or Belief and
Unbelief Reconciled*, 1832 (expanded and revised as *The Religion
of the Heart*, 1853); *The Indicator, and the Companion*, 2 vols., 1834
(a selection from these periodicals); *The Seer*, 1840–1 (a similar
selection); *Imagination and Fancy, with an essay in answer to the
question 'What is Poetry?'*, 1844; *Wit and Humour, Selected from
the English Poets, with an Illustrative Essay*, 1846; *Stories from the
Italian Poets*, 2 vols., 1846; *Men, Women, and Books*, 2 vols., 1847;
A Jar of Honey from Mount Hybla, 1848: *The Town: Its Memorable*

Characters and Events, 2 vols., 1848; *The Autobiography*, 3 vols., 1850 (a rewriting of *Lord Byron and Some of his Contemporaries*); *Table Talk*, 1851; *The Old Court Suburb, or Memorials of Kensington*, 2 vols., 1855 (enlarged ed. the same year); and *A Saunter through the West End*, 1861. Hunt contributed to many periodicals and gift-books throughout his life. No collected edition of his prose writings exists. In 1870 J. E. B[abson] collected some of his scattered essays as *A Day by the Fire*, and three years later he similarly collected *The Wishing-Cap Papers*, Boston, 1873. In 1891 there was an edition of his *Tales . . . with a . . . Memoir* by William Knight. In 1923 L. A. and E. T. Brewer collected some essays as *The Love of Books*, published at Cedar Rapids, Iowa.

There are editions of *The Autobiography*, by Thornton Hunt, '1860' (1859: 'revised'); by R. Ingpen, 2 vols., 1903; by E. Blunden, 1928 (World's Classics); and by J. E. Morpurgo, 1949 (with a useful key to corresponding passages in *Lord Byron and Some of his Contemporaries*). In 1959 S. N. Fogle published at Florida *Leigh Hunt's Autobiography: The Earliest Sketches*.

Hunt edited the following periodicals: *The Examiner, a Sunday Paper*, 1808–21 (although he ceased to be editor in 1821, Hunt continued to be an occasional contributor); *The Reflector, A Quarterly Magazine*, 1810–11 (reissued as *The Reflector, a Collection of Essays*, in 2 vols. in 1812); *The Literary Pocket-Book*, 1818–22 (an annual); *The Indicator*, 1819–21 (a weekly: reissued in 1 vol. in 1822); *The Liberal: Verse and Prose from the South*, 1822–3 (collected as 2 vols.); *The Literary Examiner*, 1823 (probably edited by John Hunt, although commonly attributed to Leigh Hunt); *The Companion*, 1828 (a weekly); *The Chat of the Week*, 1830 (also a weekly); *The Tatler: A Daily Journal of Literature and the Stage*, 1830–2; *Leigh Hunt's London Journal*, 1834–5 (a weekly); *The Monthly Repository*, 1837–8; and *Leigh Hunt's Journal*, 1850–1 (distinct from Leigh Hunt's *London Journal*, though also a weekly). Many of Hunt's numerous contributions to other periodicals are mentioned in the *CBEL* and in the bibliographies mentioned at the end of this entry.

Books edited by Leigh Hunt include *Classic Tales . . . with Critical Essays on the . . . Authors*, 5 vols., 1806–7; *The Masque of Anarchy, a Poem by . . . Shelley*, 1832; *The Dramatic Works of R. B. Sheridan*, 1840; *The Dramatic Works of Wycherley, Congreve, Vanbrugh and Farquhar*, 1840; *One Hundred Romances of Real Life*, 1843; *The Foster Brother*, 3 vols., 1845 (by Thornton Hunt:

introduction by Leigh Hunt); *Readings for Railways*, 1849 (series 2, 1853, with J. B. Syme); *A Book for a Corner*, 2 vols, 1849; *Beaumont and Fletcher . . . selected*, 1855; and *The Book of the Sonnet*, edited by Leigh Hunt and S. Adams Lee, 2 vols., Boston, 1867 (contains an essay on the sonnet by Leigh Hunt).

Hunt's *Dramatic Criticism, 1808–31*, was collected by L. H. and C. W. Houtchens in 1949, much of his uncollected *Literary Criticism* by the same scholars in 1956 (with a long essay on Hunt as a man of letters by C. D. Thorpe), and his *Political and Occasional Essays* in 1962. *Shelley—Leigh Hunt: How Friendship Made History*, ed. R. Brimley Johnson, 1928 (revised edition, 1929), is a useful book which reprints the reviews of Shelley's poems in the *Examiner*, as well as a great many political articles from the same periodical, with other relevant material. Selections are also to be found in *Leigh Hunt's 'Examiner' Examined*, by E. Blunden, 1928.

The Correspondence of Leigh Hunt was edited by his eldest son in 2 vols. in 1862. In 1874–5 S. R. Townshend Mayer published anonymously selections from Leigh Hunt's correspondence with B. R. Haydon, Charles Ollier, and Southwood Smith in the *St. James's Magazine*, while in 1876 he published 'Leigh Hunt and Lord Brougham: With Original Letters', in *Temple Bar*, xlvii. *Six Letters . . . to W. W. Story, 1850–6*, were printed in 1913. Vol. ii of L. A. Brewer's *My Leigh Hunt Library* contains *The Holograph Letters* (1938), many of which had been privately printed earlier by the same collector. Many of the letters in Brewer's collection are still unpublished. In 1934 A. N. L. Munby published *Letters to Leigh Hunt from his Son Vincent*. Other letters of Hunt's may be found in many different books and articles, and in *Shelley and his Circle* (p. 615 below).

Of the numerous volumes of selections only a few can be mentioned. Those consisting wholly of prose, often with good introductions, include *A Tale for a Chimney Corner*, ed. E. Ollier [1869]; *Essays*, ed. A. Symons, 1887 (enlarged ed., 1903); *Dramatic Essays*, ed. W. Archer and R. W. Lowe, 1894; *Essays and Sketches*, ed. R. B. Johnson [1907]; *Prefaces . . . mainly to his Periodicals*, ed. R. B. Johnson, 1927 (not limited to the prefaces); and *Essays*, ed. J. B. Priestley, 1929 (Everyman's Library). Others include both verse and prose, notably *Leigh Hunt as Poet and Essayist*, ed. C. Kent, 1889; *Essays, and Poems*, ed. R. B. Johnson, 2 vols., 1891; *Selections*, ed. J. H. Lobban,

1909; and *Leigh Hunt*, ed. E. Storer [1911]. In 1893 A. S. Cook published *An Answer to the Question 'What is Poetry?'* with notes and other relevant material.

Since Hunt knew many of the leading men of letters from the time of Byron to that of Dickens, information about him is to be found in a great many books of the period, as well as in later biographies. The best general study remains E. Blunden's *Leigh Hunt*, 1930, an admirable book in spite of a few minor inaccuracies. L. Landré's *Leigh Hunt . . . Contribution à l'histoire du Romantisme anglais*, 2 vols., 1935–6, is an excellent scholarly study. The author makes use of some of the manuscript material in America, and provides a full bibliography. The earlier biographies by W. C. Monkhouse (1893) and R. Brimley Johnson (1896) retain a slight value. Blunden's study, *Leigh Hunt's 'Examiner' Examined* and Brimley Johnson's *Shelley—Leigh Hunt: How Friendship Made History* (both 1928) have already been mentioned. There is a monograph, *The Political History of Leigh Hunt's Examiner*, by G. D. Stout, St. Louis, 1949. Two German studies are *Leigh Hunts Kritik der Entwicklung der englischen Literatur bis zum Ende des 18. Jahrhunderts*, by O. Moebus, Straßburg, 1916, and *Hunt und die italienische Literatur*, by E. Fisher, Freiburg, 1936.

There are numerous articles and other studies which throw light on Hunt's life and writings. Thornton Hunt wrote on his father in 'A Man of Letters of the Last Generation', *Cornhill Magazine*, 1860, and in the introduction to his edition of his father's *Autobiography*, '1860' (1859). J. D. Campbell published Hunt's 'Attempt . . . to Estimate his Own Character' in the *Athenaeum* for 25 March 1893. Several recent scholars have investigated the attacks of the reviewers on 'The Cockneys': see particularly P. M. Wheeler, 'The Great Quarterlies . . . and Leigh Hunt', *South Atlantic Quarterly*, 1930; G. D. Stout, 'The Cockney School', *TLS*, 7 February 1929; A. L. Strout, 'Hunt, Hazlitt, and *Maga*', *ELH* iv, 1937, and the same writer's article in *Studia Neophilologica*, 1953–4. Other articles of primarily biographical importance include Monica C. Grobel, 'Leigh Hunt and "The Town"', *MLR*, xxvi, 1931 (Hunt, Charles Knight, and the Useful Knowledge Society); and J. P. Brawner, 'Leigh Hunt and his wife Marianne', *W. Virginia Univ. Stud.*, 1937. Sylva Norman's book on the reputation of Shelley, *Flight of the Skylark*, 1954, deals with Hunt's relations with Mary Shelley from 1822. H. E. Rollins deals usefully with Hunt and Keats in

The Keats Circle, 2 vols., 1948. J. R. MacGillivray discusses Hunt's importance in the introductory essay to his *Keats: A Bibliography and Reference Guide*, Toronto, 1949. On Hunt's role in *The Liberal* see W. H. Marshall, *Byron, Shelley, Hunt, and 'The Liberal'*, Philadelphia, 1960. Nettie S. Tillett's 'Elia and "The Indicator" ', *South Atlantic Quarterly*, 1934, deals with Hunt's relations with Lamb. P. P. Howe's *Life of William Hazlitt*, 1922 (3rd ed., 1947), and R. W. Armour's *Barry Cornwall*, Boston, 1935, give good accounts of two other important friendships. For similar studies see D. Hudson, *Thomas Barnes of 'The Times'*, 1943; R. D. Altick, *The Cowden Clarkes*, 1948; and C. R. Woodring's *Victorian Samplers: William and Mary Howitt*, 1952. S. F. Fogle's 'Skimpole Once More', *Nineteenth-Century Fiction*, 1952, is a fair summary of the Dickens affair; but also see G. D. Stout, 'Leigh Hunt's Money Troubles: Some New Light', *Washington University Studies*, and K. J. Fielding, 'Skimpole and Leigh Hunt Again', *NQ*, 1955.

Saintsbury wrote on Hunt in *Essays in English Literature, 1780–1860*, 1890, as well as in his *History of English Prosody*, 1910, and his *History of Criticism*, vol. iii, 1904. Reference may also be made to 'Italian Influence on English Scholarship and Literature during the "Romantic Revival", Part iii', by R. W. King, *MLR*, xxi, 1926; 'Leigh Hunt e "The Examiner" (1808–1812)', by B. Cellini, in *Studi sul romanticismo inglese*, 1932; 'Leigh Hunt's Place in the Reform Movement, 1808–1810', by M. Roberts, *RES*, xi, 1935; *Mythology and the Romantic Tradition in English Poetry*, by D. Bush, Cambridge, Mass., 1937; 'Leigh Hunt and *The Rambler*', by W. W. Pratt, *Texas Studies in English*, 1938; *The Dissidence of Dissent*, by F. E. Mineka, Chapel Hill, 1944 (Hunt and the *Monthly Repository*); 'The *Spectator* Tradition and the Development of the Familiar Essay', by M. R. Watson, *ELH*, xii, 1946; 'Hunt's Review of Shelley's Posthumous Poems', by P. C. Gates, *Papers of the Bibliographical Society of America*, xlii, 1948; *English Poetic Theory, 1825–1865*, by A. H. Warren, 1950; *Dante's Fame Abroad, 1350–1850*, by W. P. Friederich, 1950; 'Leigh Hunt's Shakespeare: A "Romantic" Concept', by G. D. Stout, *Studies in Memory of F. M. Webster*, 1951; 'Hunt's *Horace*', by F. H. Ristine, *MLN* lxvi, 1951; 'Leigh Hunt, Moore and Byron', by Sylva Norman, *TLS*, 2 January 1953; 'A Leigh Hunt–Byron Letter', by P. C. Gates. *K.-Sh.J.* ii, 1953; and 'Leigh Hunt's Shakespearean Criticism', by J. Fleece, *Essays in Honor of W. C. Curry*, 1955.

For bibliographical information one may consult the *CBEL*, Landré, and the article in *ERPE*. Milford's edition of the poems has a useful bibliography. L. A. Brewer's *My Leigh Hunt Library: The First Editions*, Iowa, 1932, is also useful. Many of the books with annotations by Hunt now in the United States are listed in 'Leigh Hunt's Marginalia', by W. J. Burke, *Bulletin of the New York Public Library*, 1933.

JEFFREY, FRANCIS, LORD JEFFREY, 1773–1850.

Jeffrey wrote *Observations on Mr. Thelwall's Letter to the Editor of the Edinburgh Review*, 1804; *A Summary View of the Rights and Claims of the Roman Catholics of Ireland*, 1808 (reprinted from the *Edinburgh Review*); a Memoir published in *The Works of John Playfair* [ed. J. G. Playfair], 4 vols., 1822; *Combinations of Workmen: A Speech*, 1825; and *Corrected Report of the Speech of the Lord Advocate of Scotland upon . . . Reform of Parliament*, 1831.

Jeffrey contributed an 'Essay on Beauty' to the *Encyclopaedia Britannica Supplement*, 1824 (being a revised reprint from the *Edinburgh Review*) and also a 'Eulogium of James Watt' (reprinted from the *Encyclopaedia Britannica* in D. F. J. Arago's *Life of Watt*, 1839). His speeches as Rector of Glasgow University may be found in *Inaugural Addresses*, ed. J. B. Hay, Glasgow, 1839. He published a selection from his *Contributions to the Edinburgh Review* in 4 vols. in 1844 (3 vols., 1846, 1853). After his death there appeared two pamphlets, *Samuel Richardson* and *Jonathan Swift*, both 1853; and a story, *Peter and his Enemies*, 1859 ('2nd ed.').

In the 'New Universal Library' there is a selection, *Essays on English Poets and Poetry From the Edinburgh Review, by Francis Jeffrey*, n.d. In 1910 D. Nichol Smith edited selections from *Jeffrey's Literary Criticism*, with a list of his articles in the *Edinburgh Review*; and in 1934 J. Purves edited *The Letters of Francis Jeffrey to Ugo Foscolo*.

In 1852 Lord Cockburn published his *Life of Lord Jeffrey with a Selection from his Correspondence*, in 2 vols. (including a list of Jeffrey's articles in the *Edinburgh Review*), a biography which has not yet been superseded. There are four other books or pamphlets about Jeffrey: James Taylor, *Lord Jeffrey and Craigcrook*, 1892; R. Elsner, *Francis Jeffrey und seine kritischen Prinzipien*, Berlin, 1908; R. Noyes, *Wordsworth and Jeffrey in Controversy*,

Bloomington, 1941; and J. A. Greig, *Francis Jeffrey of the Edinburgh Review*, 1948 (an uncritical survey of his criticism).

Material may also be found in the following books and studies: G. Gilfillan, *A Gallery of Literary Portraits*, ii, 1850; T. Carlyle, 'Lord Jeffrey', in *Reminiscences*, ed. J. A. Froude, 2 vols., 1881 (a penetrating portrait; also see Carlyle's letters); L. E. Gates, *Three Studies in Literature*, New York, 1899 (still of value); M. Y. Hughes, 'The Humanism of Francis Jeffrey', *MLR* xvi, 1921; J. M. Beatty, 'Lord Jeffrey and Wordsworth', *PMLA* xxxviii, 1923; R. C. Bald, 'Francis Jeffrey as a Literary Critic', *Nineteenth Century*, xcvii, 1925; Leslie Stephen, *Hours in a Library*, ii, 1876; Sir G. O. Trevelyan, *The Life and Letters of Lord Macaulay*, 2 vols., 1876; M. H. Goldberg, 'Jeffrey: Mutilator of Carlyle's "Burns" ', *PMLA* lvi, 1941, and 'Carlyle, Pictet and Jeffrey', *MLQ* vii, 1946; R. Daniel, 'Jeffrey and Wordsworth: the Shape of Persecution', *Sewanee Review*, l (50), 1942; R. Derby, 'The Paradox of Jeffrey: Reason versus Sensibility', *MLQ* vii, 1946; and B. Guyer, 'Jeffrey's "Essay on Beauty" ', *HLQ* xiii, 1950, and 'The Philosophy of Jeffrey', *MLQ* xi, 1950. Jeffrey's criticism is sympathetically discussed by R. Wellek (see p. 475 above). See also *Edinburgh Review*, on p. 470–3 above.

WILLIAM JERDAN, 1782–1869.

From 1817 to 1850 Jerdan edited the *Literary Gazette*, an influential periodical later eclipsed by the *Athenaeum*. Earlier he had edited a number of other journals, including the *Satirist* (which he edited from 1812 to 1814) and the *Sun*. His *Foreign Literary Gazette*, 1831, was short-lived. His other writings include *Six Weeks in Paris, by a late Visitant*, 3 vols., 1818 (2nd ed.); *Personal Narrative of a Journey overland from the Bank to Barnes*, 1829 (a skit on the vogue for travel books); *The National Portrait Gallery of the Nineteenth Century*, 5 annual vols., 1830–4; *Illustrations of the Plan of a National Association for the Encouragement and Protection of Authors and Men of Talent and Genius*, 1839; and a handbook for the South-Eastern Railway Company (*Manual No. 1. Main Line to the Coast and Continent*, 1854). His *Autobiography* appeared in 4 vols. in 1852–3, and was supplemented by *Men I have Known*, 1866. He contributed to many periodicals, including *Fraser's*, the *Gentleman's Magazine*, and *Notes and Queries* (as 'Bushey Heath'). In 1831 he contributed to *The Club Book*, ed. Andrew Picken, vol. ii. He edited the

Rutland Papers and the Perth Correspondence for the Camden Society.

There is a useful account of Jerdan's career, which is of interest as that of a typical man of letters of the day, in the *DNB*. Information about the *Literary Gazette* may also be found in *The Athenaeum: A Mirror of Victorian Culture*, by L. A. Marchand, Chapel Hill, 1941.

JOHN KEATS, 1795–1821.

Keats published three volumes: *Poems*, 1817; *Endymion: A Poetic Romance*, 1818; and *Lamia, Isabella, The Eve of St. Agnes, and Other Poems*, 1820. The first attempt at a collection of his poems is to be found in *The Poetical Works of Coleridge, Shelley, and Keats*, Paris, 1829. Neither this nor *The Poetical Works* of 1840 had any authority. In 1848 there appeared the *Life, Letters, and Literary Remains, of John Keats*, edited by Richard Monckton Milnes, in 2 vols. Vol. II contains unpublished poems. There is a reprint of Milnes's book, without the poems, in Everyman's Library, 1927. In 1856–7 Milnes (Lord Houghton) published *Another Version of Keats' 'Hyperion'*. Since this time some forty-two further short pieces have come to light.

In 1909 M. Robertson edited a facsimile of *Lamia*, &c. There are also Noel Douglas facsimiles of the volumes of 1817 and 1820 (both 1927). There is a facsimile of *Endymion* in two different forms, with and without an introduction by H. Clement Notcutt (1927). There are also American facsimiles of the volumes of 1817 and 1820, New York, 1934.

The standard modern edition of *The Poetical Works* is that of H. W. Garrod, 1939, revised 1958. The same text is given with a less elaborate apparatus in the Oxford Standard Authors edition, also ed. Garrod (new ed., 1956). Of innumerable other editions mention may be made of the edition of *The Poems* in Everyman's Library, ed. G. Bullett, 1944, and of the *Complete Poetry and Selected Prose*, ed. H. E. Briggs, New York, 1951. For explanatory notes one must refer to E. de Sélincourt's edition, 1905, revised 1907 and 1926. The Hampstead Edition of Keats's *Works*, ed. H. B. and M. Buxton Forman, 8 vols., 1938, is an amplification of H. B. Forman's *Complete Works*, 5 vols., Glasgow, 1900–1, and still contains a little material not readily available elsewhere.

The standard edition of the letters was for many years that

of M. Buxton Forman, 2 vols., 1931, 4th edition (1 vol.) 1952. This has now been superseded by *The Letters of John Keats 1814–1821*, ed. H. E. Rollins, 2 vols., 1958.

Only a few of the more recent of the numerous volumes of selections from the poems and the letters can be mentioned: *Keats: Poetry and Prose*, ed. H. Ellershaw, 1922; *Selected Poetry and Letters*, ed. R. H. Fogle, New York, 1951; *Selected Letters of John Keats*, ed. L. Trilling, New York, 1951, enlarged ed. 1955 (with a notable essay mentioned on p. 563 below); *Selected Letters and Poems of John Keats*, ed. J. H. Walsh, 1954; and *John Keats: Selected Poems and Letters*, ed. D. Bush, New York, 1959. There is also a volume of *Letters of John Keats*, ed. F. Page, in the World's Classics series, 1954.

The Keats Circle: Letters and Papers, 1816–78, ed. H. E. Rollins, 2 vols., Cambridge, Mass., 1948, contains a great deal of material about Keats, including reprints of a number of the writings mentioned in the next paragraph. *More Letters and Poems of the Keats Circle*, 1955, is a small supplement by the same editor. F. Edgcumbe edited *The Letters of Fanny Brawne to Fanny Keats*, 1937.

Charles (Armitage) Brown's unpublished *Life of John Keats* was edited by Dorothy H. Bodurtha and W. B. Pope in 1937. R. M. Milnes printed about eighty letters in the *Life, Letters, and Literary Remains* of 1848. Sir Sidney Colvin's *John Keats: His Life and Poetry, His Friends, Critics, and After-Fame*, 1917, revised 1925, still remains one of the best general books on Keats, in spite of all the material that has become available more recently. Colvin's briefer *Keats* in the English Men of Letters series, 1887, gave him the incentive to write the fuller work. Amy Lowell's *John Keats*, 2 vols., 1925, is enthusiastic but unreliable. C. L. Finney's *The Evolution of Keats's Poetry*, 2 vols., Cambridge, Mass., 1936, also deals with the life as well as the poetry and remains of considerable value. Dorothy Hewlett published *Adonais: A Life of John Keats* in 1937: a revised edition, *A Life of Keats*, appeared in 1949. B. Ifor Evans's *Keats*, 1934, is very brief but sensible. *John Keats: The Living Year*, 1954, by R. Gittings, is a brilliant foray into the field of biographical and interpretative conjecture. (See also *The Mask of Keats: A Study of Problems*, 1956, by the same writer.) The best biography is now *John Keats: The Making of a Poet*, by Aileen Ward, 1963.

Other material of biographical relevance may be found in

E. Blunden's useful compilation, *Shelley and Keats as they Struck their Contemporaries*, 1925, in the same writer's *Keats's Publisher*, 1936, and in Joanna Richardson's *Fanny Brawne*, 1952. In 1938 Sir William Hale White published *Keats as Doctor and Patient*; see also *John Keats's Anatomical Notebook*, ed. M. B. Forman, 1934.

Articles of biographical importance include 'John Keats and Benjamin Robert Haydon', by C. Olney, *PMLA* xlix, 1934; 'Keats and Wordsworth: A Study in Personal and Critical Impressions', by C. D. Thorpe, *PMLA* xlii, 1927; and 'Keats and Hazlitt: A Record of Personal Relationship and Critical Estimate', by the same writer, *PMLA* lxii, 1947 (on this topic see also *John Keats' Fancy*, by J. R. Caldwell, mentioned below).

The history of Keats's reputation is surveyed in the introduction to J. R. MacGillivray's *John Keats: A Bibliography and Reference Guide*, Toronto, 1949. See also 'Keats and the Periodicals of his Time', by G. L. Marsh and N. I. White, *MP* xxxii, 1934; *Keats and the Victorians . . . 1821–1895*, by G. H. Ford, New Haven, 1944; and *Keats' Reputation in America to 1848*, by H. E. Rollins, Cambridge, Mass., 1946. *Keats and the Bostonians*, by H. E. Rollins and S. M. Parrish, Cambridge, Mass., 1951, is concerned with collectors rather than the poet himself.

The books by J. Middleton Murry are both biographical and critical in their scope. The most remarkable remains *Keats and Shakespeare*, 1925, a brilliant example of interpretative criticism of the most hazardous kind. His evolving views may be followed in the various versions of his subsequent essays on Keats, *Studies in Keats*, 1930, 1939, 1949 (as *The Mystery of Keats*), 1955 (*Keats*).

Apart from the books by Colvin, Finney, and Middleton Murry already mentioned, the most helpful critical studies are those by Garrod (*Keats*, 1926, revised 1939), E. C. Pettet (*On the Poetry of Keats*, 1957), and W. J. Bate (*John Keats*, 1963). A few of the numerous other studies may also be mentioned. An early book still of some interest is *John Keats, A Study*, by Mrs. F. M. Owen, 1880. *The Mind of John Keats*, by C. D. Thorpe, New York, 1926, deals particularly with Keats's aesthetic ideas. *The Genius of Keats*, by A. W. Crawford, 1932, supports the view that Keats was a strenuously intellectual poet. *Keats's Shakespeare*, by Caroline F. E. Spurgeon, 1928 (2nd edition, 1929) is a close study of his marginalia on certain of Shakespeare's plays. W. J. Bate's *The Stylistic Development of John Keats*, 1945, may be read with *Keats's Craftsmanship*, by M. R. Ridley, 1933. Bate's *Negative*

Capability: The Intuitive Approach in Keats, Cambridge, Mass., 1939, is another intelligent study. *John Keats' Fancy,* by J. R. Caldwell, Ithaca, New York, 1945, incorporates a good deal of the material in his *Beauty is Truth* . . . (*University of California Publications in English,* 1940), and explores his relation to the associationist aestheticians of the eighteenth century. Two careful German studies are *Die Anschauungen von John Keats über Dichter und Dichtkunst,* Marburg, 1946 (Habilitationsschrift), by H. Viebrock, and *Zum magischen Realismus bei Keats und Novalis,* by G. Bonarius, Giessen, 1950. *Keats and the Daemon King,* by W. W. Beyer, 1946, makes a great deal of the influence of Wieland's *Oberon. The Prefigurative Imagination of John Keats,* by N. F. Ford, Stanford, 1951, deals with the 'Beauty-Truth Identification and its Implications'. *The Finer Tone: Keats's Major Poems,* by E. R. Wasserman, Baltimore, 1953, offers an ambitiously philosophical reading of certain of the major poems. L. J. Zillman's *Keats and the Sonnet Tradition in English,* Los Angeles 1939, throws more light on Keats than does G. Shuster's *The English Ode from Milton to Keats,* 1940. In *Keats and Mrs. Tighe,* New York, 1928, E. V. Weller made too much of interesting resemblances between the poems of Keats and Mrs. Tighe's once-famous *Psyche,* only to be demolished by D. Bush, in his 'Notes on Keats's Reading', *PMLA* l (50), 1935. *John Keats: A Reassessment,* ed. K. Muir, Liverpool, 1959, contains a collection of essays by various hands. *The Consecrated Urn,* by B. Blackstone, 1959, is an eccentric and occasionally illuminating attempt to present 'An Interpretation of Keats in Terms of Growth and Form'.

The following books contain important sections or chapters on Keats: *Mythology and the Romantic Tradition in English Poetry,* by D. Bush, Cambridge, Mass., 1937; *The Starlit Dome,* by G. Wilson Knight, 1941; *English Bards and Grecian Marbles,* by S. A. Larrabee, New York, 1943; the books by H. N. Fairchild mentioned above on p. 494; *The Romantic Comedy,* by D. G. James, 1948; *Major Adjectives in English Poetry from Wyatt to Auden,* by Josephine Miles, 1946; *The Imagery of Keats and Shelley: A Comparative Study,* by R. H. Fogle, Chapel Hill, 1949; and *The Quest for Permanence: The Symbolism of Wordsworth, Shelley and Keats,* by D. Perkins, Cambridge, Mass., 1959. Five important essays on Keats, by Bush, W. J. Bate, Cleanth Brooks, E. Wasserman, and R. H. Fogle, are to be found in the collection of essays edited by M. H. Abrams mentioned on p. 467 above.

Important essays and articles with a general bearing include: 'John Keats', by Matthew Arnold, *Essays in Criticism*, 2nd series, 1888 (reprinted from *The English Poets*, ed. T. H. Ward, iv, 1880); *A Critical Introduction to Keats*, by Robert Bridges, in his *Collected Essays*, iv, 1929 (first privately printed in 1895, and published in the Muses' Library *Keats*, 1896); 'The Letters of Keats', by Andrew Bradley, in his *Oxford Lectures on Poetry*, 1909; the same writer's 'Keats and "Philosophy"', *A Miscellany*, 1929; 'Keats', by E. de Sélincourt, 1921 (British Academy Lecture, reprinted in *The John Keats Memorial Volume*, ed. G. C. Williamson, 1921), a volume which contains other interesting essays; 'Keats's Epithets', by D. W. Rannie, *ESEA*, 1912; 'Keats', by F. R. Leavis, *Revaluation*, 1936; 'From Good to Bright: A Note in Poetic History', by Josephine Miles, *PMLA* lx, 1945; 'The Validity of the Poetic Vision: Keats and Spenser', by E. E. Stoll, *MLR* xl, 1945; 'Romanticism and Synaesthesia: . . . Sense Transfer in Keats and Byron', by S. De Ullmann, *PMLA* lx, 1945; 'Empathic Imagery in Keats and Shelley', by R. H. Fogle, *PMLA* lxi, 1946; 'A Reading of Keats', by Allen Tate, *The American Scholar*, xv, 1946; 'Of Beauty and Reality in Keats', by R. D. Havens, *ELH* xvii, 1950; 'Coleridge, Keats and the Modern Mind', by A. Gérard, *EC* i, 1951; 'Keats the Apollonian: The Time-and-Space Logic of his Poems as Paintings', by R. W. Stallman, *UTQ* xvi, 1947; 'The Poet as Hero: Keats in his Letters', by L. Trilling, in *The Opposing Self*, New York, 1950; 'Keats and William Browne', by Joan Grundy, *RES*, n.s., vi, 1955; and *Keats and Reality*, by John Bayley, 1962 (British Academy Lecture).

Only a few of the articles on individual poems can be mentioned here. On poems in the volume of 1817 one may consult 'Keats's Approach to the Chapman Sonnet', by B. Ifor Evans, *ESEA* xvi, 1930; 'Keats's Realms of Gold', by J. W. Beach, *PMLA* xlix, 1934; and 'The Realm of Flora in Keats and Poussin', by I. Jack, *TLS*, 10 April 1959. There are notable discussions of *Endymion* by L. Brown ('The Genesis, Growth, and Meaning of *Endymion*', *SP* xxx, 1933); N. F. Ford ('*Endymion*: a Neo-Platonic Allegory?', *ELH* xiv, 1947, and 'The Meaning of "Fellowship with Essence" in *Endymion*', *PMLA* lxii, 1947); J. D. Wigod ('The Meaning of *Endymion*', *PMLA* lxviii, 1953); G. O. Allen ('The Fall of Endymion: A Study in Keats's Intellectual Growth', *K.-Sh.J.* vi, 1957); and S. M. Sperry, 'The Allegory of *Endymion*', *SR* ii, 1962.

On the Tales in the 1820 volume see J. H. Roberts, 'The Significance of *Lamia*', *PMLA* l (50), 1935; H. G. Wright, 'Possible Indebtedness of Keats's *Isabella* to the *Decameron*', *RES*, N.S., ii, 1951; and the discussion between H. G. Wright and M. Whitely on the question whether *The Eve of St. Agnes* has a tragic ending (*MLR* xl and xlii, 1945 and 1947).

On the Odes in general, which are of course discussed in most of the critical studies of Keats, one may also consult H. M. McLuhan's 'Aesthetic Pattern in Keats's Odes', *UTQ* xii, 1943; the article by T. E. Connolly in *ELH* xvi, 1949; the essay by J. Holloway in the *Cambridge Journal*, v, 1952 (reprinted in *The Charted Mirror*, 1960); 'Keats's Odes and Letters: Recurrent Diction and Imagery', by D. Perkins, *K.-Sh.J.* ii, 1953; and 'Keats's Odes: Further Notes', by E. Blunden, *K.-Sh.J.* iii, 1954. The 'Grecian Urn' has been discussed by K. Burke in *A Grammar of Motives*, 1945; by Cleanth Brooks in *The Well Wrought Urn*, New York, 1947; by A. Whitley in *K.-Sh.B.* iii, 1952; and by C. Patterson in *ELH* xxi, 1954. On the 'Nightingale' we may consult R. H. Fogle in *MLQ* viii, 1947, and *PMLA* lxviii, 1953; A. Gérard in the *Yale Review*, 1944; and Janet Spens in *RES*, N.S., iii, July 1952. There are discussions of 'Autumn' by E. J. Lovell in *Texas Studies in English*, xxix, 1950; by R. A. Brower in *The Fields of Light*, 1951; and by B. C. Southam in *K.-Sh.J.* ix, 1960.

On 'Hyperion' there are important articles by Martha Hale Shackford, *SP*, xxii, 1925; Helen Darbishire, *RES* iii, 1927 ('Keats and Egypt'); D. Bush, *MLN* xlix, 1934 ('The Date of Keats's *Fall of Hyperion*'); J. R. Caldwell, *PMLA* li, 1936 ('The Meaning of *Hyperion*'); J. Livingston Lowes, *PMLA* li, 1936 ('Moneta's Temple'); K. Muir, *EC* ii, 1952 ('The Meaning of *Hyperion*', reprinted in his *John Keats: A Reassessment*, Liverpool, 1958); and S. M. Sperry ('Keats, Milton, and *The Fall of Hyperion*', *PMLA* lxxvii, 1962).

The lines to Fanny, 'What can I do to drive away', are discussed by H. E. Briggs in 'Keats, Robertson and "That Most Hateful Land" ', in *PMLA* lix, 1944. 'The Meaning of Keats's "Eve of St. Mark" ' is the subject of an article by W. E. Houghton, in *ELH* xiii, 1946. Gittings's dating of the 'Bright Star' sonnet is rejected by Aileen Ward in an article in *SP* lii, 1955.

Those wishing more complete information about the work that has been done on Keats may refer to the *CBEL*; to J. R. MacGillivray's *John Keats: A Bibliography and Reference Guide*,

Toronto, 1949; and to the chapter by C. D. Thorpe in *ERP*. The *K.-Sh.J.* contains annual bibliographies.

There is a *Concordance*, ed. D. L. Baldwin, J. W. Hebel, L. N. Broughton, and others, Washington, 1917. Also of use is *The Keats Letters, Papers, and Other Relics forming the Dilke Bequest in the Hampstead Public Library*, ed. G. C. Williamson, 1914. There are several articles on manuscript material, notably Mabel A. E. Steele, 'The Woodhouse Transcript of the Poems of Keats', *Harvard Library Bulletin*, iii, 1949, and her 'Three Early Manuscripts of Keats', *K.-Sh.J.* i, 1952; W. A. Coles, 'The Proof Sheets of Keats's "Lamia"', *Harvard Library Bulletin*, 1954; and H. E. Rollins, 'Unpublished Autograph Texts of Keats', *Harvard Library Bulletin*, vi, 1952. In 1905 E. de Sélincourt edited *Hyperion: A Facsimile of Keats's Autograph Manuscript with a Transliteration of the Manuscript of The Fall of Hyperion A Dream.*

CHARLES KNIGHT, 1791–1873.

Only a few of the productions of Knight's long and useful life can be recorded here. He wrote *Arminius, or The Deliverance of Germany. A Tragedy*, Windsor, 1814; *The Bridal of the Isles, A Mask*, 1817 (2nd ed.); *The Menageries*, 3 vols. (Society for the Diffusion of Useful Knowledge), 1829–40 (anon.); *The Working-Man's Companion: The Rights of Industry*, 2 parts (*Capital and Labour*, and *The Results of Machinery*), 1831 (anon.); *Trades' Unions and Strikes*, 1834 (anon.); *William Shakspere: A Biography*, 1842 (1850, as *Studies and Illustrations of the Writings of Shakspere*, vol. i); *William Caxton. A Biography*, 1844; *Studies and Illustrations of the Writings of Shakspere*, 3 vols., 1850; *The Struggles of a Book against Excessive Taxation* ([1850], 2nd ed.); *The Case of Authors as regards the Paper Duty*, 1851; *Once upon a Time*, 2 vols., 1854 (essays); *The Old Printer and the Modern Press*, 1854; *The Popular History of England*, 8 vols., 1856–62; *Passages of a Working Life*, 3 vols., 1864–5; *Shadows of the Old Booksellers*, 1865; and *Begg'd at Court: A Legend of Westminster* (novel), 1867.

Knight also contributed editorial information to an edition of Fairfax's translation of Tasso, Windsor, 2 vols., 1817. He edited *The Pictorial Edition of the Works of Shakspere*, 7 vols., [1839–]41, rev. ed., 5 vols. 1867; and wrote on 'Shakspere and his Writings', in *Knight's Store of Knowledge*, 1841. He contributed a great deal to *London*, a 6-vol. work which he edited in 1841–4 (rev. E. Walford, 6 vols. [1875–7]).

In 1823–4 he edited *Knight's Quarterly Magazine*, continued in 1825 as *The Quarterly Magazine, New Series*. In 1828–9 he was editor of the *London Magazine*. From 1832 he edited *The Penny Magazine of the Society for the Diffusion of Useful Knowledge*. He collaborated with Harriet Martineau in *The Land We Live In*, 1847.

In 1892 A. A. Clowes published *Charles Knight, A Sketch*, with a bibliography. Otherwise the main source of information remains Knight's *Passages of a Working Life*, though a good deal of information may also be found in *Harriet Martineau's Autobiography*, 3 vols., 1877; in *Recorder of Birmingham: A Memoir of Matthew Davenport Hill*, by his daughters, 1878; and in *The English Common Reader*, by R. D. Altick, Chicago, 1957. Many of the publications for which Knight was responsible are mentioned in Lowndes and the *DNB*.

JAMES SHERIDAN KNOWLES, 1784–1862.

Knowles's first play, *Leo; or, The Gypsy*, was performed at Waterford in 1810: see *The Life of Edmund Kean*, by B. W. Procter, 2 vols., 1835. His second, *Brian Boroihme; or, The Maid of Erin*, was performed in 1811 and first published in B. N. Webster's *The Acting National Drama*, vol. viii, in the 1840's. For his later plays only the date of separate publication is here given (Allardyce Nicoll also gives dates of performance): *Virginius*, Glasgow, 1820; *Caius Gracchus*, Glasgow, 1823; *The Fatal Dowry* (from Massinger), 1825; *William Tell*, 1825; *The Beggar's Daughter of Bethnal Green*, 1828; *Alfred the Great*, 1831; *The Hunchback*, 1832; *The Vision of the Bard*, 1832; *The Wife*, 1833; *The Daughter*, 1837; *The Bridal*, [1837] (from *The Maid's Tragedy*, by Beaumont and Fletcher); *The Love-Chase*, 1837; *Woman's Wit*, 1838; *The Maid of Mariendorpt*, 1838; *Love*, 1840; *John of Procida*, 1840; *Old Maids*, 1841; *The Rose of Arragon*, 1842; *The Secretary*, 1843; and *The Rock of Rome*, 1849. *True unto Death* was published in 1863.

Knowles published his *Dramatic Works* in 3 vols. in 1841–3. This collection includes fifteen plays. R. Shelton Mackenzie had provided a Memoir for a previous collection, published at Baltimore in 1835. In 1874 there was a privately printed edition of *Various Dramatic Works of James Sheridan Knowles*, in 2 vols.

Knowles also wrote: *The Welch Harper: A Ballad*, 1796; *Fugitive Pieces*, 1810; *The Elocutionist* (an anthology for reading aloud), Belfast [? 1823]; *Fortescue: A Novel,* 3 vols., 1847 (first published serially, in *The Sunday Times,* 1846, and privately printed in the same year); *George Lovell: A Novel,* 3 vols., 1847; *The Rock of Rome, or the Arch Heresy,* 1849; *The Idol demolished by its own Priest: An Answer to Cardinal Wiseman's Lectures on Transubstantiation,* 1851; *The Gospel attributed to Matthew is the Record of the whole original Apostlehood,* 1855; 'Old Adventures', in *The Tale Book,* by Knowles and others, Königsberg, 1859; *Lectures on Dramatic Literature,* ed. S. W. Abbott and F. Harvey, 2 vols., 1873 (privately printed); and *Tales and Novelettes,* revised and edited by F. Harvey, 1874 (privately printed).

On Knowles see the last paragraph of Hazlitt's *The Spirit of the Age,* 1825; R. H. Horne's *A New Spirit of the Age,* vol. ii, 1844; *Blackwood's Magazine,* xciv, 1863; *The Life of James Sheridan Knowles,* by R. B. Knowles, revised and edited by F. Harvey, 1872 (privately printed: only twenty-five copies); W. Maginn, *A Gallery of Illustrious Literary Characters,* ed. W. Bates [1873]; L. Hasberg, *James Sheridan Knowles' Leben und dramatische Werke,* Lingen, 1883; W. Klapp, *Sheridan Knowles' Virginius und sein angebliches französisches Gegenstück,* Rostock, 1904; *The Diaries of W. C. Macready, 1833–1851,* ed. W. Toynbee, 2 vols., 1912; and L. H. Meeks, *Sheridan Knowles and the Theatre of his Time,* Bloomington, Indiana, 1933 (with bibliography).

CHARLES LAMB, 1775–1834 (AND MARY LAMB, 1764–1847).

A handful of poems by Lamb may be found in *Poems on Various Subjects,* by S. T. Coleridge, 1796; in a privately printed collection of sonnets, without a title, produced by Coleridge in the same year; and in *Poems on the Death of Priscilla Farmer,* by Charles Lloyd, 1796. Lamb helped James White with *Original Letters, &c. of Sir John Falstaff and his Friends,* 1796. The second edition of *Poems,* by S. T. Coleridge, Bristol, 1797, includes poems by Lamb on pp. 215–40. In 1798 Lamb published *A Tale of Rosamund Gray and Old Blind Margaret* at Birmingham, and *Blank Verse,* by Charles Lloyd and Charles Lamb. *John Woodvil* appeared in 1802. *Mr. H., or Beware a Bad Name* was published without authority in Philadelphia in 1813. Lamb contributed to *The Poetical Recreations of 'The Champion',* 1822, published *Album Verses* in 1830, and *Satan in Search of a Wife* the following year.

Specimens of English Dramatic Poets first appeared in 1808. *Elia:*

Essays which have appeared under that Signature in the London Magazine, was published in 1823 (some copies being issued in 1822). *The Last Essays of Elia* came out in 1833, the two series being collected in 1835. The 1828 Philadelphia edition of the two series was unauthorized. The 1835 Paris edition, also unauthorized, included other prose of Lamb's. *Eliana: Being the Hitherto Uncollected Writings*, was edited by [J. E. Babson], Boston, 1864. *Recollections of Christ's Hospital*, published in the *Gentleman's Magazine* in 1813, was issued separately in 1835.

Lamb also published a number of books for children: *The King and Queen of Hearts*, 1805 (facsimile edition, ed. E. V. Lucas, 1902); *Tales from Shakespear*, 2 vols., 1807 (with Mary Lamb); *Mrs. Leicester's School*, 1807; *The Adventures of Ulysses*, 1808; *Poetry for Children*, 1809; *Prince Dorus*, 1811; and *Beauty and the Beast*, 1811.

Apart from the *London Magazine*, Lamb contributed to a great many journals, including the *Reflector*, the *Examiner*, the *Indicator*, the *New Monthly Magazine*, Hone's *Every-Day Book*, *Table-Book*, and *Year Book*, *Blackwood's Magazine*, Moxon's *Englishman's Magazine*, the *Athenaeum*, and several newspapers. He also helped G. Burnett with his *Specimens of English Prose-Writers*, 3 vols., 1807.

His letters were first published in 1837, in *Letters of Charles Lamb, with a Sketch of his Life*, ed. Sir T. N. Talfourd, 2 vols. In 1848 Talfourd published *Final Memorials of Charles Lamb* in 2 vols. Later editions have contained more letters, for example those of W. C. Hazlitt, 2 vols., 1886; A. Ainger, 2 vols., 1888; and W. Macdonald, 2 vols., 1903, and 2 vols., 1906 (Everyman's Library). E. V. Lucas first edited the *Letters* in 2 vols. in 1905. His 3-vol. edition of 1935, which includes the letters of Mary Lamb, is at present the standard edition (but see the comments of G. L. Barnett in *MLQ* ix, 1948, and *HLQ*, 1955, and those of P. F. Morgan in *NQ* for December 1956). There is a 2-vol. selection from the letters in Everyman's Library, ed. G. Pocock, 1945, and a selection in a 1-vol. edition by G. Woodcock, 1950.

Lamb published his *Works* in 2 vols. as early as 1818. An unauthorized edition of *The Poetical Works* of Rogers, Lamb, and others appeared at Paris in 1829. There was a 3-vol. edition of *The Prose Works* in 1835. Talfourd edited the *Works* (prose and verse) in five parts in 1840. Later editions of the *Works* include those edited by R. H. Shepherd, 1874, A. Ainger, 1878–88 (7 vols., also *Life and Works*, 12 vols., 1899–1900), and W. Macdonald, 1903–4 (12 vols.) The standard edition is that in 7 vols., edited by E. V. Lucas in 1903–5 (reissued in 6 vols. in 1912 with a revised edition of the letters now in turn superseded by the edition mentioned in the previous paragraph, but without the *Dramatic Specimens*). In [1908] T. Hutchinson produced a convenient smaller edition in 2 vols. (1 vol., 1924), which contains useful bibliographical information.

There are numerous volumes of selections. Mention may be made of *The Best of Lamb*, ed. E. V. Lucas, 1914; *Charles Lamb: Prose and Poetry*, ed. George Gordon, 1921; *Lamb's Criticism*, ed. E. M. W. Tillyard, 1923; *Charles Lamb: Essays and Letters*, ed. J. M. French, New York, 1937; and *The Portable Lamb*, ed. J. M. Brown, New York, 1949. Of the many separate editions of the *Essays of Elia*, one of the most recent, which gives both series, is that edited by M. Elwin, 1952.

Since Lamb published so much anonymously in periodicals it is not surprising that many ascriptions should have been made. Some of these are mentioned in the *CBEL* iii, 633–4, while there is a brief discussion in *ERPE*, pp. 37–38.

The best biography is still *The Life of Charles Lamb*, by E. V. Lucas, 2 vols., 1905, revised edition, 1 vol., 1921. For earlier accounts we may go to the *New Monthly Magazine* for 1835 (Lamb's brief 'Autobiographical Sketch', written in 1827); Leigh Hunt's *Lord Byron and Some of his Contemporaries*, 2 vols., 1828, and his *Autobiography*, 1850; Sir T. N. Talfourd's *Letters of Charles Lamb, with a Sketch of his Life*, 2 vols., 1837 (on his reliability see R. S. Newdick, *The First Life and Letters of Charles Lamb—A Study of Talfourd as Editor and Biographer*, Ohio State University, 1935); P. G. Patmore, *My Friends and Acquaintances*, 3 vols., 1855; *Love's Last Labour Not Lost*, by George Daniel, 1863; *Charles Lamb: A Memoir*, by Barry Cornwall (B. W. Procter), 1866 (see also his *Autobiographical Fragment*, 1877); *Charles Lamb—His Friends, His Haunts, and His Books*, by Percy Fitzgerald, 1866; A. Ainger, *Charles Lamb*, 1882 (English Men of Letters); and *The Lambs: Their Lives, Their Friends, and Their Correspondence*, by W. C. Hazlitt, 1897.

There are a great many references to Lamb in the letters and memoirs of his contemporaries. See, for example, *Henry Crabb*

Robinson on Books and Their Writers, ed. Edith J. Morley, 3 vols., 1938. The comments of Hazlitt and De Quincey may be found scattered throughout their writings. There is a useful collection by E. Blunden, *Charles Lamb: His Life Recorded by his Contemporaries*, 1934, which complements S. M. Rich's *The Elian Miscellany*, 1931. There are also several volumes which throw particular light on Lamb and his friends: for example, *Lamb and Hazlitt*, by W. C. Hazlitt, 1900; *The Letters of Thomas Manning to Charles Lamb*, ed. G. A. Anderson, 1925; E. V. Lucas, *Charles Lamb and the Lloyds*, 1898; *Lamb's Friend the Census-Taker: Life and Letters of John Rickman*, by O. Williams, 1911; *Thomas Hood & Charles Lamb*, by W. Jerrold, 1930; E. C. Ross, *Charles Lamb and Emma Isola* (Charles Lamb Society Booklet, 1950); and 'Charles Lamb's "Companionship...in Almost Solitude"', *Princeton University Library Chronicle*, vi, 1945, by J. S. Finch (an article which gives details of MSS. at Princeton).

Also worth mentioning are F. V. Morley, *Lamb Before Elia*, 1932; J. Derocquigny's intelligent *Charles Lamb: sa vie et ses œuvres*, Lille, 1904; W. Jerrold's *Charles Lamb*, 1905, an introduction; and three contributions by E. Blunden: his British Council pamphlet (Writers and their Work, no. 56); *Charles Lamb and his Contemporaries*, 1933, his Clark Lectures; and 'Elia and Christ's Hospital', *ESEA* xxii, 1937. Two specialized studies are B. Lake's *Introduction to Charles Lamb . . . With a . . . Study of His Relation to Robert Burton*, Leipzig, 1903, and J. S. Iseman's *A Perfect Sympathy: Charles Lamb and Sir Thomas Browne*, Cambridge, Mass., 1937.

Carlyle's unfavourable view of Lamb is expressed in his *Reminiscences*, ed. J. A. Froude, 2 vols., 1881, and elsewhere. The following books also contain interesting discussions of Lamb: *Miscellanies*, by A. C. Swinburne, 1886; *Appreciations*, by Walter Pater, 1889; *Shelburne Essays*, 2nd and 4th series, by Paul Elmore More, 1905–6; *Determinations*, ed. F. R. Leavis, 1934 ('Our Debt to Lamb', a rather humourless essay on Lamb's influence by Denys Thompson); *Selected Essays*, by A. R. Orage, ed. H. Read and D. Saurat, 1935 ('The Danger of the Whimsical'); *The Liberal Imagination*, by L. Trilling, 1950 ('The Sanity of True Genius'); *A History of Modern Criticism: 1750– 1950*, vol. ii, *The Romantic Age*, by R. Wellek, 1955; and *The Hero in Eclipse in Victorian Fiction*, by M. Praz, 1956.

Articles include 'The Equation of the Essay', by G. Williamson, *Sewanee Review*, 1927; 'Charles Lamb Sees London', by A. D. McKillop, *Rice Institute Pamphlet*, 1935; 'Lamb and Coleridge', by Edith C. Johnson, *American Scholar*, 1937; 'Charles Lamb, Marston, and Du Bartas', by M. P. Tilley, *MLN* liii, 1938; 'Antiquarian Interest in Elizabethan Drama Before Lamb', by R. D. Williams, *PMLA* liii, 1938 (for a fuller background see E. R. Wasserman's *Elizabethan Poetry in the Eighteenth Century*, 1947); 'A Chip from Elia's Workshop', by J. M. French, *SP* xxxvii, 1940; 'The Character in the Elia Essay', by V. Lang, *MLN* lvi, 1941; 'History of Ideas versus Reading of Poetry', by L. Spitzer, *Southern Review*, 1941 (a discussion of how to read 'The Old Familiar Faces'); 'Romantic Apologiae for Hamlet's Treatment of Ophelia', by A. P. Hudson, *ELH* ix, 1942; 'Lamb's Criticism of Restoration Comedy', by W. E. Houghton, *ELH* x, 1943; 'Dating Lamb's Contributions to the *Table Book*', by G. L. Barnett, *PMLA* lx, 1945; 'Lamb and the Elizabethans', by R. C. Bald, *Studies in Honor of A. H. R. Fairchild*, Columbia, Missouri, 1946; 'Yorick and Elia', by J. V. Logan, *Charles Lamb Society Bulletin*, lxxxv–lxxxvi, 1948; 'Lamb's Insight into the Nature of the Novel', by C. I. Patterson, *PMLA* xlvii, 1952; 'Lamb's Latinity', a correspondence in the *TLS* by P. Legouis, I. P. M. Chambers, and R. G. C. Levens, 10 and 24 June and 11 August 1952; 'Charles Lamb's Contribution to the Theory of Dramatic Illusion', by S. Barnet, *PMLA* xlix, 1954; 'The Mind of Elia', by B. Jessup, *JHI*, 1954; and 'Charles Lamb and the Tragic Malvolio', by S. Barnet, *PQ*, 1954.

Lamb's method of working is discussed with reference to the manuscripts in G. L. Barnett's unpublished study, 'The Evolution of Elia', a Princeton dissertation (1942) available on microfilm.

The best bibliographies are those in *CBEL* and *ERPE*, which may be supplemented by the annual bibliographies in *PQ*. J. C. Thomson's *Bibliography*, 1908, lists many of Lamb's contributions to periodicals. W. C. Hazlitt's *Mary and Charles Lamb: Poems, Letters, and Remains*, 1874, lists the books sold from Lamb's library. See also 'The Scribner Lamb Collection', by J. S. Finch, *Princeton University Library Chronicle*, vii, 1946.

There is a separate *Life of Mary Lamb*, by Anne Gilchrist, ed. J. H. Ingram, 1883, which has been rendered obsolete by E. C. Ross's *The Ordeal of Bridget Elia*, Norman, Oklahoma, 1940. See also 'The Tragedy of Mary Lamb', by W. R. Riddell,

Transactions of the Royal Society of Canada, 1928. Florence V. Barry sets the Lambs' writings for children in perspective in *A Century of Children's Books*, 1922.

LETITIA ELIZABETH LANDON (afterwards Maclean, 'L.E.L.'), 1802–38.

In verse 'L.E.L.' published *The Fate of Adelaide: A Swiss Romantic Tale; and other Poems*, 1821; *The Improvisatrice*, 1824; *The Troubadour, Catalogue of Pictures, and Historical Sketches*, 1825; *The Golden Violet, with its Tales of Romance and Chivalry*, 1827; *The Venetian Bracelet, The Lost Pleiad, A History of the Lyre, and other poems*, 1828; *The Vow of the Peacock*, 1835; *A Birthday Tribute, addressed to the Princess Alexandrina Victoria*, [1837]; *Flowers of Loveliness . . . with Poetical Illustrations by L.E.L.*, 1838; and *The Easter Gift: A Religious Offering*, [1838]. *The Zenana, and Minor Poems of L.E.L. With a Memoir by Emma Roberts* appeared in 1839. *The Miscellaneous Poetical Works* had appeared in 1835. There were various editions of *The Works*, the first appearing at Philadelphia in 2 vols. in 1838. *The Poetical Works* appeared in 4 vols. in 1839 and in 2 vols. in 1850 (with a Memoir). W. B. Scott produced an edition in [1873].

L.E.L. also wrote four three-volume novels: *Romance and Reality*, 1831; *Francesco Carrara*, 1834; *Ethel Churchill: or, The Two Brides*, 1837; and *Lady Anne Granard; or Keeping Up Appearances*, 1842. She 'edited' *The Heir-Presumptive*, by Lady Stepney, 3 vols., 1835, and *Duty and Inclination* (no author given), 1838.

Of her numerous other writings mention may also be made of *Traits and Trials of Early Life*, 1836 (tales, with some poems). She contributed to Jerdan's *Literary Gazette*, the *New Monthly Magazine*, and other periodicals. She edited *Fisher's Drawing Room Scrap Book: with Poetical Illustrations by L.E.L.* from 1832 to 1838, and *The Book of Beauty* for 1833.

S. L. Blanchard's *Life and Literary Remains of L.E.L.*, 2 vols., 1841, contains a good deal of unpublished writing. In 1841 S. S[heppard] published *Characteristics of the Genius and Writings of L.E.L.* In 1928 D. E. Enfield produced his *L.E.L.: A Mystery of the Thirties*. See also A. K. Elwood, *Memoirs of the Literary Ladies of England*, vol. ii, 1843; *A Book of Memories*, 1871, by S. C. Hall; 'Memories of Authors: Miss Landon', by S. C. and A. M. Hall, *Atlantic Monthly*, xv, 1865; J. Le Fèvre-Deumier,

Célébrités anglaises, Paris, 1895; W. Maginn, *A Gallery of Illustrious Literary Characters*, ed. W. Bates [1873]; the *Autobiography* of W. Jerdan, 4 vols., 1852–3; *Thirty Years' Musical Recollections*, by H. F. Chorley, 2 vols., 1862 (ed. E. Newman, 1926); *My Life and Recollections*, by Grantley Berkeley, 4 vols., 1864–6; *The Literary Life and Correspondence of the Countess of Blessington*, by R. R. Madden, 3 vols., 1855; and the letters of Mary Russell Mitford. Information may also be found in the two books by M. Sadleir mentioned on p. 474 above.

Robert Eyres Landor, 1781–1869.

R. E. Landor published *An Essay on the Character and Doctrines of Socrates*, 1802; *The Count Arezzi, A Tragedy*, 1824; *The Impious Feast: a Poem in Ten Books*, 1828; *The Earl of Brecon: a Tragedy*, 1841 (also contains two other tragedies, *Faith's Fraud* and *The Ferryman*); and two novels, *The Fawn of Sertorius*, 1846, and *The Fountain of Arethusa*, 2 vols., 1848.

The only book about Landor is *Robert Eyres Landor: Selections from his Poetry and Prose with an Introduction Biographical & Critical* by E. Partridge, 1927. Information about R. E. Landor is mainly to be found in accounts of his brother. In 'The Authorship of "Guy's Porridge Pot" and "The Dun Cow"', *The Library*, 5th series, v, 1950, R. H. Super disputes two of Partridge's attributions.

Walter Savage Landor, 1775–1864.

Landor's poems and plays are outside our scope, as are his minor and privately printed works. The most nearly complete edition of his writings is *The Complete Works*, ed. T. Earle Welby and S. Wheeler, 16 vols., 1927–36, although the editing of the prose writings (vols. i–xii, ed. Welby) is far from satisfactory. Landor himself had published his *Works* in 2 vols. in 1846, vol. i containing the prose. This he supplemented with *Last Fruit off an Old Tree* in 1853. In 1876 John Forster produced an edition in 8 vols., vol. i being a condensation of his 1869 biography. In 1891 C. G. Crump published an edition of the *Imaginary Conversations* in 6 vols., with some of the poems and longer prose works in four further volumes, 1891–3. This remains the best edition of Landor's prose.

Imaginary Conversations of Literary Men and Statesmen had

appeared in 3 vols. in 1824–8, vols. i and ii being 'corrected and enlarged' in 1826. A Second Series was published in 2 vols. in 1829. *The Pentameron and Pentalogia* followed in 1837, being reprinted in *Last Fruit off an Old Tree. Imaginary Conversations of Greeks and Romans* appeared in 1853. *Last Fruit off an Old Tree*, 1853, includes the *Imaginary Conversation of King Carlo-Alberto and The Duchess Belgioioso*, 1848, and eighteen further Conversations. *Savonarola e il Priore di San Marco* was published at Florence in 1860.

The Citation and Examination of William Shakspeare was published in 1834, *Pericles and Aspasia* in 1836 (in 2 vols.). Other prose works were as follows: *Three Letters, Written in Spain, to D. Francisco Riguelme*, 1809; *Commentary on* [J. B. Trotter's] *Memoirs of Mr. Fox*, 1812 (suppressed by Landor, ed. S. Wheeler, 1907); *Letters Addressed to Lord Liverpool . . . on the Preliminaries of Peace: By Calvus*, 1814 (suppressed by Landor); *Letters of a Conservative*, 1836; *Popery: British and Foreign*, 1851 (reprinted in *The Last Fruit off an Old Tree*, 1853); *Letters of an American, mainly on Russia and Revolution*, 1854; and a *Letter from W. S. Landor to R. W. Emerson*, Bath [1856] (reprinted in *Literary Anecdotes of the Nineteenth Century*, ed. W. Robertson Nicoll and Thomas J. Wise, vol. ii, 1896).

Four new *Imaginary Conversations* were printed from manuscript by M. F. Ashley-Montagu in the *Nineteenth Century* in 1930–1. The same scholar published further 'waifs' in *RES* viii, 1932, and the *Nineteenth Century* for 1939.

S. Wheeler edited *Letters and Other Unpublished Writings* in 1897 (an unreliable book), and *Letters of Walter Savage Landor Private and Public* two years later. H. C. Minchin published *Walter Savage Landor: Last Days, Letters and Conversations* in 1934. Many of Landor's letters had been published during his lifetime in *The Literary Life and Correspondence of the Countess of Blessington*, by R. R. Madden, 3 vols. The second of the two editions of 1855 is the better, but A. Morrison's *The Blessington Papers*, 1895, is much more reliable. Further letters from Landor to Lady Blessington may be found in *Literary Anecdotes of the Nineteenth Century* (above), vol. i, 1895. The article in *ERPE* records the publication of other letters in various books and journals.

There are selections by Sir S. Colvin, 1882 (Golden Treasury series); E. de Sélincourt, 1915 (World's Classics: prose only); H. Ellis, 1933 (Everyman's Library); and E. K. Chambers,

1946. There is also a selected edition of the *Imaginary Conversations*, chosen by T. Earle Welby and edited by F. A. Cavenagh and A. C. Ward, 1934.

John Forster's *Walter Savage Landor: A Biography*, 2 vols., 1869, was for a long time the authoritative Life. His 1-vol. edition of 1876 (reprinted 1895) is abbreviated, though occasionally corrected. Sir S. Colvin's volume in the English Men of Letters series appeared in 1881. The standard modern studies are *Savage Landor*, by M. Elwin, New York, 1941; *Walter Savage Landor: A Biography*, by R. H. Super, New York, 1954 (English ed., 1957); and *Landor: A Replevin*, by M. Elwin, 1958. There is an essay by George Rostrevor Hamilton ('Writers and their Work', no. 126, 1960).

Early accounts of Landor, sometimes based on information provided by himself, may be found in S. C. Hall's *Book of Gems*, 3rd series, 1838; the same writer's *Book of Memories*, 1871; *A New Spirit of the Age*, by R. H. Horne, vol. i, 1844; and *Homes and Haunts of the Most Eminent British Poets*, by W. Howitt, 1847 (the 1857 ed. has corrections by Landor). 'The Life and Opinions of Walter Savage Landor', by E. Spender, *London Quarterly Review*, 1865, utilized information given by Robert Landor (see R. H. Super's account of Robert Landor's marginal comments in *MLN* lii–liii, 1937–8). There are numerous references to Landor in the writings of Crabb Robinson, De Quincey and Browning. Emerson wrote about him in *English Traits*, 1856, while Boythorn in *Bleak House* is partly based on him.

We may also refer to E. Quillinan's 'Imaginary Conversation, between Mr. Walter Savage Landor and the Editor', *Blackwood's Magazine*, 1843; 'Last Days of Walter Savage Landor', by Kate Field, *Atlantic Monthly*, 1866; Dickens's review of Forster in *All the Year Round*, 24 July 1869; 'Reminiscences of Walter Savage Landor', by E. Lynn Linton, *Fraser's Magazine*, July 1870; *Monographs, Personal and Social*, by R. M. Milnes (Lord Houghton), 1873; 'Landor's Imaginary Conversations', by Leslie Stephen, in *Hours in a Library*, 2nd series, 1876 (an admirable, and severe, critique); 'Reminiscences of Walter Savage Landor', by R. Bulwer Lytton (Lady Lytton), *Tinsley's Magazine*, June 1883; Swinburne's *Miscellanies*, 1886; *Red-Letter Days of my Life*, by Mrs. A. Crosse, 1892; 'Landor', by Francis Thompson, *The Academy*, 27 February 1897; and 'The Llanthony Maze' in E. Betham's *A House of Letters*, 1905.

The discussion of 'The Rhetoric of Landor' in *The Handling of Words*, by 'Vernon Lee', 1923, forms an intelligent companion-study to Leslie Stephen's essay. In his *History of English Prose Rhythm*, 1912, Saintsbury had been more laudatory. The following are mostly articles in learned journals: 'The Classicism of Walter Savage Landor', by Elizabeth Nitchie, *Classical Journal*, 1918; 'Walter Savage Landor as a Critic of Literature', by S. T. Williams, *PMLA* xxxviii, 1923; 'Walter Savage Landor und seine "Imaginary Conversations" ', by H. M. Flasdieck, *Englische Studien*, 1924; 'The Spanish Adventure of Walter Savage Landor', by C. P. Hawkes, *Cornhill Magazine*, lxxiv, 1933; 'Three Unknown Portraits of Landor', by M. F. Ashley-Montagu, *Colophon*, ii, 1937; 'Landor's Political Purpose', by G. J. Becker, *SP* xxxv, 1938; 'Landor's Treatment of his Source Materials in the "Imaginary Conversations of Greeks and Romans" ', by Doris E. Peterson, unpublished dissertation at the University of Minnesota, 1942; the same writer's 'Note on a Probable Source of Landor's "Metellus and Marius" ', *SP* xxxix, 1942; 'A New Landorian Manuscript', by R. F. Metzdorf, *PMLA* lvi, 1941; 'Landor's Critique of *The Cenci*', by K. G. Pfeiffer, *SP* xxxix, 1942 (see also R. H. Super in *SP* xl, 1943); 'Landor and Ireland', by M. J. Craig, *Dublin Magazine*, 1943; 'Some New Letters of Landor', by J. B. Hubbell, *Virginia Magazine of History and Biography*, li, 1943; 'Some Notes on Landor', by Sir E. K. Chambers, *RES* xx, 1944; 'Landor's Prose', by E. de Sélincourt, *Wordsworthian and Other Studies*, 1947; and 'Leigh Hunt, Landor and Dickens', by M. Fitzgerald, *TLS*, 26 October 1951 (see also a letter from G. Artom Treves, 28 December 1951). The numerous articles by R. H. Super are not listed here, as most of the information that they contain is included in his biography.

In *Southey und Landor*, 1934, E. Erich regarded Landor as a Fascist. The book contains some new information. Giuliana Artom Treves's *Anglo-fiorentini di cento anni fa*, 1953 (English translation, *The Golden Ring*, 1956), also embodies some fresh research. H. W. Rudman's *Italian Nationalism and English Letters*, 1940, throws light on Landor's political activities.

There are a number of bibliographical aids. The catalogue of books and manuscripts bequeathed to the Victoria and Albert Museum by John Forster (1888–93) is still of use. The 1919 *Bibliography* by S. Wheeler and Thomas James Wise remains indispensable. Wise's *A Landor Library*, 1928, supplements it. *The Publication of Landor's Works*, by R. H. Super (London: The Bibliographical Society, 1954 for 1946), is an admirable guide through the labyrinth, although (as the author points out) it does not include research after 1949. 'Landor's Unrecorded Contributions to Periodicals', *NQ*, 8 November 1952, by Super, is a useful supplement to the information in Wise and Wheeler. His article in *ERPE* surveys the field of Landor scholarship and provides more detailed bibliographical information.

JOHN LINGARD, 1771–1851.

His principal works include *The Antiquities of the Anglo-Saxon Church*, 2 vols., Newcastle-upon-Tyne, 1806 (entirely recast as *The History and Antiquities of the Anglo-Saxon Church* in 2 vols. in 1845); *A History of England from the First Invasion by the Romans to the Accession of Henry VIII*, 3 vols., 1819; 8 vols. (to 1688), 1819–30; 13 vols., 1837, 1839 (revised); 10 vols., 1854–5 (further revised); *A Vindication of Certain Passages in the Fourth and Fifth Volumes of the History of England*, 1826; and *A Collection of Tracts, on . . . the Civil and Religious Principles of Catholics*, 1826.

A full list of Lingard's works may be found in *The Life and Letters* by M. Haile and E. Bonney, [1911]. See also H. Phillpotts, *Letters to Charles Butler, with Remarks on . . . Dr. Lingard*, 1825; J. Fletcher, *John Lingard* (reprinted from *The Dublin Review*), Lingard Society, 1925; J. Lechmere, 'A Great Catholic Historian', *Ecclesiastical Review*, xciv, 1926; and C. Hollis in *Great Catholics*, ed. C. C. H. Williamson, 1938. The *DNB* mentions other writings relating to Lingard.

THOMAS HENRY LISTER, 1800–42.

Lister published three novels, *Granby*, 3 vols., 1826 (1838, with a preface); *Herbert Lacy*, 3 vols., 1828; and *Arlington*, 3 vols., 1832. He also edited *Anne Grey*, 3 vols., 1834, an (anonymous) novel by his sister Lady Harriet Cradock. The other novels attributed to him in *CBEL* are authoritatively rejected by Sadleir (*XIX Century Fiction*, 1951, i, 212).

Lister also published *Epicharis: An Historical Tragedy*, 1829; *The Life and Administration of Edward, First Earl of Clarendon . . .*, 3 vols., 1837–8 (a valuable study); and *An Answer to the Misrepresentations . . . in an Article on the Life of Clarendon* (by Croker in the *Quarterly Review*), 1839.

Information about Lister may be found in the *DNB* and in *Bulwer and his Wife: a Panorama, 1803–1836*, by M. Sadleir, 1933.

JOHN GIBSON LOCKHART, 1794–1854.

Lockhart published *Peter's Letters to his Kinsfolk* anonymously in 3 vols. in 1819 (nominally 'Second Edition'), and then four novels: *Valerius. A Roman Story*, 3 vols., 1821 (rev. ed. 1842); *Some Passages in the Life of Mr. Adam Blair*, 1822 (ed. D. Craig, 1963); *Reginald Dalton*, 3 vols., 1823; and *The History of Matthew Wald*, 1824.

His principal other publications were *Ancient Spanish Ballads: Historical and Romantic, Translated*, 1823 (revised ed., 1841); *Janus, or the Edinburgh Literary Almanack*, 1826 (ed. by Lockhart); *Life of Robert Burns*, 1828 (reprinted several times, and reissued in Everyman's Library in 1907); *The History of Napoleon Buonaparte*, 1829 (reprinted several times, including Everyman's Library, 1906); *The History of the late War . . . For Children*, 1832; *Memoirs of the Life of Sir Walter Scott, Bart.*, 7 vols., 1837–8; 2nd ed., 10 vols., 1839 (followed by other reprints and several abridgements); *The Ballantyne-Humbug Handled*, 1839; and *Theodore Hook, A Sketch*, 1852 (first published in the *Quarterly Review*, May 1843). Lockhart edited the 12-volume edition of Scott's *Poetical Works*, 1833–4. A. L. Strout edited and attributed to Lockhart *John Bull's Letter to Lord Byron*, 1821, in 1947 (Norman, Oklahoma). Lockhart also translated F. Schlegel's *Lectures on Ancient and Modern Literature*, 1815; provided an essay on Cervantes, and notes, for a reprint of Motteux's *Don Quixote*, 5 vols., 1822; played a part in some of the earlier papers in the *Noctes Ambrosianæ* (see John Wilson below); and contributed regularly to *Blackwood's* and other periodicals, as well as editing the *Quarterly Review* from 1825 to 1853. M. C. Hildyard edited *Lockhart's Literary Criticism* in 1931 and included a list of his contributions to periodicals.

A. Lang's *Life and Letters of John Gibson Lockhart*, 2 vols., 1897, has not yet been wholly superseded, although Lang was denied access to some important material. A great deal of information about Lockhart is to be found in Scott's letters and in books about Scott, in S. Smiles, *A Publisher and his Friends*, 2 vols., 1891, and in articles on the *Quarterly Review*. The pamphlet which occasioned *The Ballantyne-Humbug Handled* was entitled, *Refutation of the Mistatements* [sic] *and Calumnies contained in Mr. Lockhart's Life of Sir Walter Scott, Bart. respecting the Messrs. Ballantyne: By the Trustees and Son of the late Mr. James Ballantyne,* 1838. The same authors published their *Reply to Mr. Lockhart's Pamphlet* in 1839.

See also the *Quarterly Review*, October 1864 [by G. R. Gleig]; W. Maginn, *A Gallery of Illustrious Literary Characters*, ed. W. Bates, [1873]; *The Croker Papers*, L. J. Jennings, 3 vols., 1884; M. C. Hildyard, 'J. G. Lockhart', *Cornhill Magazine*, lxxii, 1932; F. Ewen, 'J. G. Lockhart, Propagandist of German Literature', *MLN* xlix, 1934; Elsie Swann, *Christopher North*, 1934; G. Macbeth, *John Gibson Lockhart: A Critical Study* (Urbana, 1935, with bibliography); and a long series of useful snippets of information and unpublished letters by A. L. Strout listed in *CBEL* (iii, 676 and v, 664).

See also W. M. Parker, 'Lockhart and Scott', *TLS*, 1 October 1938, and 'Lockhart's Obiter Dicta', *TLS*, 5 and 12 February 1944; C. L. Cline, 'D'Israeli and Lockhart', *MLN*, lvi, 1941; 'L.F.', 'Lockhart's Novels', *NQ*, 15 March and 5 April 1941; M. F. Brightfield, 'Lockhart's Quarterly Contributors', *PMLA* lix, 1944; C. O. Parsons, 'The Possible Origin of Lockhart's "Adam Blair" ', *NQ*, 17 November 1945; and Virginia Woolf, 'Lockhart's Criticism', in *The Moment and Other Essays*, 1947. M. Lochhead's *Lockhart*, 1954, contains a little new material.

There is a long-standing controversy on the authorship of 'The Lone Shieling', a lyric which appeared in *Blackwood's* in September 1829 with the description: 'Canadian Boat-song—(from the Gaelic).' This famous poem, which is neither a boat-song (in any usual sense) nor a translation from the Gaelic, has been attributed to Scott, 'Christopher North', Hogg, and others. In *The Lone Shieling*, Toronto, 1941, G. H. Needler argued at some length that it was written by D. M. Moir, inspired by Galt's work for the Canada Company. A full bibliography of the controversy cannot be included here, but Francis R. Hart argued well in the *TLS* for 27 February 1959 that the poem is the work of Lockhart. Mr. Hart is the author of an important unpublished study of Lockhart. He has written on the significance of the corrected proof sheets of Lockhart's *Scott* in *Studies in Bibliography*, vol. xiv (Charlottesville, Virginia).

HENRY LUTTRELL, ?1765–1851.

Henry Luttrell, who was a natural son of Lord Carhampton,

published *Lines written at Ampthill-Park, in the Autumn of 1818* in
1819. *Advice to Julia: A Letter in Rhyme*, a witty poem admired by
Byron, appeared in 1820. *Letters to Julia, in Rhyme*, 3rd ed., 1822,
includes *Lines written at Ampthill-Park* as well as a revised form of
the main poem. *Crockford-House, a Rhapsody: In Two Cantos* [with]
A Rhymer in Rome, appeared in 1827.

A. Dobson's 'A Forgotten Poet of Society' (*St. James's Magazine*, xxxiii, January 1878) is reprinted as 'Luttrell's Letters to
Julia', in *A Paladin of Philanthropy*, 1899. See also A. Crosse, 'An
Old Society Wit', *Temple Bar*, civ, 1895. Luttrell was a great
wit and diner-out. There are numerous references to him in
The Greville Memoirs (see p. 490 above), as well as in the letters
and journals of Samuel Rogers (and see P. W. Clayden, *Rogers
and his Contemporaries*, 2 vols., 1889), Moore, Sydney Smith, and
other members of the Holland House circle.

WILLIAM MAGINN, 1793–1842.

Maginn's *Miscellaneous Writings* were edited by R. Shelton
Mackenzie, 5 vols., New York, 1855–7. A 2-vol. collection,
Miscellanies: Prose and Verse, ed. R. W. Montagu [Johnson],
with a Memoir, appeared in 1885; *Ten Tales*, with a preface
signed 'W. B.', appeared in 1933.

Throughout his life Maginn contributed to numerous periodicals, notably *Blackwood's* (he was one of the writers of the *Noctes
Ambrosianæ*: see John Wilson below) and *Fraser's*. Apart from
uncertain attributions (such as *The Red Barn: A Tale, Founded
on Fact*, 1828), the following includes all his writings published
in book form, mostly after his death: *Whitehall, or The Days of
George IV*, [1827]; *Magazine Miscellanies*, [1840]; *John Manesty,
the Liverpool Merchant*, 2 vols., 1844; *Maxims of Sir Morgan
O'Doherty, Bart.*, 1849; *Homeric Ballads: with Translations and
Notes*, 1850; *Shakespeare Papers: Pictures Grave and Gay*, 1859
(1860, adds an essay on *Hamlet*); and *A Gallery of Illustrious
Literary Characters (1830–1838). Drawn by . . . Daniel Maclise . . .
with Notices chiefly by . . . William Maginn*, ed. by W. Bates, [1873].
A Story without a Tale, first published in *Blackwood's Magazine*,
April 1834, and reprinted in *Tales from Blackwood*, ii, was
separately issued with a preface by G. Saintsbury in 1928 as
no. 4 of the 'Baskerville Series'. Maginn contributed four tales
to vol. i of T. Crofton Croker's *Fairy Legends and Traditions of the*

South of Ireland (3 vols., 1825–8). One or two other short stories
and possible attributions are mentioned in the *CBEL*.

The list of Maginn's writings in Appendix IV of Michael
Sadleir's *Bulwer and his Wife: A Panorama, 1803–1836*, 1933,
should be checked against that in vol. i of the same writer's
XIX Century Fiction. The fullest recent account of Maginn is that
by Miriam M. H. Thrall in *Rebellious Fraser's*, New York, 1934.
See also 'The Doctor', in *Fraser's Magazine*, January 1831 (by
Lockhart: reprinted in *A Gallery of Illustrious Literary Characters*,
ed. W. Bates, [1873]); E. V. Kenealy and D. M. Moir, 'William
Maginn, LL.D.', *Dublin University Magazine*, xxiii, 1844; S. C.
Hall, *A Book of Memories*, 1871; M. Elwin, *Victorian Wallflowers*,
1934; *TLS*, 22 August 1942 ('Tragedy of a Writer: Maginn');
and R. M. Wardle, 'Outwitting Hazlitt', *MLN* lvii, 1942.

CHARLES ROBERT MATURIN, 1782–1824.

Maturin published the following works of prose fiction: *Fatal
Revenge, or the Family of Montorio*, 3 vols., 1807; *The Wild Irish
Boy*, 3 vols., 1808; *The Milesian Chief*, 4 vols., 1812; *Women, or
Pour et Contre*, 3 vols., 1818; *Melmoth the Wanderer*, 4 vols., 1820;
and *The Albigenses*, 4 vols., 1824.

Maturin also published three tragedies, *Bertram, or The Castle
of St Aldobrand*, 1816; *Manuel*, 1817; and *Fredolfo*, 1819; and
Sermons, 1819. 'Extracts from some Unpublished Scenes of
Manuel' appeared in the *New Monthly Magazine*, xi, 1819, and
Six Sermons of the Errors of the Roman Catholic Church at Dublin
in 1824.

Tales of Mystery, ed. G. Saintsbury, 1891, contains selections
from Maturin, as well as from Mrs. Radcliffe and M. G. Lewis.

Early essays may be found in the *Edinburgh Review*, July 1821
(a review of Melmoth, partly reprinted in *Famous Reviews*, ed.
R. B. Johnson, 1914); 'The Writings of Maturin', *London Magazine*, iii, 1821; 'The Conversations of Maturin', *New Monthly
Magazine*, xix, 1827. See also the 3-vol. reprint of *Melmoth*
published in 1892, which contains a Memoir, a critical essay,
and a bibliography; O. Elton, *A Survey of English Literature
1780–1830*, vol. i, 1912; 'Maturin and the Novel of Terror',
TLS, 26 August 1920; Edith Birkhead, *The Tale of Terror*, 1921;
N. Idman, *Charles Robert Maturin, his Life and Works*, Helsingfors, 1923; W. Scholten, *Charles Robert Maturin, the Terror-
Novelist*, Amsterdam, 1933; and E. A. Baker, *The History of the*

English Novel, v, 1934. In his early years Balzac was much influenced by *Melmoth*, which was translated into French in 1821. In 1835 he published *Melmoth réconcilié*, one of the 'Études philosophiques' of his *Comédie humaine*. See G. T. Clapton, 'Balzac, Baudelaire and Maturin', *French Quarterly*, June and September 1930.

THOMAS MEDWIN, 1788–1869.

An early poem, *The Pindarries* (afterwards affixed to *The Angler in Wales*), seems to have been published *c.* 1815. *Sketches in Hindoostan with Other Poems* appeared in 1821. *Ahasuerus the Wanderer*, a dramatic legend in six parts, was published in London in 1823. His *Journal of the Conversations of Lord Byron . . . at Pisa* appeared in 1824. In 1832 he published a translation of the *Agamemnon* of Aeschylus. *The Shelley Papers*, containing the *Memoir of Percy Bysshe Shelley: By T. Medwin, Esq.*, were published in 1833. *The Angler in Wales, or Days and Nights of Sportsmen* came out in 2 vols. in 1834 (vol. ii contains a good deal relating to Byron). *Lady Singleton, or the World as It Is*, a novel in 3 vols., was published in 1842. Medwin's *Life of Shelley* was published in 2 vols. in 1847 (ed. H. B. Forman, 1913). Four of his contributions to *Bentley's Miscellany*—'Mascalbruni', 'The Contrabandista', 'Pasquale', and 'The Quarantine'—are reprinted in *Tales from Bentley*, 1859–60.

The reliability of the *Conversations of Lord Byron* is discussed in studies of Byron: for early treatments of the matter see *Blackwood's Magazine*, November 1824; the *Gentleman's Magazine*, November 1824; John Murray's privately printed *Notes on Capt. Medwin's Conversations of Lord Byron*, 1824 (reprinted in *The Works of Lord Byron*, Murray, 1829); and *Capt. Medwin Vindicated from the Calumnies of the Reviewers by Vindex*, 1825. Medwin's account of Shelley is examined by N. I. White and other writers on Shelley. There is a biographical study, *Captain Medwin: Friend of Byron and Shelley*, by E. J. Lovell, Austin, Texas, 1962.

JOHN HERMAN MERIVALE, 1779–1844.

Poems Original and Translated, now first Collected, appeared in 2 vols. in 1828–38, and 'corrected' in 1844. There may have been a separate edition of *The Minstrel, Book III: In Continuation of Dr. Beattie's Poem*, which is included in *Poems Original and*

Translated. Apart from contributions to the *Quarterly Review*, the *New Monthly Magazine* and the *Gentleman's Magazine*, and some writings on legal subjects, Merivale also published *Translations chiefly from the Greek Anthology, with Tales and Miscellaneous Poems*, 1806 (with R. Bland); *Collections from the Greek Anthology: By R. Bland and Others*, 1813; *Orlando in Roncesvalles, a Poem*, 1814 (based on the *Morgante Maggiore* of Pulci); *The Two first Cantos of Richardetto, from the Original of N. Fortiguerra*, 1820; and *The Minor Poems of Schiller, translated*, 1844 (partly reprinted from the *New Monthly Magazine*). In 1911 E. H. A. Koch edited *Leaves from the Diary of a Literary Amateur* (published at Hampstead). Merivale was a friend of Byron's, and his name crops up in memoirs of the time. See also *Blackwood's Magazine*, xxxiii–iv; the *Quarterly Review*, xlix, 1833 (H. N. Coleridge on his Greek translations); C. Merivale's article in *Transactions of the Devonshire Association*, 1884; and the article in the *DNB*. Merivale's translations are mentioned in the books on Italian influence by R. Marshall and C. P. Brand mentioned above on p. 478.

JAMES MILL, 1773–1836.

Mill's main publications were *The History of British India*, 3 vols., 1817; *Elements of Political Economy*, 1821; *Essays on Government, Jurisprudence, Liberty of the Press* [etc.] . . . *Reprinted from the Supplement to the Encyclopaedia Britannica* (privately printed, [1825]: other articles, those on 'Caste', 'Economists', and 'Beggars', were not reprinted: the *Essay on Government* was edited by E. Barker, 1937); *Analysis of the Phenomena of the Human Mind*, 2 vols., 1829 (ed. J. S. Mill, 2 vols., 1869); *A Fragment on Mackintosh*, 1835; and *The Principles of Toleration* (reprinted from the *Westminster Review*, July, 1829), 1837.

A. Bain published *James Mill: A Biography* in 1882, G. S. Bower's *Hartley and James Mill* having appeared the previous year. A great deal of information about Mill is to be found in the books on the Utilitarians listed above on pp. 488–9. His son's *Autobiography* is, of course, a primary source. See also *Benthamite Reviewing*, by G. L. Nesbitt, New York, 1934; *The Life of John Stuart Mill*, by M. St. J. Packe, 1954; *The English Utilitarians and India*, by E. Stokes, 1959; *Works and Correspondence of David Ricardo*, ed. P. Sraffa, vols. vi–ix, 1952 (Mill's letters to Ricardo); *Selections from the Correspondence of Macvey*

Napier, privately printed, 1877; D. Forbes, 'James Mill and India', *Cambridge Journal*, v, 1951; and W. J. Burston, 'James Mill on the Aims of Education', *Cambridge Journal*, vi, 1952.

HENRY HART MILMAN, 1791–1868.

In verse Milman published *Fazio. A Tragedy*, 1815 (1821, with *The Belvidere Apollo* [a Prize Poem, first published 1812], &c.); *Samor, Lord of the Bright City: An Heroic Poem*, 1818; *The Fall of Jerusalem: A Dramatic Poem*, 1820; *The Martyr of Antioch: A Dramatic Poem*, 1822; *Belshazzar: A Dramatic Poem*, 1822; and *Anne Boleyn: A Dramatic Poem*, 1826. The *Poetical Works of Milman, Bowles, Wilson, and Barry Cornwall* appeared in Paris in 1829. Milman's *Poetical Works* were collected in 3 vols. in 1839. Milman also translated *Nala and Damayanti and Other Poems . . . from the Sanscrit into English Verse*, 1835, and was responsible for the translation of the *Bacchae* in *The Agamemnon of Æschylus and the Bacchanals of Euripides, &c.*, translated, 1865 (1888, *Bacchae* only). He contributed a number of hymns to Reginald Heber's collection.

His principal writings in prose were *The History of the Jews*, 3 vols., 1829–30 (revised in later editions; 'Everyman's Library', 2 vols., 1909); *The History of Christianity, to the Abolition of Paganism in the Roman Empire*, 3 vols., 1840 (3 vols., 1863, revised); and the *History of Latin Christianity; including that of the Popes to Nicolas V*, 6 vols., 1854–5.

He also provided notes for Gibbon's *Decline and Fall*, 12 vols., 1838–9, and edited *The Life of Edward Gibbon, with Selections from his Correspondence*, 1839, and *The Works of Q. Horatius Flaccus illustrated . . . from the Remains of Ancient Art*, 1849 (with a Life by Milman).

His obituary of Macaulay, first published in *Proceedings of the Royal Society*, xi, 1862, appeared as a pamphlet in 1862 and was reprinted in vol. viii of Macaulay's *History* the same year. He contributed to the *Quarterly Review*, from which *Savonarola, Erasmus, and other Essays* were reprinted in 1870. His minor writings include *Annals of S. Paul's Cathedral*, 1868, sermons, and two prize essays.

There is a biography by A. Milman, *Henry Hart Milman: A Biographical Sketch*, 1900. C. Venatier's *Milman's Fall of Jerusalem*, Breslau, 1893, is a dissertation. See also A. P. Stanley, 'The Late Dean of St. Paul's', *Macmillan's Magazine*, January

1869; and C. H. E. Smyth, *Dean Milman*, 1949. In the *TLS*, 29 June 1962, F. May claims for Milman some translations from Petrarch in Foscolo's *Essays on Petrarch*.

MARY RUSSELL MITFORD, 1787–1855.

In verse she published *Poems*, 1810 (with additions, 1811); *Christina: The Maid of the South Seas. A Poem*, 1811; *Blanche of Castile*, 1812; *Watlington Hill*, 1812; *Narrative Poems on the Female Character*, vol. i, 1813 (the only volume); *Julian: A Tragedy*, 1823; *Foscari: A Tragedy*, 1826 (together as *Foscari and Julian*, 1827); *Dramatic Scenes, Sonnets, and Other Poems*, 1827; *Rienzi: A Tragedy*, 1828; *Mary, Queen of Scots: A Scene in English Verse*, 1831; *Charles the First: An Historical Tragedy*, 1834; and *Sadak and Kalasrade, or the Waters of Oblivion: A Romantic Opera*, 1835. Her *Dramatic Works* appeared in 2 vols. in 1854, with an interesting autobiographical introduction.

Our Village: Sketches of Rural Character and Scenery appeared in 5 vols. between 1824 and 1832. Some of the Sketches had been turned down by Campbell for the *New Monthly Magazine*, but many of them had been published in *The Lady's Magazine* and other 'respectable publications'. According to information supplied by Mr. S. H. Horrocks (of Reading Public Libraries) the most complete edition ever published after the original editions was the Bohn edition, which first appeared in 1848 and which 'lacks only two items from the original 5 vols.'. Most later 'editions' of *Our Village* consist in fact of selections. *Belford Regis: or Sketches of a Country Town* appeared in 3 vols. in 1835, and *Country Stories* in 1837. A collection, *Atherton and Other Tales*, appeared in 3 vols. in 1854. Miss Mitford also contributed a number of stories to *The Edinburgh Tales*, ed. C. I. Johnstone, 3 vols., 1845–6; to *Finden's Tableaux*, 1838, 1839, and 1841; and to numerous Annuals.

Miss Mitford edited *Stories of American Life by American Writers*, 3 vols., 1830; *Lights and Shadows of American Life*, 3 vols., 1832; and two series of *American Stories for Little Boys and Girls*, 1831–2.

Recollections of a Literary Life; or Books, Places, and People appeared in 3 vols. in 1852. Letters have been published in *The Life of Mary Russell Mitford . . . in a Selection from her Letters*, ed. A. G. L'Estrange, 3 vols., 1870 ('Second and Revised Edition'); *Letters of Mary Russell Mitford*, 2nd series, ed. H. Chorley, 2 vols., 1872; *The Friendships of Mary Russell Mitford in Letters from her*

Literary Correspondents, ed. A. G. L'Estrange, 2 vols., 1882; *Mary Russell Mitford: Correspondence with Charles Boner & John Ruskin*, ed. Elizabeth Lee, 1914; and R. M. Kettle, *Memoirs and Letters with Letters of Mary Russell Mitford to him during Ten Years*, 2 vols., 1871. In 1925 R. B. Johnson published a selection from her letters.

There are several books about her: W. J. Roberts, *Mary Russell Mitford: The Tragedy of a Blue Stocking*, 1913; Constance Hill, *Mary Russell Mitford and her Surroundings*, 1920; Marjorie Astin, *Mary Russell Mitford: her Circle and her Books*, 1930; and Vera Watson, *Mary Russell Mitford*, [1949]. There are early impressions by M. O. Oliphant, *Blackwood's Magazine*, June 1854 and March 1870 ('Miss Austen and Miss Mitford'); W. Maginn, *A Gallery of Illustrious Literary Characters*, ed. W. Bates, [1873]; and H. Martineau, *Biographical Sketches, 1852–1875*, 1877. Further information may be found in *The Literary Life of the Rev. William Harness*, by A. G. L'Estrange, 1871; *Memorials of Mrs. Hemans*, by H. F. Chorley, 2 vols., 1836; *Thirty Years' Musical Recollections*, 2 vols., 1862, by the same author; *Some Literary Recollections*, by J. Payn, 1884; and *Elizabeth Barrett to Miss Mitford*, ed. Betty Miller, 1954. More recent notes and essays include M. Kent, 'Mary Mitford's Letters', *Cornhill Magazine*, clix, 1936; 'R. H. Horne on Miss Mitford after Forty Years', *NQ*, 9 March 1946; V. G. Watson, *NQ*, 11 June 1949; and M. H. Dodds, 'Mary Russell Mitford and Jane Austen', *NQ*, 29 April 1950. See also J. Carter and G. Pollard, *An Enquiry into the Nature of Certain XIX Century Pamphlets*, 1934.

Reading Public Libraries published a brief catalogue of their centennial exhibition, *Mary Russell Mitford: 1787–1855*, compiled by Miss D. J. Phillips. This contains information about manuscripts and a list of the individual Tales. There is a useful article by W. A. Coles in *Studies in Bibliography, Published by the University of Virginia*, 1959: 'Magazine and other Contributions by Mary Russell Mitford and T. N. Talfourd.'

DAVID MACBETH MOIR ('Δ'), 1798–1851.

In 1816 Moir published *The Bombardment of Algiers, and Other Poems*, and in 1824 *The Legend of Geneviève: With other Tales and Poems*, (by 'Delta'). *The Life of Mansie Wauch*, first published in *Blackwood's*, appeared as a book in 1828 (the 1839 edition was revised, and illustrated by Cruikshank). *Domestic Verses: By Δ*, came out in 1843. *Sketches of the Poetical Literature of the Past Half-*

Century, in Six Lectures, were published in 1851. Moir's *Poetical Works* were edited with a Memoir by T. Aird in 2 vols. in 1852.

Moir also wrote the final chapters of Galt's *The Last of the Lairds*, 1826; contributed an interesting Memoir of Galt to the [1841] edition of *The Annals of the Parish and The Ayrshire Legatees*, ('Blackwood's Standard Novels'); wrote 'School Recollections' in *Friendship's Offering*, 1829, and 'The Bridal of Borthwick', in *The Club Book*, ed. Andrew Picken, 3 vols., 1831; and contributed the account of the Roman Antiquities of Inveresk in the *Statistical Account of Scotland*, 1845 (the account was published separately in 1860).

Moir began contributing to periodicals when he was about fourteen, and soon he was writing in the *Scots Magazine*. Throughout his life he wrote a great deal in periodicals, including Constable's *Edinburgh Magazine, Fraser's*, and the *Edinburgh Literary Gazette*. A list of nearly 400 of his contributions to *Blackwood's* is printed on pp. 128–30 of the *General Index* to the first fifty volumes, 1855. In 1826 he contributed to *Janus, or the Edinburgh Literary Almanack*, ed. Lockhart. He also wrote several medical books and a number of memoirs, including that of Mrs. Hemans in the 1848 edition of her poems. The view that he wrote 'The Canadian Boat Song', advanced by E. MacCurdy in *A Literary Enigma*, Stirling, 1935, was supported by G. H. Needler but rejected by F. R. Hart (see Lockhart above).

On Moir see W. Maginn's *Gallery of Illustrious Literary Characters*, ed. W. Bates, [1873]; *Blackwood's Magazine*, lxx, 1851; *Eclectic Review*, xcvi, 1852; G. Gilfillan, *A Gallery of Literary Portraits*, vol. ii, 1850; Sir G. Douglas, *The Blackwood Group* [1897]; and E. H. A. Robson, *A Preparation for a Study of Metropolitan Scots of the . . . Nineteenth Century as exemplified in 'Mansie Wauch'*, 1937.

Information about Moir may be found in the *DNB* and in books about Galt, De Quincey, and the *Blackwood's* group.

ROBERT MONTGOMERY, 1807–55.

Montgomery's main publications in verse include *The Stage-Coach*, 1827; *The Age Reviewed: A Satire*, 1827 (1828, rev. ed.); *The Omnipresence of the Deity*, 1828 (28 editions by 1855); *The Puffiad: A Satire*, 1828; *A Universal Prayer; Death; A Vision of Heaven; and a Vision of Hell*, 1828; *Satan*, 1830; *Oxford*, 1831 (4th ed., Oxford, 1835, adds recollections of Shelley); *The Messiah*,

1832; *Woman, the Angel of Life*, 1833; *Ellesmere Lake: Poems*, 1836; *Sacred Meditations in Verse*, 1842; *Luther*, 1842; *Scarborough: A Poetic Glance*, 1846; *The Christian Life: A Manual of Sacred Verse*, 1849; *The Hero's Funeral*, 1852; and *The Sanctuary: A Companion in Verse for the Prayer Book*, 1855. Montgomery's sermons and theological writings are not listed here.

The *Poetical Works* appeared in 6 vols. in 1839–40, and again in 1841–3. In 1853 there was an edition by J. Twycross. *Selections* were published in 1836, with an introduction. *The Poetical Works*, 3 vols., Glasgow, 1839, is a full selection. See also *Religion and Poetry*, ed. S. J. H., 1847; *Lyra Christiana*, 1851 (Montgomery's own selection); and *Christian Poetry*, ed. E. Farr, [1856].

Macaulay attacked *The Omnipresence of the Deity* in the *Edinburgh Review*, li, 1830, his essay being reprinted in his *Critical and Historical Essays*, 1843, &c. See also E. Clarkson, *Robert Montgomery and his Reviewers*, 1830; the same writer's *The Reviewers Reviewed*, [? 1830]; R. H. Horne, *A New Spirit of the Age*, vol. ii, 1844; W. Maginn, *A Gallery of Illustrious Literary Characters*, ed. W. Bates, [1873]; and *The London Quarterly and Holborn Review*, ed. J. Alan Kay, April 1954. There is a fuller list of Montgomery's writings in the *Gentleman's Magazine*, 1856, i, p. 312. Further information may be found in the *DNB*. An accurate bibliography of Montgomery would be very difficult to compile; for, as Lowndes observes, 'this author was extremely anxious to make his books appear very popular, and therefore constantly changed his title pages, and even cancelled or sold off almost as waste one edition for the sake of printing another'.

THOMAS MOORE, 1779–1852.

Moore's main publications in book form were *Odes of Anacreon, translated into English Verse*, 1800; *The Poetical Works of the late Thomas Little, Esq.*, 1801; *Oh Lady Fair: A Ballad*, 1802; *A Candid Appeal to Public Confidence*, 1803; *Sequel to Oh Lady Fair!*, 1804; *Songs and Glees*, 1804; *A Canadian Boat-Song, arranged for three Voices*, 1805; *Epistles, Odes, and other Poems*, 1806; *A Selection of Irish Melodies*, 10 parts and supplement [1808–34]; *Irish Melodies*, 1821 (first authorized edition of the words alone); *Corruption and Intolerance: Two Poems*, 1808; *The Sceptic: a Philosophical Satire*, 1809; *A Letter to the Roman Catholics of Dublin*, Dublin, 1810; *M. P.; or, The Blue Stocking: a Comic Opera*, 1811 (libretto and music by Moore); *A Melologue upon National*

Music, 1811 (reprinted with *Irish Melodies*); *Parody of a Celebrated Letter*, 1812 (privately printed); *Intercepted Letters; or, The Two-penny Postbag*, 1813; *Sacred Songs*, 2 parts, 1816–24; *Lines on the Death of* — [Sheridan], 1816; *Lalla Rookh; an Oriental Romance*, 1817; *National Airs*, 6 parts, 1818–27; *The Fudge Family in Paris*, 1818; *Melodies, Songs, and Sacred Songs*, 1818; *The World at Westminster*, 2 vols., 1818; *Tom Crib's Memorial to Congress*, 1819; *The Loves of the Angels*, 1823; *Fables for the Holy Alliance; Rhymes on the Road, &c., &c.*, 1823; *Memoirs of Captain Rock, the celebrated Irish Chieftain*, 1824; *Memoirs of . . . Sheridan*, 1825 (5th ed., 1827, with new preface); *Evenings in Greece*, 2 parts, 1826–32; *The Epicurean: A Tale*, 1827; *A Set of Glees*, 1827; *Odes upon Cash, Corn, Catholics, and other Matters*, 1828; *Legendary Ballads*, 1828; *Letters and Journals of Lord Byron; with Notices of his Life*, 2 vols., 1830; *The Life and Death of Lord Edward FitzGerald*, 2 vols., 1831; *The Summer Fête*, 1831; *Travels of an Irish Gentle-man in Search of a Religion*, 2 vols., 1833; *Vocal Miscellany*, 2 nos., 1834–5; *The Fudges in England*, 1835; *History: Ireland* (in D. Lardner's *The Cabinet Cyclopaedia*, 4 vols., 1835–46); *Alciphron: a Poem*, 1839. In 1878 R. H. Shepherd edited *Prose and Verse . . . with Suppressed Passages from the Memoirs of Lord Byron*.

Throughout his life Moore contributed a great deal to numerous periodicals, including *The Times* and the *Edinburgh Review*.

The Poetical Works of Thomas Moore, Collected by Himself appeared in 10 vols. in 1840–1, superseding earlier unauthorized editions. Shepherd's *Prose and Verse*, mentioned above, contains some other poems. In 1910 A. D. Godley edited the Oxford edition, *The Poetical Works*. *Poetry of Thomas Moore*, ed. C. L. Falkiner, 1903, is a selection in the Golden Treasury series, with an interesting preface. In 1929 S. O'Fáolain edited another selection, *Lyrics and Satires from Tom Moore*, Dublin.

Moore's *Memoirs, Journal, and Correspondence* were edited by Lord John Russell in 8 vols. in 1853–6. *Tom Moore's Diary*, ed. J. B. Priestley, 1925, consists of selections from these volumes. Other letters by Moore are to be found in numerous books, notably in *Notes from the Letters of Thomas Moore to His Music Publisher, James Power*, ed. T. C. Croker, New York [? 1854], an inaccurate volume. A series of manuscript letters from Moore to Mary Shelley was sold at Sotheby's in 1962. Professor W. S. Dowden of the Rice Institute is now completing an edition of

Moore's letters. Much the best biography is H. M. Jones's *The Harp that Once* —, New York, 1937. Other general books of varying merit are G. Vallat's *Étude sur la vie et les œuvres de Thomas Moore*, 1886; Stephen Gwynn's *Thomas Moore*, 1905 (English Men of Letters); L. A. G. Strong's *The Minstrel Boy*, 1937; A. Stockmann, *Thomas Moore, der irische Freiheitssänger*, 1910; and W. F. Trench, *Tom Moore*, 1934 (a sensible brief study). A great deal of information is to be found in books by his contemporaries, such as *Conversations of Lord Byron with the Countess of Blessington*, 1834; Leigh Hunt's *Lord Byron and Some of his Contemporaries* (1828) and *Autobiography* (1850); N. P. Willis's *Pencillings by the Way*, 3 vols., 1835; W. Gardiner's *Music and Friends*, 1838–53; Lockhart's *Memoirs of Scott*, 1837–8; and Crabb Robinson's journals.

The *Irish Melodies* have often been discussed, notably in C. V. Stanford's *The Irish Melodies of Thomas Moore: The Original Airs Restored and Arranged for the Voice*, 1895; *The Minstrelsy of Ireland*, by A. Moffat, 1897; and D. J. O'Sullivan's 'The Bunting Collection of Irish Folk Music and Songs', ed. for the *Journal of the Irish Folk Song Society*, 1926–32.

A good deal has been written on Moore's influence abroad. See particularly A. B. Thomas, *Moore en France . . . 1819–1830*, 1911; F. Baldensperger, 'Thomas Moore et Alfred de Vigny', *MLR*, i, 1906; K. Campbell, *The Poems of Edgar Allan Poe*, 1917, and 'Poe's Reading', *University of Texas Studies in English*, 1925; H. H. Jordan, 'Poe's Debt to Thomas Moore', *PMLA* lxiii, 1948; and T. O. Mabbott, 'Poe's "The Sleeper" Again', *American Literature*, 1949.

Hazlitt often wrote about Moore, notably in *The Spirit of the Age*, 1825. Peacock's attack on *The Epicurean* was first published in the *Westminster Review*, viii, 1827, and is now in vol. ix (1926) of his *Works*, ed. H. F. B. Brett-Smith and C. E. Jones. Leigh Hunt wrote well on *M. P.; or, The Blue Stocking* (see his *Dramatic Criticism*, ed. L. H. and C. W. Houtchens, 1949).

Also worth noting are W. C. Brown, 'Thomas Moore and English Interest in the East', *SP* xxxiv, 1937; H. O. Brogan, 'Thomas Moore, Irish Satirist and Keeper of the English Conscience', *PQ* xxiv, 1945; W. F. P. Stockley, 'Moore's Satirical Verse', *Queen's Quarterly*, 1905, and his study in *Essays in Irish Biography*, Cork, 1933; J. Hennig, 'Thomas Moore and the Holy Alliance', *Irish Monthly*, 1946. The fullest discussion of his

Letters and Journals of Lord Byron is in Doris Langley Moore's *The Late Lord Byron*, 1961. H. H. Jordan's 'Byron and Moore', *MLQ* ix, 1948, is a useful study of Moore's influence on Byron. R. Birley discusses *Lalla Rookh* in *Sunk Without Trace*, 1962.

Apart from *CBEL*, the following present bibliographical assistance: M. J. MacManus, *A Bibliographical Hand-List of the First Editions of Thomas Moore*, Dublin, 1934; P. H. Muir, 'Thomas Moore's Irish Melodies, 1808–1834', *Colophon*, no. 15, 1933; and H. H. Jordan in *ERPE* (a useful account of scholarly work on Moore). In 'Thomas Moore and the Review of *Christabel*', *MP*, liii, 1956, Jordan argues against Moore's authorship, maintained by Elisabeth Schneider in *MLN* lxi, 1946. H. G. Wright has made another attribution in 'Thomas Moore as the Author of *Spirit of Boccaccio's Decameron*', *RES* xxiii, 1947.

MORGAN, LADY (SYDNEY OWENSON), 1776–1859.

Lady Morgan published the following works of prose fiction: *St. Clair, or the Heiress of Desmond*, 1803 (3rd edition, much revised, 2 vols., 1812); *The Novice of St. Dominick*, 4 vols., 1805; *The Wild Irish Girl: a National Tale*, 3 vols., 1806; *Woman, or Ida of Athens*, 4 vols., 1809; *The Missionary: an Indian Tale*, 3 vols., 1811; *O'Donnel: a National Tale*, 3 vols., 1814; *Florence Macarthy: an Irish Tale*, 4 vols., 1818; *The O'Briens and the O'Flahertys: a National Tale*, 4 vols., 1827; *The Princess, or The Beguine*, 3 vols., 1835; *Woman and her Master*, 2 vols., 1840.

Her other writings include *Poems*, Dublin, 1801; *The Lay of an Irish Harp, or Metrical Fragments*, 1807; *Patriotic Sketches of Ireland*, 2 vols., 1807; *France*, 1817; *France in 1829–30*, 2 vols., 1830; *Italy*, 2 vols., 1821 (slightly different edition, in 3 vols., the same year); *The Mohawks: a Satirical Poem* (with Sir Charles Morgan) 1822; *The Life and Times of Salvator Rosa*, 2 vols., 1824; *Absenteeism*, 1825; *The Book of the Boudoir*, 2 vols., 1829; *The Book without a Name* (with Sir Charles Morgan), 2 vols., 1841; and *An Odd Volume, extracted from an Autobiography*, 1859. Lady Morgan's *Memoirs: Autobiography, Diaries and Correspondence* [ed. by W. Hepworth Dixon] appeared in 2 vols. in 1862.

There is a modern study by L. Stevenson, *The Wild Irish Girl*, 1936. See also the characteristic attacks by Croker in the *Quarterly Review*, xvii (1817) and xxv (1821); *The Friends, Foes, and Adventures of Lady Morgan*, by W. J. Fitzpatrick, Dublin, 1859; 'Lady Morgan', by G. E. Jewsbury, *Cornhill Magazine*, vii,

1863; *English Women of Letters*, by J. Kavanagh, vol. ii, 1863; *A Gallery of Illustrious Literary Characters*, by W. Maginn, ed. W. Bates, [1873]; *Little Memoirs of the Nineteenth Century*, by 'George Paston', 1902; and *These were Muses*, by Mona Wilson, 1924.

JAMES JUSTINIAN MORIER, 1780–1849.

Morier wrote the following works of prose fiction: *The Adventures of Hajji Baba of Ispahan*, 3 vols., 1824 (2nd ed., 3 vols., 1824, with long preface: rev. eds. 1835 and 1863: numerous other editions and reprints including editions in 'Everyman's Library', 1914, and 'World's Classics', 1923); *The Adventures of Hajji Baba of Ispahan in England*, 2 vols., 1828 (rev. ed. 1835; 'World's Classics' ed. 1925); *Zohrab the Hostage*, 3 vols., 1832 (revised with notes, 1833); *Ayesha: The Maid of Kars*, 3 vols., 1834; *Abel Allnutt: a Novel*, 3 vols., 1837; *An Oriental Tale*, Brighton, 1839 (privately printed); *The Mirza*, 3 vols., 1841; *Misselmah: A Persian Tale*, Brighton, 1847; *Martin Toutrond: A Frenchman in London in 1831*, 1849 (two issues, one anonymous).

Morier also wrote a *Journey through Persia, Armenia and Asia Minor to Constantinople, 1808–9 . . .*, 1812; *Second Journey through Persia, Armenia and Asia Minor . . . 1810–16 . . .*, 1818; *The Adventures of Tom Spicer, who advertised for a Wife*, 1840 (privately printed); and contributed to *Literary Contributions by Various Authors in aid of . . . The Hospital . . . at Brompton*, 1846. He 'edited' *The Banished*, 3 vols., 1839 (from the German of Hauff), and *St. Roche: A Romance, from the German*, 3 vols., 1847.

Scott wrote an anonymous review of *Hajji Baba* in the *Quarterly Review*, xxxix, 1829. See also 'James Morier', *Fraser's Magazine*, vii, 1852; W. Maginn, *A Gallery of Illustrious Literary Characters*, ed. W. Bates, [1873]; F. W. Chandler, *The Literature of Roguery*, vol. ii, Boston and New York, 1907; K. J. Zeidler, *Beckford, Hope und Morier als Vertreter des orientalischen Romans*, Leipzig, 1909; 'The Sun and the Pen', *TLS*, 22 July 1949; and 'Orientals in Picaresque: A Chapter in the History of the Oriental Tale in England', by Fatma Moussa-Mahmoud, in *Cairo Studies in English*, ed. M. Wahba, Cairo, 1961–2.

JOHN MOULTRIE, 1799–1874.

In verse Moultrie published *Poems*, 1837; *The Dream of Life, and other Poems*, 1843; *Saint Mary, the Virgin and the Wife*, 1850; *The Black Fence, a Lay of Modern Rome*, 1850; *The Song of the*

Rugby Church-Builders, [1851]; *A Pentecostal Ode*, 1852; and *Altars, Hearths, and Graves*, 1854.

He also contributed to *The Etonian*, 1820–1, and to Knight's *Quarterly Magazine*, 1823–4. He compiled *Psalms and Hymns*, 1851, which contains a number of his own hymns, and edited *The Poetical Remains of W. S. Walker*, with a Memoir, 1852. He edited Gray's *Poetical Works*, Eton, 1847 (2nd ed.). He published a volume of *Sermons* in 1852.

His *Poems, with a Memoir by Prebendary* [*Derwent*] *Coleridge* appeared in 2 vols. in 1876.

J. Julian's *Dictionary of Hymnology*, 1892, contains information about Moultrie's hymns. Further sources of information are mentioned in the *DNB*. Praed, Macaulay, and Thomas Arnold were among his friends.

Edward Moxon, 1801–58.

Moxon published *The Prospect, and Other Poems*, 1826; *Christmas, A Poem*, 1829; *Sonnets*, 2 parts, 1830–5 (reprinted 1837, 1843, and 1871); and *Charles Lamb*, 1835 (privately printed). He published and edited *The Englishman's Magazine*, August–October, 1831.

Lamb's *Athenaeum* review of the sonnets (13 April 1833) is reprinted in his *Works*, ed. E. V. Lucas, i, 1903. Croker attacked the sonnets in the *Quarterly* in 1837 (vol. lix). Information about Moxon is to be found in books about Lamb (whose adopted daughter, Emma Isola, Moxon married), Wordsworth, Samuel Rogers, and other men of letters of the time. Crabb Robinson often refers to him. See also N. I. White, 'Literature and the Law of Libel', *SP* xxii, 1925 (an account of Moxon's trial for blasphemous libel in 1841: see *State Trials*, new series, iv, 693–722); E. G. Wilson, 'Edward Moxon and the First Two Editions of Milnes's Biography of Keats', *Harvard Library Bulletin*, v, 1951; and particularly H. G. Merriam, *Edward Moxon, Publisher of Poets*, New York, 1939.

Sir William Francis Patrick Napier, 1785–1860.

The *History of the War in the Peninsula and in the South of France* appeared in 6 vols. in 1828–40, and in a revised edition in 6 vols. in 1851. Apart from other editions, there was an edition abridged by Napier himself and entitled *English Battles and Sieges in the Peninsula*, 1852. He also wrote *The Conquest of Scinde*, *with some Introductory Passages in the Life of* . . . *Sir Charles Napier,* 2 vols., 1845; *History of Sir Charles Napier's Administration of Scinde, and Campaign in the Cutchee Hills,* 1851; *Defects, Civil and Military, of the Indian Government, by Sir Charles Napier,* 1853 (edited, with supplementary chapter, by Sir W. Napier); and *The Life and Opinions of General Sir C. J. Napier,* 4 vols., 1857. Napier was an untiring controversialist. Many of his pamphlets and other controversial writings, usually in defence of his own historical works, are listed in the *CBEL* and the *DNB.*

See Sir James Outram, *The Conquest of Scinde: A Commentary,* 1846; G. Buist, *Corrections of a Few of the Errors contained in Sir Wm. Napier's Life of Sir Charles Napier,* 1857; H. A. Bruce (Baron Aberdare), *Life of Sir William Napier,* 2 vols., 1864 (edited by Aberdare); the Hon. Sir J. W. Fortescue, *The Last Post,* 1934; 'General John Jacob's Notes on Sir William Napier . . .', ed. Sir P. R. Cadell, *Journal of Sind Historical Society,* iii, 1938; and M. G. T. Lambrick, *Sir Charles Napier and Sind,* 1952.

SIR NICHOLAS HARRIS NICOLAS, 1799–1848.

Observations on the State of Historical Literature appeared in 1830. It is often bound up with Nicolas's *Refutation of Mr. Palgrave's 'Remarks in Reply to "Observations on the State of Historical Literature"',* 1831, which contains an appendix relative to the dispute between the two men. Of Nicolas's other numerous and important historical and antiquarian publications only a few can be mentioned here: *Life of William Davison, Secretary of State . . . to Queen Elizabeth,* 1823; *The History of the Battle of Agincourt,* 1827; *History of the Orders of Knighthood of the British Empire,* 4 vols., 1841–2; *A History of the Royal Navy,* 2 vols., 1847 (uncompleted); and *Memoirs of the Life and Times of Sir Christopher Hatton,* 1847. Nicolas also edited *The Literary Remains of Lady Jane Grey,* 1825; *The Poetical Rhapsody of Francis Davison,* 2 vols., 1826; *Private Memoirs of Sir Kenelm Digby,* 1827; *The Letters of Joseph Ritson,* 2 vols., 1833 (with a Memoir of Ritson by Nicolas); *The Complete Angler of Izaak Walton and Charles Cotton,* 2 vols., 1836; and other works. He was responsible for a number of volumes in the Aldine series. With H. Southern, Nicolas was editor of *The Retrospective Review,* 2nd series, 1827–8. He also contributed frequently to the *Gentleman's Magazine, Archaeologia,* and other periodicals. A fuller account of his writings may be found in the *DNB.*

PETER GEORGE PATMORE, 1786–1855.

Patmore published *Letters on England* ('By Victoire, Count de Soligny'), 1823; *British Galleries of Art*, 1824; *Mirror of the Months*, 1826 (a novel); *Rejected Articles*, 1826 (parodies which reached a 4th edition in 1844 under the title, *Imitations of Celebrated Authors*); *Sir Thomas Lawrence's Cabinet of Gems, with . . . Memorials by Peter George Patmore*, 1837; *Finden's Gallery of Beauty, or the Court of Queen Victoria*, ed. Patmore, [1841]; *Chatsworth, or the Romance of a Week*, 3 vols., 1844 [ed. by R. Plumer Ward]; *Marriage in May Fair: A Comedy*, 1854 (2nd ed.); and *My Friends and Acquaintances*, 3 vols., 1855.

Patmore edited the *New Monthly Magazine* from 1841 to 1853, and contributed largely to numerous periodicals. His 'Reminiscences of Charles Lamb, with Original Letters', appeared in the *Court Magazine*, March and December 1835. Hazlitt's *Liber Amoris* was partly based on letters to Patmore.

Information about Patmore may be found in many memoirs of the time, in biographies of his son, Coventry Patmore, and in *Portrait of my Family*, by D. Patmore, 1935.

THOMAS LOVE PEACOCK, 1785–1866.

In verse Peacock published *The Monks of St. Mark*, 1804; *Palmyra, and other Poems*, 1806; *The Genius of the Thames*, 1810 (reissued in 1812 with *Palmyra, and other poems*); *The Philosophy of Melancholy*, 1812; *Sir Hornbook; or, Childe Launcelot's Expedition. A Grammatico-allegorical Ballad*, 1814; *Sir Proteus: A Satirical Ballad* (by 'P. M. O'Donovan, Esq.'), 1814; *The Round Table; or, King Arthur's Feast* [1817]; *Rhododaphne: or The Thessalian Spell*, 1818; and *Paper Money Lyrics, and Other Poems*, 1837 (privately printed). *A Bill for the Better Promotion of Oppression on the Sabbath Day* was privately printed in 1926.

Peacock's seven works of prose fiction appeared as follows: *Headlong Hall*, 1816; *Melincourt*, 3 vols., 1817, 1856 (with new preface); *Nightmare Abbey*, 1818; *Maid Marian*, 1822; *The Misfortunes of Elphin*, 1829; *Crotchet Castle*, 1831; and *Gryll Grange*, 1861 (first published serially in *Fraser's Magazine*, lxi and lxii, 1860).

In 1837 *Headlong Hall*, *Nightmare Abbey*, *Maid Marian*, and *Crotchet Castle* were republished as vol. 57 of 'Bentley's Standard Novels', with a new preface.

Peacock also wrote 'The Four Ages of Poetry', in *Ollier's Literary Miscellany*, no. 1 (only issue), 1820 (ed. H. F. B. Brett-Smith, 1921, with Shelley's *Defence* and Browning's *Essay on Shelley*); 'Memoirs of Percy Bysshe Shelley', in *Fraser's Magazine*, July 1858 and January 1860, with a supplementary notice in March 1862 (ed. H. F. B. Brett-Smith, 1909); and *Gl'Ingannati: the Deceived ... and Aelia Laelia Crispis*, 1862.

Peacock's *Works* were edited by H. Cole in 3 vols. in 1875, with a preface by Lord Houghton and a biographical notice by his granddaughter, Edith Nicolls. This edition includes his principal contributions to periodicals. The *Novels, Calidore and Miscellanea* were edited by R. Garnett in 10 vols. in 1891: the *Novels and Rhododaphne* by G. Saintsbury in 5 vols. in 1895–7. An edition of the *Poems* appeared in [1906], edited by R. B. Johnson. *Plays published for the First Time* were edited by A. B. Young, 1910. Peacock's *Letters to Edward Hookham and Percy B. Shelley with Fragments of Unpublished MS.* were edited by R. Garnett, Boston, 1910. All these were superseded by the Halliford Edition, ed. H. F. B. Brett-Smith and C. E. Jones, 10 vols., 1924–34. Vol i is a dry but accurate biography. For further material see *Shelley and his Circle* (p. 615 below).

There is an excellent one-volume edition of *The Novels*, ed. D. Garnett, 1948. There are numerous reprints of the individual novels.

Selections were edited by H. F. B. Brett-Smith in 1928 and by B. R. Redman in 1947 (*The Pleasures of Peacock*, New York).

The best critical study is J.-J. Mayoux's *Un Épicurien anglais: Thomas Love Peacock*, 1933. J. B. Priestley's *Thomas Love Peacock* (English Men of Letters, 1927) is a good introduction. Of the numerous other books mention may be made of *The Life of T. L. Peacock*, by C. van Doren, 1911; A. M. Freeman, *T. L. Peacock: A Critical Study*, 1911; A. H. Able, *Meredith and Peacock: A Study in Literary Influence*, Philadelphia, 1933; and B. Cellini, *T. L. Peacock*, Rome, 1937.

Essays and articles worth mentioning are the article in the *Edinburgh Review*, lxviii, 1839 [by J. Spedding], and that in cxlii, 1875; J. Davies, 'Thomas Love Peacock', *Contemporary Review*, xxv, 1875; R. Buchanan, 'Thomas Love Peacock: A Personal Reminiscence', *New Quarterly Magazine*, iv, 1875; H. Paul, 'The Novels of Peacock', *Nineteenth Century*, liii, 1903 (reprinted in *Stray Leaves*, 1906); Sir H. Newbolt, 'Peacock,

Scott and Robin Hood', *Transactions of the R. Society of Literature*, iv, 1924; H. Wright, 'The Associations of Thomas Love Peacock with Wales', *ESEA* xii, 1926; A. Digeon, 'T. L. Peacock, Ami de Shelley', *Revue anglo-américaine*, February 1928; F. Dannenberg, 'Peacock in seinem Verhältnis zu Shelley', *Germanisch-Romanische Monatszeitschrift*, xx, 1932; H. F. B. Brett-Smith, 'The L'Estrange–Peacock Correspondence', *ESEA* xviii, 1933; H. R. Fedden, 'Peacock', in *The English Novelists*, ed. D. Verschoyle, 1936; F. J. Glasheen, 'Shelley and Peacock', *TLS*, 18 October 1941; R. Mason, 'Notes for an Estimate of Peacock', *Horizon*, ix, 1944; H. House, 'The Works of Peacock', *The Listener*, 8 December 1949; and F. L. Jones, 'Macaulay's Theory of Poetry in "Milton" ', *MLQ* xiii, 1952.

The Critical Reputation of Thomas Love Peacock, by B. Read (Boston, 1960, available on microfilm and as Xerox book), gives a survey of his reputation and a list of his writings and of criticism on him.

JOHN WILLIAM POLIDORI, 1795–1821.

Polidori wrote a Latin thesis on nightmare, 1815; 'On the Punishment of Death', *The Pamphleteer*, vol. viii, 1816; *An Essay upon the Source of Positive Pleasure*, 1818; *Ximenes, The Wreath, and Other Poems*, 1819; *The Vampyre: A Tale*, 1819 (first published in the *New Monthly Magazine*, April 1819: attributed to Byron); *Ernestus Berchtold, or the Modern Œdipus: A Tale*, 1819; and *The Fall of the Angels*, 1821.

Information about Polidori is to be found in books about Byron, Shelley, and the Rossettis (since one of his sisters became the mother of Dante Gabriel and Christina Rossetti), and in *NQ*, 3rd series, vols. vii, ix, and x.

ROBERT POLLOK, 1798–1827.

Pollok's main publications were *Ralph Gemmel, a Tale* (prose), [? 1825]; *Helen of the Glen, a Tale for Youth* (prose) [? 1825]; *The Course of Time: a Poem in Ten Books*, 2 vols., 1827 (25 editions by 1867); and *Tales of the Covenanters* (prose), 1833 (ed. A. Thomson, 1895).

See D. Pollok's *Life of Robert Pollok*, 1843, and R. O. Masson's *Pollok and Aytoun*, [1898]. There are selections from his verse in Miles, x (xi).

Winthrop Mackworth Praed, 1802–39.

In English verse Praed published *Lillian, a Fairy Tale*, 1823; *Australasia*, 1823, and *Athens*, 1824 (both reprinted in *Cambridge Prize Poems*, 4th edn., 1828); *The Ascent of Elijah, A Poem*, 1831; *Intercepted Letters about the Infirmary Bazaar* (n.d., four four-page pamphlets in verse) and *Trash dedicated without Respect to J. Halse, Esq. M.P.*, Penzance, 1833. In 1832 he published his *Speech . . . on the Reform Bill*.

The Poetical Works, now first collected by R. W. Griswold, appeared at New York in 1844. *Lillian and Other Poems, now first collected*, by the same editor, appeared there in 1852. Another American edition of *The Poetical Works* was edited by W. A. Whitmore in 1859. At last an authorized edition, *The Poems, with a Memoir by Derwent Coleridge*, was published in 2 vols. in 1864. (In 1885 *Poems: Revised and Complete Edition* was published at New York in 2 vols.)

There were several volumes of Selections, including that of A. D. Godley, 1909, and *Selected Poems*, with an excellent introduction, by K. Allott, 1953 ('Muses' Library'). Praed's *Essays* were edited by Sir G. Young in 1887 (Morley's Universal Library).

In his lifetime Praed published mainly in periodicals. With W. Blunt he was the editor and chief contributor to *The Etonian*, 2 vols., 1820–1. He contributed largely to Knight's *Quarterly Magazine*, 1823–4, and to the *Brazen Head*, 1826 (four numbers only). His poems were often printed in the Annuals, and he also contributed to the *Albion*, 1830–2, the *Morning Post*, 1832–4, *The Times*, and other papers.

D. Hudson's *A Poet in Parliament: The Life of . . . Praed*, 1939, is a useful biography (with an appendix on 'The Editing of Praed's Poems'). See also G. Saintsbury, *Essays in English Literature, 1780–1860*, 1890; M. Kraupa, *W. M. Praed, sein Leben und seine Werke*, Vienna, 1910; 'Letters of Praed', *Etoniana*, 1 July 1941–28 December 1943 (67 letters); D. Hudson, 'W. M. Praed', *NQ*, 3 January 1942; and K. Allott, 'The Text of Praed's Poems', *NQ*, March 1953.

Bryan Waller Procter ('Barry Cornwall'), 1787–1874.

In verse Procter published *Dramatic Scenes and Other Poems*, 1819 (enlarged, and illustrated by Birket Foster, Tenniel, and others, 1857); *A Sicilian Story . . . and Other Poems*, 1820; *Marcian*

Colonna, An Italian Tale with Three Dramatic Scenes . . ., 1820; *Mirandola, A Tragedy,* 1821; *The Flood of Thessaly, the Girl of Provence, and Other Poems,* 1823; and *English Songs,* 1832 (new eds., 1844, 1851). His *Poetical Works* were collected in 3 vols. in 1822. *The Poetical Works of Milman, Barry Cornwall* [and others] appeared at Paris in 1829.

He also published *Effigies Poeticae, or the Portraits of the British Poets,* 1824; *The Life of Edmund Kean,* 2 vols., 1835; *The Works of Ben Jonson, with a Memoir,* 1838; *The Works of Shakespeare, with a Memoir and Essay on his Genius* (by Procter), 1843; *Essays and Tales in Prose,* 2 vols., Boston, 1853; *Selections from Robert Browning* [ed. B. W. Procter and J. Forster], 1863; and *Charles Lamb: a Memoir,* 1866 (reprinted in *Essays of Elia, with a Memoir of Lamb,* 1879). See also *Bryan Waller Procter: An Autobiographical Fragment,* ed. C. P[atmore], 1877.

Procter contributed to many periodicals, including the *Literary Gazette,* the *Edinburgh Review,* the *London Magazine,* the *New Monthly Magazine,* and the *Athenaeum.*

See J. T. Fields, *Old Acquaintance: Barry Cornwall and Some of his Friends,* Boston, 1876; F. Becker, *Bryan Waller Procter,* Vienna, 1912; and R. W. Armour, *Barry Cornwall: A Biography* . . . *with* . . . *hitherto unpublished letters,* Boston, 1935. Jeffrey noticed *A Sicilian Story* in the *Edinburgh Review,* xxxiii, 1820. Lamb reviewed *Marcian Colonna* in the *New Times,* 22 July 1820; while Darley attacked Procter in 'The Characteristic of the Present Age of Poetry', *London Magazine,* ix, 1824. H. Martineau has an essay on him in her *Biographical Sketches, 1852-75,* 1877. Recent notes and articles include F. Price, 'Barry Cornwall and Patmore on Child-Love', *NQ,* 14 August 1943; G. H. Ford, 'Keats and Procter: a Misdated Acquaintance', *MLN* lxvi, 1951; R. G. Townend, 'Barry Cornwall's Memoir of Charles Lamb', *Charles Lamb Society Bulletin,* March 1953; and E. L. Brooks, 'B. W. Procter and the Genesis of Carlyle's *Frederick the Great*', *Harvard Library Bulletin,* vii, 1953.

JOHN HAMILTON REYNOLDS, 1794–1852.

Reynolds published *Safie: An Eastern Tale,* 1814; *The Eden of Imagination,* 1814; *An Ode,* 1815; *The Naiad: a Tale,* 1816; *Peter Bell: A Lyrical Ballad,* 1819 (signed 'W. W.', a parody of Words-worth's poem then on the point of publication); *Benjamin, the Waggoner* . . . *A Fragment,* 1819 (another parody); *The Fancy:*

A Selection from the Poetical Remains of the late Peter Corcoran, 1820; *The Garden of Florence, and Other Poems* (by 'John Hamilton'), 1821; *Odes and Addresses to Great People*, 1825 (in collaboration with Thomas Hood); *One, Two, Three, Four, Five: by Advertisement, a Musical Entertainment* (acted 1815: published anonymously in J. Cumberland's *British Theatre*, vol. xxxi, 1829); and *Confounded Foreigners: A Farce in One Act* [1838].

There is no collected edition of Reynolds's poems. J. Masefield edited a reprint of *The Fancy* in 1905. The only modern edition is *John Hamilton Reynolds: [Selected] Poetry and Prose, with an Introduction and Notes*, by G. L. Marsh, 1928.

Reynolds contributed to numerous periodicals, including the *Champion*, the *London Magazine*, the *Edinburgh Review*, the *Westminster Review*, the *Retrospective Review*, the *Athenaeum*, and the *New Monthly Magazine*. On this and other topics Marsh's introduction is supplemented by his important articles in *SP* xxv, 1928; *MP* xl, 1943; and *K.-Sh.J.* i, 1952. Some information may be found in *The Keats Circle*, ed. Rollins, 2 vols., 1948, and *The Letters of John Keats*, ed. Rollins, 2 vols., 1958. According to a note on p. 84 of vol. i of *The Letters* 'by far the best biography' of Reynolds is that in an unpublished Harvard dissertation by W. B. Pope (1932). Further views and information may be found in the memoirs of Reynolds's friends, and in C. W. Dilke's *Papers of a Critic*, 2 vols., 1875; Sir E. Gosse, *Gossip in a Library*, 1891; H. C. Shelley, *Literary By-Paths in Old England*, 1909; A. E. H. Swaen, 'Peter Bell', *Anglia*, xlvii, 1923; W. B. Gates, 'A Sporting Poet of the Regency', *Sewanee Review*, xxxv, 1927; J. M. Turnbull, 'Keats, Reynolds, and *The Champion*', *London Mercury*, xix, 1929; E. Blunden, 'Friends of Keats', in *Votive Tablets*, 1931; and W. B. Pope, 'J. H. Reynolds', *Wessex*, iii, 1935. See also P. Kaufman's article, 'The Reynolds–Hood Commonplace Book: A Fresh Appraisal', *K.-Sh.J.* x, 1961.

HENRY CRABB ROBINSON, 1775–1867.

In 1838 Robinson edited *Strictures* [by T. Clarkson] *on a Life of W. Wilberforce* and in 1840 he published his *Exposure of Misrepresentations contained in the Preface to the Correspondence of William Wilberforce*. Throughout his life he was a prolific contributor to *The Times* and to many other periodicals, often on Germany and German literature. But he is remembered because of his Diary. The *Diary, Reminiscences, and Correspondence* were first edited by

T. Sadler in 3 vols. in 1869. Sadler's edition of 1872, in 2 vols., also contains A. De Morgan's 'Recollections' of Robinson. In 1922 Edith J. Morley published at Manchester *Blake, Coleridge, Wordsworth, etc., being Selections from the Remains of Henry Crabb Robinson*, and in 1938 she edited *Henry Crabb Robinson on Books and their Writers*, an invaluable collection in 3 vols. Edith Morley also edited *The Correspondence of Henry Crabb Robinson with the Wordsworth Circle (1808–66)*, 2 vols., 1927, and *Crabb Robinson in Germany, 1800–5: Extracts from his Correspondence*, 1929.

The fullest account of Crabb Robinson is Edith J. Morley's *The Life and Times of Henry Crabb Robinson*, 1935. There is a good essay (reprinted in Edith J. Morley's biography) by W. Bagehot in *Literary Studies*, ii, 1879. See also H. G. Wright, 'Henry Crabb Robinson's "Essay on Blake"', *MLR* xxii, 1927; R. W. King, 'Crabb Robinson's Opinion of Shelley', *RES* iv, 1928; D. G. Larg, 'Mme de Staël et Henry Crabb Robinson', *Revue de la littérature comparée*, viii, 1928; 'Henry Crabb Robinson and Mme de Staël', by the same writer *RES* v, 1929; P. Norman, 'Henry Crabb Robinson and Goethe', 2 parts, *English Goethe Society*, 1930–1; B. J. Morse, 'Crabb Robinson and Goethe in England', *Englische Studien*, lxvii, 1932; J. M. Baker, *Henry Crabb Robinson of Bury, Jena, the 'Times' and Russell Square*, 1937; and M. E. Gilbert, 'Two Little-known References to Henry Crabb Robinson', *MLR* xxxiii, 1938. An *Index to the Henry Crabb Robinson Letters in Dr. Williams's Library*, compiled by Inez Elliott, supplements Edith Morley's edition.

WILLIAM STEWART ROSE, 1775–1843.

Rose's writings include *A Naval History of the late War*, vol. i (no more published), 1802; *Amadis de Gaul: Freely translated from the First Part of the French version*, 1803; *Partenopex de Blois: Freely translated*, 1807; *The Crusade of St Lewis, and King Edward the Martyr*, 1810 (ballads); *The Court and Parliament of Beasts freely translated from The Animali Parlanti of Giambattista Casti*, 1819 (anon. ed., 1816); *Letters from the North of Italy. Addressed to Henry Hallam, Esq.*, 2 vols., 1819; *The Orlando Innamorato: Translated into Prose*, 1823 (abridged); *The Orlando Furioso Translated into English Verse*, 8 vols., 1823–31 (2 vols., 1858, with a brief Memoir by C. Townsend); *Thoughts and Recollections*, 1825; and *Rhymes*, Brighton, 1837 (privately printed).

Rose became a linguist at Eton, contributing to *Musæ*

Etonenses. Later in life he became a friend of Scott's. There is a brief account of him in the *DNB*, apart from Townsend's Memoir mentioned above. C. R. Leslie's *Autobiographical Recollections*, 1860, give an account of his stay at Abbotsford.

FRANCIS BARRY ST. LEGER, 1799–1829.

As Sadleir remarks in *XIX Century Fiction: A Bibliographical Record*, 1951, St. Leger was 'a writer of great promise, whose mature work might well have been of importance'. He printed *Remorse and Other Poems* privately in 1821. *Some Account of the Life of the late Gilbert Earle, Esq. Written by Himself*, 1824 (fiction); *Mr. Blount's MSS.: Being Selections from the Papers of a Man of the World*, 2 vols., 1826; *Tales of Passion*, 3 vols., 1829; and (posthumously) *Stories from Froissart*, 3 vols., 1832. He collaborated with Charles Knight in editing a periodical called the *Brazen Head*, and himself edited an interesting quarterly periodical, *The Album*, 4 vols., 1822–3. On St. Leger see Charles Knight, *Passages of a Working Life*, 3 vols., 1864–5. He was a friend of Praed, who contributed to the *Album*.

JOHN SCOTT, 1783–1821.

At different times Scott edited a number of periodicals, including the *Morning Advertiser*, the *Day*, the *News* (a weekly), and the *Statesman* (an evening paper, 1809–14). He is remembered primarily as the editor of the *Champion, A Weekly Political and Literary Journal*, and the *London Magazine* (1820–1). He also wrote a poem, *The House of Mourning*, 1817, and two interesting travel books: *A Visit to Paris in 1814; being a Review of the Moral, Political, Intellectual, and Social Condition of the French Capital*, 1815, and *Paris Revisited, in 1815, by Way of Brussels: including A Walk over the Field of Battle at Waterloo*, 1816. He wrote the English letterpress for *Picturesque Views of Paris and its Environs: Drawings by Frederick Nash*, 1820–3. After his death there appeared *Sketches of Manners* [and] *Scenery in the French Provinces, Switzerland, and Italy*, 1821.

There is no Life of John Scott. Information must be sought in studies relating to the *London Magazine* (p. 472 above), and in letters and memoirs of the time. See, e.g., *My Friends and Acquaintances*, by P. G. Patmore, 1855, ii, 283–7; the letters of Sir Walter Scott; and Andrew Lang's *Life and Letters of John Gibson Lockhart*, 2 vols., 1897. There is a brief Memoir by Horace Smith in the *New Monthly Magazine*, lxxxi, 1847, 415–18.

SIR WALTER SCOTT, 1771–1832.

The poems and the *Minstrelsy of the Scottish Border* are outside the scope of this volume, which confines itself to the Waverley Romances and Scott's other work in prose. The dates of the main works of prose fiction are as follows: *Waverley, or 'Tis Sixty Years Since*, 3 vols., 1814; *Guy Mannering, or The Astrologer*, 3 vols., 1815; *The Antiquary*, 3 vols., 1816; *Tales of my Landlord*, 4 vols., 1816 (*The Black Dwarf* and *Old Mortality*); *Rob Roy*, 3 vols., 1818; *Tales of my Landlord: Second Series*, 4 vols., 1818 (*The Heart of Mid-Lothian*); *Tales of my Landlord: Third Series*, 4 vols., 1819 (*The Bride of Lammermoor* and *A Legend of Montrose*); *Ivanhoe: A Romance*, 3 vols., 1820; *The Monastery: A Romance*, 3 vols., 1820; *The Abbot*, 3 vols., 1820; *Kenilworth: A Romance*, 3 vols., 1821; *The Pirate*, 3 vols., 1822; *The Fortunes of Nigel*, 3 vols., 1822; *Peveril of the Peak*, 4 vols., 1822; *Quentin Durward*, 3 vols., 1823; *St. Ronan's Well*, 3 vols., 1824; *Redgauntlet: A Tale of the Eighteenth Century*, 3 vols., 1824; *Tales of the Crusaders*, 4 vols., 1825 (*The Betrothed* and *The Talisman*); *Woodstock: or, The Cavalier: A Tale of the Year Sixteen Hundred and Fifty-One*, 3 vols., 1826; *Chronicles of the Canongate*, 2 vols., 1827 (*The Highland Widow, The Two Drovers*, and *The Surgeon's Daughter*, with an introduction in which Scott acknowledges the authorship of *Waverley* and its successors); *Chronicles of the Canongate: Second Series*, 3 vols., 1828 (*St. Valentine's Day: Or, The Fair Maid of Perth*); *Anne of Geierstein: or The Maiden of the Mist*, 3 vols., 1829; and *Tales of my Landlord: Fourth and Last Series*, 4 vols., 1832 (*Count Robert of Paris* and *Castle Dangerous*). Of his other separate works in prose the following are the most important: the introduction (1817) to *The Border Antiquities of England and Scotland*, 2 vols., 1814–17; *Paul's Letters to his Kinsfolk*, 1816; *Provincial Antiquities of Scotland*, 10 parts, 1819–26 (2 vols., 1826); Lives of the Novelists, prefixed to *Ballantyne's Novelist's Library*, 10 vols., 1821–4 (2 vols., Paris, 1825; ed. G. Saintsbury, Everyman's Library, 1910); *The Life of Napoleon Buonaparte, Emperor of the French: With a Preliminary View of the French Revolution*, 9 vols., 1827; *Religious Discourses: By a Layman*, 1828; *Tales of a Grandfather: Being Stories taken from Scottish History*, 9 vols., 1828–30; *History of Scotland*, 2 vols., 1829–30 (Lardner's *Cabinet Cyclopaedia*); *Letters on Demonology and Witchcraft*, 1830; and *Tales of a Grandfather: Being Stories taken from the History of France*, 3 vols., 1831. His essays on chivalry, romance, and the drama first appeared in the *Encyclopaedia*

Britannica, 1818–24, and were first republished in the *Miscellaneous Prose Works*, 1827.

Of the many works edited by Scott mention may be made of *Original Memoirs written during the Great Civil War*, 1806; *The Works of John Dryden . . . with . . . a Life of the Author*, 18 vols., 1808 (50 copies of Scott's fine *Life of Dryden* were printed separately for presentation: on this biography see *John Dryden: Some Biographical Facts and Problems*, by J. M. Osborn, New York, 1940); *Queenhoo-Hall, a Romance; and Ancient Times, a Drama*, by the late Joseph Strutt, 4 vols., 1808; *Memoirs of Capt. George Carleton, written by himself*, 1808; *Memoirs of Robert Cary . . .*, 1808; *A Collection of Scarce and Valuable Tracts*, 13 vols., 1809–15 (known as the *Somers' Tracts*); *English Minstrelsy: Being a Selection of Fugitive Poetry . . .*, 2 vols., 1810; *The Poetical Works of Anna Seward: With Extracts from her Literary Correspondence*, 3 vols., 1810; *Secret History of the Court of James the First*, 2 vols., 1811; *The Works of Jonathan Swift. . . . With notes and a life of the Author*, 19 vols., 1814 (the *Memoirs of Swift* were published separately at Paris in 1826); *Memorie of the Somervilles*, 2 vols., 1815; and *Memorials of the Haliburtons*, 1820 (privately printed).

Scott began to produce a collected edition of the *Waverley Novels* in 1829. It was completed in 1833, in 48 vols. This edition, 'The Magnum', has long and interesting prefaces dealing with the sources and historical background of the books. The best of the innumerable subsequent editions is the Dryburgh Edition, 25 vols., 1892–4. There is still no scholarly edition, but the first volume of such an edition is due to appear shortly, under the editorship of Dr. J. C. Corson.

In 1827 Scott produced a 6-vol. collection of his *Miscellaneous Prose Works*. Lockhart collected *The Miscellaneous* [Prose] *Works* in 28 vols. in 1834–6. Two further volumes, containing the *Letters on Demonology and Witchcraft*, the *Religious Discourses*, and the *Memoir of George Bannatyne*, were added in 1871.

There is a good edition of *The Heart of Mid-Lothian*, ed. D. Daiches, New York, [1948]. Lord David Cecil has edited *Short Stories by Scott* in the World's Classics series, 1934. *Private Letters of the Seventeenth Century*, ed. D. Grant, 1947, are bogus letters by Scott himself which were the germ of *The Fortunes of Nigel*. (W. M. Parker had written on the matter in his article, 'The Origin of Scott's *Nigel*', *MLR*, xxxiv, 1939.)

Earlier collections of Scott's letters were rendered obsolete by

The Letters of Sir Walter Scott, ed. by H. J. C. Grierson, assisted by D. Cook, W. M. Parker, and others, 12 vols., 1932–7. It is a scandal that no index has been published. An index on cards, by Mr. W. M. Parker, may be consulted in the National Library of Scotland. The originals or copies of the many Scott letters which were rejected by Grierson or which have turned up since his edition are kept in the library. Articles relating to such letters are listed in the *CBEL* and in *ERPE*: no mention is made of them here. See also *The Correspondence of Sir Walter Scott and C. R. Maturin*, ed. F. E. Ratchford and W. H. McCarthy, Austin, Texas, 1937; and W. Partington's *The Private Letter-Books of Sir Walter Scott*, 1930, and his *Sir Walter's Post-Bag: More stories and sidelights from his unpublished Letter-Books*, 1932.

The Journal of Sir Walter Scott was edited by D. Douglas in 2 vols. in 1890 (1891, 1910, 1 vol.). There is a better text in 3 vols., by J. G. Tait, 1939–46 (1 vol., 1950), but Douglas's annotations remain valuable.

Of the numerous accounts of Scott that appeared before Lockhart's biography mention may be made of G. Allan's *Life . . . with Critical Notices of his Writings*, 5 parts, 1832–4 (the part dealing with Scott's early life is by William Weir); of J. Hogg's *Domestic Manners and Private Life of Sir Walter Scott*, Glasgow, 1834; and of the *Life* by Robert Chambers first published in *Chambers's Edinburgh Journal* in 1832 which formed the basis of his *Life* of 1871. Another early account was published in Toronto by G. H. Needler in 1953 and in this country by J. C. Corson in 1957 as *Reminiscences of Sir Walter Scott in Italy by Sir William Gell*.

Lockhart's *Memoirs of the Life of Sir Walter Scott, Bart.*, were published in 7 vols. in 1837–8 and in 10 vols. (slightly revised) in 1839. It includes Scott's brief autobiography in Chapter I. (See also *The Ballantyne-Humbug*, under Lockhart.) A. W. Pollard's edition, 5 vols., 1900, contains additional material from Lockhart's 2nd edition and from his abridged *Narrative* of 1848. The only major biographical study to appear since Lockhart's is Sir Herbert Grierson's *Sir Walter Scott, Bart., A New Life supplementary to, and corrective of, Lockhart's Biography*, 1938. A great deal of information about Scott may be found in memoirs and other books of the period, and in the histories of the publishing firms of Constable and John Murray listed above on p. 483. R. H. Hutton's volume in the English Men of Letters series (1878) is concise and reasonable. Other books and monographs of biographical interest include *Sir Walter Scott's Friends*, by Florence MacCunn, 1909; *Sir Walter Scott's Congé*, by C. N. Johnston (Lord Sands), 3rd edition, 1931 (an account of Scott's unsuccessful love for Williamina Belsches); *Sir Walter: A Four-Part Study in Biography*, by D. Carswell, 1930; *Sir Walter Scott*, by John Buchan, 1932; *The Laird of Abbotsford*, by Una Pope-Hennessy, 1932; and *Sir Walter Scott's Journal and its Editors*, by J. G. Tait, 1938. Professor Edgar Johnson is at work on a full-scale study on the same lines as his fine biography of Dickens.

Essays and articles of primarily biographical interest include 'The Story of Scott's Ruin', by Sir Leslie Stephen, *Studies of a Biographer*, ii, 1898; 'The Early Literary Life of Sir Walter Scott', three articles by O. F. Emerson, *JEGP*, xxiii, 1924; 'Lockhart's Treatment of Scott's Letters', by D. Cook, *The Nineteenth Century*, September, 1927; *Lang, Lockhart and Biography*, by H. J. C. Grierson, 1934 (reprinted in *Essays and Addresses*, 1940); and 'James Hogg's Familiar Anecdotes of Sir Walter Scott', by A. L. Strout, *SP* xxxiii, 1936.

Much intelligent criticism of *Waverley* and its successors may be found in contemporary reviews. Some of these are reprinted in the books mentioned above on pp. 475, in Jeffrey's *Contributions to the Edinburgh Review*, 4 vols., 1844, and in *Essays on Fiction*, by Nassau Senior, 1864. *Letters to Richard Heber, Esq.*, in which J. L. Adolphus (anonymously) identified the author of the prose romances with the famous poet, contain some shrewd criticism in the course of their argument. Two early studies still of some interest are *Illustrations, Critical, Historical, Biographical, and Miscellaneous, of Novels by the Author of Waverley*, 3 vols., 1821–4, by R. Warner, and *Illustrations of the Author of Waverley: being Notices and Anecdotes of Real Characters, Scenes, and Incidents, supposed to be Described in his Works*, by Robert Chambers, 2nd ed., 1825. Hazlitt has a brilliant chapter in *The Spirit of the Age*, 1825. The severe views of Carlyle and Harriet Martineau may be found in Carlyle's *Critical and Miscellaneous Essays*, 4 vols., 1839, and Harriet Martineau's *Miscellanies*, 2 vols., [Boston], 1836.

The following books contain, criticism or background information about Scott's writings: *The Influence of 'Gothic' Literature on Sir Walter Scott*, by W. Freye, 1902; *The Waverley Novels: An Appreciation*, by C. A. Young, Glasgow, 1907; *Sir Walter Scott as a Critic of Literature*, by Margaret Ball, New York, 1907; *The Scott Originals*, by W. S. Crockett, 1912; *Scott and Goethe:*

German Influence on the Writings of Sir Walter Scott, by W. Macintosh, 1925; *Sir Walter Scott's Novels on the Stage*, by H. A. White, New Haven, 1927; *Scott Centenary Articles*, by T. Seccombe, W. P. Ker, and others, 1932; *Sir Walter Scott Today: Some Retrospective Essays and Studies*, ed. Sir H. J. C. Grierson, 1932; *Religious Creeds and Philosophies* [of] *Characters in Scott's Works and Biography*, By K. Bos, Amsterdam, 1932; *The Waverley Novels and their Critics*, by J. T. Hillhouse, Minneapolis, 1936; *Scott and Scotland: The Predicament of the Scottish Writer*, by Edwin Muir, 1936; *Die romantische Landschaft bei Walter Scott*, by J. Möller, 1936; *Scott, Hazlitt and Napoleon*, by M. F. Brightfield (*University of California Publications in English*, Berkeley, 1943); and *Goethe and Scott*, by G. H. Needler, Toronto, 1950. *The Historical Novel*, by G. Lukács (Eng. trans., 1961) throws a great deal of light on Scott. See also *The Hero of the Waverley Novels*, by A. Welsh, New Haven, 1963.

Sir Walter Scott Lectures 1940–1948, with an introduction by W. L. Renwick, 1950, includes important lectures delivered at the University of Edinburgh by Grierson, Edwin Muir, G. M. Young, and S. C. Roberts. Subsequent lectures, by D. Nichol Smith, J. R. Sutherland, J. C. Corson, and Mary Lascelles may be found in the *Edinburgh University Journal*. Those by Dr. J. C. Corson constitute a useful survey of 'Scott Studies' (*EUJ*, autumn 1955 and summer 1956).

When we turn to essays and articles we encounter right away Sir Leslie Stephen's admirable study in *Hours in a Library*, i, 1874, and Walter Bagehot's essay in *Literary Studies*, ii, 1879 (first published in 1858, also reprinted in his *Estimations in Criticism*). Ruskin's interesting criticisms of Scott may be found in his *Works*, but most of them are usefully assembled in *Ruskin as Literary Critic*, ed. A. H. R. Ball, 1928. Mrs. Oliphant's chapter in her *Literary History of England in the End of the Eighteenth and Beginning of the Nineteenth Century*, 3 vols., 1882, is still worth reading. J. M. Collyer wrote interestingly on ' "The Catastrophe" in *St. Ronan's Well*' in the *Athenaeum* for 4 February 1893, referring to a cancelled sheet which reveals the original ending. Paul Elmer More's 'The Scotch Novels and Scotch History', in *Shelburne Essays*, iii, 1905, may serve as a bridge to more recent studies.

A number of essays and pamphlets attempt a general assessment of Scott as a writer of fiction. They include Lord David

Cecil's *Sir Walter Scott*, 1933, a long and interesting essay reprinted from the *Atlantic Monthly*, 1932; Edwin Muir's essays in *The English Novelists*, ed. D. Verschoyle, 1936, and *From Anne to Victoria*, ed. B. Dobrée, 1937; V. S. Pritchett's brief yet illuminating essay in *The Living Novel*, 1946; David Daiches's fine assessment, 'Scott's Achievement as a Novelist', reprinted from *Nineteenth-Century Fiction*, vi, 1951, in his *Literary Essays*, 1956; I. Jack's British Council pamphlet, 1958 ('Writers and their Work', no. 103); and an essay in C. S. Lewis's *They Asked for a Paper*, 1962.

The following essays and articles, usually on more limited topics, also deserve attention: three essays in vol. i of the *Collected Essays of W. P. Ker*, ed. C. Whibley, 2 vols., 1925; 'Ivanhoe and its Literary Consequences', by G. H. Maynadier, *Essays in Memory of Barrett Wendell*, 1926; 'Sir Walter Scotts Beziehungen zu Deutschland', by J. Koch, *Germanische-romanische Monatsschrift*, 1927 (2 parts); 'Scott and Carlyle', by H. J. C. Grierson, *ESEA*, 1928 (reprinted in *Essays and Addresses*, 1940); 'Sir Walter Scott and the Sagas', by Edith Batho, *MLR* xxiv, 1929; 'The Chapter-Tags in the *Waverley Novels*', by T. B. Haber, *PMLA* xlv, 1930; 'Sir Walter Scott and *Emma*', by C. B. Hogan, *PMLA* xlv, 1930 (proves Scott's authorship of the review in the *Quarterly*); 'Witchcraft in the Novels of Sir Walter Scott', by M. C. Boatright, *Texas Studies*, xiii–xiv, 1933–4; and 'Scott's Theory and Practice concerning the Use of the Supernatural in Prose Fiction in Relation to the Chronology of the *Waverley Novels*', by the same author, *PMLA*, l (50), 1935; 'Character Names in the *Waverley Novels*', by C. O. Parsons, *PMLA* xlix, 1934; 'Sir Walter Scott und die Geschichte', by Max Korn, *Anglia* lxi, 1937; 'The *Waverley Novels*, or A Hundred Years After', by P. N. Landis, *PMLA* lii, 1937; 'Scott's Unpublished Translations of German Plays', by D. M. Mennie, *MLR* xxxiii, 1938; 'Sir Walter Scott and the Development of Historical Study', by D. Munroe, *Queen's Quarterly*, 1938; 'Critics of *The Bride of Lammermoor*', by E. Owen, *Dalhousie Review*, xviii, 1938; 'Shakespeare and Some Scenes in the *Waverley Novels*', by R. K. Gordon, *Queen's Quarterly*, 1938 (see also his contributions to *MLR*, 1942 (Scott and *Henry IV*) and to *Transactions of the Royal Society of Canada*, 1945 (Scott and Shakespeare's tragedies)); 'Scott and Shakespeare', by J. C. Smith, *ESEA* xxiv, 1938; 'Scott's *Letters on Demonology and Witchcraft:* Outside Contributors', by C. O. Parsons, *NQ*, 21 and 28 March and 5 December

1942; 'Scott's Antiquary', by R. W. Chapman, *RES* xix, 1943; 'The Original of the Black Dwarf', by C. O. Parsons, *SP* xl, 1943; 'The Power of Memory in Boswell and Scott', by F. A. Pottle, in *Essays on the Eighteenth Century Presented to David Nichol Smith*, 1945; 'The Chronology of the *Waverley Novels*: The Evidence of the Manuscripts', by R. D. Mayo, *PMLA* lxiii, 1948 (a refutation of the theory of Dame Una Pope-Hennessy, D. Carswell, and M. C. Boatright that some of the later novels were written before *Waverley*); '*Waverley* and the "Unified Design" ', by S. S. Gordon, *ELH* xviii, 1951; 'The Rationalism of Sir Walter Scott', by D. Forbes, *Cambridge Journal*, 1953; 'Sir Walter Scott's Contributions to the English Vocabulary', by P. Roberts, *PMLA* lxviii, 1953; 'Providence, Fate and the Historical Imagination in Scott's *Heart of Mid-Lothian*', by P. F. Fisher, *Nineteenth-Century Fiction*, x, 1955; 'Sir Walter Scott', in *The Hero in Eclipse in Victorian Fiction*, by M. Praz, 1956; and 'Scott's *Redgauntlet*', by D. Daiches, in *From Jane Austen to Joseph Conrad: Essays . . . In Memory of James T. Hillhouse*, ed. R. C. Rathburn and M. Steinmann, jun., 1958.

Bibliographical information may be found in the *CBEL* (which has numerous inaccuracies), in *ERPE*, and in *A Bibliography of Sir Walter Scott: A Classified and Annotated List of Books and Articles . . . 1797–1940*, by J. C. Corson, 1943. G. Worthington's *Bibliography of the Waverley Novels*, 1931, is strictly limited in its scope. Two useful books are M. F. A. Husband's *Dictionary of the Characters in the Waverley Novels*, 1910, and Allston Burr's *Sir Walter Scott: An Index Placing the Short Poems in His Novels and in His Long Poems and Dramas*, 1936. Gillian Dyson's useful census of the manuscripts and proof sheets of the *Waverley Novels* may be found in *Edinburgh Bibliographical Society Transactions*, vol. iv, part i (Session 1955–6), 1960. The catalogue of Scott's Library at Abbotsford, edited by J. G. Cochrane and published by the Bannatyne Club, appeared in 1838.

JOSEPH SEVERN, 1793–1879.

Severn published 'The Vicissitudes of Keats's Fame' in the *Atlantic Monthly*, xi, 1863. Specimens of his attempts at fiction may be found in W. Sharp's *Life and Letters of Joseph Severn*, 1892, the best (though unsatisfactory) biography. *Against Oblivion*, 1943, by the Countess of Birkenhead, is another study of Severn's life.

Some information may be found in *The Keats Circle*, ed. H. E. Rollins, 2 vols., 1948, and *The Letters of John Keats*, ed. H. E. Rollins, 2 vols., 1958.

RICHARD LALOR SHEIL, 1791–1851.

Sheil published four plays, one of them an adaptation. They were *Adelaide, or the Emigrants*, Dublin, 1814; *The Apostate*, 1817; *Bellamira, or the Fall of Tunis*, 1818; and *Evadne, or The Statue* (adapted from Shirley's *The Traitor*), 1819. He altered and prepared for the stage *Damon and Pythias*, by John Banim, 1821. In 1824 Sheil adapted Massinger's *Fatal Dowry* for Drury Lane. Two of his plays were unprinted: *Montoni, or the Phantom* (Covent Garden, 1820), and *The Huguenot* (Covent Garden, 1822). Sheil's *Speeches* were edited with a memoir by T. Mac-Nevin, Dublin, 1845. He was joint author of *Sketches of the Irish Bar*, ed. R. S. Mackenzie, 2 vols., New York, 1854–6 (first published in the *New Monthly Magazine*. W. H. Curran was the other author. Sheil's contributions, with other papers, were reprinted in 1855 in 2 vols. as *Sketches, Legal and Political*. ed. M. W. Savage.)

See 'The Tragic Drama—The Apostate', [by Maturin and Gifford], *Quarterly Review*, xvii, 1817; 'Richard Lalor Sheil', *Fraser's Magazine*, xxxiii, 1846; and W. T. MacCullagh (later MacCullagh Torrens), *Memoirs of the Rt. Hon. Richard Lalor Sheil*, 1855.

MARY WOLLSTONECRAFT SHELLEY, NÉE GODWIN, 1797–1851.

Mary Shelley published six long works of prose fiction: *Frankenstein or the Modern Prometheus*, 1818 (many reprints); *Valperga or the Life and Adventures of Castruccio Prince of Lucca*, 3 vols., 1823; *The Last Man*, 3 vols., 1826 (reprinted 1954); *The Fortunes of Perkin Warbeck: A Romance*, 3 vols., 1830 (2 eds., the later 'revised, corrected, and illustrated with a new introduction by the author'); *Lodore*, 3 vols., 1835; and *Falkner: A Novel*, 3 vols., 1837. See also 'The Swiss Peasant' in *The Tale Book*, by C. A. Bowles, J. S. Knowles, M. W. Shelley, &c., Königsberg, 1859, and *Tales and Stories by Mary Wollstonecraft Shelley, now first collected with an Essay by R. Garnett*, 1891.

She also wrote a *History of a Six Weeks' Tour through a Part of France, Switzerland, Germany, and Holland*, 1817 (anon.: with P. B. Shelley); *Lives of the Most Eminent Literary and Scientific*

Men of Italy, Spain and Portugal (with others: in D. Lardner's *Cabinet Cyclopaedia*, 3 vols., 1835–7); *Lives of the Most Eminent Literary and Scientific Men of France* (with others: also in D. Lardner's *Cabinet Cyclopaedia*, 1838); and *Rambles in Germany and Italy . . ., 1840–3*, 2 vols., 1844. After her death there appeared 'The Choice: A Poem on Shelley's Death', ed. H. B. Forman, 1876 (privately printed); *Proserpine & Midas: Two unpublished Mythological Dramas*, ed. A. Koszul, 1922; and *Mathilda*, ed. E. Nitchie, North Carolina, 1959.

For her editions of the works of P. B. Shelley see next entry.

Some letters were published in *The Romance of Mary W. Shelley, John Howard Payne and Washington Irving*, Boston, 1907, and *Letters, mostly Unpublished*, ed. H. H. Harper, Boston, 1918. F. L. Jones produced a scholarly edition of *The Letters* in 2 vols. in 1944 and of the *Journal* in 1947 (both Norman, Oklahoma). E. Nitchie edited some further letters in the *K.-Sh.B.* iii, 1950. M. Spark and D. Stanford edited *My Best Mary: Selected Letters*, in 1953. Much relevant material may also be found in *Shelley and his Circle 1773–1822*, ed. K. N. Cameron, 8 vols., 1961– (in progress).

There are books on Mary Shelley by Helen Moore, Philadelphia, 1886; F. A. Marshall, 2 vols., 1889 (*Life and Letters*); L. M. Rossetti, 1890; M. Vohl (*Die Erzählungen der Mary Shelley und ihre Urbilder*, Heidelberg, 1912); R. Church, 1928; C. I. Dodd, 1933 (*Eagle-Feather*, a biography); R. Glynn Grylls, 1938; Muriel Spark, 1951 (*Child of Light: A Reassessment*); and Elizabeth M. S. Nitchie, Rutgers, 1953.

See also G. Gilfillan, *Galleries of Literary Portraits*, vol. i, 1856; T. J. Wise, *A Shelley Library*, 1924; F. L. Jones, 'Letters of Mary W. Shelley in the Bodleian Library', *Bodleian Quarterly Record*, viii, 1937; F. L. Jones, 'Mary Shelley and Claire Clairmont', *South Atlantic Quarterly*, xlii, 1943, and 'Unpublished Fragments by Shelley and Mary', *SP* xlv, 1948; B. A. Booth, ' "The Pole": A Story by Claire Clairmont?', *ELH* v, 1938; Sylva Norman, *On Shelley*, 1938; E. Nitchie, 'The Stage History of *Frankenstein*', *South Atlantic Quarterly*, xli, 1942, 'Mary Shelley's "Mathilda": An Unpublished Story and its Biographical Significance', *SP* xl, 1943, and 'Mary Shelley, Traveller', *K.-Sh.J.* ix, 1960; T. G. Ehrsam, 'Mary Shelley in her Letters', *MLQ* vii, 1946; 'Mary Shelley and G. H. Lewes', *TLS* 12 January 1946; M. Millhauser, 'The Noble Savage in . . . *Frankenstein*', *NQ* 15 June

1946; C. L. Cline, 'Two Mary Shelley Letters', *NQ* 28 October 1950; E. J. Lovell, 'Byron and the Byronic Hero in the Novels of Mary Shelley', *Texas Studies in English*, xxx, 1951, and 'Byron and Mary Shelley', *K.-Sh.J.* ii, 1953.

PERCY BYSSHE SHELLEY, 1792–1822.

Four *juvenilia* before *Queen Mab* may first be mentioned: *Original Poetry; By Victor and Cazire* (P. B. Shelley and Elizabeth Shelley), Worthing, 1810; *Posthumous Fragments of Margaret Nicholson*, ed. 'John Fitz-Victor', Oxford, 1810; *A Poetical Essay on the Existing State of Things: By a Gentleman of the University of Oxford*, 1811; and *The Devil's Walk; a Ballad* [1812: broadside]. *Queen Mab; a Philosophical Poem*, was published in 1813, and followed by: *Alastor; or, The Spirit of Solitude: and Other Poems*, 1816; *Laon and Cythna; or, The Revolution of The Golden City: A Vision of the Nineteenth Century: In The Stanza of Spenser*, 1818 (printed 1817: suppressed and reissued, in revised form, as *The Revolt of Islam*, 1818); *Rosalind and Helen, A Modern Eclogue; with Other Poems*, 1819; *The Cenci: A Tragedy, in five acts*, Italy, 1819; *Prometheus Unbound A Lyrical Drama in four acts With Other Poems*, 1820; *Oedipus Tyrannus; or, Swellfoot the Tyrant. . . . Translated from the Original Doric*, 1820; *Epipsychidion*, 1821; *Adonais An Elegy on the Death of John Keats*, Pisa, 1921; and *Hellas A Lyrical Drama*, 1822. After his death there appeared *Poetical Pieces*, 1823; *Posthumous Poems* [ed. M. W. Shelley], 1824; *The Masque of Anarchy*, with a Preface by Leigh Hunt, 1832; and *Relics of Shelley*, ed. R. Garnett, 1862.

There are facsimiles of *Alastor* (ed. B. Dobell, 1885); *Rosalind and Helen* (ed. H. B. Forman, 1888); *Epipsychidion* (ed. S. A. Brooke, A. C. Swinburne, and R. A. Potts, 1887); *Adonais* (type-facsimile edition, ed. T. J. Wise, 1886; photo-facsimile, 1927); and *The Masque of Anarchy* (facsimile of the MS., ed. H. B. Forman, 1887).

Mention should also be made of editions of *Original Poetry*, ed. R. Garnett, 1898; *Posthumous Fragments of Margaret Nicholson*, ed. H. B. Forman, 1877 (privately printed); *The Cenci*, ed. A. and H. B. Forman, 1886, ed. G. E. Woodberry, Boston, 1909; *Prometheus Unbound*, ed. G. L. Dickinson, 1898, ed. A. M. D. Hughes, 1910 (the poems of 1820: rev. ed., 1957), and ed. L. J. Zillman, Washington, 1959; *Adonais*, ed. W. M. Rossetti and A. O. Prickard, 1903; and *Hellas*, ed. T. J. Wise, 1886.

The Daemon of the World . . . (the second part being printed from the MS.) was privately printed by H. B. Forman, 1876; and *The Wandering Jew* was edited by B. Dobell, 1887. *Shelley's Skylark, A Facsimile of the Original MS., with a Note on Other MSS. of Shelley in Harvard College Library*, was published at Cambridge, Mass., in 1888.

The best text of 'The Triumph of Life' may be found in *Studia Neophilologica*, xxxii, 1960, ed. G. M. Matthews. See the same scholar's article in the *TLS*, 5 August 1960, 'The "Triumph of Life" Apocrypha'.

Shelley published the following prose works: *Zastrozzi, A Romance: By P. B. S.*, 1810; *St. Irvyne; or, The Rosicrucian: A Romance: By a Gentleman of the University of Oxford*, 1811; *The Necessity of Atheism*, Worthing [1811]; *An Address to the Irish People*, Dublin, 1812 (ed. T. J. Wise, 1890); *Proposals for an association of . . . philanthropists*, Dublin [1812]; *Declaration of Rights* [Dublin], 1812 (broadsheet: reprinted *Philobiblon Society Miscellany*, vol. xii, 1868–9); *A Letter to Lord Ellenborough* [1812]; *A Vindication of Natural Diet*, 1813 (reprinted 1884); *A Refutation of Deism, in a Dialogue*, 1814; *A Proposal for Putting Reform to the Vote throughout the Kingdom: By the Hermit of Marlow*, 1817 (facsimile of the MS., ed. H. B. Forman, 1887); *An Address to the People on the Death of the Princess Charlotte* [1817] (reprinted [1843?]); and *History of a Six Weeks' Tour*, 1817 (ed. C. I. Elton, 1894: written with Mary Shelley). 'A Defence of Poetry', part of a longer essay designed as a reply to Peacock's 'Four Ages of Poetry', was first published in *Essays, Letters from Abroad*, &c., 1840 (see below). It has been reprinted several times, notably in 'The Percy Reprints', No. 3 (with Peacock's essay), ed. H. F. B. Brett-Smith, 1921, in the edition of A. S. Cook, New York, 1890, and in *English Critical Essays: Nineteenth Century*, ed. E. D. Jones, 1916 (World's Classics: plain text). Other prose writings which appeared after Shelley's death include *Notes on Sculptures in Rome and Florence*, ed. H. B. Forman, 1879 (privately printed); *Review of Hogg's Memoirs of Prince Alexy Haimatoff*, &c., ed. E. Dowden and T. J. Wise, 1886; *A Philosophical View of Reform*, ed. T. W. Rolleston, 1920 (also privately printed by W. E. Peck, 1930, and reprinted, with 'A Defence of Poetry', in *Political Tracts of Wordsworth, Coleridge and Shelley*, ed. R. J. White, 1953); *On the Vegetarian System of Diet*, ed. R. Ingpen, 1929 (privately printed); and *Plato's Banquet translated from the*

Greek, &c., revised and enlarged from manuscripts, ed. R. Ingpen, 1931 (privately printed).

Mary Shelley published *Essays, Letters from Abroad, Translations and Fragments* in 2 vols. in 1840 (reprinted 1852). Letters by Shelley were also published in various other books: most of them were collected by R. Ingpen in *The Letters*, 2 vols., 1909 (revised edition, 1914). This has been superseded by the edition of F. L. Jones, 2 vols., 1964. We may also refer to *The Shelley Correspondence in the Bodleian Library*, ed. R. H. Hill, 1926; C. D. Locock's *Examination of the Shelley MSS. in the Bodleian Library*, 1903; *Shelley's Prose in the Bodleian Manuscripts*, ed. A. H. Koszul, 1910; *The Shelley Notebook in the Harvard College Library*, ed. G. E. Woodberry, Cambridge, Mass., 1930; *Note Books of . . . Shelley*, ed. H. B. Forman, 3 vols., Bibliophile Society, Boston, 1911; *Shelley's Lost Letters to Harriet*, ed. L. Hotson, 1930; and *New Shelley Letters*, ed. W. S. Scott, 1948 (first published as three small volumes, in limited editions, as *The Athenians, Harriet and Mary*, and *Shelley at Oxford*, 1943–4). Other unpublished passages may be found in *SP* xlv, 1948, ed. F. L. Jones, and *The Platonism of Shelley*, by J. A. Notopoulos (below).

There is a useful collection of *Shelley's Prose*, excluding the letters and the two romances, edited by D. L. Clark, Albuquerque, 1954. Another useful collection, on a smaller scale, is *Shelley's Literary and Philosophical Criticism*, ed. J. Shawcross, 1909.

In 1888 R. H. Shepherd ed. *The Poetical Works* in 3 vols. and *The Prose Works* in 2 vols. The most nearly complete edition of Shelley, *The Complete Works*, ed. R. Ingpen and W. E. Peck, appeared in 10 vols. in 1926–30 (the Julian Edition). It may be supplemented by *Verse and Prose from the Manuscripts of Percy Bysshe Shelley*, ed. Sir J. C. E. Shelley-Rolls and R. Ingpen, 1934 (privately printed). Earlier editions of *The Works* had included that of Mary Shelley in 2 parts in 1847; that of R. H. Shepherd (with a Memoir by Leigh Hunt) in 4 series in 1871–5; and that of H. B. Forman in 8 vols. in 1880.

An early attempt at a collected edition of the poems, for which some assistance was afforded by Mary Shelley, was *The Poetical Works of Coleridge, Shelley and Keats*, Paris, 1829 (with a Memoir by Cyrus Redding). Mary Shelley published her own authoritative edition of *The Poetical Works*, with a preface and important notes, in 4 vols. in 1839. Other editions that may be mentioned are those of W. M. Rossetti, 2 vols., 1870 (and 3 vols., 1878); H. B. Forman, 4 vols., 1876 (and 2 vols., 1882, and 5 vols., 1892 (Aldine Edition)); R. H. Shepherd, 3 vols., 1888 (and 2 vols., 1912); E. Dowden, 1890; G. E. Woodberry, 4 vols., 1892 (annotated); and T. Hutchinson, 1905—often regarded as the standard edition. There is a 4-vol. edition, 1906, ed. by C. D. Locock. Locock's edition of 1911, in 2 vols., has useful notes and an introduction by A. Clutton-Brock.

Among the fullest of the many volumes of selections, usually with notes and often with passages from the prose, there are *The Best of Shelley*, ed. N. I. White, New York, 1932; *The Reader's Shelley*, ed. C. H. Grabo and M. J. Freeman, New York, 1942, and the Nonesuch *Shelley* (ed. A. S. B. Glover, 1951). There are other good volumes of selections edited by A. M. D. Hughes, 1931; E. Barnard, New York, 1944; C. Baker, New York, 1951; and K. N. Cameron, New York and Toronto, 1951.

Of the unreliable yet invaluable early accounts of Shelley only a few can be mentioned: T. Medwin's *The Shelley Papers: Memoir of Percy Bysshe Shelley . . . And Original Poems and Papers by Shelley*, 1833; the same writer's *Life of Percy Bysshe Shelley*, 2 vols., 1847 (rev. ed., with introduction and commentary by H. B. Forman, 1913); T. J. Hogg's *Life of Percy Bysshe Shelley*, 2 vols., 1858, ed. E. Dowden, 1906 (and *Shelley at Oxford*, reprinted from the *New Monthly Magazine*, 1832–3, ed. R. A. Streatfeild, 1904); E. J. Trelawny's *Recollections of the Last Days of Shelley and Byron*, 1858 (ed. E. Dowden, 1906: revised in 1878 as *Records of Shelley, Byron, and the Author*); *Shelley Memorials: from authentic sources*, ed. Lady [Jane] Shelley, 1859; and the book now known as Peacock's *Memoirs of Shelley*, edited (with Shelley's letters to Peacock) by H. F. B. Brett-Smith, 1909, but first published in *Fraser's Magazine*, 1858–62. See also *Lord Byron and Some of his Contemporaries*, 1828, and the *Autobiography of Leigh Hunt*, 3 vols., 1850. Much early documentation may be found in *Shelley and his Circle 1773–1822*, ed. K. N. Cameron, 8 vols., Cambridge, Mass., 1961– (in progress). In *Shelley–Leigh Hunt: How Friendship Made History*, 1928, R. Brimley Johnson reprinted reviews from *The Examiner*, with correspondence between the Shelleys and Leigh Hunt.

Later biographies include: *Shelley*, by J. A. Symonds, 1878 (revised edition, 1887: English Men of Letters Series); *The Real Shelley*, by J. C. Jeaffreson, 2 vols., 1885; *The Life of Percy Bysshe*

Shelley, by E. Dowden, 2 vols., 1886 (rev. and condensed ed., 1896); *Percy Bysshe Shelley: Poet and Pioneer*, by H. S. Salt, 1896; *Life of Shelley*, by W. Sharp (with bibliography), 1887; *La Jeunesse de Shelley*, by A. Koszul, 1910; *Shelley in England: New Facts and Letters*, by R. Ingpen, 1917; *Ariel, ou la vie de Shelley*, by A. Maurois, 1923 (Eng. trans. 1924: of no scholarly value); *Shelley His Life and Work*, by W. E. Peck, 2 vols., 1927 (of little value); *Shelley*, by N. I. White, 2 vols., New York, 1940 ('corrected', 2 vols., London, 1947: an authoritative work, abbreviated as *Portrait of Shelley*, New York, 1945); and *Shelley A Life Story*, by E. Blunden, 1946. See also *Byron, Shelley, Hunt, and 'The Liberal'*, by W. H. Marshall, Philadelphia, 1960. There is a biography of *Harriet Shelley*, by L. S. Boas, 1961, discussed in correspondence in the *TLS*, February 1961.

The Nascent Mind of Shelley, by A. M. D. Hughes, 1947, is both biographical and interpretative and forms an admirable introduction to Shelley's life and work.

There are studies of Shelley's reputation by N. I. White (*The Unextinguished Hearth: Shelley and his Contemporary Critics*, Durham, N. Carolina, 1938); and by Sylva Norman (*Flight of the Skylark*, 1954). See also E. Blunden's *Shelley and Keats as they Struck their Contemporaries*, 1925. *The Shelley Legend*, by R. M. Smith and others, was published at New York in 1945. N. I. White, F. L. Jones and K. N. Cameron demolished it in *An Examination of The Shelley Legend*, Philadelphia, 1951.

The principal interpretative and critical studies include the following: *Shelley*, by G. Barnett Smith, 1877; *Shelley*, by Francis Thompson, 1909 (first published in the *Dublin Review*); *Shelley: An Essay*, by A. A. Jack, 1904; *Shelley, Godwin and their Circle*, by H. N. Brailsford, 1913; *Shelley and the Unromantics*, by O. W. Campbell, 1924; *Mad Shelley*, by J. R. Ullman, Princeton, 1930; *Desire and Restraint in Shelley*, by F. Stovall, Durham, N. Carolina, 1931; *Toward the Understanding of Shelley*, by B. Weaver, Ann Arbor, 1932; *The Pursuit of Death: A Study of Shelley's Poetry*, by B. P. Kurtz, New York, 1933; *Shelley*, by R. Bailey, 1934; *The Magic Plant: The Growth of Shelley's Thought*, by C. Grabo, Chapel Hill, 1936 (and see next paragraph); *Shelley's Major Poetry: The Fabric of a Vision*, by Carlos Baker, 1948; *The Young Shelley: Genesis of a Radical*, by K. N. Cameron, 1951; *Shelley's Idols of the Cave*, by P. H. Butter, 1954; *The Deep Truth: A Study of Shelley's Scepticism*, by C. E. Pulos, Lincoln, Nebraska, 1954; *Shelley at Work*, by N. Rogers, 1956; *Shelley's Later Poetry: A Study of his Prophetic Imagination*, by M. Wilson, New York, 1959; *Shelley's Mythmaking*, by H. Bloom, New Haven, 1959; and *Shelley: Poète des Éléments*, by Hélène Lemaitre, 1962.

The following are more specialized in their scope: *Studien zu Shelleys Lyrik*, by H. Huscher, Leipzig, 1919; *Shelley: His Theory of Poetry*, by M. T. Solve, Chicago, 1928; three studies by C. Grabo, published at Chapel Hill—*A Newton among Poets: Shelley's Use of Science in Prometheus Unbound*, 1930, *Prometheus Unbound: An Interpretation*, 1935, and *The Meaning of 'The Witch of Atlas'*, 1935; *An Odyssey of the Soul: Shelley's Alastor*, by H. L. Hofman, New York, 1933; *A Classification of Shelley's Metres*, by J. B. Mayor, 1888; *An Analytical Study of Shelley's Versification*, by L. Probst (*University of Iowa Studies*, v. 1932); *Shelley et la France*, by H. Peyre, 1935; *Shelley's Religion*, by E. Barnard, Minneapolis, 1937; *Shelleys Geisterwelt*, by W. Clemen, Frankfurt, 1948; *The Platonism of Shelley*, by J. A. Notopoulos, Durham, North Carolina, 1949; *The Imagery of Keats and Shelley: A Comparative Study*, by R. H. Fogle, Chapel Hill, 1949; and *Il pensiero religioso di Shelley*, by B. Chiappelli, Rome, 1956. For *The Early Collected Editions*, by C. H. Taylor, see p. 621 below.

Important studies of Shelley may be found in the following books: *Shelley and Calderón and Other Essays*, by S. de Madariaga, 1920; *Mythology and the Romantic Tradition in English Poetry*, by D. Bush, Cambridge, Mass., 1937; *Revaluation*, by F. R. Leavis, 1936 (the most influential of all the attacks); *Rehabilitations and Other Essays*, by C. S. Lewis ('Shelley, Dryden, and Mr. Eliot'), 1939; *In Defence of Shelley and Other Essays*, by H. Read, 1936 (revised in *The True Voice of Feeling*, 1953); *The Starlit Dome*, by G. Wilson Knight, 1941; *English Bards and Grecian Marbles*, by S. A. Larrabee, New York, 1942; *English Poetry and its Contribution to the Knowledge of a Creative Principle*, by L. Vivante, 1950; *The Romantic Poets*, by G. Hough, 1953; *The Discipline of Letters*, by G. S. Gordon, 1946 ('Shelley and the Oppressors of Mankind', British Academy lecture, 1922); *Purity of Diction in English Verse*, by D. Davie, 1952 (the chapter on Shelley is reprinted in *English Romantic Poets: Modern Essays in Criticism*, ed. M. H. Abrams, New York, 1960); *Poets' Grammar*, by F. Berry, 1958 ('Shelley and the Future Tense'); and *The Quest for Permanence: The Symbolism of Wordsworth, Shelley and Keats*, by D. Perkins, Harvard, 1959. *The Subtler Language*, by

E. R. Wasserman, Baltimore 1959, contains three essays on Shelley.

Browning's *Essay on Shelley* was prefixed to an edition of *Letters of Shelley*, most of which were spurious, in 1852. It has been edited by W. T. Harden, 1888, R. Garnett, 1903, and H. F. B. Brett-Smith, 1921 (with essays by Peacock and Shelley). There is an intelligent essay by W. Bagehot in *Literary Studies*, i, 1879. Arnold's essay, which hardly shows him at his best, is in *Essays in Criticism*, 2nd series, 1888. Leslie Stephen has an essay on 'Godwin and Shelley' in *Hours in a Library*, iii, 1879. Yeats wrote on Shelley more than once: see particularly 'The Philosophy of Shelley's Poetry', in *Ideas of Good and Evil*, 1903. Bradley also wrote on Shelley several times: see 'Shelley's View of Poetry', in *Oxford Lectures on Poetry*, 1909, and three essays in his *A Miscellany*, 1929. 'The Case of Shelley', by F. A. Pottle was published in *PMLA* lxvii, 1952, and revised for *English Romantic Poets: Modern Essays in Criticism*, ed. M. H. Abrams, New York, 1960 (see also Pottle's essay in *MP*, February 1958, formally a review of the book by N. Rogers). C. Baker wrote on 'The Permanent Shelley' in the *Sewanee Review*, xlviii, 1940.

There are important articles as follows: 'The Early Reviews of Shelley', by G. L. Marsh, *MP* xxvii, 1929; 'Peterloo, Shelley, and Reform', by A. S. Walker, *PMLA* xl, 1925; 'Shelley and the Active Radicals of the Early Nineteenth Century', *South Atlantic Quarterly*, xxix, 1930, by N. I. White; and three articles by K. N. Cameron in *JEGP* xlii, 1943 ('Shelley, Cobbett, and the National Debt'), *Sewanee Review*, l (50), October 1942 ('The Social Philosophy of Shelley'), and *ELH* xii, 1945 ('Shelley and the Reformers'). For the influence of Bacon on Shelley see D. L. Clark in *PMLA* xlviii, 1933. On Shakespeare and Shelley see D. L. Clark in *PMLA* liv, 1939, B. Langston in *HLQ* xii, 1949, and F. L. Jones in *PMLA* lix, 1944. In 'Shelley's "Disinterested Love" and Aristotle', *PQ* xxxii, 1953, J. A. Notopoulos pursues his study of Shelley's thought. Also of interest are 'Hogg and *The Necessity of Atheism*', by F. L. Jones, *PMLA* lii, 1937; 'Shelley, Godwin, Hume, and the Doctrine of Necessity', by F. B. Evans, *SP* xxxvii, 1940; 'How Poetic is Shelley's Poetry?', by G. R. Elliott, *PMLA* xxxvii, 1922; the articles on Shelley and Spenser, and Shelley and Milton, by F. L. Jones, in *SP* xxxix, 1942, and xlix, 1952; 'Latter-Day Critics of Shelley', by W. Warren Beach, *Yale Review*, 1922;

'Shelley Once More', by C. B. Tinker, *Yale Review*, xxxi, 1941 (reprinted in *Essays in Retrospect*, New Haven, 1948); 'Structure and Prosodic Pattern in Shelley's Lyrics', by R. D. Havens, *PMLA* lxv, 1950; three articles by R. H. Fogle—'The Abstractness of Shelley', *PQ* xxiv, 1945, 'Empathic Imagery in Keats and Shelley', *PMLA* lxi, 1946, and 'Romantic Bards and Metaphysical Reviewers', *ELH* xii, 1945; 'Shelley's Eccentricities', by C. Grabo (*University of New Mexico Publications*, no. 5, Albuquerque, 1950); and 'Shelley and Calderón', by E. J. Gates, *PQ* xvi, 1937.

A few of the innumerable articles on individual poems may be singled out: 'Shelley's *Queen Mab* und Volney's "Les Ruines" ', by L. Kellner, was published in *Englische Studien*, xxii, in 1895. Many critics have considered the problems set by the interpretation of *Alastor*: see particularly 'Shelley's *Alastor*', by R. D. Havens, *PMLA* xlv, 1930; 'Wordsworth as the Prototype of the Poet in Shelley's *Alastor*', by P. Mueschke and E. L. Griggs, *PMLA* xlix, 1934; '*Rasselas* and *Alastor*: A Study in Transmutation', by K. N. Cameron, *SP* xl, 1943; 'The Inconsistency of Shelley's *Alastor*', by F. L. Jones, *ELH* xiii, 1946, and his 'The Vision Theme in Shelley's *Alastor* and Related Works', *SP* xliv, 1947; '*Alastor*: A Reinterpretation', by E. K. Gibson, *PMLA* lxii, 1947; '*Alastor*', by A. M. D. Hughes, *MLR* xliii, 1948; and '*Alastor*, or the Spirit of Solipsism', by A. Gerard, *PQ*, 1954.

On *The Revolt of Islam* see 'The Revision of *Laon and Cythna*', by F. L. Jones, *JEGP* xxxiii, 1933; 'A Major Source of *The Revolt of Islam*', by K. N. Cameron, *PMLA* lvi, 1941; 'Shelley's Use of Metempsychosis in *The Revolt of Islam*', by W. S. Dowden (*Rice Institute Pamphlets*, xxxviii, 1951); and 'Canto I of *The Revolt of Islam*', by F. L. Jones, *K.-Sh.J.* ix, 1960. R. D. Havens has written on *Julian and Maddalo* in *SP* xxvii, 1930, as have C. Baker ('Shelley's Ferrarese Maniac') in *English Institute Essays*, 1946, and J. E. Saveson in *K.-Sh.J.* x, 1961.

Apart from the discussions of *Prometheus Unbound* in book form and in the various editions, culminating in Zillman's, one may consult 'Shelley's *Prometheus Unbound*, or Every Man his Own Allegorist', by N. I. White, *PMLA* xl, 1925; 'The Political Symbolism of *Prometheus Unbound*', by K. N. Cameron, *PMLA* lviii, 1943; 'The Unbinding of Prometheus', by J. S. Thomson, *UTQ* xv, 1945; and 'Image and Imagelessness: A Limited Reading of *Prometheus Unbound*', by R. H. Fogle, *K.-Sh. J.* i, 1952. See also B. Weaver's study, Michigan, 1957. K. N. Cameron and H. Frenz have written on 'The Stage History of Shelley's *The Cenci*', in *PMLA* lx, 1945. D. L. Clark has an article on 'Literary Sources of Shelley's *The Witch of Atlas*', in *PMLA* lvi, 1941, while J. E. Jordan has written on 'Wordsworth and *The Witch of Atlas*', in *ELH* ix, 1942. K. N. Cameron has studied 'The Planet-Tempest Passage in *Epipsychidion*', in *PMLA* lxviii, 1948. On *Adonais* one may consult 'Spenser and Shelley's *Adonais*', by T. P. Harrison (*Texas Studies in English*, 1933); *Shores of Darkness*, by E. B. Hungerford, New York, 1941; 'The Thematic Unity of *Adonais*' by M. R. Watson, *K.-Sh.J.* i, 1952; and '*Adonais*: Progressive Revelation as a Poetic Mode', by E. Wasserman, *ELH* xxi, 1954. *Hellas* and *Charles I* have been discussed by R. D. Havens in *SP* xliii, 1946.

Of the numerous studies of 'The Triumph of Life' we may mention that by M. Stawell in *ESEA*, v, 1914; that by Bradley in *A Miscellany*, 1929, mentioned above; that by W. Cherubini in *SP* xxxix, 1942 ('Shelley's Own Symposium . . .'); and that by P. H. Butter, *RES*, n.s., xiii, 1962. On the text see G. M. Matthews, as above on p. 613.

The most discussed of the shorter poems has been the 'Ode to the West Wind': see the articles by I. J. Kapstein, *PMLA* li, 1936; R. H. Fogle, *ELH* xv, 1948; and S. C. Wilcox, *SP* xlvii, 1950. See also the discussion by F. Berry in *Poets' Grammar*, already mentioned. Of the numerous discussions of 'To a Skylark' the following deserve particular mention: 'The Symbolism of Shelley's "To a Skylark"', by E. W. Marjarum, *PMLA* lii, 1937; 'The Sources, Symbolism and Unity of Shelley's "Skylark"', by S. C. Wilcox, *SP* xlvi, 1949; and 'Shelley and the Skylark', by N. Rogers, *TLS*, 24 July 1953.

I. J. Kapstein and C. H. Vivian have written on 'Mont Blanc', in *PMLA* lxii, 1947, and *K.-Sh.J.* iv, 1955; D. W. Thompson, J. G. Griffiths, and J. Parr on 'Ozymandias', in (respectively) *PQ* xvi, 1937, *MLR* xliii, 1948, and *MLR* xlvi, 1951. B. Weaver wrote 'Shelley Works out the Rhythm of *A Lament*', in *PMLA* xlvii, 1932. N. Rogers has considered the poem 'On the Medusa of Leonardo da Vinci' in 'Shelley and the Visual Arts', *K.-Sh.B.* xii, 1961. See also 'Two Notes on Shelley', by J. A. Notopoulos, *MLR* xlviii, 1953 (on *Adonais* and 'Ozymandias'). On the 'Lines Written Among the Euganean Hills' see D. H. Reiman in *PMLA* lxxvii, 1962.

K. N. Cameron wrote on 'A New Source for Shelley's *A*

Defence of Poetry [*Rasselas*]', in *SP* xxxviii, 1941 (and see also L. Verkoren's full study of the *Defence*, Amsterdam, 1937).

Two valuable aids are *A Lexical Concordance to the Poetical Works*, ed. F. S. Ellis, 1892, and *The Early Collected Editions of Shelley's Poems*, by C. H. Taylor, New Haven, 1959. Earlier works which retain some value are *The Shelley Library*, by H. B. Forman, 1886; *A Descriptive Catalogue of the First Editions of Shelley*, by R. S. Grannis, New York, 1923; *A Shelley Library*, by T. J. Wise, 1924; and *A Bibliography of Shelley's Letters*, by S. A. de Ricci, Paris, 1927 (privately printed). Since so much has been written on Shelley a particular warning must be given that this selective bibliography may be supplemented by *CBEL* iii and v, by the article by B. Weaver in *ERP*, and by the annual bibliographies in the *K.-Sh.J.*

Shelley's 'Esdaile Notebook', which contains some 2,000 lines of unpublished juvenile verse, is to be edited by Mr. N. Rogers, as a forerunner to his Oxford edition of *The Poetical Works*.

HORATIO (HORACE) SMITH, 1779–1849.

(For *Rejected Addresses* and *Horace in London* see next entry.)

In prose Smith published *A Family Story*, 3 vols., 1799; *The Runaway, or the Seat of Benevolence*, 4 vols., 1800; *Trevanion, or Matrimonial Errors*, 4 vols., 1801; *Horatio, or Memoirs of the Davenport Family*, 4 vols., 1807; *Gaieties and Gravities*, 3 vols., 1825 (prose and verse, mainly reprinted from the *London Magazine* and the *New Monthly Magazine*); *The Tor Hill*, 3 vols., 1826; *Brambletye House, or Cavaliers and Roundheads*, 3 vols., 1826; *Reuben Apsley*, 3 vols., 1827; *Zillah: A Tale of the Holy City*, 4 vols., 1828; *The New Forest: A Novel*, 3 vols., 1829; *Walter Colyton: A Tale of 1688*, 3 vols., 1830; *The Midsummer Medley for 1830: A Series of Comic Tales* (prose and verse), 2 vols., 1830; *Tales of the Early Ages*, 3 vols., 1832; *Gale Middleton: A Story of the Present Day*, 3 vols., 1833; *The Involuntary Prophet: A Tale of the Early Ages*, 1835; *Jane Lomax, or a Mother's Crime*, 3 vols., 1838; *The Moneyed Man, or the Lesson of a Life*, 3 vols., 1841; *Massaniello: A Historical Romance*, 3 vols., 1842; *Adam Brown, the Merchant*, 3 vols., 1843; *Arthur Arundel: A Tale of the English Revolution*, 3 vols., 1844; and *Love and Mesmerism*, 3 vols., 1845. Smith edited *Oliver Cromwell: An Historical Romance*, 3 vols., 1840.

He also wrote *First Impressions, or Trade in the West: A Comedy*, 1813; *Amarynthus the Nympholept: A Pastoral Drama . . . With other*

Poems, 1821; *Festivals, Games, and Amusements, Ancient and Modern*, 1831; and *The Tin Trumpet, or Heads and Tales for the Wise and Waggish. To which are added Poetical Selections by the late Paul Chatfield, M.D.* ('ed. Jefferson Saunders, Esq.'), 2 vols., 1836. He contributed to *Literary Contributions by Various Authors in aid of . . . The Hospital . . . at Brompton*, 1846. His *Poetical Works* appeared in 2 vols. in 1846. His edition of his brother's *Memoirs, &c.*, is mentioned below.

There is a book by A. H. Beavan, *James and Horace Smith*, 1899. See also P. G. Patmore, *My Friends and Acquaintances*, 3 vols., 1855.

JAMES SMITH, 1775–1839.

Rejected Addresses: or The New Theatrum Poetarum, the work of the two brothers, first appeared anonymously in 1812. The 2nd edition, 1812, was carefully revised. There are editions by P. Cunningham, 1851, E. Sargent, New York, 1871, P. Fitzgerald, 1890, A. D. Godley, 1904, and A. Boyle, 1929 (with a bibliography). *Horace in London: consisting of Imitations of the First Two Books of the Odes of Horace* appeared in 1813 (the translations are reprinted from *The Monthly Mirror*, and are mainly the work of James Smith). Horace Smith edited *Comic Miscellanies in Prose and Verse by the late James Smith*, in 2 vols. in 1840. James Smith had also contributed to various periodicals and written the text for Charles Mathews's comic entertainments, 'The Country Cousin', 'The Trip to France', and 'The Trip to America' (1820–2).

Apart from the books by Beavan and P. G. Patmore mentioned above, see the *Edinburgh Review*, xx, 1812 (Jeffrey on the *Rejected Addresses*); A. Hayward, *Biographical and Critical Essays*, vol. i, 1858; R. W. Lowe, 'The Real Rejected Addresses', *Blackwood's Magazine*, cliii, 1893; W. C. Jerrold, 'The Centenary of the *Rejected Addresses*', *Fortnightly Review*, xciv, 1912; E. Blunden, 'The Rejected Addresses', in *Votive Tablets*, 1931; and G. Kitchin, *A Survey of Burlesque and Parody in English*, 1931.

SYDNEY SMITH, 1771–1845.

Smith published *Six Sermons*, 1800 (enlarged edition, 2 vols., 1801); *Elementary Sketches of Moral Philosophy*, 1804, 1805, 1806 (lectures: privately printed), 1850 (public edition); *The Letters of Peter Plymley to* [his] *Brother Abraham who lives in the Country*, 1807–8; 1808 (collected edition), ed. H. Morley, 1886 (with *Selected*

Essays), ed. G. C. Heseltine, 1929 (with other writings); *A Sermon upon . . . Conduct . . . towards Catholics . . .*, 1807; *Extracts from the Edinburgh Review*, [1810?]; *The Lawyer that tempted Christ: A Sermon*, York, 1824 (privately printed); *Catholic Claims: A Speech*, 1825; *A Sermon on Religious Charity*, York, 1825; *A Letter to the Electors, upon the Catholic Question*, York, 1826; *Mr. Dyson's Speech to the Freeholders on Reform*, 1831; *Speech at the Taunton Reform Meeting*, 1831; *The New Reign: The Duties of Queen Victoria: A Sermon*, 1837; *A Letter to Archdeacon Singleton, on the Ecclesiastical Commission*, 1837; *A Letter to Lord John Russell on the Church Bills*, 1838; *Second Letter to Archdeacon Singleton . . .*, 1838; *Third Letter to Archdeacon Singleton*, 1839; *Ballot*, 1839; *Letters on American Debts*, 1844 (reprinted from the *Morning Chronicle*); and *A Fragment on the Irish Roman Catholic Church*, 1845.

After his death there appeared *Essays, 1802–[1827]*, 2 vols., 1874–80 (reprinted from the *Edinburgh Review*); *Essays, Social and Political, 1802–1825*, 1874, 1877 (much fuller); and *Nine Letters*, ed. E. Cheney, *Philobiblon Society Miscellany*, vol. xv, 1877–84.

His *Works* appeared in 4 vols., 1839–40, and in subsequent editions. *Selections* appeared in 2 vols. in 1855. *Wit and Wisdom of the Rev. Sydney Smith*, ed. E. A. Duychuick, New York, 1858, contains extracts from his main writings. *The Wit and Wisdom*, 1860, is a different (English) volume of selections. E. Rhys, also edited *Selections* in 1892. See also *Bon-Mots of Sydney Smith and R. Brinsley Sheridan*, ed. W. Jerrold, 1893; *The Letters of Peter Plymley*, &c., ed. G. C. Heseltine, 1929 (as above); and W. H. Auden, *Selected Writings*, 1957.

The Letters of Sydney Smith were edited in 2 vols. in 1953, by Nowell C. Smith (but see *TLS*, 11 December 1953, and John Butt in *RES*, new series, vol. v, 1954).

The principal book is Lady Holland's *Memoir of the Reverend Sydney Smith . . . with a Selection from his Letters*, ed. Mrs. Austin, 2 vols., 1855 (with a list of his articles in the *Edinburgh Review*). There are other books by S. J. Reid (*A Sketch of the Life and Times of the Rev. Sydney Smith*, 1884); A. Chevrillon (*Sydney Smith et la renaissance des idées libérales en Angleterre au XIXe siècle*, 1894); G. W. E. Russell (English Men of Letters Series, 1905); O. Saint Clair (*Sydney Smith: A Biographical Sketch*, 1913); O. Burdett (*The Rev. Smith, Sydney*, 1934); Hesketh Pearson (*The Smith of Smiths*, 1934); and G. Bullett (*Sydney Smith: a Biography and a Selection*, 1951).

See also R. H. Horne, *A New Spirit of the Age*, vol. i, 1844;
G. Gilfillan, *Galleries of Literary Portraits*, vol. ii, 1856; R. A.
Vaughan, *Essays and Remains*, 2 vols., 1858; W. Maginn, *A
Gallery of Illustrious Literary Characters*, ed. W. Bates [1873];
R. M. Milnes (Lord Houghton), *Monographs*, 1873; Abraham
Hayward, *Selected Essays*, vol. i, 1878; Sir H. C. Biron, 'A
Victorian Prophet', *Fortnightly Review*, January 1921; S. T. Wil-
liams, 'The Literary Criticism of Sydney Smith', *MLN* xxxviii,
1923; J. Murphy, 'Some Plagiarisms of Sydney Smith', *RES* xiv,
1938; and 'The Smith of Smiths', *TLS*, 24 February 1945.
    See also the entry for the *Edinburgh Review* on pp. 470–3 above.

HENRY SOUTHERN, 1799–1853.

    Southern edited the *Retrospective Review*, series i, 1820–6, and
series ii, 1827–8 (assisted by Sir N. H. Nicolas). From 1825 to
1828 he edited the *London Magazine*. He was also literary editor
of the *Westminster Review* for its first three years or so, as well as
contributing at various times to the *Atlas*, the *Spectator*, and the
Examiner. Information about him may be found in Crabb
Robinson, in G. L. Nesbitt's *Benthamite Reviewing*, New York,
1934, and in Josephine Bauer's study, *The London Magazine
1820–29*, Copenhagen, 1953 (*Anglistica*, vol. i).

JOHN TAYLOR, 1781–1864.

    Taylor is important because of his work as a publisher and on
account of the *London Magazine*, which he edited from 1821 to
1824 and to which he himself contributed. But he also wrote a
great many books and pamphlets. A fairly full list may be found
in E. Blunden, *Keats's Publisher: A Memoir of John Taylor*, 1936.
No mention need be made here of most of his pamphlets on
financial questions, but some of his other publications may be
recorded: *A Discovery of the Author of the Letters of Junius*, 1813;
*The Identity of Junius with a Distinguished Living Character Estab-
lished*, 1816 (in the 2nd ed., 1818, Taylor argues for the author-
ship of Sir Philip Francis, having earlier suggested his father,
Dr. Francis, possibly helped by his son); *A Supplement to Junius
Identified, consisting of Facsimiles of Hand-Writing*, 1817; *What is the
Power of the Greek Article, and How may it be expressed in the English
Version of the New Testament?*, 1842; *The Case of the Industrious
Classes Briefly Stated*, 1843; *Propositions Concerning the Cause and
Remedy of the Present Distress*, 1843; *Emancipation of Industry*, 1844;

The Gemini Letters, 1844; *The Astronomy of an Ancient Carthaginian Tablet*, 1850; *Cinderella and her Glass Slipper: a Story of Ancient Astronomical Mythology*, 1850; *The Emphatic New Testament . . . With an Introductory Essay on Greek Emphasis by J. Taylor*, 1852–4; *The Revised Liturgy of 1689*, ed. J. Taylor, 1855; *The Great Pyramid; Why was it Built? and Who Built It?*, 1859; *The Battle of the Standards: The Ancient, of Four Thousand Years, Against the Modern, of the Last Fifty Years—The Less Perfect of the Two*, 1864; and *Light Shed on Scripture Truth by a more uniform Translation*, 1864. Taylor wrote the prefaces to Clare's *Poems Descriptive of Rural Life and Scenery*, 1820, and *The Village Minstrel*, 2 vols., 1821. A mass of papers relating to Taylor has been dispersed, but much remains in the British Museum. Commonplace books and manuscript poems by Taylor were sold at Sotheby's in 1961.

WILLIAM TAYLOR OF NORWICH, 1765–1836.

Taylor's *Historic Survey of German Poetry: Interspersed with Various Translations* appeared in 3 vols. in 1830, and was severely reviewed by Carlyle in the *Edinburgh Review* for March 1831. Throughout his life he was an astonishingly prolific contributor to periodicals, particularly the *Monthly Review* from 1793 to 1824. He produced the following separate translations: Lessing's *Nathan the Wise*, Norwich, 1791 (privately printed), 1805, 1886 (ed. H. Morley); Goethe's *Iphigenia in Tauris*, 1793 (privately printed), 1794; Wieland's *Dialogues of the Gods*, 1795; Bürger's *Ellenore*, 1796 (reprinted in revised form from the *Monthly Magazine*, March 1796); *Select Fairy Tales from the German of Wieland*, 1796; and *Tales of Yore*, 3 vols., 1810 (from French and German). He also published *A Letter concerning the Two First Chapters of Luke*, 1810; *English Synonyms Discriminated*, 1813; 'Some Biographic Particulars of the late Dr. Sayers' (prefixed to Frank Sayers's *Collective Works*, Norwich, 1823); and *A Memoir of the late Philip Meadows Martineau, Surgeon* (with F. Elwes), 1831.

There is a *Memoir* by J. W. Robberds, 2 vols., 1843, containing many letters and lists of his contribution to periodicals; and a study, by G. Herzfeld, *William Taylor of Norwich: Eine Studie über den Einfluß der neueren deutschen Literatur in England*, Halle, 1897. See also Section IV, 7 above.

EDWARD JOHN TRELAWNY, 1792–1881.

Trelawny published *The Adventures of a Younger Son*, 3 vols.,

1831 (ed. E. Garnett, 1890: ed. H. N. Brailsford, 1914: ed. E. C. Mayne, 1925, World's Classics), and *Recollections of the last Days of Shelley and Byron*, 1858 (1878, with additions, as *Records of Shelley, Byron and the Author*); ed. E. Dowden, 1906; ed. J. E. Morpurgo, 1952.

His *Letters* were edited by H. Buxton Forman in 1910. *The Relations of Percy Bysshe Shelley with his Two Wives, Harriet and Mary, and a Comment on the Character of Lady Byron*, and *The Relations of Lord Byron and Augusta Leigh* (4 letters), were both privately printed in 1920.

There are several books about Trelawny: R. Edgcumbe, *Edward Trelawny: A Biographical Sketch*, Plymouth, 1882; Joaquin Miller, *Trelawny with Shelley and Byron*, 1922; H. J. Massingham, *The Friend of Shelley: A Memoir of Edward John Trelawny*, 1930; M. Armstrong, *Trelawny: A Man's Life*, New York, 1940; and R. G. Grylls, *Trelawny*, 1950. See also R. Garnett, 'Shelley's Last Days', *Fortnightly Review*, xxix, 1878; Mathilde Blind, *Whitehall Review*, 10 January 1880 (a record of Trelawny's conversation); and W. M. Rossetti, 'Talks with Trelawny, 1879–1880', *Athenaeum*, 15 and 29 July and 5 August 1882. There is also a good deal about Trelawny in William Sharp's *The Life and Letters of Joseph Severn*, 1892. His (un)reliability as a witness is discussed in studies of Byron and Shelley and (with new evidence) in the *K.-Sh.J.* v, 1956, by Lady Anne Hill.

PATRICK FRASER TYTLER, 1791–1849.

Fraser Tytler published the *Life of James Crichton of Cluny, the Admirable Crichton*, 1819; *An Account of the Life and Writings of Sir Thomas Craig* (reprinted from *Blackwood's Magazine*), 1823; *The Life of John Wickliff*, 1826; a *History of Scotland*, 9 vols. (and index), 1828–43 (and later editions); *Lives of Scottish Worthies*, 3 vols., 1831–3; a *Historical View of the Progress of Discovery on the More Northern Coasts of America*, 1832; a *Life of Sir Walter Raleigh*, 1833; a *Life of King Henry the Eighth*, 1837; *England under the Reigns of Edward VI and Mary*, 2 vols., 1839; and 'Scotland' in the 7th (1839) and some later editions of the *Encyclopaedia Britannica*. This article was later enlarged and published separately. He contributed occasionally to *Blackwood's Magazine*. With Scott and others he was one of the founders of the Bannatyne Club, whose poet-laureate he became. In 1833 he and others edited for the club Hugh Mackay's *Memoirs . . . 1689–91*.

There is a Memoir by the Rev. J. W. Burgon, *The Portrait of a Christian Gentleman: A Memoir of Patrick Fraser Tytler*, 1859. The *DNB* mentions a few minor writings.

THOMAS GRIFFITHS WAINEWRIGHT, 1794–1847.

Wainewright's *Essays and Criticisms* were edited by W. Carew Hazlitt in 1880, most of them having been published in the *London Magazine*. A list of his contributions is included in Jonathan Curling's *Janus Weathercock: The Life of Thomas Griffiths Wainewright*, 1938, the best study. Little is added by J. Lindsey's *Suburban Gentleman*, 1942, or R. Crossland's *Wainewright in Tasmania*, Melbourne, 1954. Some reminiscences may be found in B. W. Procter's *Autobiographical Fragment*, 1877, and in the writings of other members of the *London* group. (See also Josephine Bauer's *The London Magazine 1820–29*, Copenhagen, 1953.) Dickens, Bulwer Lytton, and Oscar Wilde were all fascinated by Wainewright: *For the Term of his Natural Life*, by Marcus Clarke, owes something to Wainewright's career, as do Dickens's *Hunted Down* and Lytton's *Lucretia, or The Children of Night*, 1846.

WILLIAM SIDNEY WALKER, 1795–1846.

Walker published *Gustavus Vasa, and other Poems*, 1813; *The Heroes of Waterloo: An Ode*, 1815; *Poems from the Danish*, 1815; and *The Appeal of Poland: An Ode*, 1816. He edited a *Corpus Poetarum Latinorum*, 1828, and Milton's *De Doctrina Christiana*, 1825 (nominally ed. by C. R. Sumner). The *Poetical Remains* were edited with a long Memoir by his friend J. Moultrie in 1852. See also *Shakespeare's Versification and its Apparent Irregularities Explained*, ed. W. N. Lettsom, 1854, and *A Critical Examination of the Text of Shakespeare*, ed. W. N. Lettsom, 3 vols., 1860. As a young man Walker had contributed to *The Etonian*, 1820–1, and later he wrote in Knight's *Quarterly Magazine* and the *Classical Journal*. He was a friend of Praed.

ROBERT (LATER PLUMER) WARD, 1765–1846.

This tedious writer produced five works of fiction: *Tremaine, or the Man of Refinement*, 3 vols., 1825; *De Vere, or the Man of Independence*, 4 vols., 1827; *Illustrations of Human Life*, 3 vols., 1837; *Pictures of the World at Home and Abroad*, 3 vols., 1839; and *De Clifford, or the Constant Man*, 4 vols., 1841. He edited P. G. Patmore's anonymous *Chatsworth, or the Romance of a Week*, 3 vols., 1844. His other prose works have little literary interest.

Memoirs of . . . Robert Plumer Ward with letters and unpublished remains were edited by E. Phipps in 2 vols. in 1850. See also P. G. Patmore's *My Friends and Acquaintances*, 3 vols., 1855, and 'Robert Plumer Ward', in *Bentley's Miscellany*, xxviii, 1850. As Michael Sadleir pointed out in *Bulwer and his Wife: a Panorama 1803–1836*, 1933, both Disraeli and Bulwer Lytton were influenced by Ward.

ALARIC ALEXANDER WATTS, 1797–1864.

As writer and editor, Watts was responsible for a great many productions. Of his own books mention may be made of *Poetical Sketches*, 1822 (privately printed); *Poetical Sketches: The Profession; The Broken Heart, etc.*, 1823; *Scenes of Life and Shades of Character*, 2 vols., 1831 (prose); and *Lyrics of the Heart*, 1851. In 1828–9 he produced a most interesting two-volume anthology of contemporary poetry, *The Poetical Album*, followed by *The Lyre* and *The Laurel* (reprinted together in 1867 as *The Laurel and the Lyre*).

He helped to edit the *New Monthly Magazine* from about 1815 to 1819, and the *Literary Souvenir* from 1825 to 1835. He wrote a good deal for the *Literary Gazette*. He also edited the *Leeds Intelligencer*, 1822–5; the *Manchester Courier*, 1825–6 (at first a weekly); the *Standard* (1827); and the *United Service Gazette* (1833–41). He was responsible for the *Cabinet of British Art*, 1835–8 (a sequel to the *Literary Souvenir*), and *Men of the Time*, 1856, which includes an article on Watts himself three times as long as that on Tennyson.

His son Alaric Alfred Watts published *Alaric Watts: A Narrative of his Life* in 2 vols. in 1884. See also Watts's own entertaining article, 'Some Passages in the Life of a Magazine Editor', in the *Literary Magnet*, 1826.

CHARLES JEREMIAH WELLS, 1800–79.

Wells published a volume of prose, *Stories after Nature*, in 1822 (ed. W. J. Linton, 1891), and *Joseph and his Brethren, a Scriptural Drama*, in '1824' (really December 1823: by 'H. L. Howard': ed. A. C. Swinburne, 1876, reprinted in 1908 in the World's Classics). He wrote two papers in *Fraser's Magazine* and contributed a tale, 'Claribel', to Linton's *Illuminated Magazine* for 1845. Swinburne's essay, first published in the *Fortnightly Review* for February 1875, was just too late to prevent Wells from burning a great mass of his unpublished writings. 'A Dramatic Scene', ed. H. B. Forman, was printed in *Literary Anecdotes of the Nineteenth Century*, ed. W. Robertson Nicoll and Thomas J. Wise, vol. i, 1895.

Miles's *Poets and Poetry of the Century*, iii, contains a selection and a brief critique by H. B. Forman. See also Sir E. Gosse's obituary in the *Academy*, 1 March 1879, and the notice in the *DNB*.

JEREMIAH HOLMES WIFFEN, 1792–1836.

With T. Raffles and J. B. Brown, Wiffen published *Poems by Three Friends*, 1813. With his brother, Benjamin Barron Wiffen, he published *Elegiac Lines* in 1818. On his own he then published *Aonian Hours and other Poems*, 1819; *Julia Alpinula, with The Captive of Stamboul, and other Poems*, 1820; *Jerusalem Delivered: Book the Fourth*, 1821 (a specimen of his projected translation of Tasso, with a critique of earlier translations); *The Works of Garcilasso de la Vega, translated*, 1823; *Jerusalem Delivered. . . . Translated into English Spenserian Verse . . .*, 2 vols., 1824–5; *Verses on the Alameda at Ampthill Park*, 1827 (privately printed); *Historical Memoirs of the House of Russell*, 2 vols., 1833; *Appeal for the Injured African*, Newcastle upon Tyne, 1833 (verse); and *Verses Written at Woburn Abbey*, 1836 (privately printed).

He also published a number of reviews and other writings in prose. He wrote on 'The Character and Poetry of Lord Byron' in the *New Monthly Magazine* for May 1819.

The Brothers Wiffen: Memoirs and Miscellanies, ed. S. R. Pattison, 1880, includes a selection from their poems. The *Quarterly Review*, xxxiv, 1826, contains an interesting review of Wiffen's *Tasso*.

JOHN WILSON ('CHRISTOPHER NORTH'), 1785–1854.

In verse he published *A Recommendation of the Study of the Remains of Ancient . . . Architecture . . . A Prize Poem*, Oxford, 1807; *Lines Sacred to the Memory of the Rev. James Grahame*, 1811; *The Isle of Palms*, 1812; *The Magic Mirror*, 1812; and *The City of the Plague*, 1816. His *Poems* were published in 2 vols. in 1825, and there were subsequent editions.

His principal writings in prose include *Translation From an Ancient Chaldee Manuscript* (with Lockhart: reprinted from *Blackwood's Magazine*, October 1817); *Lights and Shadows of Scottish*

Life (by 'Arthur Austin'), 1822; *The Trials of Margaret Lyndsay*, 1823; *The Foresters*, 1825; *Tales*, 1865 (the last three books together); *Janus, or the Edinburgh Literary Almanack* (ed. by Lockhart: contains contributions by Wilson), 1826; *Some Illustrations of Mr. M'Culloch's Principles of Political Economy* (by 'Mordecai Mullion'), 1826; *The Recreations of Christopher North*, 3 vols., 1842; *The Noctes Ambrosianæ of 'Blackwood'*, ed. R. Skelton Mackenzie, 5 vols., New York, 1854, revised 1863 (fullest edition); 4 vols., 1864; selected edition, ed. J. Scott Moncrieff, n.d., New Universal Library (mainly the work of North, but with collaboration from Hogg, Lockhart, and others); *Specimens of the British Critics*, Philadelphia, 1846; and *Essays Critical and Imaginative*, 4 vols., 1866. *The Works of Professor Wilson*, in 12 vols., ed. Professor Ferrier, appeared between 1855 and 1858.

The fullest accounts are to be found in Mary Gordon's *Christopher North: A Memoir*, 2 vols., 1862, and Elsie Swann's *Christopher North*, 1934. See also J. G. Lockhart, *Peter's Letters to his Kinsfolk*, 3 vols., 1819; G. Gilfillan, *Galleries of Literary Portraits*, ii, 1856; J. Hannay, 'Professor Wilson', in *Characters and Criticisms*, 1865; W. Maginn, *A Gallery of Illustrious Literary Characters*, ed. W. Bates, [1873]; G. Saintsbury, *Essays in English Literature, 1780–1860*, ser. i, 1890; D. Masson, 'Christopher North', in *Memories of Two Cities*, 1911; H. von Struve, *John Wilson . . . als Kritiker*, Leipzig, 1922; M. Elwin, 'Christopher North', in *Victorian Wallflowers*, 1934; and a series of brief articles by A. L. Strout, as follows: *MP* xxxi, 1934; *ELH* ii, 1935; *MLN* li, 1935 (and *RES* xiii, 1937, pp. 46–63 and 177–89); *Shakespeare Jahrbuch*, lxxii, 1936; *RES* xiv, 1938; *NQ* 11 March 1939, 1 April 1939; *PMLA* lv, 1940; *NQ* 6 June and 1 August 1942. R. M. Wardle's 'The Authorship of the "Noctes Ambrosianæ"' (*MP* xlii, 1944–5) was supplemented by Strout in *The Library*, ser. v, vol. xii, no. 2 (June 1957). See also 'An Unknown Castigator of Christopher North', by N. S. Aurnor, in *If by Your Art: Testament to Percival Hunt*, Pittsburgh, 1948; and M. P. Alekseev's essay on *The City of the Plague* in *Iz istorii angliyskoy literatury*, Moscow and Leningrad, 1960. See also the section on *Blackwood's Magazine* on pp. 470–3 above.

FRANCIS WRANGHAM, 1769–1842.

The Lyrics of Horace: being the First Four Books of his Odes, translated by Wrangham, was published in 1821. (The previous year Wrangham had published *Q. Horatius Flaccus: Carmina . . . Specimens of a version of Book III.*) His other work in verse (often Cambridge prize poems) includes *The Restoration of the Jews*, 1795; *The Destruction of Babylon*, 1795; *Poems* (privately printed 1795, but not published till *c.* 1802); *The Holy Land*, 1800; *The Raising of Jaïrus' Daughter*, 1804; *A Poem on the Restoration of Learning in the East*, 1805; *A Volunteer Song*, York, [? 1806] (11 pieces in verse); *The Sufferings of the Primitive Martyrs*, 1812; *Joseph Made Known to his Brethren*, 1812; *Death of Saul and Jonathan*, 1813; *Poetical Sketches of Scarborough* (by Wrangham and others), 1813; *Poems*, [? 1814] (privately printed); *Virgil's Bucolics*, Scarborough, 1815; *A Few Sonnets Attempted from Petrarch in Early Life*, Lee Priory, 1817; *Scarborough Castle*, Scarborough, 1823; *Psychae; or Songs on Butterflies, by T. H. Bayly, attempted in Latin Rhyme*, 1828; *Homerics*, 1834 (translation of *Odyssey* v, and *Iliad* III); *Epithalamia tria Mariana*, &c., Chester, 1837 (translations); and *A Few Epigrams: Attempted in Latin Translation*, Chester, 1842.

In 1792 he had published *Reform: A Farce Modernised from Aristophanes . . . By S. Foote Jr.* He produced several editions of Langhorne's *Plutarch*. *The British Plutarch, containing the Lives of the most Eminent Divines, &c.*, 6 vols., 1816, a revision by Wrangham of Thomas Mortimer's book, is a quite distinct work. For an account of Wrangham, with a detailed list of these and of other publications of religious interest, see Michael Sadleir, *Archdeacon Francis Wrangham 1769–1842*, Bibliographical Society, 1937 (Supplement no. 12).

INDEX

Main entries are in bold figures. An asterisk indicates a biographical footnote. The index excludes the Bibliography, except in the case of a few minor writers who are not mentioned in the text, or mentioned only in passing.